What people are saying about
The Graham Harman Reader

Overcoming the war of religion between analytics and continentals
with a brand-new metaphysical insight, Graham Harman has
restored to philosophy its greatness and value.
Maurizio Ferraris, Italian continental philosopher and author
of the *Manifesto of New Realism*

I don't read a lot of metaphysics, but *The Graham Harman Reader*
is metaphysics that I read.
Bruce Sterling, science fiction author

THE GRAHAM HARMAN READER

Edited by Jon Cogburn and Niki Young

Winchester, UK
Washington, USA

JOHN HUNT PUBLISHING

First published by Zero Books, 2023
Zero Books is an imprint of John Hunt Publishing Ltd., No. 3 East St., Alresford,
Hampshire SO24 9EE, UK
office@jhpbooks.com
www.johnhuntpublishing.com
www.zero-books.net

For distributor details and how to order please visit the 'Ordering' section
on our website.

Paperback ISBN: 978-1-80341-240-5
eBook ISBN: 978-1-80341-241-2
PCN: 2022936588

A CIP catalogue record for this book is available from the British Library.

Design credit(s): Lapiz Digital

UK: Printed and bound by CPI Group (UK) Ltd, Croydon, CR0 4YY
Printed in North America by CPI GPS partners

We operate a distinctive and ethical publishing philosophy in all areas
of our business, from our global network of authors to production and
worldwide distribution.

TABLE OF CONTENTS

EDITORS' INTRODUCTION

1. Why Harman?

Great philosophers have always subverted widely presupposed dualisms, in the Western tradition starting with the Greek concepts of *nomos* and *physis*, which are roughly what we mean today by "convention" and "nature."[1] Is the division of practices, beliefs, and objects according to this dualism itself merely conventional? Or is it natural in the sense that one can objectively get it right or wrong? Is there anything more to truth than what people can be convinced to believe? The Egyptians do things one way and the Athenians another. Is it ever the case that one is better as a matter of nature? Or is that also merely human convention?

Such dichotomies are reflected in social division, for example with team *physis* represented by bean-abstaining, number-worshipping mystics and team *nomos* represented by those who worship power. Must one choose sides? Socrates, Plato, and Aristotle thought not. And if there is anything currently analogous to that which confronted Socrates, it is surely the division between science on the one hand and subjectivist irrationalism on the other, a dualism that during the era of pandemic and environmental collapse works itself out in ways nearly too depressing to contemplate. Science gives us life-saving vaccines but also a worldview that recognizes no intrinsic value in the ecosystem being rendered inhospitable by other

---

[1] This is, if anything, *clearer* in the main philosophical traditions of the Indian subcontinent, where disputes about the distinction between conventional (*saṁvṛti*) and ultimate (*paramārtha*) truth form a reliable dialectical engine. See for example Dan Arnold, *Buddhists, Brahmins, and Belief*.

technological offspring of that same science. And team anti-science is no better. While the editors were writing this, the annual rate of death from all causes in American counties that strongly vote for the political party which marries irrationalist religious and political extremism with anti-scientific subjectivism was over *five times* that of those which vote for the nominally pro-science party, whose members don't organize their lives around the assumption that intercessory prayer and nutritional supplements obviate the need for vaccines. And yet, under the aegis of "follow the science," the early Biden administration allowed scientific advisory boards to make a set of political decisions which had the effect (despite desperate collective pleading by the American Academy of Pediatrics) of unnecessarily slowing down the approval of childhood vaccinations and booster shots by over half a year.

But philosophers cannot merely register a reigning dichotomy as false and move on the same as before; philosophy demands a willingness to subvert everything (including subversion itself).[2] For example, Kant did not merely reject "Hume's fork," the division of propositions into "relations of ideas" and "matters of fact," but also used this rejection to raise the question of how we could have knowledge of propositions made true by things in the world when they so clearly weren't made true by those things in the world that we directly experience with our senses. The claims that we ought not lie or that every even number is the sum of two primes or every event has a cause are all *about* the world we experience, yet our sensory experience does not seem to justify them. It was in trying to figure out how this worked that Kant developed a philosophy so systematic that it has something non-trivial to say about everything, including itself.[3]

For Graham Harman, the analogous question concerns how we can have access to things in the world independently from the caricatures we

---

[2]   In "What is Philosophy?" Graham Priest argues that this kind of self-reference is characteristic of philosophy as such. One of us has shown (in Cogburn, *Garcian Meditations*) how Harman's account of allure and theory as both epistemological and metaphysical relations allows him to give a satisfying account of the epistemic status of his own epistemology. With the exceptions of Priest and A.W. Moore (cf. *The Evolution of Modern Metaphysics*), contemporary analytic and continental philosophers ignore this issue, in the former case due to the mistaken views that there is no philosophical problem with empirical justification and that all justification is empirical, and in the latter due to the equally mistaken view that such problems were forever bracketed by Saint Edmund. This is all to say that analytic philosophers learn wrongly from pragmatism that science thinks, and continental philosophers learn wrongly from phenomenology that philosophy doesn't need to.

[3]   This is clearly a Whig history which elides Kant's usual, but by no means universal, elision of semantic and epistemic issues. This kind of thing is the price of conversing with the mighty dead.

construct in our theoretical and practical engagements. If there is more to the vase than what science or phenomenology theoretically describes, what is it? If there is more to the vase than a caricature sufficient for our pragmatic use, what is it? And how could we be sensitive to something that transcends the theoretical and practical?

While an army of retrograde academic neo-Kantians still perversely tries to convince us that these questions are naïve, or even retrograde and politically rebarbative, they are in fact pressing in all of the ways that should matter to us: existentially, morally, politically, spiritually, aesthetically, etc.[4] To see this, just attend to the fact that there is all the difference in the world between loving your spouse and merely loving how they look to you or what they do or what you can do with them. But if all we have is access to the phenomenal experience engendered by those we love, or alternatively the scientific picture which allows us some imperfect level of prediction and control over those phenomena, there is no difference!

One cannot "follow the science" into a loving relationship any more than science can directly tell you how to act politically. But that does not mean that loving (or politics for that matter) is whatever you want it to be. Against team anti-science, we must affirm that contradicting science courts disaster, but against team science we must affirm that so does thinking that science is something that can be followed. *Objects of love* (and by objects of love we include ecosystems, theorems, marsupials, paintings, chrysanthemums, suckling pigs, fabled ones, those who have just broken the vase, etc.) *obligate the lover*.

But how does one go beyond a theoretical or pragmatic caricature to respond appropriately to things themselves? Only a sophist could pretend that there is a simple answer to this question. No. It demands systematic philosophy. And, to repeat, systematic philosophy is called into being precisely by those questions which subvert reigning dualisms and which

---

[4] The philosophers that Quentin Meillassoux called "correlationists" were all idealists pretending to be beyond the idealism/realism dualism. The cancer in continental philosophy was weirdly analogous to Quineans in analytic philosophy pretending to have subverted the analytic/ synthetic dualism when in fact they always just held that all propositions are synthetic. Since verificationism is the analytic philosophy version of idealism, and Quine himself was a holistic verificationist, these are arguably the same cancers. See Harman's early *Quentin Meillassoux: Philosophy in the Making* for the definitive typology of correlationisms, one that makes sense of the transition from Kant to German Idealism, the agony of contemporary continental philosophy, and how Meillassoux's arguments actually show the collapse of correlationism into idealism. See also Harman's *Speculative Realism: An Introduction*, divided into chapters on Ray Brassier, Iain Hamilton Grant, Harman himself, and Meillassoux.

as such have no simple answer. And just as for Kant the question of the synthetic *a priori* both follows from his subverting Hume's dualism and is the key to the development of his (anti-)metaphysics, for Harman the question of accessing the inaccessible is key to his subversion of our reigning, terrible dualism, this stupid yet ultimately horrifying war between scientism and irrationalism. As with Kant on the synthetic *a priori*, it is key to Harman's Object-Oriented Ontology (OOO) with its attendant fourfold metaphysics, epistemic theory of sincerity and allure, and his fundamental rethinking of art, science, truth, knowledge, and politics in terms of these categories.[5]

2. Apophasis: Harman's *Via Negativa*

Failure is the great teacher, and for good and bad, the history of twentieth-century philosophy was largely the history of failures of pragmatic, phenomenal, phenomenological, and finally scientistic reductions, all of which, if successfully prosecuted, would have foreclosed the possibility of answering Harman's question.[6] That is, *defining* objects in terms of how they are accessed by (able-minded, adult, but not too old) human twentieth-century philosophers is not only myopic in the usual post-Cartesian ableist and speciesist ways, it also absolutely precludes an account of how we (and by "we" the editors include creatures with different phenomenologies than writers of philosophy) access the inaccessible, how we respond correctly to things, not merely how we manipulate them using the dumb caricatures constructed out of the whirling effluvia produced by our sensory upstream and cognitive/pragmatic downstreams.[7]

---

[5] As far as we know, Levi Bryant came up with the name "OOO" to denote a group of thinkers thinking within the framework established by Harman in his 2002 *Tool-Being: Heidegger and the Metaphysics of Objects*. See especially Harman's own discussion of Ian Bogost, Levi Bryant, Timothy Morton, and Tristan Garcia in his *Object-Oriented Ontology: A New Theory of Everything* as well as the discussions in his *Skirmishes: With Friends, Enemies, and Neutrals*.

[6] For the standard account of the history of analytic philosophy as the failure of such reductions, see Scott Soames's two-part *Philosophical Analysis in the Twentieth Century*. If one separates out the alleged bugs from the features in a different manner from the author (to be fair, one must do this with some of Soames's texts as well), Lee Braver's *A Thing of This World: A History of Continental Anti-Realism* beautifully accomplishes the same for the continental tradition.

[7] In the opening sections of *Object-Oriented Ontology: A New Theory of Everything*, Harman isolates physicalism, smallism, anti-fictionalism, and literalism as the dominant correlationist metaphysical prejudices of our day. With respect to literalism, Harman is able to show that an astonishing number of contemporary philosophers (and his critique applies to Robert Brandom

2.1. *Nomos* and *Physis* as Scylla and Charybdis

In twentieth-century philosophy, the more obviously correlationist reductions were usually opposed by physicalists, who were (as is the nature of all such movements) once *avant* and now old guard(*e*). Physicalists take objects to be *physical* things such as chairs and cups, or perhaps only the smallest physical entities such as quarks or neutrinos which compose chairs and cups. Physicalist ontologies require that one reduce, exclude, or eliminate non-physical entities such as numbers, nations, possibilities, the Dutch East India Company, feelings, political parties, fictional characters, minds, obligations, probabilities, angels, moods, dispositions, etc. etc. etc. However, after decades of furious work to the contrary by some of the best minds of the previous generation, it is at this point impossible to imagine how such entities could be reduced to anything commonsensically physical or to their tiniest component physical parts. Indeed, if there is any moral to twentieth-century analytic philosophy of science it is this: reductionism fails and physicalism always relies in the end on the *elimination* of a vast array of objects which do not conform to its restrictive definition. For the honest physicalist, none of the entities we just listed (numbers, nations …) *really* exist, after all.[8]

In contrast to such positions, OOO is committed to a pluralist view of objects, according to which Geppetto, prime numbers, Mickey Mouse, possible worlds, the island of Comino, states of grace, the World Health Organization, etc. are no more (or no less) objects than neutrinos, atoms, cups, and chairs. All such objects are all in fact equally objects for OOO, even if — and as we shall see — not all of them are equally real.

2.2. Undermining and Overmining

Harman names the attempt to reduce an object to its constituent pieces "undermining."[9] Undermining philosophies deny the existence of all sorts of entities by alleging that they are *nothing more than* — say, in the case of a

---

and all extant schools of modal actualism in analytic philosophy) to commit a metaphysical version of what the New Critics called "the paraphrastic fallacy." See the essays in "IV. Aesthetics as First Philosophy," this volume.

[8] There is an *enormous* philosophical literature on reduction which merely in the end supports the following claim: for all *x*, *y*, and *z*, if *x* is a formal model of reducibility put forward by analytical philosophers, and *y* some entity or proposition that might be reducible to *z*, then by the model *x*, *y* will not reduce to *z*. With respect to this point, see the discussions in Cogburn, *Garcian Meditations*, on reductionism, emergence, and the relevance of "the Stanford School" philosophers of science to Object-Oriented Ontology.

[9] See the papers in "I. Anti-Mining and the Return to Metaphysics" in this volume.

bicycle — basic particles arranged "bicyclewise." In this way, the underminer reduces the reality of the bicycle to an epiphenomenal manifestation of its more basic parts. Things are complicated a bit by the crookedness of the game, however. For undermining, like newspaper astrology, cannot be falsified! If the reduction were to succeed, then the underminer has shown that we need not be ontologically committed to bicycles, only their basic parts. And so bicycles do not *really* exist.[10] But if it fails, then the committed physicalist (under the guise of eliminative materialism) can also conclude: so much the worse for bicycles![11] The standard materialist holds that if bicycles are reducible to their parts, then there is a sense in which they don't really exist over and above their parts. The eliminative materialist holds that if bicycles are not reducible to their parts, then they are in some sense fictional: they do not exist. Heads I win, tails you lose.

To be sure, Harman does not deny that objects are comprised of sub-components, and he even entertains the possibility of an indefinite regress of part-to-whole relations. Nevertheless, he also claims that undermining cannot account for a phenomenon known in philosophy as "emergence," which denotes the fact that objects unify their parts in such a way that they can generate new properties not found in their individual pieces.[12] The most important such property in this context is the ability of an emergent whole to retroactively affect its parts. For instance, the bicycle as an emergent whole is able to affect each of its parts in order to allow for locomotion. The artist's property of being creative determines the movement of all her parts while painting, writing and playing guitar, but it is not a property of any of those moving parts. But by reducing all entities to their most basic subcomponents, the underminer cannot account for such emergent features.

Harman also identifies a second way that thinkers attempt to do away with the reality of objects, that is, by reducing them "upwards" to their effects and affects rather than to their constituent parts. He calls such philosophers "overminers," all of them claiming in some respect that an object is *nothing more than* its surface affect: a mere fleeting epiphenomenal

---

10 The Abhidharma school of early Buddhist philosophy in fact used this kind of eliminativist atomism to teach that there was no self. The philosophers coming out of the later Mahayana tradition in various ways tend to reject the move. See Mark Siderits, *Buddhism as Philosophy* and Jay Garfield's, *Engaging Buddhism: Why it Matters to Philosophy.*
11 See Patricia Churchland *Neurophilosophy: Toward a Unified Science of Mind-Brain* for what was perhaps the high-water mark of eliminative materialism with respect to the mind.
12 See Niki Young, "Object, Reduction, and Emergence: An Object-Oriented View," and Jon Cogburn & Mark Silcox, "Computability Theory and Ontological Emergence."

expression produced through its relations. Harman argues that this mode of explanation is constitutively unable to account for change. Going back to our trusty bicycle example, if the latter were *entirely* determined by the relations to the earth and lanes as well as its effects on the rider, it would be impossible to imagine how these relations could be disrupted such that the bicycle could then enter into new relations and have new effects without ceasing to be itself. Again, Harman does not deny that objects enter into affective and effective relations. Nevertheless, he thinks that such relations are products of objects rather than being constitutive of them. Stated differently, for Harman, the object *acts because it is* rather than the reverse.

One of Harman's most interesting claims is that the rejected disjunction between undermining and overmining is not itself exclusive. In fact, he shows that they rarely exist in isolation. Rather, one of the poles is often quick to supplement itself with its other. For instance, if an underminer were challenged with the claim that familiar everyday entities do in fact manifestly exist, they would respond that these objects do indeed *seemingly* exist, but that they do so only in relation to a human observer. In this way, they supplement their undermining strategy with an overmining move according to which individual entities only exist in relation to the almighty human who is able to "carve up nature at the joints." Similarly, when confronted with the problem of change, an overminer will often postulate a hidden layer of reality responsible for alteration.

In addition to undermining and overmining, Harman notes that there is also a position which under- and overmines objects *simultaneously* rather than using one side of the poles as a supplement for the other. He calls such positions "duomining." Duominers concurrently claim (a) that objects are nothing but their most basic elements, and (b) that the latter are exhaustively characterized by our models of them. Typical of such positions would be the scientific materialists of our time who claim both that a base layer of indefinite "matter" exhausts all of reality, and that it is possible to come to know this ultimate layer through mathematical modeling. Needless to say, Harman rejects duomining due to the fact that it possesses the sum total of vices present in both under- and overmining, namely it is unable to account for both change and emergence.[13]

---

[13] This is not to align with team anti-science! Nothing in the rejection of duomining either legitimates pseudo-science or delegitimates the manner in which scientific explanation allows us to understand those aspects of objects which allow their manipulation.

3. Cataphasis I: Sensual and Real Objects

Harman's critique of undermining and overmining gives us two negative criteria for objects, as things reducible neither to (i) their constituent parts, nor (ii) their relations to other objects, including their affects and effects. We can perhaps best understand the route to Harman's positive theses, (iii) unity and (iv) autonomy, if we first consider the moral, political, and existential role played by their denials.

3.1. Unity and the Sensual Object

Any sufficiently reflective person hopes on their deathbed to be able to make a kind of narrative of what has come before. That is, we don't merely want to have realized large quantities of the true, the good, and the beautiful, but want these things to have unfolded in a unique manner.[14] But for this to minimally scan, there must be some sense in which the person on the deathbed looking back is the same person as the adolescent setting forth on a life of projects. And these projects must be interconnected in a meaningful way.[15]

This is political. Modes of social organization that reduce us to atomistic moments of intermittent craving and satiation can only be seen as natural to people for whom undermining is metaphysical common sense. But all of us, not just the saints, sages, and artists among us, are more than the mere sum of our purchases or labor contributions. And for that matter, political collectives such as society are not merely the sum of their parts either.[16]

---

[14] This is what is interesting and distinctive about stereotypical Western theodicies, where for example the hiddenness of the divine is explained in terms of the idea that too much divine presence is overwhelming to the point of us not developing (even in a Western case, perhaps over several incarnations) into the unique creatures we are. Buddhism is not inconsistent with this, but rather in just this context teaches the Aristotelian paradox of happiness, where trying to be happy (as opposed to realizing the true, the good, and the beautiful *for their own sake*) leads to unhappiness.

[15] In Mahayana Buddhism, the main soteriological figure is not the atman who disappears into Nirvana, but rather the bodhisattva who rejects Nirvana and embraces rebirth. But, and this is a very Mahayana point, even the atman who realizes the emptiness of "self" must tell a story about becoming the kind of self that rejects the self.

[16] This is why Harman's view does not fall into the kind of neo-liberal atomism that existentialism and post-structuralism always tended towards. For Harman, just as human individuals are unified, autonomous entities, so are hybrid objects such as the Dutch East India Company, which combine human and non-human objects. And contra the bad metaphysics of Margaret Thatcher, so is society. See particularly Harman's *Immaterialism*, which also contains a fascinating discussion of the stages of life of hybrid objects, as well as the essays in Section V of this volume.

For the political overminer, on the other hand, you are nothing more than a node in some supposedly liberating, or perhaps nakedly reactionary, collective project. Here, as Tristan Garcia argues in *Form and Object*, the politics freak who relies on class for a complete understanding of the social world has more in common with the racist than one might suppose. For the murderous essence of both is the inability to see people of a given type as anything but instances of that type. This is what happens when Charles Swann's aristocratic friends decide that even though he is a fine gourmet and member of the Jockey Club, he is in the end nothing more than a Jew, who as such can neither be French nor honorable. This is what is behind mass famines justified by the necessary liquidation of the kulaks. This is why, during the period from 1890 until 1960, when on average every four days in the United States one Black man was lynched in a public orgy of torture that would have shamed King Louis XV, it didn't matter whether the victim had actually perpetrated a crime. To racist bullies, the victim is in the end always nothing more than an instance of Blackness. Our ability to resist undermining and overmining is thus the essential metaphysical fact about us that renders every "-ism" not merely morally opprobrious but false as well. And according to Harman, this fact about us must also be understood as an instance of something instantiated by *all* objects. This is a radical, radical idea.

Harman first developed his speculative account of unity in *Guerilla Metaphysics*, where he realized that Edmund Husserl's greatest philosophical contribution was the phenomenological claim that we do not perceive objects as bundles of qualities but rather as stable, unified entities that are self-identical through change. And the continuing importance of this reading of Husserl can hardly be overstated.[17] For the Humean bundle theory of perception is not mere philosophical folklore, but continues to be presupposed with varying levels of implicitness by nearly everyone working in modern consciousness studies, for whom the task of the brain is first and foremost to construct objects out of a synthesis of immediately perceived qualities.[18] And, as a piece of speculative metaphysics, the inheritor of the

---

[17] Patricia Kitcher's *Kant's Transcendental Psychology* can in some ways be seen as a precursor to Harman's reading of Husserl, though the analogous argument she finds in Kant's transcendental deduction is focused on the perceiver and not the perceived. That is, what Kitcher's Kant does against David Hume's deconstruction of the perceiving subject is exactly what Harman's Husserl does against Hume's deconstruction of the perceiving object.

[18] See Susan Blackmore & Emily T. Troscianko, *Consciousness: An Introduction*, which is also an introduction to nearly all of the extant theories of consciousness developed and used by brain researchers (the only two not considered are recent theories of consciousness as field phenomena

bundle theory is the Geach/Kraut/Garcia view of individuation as always being relative to a sortal.[19] Here it makes no sense to say that there is one object in front of you, but only one instance of a given sort, such as one telephone. But for Harman, an object's unity, its oneness, is not a function of the qualities it has.

For Harman, *all* objects have a unity, and moreover, this unity is something that we immediately perceive in ordinary perception, both in terms of perceiving the object as unified over change and the way that the object is a locus for how its qualities are perceived. An object is not a bundle of qualities in part because as a whole it adds flavor to each of the qualities. The red of a Rothko or black of an executioner's hood is perceived differently from the red spot on a spider's back or its otherwise black carapace.[20] The fact that we immediately perceive these things is why such objects and their qualities are called by Harman *sensual* objects and *sensual* qualities. Finally, we noted above how Harman's reappraisal of Husserl can be seen as speculative in the sense that important existential themes from the philosophical tradition (the unity of the human being) are understood in terms of the occurrence of the category (unity) in non-human cases, here sensual objects. While this is radical, as it minimally commits us to a rethinking of contemporary consciousness studies, it is nowhere near as radical as Harman's other speculative move involving unity.

The second move is more difficult, so note first that I as a perceiver am not a mere sensual object. In my game, I am not merely a non-player character, but am a real object with my own sensorium. But what about

---

as well as non-Humean Huxleyan views of perception as gating, along with the relating cosmopsychic metaphysics). All of those discussed are Humean. One might conclude "well, so much the worse for Harman" were it not for the fact that the field is a mess. *Every* significant claim of localization in the brain comes with equally significant caveats and counterexamples. As a result, Blackmore and Troscianko in the end support a Dennettian eliminativism about consciousness! But is it not far more reasonable to conclude, with Harman, "so much the worse for Hume"?

19 See the discussion in Cogburn's *Garcian Meditations*. In this respect, Harman and Graham Priest are on one side and Tristan Garcia, Peter Geach, and Robert Kraut on the other, which is interesting in part because Garcia endorses Harman's critique of mining.

20 Cognitive science on perception is much closer to Harman, in this regard at least, than one might think. For example, the "push-pull effect" names the radical way that perception of a given color sample is highly dependent on context. Video game designers who rely on the kind of color theory taught in high school (as opposed to using actual artists with an instinct for context) end up producing what is known in the industry as "angry fruit salad." See the discussion in Jon Cogburn & Mark Silcox, *Philosophy Through Video Games*.

the objects in my sensorium? Do I appear as a sensual object with shifting qualities in their sensoria?

Certainly, with the human and animal sensual objects, the relation is reciprocal. And this presupposes they too are real objects, player characters in their own worlds. But Harman extends this, so that his most radical suggestion is that the same holds for the inanimate objects I perceive. This cotton ball also has an interior life, as does this plate on which it rests. For both of them, I am a sensual object. For each of them, the other is. And pick your litany. It is well known that Johnny Cash wrote songs about horses, railroads, land, Judgment Day, family, hard times, whiskey, courtship, marriage, adultery, separation, murder, war, prison, rambling, damnation, home, salvation, death, pride, humor, piety, rebellion, patriotism, larceny, determination, tragedy, rowdiness, heartbreak, and love. And Mother and God. But, as is also well known from his songs, when you stare into the home, the home stares into you.

3.2. Autonomy and the Real Object

What, in the end, does all of this really have to do with mountains and trees, billiard balls and oceans? Why should it matter if, as underminers, we see the mountain as nothing more than the sum of its parts, or as overminers, as nothing more than one more interchangeable mountain-for-us? Actually, everything hangs on this, but to see why we must turn to (iv) autonomy.

When philosophers talk about autonomy, they typically denote the capacity of humans to make informed and rational decisions. And at least since Aristotle, it has been clear that we can't be rational while under great physical or emotional duress or if we lack beliefs relevant to our deliberation. So respecting other people's autonomy minimally means not coercing or misleading them. Arguably, it also means working to help them thrive.[21]

Clear enough, but we tend to misidentify what is going wrong when human autonomy is violated. That is, the dumbest thing we say about sadists and bullies is that they "objectify" their victims. This is mistaken for three reasons. First, most sadists delight in causing the kind of psychological and physical suffering that non-living objects don't seem to possess. In this

---

[21] See James Sterba, "From Liberty to Welfare," for the dispositive case that respect for negative liberties such as freedom from coercion entail the existence of positive liberties such as welfare. See also James Rocha, "Autonomy Within Subservient Careers," for an analogous introduction of substantive teleological considerations into Kantian debates about autonomy. We speculate that it is only due to dumb metaphysical prejudice that Rocha's radical, yet equally convincing, conclusion has been resisted by Kantians who have no problem with Sterba's.

sense, bullies never objectify the rest of us; objectification in this sense is the province of the assassin. Second, narcissistic sadists want their victims to become complicit in their own immiseration. "Look what you made me do!" Again, there is no point in saying something like this to a non-living object. Third, and most important for our purposes, the view that the *summum bonum* of human depravity is "objectification" betrays a commitment to the perfectly hideous view that one should be able do whatever one wants with mere objects.

But note that when philosophers equate the injunction to respect the autonomy of humans with not interfering with, or perhaps promoting, their ability to rationally deliberate and freely chose, they do this only because of a prior commitment to the view that rational choice is what is in some sense proper to human beings. Respecting human autonomy, then, is really just not interfering with, and perhaps promoting, the good for humans. And this requires neither theoretically or actively undermining or overmining human beings. Likewise, respecting the autonomy of any object (say a mountain or ecosystem) involves not interfering with, and perhaps promoting, the good for that object.

We thus return to the concerns that opened this introduction. Team science is complicit in environmental collapse because science constitutively abstracts the qualities of things which can be mathematized and manipulated. The philosophical naturalist, or physicalist, thus lives in a universe where all that exists is there to be controlled. There is no good of the mountain in such a universe.[22] This is not to say that it is trivial to discern the good for a mountain. And Harman's system accurately reflects this difficulty both insofar as we only have direct access to the sensual mountain and its sensual properties and insofar as the issue of indirect contact with the real mountain, a contact which Harman calls allure, is a major research area in object-oriented ontology.

Philosophers should want to get what is right about the Zen artist who stares intently at the rose, hand gently cradling the large ink brush, until she finally begins to caress the rice paper with the glistening sable hair. When we ask her how she managed to so quickly represent the rose in negative space, she invariably tells us that she did not begin to paint until she and the rose were one. But how did she and the rose connect beyond the mere sensory?

---

22 For an extended meditation on this point in the service of OOO epistemology, arrived at by presenting John McDowell's myth of the given argument as an inclosure paradox, see Jon Cogburn, "Be(ing) Here Now." All of this must be read with the background of the essays in "VI. Epistemology, Mind, and Science," this volume.

How did this impossible connection result in a new rose? Shockingly, of *all* extant theories of metaphysics and aesthetics in the Western tradition, only Harman's has anything at all to say to this process, arguably universal in aesthetics, ethics, and human psychology.[23] Zen artists, as one would predict, are perhaps only distinctive in being a little more aware about what is really going on when the connection is made.[24]

But we will never get insight into how real objects relate until we get insight into what those objects are in the first place. Harman initially approached this in a systematic way in his fundamental rethinking of Martin Heidegger, *Tool Being: Heidegger and the Metaphysics of Objects*, where he characterized real objects in terms of their withdrawal from their sensory qualities perceived by others. This withdrawal is why, for Harman, there is a sense in which a real object is distinct from the sensual objects which instantiate the sensual qualities of that object.[25] Why the distinction, though? Remember our example of objects of love. Loving requires respecting the autonomy of the beloved object. This is not possible if you only love how the object looks to you or what you can do with the object. The extraction industry executive does not love the mountain, which they are instrumental in destroying. And for the rest of us, though one can and does love the sensual object, one cannot *merely* love the sensual object. Thus, we see through allure the constitutive connection between autonomy and the withdrawn real.

---

[23] Here there are mainstream areas of cognitive science more consistent with Harman's view, as simulation theorists explain our ability to understand others as rooted in our ability to mentally mimic them, and this mental simulation is not reducible to the kind of purported tacit propositional knowledge in which theorists of folk psychology trade. See the discussion in *Consciousness: An Introduction* as well as the citations in the following footnote.

[24] See the essays in "IV: Aesthetics as First Philosophy" of this volume, as well as Harman's recent *Art and Objects*, which — although concerned primarily with ontological questions about the artwork itself and spectatorship — contains much that is necessary for understanding this issue.

[25] This issue is a bit underdetermined in Harman's work. One can imagine a radical version of OOO, where the sensual and real object are the same object, just considered differently. This is what Henry Allison (in *Kant's Transcendental Idealism: An Interpretation and Defense*) influentially argues about Kant's phenomenal and noumenal objects. The version of Kant we get from P.F. Strawson, Jonathan Bennett, and Paul Guyer on the other hand, in effect treats phenomenal and noumenal objects as distinct, so the noumenal paperclip in some sense co-produces all of its directly perceived phenomenal paperclips (which are distinct objects) with everyone indirectly viewing the real paperclip. One of us tends towards an Allisonian and the other towards a Strawsonian Harman, though both of us recognize that the Strawsonian Harman has more exegetical plausibility.

4. Cataphasis 2: The New Fourfold[26]

Harman's flat ontology instantiates the claim that all objects are equally objects. He rejects presupposed dualisms — or what he calls "onto-taxonomies" — which postulate a hierarchical distinction between, say, the human and nonhuman, natural and artificial, or the real and fictional.[27] Nevertheless, his ontology is also *quasi*-flat to the extent that he does not claim that all objects are equally *real*. Instead, as should be clear from the previous section, he distinguishes between two varieties of objects, namely real ones and sensual ones.

Throughout his works, Harman provides two definitions of the real object. The first of these is couched in terms of the concept of "withdrawal," a notion that emphasizes the manner in which each real object contains a non-relational surplus beyond any of its current or possible associations. This specific notion performs two important tasks in OOO. First, it accounts for the aforementioned autonomy of the real object, since it entails that the latter is never defined by or reducible to its external relations with other entities. Second, it entails that a real object cannot make direct contact with another, to the effect that any possible relations entertained between objects must occur in a mediated — or what Harman terms "vicarious" — manner (as we shall see in the following section).

The second definition is articulated in terms of the notion of emergence discussed earlier. In this context, Harman defines any real object as an *emergent entity* which *generates new real qualities* by virtue of the *unification of its parts*. This characterization performs a further twofold task in OOO: first, it underlines that a real object is always an emergent entity in virtue of sustaining relations between the component parts which support it. In this way, once a real object emerges into being, it becomes a *unified whole* rather than an aggregate sum of its parts, and this whole in turn generates individual real qualities (or RQ) of its own. In a similar manner to that between the sensual object and its properties, Harman maintains that the real object is not composed of or reducible to its real qualities. Rather, there exists a *tension* between a real object and its real qualities, and this produces what is known as the "essence" of the object. The latter is, however, not a universal, but rather an individual essence belonging to the irreplaceable and

---

26   Rather than attempting to give citations for all the philosophical theses in this section, which is of necessity more finely grained than the previous one, we must simply direct the reader to "II. The Fourfold Object," in this volume.

27   See, especially, Harman, "The Only Exit from Modern Philosophy," in this volume, and Niki Young, "Only Two Peas in a Pod: On the Overcoming of Ontological Taxonomies."

irreducible particular. In other words, this is not an essentialism according to which one can discover an entity's nature by figuring out the alleged set to which it belongs. The real object withdraws from relations, to the effect that direct interaction between objects is precluded *a priori* in OOO.

Nevertheless, this does not imply that objects do not interact at all. It's rather that, as with the Zen artist and the rose, contacts between real objects necessitate the breakdown of the sensual and the creation of something new. But this is not inconsistent with the claim that objects interact with other real ones obliquely, via the mediation of sensual objects (SOs). In this context, a sensual object refers to any unified entity which only exists within the experience — or "sincerity" — of a real object. Crucially, in the present context, the signifier "experience" is not to be conflated with consciousness, and thus should not be limited to living or sentient beings. Rather, OOO maintains that all real objects are capable of experience insofar as all entities translate other ones into their own terms. In other words, "experience" here simply means that a real object RO_1 relates to another object RO_2 obliquely by way of a translation. This translation is the sensual object SO_2.

More specifically, and if, following the phenomenological tradition out of which OOO first emerged, we define *intentionality* in terms of "aboutness of experience" or "directedness towards an object," then it follows that a real object always *intends* another real object, since experience always points to something outside it rather than to itself pure and simple. Nevertheless, the real object *relates* to the real indirectly, via a sensual translation, since it can only ever translate the real into its own terms given its finite capacities defined by its being the kind of real object it is.

Now let us return to the beginning of this discussion, where we noted that any great philosophy subverts widely presupposed dualisms. Harman's distinction between the real and the sensual seemingly brings us back to a standard "two-world" dualism exemplified, for instance, in the philosophy of Plato through the distinction between reality and appearance, or in Kant's distinction between things-in-themselves (or noumena) and phenomenal things as they appear to us. This characterization, however, is mistaken. Contra Kant, for Harman there is not one noumenal tier opposed to the level of phenomenal (human) experience. Rather, following the thesis of withdrawal, every real object is in fact a thing-in-itself for every other, insofar as the world is replete with objects which cannot be absorbed into their relations and interactions. Furthermore, against Plato, Harman would claim that the sensual is not an illusion opposed and subservient to a truer realm.

5. Effective Affection[28]

Harman's crisscrossing two categories (real versus sensual, object versus quality) leave us with the following definition: in OOO the term "object" refers to any irreducible unified and autonomous entity existing in tension with its respective real and sensual qualities. As we have also seen, real objects cannot entertain direct relations with other real objects, even if they do indirectly "experience" one another via the mediation of a sensual ether. This kind of indirect relation is, however, not strictly speaking causal in the OOO sense, since sensual objects cannot bring about significant change at the level of the real. This raises the question of how change occurs at the level of the real. The solution to this conundrum lies in the distinction between two modalities of relation in OOO, namely what Harman calls "sincerity" and "allure." Let us consider each of these terms in more detail.

Sincerity may be described as an ordinary state of inter-objective (indirect) relation, and is roughly the analogue of what we have earlier designated under the name "experience." As we have already stated earlier, in cases of sincerity — or "ordinary experience" — a real object RO_1 *intends* another object RO_2 but nevertheless *relates* only to the translated sensual object SO^2 encrusted with its various shifting and shimmering qualities SQ_2. It should be remembered that each SQ_2 emanates from RO_2, but nevertheless also encrusts SO_2 within the experience of RO_1.

Let us, for the sake of illustration, imagine a domestic silkworm (*Bombyx Mori*) looking for food. This monophagous insect moves in the vicinity of its preferred food source, the mulberry leaf (*Morus alba*), which in turn emits small quantities of the specific chemical "cis-jasmone." This chemical is highly attractive to the larva, and activates a receptor in the worm's antennae, thereby allowing it to translate the leaf into a sensual object with sensual qualities pertinent to the worm but not, say, to a human or chair, since the experience of the leaf for these entities might be entirely different. We must remember that "experience" is not limited to sentient or even living entities in OOO, since the term simply acts as a placeholder for situations where a real entity relates to a sensual translation of another one.

It is worth noting that even though Harman often speaks of sincerity as involving "translation", it is not representationalist, at least not in any of the ways we associate with "mirroring." This is crucially important for three reasons. First, to deny literalism is to affirm that the "translated" real is neither linguistic nor linguaform. Second, representational idioms in

---

[28] Here, we direct the reader to "III. Indirect Causation," in this volume.

early analytic philosophy were in part an attempt to try to preserve some last vestige of indubitability. The idea was that though I can reasonably doubt that there is a tree in front of me, I cannot doubt the tree sense data I perceive. But nothing in Harman commits him to the view that one cannot have false beliefs about the contents of one's sensual realm. Third, and most important, is that both team science and team anti-science presuppose claims about how a linguistic medium mirrors reality. The physicalist in essence voting yes (for science), and the marketplace postmodernist voting no (for everything). But the sensual medium's job is not to succeed or fail at mirroring the real. Moreover, though this denial of mirroring (via his denial of literalism) is something Harman has in common with American pragmatists, it commits him neither to the lazy overmining relativism of many pragmatists nor the kind of undermining scientism we get from recent American philosophers, pragmatists or not, for whom "naturalize" remains a success verb.

In the case of the silkworm example, we then have a real worm in a "sincere" direct relation with a sensual leaf coupled with its sensual qualities. To be sure, the real leaf emanates its sensual qualities, for the worm cannot by definition eventually feed on a sensual leaf existing only within its experience. Nevertheless, the leaf-in-itself withdraws from direct contact due to the fact that the worm's relation to it is finite, buffered by the sensual ether.

Two points are worth emphasizing here. In the first instance, it may be noted that the real and sensual are arguably not two separate realms, since they cross paths in two crucial ways in the scenario just described: first, as discussed earlier, the sensual mulberry leaf experienced by the silkworm indirectly points to the real qualities of the leaf itself; second, the sensual qualities of the leaf emanate from the real leaf inasmuch as they are connected to a sensual one, even if the real leaf falls outside the direct purview of the worm.[29] Furthermore, it would also be vital to note that in cases of sincerity, the real object in direct contact with a sensual one — in this case the real worm and the sensual leaf with its multifarious qualities — is contained on the interior of a *total* relation which Harman dubs "containment." This container is in turn classed as a new object in its own right since it possesses the full features of an object discussed in the previous section.

---

[29] Precisely here is where one can see the import of the debate between the Allisonian and Strawsonian Harman alluded to in a previous footnote.

Harman's philosophy draws a difference between the ordinary cases of sincerity just described and what he terms "allure." Unlike cases of sincerity, allure is *occasional*. This can have one of two possible meanings. The first sense designates some rare or special event. The second, more directly philosophical meaning of "occasional" relates to the occasionalist tradition of Malebranche and the earlier Ash'arite and Māturīdite Muslim schools of the tenth century. For the purposes of this introduction, it would suffice to broadly define such positions in terms of the central claim that direct relations between substances are precluded. A third entity must act as a mediator or medium for relations. Allure is occasional in both these senses: it refers to a "special and intermittent" occurrence which unsettles the ordinary flow of experience, thereby allowing for a mediated causal relation between two real entities. To be sure, a relation of sincerity must already be present for allure to take place. In other words, we can say that sincerity — namely the contact between a real object and a sensual one within an intentional whole — is the pre-causal ether through which the deeper contact of allure is unleashed.

Allure, however, differs from sincerity insofar as it consists of a double mechanism. As we have seen in cases of ordinary sincerity, sensual qualities indirectly emanate *from* the real object, even if they are *fused* to a sensual object within the "contained" or total relation which another real object produces with a sensual one. The first mechanism of allure consists in an extraordinary event where there is a breakdown, or fission between the sensual object and its previously fused sensual qualities. Allure begins by interrupting the flow of sincerity by manifesting the tension between a sensual object and sensual qualities for the experiencing real object.

The second mechanism of allure then consists in using the sensual qualities previously associated with a sensual object to point *to* the real object. In this way, the sensual qualities — and by implication the perceiving real object itself — are *lured* towards the previously withdrawn real object such that they then *allude* to it in its absence. In this way, a real object is made *present in its absence* through the medium of sensual qualities which fill in for this absence. Thus, the breakdown works as almost a negative-theological, or perhaps Zen Buddhist, pointing towards the real object.[30]

---

[30] Better accounts of the function of koans in the Rinzai Zen tradition, such as that of Toshihiko Izutsu, say in essence that their role is to produce exactly this kind of awareness of allure, an awareness which might indeed be equated with Zen.

The double mechanism of allure allows for one real object to obliquely establish a link with another by transforming the relation of "containment" discussed earlier into an *emergent* mediated "connection" between two real objects. This compositional sense of causation expresses the principal meaning of causality for Harman, such that what we normally understand causality to entail — namely one thing exerting influence on another — is in fact a resultant by-product of an emergent connection's ability to retroactively affects its own parts.

It might be best to illustrate the mechanism of vicarious causation by making recourse to an example which Harman borrows from the Islamic occasionalist tradition, namely that of fire burning cotton. In keeping with the principle of autonomy discussed in the previous section, it is evident that the real fire never encounters the real being of cotton, since these are by default withdrawn from one another. Rather, fire necessarily encounters a sensual object displaying qualities such as flammability, namely ones which are pertinent to the fire but not to a human who might see cotton in terms of cleaning equipment. Yet this sincere relation between the real fire and sensual cotton is occasionally — in both senses outlined earlier — disrupted, thereby allowing the sensual qualities of cotton, perceived by the flame, to allude to the cotton's reality. In this way, a new emergent "burning cotton ball" entity is formed in such a way that it is then able to affect its respective parts. The event called "burning" is then none other than the *ex post facto* effect of the "connection" between fire and cotton through which the flammable qualities of fire are grafted onto the object cotton.

6. Eternal Non-Recurrence

Whew! We would like to say much more. We would like to recapitulate here what we have said. But wisdom counsels us instead to encourage those readers still with us to avail themselves of the pleasure of Harman's prose.

In lieu of a recap, let us cite the ending of *Four Quartets*, where all that preceded leads to T.S. Eliot's vision of the fire and the rose as one. Again, Harman is the only contemporary philosopher who might both accommodate and help us understand this kind of union in separation, not just with the fire and the rose, but also when one friend uncannily knows exactly how to cheer the other up, when the artist directs our attention to things previously invisible and unheard, when everything is newly illuminated by someone's equally oblique explanation of a koan, when we perceive the tragic in the denuded mountaintop bleeding poisonous slag into the valley, when we are drawn to meditative contemplation among that mountain's brothers and sisters or perhaps merely while staring at the falling snow under the orange Chicago streetlights. Making sense of making sense is not easy, but what kind of life would there be without allure?

Near the end of the poem, by way of leading up to his final mystical vision, Eliot writes, "We shall not cease from exploration // And the end of all our exploring // Will be to arrive where we started // And know the place for the first time." Typical readings equate this final knowledge with the mystical union expressed in the line about the fire and rose. But Eliot is not saying this. He is rather making a conditional claim, informing us that *if* there were an end, *then* we would finally have knowledge.

But once one reads Harman, one realizes that Eliot does not take his conditional to support a *modus ponens*. Rather, Eliot encourages us to realize in our bones that since there is no final knowledge, since the objects with which we join are still autonomous beings with their own agendas capable of surprising, since mystical joining is neither mastery nor being mastered, exploration is never finished. Harman reminds us that philosophy is *love* of wisdom, and love can never own that which it loves. And thus, we see Friedrich Nietzsche's eternal monotony replaced with surprise, something true lovers know about one another, but which we now realize as universal.[31]

And though most fail even at this, it is not enough for philosophy merely to be *consistent with* the different, the new, the uncanny. It must also balance openness to and understanding of particular kinds of uncanny entities in their particularity. Great philosophy is always itself one of the new beginnings because its general intuitions are always getting applied, extended, and transformed in confrontation with being's tapestry. And one only needs to read any of the fourteen essays in Sections IV, V, and VI of this volume to see this axiom in action. Or consider, by way of invitation, the following list of people now in their own ways continuing Harman's revolution:

Architecture: Mark Foster Gage, Ferda Kolatan, Rhett Russo, David Ruy, Peter Trummer, Tom Wiscombe, Michael Young.

---

[31] We are not being glib here; the quip about the meaning of the word "philosophy" bears immense weight when properly investigated. Allure as an epistemic relation is not an idealized absolute knowledge of an object, but something prior that makes correct practical and theoretical comportment possible, part of correct comportment here being Socratic humility. This is the point of Cogburn, "Be(ing) Here Now" which only begins to plumb the depths of, for example, Harman's "Excerpts on Unjustified True Belief," in this volume.

<u>Art</u>: Charles Ray, Egan Frantz, Joanna Malinowski, and many, many others.

<u>Archaeology</u>: Bjørnar Olsen, Christopher Witmore.

<u>Critical Theory and Environmental Studies</u>: Timothy Morton (in *Hyperobjects*).

<u>Organization Studies</u>: Participants in a day-long conference on Harman's book *Dante's Broken Hammer* at the University of Leicester.

<u>Political Science</u>: Bruno Latour (via the concept of "object-oriented politics" in *An Inquiry Into Modes of Existence*)

This is, to say the least, an incomplete enumeration for a writer ranked by The Best Schools as one of the fifty most influential living philosophers and by *ArtReview* as the seventy-fifth most powerful person in the international art world.[32]

But part of what has been so exciting about editing this anthology is that the revolution is still young. For us and other thinkers, seeking to know Harman's work is a radical beginning. And our greatest hope is that this volume will serve as something like Robert C. Tucker's *Marx-Engels Reader* did for so many generations of students. For, partly as a result of Tucker's labors, one needn't master every paragraph of all three volumes of *Das Kapital* to think and converse in the most profound way with Marx. Perhaps Harman is the only living philosopher for whom something similar can and should be achieved.

Jon Cogburn, Baton Rouge, Louisiana
Niki Young, Birguma, Malta
January 2022

---

[32] See https://thebestschools.org/magazine/most-influential-living-philosophers/ and https://www.aucegypt.edu/news/stories/graham-harman-among-most-powerful-forces-art-world/

PART I
ANTI-MINING AND THE RETURN TO METAPHYSICS

CHAPTER I
THE THIRD TABLE[33]

In recent years I have been linked with a philosophical movement called "speculative realism." But my own variant of speculative realism, known as "object-oriented philosophy," actually dates to the late 1990s. The principles of object-oriented philosophy can be summarized in a few sentences. First, philosophy must deal with every type of object rather than reducing all objects to one privileged type: zebras, leprechauns, and armies are just as worthy of philosophical discussion as atoms and brains. Second, objects are deeper than their appearance to the human mind, but also deeper than their relations to each other, so that all contact between objects must be indirect or vicarious. Third, objects are polarized in two different ways: first there is a distinction between objects and their qualities, and then there is a separate distinction between real objects withdrawn from all access and sensual objects that exist only for some observer, whether human or inhuman. Finally, the basic problems of ontology must be reformulated in terms of the fourfold structure that results from these two polarizations in the heart of objects. In a brief article like this one, there is no way to deal adequately with all of these problems. Instead, I will focus on clarifying the nature of what I have called "real objects" by way of a critical treatment of the famous theme of Eddington's two tables.

Sir Arthur Stanley Eddington was a British astrophysicist best known for his observations of a solar eclipse in 1919, which confirmed Einstein's general theory of relativity. Raised as a Quaker, he also had a brief dissident

---

[33] "The Third Table" originally appeared in 2012 in *The Book of Books*, ed. C. Christov-Bakargiev, pp. 540–542.

career as a conscientious objector to British participation in the First World War. Eddington's primary gift to philosophy, however, is his well-known parable of the two tables. In the Introduction to his 1927 Gifford Lectures in Edinburgh, he describes the situation as follows: "I have settled down to the task of writing these lectures and have drawn up my chairs to my two tables. Two tables! Yes; there are duplicates of every object about me — two tables, two chairs, two pens."[34] As the reader may guess, the two tables in question are the familiar table of everyday life and the same table as described by physics. We have long been accustomed to C.P. Snow's concept of the "two cultures" distinguishing natural scientists from so-called literary intellectuals.[35] Eddington's sympathies are squarely with his own group, the first. But he admits that the second cannot be effaced:

> I need not tell you that modern physics has by delicate test and remorseless logic assured me that my second scientific table is the only one which is really there — wherever "there" may be. On the other hand I need not tell you that modern physics will never succeed in exorcising that first table — strange compound of external nature, mental imagery and inherited prejudice — which lies visible to my eyes and tangible to my grasp. We must bid good-bye to it for the present for we are about to turn from the familiar world to the scientific world revealed by physics. This is, or is intended to be, a wholly external world.[36]

Against this attitude, the humanities might be tempted to reverse Eddington's conclusions and claim that the table of everyday life is just as real, or even more real, than the scientific table. The first table and first culture would thereby be opposed to the second, and the result would be the usual trench war between science and the humanities. My contrary view is that both groups are equally wrong about the table, and for precisely the same reason. When weighing the respective merits of the everyday and scientific tables, we will find that both are *equally unreal,* since both amount simply to opposite forms of reductionism. The scientist reduces the table downward to tiny little particles invisible to the eye; the humanist reduces it upward to a series of effects on people and other things. To put it bluntly, both of

---

[34] A.S. Eddington, *The Nature of the Physical World*, p. ix.
[35] C.P. Snow, *The Two Cultures*.
[36] Eddington, *The Nature of the Physical World*, p. xii.

Eddington's tables are utter shams that confuse the table with its internal and external environments, respectively. The real table is in fact a third table lying between these two others. And if Eddington's two tables provided the moral support for Snow's "two cultures" of scientists and humanists, our third table will probably require a third culture completely different from these two. This is not to say that the third culture is a completely new one: perhaps it is the culture of the *arts*, which do not seem to reduce tables either to quarks and electrons, or to table-effects on humans.

What we call the third table cannot be reduced downward to the scientific one. As Eddington describes it, "[the] scientific table is mostly emptiness. Sparsely scattered in the emptiness are numerous electric charges rushing about with great speed; but their combined bulk amounts to less than a billionth of the bulk of the table itself."[37] In this way, the familiar household table is dissolved into rushing electrical charges and other tiny elements. But while the natural sciences must be admired for having discovered all these minuscule entities, it does not follow that the everyday table can be eliminated outright and replaced by these particles. First, note the table as a whole has features that its various component particles do not have in isolation. These are often called "emergent" properties, and there need not be anything mystical about them. The point is not that the passage from quarks and electrons to tables is miraculous (quantum theory can explain such transitions fairly well) but simply that the table has an autonomous *reality* over and above its causal subcomponents, just as individual humans cannot be dissolved back into their parents. Notice that we can replace or outright remove a certain number of the table's subcomponents without destroying the table. I am inclined to agree that all entities are composite, made of smaller things rather than being simple and indivisible, but in no way does this prove that only the *smallest* things are real, though this prejudice goes back to the days of pre-Socratic philosophy. But even if every physical thing is made of atoms, every basketball game is also made of individual plays —yet objects are not just sets of atoms any more than a game is just a set of plays, or a nation just a set of individuals. The death of an Egyptian in combat on Mohamed Mahmoud Street is tragic, yet it does not mean the death of Egypt —indeed, quite the contrary.

Having defended the existence of tables against their scientific dissolution, it might be assumed that we are defending the rights of Eddington's *first* table, the one of everyday use. As he describes this everyday table, "[it]

---

[37] Eddington, *The Nature of the Physical World*, p. x.

has been familiar to me from my earliest years. It is a commonplace object of that environment that I call the world …. It has extension; it is comparatively permanent; it is coloured; it is above all *substantial*."[38] We ignore for now the word "substantial," which Eddington uses in a confusing and philosophically imprecise way. What is important for the moment is that Table Number One is identified with the table of everyday use: the one we see, the one at which we sit, the one we can pound or lovingly stroke. Yet this first table is still not the one we are seeking. Surprisingly enough, the one who tells us why is Martin Heidegger, even though he is often viewed as a champion of everyday utensils against a science that "does not think."[39]

The phenomenology of Edmund Husserl asks us to avoid all scientific theories about reality not directly seen; we are requested to shun Eddington's favored second table and simply describe what appears to consciousness. Heidegger counters that most of our dealings with things are not a matter of conscious experience at all. Blood circulates freely, and vehicles and floors function smoothly, until these malfunction and thus gain our notice.[40] Restated in terms of Eddington's example, the table I see is derivative of the table that is invisibly used as I go about my daily business. But even this formulation does not go deep enough. After all, even the table encountered in *practical use* does not exhaust the table's reality. In one moment it reliably supports paperweights and our midday meal; in the next it collapses to the ground, shattering everything. This shows that just as the table could not be identified with the one we *saw*, it was also not the same as the one we *used*. The real table is a genuine reality deeper than any theoretical or practical encounter with it. And beyond this, if rocks or other weights slam into the table, they fail to exhaust its inner depths as well. The table is something deeper than any relations in which it might become involved, whether with humans or inanimate entities. In short, Eddington's everyday Table Number One is no better than his scientific Table Number Two. Just as we cannot reduce the table downward to electric charges rushing through empty space, we also cannot reduce it upward to its theoretical, practical, or causal effects on humans or on anything else.

We have now isolated the location of the third table — the only *real* one. Eddington's First Table ruins tables by turning them into nothing but their everyday effects on us or on someone else. Eddington's Second Table ruins

---

38 Eddington, *The Nature of the Physical World*, p. ix.
39 Martin Heidegger, *What is Called Thinking?* p. 8.
40 Martin Heidegger, *Being and Time*.

tables by disintegrating them into nothing but tiny electrical charges or faint material flickerings. Yet the Third Table lies directly between these other two, neither of which is really a table. Our third table *emerges* as something distinct from its own components, and also *withdraws* behind all its external effects. Our table is an intermediate being found neither in subatomic physics nor in human psychology, but in a permanent autonomous zone where objects are simply themselves. And in my view, *this* is the genuine meaning of the word "substance," which Eddington uses too loosely to refer to Table Number One as found in human experience. In the Aristotelian tradition, the term "substance" (*ousia*) refers to the autonomous reality of individual things. Unlike in Plato, for whom there is one table-form in which countless tables "participate," for Aristotle each table is its own form: a *substantial* form, rather than a form existing only through its relation to a perceiver or some other thing. It might seem strange to wave the flag of Aristotle, since he is widely viewed as a boring, middle-aged reactionary whose medieval enforcers were overthrown in liberating revolution by Descartes and other moderns. But what is most fascinating about Aristotle's concept of substance is how much it has in common with our third table, provided Aristotle is given a properly weird interpretation. For on the one hand, Aristotle does not reduce individual things downward to tiny component pieces. And on the other, contrary to popular belief, he does not reduce substances upward to what humans can grasp of them using reason. After all, things are always individuals, but knowledge is only of universals (green, heavy, square) and universals belong to many things.[41] This entails that even for Aristotle, the reality of things lies outside the grasp of human knowledge.

By locating the third table (and to repeat, this is the only *real* table) in a space between the "table" as particles and the "table" in its effects on humans, we have apparently found a table that can be verified in no way at all, whether by science or by tangible effects in the human sphere. Yes, and that is precisely the point. Any philosophy is unworthy of the name if it attempts to convert objects into the conditions by which they can be known or verified. The term *philosophia*, possibly coined by Pythagoras, famously means not wisdom but *love* of wisdom. The real is something that cannot be known, only loved. This does not mean that access to the table is impossible, only that it must be *indirect*. Just as erotic speech works only when composed of hint, allusion, and innuendo rather than of declarative

---

[41] Aristotle, *Metaphysics,* p. 145.

statements and clearly articulated propositions, and just as jokes or magic tricks are easily ruined when each of their steps is explained, thinking is not thinking unless it realizes that its approach to objects can only be oblique. We cannot be downward scientific reducers, nor can we be upward humanistic reducers. We can only be *hunters of objects*, and must even be non-lethal hunters, since objects can never be caught. The world is filled primarily not with electrons or human praxis, but with ghostly objects withdrawing from all human and inhuman access, accessible only by allusion and seducing us by means of *allure*. Whatever we capture, whatever table we sit on or destroy, is not the real table.

But if the first and second table are both unreal, then there is a sense in which the "two cultures" of C.P. Snow are both failures. Whatever the practical successes in their own domains of scientific realism and social constructionism, they are both complete failures as philosophy. This was vividly seen two decades ago by Bruno Latour, in his famous polemic against the modern divide between nature and culture.[42] However, there is a sense in which Latour retains Eddington's first table (the everyday one), merely expanding its scope so that all electrons, cartoon characters, and real and fictional tables are placed on the same footing. The reason for this is that an object (or "actor") for Latour is to be defined only by how it transforms, modifies, perturbs, or creates some other actor.[43] In his philosophy, nothing is hidden in the depths, since everything is fully deployed in duels and negotiations with other things. By contrast, the Philosophy of the Third Table that I advocate is committed to tables that do exist at a deeper level than all possible transformations, modifications, perturbations, or creations.

I have also suggested in passing that a "third culture" corresponding to the third table might not need to be created from scratch. Nor is it sufficient (though it may be interesting) to award the "third culture" title to natural scientists who happen to brush up against philosophical problems, thereby mixing the worlds of Eddington's two tables. John Brockman reflects this prejudice when he says, in his otherwise fascinating anthology, that "the third culture consists of those scientists and other thinkers in the empirical world who, through their work and expository writing, are taking the place of the traditional intellectual in rendering visible the deeper meanings of our lives, redefining who and what we are."[44] Far from a true third culture,

---

[42] Bruno Latour, *We Have Never Been Modern*.
[43] Bruno Latour, *Pandora's Hope*, p. 122.
[44] This phrase occurs in the Table of Contents of John Brockman, ed., *The Third Culture*.

Brockman is merely calling for total victory of the second, scientific one, though in somewhat sexier and less nihilistic form. At best, the authors in his collection are trying to make Eddington's two tables communicate, not hunting the elusive Table Number 3, emerging from its components while withdrawing from all direct access. But as stated earlier, it may be artists (in all genres) who best meet this description. For on the one hand, art does not function by dissolving white whales, mansions, rafts, apples, guitars, and windmills into their subatomic underpinnings. Quite obviously, artists do not provide a theory of physical reality, and Eddington's second table is the last thing they seek. But on the other hand, they also do not seek the first table, as if the arts merely replicated the objects of everyday life or sought to create effects on us. Instead, there is the attempt to establish objects deeper than the features through which they are announced, or allude to objects that cannot quite be made present. For centuries, philosophy has aspired to the conditions of a rigorous science, allying itself at various times with mathematics or descriptive psychology. Yet what if the counter-project of the next four centuries were to turn philosophy into an art? We would have "Philosophy as Vigorous Art" rather than Husserl's "Philosophy as Rigorous Science." In being transformed from a science into an art, philosophy regains its original character as *eros*. In some ways this erotic model is the basic aspiration of object-oriented philosophy: the only way, in the present philosophical climate, to do justice to the *love* of wisdom that makes no claim to be an actual wisdom.

CHAPTER 2
UNDERMINING, OVERMINING, AND DUOMINING: A CRITIQUE[45]

The French philosopher Tristan Garcia holds that objects must be understood in two directions, according to "that which is in them" and "that in which they are."[46] We are already familiar with what Garcia is talking about. One way of understanding a thing is to determine what it is made of, such as when we discover that water is H_2O or that Finnish and Hungarian stem from the same linguistic family. Another type of understanding comes from knowing not what components a thing is made of, but what effects it has on other things. We understand something of Napoleon by knowing that he won victories at Austerlitz and Jena while suffering defeats at Leipzig and Waterloo. In fact, for all entities we seek *both* kinds of knowledge. Water is known by learning not only its chemical formula, but also the various uses to which it can be put and the various effects it has on other chemical compounds, how it behaves at freezing and boiling temperatures, or under zero-gravity conditions on spacecraft. Likewise, in Napoleon's case we not only learn about his successful and unsuccessful interactions with other historical agents, but can also learn about that of which Napoleon is made: the ancestral history of the Buonaparte family, the conditions in Corsica

---

[45] "Undermining, Overmining, and Duomining" originally appeared in 2013 in *ADD Metaphysics*, ed. Jenna Sutela, pp. 40–51.
[46] Tristan Garcia, *Form and Object*, p. 13.

and post-Revolution France that enabled his rise, and perhaps even some medical information about the specific composition of his body. We seek to know everything either by looking downward to what it came from, or upward to where it is going. For Tristan Garcia, things are the *difference* between these two poles of their reality, between that which composes them and that which they cause to happen. In my philosophy, by contrast, things are *neither* of these two extremes, but irreducible to both. The goal of this article is to explain my position briefly and draw some consequences from it.

As we have seen, it is possible to gain information about anything by determining either its constituent elements or its effects on the environmental context it inhabits. But some observers go further than this, and claim that a thing is *nothing more* than its constituent elements, or *nothing more* than its environmental situation. Both of these gestures count as reductive strategies, since they reduce the thing to something else by moving either upward, downward, or both at once. In 2009, I began to use the paired terms "undermining" and "overmining" to refer to these two reductive strategies.[47] Let's recall briefly how they function.

Undermining in philosophy begins with the pre-Socratic thinkers. Naïve common sense believes it is surrounded by macroscopic entities such as tables, chairs, pottery, and ships. The pre-Socratic philosophers, who also count as the first natural scientists in the West, tried to show that these macroscopic objects are built of something more basic. One type of pre-Socratic thinker tries to find the privileged physical element or elements to which all else can be reduced. Thales of Miletus launched this tradition in roughly 600 B.C.E., by saying that water is the first principle of everything, perhaps thinking of the vastness of the oceans and the dependence of all life on moisture. He was followed by Anaximenes, who countered that colorless, odorless air is a better choice for the root stuff of reality. Some of the fragments of Heraclitus suggest that he granted a similar role to fire. Empedocles, sensing difficulty in allowing any one element to serve as the basis of the world, developed a more intricate system that we now know as the four traditional Greek elements: air, earth, fire, and water, joined by love and separated by hate. An even more modern theory can be found in the later atomistic philosophy of Leucippus and Democritus, in which atoms of different sizes move through an empty void. For all these theories, macroscopic objects have no autonomous reality but can be boiled down to some privileged, simple, eternal element from which they are made.

---

[47] Graham Harman, "On the Undermining of Objects."

In parallel with this tradition, there was always a second pre-Socratic trend at work, that of the so-called *apeiron*. According to this view, since the world consists of numerous opposite qualities — cold and hot, wet and dry, justice and injustice — the ultimate reality must be something less determinate than any of them. They all must emerge from something boundless and indefinite, a sort of blob-like indeterminacy from which anything specific would arise as a derivative product. This tradition began not long after Thales, in the thinking of Anaximander. For Anaximander, the existence of opposite qualities counts as a kind of "injustice" that will be healed by time, as everything collapses into the indefinite *apeiron* (there seems to be a clear influence here on Karl Marx, who did his doctoral work on these early Greek thinkers). In short, the *apeiron* does not exist now, but will exist in some distant *future*. A different tack is taken by Parmenides, who speaks of "being" rather than the *apeiron*, but means roughly the same thing by it: something that is one, real, and indeterminate as to specific qualities. For Parmenides, it exists in the *present* rather than the future; we are simply deceived by the senses into thinking otherwise. That leaves the final option that the *apeiron* exists not in the future or present but in the *past*, and two philosophers did choose this option. For the mysterious Pythagoras, there was once an *apeiron* but it inhaled the void, and as a result broke into numerous separate pieces. For Anaxagoras the *apeiron* was shattered into pieces after being rotated rapidly through the thinking of a powerful *Nous*, or mind. Here once more, we have a theory which holds that individual objects exist only in derivative fashion when compared with some deeper, primordial thing. Both kinds of pre-Socratics (the "element" kind and the "*apeiron*"kind) undermine objects by claiming that they are too shallow to be real.

But reduction is also possible in the opposite direction. Instead of saying that objects are too shallow to be real, it might also be said that they are too deep to be real. This approach became more common in the modern era, and might be called "overmining," to coin a new term. One such case would be outright idealism, which holds that there is nothing hiding beneath whatever appears to the mind. We also find overmining in the various philosophies of social constructionism, for which there is no independent reality outside the system of language, discourse, or power. Philosophies which hold that there are only events, not objects, also adopt an overmining strategy. So too does a philosophy such as that of Whitehead, which claims that the reality of things is exhausted by their relations with other things.[48]

---

[48]   Alfred North Whitehead, *Process and Reality*.

We should note that the view that reality is exhaustively mathematizable is also an overmining position, since objects are thereby made interchangeable with what can be known about them. A daring attempt in this direction was made recently by Quentin Meillassoux.[49]

But what is perhaps most interesting about the undermining and overmining positions is that they rarely occur in isolation, as if both realized that they needed the hidden support of the other. Let's borrow the recent computer science term "duomining" to refer to this simultaneous twofold employment of overmining and undermining.[50] The first instance of duomining in the history of philosophy may be that of Pythagoras, who on the one hand views the world as having originated in an *apeiron* destroyed by inhaling (undermining), but on the other is the textbook case of a philosopher who treats the world as consisting of its mathematizability (overmining). An even better example might be Parmenides, who undermines objects by calling them less real than unified, motionless being and overmines them by identifying individual things with the delusions of sense and opinion. The whole of modern science is a duomining project, since it aims both to reduce objects downward to the most basic tiny constituents *and* to claim that these things are, in principle, knowable through mathematization. Meillassoux's is a classic duomining position, since he holds that the primary qualities of things are those which can be mathematized *and* denies that he is a Pythagorean, insisting that numbers do not exhaust the world but simply point to some sort of "dead matter" whose exact metaphysical status is never clarified. And even Garcia, whose position is otherwise close to my own, duomines objects by dissolving them simultaneously in two directions.

Now, it might be asked what is wrong with undermining and overmining in the first place, given that both techniques are so useful. My response is that usefulness and reality are not the same thing, and that useful intellectual methods are generally those that adopt a powerful exaggeration as their primary tool.[51] The problem with undermining is that it fails to account for emergence. The fact that my body is made of atoms, and that I presumably could not exist if those atoms were suddenly vaporized, does not entail that I am nothing over and above those atoms. The proof of this is that

---

[49] Quentin Meillassoux, *After Finitude*.

[50] The industrial use of the term refers to the simultaneous use of data mining and text mining, but I take the liberty of reshaping it for philosophical use. On the industrial use of the term see Aditi Chawla & Deepty Sachdeva, "Impact of Duomining in Knowledge Discovery Process."

[51] In the original version of this article, "truth" occurred here in place of "reality." I have changed it for the sake of consistency with my later terminology — G.H.

not all changes in these atoms would lead to changes in me; various atoms could be moved, replaced, or destroyed though I would still remain who I am. Meanwhile, what is wrong with overmining is that it cannot explain change. If there is nothing but appearance, relation, event, or interaction with nothing lying beneath, then there is no reason why anything could possibly alter. The reality of the world would be exhaustively deployed in its current state, with no hidden surplus or reserve that might surge forth and generate novelty. What is wrong with duomining is that it combines the weaknesses rather then the strengths of both positions.

A table is not the pieces of which it is made, nor the effects it has on users. Neither is it the difference between these two extremes. Instead, it is that which is *cut off* from total dependence in either direction. The table can withstand numerous changes in its pieces and countless movements in three-dimensional space without becoming something other than itself. If what we call "knowledge" is an attempt to reduce the table either downward or upward, then we can get at the table only through something that is not a form of knowledge. Earlier this year I suggested that *art* has a special capacity for dealing with the "third table" lying between the first table (table-particles) and second table (table-events).[52] But this is also the founding insight of philosophy, as *philo-sophia*, or love of wisdom rather than wisdom itself. We cannot know the world directly, whether through undermining, overmining, or duomining, but must approach it obliquely in the manner of Socrates or Picasso.

Experimental School Assignment to go with Graham Harman, "Undermining, Overmining, and Duomining: A Critique"

The purpose of the assignment is to reinforce the sense that objects are independent both of their constituent pieces and their effects on other things.

1 The independent reality of a thing is appreciated if we imagine it inhabiting other situations or having other effects than it currently does. These are known as "counterfactuals."

---

[52] Graham Harman, "The Third Table."

2. The independent reality of a thing is also appreciated if we imagine that it were composed of different elements. Coining a new term, we can call these "countercompositionals."

The assignment is to explore both counterfactuals and countercompositionals for any given object, in order to better appreciate the autonomous reality of those objects.

STEP 1: Each student is given a slip of paper and writes the name of an object, which can be a person, an animal, a thing, a fictional character, a corporation — indeed, anything at all. The slips of paper are then put into a container.

STEP 2: Each student draws one of the slips of paper, and must work with the object mentioned on it.

STEP 3: The student should determine the counterfactuals for this object. Start by asking: "In what situation do we usually find this object?" Then, the student should imagine other possible situations for the object, starting simply and working towards more and more imaginative scenarios. What surprises result from this exercise? Is this object capable of things that we never realized? How would the world need to change in order for this object to become either extremely important or extremely unimportant?

STEP 4: The student should now determine the countercompositionals for the object. How could we rebuild this object using different materials or components? What is the greatest number of changes we could make while still having the object remain roughly the same thing? What is the smallest change we could make that would destroy the object or turn it into something else altogether?

STEP 5: Students should now discuss all of their results together. Are any of the results especially funny? Especially surprising? Especially frightening?

CHAPTER 3
THE FERRIS WHEEL[53]

Imagine a gigantic Ferris wheel of many miles in diameter. The wheel would be lodged in a massive trench in the earth, with the hub at ground level. At all times, half of the wheel would be above ground and half beneath the surface. Over the course of twelve or fourteen hours, the wheel would make a complete circuit high in the air and deep beneath the soil. It would carry thousands of separate cars, each of them loaded with various objects. Some would contain printed documents, or zinc and molybdenum Buddhas. Others would be loaded with colorful flags, electric generators, reptiles and birds, miniature explosive charges, bottles of wine, tap dancers, brass bands playing military music, and other entities circling day and night. We will suppose that the wheel itself is made of an unspecified indestructible material not affected by anything that happens in the myth.

The reader should pause for several moments and fix this image firmly in mind: a giant rotating wheel, carrying thousands of beings in a long arc ascending to the clouds and vanishing into the darkness of the earth. Let it spin dozens of times in your mind before we move on from this beautiful spectacle. Imagine the faint machinic whirr of its concealed engine, the creaking of its bolts, and the varied sounds emitted by the objects riding in its cars: from neighing horses to mournful woodwind ensembles. Imagine too the ominous mood in the vicinity as its cars plunge deep into the earth. Picture the wheel loaded with animals, bombs, and religious icons. Picture it creaking under the weight of its cargo and emitting a ghostly light as it spins along its colossal circuit. Imagine the artists and engineers of genius

---

[53] From Graham Harman, *Circus Philosophicus*, pp. 1–12.

who designed such a thing. And consider the human culture that would arise nearby, with the wheel as its sacred point of reference.

• • •

We now add a few new elements to the myth of the Ferris wheel, burning the image ever more deeply into the reader's mind. Above ground, thousands of people would live in the vicinity of the wheel: some applauding it, others terrified by the sight, with a few insensitive souls bored by the wheel as by a commonplace. Some of the residents would observe its rotations minutely through binoculars, while others would go about their business with no more than occasional glances at the machine. A number of dogs would bark angrily at the wheel, and crows or eagles would sometimes approach for a closer look.

We might stipulate further that numerous chambers have been constructed along the underground path of the wheel. Every ten feet its cars would pass by one of these dimly lit spaces. Some of the underground rooms are filled with people, while others house devices of various sorts. It should be clear that the objects inhabiting each of these rooms will react with especial intensity only to *some* of the entities riding in the wheel. For instance, one of the rooms would be occupied by the members of a secret society or labor union. They have assembled perhaps for a celebration, but are under strict orders to wait calmly and quietly until the special flag of their group passes by. When at last it does, they cheer wildly and erupt into violent revelry. There are poets writing verse in some of the rooms, their moods affected deeply by all passing objects, but especially by the various musical ensembles that circle past. As they hear the music passing their chambers, the character of their poems is altered by the style of what they hear.

A few more examples will clarify the upheavals brought about by the rotation of the wheel. Some of the rooms contain rabid dogs that bark at all passing objects, but especially at the cats and foxes that sometimes circle past, pushing the dogs toward a state of frenzy. Another room is a holding cell for a condemned prisoner, who endures additional torment as portraits of deceased family members pass. Let's suppose as well that one of these underground chambers contains the main power generator for the town above. From time to time a huge electromagnetic coil circles in one of the cars past this room, disrupting the town's energy supply for several minutes, though the wheel continues to circle through an alternate source of power whose nature need not concern us. Whenever this disruption occurs, the observers milling in the streets begin to curse and lament, forgetting the wheel altogether until energy is restored and life returns to what it was.

With the exception of the eternal wheel itself, each of the entities in this myth faces a certain degree of danger. After all, some of the cars contain explosive devices; no one knows when they might detonate, or how powerfully. If these explode while transiting underground, the chambers closest to them will be annihilated without hope of survivors. If the bombs explode while circling in the air, then so much the worse: for in this case they rain lethal debris over the entire town. Yet the danger also works in reverse, with some of the underground rooms posing a threat to the objects riding the wheel. For instance, a number of the subterranean rooms might be equipped with dormant furnaces. Most of the time these will be inactive. But at sporadic intervals and random temperatures, jets of flame suddenly erupt from the room toward the car that is passing by, spraying fire on whatever entity it contains. Occasionally the flames are hot enough to melt even the metallic images of the Buddha loaded in some of the cars.

Finally, it is clear that the rotating objects will have a profound effect on the crowd in the streets, harming or pleasing them on various occasions. The higher the objects move toward the summit of the wheel, the less visible they are to the townspeople. But when they first emerge from the earth, and again when descending to a point near the ground, they are recognized even by children. Indeed, children would surely assemble near the entry and exit points of the wheel, delighted by the sudden emergence or disappearance of surprising things. Each of the objects riding the wheel has a potentially serious impact upon local morale. Some strike the townspeople as comical, provoking sarcastic remarks. Others are melancholy reminders of human frailty: a lonely skull, or the portrait of a reviled former statesman. At such moments the mood in the streets veers toward the tense and the somber. But some of the objects strike different people in different ways, as when a whining kitten circles past, provoking mockery in some and empathy in others. There will also be moments when heavy explosives circle past: these are frightening times for even the most hardened cynics in the town. Some of the cars might even contain loudspeakers emitting religious or political messages. A few observers take these messages seriously and plan conversion or revolution, while others dismiss them with a wave of the hand.

This image of a revolving wheel is a picture of our world. In it, the dramatic interplay of object and network becomes visible. Countless entities circle into and out of our lives, some of them threatening and others ludicrous.

The objects in the cars and those on the ground or in the chambers affect one another, coupling and uncoupling from countless relations — seducing, ignoring, ruining, or liberating each other. This process is anything but a game: in it, our happiness and even physical safety are at stake. It would be easy to follow tradition and speak of a Wheel of Fortune. But in keeping with the metaphysical nature of this book, it is better to call it the Wheel of Events, the Wheel of Contexts, or the Wheel of Relations. As the Ferris wheel circles, new and surprising events are summoned into existence. Bombs detonate; solid Buddhas are liquefied; lackluster crowds become howling mobs; depressive writers are inspired by music; power outages are caused by disruptive magnetic fields. By affecting one another in this way, the interacting things generate new realities, each just as real as the basic elements circling in the wheel.

Let's develop an example already mentioned, and say that one of the underground chambers houses a union of steelworkers. As they await the appearance of their familiar gray flag with its black crescents and diamonds, the workers and the flag are two utterly separate realities. But once the banner moves into view, the room erupts in raucous celebration. Now, we cannot agree with the classical theory which holds that the piece of cloth is a substance and each of the workers also a substance, but the celebration itself just an accidental intersection of two entities. No, the celebration is not a mere aggregate, for it is every bit as real as the physical piece of cloth or the human workers themselves. We admit that the celebration is unlikely to last for more than a few hours, while the flag and the workers may endure for decades to come. But this familiar criterion of durability is irrelevant to the *metaphysical* question of what can be regarded as a substance. For as everyone who has taken part in especially intense gatherings knows, a celebration is a force to be reckoned with: a new entity to be taken into account by all other things. The workers may find themselves carried away by the mood of the party — a mood that exists somewhere beyond each of the individuals, as a reservoir of surplus energy. Riot police may be summoned should the atmosphere deteriorate, and the celebration might resist police efforts to control it. Even the union flag that triggered the party will be affected by the celebration-entity of which it is a key component. For it may gain historic value from being the very flag that triggered this particular riot; it could become outlawed, and thereby attain wide popularity as a symbol of resistance. In addition, the flag can be physically altered by the smoky fumes or spray of champagne that the party unleashes. In short, the party seems to have all the features of a genuine entity. We cannot use physical duration as a standard of what is real and what is accidental. Chemists are aware of this fact, and feel no shame in using the same periodic table both for the artificial heavy elements that last for fractions of a second *and* for the hydrogen and helium that have endured since nearly the dawn of time. The difference between substance and accident is not decided by stopwatch or calendar. If we provisionally accept that reality equals resistance (an idea I will shortly reject for other reasons), then the steelworkers' celebration is very much a substantial reality, as any riot officer will testify.

Nor does the myth of the wheel require the presence of human beings or other sentient organisms. One can easily imagine a toxic spill in the area. The town and the underground chambers would be evacuated, and all living creatures removed from the wheel until the situation is clarified. As a precaution, it now circles with only inanimate objects riding aboard. Now let us suppose that one of the cars contains a barrel of seashells, and one of the underground chambers is a jet that sprays acid at random intervals. If the acid is sprayed just as the shells circle past, there will be a reaction between them resulting in a very different set of substances. Here again, one cannot say that acid and shells are real and their conjunction only an accident. The example can be pushed further by imagining that some of the cars contain subatomic particles, and that several underground rooms are able to split these tiny things by channeling powerful beams into their midst, even though no one is watching.

For those who feel distracted by such bizarre examples, more prosaic scenarios are possible. We can assume that the entire complex of underground chambers has been shut down, all of them decommissioned and filled with cement. This having been done, the objects riding the wheel have nothing to hope for and nothing to fear when underground. They do nothing but circle, orbiting forever down into the earth and up into the sky. But even here there is a sense in which the objects change. If nothing else, they will tend to become cold at the top of the wheel as they approach the jet stream, but hot and moist at the bottom as they descend through the dank underground channel. Moreover, their relations with everything found in the outer landscape will change continually, depending on how high or low they are at any moment. For these changes are real, and describe vastly different events. A zinc Buddha at the top of the wheel is involved in a different set of relations from the same Buddha at the bottom. The fact that these statues never remain in one place for long does not mean that their specific position at any moment is of less importance than the timeless metal of which they are forged.

This concludes part one of the myth of the wheel. So far, I have used this image to *defend* the model of reality presented by such figures as Alred North Whitehead and Bruno Latour, for whom the interrelation of things is so pervasive that they discount the very existence of individual entities outside their relational effects. There is surely some truth in this outlook, since it is difficult to think of an object apart from the varied relations in which it participates. The labor union, the seashells, and the magnetic coils are so thoroughly defined by the incidents in which they take part that their reality might seem identical with the *events* to which the wheel gives rise. The objects riding in the wheel seem no better than pawns of their interactions with other things. Some might call it naïve to think of some Buddha-in-itself or electrical coil *an sich* apart from the events in which these objects are involved. In this way the myth suggests that there is no such thing as an "accident" as opposed to substance, and also no such thing as mere "relations" that would be less real than the component parts of which they are built. The various flags, machines, cats, and foxes in the myth would not be substances undergoing accidental interplay with other objects. They would only be concrete events, deployed in specific relations with all other things.

Nonetheless, the myth also shows the limitations of this philosophy of relations or events. It is certainly true that all of the human and inhuman objects in the myth — those that ride the wheel, live in the underground chambers, or mill around in the streets — are closely linked with the wider series of events in which they are involved. Even so, none of the objects are reducible to the events in which they participate. This becomes clear if we add some additional twists to the story. Along with the banner of the steelworkers' union, we can stipulate that the wheel carries an additional flag — say, a purple lozenge on a field of amber. Once upon a time, this flag would have triggered additional celebration by the union of arrowsmiths. Yet this guild was disbanded long before the wheel was constructed, and therefore never arrived in the underground room reserved for its festival. If the union still existed, the flag would have triggered a memorable event, but this is now destined never to occur. As things stand, the flag is recognized by no one. It is left to circle as a mere piece of fabric or an aesthetic curiosity, with no one aware of its depth of symbolic resonance. Since the flag with the purple lozenge never triggers celebration, some might try to reduce it to its current status amidst the network of things: the state of being viewed with indifference. Yet there is a certain reality possessed by this flag, no matter how cruelly ignored, and someday a new throwback union may arise to adopt it as an emblem once more.

Let's simplify the example somewhat, so that only a handful of objects remain in the cars: a plastic cup, a gyroscope, an aircraft engine, and a chunk of plutonium. Now, let's evacuate the underground chambers and fill them with new entities never previously there. What do we learn from such variation? First of all, any living creature in the chambers will be exterminated by the plutonium. But elsewhere, different dramas unfold. There may be an object in one of the chambers that causes the gyroscope to move differently from before. So too, the aircraft engine may be affected in unique ways by some of the entities that have been placed in the various rooms. A few turns of the wheel, and we become bored with these permutations. So let's empty the rooms once more and fill them with hundreds of new objects. Here once more, we generate a world of new relations that have never previously walked the earth. And no matter how often we are sated with the multitude of combinations between the wheel and the chambers, the supply of novelties is limitless. For as long as there are unlimited funds at our command (and this we suppose as a condition of the myth), there is a limitless number of entities that can be placed in the emptied chambers and the vacant cars of the wheel.

It must be said that there is something to the plutonium, the plastic cup, and the gyroscope that is never exhausted by the various events that occur. New pairings of these objects with other things can always be dreamed up or even put into effect. And this is where most philosophers would invoke a traditional concept that can only be regarded as misleading: potentiality. For as soon as the specter of potential is raised, the key point has been evaded. It will be said that the various new events involving the plutonium, the plastic cup, and the gyroscope tell us nothing new about the actuality of these objects. Instead, these events only make clear that every object has the *potential* to affect other things in certain ways. On this point the classical and twentieth-century theories are in reciprocal agreement. Namely, the classical models invoke potentiality *in order to shut relations out of substance*, since if a single hammer has the potential to build a church, a weapon, or a coffin, it might seem possible to forgive its accidental entanglements in any of these activities while maintaining its private integrity. Conversely, the twentieth-century theories invoke potentiality *in order to shut substance out of relations*, since if the hammer is defined by its totality of relations, to speak of its unactualized future states as "potentials" frees us from having to determine where these potentials are located, thereby denying any actuality outside of explicit current relations.

Both the classical and recent theories appeal to "potential" as a disingenuous way of equating the actual with the relational. For if we only say that plutonium has the *potential* to kill whatever creatures enter the underground room, we have betrayed our obligation to decide in what the *actuality* of the plutonium consists. To define a thing as potential is to view it solely from the outside, in terms of the effects it might one day have on other things, and this avoids the very question under dispute. For let us now establish a variation on the myth in which no living creatures are in the underground chambers at all, so that the plutonium only circles past metallic, wooden, and cotton items. Here the lethal character of the plutonium is never triggered, yet this deadliness remains a part of its actuality. The plutonium's act of killing will surely exist only in relation to a living thing, but this misses the point. For I speak here not of the killing (which is obviously a relation) but of that lethal portion of the plutonium's reality that is never manifest in cases where nothing is killed. Even the most ardent philosopher of networks would not deny that there is more to the plutonium than is expressed in any given instant. One will concede that the plutonium has an actuality apart from its relations. Yet there is also a disappointing habit of assuming that this extra portion of reality is simply a material substratum supporting many properties not currently expressed. It will be thought that the real action lies on the side of *perception*, of our tortuous and subtle human awareness, which finds ways to add spice to bland slabs of objective material stuff. The high ground of philosophy is given over to a dogmatic brand of materialism, even by those who claim to despise material reality. Against this, I hold that it remains a mystery where and what the actuality of the plutonium really is. It cannot be defined by its current relations, because the reality of the plutonium is precisely what exceeds those relations. What needs to be discovered is an actuality different from all events, but one that belongs to armies, flocks of geese, and Hindu epics no less than to atoms.

And this is the possibly misleading point in our myth. As the various passenger objects rise and fall with the motion of the wheel, they trigger a multitude of events. This seems to lead to a twofold ontology in which we have solid physical entities riding in the cars and immaterial events that are triggered by the various interactions. But this is inadequate. For in a sense even the physical objects riding the cars of the wheel are themselves events, since each involves a special configuration of various subcomponents.

In order to do justice to the ontology of the world, we must not think of the cats, foxes, or bombs riding the wheel as simple unified lumps. Instead, we must imagine that each of these entities is itself produced by a smaller Ferris wheel riding in each car, to represent the interaction of the components of any cat, fox, or bomb. And all these pieces should be imagined in turn as products of still smaller wheels, these by even tinier wheels, the tiny wheels by minuscule ones, minuscule wheels by micro-wheels, and so on to infinity. Nor does the movement occur only in a downward direction. To complete the myth, we also need to imagine each of the events triggered by our Ferris wheel as loaded into a larger wheel in turn, spinning through a different landscape from its components. For instance, the celebration of the steelworkers is a potential ingredient in further events, no less than are the flag and workers themselves. As for the crowds milling around in the street, each of them might be considered as made of an interlocking and infinitely regressing series of Ferris wheels, stretching to the depths of hell and beyond. No point in reality is merely a solid thing, and no point is an ultimate concrete event unable to act as a component in further events. In this respect, the cosmos might be described as a vast series of interlocking Ferris wheels. Let these trillions of wheels spin in your mind. Let them sink into your heart and enliven your mood. And savor these countless wheels before moving on to the myths still to come.

CHAPTER 4

THE ONLY EXIT FROM MODERN PHILOSOPHY[54]

1. Against Onto-Taxonomy

Two of the most interesting philosophers at work today live just a mile apart on the Left Bank in Paris, though separated in age by twenty years: Bruno Latour (b. 1947) and Quentin Meillassoux (b. 1967). In some ways they have very little in common. A Venn diagram of their respective readerships would show minuscule intersection, mostly covering a small circle of authors working on object-oriented ontology (OOO). Latour and Meillassoux are not even especially interested in each other's work, although they did share some kind words after a salon for Meillassoux held at Latour's Latin Quarter flat in 2006.[55] Meillassoux is an unapologetic rationalist from the school of Alain Badiou, one who takes René Descartes as our model for forward progress; Latour is a vehement non-modernist whom many rationalists dismiss as seeing no difference in kind between particle physics and witchcraft.[56] Nonetheless, the two are united in their view that Immanuel

---

[54] "The Only Exit from Modern Philosophy" originally appeared in 2020 in the journal *Open Philosophy*.
[55] Latour's initial enthusiastic remarks about Meillassoux can be found in Graham Harman, *Quentin Meillassoux*, p. 2. Two years later, he provided a largely positive back jacket endorsement for Meillassoux's debut book *After Finitude*. Meillassoux also spoke kind words about Latour to me in person, though a sample of his mostly critical attitude in print can be found in the transcript of the 2007 Speculative Realism workshop at Goldsmiths in Ray Brassier et al., "Speculative Realism," p. 423.
[56] The originally published version of this sentence had "anti-modernist" in place of "non-modernist." That was an infelicitous choice on my part, since Latour distances himself completely

Kant is still the most dangerous influence on contemporary philosophy.[57] In *After Finitude*, Meillassoux explicitly charges Kant's so-called Copernican Revolution with being a "Ptolemaic Counter-Revolution"; Latour had said much the same thing a generation earlier in *We Have Never Been Modern*.[58] Given that Kant still provides the basic background assumptions for most present-day philosophy — whether of an analytic or continental stripe — this point alone is already worthy of interest. What is even more interesting is that the two philosophers reject Kant for opposite reasons:

1 For Meillassoux, Kant collapses the independence of thought and world into a *correlation* when they really ought to be kept separate from each other. Meillassoux implements such a separation with his concepts of "ancestrality" and "diachronicity," which refer to the existence of the world prior to the existence of conscious life and after its possible disappearance. He pushes it further with his view that mathematics is able to index the primary qualities of things outside their presence to thought. The problem with Kant — and already with David Hume — was that he left us with no possibility of thinking the separation of thought and world, thereby leading us inexorably into "correlationism," the dominant philosopheme of our time.[59]

2 In Latour's eyes, Kant has precisely the opposite problem: namely, he tries to *purify* thought and world from each other. Far from being a problem with Kant alone, Latour sees this attempted but impossible purification as the essence of modernity in all its forms. His solution, in *We Have Never Been Modern*, is to argue for just how difficult it is to separate nature from culture. Just consider such examples as the ozone hole, whales fitted with tracking devices, or a garbage dump that becomes an ecological preserve. Latour calls such entities "hybrids," and they are impossible to clarify by way of the modern concepts of nature and culture. In fact, Latour is often inclined to treat *every* entity as a hybrid. If it is true that Kant tries to separate thought from world, then the hybrid flouts the Kantian paradigm insofar as it is always made up of *both* poles: nature and culture at the same time.

---

from the term "anti-modernist." As he discusses in detail in *We Have Never Been Modern*, he reserves the designation "anti-modernist" for outright reactionaries.

57 Immanuel Kant, *Critique of Pure Reason*. See also Maurizio Ferraris, *Goodbye, Kant!*

58 Meillassoux, *After Finitude*; Bruno Latour, *We Have Never Been Modern*.

59 Meillassoux's extension of correlationism from Kant back in time to Hume can be found in the published version of his 2012 Berlin lecture "Iteration, Reiteration, Repetition," p. 91, n. 18.

I regard Latour's position to be superior due to his recognition that modern onto-taxonomy is a problem, whereas Meillassoux prefers to celebrate and even extend it. Nonetheless, Latour's solution to the nature/culture divide — namely, asserting that both terms are everywhere united — still affirms onto-taxonomy at the very moment it could have escaped. It is also noteworthy that Meillassoux and Latour follow typical early modern and late modern approaches, respectively. In early modernity, running from Descartes through Kant, everyone was concerned with *gaps* in the cosmos: gaps between mind and body, God and both mind and body, or phenomena and noumena. By insisting on a separation between thought and world, one that can supposedly be bridged by mathematical reason, Meillassoux takes the side of early modernity on this question. This will come as little surprise in view of his ultimately Cartesian inclinations. But from German Idealism onward the terrain shifted, and the worry about gaps in the world came to be seen as a naïve pseudo-problem. We see this not only in Hegel's collapse of the phenomenal/noumenal distinction into an immanent space of dialectical reason, but also in Husserl's and Heidegger's respective ways of claiming that we are "always already outside" in the world, and in the pragmatist notion that we should not artificially separate the two great poles of mind and world. This is the late modern position where Latour feels fully at home.

Stated differently, the fundamental problem with the modern taxonomy has been obscured by a side-debate over two possible kinds of response to it. Namely, it becomes a war over whether there are gaps in the world or whether these are merely illusions or "false problems." Yet in a sense this is just what Louis Althusser would call "ideology," in which a false or secondary problem serves to conceal a real one.[60] For instance, Marxists like to give the example of how American liberals obsess over racism and sexism precisely in order to avoid a purportedly more radical issue in which liberals themselves are heavily implicated: the class struggle. Whatever one thinks of this particular example, it is easy to see how the general mechanism might work in which a side problem is used to distract us from a more central one. In the present case, everything comes down to an outright rejection of onto-taxonomy, which cannot be accomplished either by avoiding correlationism or embracing hybrids. The rejection of onto-taxonomy is the only exit from modern philosophy. If we avoid this taxonomy, we escape; if

---

60 Louis Althusser, "Ideology and Ideological State Apparatuses."

we retain it, we remain stranded in an increasingly exhausted modernism.[61] If we continue to assume that thought and world are the two basic poles around which reality turns, it does not matter much whether we try to separate or combine them. Furthermore, if we claim that the problem is simply that the human side has been overemphasized and that we must now "meet the universe halfway," as in the title of Karen Barad's influential book, then we are still accepting the two terms of the modern settlement.[62] For it is philosophically fruitless to encourage two things meet halfway if they are not actually the two basic pillars of the cosmos. Notice that no one is asking reptiles and dust to "meet halfway," and the same holds for music and toothpaste.

Another important consequence of onto-taxonomy is the way it gives rise to the modern division of labor. One of the strictures implemented by Kantian philosophy is that we cannot discuss object-object interactions at all, except insofar as they are framed by the transcendental structure of human experience. That is to say, from the Kantian standpoint we are forbidden to discuss the collision of two rocks in empty space, but can only describe how this collision presents itself *to us* according to time, space, and the twelve categories of the understanding. The sciences alone are permitted to discuss interactions between inanimate things, while philosophy (like its kindred disciplines) is left to meditate on the human-world relation alone. Occasionally an effort is made to reduce all of reality to one side or the other: turning science into a merely social phenomenon, or — moving in the other direction — attempting to reduce all the "soft" disciplines either to neuroscience or subatomic physics. On the whole, however, there is general satisfaction with the aforementioned division of labor.

Now, what is most unusual is that today's Neo-Rationalist philosophers try to leverage two separate forces that flow from different springs; Meillassoux is probably the most interesting thinker of this sort. For in a first sense, he lays claim to the unsurpassable rigor of post-transcendental philosophy. To think a thing outside thought is itself already a thought, which leads to a performative contradiction; therefore, philosophical reflection must begin, at least, from within the closed circle of thought.[63] In its most rigorous form, Husserl's phenomenology, this vision of the

---

[61] See Graham Harman, "What the End of Modern Philosophy Would Look Like."

[62] Karen Barad, *Meeting the Universe Halfway*. For a fuller critique of Barad's interesting position see Graham Harman, "Agential and Speculative Realism."

[63] See Quentin Meillassoux, "Presentation by Quentin Meillassoux," in Brassier et al., "Speculative Realism."

nonsensical unthinkability of that which lies beyond thought leads science into a subordinate role: after all, no findings of the hard sciences can ever reach the supreme self-transparency of phenomenological reflection. But contemporary Neo-Rationalism will have none of this, since it badly wants to link itself with the unbroken cognitive success of the hard sciences. True enough, the most rigorous philosophy would be the sort that is grounded in the immediate self-evidence of its logical truths, but since *a priori* logical analysis is not the way that science attains its achievements, one commits to two separate principles that are fundamentally different in kind: (1) the inescapability of the circle of thought, (2) the mighty greatness of science.[64] But a third principle soon appears. For these same Neo-Rationalists also wish to associate themselves with the evident urgency of revolutionary politics. But this sort of politics — like every other — can be deduced neither from the *a priori* conditions of the circle of thought nor from scientific discovery. Instead, it arises only from the *moral* postulate of human equality. As admirable as this may sound, it cannot be derived from the same sources as either logical rigor or scientific success, which means that Neo-Rationalism now stumbles awkwardly on three separate legs, each moving at its own pace. Yet the situation soon becomes even more complicated. For if a flat ontologist argues that there is no *logical* reason why human cognition should be radically different in kind from the animal sort, and that *science* points instead toward a continuity of human and animal and perhaps even vegetable minds, and that *morality* suggests kindness toward animals no less than toward people, the Neo-Rationalist comes up with a fourth separate principle: common sense. After all, humans are obviously different in certain ways from lizards or even dolphins, and if we open up the term "thought" to include animals, then there is no stop on the slippery slope until we end up with the ridiculous idea that cotton, fire, and dust can think as well.

In this way, we see that the apparently crushing rigor of Neo-Rationalist philosophy is fully willing to give up rigor in favor of other virtues whenever the situation requires it. It brackets everyday scientific feasibility in favor of the impeccable logic of its first principles. Yet it strays beyond the circle of thought whenever necessary to borrow some of the glory of physics, neuroscience, or evolutionary biology, none of them derivable from *a priori* principles of cognition. As soon as it finds this combination of rigor and

---

[64] Traces of this fusion can be found both in Meillassoux, "Iteration, Reiteration, Repetition" and Ray Brassier, *Nihil Unbound*.

success too limiting, it claims moral superiority in postulating a human equality that can by no means be justified by way of transcendental logic or scientific discovery. Finally, once logic, science, and morality suggest that animals are no less important than humans, it appeals to our commonsensical feeling of separation from the animal kingdom as a whole. It was Latour who first discovered this hypocritical dimension of every form of modernism, which consists of feigned strengths that are really just a "tiered array of weaknesses."[65] For in what did the victory of the *Conquistadores* consist?

> They arrived *separately, each in his place and each with his purity*, like
> another plague on Egypt. The priests spoke only of the Bible, and
> to this and this alone they attributed the success of their mission.
> The administrators, with their rules and regulations, attributed
> their success to their country's civilizing mission. The geographers
> spoke only of science and its advance. The merchants attributed
> all the virtues of their art to gold, to trade, and to the London
> Stock Exchange. The soldiers simply obeyed orders and interpreted
> everything they did in terms of the fatherland. The engineers
> attributed the efficacy of their machines to progress.[66]

Latour adds that "they each believed themselves to be strong *because of their purity* …. Even so — and they knew this well — it was only because of each other that they were able to stay on the island at all."[67] And so it is with the Neo-Rationalist philosophers, who hope we will never notice that they move the shell with the ball through four different positions: logical certitude, scientific success, moral superiority, and good old common sense.

But let's focus here on the appeal to certitude, the chief philosophical support for onto-taxonomy. As we saw, this taxonomy splits the world into two and only two basic kinds of things: (1) human thought, and (2) everything else. Taken in isolation this claim would be absurd, given the distinctly puny import of our species amidst the vast universe as a whole. But of course, modern philosophy has been built by some prodigious minds, none of them parochial enough to grant humans half of philosophy simply because we happen to be humans; obviously, they will have a stronger case than this. That case can be found initially in Descartes's *Meditations on First*

---

[65] Bruno Latour, "Irreductions," p. 201.
[66] Latour, "Irreductions," p. 202.
[67] Latour, "Irreductions," p. 202.

Philosophy, in which the method of radical doubt shows that everything can be doubted other than the existence of thought itself: *cogito, ergo sum*.[68] In other words, the central case for onto-taxonomy is not that we are humans and therefore humans must be important, but that human thought is directly present and certain in a way that nothing else is. This is why onto-taxonomy places humans alone on one side of the cosmos and all the trillions of other kinds of entities on the other: for only the first side is directly accessible, while the rest is not.

To what extent is this true? In one sense, I would have to agree that some things are immediately accessible while others can only be accessed in mediated fashion: object-oriented ontology (OOO) already affirms a similar distinction between the sensual and the real, and this overlaps with the distinction between the immediately available and that which is only given in mediated form.[69] Yes indeed. But a problem arises from the further step of identifying the immediate with *my thinking* and the mediated with everything else. For the thought that thinks and the thought it thinks about are not one and the same, and therefore human thought has no privileged immediacy over anything else.[70] Whatever I think about, including myself, is given only in mediated fashion. Note that the finitude of human thought is not directly given, but only *deduced* from the fact that my thought of a table outside the mind does not actually prove it exists there: even if the table really does exist, my thought of it is still finite insofar as my thought of the table is not itself the table, which means that there is a difference between the two. Moreover, while I deduce my own finitude in this way, I deduce the finitude of all other entities in precisely the same way. Stated differently, I don't grasp human finitude simply because I happen to be human, but because I can deduce the finitude of human experience, and *for the very same reason* can deduce the finitude of horses, cats, trains, flowers, and atoms. The argument, to summarize, is that the same form can never exist in two different places. To move the form of a horse from the horse itself and bring it into my mind is not merely to extract it from "matter" — whatever that might be — but to *transform* it. The horse-form in the horse is not the horse-form in my mind.

---

[68] René Descartes, *Meditations on First Philosophy*.

[69] Graham Harman, *The Quadruple Object*.

[70] The closest predecessor to this critique of modern philosophy can be found in José Ortega y Gasset, "Preface for Germans."

2. Realism and Materialism

A number of analytic philosophers in the blogosphere have ridiculed the recent emergence of a realist trend in continental thought. In a way this is perfectly understandable, since realism has always been a live philosophical option in the analytic tradition, and can hardly seem like a great innovation to those working within it. Yet this sort of mockery can also be dangerous for those who employ it, since it is so often reversible. For all the *Sturm und Drang* over whether Saul Kripke, Ruth Barcan Marcus, or some other figure deserves to be honored for launching the "new theory of reference," a continental could always laugh and tell them to go back to Husserl's discussion of "nominal acts" or "fixed appellations" (cf. Kripke's "rigid designators") in the *Logical Investigations* six decades earlier.[71] What made Kripke's emergence in the early 1970s so exciting was not his non-existent discovery that names point at something beyond definite descriptions, but that he raised possibilities so foreign to the assumptions of his intellectual environment. The same holds for the longstanding continental attitude toward realism, which Husserl and Heidegger long ago dismissed as a "pseudo-problem." Lee Braver has even plausibly claimed that anti-realism has been at the core of continental thought since its inception.[72] To be sure, one can always point to Nicolai Hartmann as a *bona fide* realist in early twentieth-century continental philosophy, but he is the classic exception that proves the rule: until recently almost no one was working on Hartmann, and even today his influence is minimal compared with that of the more mainstream phenomenologists.

In any case, the real heyday of continental realism is upon us at this very moment. In the early 1990s in Italy, Maurizio Ferraris broke with Gianni Vattimo and his circle in the name of a robust form of realism, one that would eventually serve as a magnet for German *Wunderkind* Markus Gabriel as well.[73] In 2002, my own book *Tool-Being* offered a realist interpretation of Heidegger's philosophy, and eventually fed into the Speculative Realism

---

[71] Saul Kripke, *Naming and Necessity*; Ruth Barcan Marcus, "Modalities and Intensional Languages"; Timothy Williamson, "In Memoriam: Ruth Barcan Marcus, 1921–2012." For a discussion of nominal acts see Edmund Husserl, *Logical Investigations*, vol. 2, p. 561, and for fixed appellations see p. 685 of the same volume.

[72] Lee Braver, *A Thing of This World*. For an appreciative critique of Braver's approach see Graham Harman, "A Festival of Anti-Realism."

[73] One will immediately notice a stark contrast between a book like Ferraris's *Manifesto of New Realism* and the articles contained in Gianni Vattimo's co-edited anthology *Weak Thought*. For the work of Markus Gabriel, *Fields of Sense* is a good place to survey the breadth of his concerns.

movement launched a few years later in London.[74] In the same year, the Mexican-born New Yorker Manuel DeLanda did the same service for Gilles Deleuze and Félix Guattari, interpreting them as realist philosophers as well.[75] DeLanda begins his book by defining realists in a straightforward way as those "who grant reality full autonomy from the human mind."[76] This is a good start, and certainly a *sine qua non* of any realism with a straight face, rather than the sort that simply finesses the meaning of "realism" so that it no longer poses a threat to non-realist enterprises.[77] Nonetheless, to formulate realism as upholding the existence of something *outside the mind* concedes too much to the modern standpoint by assuming that where we stand is "the mind," with the implication that the human mind is the only thing that really has an exterior. The problem is that raindrops also have an outside, as do sunflowers, black holes, and *Moby-Dick*. Rather than realism pointing "outside the mind," where it should point is the outside of any relation at all.

The easiest way to look like a philosophical crackpot in the present day is to discuss object-object relations without passing through the official checkpoint of natural science, which was long ago granted a monopoly on this topic. To claim, by contrast, that philosophy has its own foothold in the object-object realm is apparently to retreat to some pre-contemporary version of philosophy. By "contemporary" I mean any philosophy that won't cause one to be laughed at behind one's back in mainstream philosophy departments, which basically means philosophy beginning with Hume and Kant.[78] To suggest that philosophy go straight to object-object relations is seemingly to flirt with what Meillassoux dismissed as a philosophical "hyper-physics" in the oral version of his 2012 Berlin lecture, though this seems to have been removed from the published text.[79] One symptom of this ban on discussing object-object relations is that Alfred North Whitehead, one of a handful of truly major twentieth-century philosophers, has never

---

[74] Graham Harman, *Tool-Being*; Brassier et al., "Speculative Realism."

[75] Manuel DeLanda, *Intensive Science and Virtual Philosophy*.

[76] DeLanda, *Intensive Science and Virtual Philosophy*, p. xii.

[77] One of the worst examples is surely John D. Caputo, "For the Love of the Things Themselves," whose primary interest is not in realism in its own right, but in eliminating it as a threat to his philosophical hero Jacques Derrida, who bears as much resemblance to a realist as does a rabbit to an elephant. Unfortunately, another such example is Bruno Latour in the opening pages of his otherwise marvelous *Pandora's Hope*, which is less concerned with realism as a positive doctrine than with fending off his critics in the "science wars" of the time.

[78] David Hume, *A Treatise of Human Nature*; Kant, *Critique of Pure Reason*.

[79] Meillassoux, "Iteration, Reiteration, Repetition."

been fully admitted into the canon by either the analytic *or* continental tradition, whose hidden union is perhaps best summarized by their shared transcendental allergy to object meeting object outside surveillance by human experience.[80] It is for this reason that a taste for Whitehead is usually a good sign that one also has a taste for escaping the straitjacket of modern philosophy, as we see in various remarks by Deleuze, Isabelle Stengers, and Latour.[81]

Another important duty when discussing realism is to distinguish it from materialism, which flourishes today in two separate but related senses of the term. Everyone is familiar with the classical materialism of atoms swerving through a void, which for many has simply been updated with subatomic particles, and with fields acting across what used to be considered empty space. It is the second type of materialism that might cause readers more puzzlement, as Levi Bryant notes when he tackles the topic for all of us: "materialism has become a *terme d'art* which has little to do with anything material. Materialism has come to mean simply that something is historical, socially constructed, involves cultural practices, and is contingent .... We wonder where the materialism in materialism is."[82] Part of what Bryant has in mind is Slavoj Žižek's unusual claim that "the true formula of materialism is not that there is some noumenal reality beyond our distorting perception of it. The only consistent materialist position is that *the world does not exist*."[83] As laughable as this might sound to hardcore materialists of atoms and the void, there is a sense in which the two views are close cousins.[84] For on the one hand, classical materialism reduces matter to its physical underpinnings, thereby belittling the possibility of any form of *emergent* reality not contained in the microphysical constituents of the world. And on the other, the new cultural materialisms reduce in the opposite direction, denying the existence of anything *submergent* beneath matter in its present

---

[80] Whitehead, *Process and Reality*.

[81] Gilles Deleuze, *The Fold*, pp. 86, 90, 92 ; Isabelle Stengers, *Thinking with Whitehead*; Latour, "Irreductions." For a discussion of Latour's debt to Whitehead see Graham Harman, *Prince of Networks*.

[82] Levi R. Bryant, *Onto-Cartography*, p. 2.

[83] Slavoj Žižek & Glyn Daly, *Conversations with Žižek*, p. 97. In the original version of this article, the word "materialist" was inadvertantly omitted in the final sentence of this quotation.

[84] Although Žižek provides the most photogenic quote for this form of materialism, the more emblematic versions can be sampled in the following works: Barad, *Meeting the Universe Halfway*; Rosi Braidotti, *The Posthuman*; Donna Haraway, *Staying with the Trouble*. Jane Bennett in *Vibrant Matter* is more of a *bona fide* physical materialist than these three, steering in the direction of a Deleuzian *monism* of matter. On this point see especially Jane Bennett, "Systems and Things."

cultural configuration. But this strange new sort of materialism reduces reality upward to its present manifestations or effects, thereby denying any surplus of the sort required to make things change. Aristotle already saw the problem with this when introducing his concept of "potentiality" to combat the actualism of his Megarian opponents, who claimed that no one is a house builder unless they happen to be building a house right now.[85] Elsewhere I have called the downward reduction "undermining," the upward reduction "overmining," and their combination "duomining."[86]

3. The World Without Us

Let's begin this section with an anecdote. Some years ago, I was giving a lecture on the philosophy of art at a conference in central France.[87] The organizer of the event, Tom Trevatt, asked a simple question that left me puzzled for months afterward: "What would an art without humans look like?" The motive behind his question immediately made sense. After all, the speculative realist movement in philosophy was already known for its interest in what the world is like apart from human access to it.[88] As one of the original members of that movement, I was a perfectly legitimate recipient of Trevatt's question, even though something in the phrasing of his question seemed wrong. Trevatt was not alone in seeing the relation between speculative realism and art as the need for artworks "without humans." The artist Joanna Malinowska had ventured in that direction in her 2009–2010 New York show *Time of Guerrilla Metaphysics*. In a contemporaneous interview with David Coggins, Malinowska explained one amusing work in which she left a solar-powered boombox "in the middle of absolute Arctic nowhere," heard presumably by no one and eventually sinking beneath the sea once global warming melts the ice on which it sits.[89] Along with this aesthetic exemplar of an "art without humans," there was Tristan Garcia's claim a few years later in *Form and Object* that art can be art without humans.[90]

---

[85] Aristotle, *Metaphysics*, Θ 3.

[86] Graham Harman, "On the Undermining of Objects"; Graham Harman, "Undermining, Overmining, and Duomining"; Graham Harman, "The Third Table."

[87] My lecture was entitled "Art and Paradox," and the conference was entitled "The Matter of Contradiction: Ungrounding the Object," held at Île de Vassivière, France on September 9, 2012.

[88] Graham Harman, *Speculative Realism: An Introduction*.

[89] David Coggins, "Secret Powers."

[90] Tristan Garcia, *Form and Object*, Book II, Chapter VIII.

It was some months before I realized that Trevatt's important question unknowingly played on an ambiguity in the phrase "without humans." It is true that within speculative realism, Meillassoux was preoccupied with the "ancestral" or "diachronic" realm of a time before or after the human species, and that Brassier in particular remains fascinated by the eventual extinction of our race.[91] Nonetheless, this is too limited and literal a sense of the phrase "without humans." And it is simply not applicable to OOO, which is not interested in artworks in the absence of humans, but only with what is absent in artworks even when humans are standing right there. Stated differently, the point is not to *get rid* of humans, but to realize that artworks exceed the human grasp even when we are on the scene. In other words, we need to distinguish between humans as *ingredients* of a situation and humans as *observers* of it, and to recognize that realism is only committed to opposing the second. It was DeLanda, on the opening page of his *A New Philosophy of Society*, who saw this most clearly.[92] After announcing that his book will pursue a realist theory of society, he notes that philosophical realism generally entails a commitment to the mind-independent reality of whatever it discusses. But given that societies cannot exist without minds, is it not impossible to conceive of society in a mind-independent sense? Obviously not. For what interests DeLanda is not societies of mindless zombies, but societies of mindful humans, with the proviso that human societies are still independent of human *conceptions* of them. That is to say, the realist conception of society means simply that society exceeds whatever we see or say of it, and has independent features that are not first produced by our knowledge of them. And mind-independent reality is there even when humans — far from being extinct — are staring at it directly. More than this: human comportment toward the world, even if only toward illusions, is itself a new kind of reality in its own right. There can be no question of increasing the amount of realism by *getting rid* of humans.

A good deal of recent thought has been occupied with the question of what the earth would be like if humans were no longer here. Alan Weisman wrote a best-seller called *The World Without Us*, which envisions the gradual breakdown of various human facilities after our hypothetical disappearance.[93] Eugene Thacker's *Horror of Philosophy* trilogy has earned a large following and even spawned a pop culture catchphrase ("In the Dust

---

[91] Brassier, *Nihil Unbound*.
[92] Manuel DeLanda, *A New Philosophy of Society*, p. 1.
[93] Alan Weisman, *The World Without Us*.

of This Planet") by way of reflections in a similar vein.[94] Rationalist circles have long taken Halloweenish delight in Thomas Metzinger's claim that "there is no self."[95] There is also the interpretation of speculative realism given by Deborah Danowski and Eduardo Viveiros de Castro in *The Ends of the World.*[96] Ignas Šatkauskas reports that according to these authors, "Meillassoux's speculative materialism ... lays the theoretical groundwork for a world-without-us, while offering metaphysical schemes that would be appropriate for the cognition of such reality."[97] As already mentioned, this is true for Brassier and Meillassoux's conceptions of realism, but is certainly not the case for OOO. The latter current does not seek the in-itself in some temporal region uninhabited by humans, but joins Kant in pointing to an in-itself that exists here and now but still beyond our ability to relate to it. This cuts against the grain of Meillassoux's view in particular. As he sees it, any in-itself that existed simultaneously with humans could simply be recuperated by the old German Idealist argument that to think a thing outside thought is to turn it into a thought, with the noumenal only a special case of the phenomenal.

This brings us to an important paradox in the history of philosophy. Kant is almost universally recognized as one of the greatest philosophers in Western history; his influence approaches that of Plato and Aristotle, the twin colossi standing at the entrance to our discipline. Even so, vanishingly few people today are willing to accept Kant's *central idea*: the thing-in-itself. It is often said that the *Ding an sich* is a "dogmatic residue" in Kant's position, so that the German Idealists were heroic in dispensing with it. The problem with this view is that the thing-in-itself is precisely what allows Kant to *refute* all dogmatism. If dogmatic metaphysics means the claim to be able to prove philosophical theses about how things really are, Kant rejects dogmatism precisely because reason can never make reality directly accessible. But among the new realists and their fellow travelers, who accepts this thing-in-itself? Certainly not Ferraris or Gabriel, who reject it on principle as a barrier to knowledge; certainly not Meillassoux, who reduces the thing-in-itself to something that merely outlasts us in time.

---

[94] Eugene Thacker, *In the Dust of This Planet*; Eugene Thacker, *Starry Speculative Corpse*; Eugene Thacker, *Tentacles Longer Than Night.*

[95] Thomas Metzinger, *Being No One.* For a critique see Graham Harman, "The Problem with Metzinger."

[96] Deborah Danowski & Eduardo Viveiros de Castro, *The Ends of the World.*

[97] Ignas Šatkauskas, "Where is the 'Great Outdoors' in Meillassoux's Speculative Materialism?" p. 112.

Not Latour or Whitehead, who treat the real in relational terms and allow no excess beyond relation, even if Whiteheadians tend to contest this point vigorously.[98] Not Husserl, who finds it "absurd" that anything could exist that would not — at least in principle — be the object of an intentional act. At most there is a trace of it in Heidegger, in a neglected passage near the end of his *Kant and the Problem of Metaphysics*: "What is the significance of the struggle initiated in German Idealism against the 'thing-in-itself' except a growing forgetfulness of what Kant had won ...?"[99] But the rest of his sentence ruins his remark: "namely ... the original development and searching study of the problem of human finitude?" With these additional words, he fetters the thing-in-itself in the dungeon of onto-taxonomy, where it becomes nothing more than an unknowable trauma to human thought, as happens even in Kant's great works.

That is to say, the usual manner of trying to get beyond Kant is along the lines of German Idealism. "Kant was a great genius, except for his naïvely traditional and self-contradictory and vaguely Platonic or Christian bit about the thing-in-itself. But he can be forgiven, since he did so many other important things, and luckily his successors cleaned up the thing-in-itself problem for him." These admiring critics of Kant are no less taxonomical than the master himself. As we saw earlier, whether or not there is a "gap" between thought and world, the real problem is that thought and world are taken as the two basic terms in the first place. The only way to escape this assumption, *the only exit from modern philosophy*, is to cease conceiving of the thing-in-itself as something "unknowable to humans," and to reconceive it as the excess in things beyond *any* of their relations to each other. The reason why so many are reluctant to take this step, which has been explained and promoted by OOO authors for nearly a generation, is because it so openly flouts the division of labor at the heart of modern thought. "How can philosophy say anything at all about object-object relations? This is what science already does! Philosophy should stick to the thought-world relation where it belongs." This is why some in Brassier's rationalist circle have mistakenly claimed that speculative realism is interested in science *as opposed* to the humanities, as if science had all the reality and the humanities all the illusions. Yet there is plenty of reality in the study of the Hittites, the

---

[98]   Steven Shaviro is one aficionado of Whitehead with whom I have had a long and productive dispute. See Steven Shaviro, *Without Criteria* and Steven Shaviro, "The Actual Volcano," as well as my counterpoints in Graham Harman, "Response to Shaviro" and Graham Harman, "Whitehead and Schools X, Y, and Z."
[99]   Martin Heidegger, *Kant and the Problem of Metaphysics*, pp. 251–252.

human psyche, or Warner Brother cartoons, and since at least Popper's time we have known that scientific statements are always just inches away from being overthrown as false. The real and the unreal cannot be taxonomically aligned with individual disciplines, since both the real and the unreal are present everywhere at all times.

Nowhere is the flaw of onto-taxonomy more visible than in the unfortunate fate of the word "formalism" in the modern period, especially in the arts. Like so much else in this period, the term is grounded in the ideas of Kant. As far as I am aware, he uses the term explicitly only in the Second Critique, where it means both that ethical actions must be walled off from their consequences, and that ethics has to do with the general form of the categorical imperative rather than more specific ethical rules.[100] In short, formalism means the autonomy of ethics from all impure influences, such as the wish to go to heaven or hell, or to obtain a good reputation in the business community. Although I do not recall the word "formalism" being used in the *Critique of Judgment*, it is an eminently formalist work as well. The beautiful must be walled off from both the agreeable and the politically beneficent: unlike Jean-Jacques Rousseau, Kant thinks it no obstacle to the beauty of a palace that the masses suffered to enable its construction.[101] It is no accident that Kant is considered the godfather of modern formalism in art, as represented by the American art critics Clement Greenberg and Michael Fried (even if both reject the "formalist" label).[102] Something similar occurs in the First Critique, whose central principle is the mutual independence of things-in-themselves and appearances. But despite Kant's pioneering advocacy of this formalist autonomy in several domains of philosophy, there is a flaw in the diamond. Namely, he is not interested in the theme of autonomy *per se* but only in one specific *kind* of autonomy: the independence of thought and world from each other. Kant's autonomy is spoiled by his onto-taxonomy. The same holds for much of high modernist art criticism, as in Fried's polemic against the "theatrical" blending of beholder and artwork in his 1967 "Art and Objecthood."[103] Soon enough, however, we will see that Fried took a surprising turn in the decades that followed.

The problems with Kantian formalism did not escape the notice of later thinkers, and I have argued elsewhere that each of his three Critiques

---

[100] Immanuel Kant, *Critique of Practical Reason*.
[101] Immanuel Kant, *Critique of Judgment*, p. 46.
[102] Clement Greenberg, *Homemade Esthetics*; Michael Fried, "Art and Objecthood."
[103] Fried, "Art and Objecthood."

eventually found a critic equal to the work.[104] We have seen that Kant's fixation on the gap between thought and world was skillfully dissected by Latour, even if we cannot accept the "all hybrids, all the time" flavor of his solution.[105] The best critique of Kant's ethics — among many such attempts — comes from his admirer Max Scheler, who upholds the autonomy of ethics from any external purpose, but who sees the unit of ethics less in the human ethical agent than in the *compound* formed by the agent and the objects of its loves, its *ordo amoris*.[106] And just as with Scheler's ethical insight, the central flaw of Kantian aesthetics could only be seen by an author so committed to its spirit as to reject it only with considerable reluctance. I speak here of Fried, whose turn from criticism to history did not initially change his sentiments. In his first historical work, on anti-theatrical painting in the age of Denis Diderot, Fried continued to uphold a crucial gap between the beholder of the painting on one side and the absorbed figures within it on the other.[107] Only later, under the pressure of his subject matter, did Fried come to see that the later history of French painting was by no means anti-theatrical. He first finds an "absorptive continuum" in the paintings of Gustave Courbet, who effectively paints himself into his own canvases, thereby breaking down the wall between work and beholder (with the painter himself being just a special case of the beholder).[108] But even more important is the "facingness" found in the works of Édouard Manet, that pivotal figure of modern art, in which every inch of the painting seems to confront the beholder directly rather than receding into absorptive depth.[109] The forerunner of all these anti-taxonomical authors is surely Dante, perhaps the most non-Kantian figure in Western intellectual history. Rather than conceding any sort of autonomy of thought and world from each other, Dante depicts a world of amorous agents who are not only fully deployed in their loves and hates for various people and objects, but are judged for it as well. There has never been a more "theatrical" author in Fried's sense of the term.

---

104 Graham Harman, *Dante's Broken Hammer*; Graham Harman, *Art and Objects*.
105 Latour, *We Have Never Been Modern*.
106 Max Scheler, *Formalism in Ethics and a Non-Formal Ethics of Value*.
107 Michael Fried, *Absorption and Theatricality*.
108 Michael Fried, *Courbet's Realism*.
109 Michael Fried, *Manet's Modernism*.

4. Philosophies of the Future

We have now reached a good point to speak of one of my favorite themes: "philosophies of the future." The obvious problem with maintaining that this or that author is "the future of philosophy" is that it presumes one knows where philosophy will or ought to lead next. More often than not, unless someone has an unusually sensitive nose for where certain problems are headed — and this means a nose for how contemporary lines of thought might eventually be twisted or reversed — one's conception of the future will simply be a projection of where they are standing now. To give an example that is not my central one, consider the case of Maurice Blanchot. During my doctoral student days in the early 1990s, the impression was often conveyed that Blanchot was a major piece of the philosophy of the future. Needless to say, almost thirty years have passed, but continental philosophy has not become noticeably more Blanchotian. He is still a perfectly respectable figure to study, if not to everyone's taste, and it would be strange to ridicule anyone who argued for his continued importance. Nonetheless, it is now clear that the progress of Blanchot's philosophical reputation from 1990–2020 was not what his staunchest champions would have hoped for and predicted. Paul de Man, writing much earlier than 1990, offered the following note of praise:

> When we will be able to observe the [post-war] period with
> more detachment, the main proponents of contemporary French
> literature may well turn out to be figures that now seem shadowy in
> comparison with the celebrities of the hour. And none is more likely
> to achieve future prominence than the little-publicized and difficult
> writer, Maurice Blanchot.[110]

This high regard for Blanchot was not rare in the circles frequented by de Man. Indeed, the 1992 English translation of Blanchot's *The Infinite Conversation* featured a back cover endorsement by Jacques Derrida that took the tendency to nearly histrionic extremes: "Blanchot waits for us to come, to be read and re-read ... I would say that never as much as today have I pictured him so far ahead of us."[111] Either Blanchot is still further ahead of us than we realize, or Derrida's assessment turned out to be exaggerated. I say this not to be cruel to Derrida in particular, but because it

---

[110] Paul de Man, *Blindness and Insight*, p. 61.

[111] Jacques Derrida, back cover endorsement for Maurice Blanchot, *The Infinite Conversation*.

exhibits a more general point: the human tendency to project the future as simply a more futuristic or "far-out" version of the present. Derrida and his intellectual kin ruled early 1990s continental philosophy in almost crushing fashion, in a way that is difficult for young people today to imagine. In such an environment, who would have seemed a better heir apparent for a few decades down the line than Blanchot? For in some ways he is simply a darker, eerier version of Derrida, more turbulent and paradoxical but never casting dangerous light on anything missing from Derrida himself. While the latter's expressed admiration for Blanchot was no doubt sincere, it is hard to imagine he found him the least bit threatening.

There is a particular nation, whose name I omit out of fondness for the place, that has often been called "the country of the future." In response to this, cynical observers sometimes remark that "country X is the country of the future, and always will be." Is there not a sense in which Blanchot is the future of continental philosophy, *and always will be*? I could still be proven wrong, but Blanchot has now "waited for us to come" for nearly thirty years, and it begins to seem as if our failure to come may not be entirely our own fault. A pair of related remarks from important authors come to mind. The first comes from Whitehead's under-read dialogues with Lucien Price, and dates to the immediate aftermath of World War II:

> **Price**: "Do you see any bulwark against [nuclear war]?"
> **Whitehead**: "Only the appearance of half a dozen eminent men."
> **Price**: "Can you descry half a dozen such on the horizon?"
> **Whitehead**: "*They don't appear on the horizon*; they appear in our midst and cannot at once be identified."[112]

The other relevant passage, which I am currently unable to locate, comes from Marcel Proust in his great multi-volume novel. Somewhere in those thousands of pages, Proust remarks that we tend to imagine the future as some sort of intricate variant of the present, failing to realize that the future springs from hidden factors in the present that are not currently manifest.

In any case, *Blanchot is the philosopher of the future, and always will be.* But my concern is not so much with Blanchot, whose futuristic rose has faded since my youth. Instead, I wish to propose a related maxim that might well annoy some readers: *Schelling and Merleau-Ponty are the philosophers of*

---

[112] Alfred North Whitehead & Lucien Price, *Dialogues of Alfred North Whitehead*, p. 362, emph. added.

the future, and always will be.[113] It is widely recognized that F.W.J. Schelling and Maurice Merleau-Ponty are two of the most colorful thinkers in the whole modern period.[114] Both have an aura of being on the scent of something possible and paradoxical but not yet actualized. There is still an air of the twenty-second century about them; we would not be surprised to hear science fiction characters discussing their work. Schelling always smells like the faint promise of an overturning of the largely Hegelian history of the nineteenth and twentieth centuries, and the consequent emergence of a parallel intellectual universe. How many attempted "Schelling Renaissances" have there already been, and how many more are still to come? Merleau-Ponty's various forays into the body and "the flesh" seem to promise an impending explosion of everyone else's lingering mind/matter deadlock. The more that even analytic philosophers of mind seem to become interested in him, the more this seems to verify that Merleau-Ponty is on the track of whatever has somehow always eluded us until now. The problem is that both Schelling and Merleau-Ponty are modern onto-taxonomists to the core. For as bizarre as the pages of Schelling sometimes become, it is always a question of "nature" and "spirit," the same basic twofold we find as early as Descartes. And as *outré* as Merleau-Ponty sounds in certain pages of his unfinished work *The Visible and the Invisible*, with his ostensibly scandalous notion that the world looks at me just as I look at it, this is really just Descartes's two terms observing each other reciprocally without anything else being added to the mix. Even "the body," Merleau-Ponty's theoretical bread and butter, is little more than a version of "meeting the universe halfway" in Barad's sense. DeLanda said it best when he called the body "a kind of token material object, invited to [non-realist] ontology just to include one member of a minority."[115] Restated in Whiteheadian terms, the problem is that Schelling and Merleau-Ponty are too much "on the horizon" and not enough "in our midst"; they cannot possibly be the future, because they accept too firmly the restrictions of past and present. They are projections of how we once thought the future should look, like

---

[113] Above all I mean no offense to my comrade-in-arms Iain Hamilton Grant, who has made such productive use of Schelling in his own work. Our disagreement concerns whether Schelling makes sufficient room for the role of individual objects as opposed to "nature." See Iain Hamilton Grant, *Philosophies of Nature After Schelling*. For my treatment of Grant's books see Harman, *Speculative Realism: An Introduction*, pp. 60–72 and Harman, "On the Undermining of Objects."
[114] F.W.J. Schelling, *Philosophical Inquiries Into the Nature of Human Freedom*; Maurice Merleau-Ponty, *The Visible and the Invisible*.
[115] DeLanda, in Manuel Delanda & Graham Harman, *The Rise of Realism*, p. 116.

pre-color films of 1980s Manhattan with hovercraft roaming the streets and lasers striking down villains.

Every moment has its "philosophers of the future," and for clarity's sake I will risk listing a few more names. François Laruelle has a large following among the young, but — with the proviso that I could always be wrong — I have yet to find a significant breakthrough in his position. And while I do find Gilbert Simondon more useful, his "futuristic" quality strikes me mostly as a tantalizing mirage for Deleuzeans who feel that their hourglass ran out too quickly.[116] Tell me your "philosopher of the future" and I will tell you who you are. More likely than not, your future philosopher is a phantasmatic image of the place where you already stand — as when hopeful fathers imagine their infant sons following in their professional footsteps someday, but with more success. Heidegger had some sense of this problem, as we find in one of his passages on ambiguity in *Being and Time*:

> Everyone is acquainted with what is up for discussion and what
> occurs, and everyone discusses it; but everyone also knows already
> how to talk about what has to happen first — about what is not yet
> up for discussion but "really" must be done. Already everyone has
> surmised and scented out in advance what Others have also surmised
> and scented out. This Being-on-the scent is of course based upon
> hearsay, for if anyone is genuinely "on the scent" of anything, he does
> not speak about it …[117]

Any philosophical future that merely involves some new permutation on the onto-taxonomy of thought and world — however radically it claims to have ended "Cartesian dualism" — is not much of a future, but merely an extension of the present. We need to stop looking toward the horizon, and reflect instead on the major prejudice in our midst.

5. Concluding Remarks

Why is there is only one possible exit from modern philosophy? Because modern philosophy lives and breathes from a single basic principle: the notion that thought and world are the two poles of the universe, the first of

---

[116] François Laruelle, *Philosophy and Non-Philosophy*; François Laruelle, *Principles of Non-Philosophy*; Gilbert Simondon, *Individuation in Light of Notions of Form and Information*.
[117] Martin Heidegger, *Being and Time*, pp. 217–218.

them immediate and radically certain, the latter less certain but impressively masterable by science. But in this way, the rift between immediacy and mediation — which I do accept — is wrongly identified with two specific *kinds* of beings. What is immediately knowable are entities in their sensual realities, as related not just to thought but to *anything else*. What is not immediately knowable, but only detectable by indirect means, is the surplus in any reality that is not exhausted by its relations with anything else. This surplus is not something that merely lurks beneath the human symbolic order, as in Lacan's narrowly traumatic sense of "the Real," but is always a form that can never be fully translated into any set of relations, whether animate or inanimate.[118] Moreover, we can deduce this for rocks and raindrops just as easily as we do for human thought.

It follows that non-modern (not "pre-"modern) philosophy should be non-relational in its outlook. This means it should be *non-literal* in its outlook, since to reduce anything to its pieces (undermining) and to reduce anything to its effects (overmining) are equally defective maneuvers. Literal language succeeds by ascribing properties to entities that they truly have. But since entities are more than bundles of qualities, they are never literalizable. This is why philosophy is *philosophia*, not *sophia*. To argue that philosophy should be non-relational does not mean that relations do not occur. If every entity is a compound (not necessarily a hybrid of human and non-human, as Latour claims) then every entity is formed from relations between components, without being nothing more than these relations. And if every entity can affect other entities, it does not follow that entities are nothing more than the sum of these effects.

Among other things, this is why arguments since the 1960s over formalism in the arts often seem to go nowhere. The problem is wrongly framed in terms of either "everything relates to everything" or "everything relates to nothing." The point, instead, is that most possible relations do not in fact occur, so that even the most "site-specific" work of art or architecture makes contact with only a limited number of aspects of its site. The work with its small circle of relations actively fends off any probings from the outside, so that further relations require genuine labor. The reason why things are inherently non-relational, even when they relate, is that no form can be moved from one place to another without change. A philosophy like Meillassoux's, which holds that we gain access to entities through mathematical formalization, ultimately relies on an ill-defined "matter"

---

[118] Jacques Lacan, *Écrits*.

that supports the same forms extracted and moved without alteration into the mind. Against this notion, OOO holds with Latour that there is no transport without transformation.[119] A form does not move — whether from the thing to the mind or in any other manner — without undergoing some sort of translation. In this age of resurgent materialism, we need less materialism and more formalism.

---

[119] Bruno Latour, *Aramis*, p. 119.

CHAPTER 5

OBJECT-ORIENTED PHILOSOPHY VS. RADICAL EMPIRICISM (FROM *BELLS AND WHISTLES*)[120]

In 2010 I had struck up a friendship with the Warsaw-based editors of the journal Kronos, Marcin Rychter in particular. Kronos has translated numerous philosophical essays into Polish for the first time, including quite a number of Speculative Realist writings. Rychter commissioned this piece especially for Kronos, with the understanding that it would be published in English at a later date. He specifically requested an essay on William James's most metaphysical work, Essays in Radical Empiricism. While on vacation in Malta in early November 2011, I reread that book and wrote the following article. Although several readers have kindly compared my writing style with that of James, and despite my deep admiration for the witty and eloquent American thinker, there turns out to be considerable incompatibility in metaphysical principles between Radical Empiricism and OOO, as this essay explains. In conclusion, I propose an object-oriented method to counter the overly celebrated pragmatic one: unless an object has reality over and above its consequences for thought, then it is not a real object.

William James (1842–1910) is well established as one of the leading philosophers to emerge from the United States, often accompanied on such lists by Charles Sanders Peirce, John Dewey, and Willard Van Orman Quine.

---

[120] This article originally appeared in 2012 in Polish in the journal *Kronos*, under the title "Filozofia zwrócona ku przedmiotom contra radykalny empiryzm."

As a writer, James is clearly superior to these others and is perhaps rivaled in this respect only by George Santayana. It hardly needs to be mentioned that literary talent ran deep in the James family: William's father, Henry Sr., was a prominent theological writer, younger brother Henry Jr. is one the nation's most celebrated novelists, and younger sister Alice has gained increased attention as a diarist. Though born into wealth and privilege, William James struggled with nervous disorders and procrastinating tendencies. His personality began to stabilize following marriage at the age of thirty-six, yet he was still unable to produce his first book (the landmark *Principles of Psychology*) until he was nearly fifty years old, in an era when fifty verged on old age.[121] Perhaps the chief intellectual merit of James was his complete lack of provincialism. Born in a period when intellectual life was dominated by Europe, the New York native James was unnaturally alert to the ideas of such continental European figures as Bergson, Fechner, and Lotze. But far from being merely receptive, James gave Europe much in return: his innovative psychological theories had an impact on such giants as Bergson, Freud, and Husserl. James's strictly philosophical impact on Europe was less pronounced, but has increased in recent years, with Bruno Latour and the younger Deleuzians frequently expressing their admiration for James.[122] While *Pragmatism* is the most widely read of James's philosophy books, his most significant metaphysical work is surely *Essays in Radical Empiricism*, which only appeared posthumously in 1912 despite having been assembled by James himself five years earlier.[123] At the request of the editors of *Kronos*, I have written this essay to summarize my views on James's radical empiricism and contrast his metaphysical views with my own.

I. The Object-Oriented Position

Many different roads can lead to the same city. But since I reached the object-oriented standpoint by way of phenomenology, it seems best to retrace that road here. The following summary will be brief, partly because I have told the story many times before, and partly because our real interest in this article is William James.

The charismatic ex-priest Franz Brentano opened a new chapter in philosophy in 1874 with his revival of the medieval term "intentionality."

---

[121] William James, *Principles of Psychology*, 2 vols.
[122] See above all David Lapoujade, *William James*.
[123] William James, "Pragmatism"; William James, *Essays in Radical Empiricism*.

Unlike physical reality, all mental reality is aimed at some object: to see is to see something; to judge is to judge some object; to love is to love someone or something. But the things at which mental life aims, according to Brentano, are not real objects outside the mind. Instead, intentionality refers to "immanent objectivity," or objects that exist only inside the mind. Clearly I can love centaurs and hate unicorns, make damning judgments about square circles, and hallucinate golden mountains, even though none of these objects exist outside my act of intending them. As for the status of real objects in the real world, Brentano initially left this issue unclarified. It was his great Polish student, Kasimir Twardowski, who insisted that the problem be addressed by distinguishing between an *object* lying outside the mind and a *content* inside the mind. This was done in Twardowski's brilliant 1894 habilitation thesis, *On the Content and Object of Presentations*.[124]

As I see it, Twardowski's argument was the most immediate impetus for Husserl's development of phenomenology. From scattered references in publications and letters, we can see that Husserl reacted with a mixture of fascination, rejection, and competitiveness in response to the arguments of Twardowski, who was seven years younger but in some ways philosophically riper. Ultimately, Husserl's response was to reject the notion of a separate reality outside the mind. The candle I see and the real candle burning in the room are one and the same thing, not two. The mind is capable of direct contact with reality, and there is no reality unobservable in principle by the mind. Eventually this pushed Husserl towards his later full-blown idealism, in which the world contains no dark residue unexhausted by the mind.

While I find Husserl's idealist turn lamentable, it did yield excellent fruits. Precisely because Husserl became so limited to a sphere of phenomenal appearance, he devoted himself all the more to uncovering more relief and drama than had ever been found within the mental sphere. The empiricist view of mental content had always treated it as made up of discrete qualities packed together in bundles; an object of the senses was nothing more than all of its content combined. Husserl's ingenuity on this point consisted in not simply rejecting Twardowski's distinction between an object outside the mind and a content inside it, but in collapsing *both* terms into the immanent sphere of the mind. No longer was mental life a matter of definite content alone; instead, it was a duel between object and content *within* the mind. This point is so important that it actually forms the backbone of phenomenology. The experienced world is made up of numerous objects

---

[124] Kasimir Twardowski, *On the Content and Object of Presentations*.

at any given moment — apples, sailboats, animals, castles, icebergs, and moons. Each of these objects is seen very concretely in each moment, from a definite angle and distance and under certain specific lighting conditions. All the details of my experience of these objects belongs to the *content* of my experience. Yet there is more to any experience than its explicit content. I can take an apple and turn it in my hands, take a bite from it, and then throw it off into the distance. As I do each of these things the "content" of my experience changes, yet it always remains the same *object* in my experience; never do I think the apple is a different apple just because it shows new facets and features from one moment to the next. An intentional object is not a bundle of qualities, as the British Empiricists and even Brentano still held. Instead, the truth is the reverse: the qualities we experience are always qualities *of the object*. Phenomenological analysis does nothing more than sift through the various changing adumbrations of intentional objects in an attempt to reach the qualities that *cannot* be removed from the object, under penalty of its no longer being the same object. Twardowski's duel between object and content survives at the heart of Husserl's system, but is now completely imploded into the immanent zone of intentional consciousness. By refusing to identify an object of experience with its bundle of qualities here and now, Husserl takes a fresh step in the history of philosophy, one that as far as I know was never approached by any earlier thinker. Those who continue to hammer Husserl for his idealism overlook the additional fact that Husserlian idealism is nonetheless object-oriented to the core.

One of the motives for Husserl's idealism was the need to preserve a space for philosophy where the advancing natural sciences could not intrude. In order to prevent philosophy from decaying into a branch of experimental psychology, it was important for Husserl to bracket off the naturalistic conception of the world and treat the mental sphere as fundamental. All scientific theory must be grounded in what lies present before the mind, the ultimate yardstick of reality. This was the point where young Martin Heidegger intervened, rebelling against Husserl just as Husserl rebelled against Brentano and Twardowski. Heidegger noted that for the most part we *do not* deal with objects as directly present to us. Quite the contrary: in our dealings with hammers, buses, chairs, floors, bodily organs, oxygen, grammar, and everything else, we usually do not notice these objects at all unless they malfunction or go missing. Usually, objects are hidden. They "withdraw" (*sich entziehen*), to use Heidegger's term. Whereas objects in consciousness are present-at-hand, the status of most objects at most times is to be ready-to-hand, withdrawn into the shadows of the world.

And here we encounter a point that is crucial for object-oriented philosophy. Husserl's objects never "hide." The blackbirds and sailboats of Husserl's world are not absent from view, but are always immediately there as soon as I acknowledge them. It is true that these objects are always seen only in a certain partial profile at any given moment, but these profiles do not conceal the bus or sailboat as a whole — instead, these profiles are "bonus information" encrusted onto the surface of objects already grasped as the target of our intentional acts. By contrast, Heidegger is interested in the *real* bus or sailboat, deeper than any perception of them. These real objects are the ones that withdraw. The bus as an intentional object can be observed but cannot take me anywhere; the bus as a real object can take me anywhere I please, if only it is properly fuelled.

The usual reading of Heidegger is that he teaches that all explicit theory is grounded in implicit background practices. Before I can develop a geological theory, I must have a pre-theoretical experience of mountains and earthquakes. But this is a misreading, even if one that Heidegger sometimes falls into himself. It is true that all of our best geological theories do not exhaust the dark background of mountains, crevices, fault-blocks, canyons, and sedimentary layers that they attempt to describe. Yet it is equally true that our *practical* dealings with these things do not exhaust them to their depths, meaning that praxis is ultimately no deeper than theory. We must also push our reading one step further and see that objects fail to exhaust *each other* as well, despite their probable lack of consciousness. A glacier that grinds through rock and soil does not make contact with all of the features of these entities any more than our geological theories or practical use of the soil are able to do. In this way, real objects turn out to be radically *non-relational*. Admittedly, Heidegger seems to say just the opposite. He tries to convince us that whereas the objects of the mental sphere seem to be discrete individuals cut off from one another, the real objects of the pre-conscious landscape are entirely defined by their mutual interrelations. But if this were true then objects could never break, nor could they surprise us in any way at all. Objects would be entirely defined by their relations with all other objects *hic et nunc*, and there would be no reason for anything ever to change from its current state. There must be some residue or surplus held in reserve behind any current state of the world, in order for the world to be able to sway and shift, or to change its state in any manner. But if objects are radically non-relational, we also need to know how they are able to relate at all, a question already posed by the occasionalist philosophers of medieval and modern times.

The basic model of object-oriented philosophy is thus seen to be as follows. The world is crossed by two dualisms. First there is the difference between the real and the intentional (or the "sensual," as I prefer to call it), and second there is the difference between objects and qualities. Husserl shows us that the sensual realm is torn apart between objects and their constantly shifting contents, while it is Leibniz rather than Heidegger who notes that real objects must all have distinct qualities or they would all be interchangeable, as clearly they are not. (At times Heidegger tends to treat the world itself as a single initial lump that is broken into pieces only derivatively.) But these ideas are familiar to anyone who has read my books, and those books can easily be read by anyone not yet familiar with the ideas.[125] Our real interest here is the radical empiricism of William James, which in many respects could hardly seem more different from object-oriented philosophy.

2. Radical Empiricism

Object-oriented philosophy is based on two overlapping dualisms: object vs. quality and real vs. sensual. William James shows no awareness of the first of these dualisms, and flatly rejects the second. In a theory reminiscent of Bergson's global doctrine of "images" in the slightly earlier *Matter and Memory*, James proposes a model in which all thoughts and things occupy a single plane of reality.[126]

The first chapter of *Essays in Radical Empiricism* is entitled "Does Consciousness Exist?" James wastes no time in giving us his answer. On the second page of the book, he frankly declares that consciousness "is the name of a nonentity, and has no right to a place among first principles."[127] [2] And further: "for twenty years past I have mistrusted 'consciousness' as an entity; for seven or eight years past I have suggested its non-existence to my students .... It seems to me that the hour is ripe for it to be openly and universally discarded." [3] What James wishes to discard is not just the reification of thinking substance. Instead, he attacks the very dualism between thoughts and things, which is precisely what object-oriented philosophy endorses in its distinction between sensual and real. "There is,

---

[125] The simplest summary of the object-oriented model so far can be found in Graham Harman, *The Quadruple Object*, which was originally published in French as *L'objet quadruple*.

[126] Henri Bergson, *Matter and Memory*.

[127] In what follows, all page numbers in square brckets refer to James, *Essays in Radical Empiricism*.

I mean, no aboriginal stuff or quality of being, contrasted with that of which material objects are made, out of which our thoughts of them are made ...." [3] Instead, thought must be viewed "functionally," in terms of its capacity for knowing. Instead of the dualism between real and sensual, James suggests the apparently more radical thesis that "there is only one primal stuff or material in the world, a stuff of which everything is composed, and if we call that stuff 'pure experience,' then knowing can easily be explained as a particular sort of relation towards one another into which portions of pure experience may enter." [4] The knower and the known are both parts of "pure experience," and enter into a certain relation that establishes their separate roles. In this way, philosophy can oppose the "neo-Kantism" [5] that views the world as inherently dualistic.

James credits Locke and Berkeley with introducing the term "idea" to mean both thing and thought, [10] just as Alfred North Whitehead would do again two decades later. James's "experience" can be viewed "as subjective and objective both at once." [10] Although James initially seems to be far less of an idealist than Husserl, he sounds much like Husserl opposing Twardowski when he says of physical things that "it is just *those self-same things* which his mind, as we say, perceives ...." [11] The whole philosophy of perception since ancient Greece seems to amount to "the paradox that what is evidently one reality should be in two places at once, both in outer space and in a person's mind." [11] And here James makes a concession, admitting that philosophies which distinguish between thought and thing seem to be more logically consistent in addressing this paradox. Nonetheless, he shuns this easy consistency for the reason that such theories "violate the reader's sense of life, which knows no intervening mental image but seems to see the room and the book immediately just as they physically exist." [12] Just as a single point can belong to two distinct lines if it is their point of intersection, so too a room can belong to a house but also to my own biography. [12] Much like Bergson, James is deeply committed to the intuition that we have a direct and immediate contact with reality rather than a mediated representational one. We will soon see how steep a price he is willing to pay for this view.

Any experience, he tells us, "is a member of diverse processes that can be followed away from it along entirely different lines. The one self-identical thing has so many relations to the rest of experience that you can take it in disparate systems of association, and treat it as belonging with opposite contexts." [12–13] He holds to this theory even as the difficulties begin to mount. The room in my mind is easy to destroy, he concedes, while the room in the real world needs "an earthquake, or a gang of men, and in any case a certain amount of time, to destroy." [14] The room in the real world cannot be lived in without paying rent, while the room in my mind can be lived in rent-free. Oddly enough, James concludes that "so far, all seems plain sailing," [15] despite the vast differences he himself has already noted between the mental and physical room. The only complication, as he sees it, comes when we stop thinking of the mental side of perceptions and turn instead towards sheer *concepts* devoid of perceptual underpinnings. To deal with this new situation, James cites the psychologist Hugo Münsterberg in defense of a position that here resembles that of Husserl [18–19]: even the centaurs and golden mountains of my thought exist not just inside me, but also outside me as objects thought about. [20] We thus arrive at what seems to be a flat ontology in which physical rooms, perceptions of rooms, and concepts of rooms are all on the same footing, all equally "outside" the mind. The reason they all seem so different to us is simply because "some couplings have the curious stubbornness, to borrow [Josiah] Royce's term, of fact; others show the fluidity of fancy — we let them come and go as we please." [21] A house tends to cohere with its town, owner, builder, and market price, "while to other houses, other towns, other owners, etc., it shows no tendency to cohere at all." [22] As a rule we tend to call the stubborn associations "external" realities and the loose associations "internal" ones. The absolute gap between thought and thing turns out to dissolve into a shaded continuum of greater and lesser stubbornness.

James closes the chapter by openly confronting the most obvious objection to his position, which "sounds quite crushing when one hears it first." [27] Namely, if the real burning candle and my thought of a burning candle are of the same order of being, then how can the attributes of the two be so different? The real candle illuminates the room, might set it on fire, cost perhaps three dollars at the time of purchase, and burns out after a certain number of hours. But the candle in my mind has none of these properties; in fact, it ceases to exist as soon as I fall asleep or die. James's first response is to call this objection commonsensical, and to suggest that thought and thing are not quite as different as might be suspected. [28] James does make a number of interesting points in noting that thought and thing both exist in time, both have a part-whole structure, both exist spatially, and other ontological similarities. He also makes the clever observation that if subject and object were so different, it should not be as hard as it normally is to determine what is objective and what is subjective in various situations. [29] James repeats his earlier claim that "the difference between objective and subjective ... is one of relation to a context solely," [30] and again the difference turns out to hinge on degrees of relative stubbornness: "in the mind the various [pieces of extension] maintain no necessarily stubborn order relatively to each other, while in the physical world they bound each other stably, and, added together, make the great enveloping Unit which we believe in and call real Space." [30–31] Thus there is no great difference in ontological kind here, but a pragmatic difference to be determined empirically: a real house stubbornly resists my imaginative powers in a way that the mental house does not.

James makes the counterintuitive claim that *thoughts* of hot and wet things are also hot or wet, just as the things themselves are. He also goes on to cite a number of facts as if they were bolstering his case though in fact they severely undercut it: "as the general chaos of our experience gets sifted, we find that there are some fires that will always burn sticks and always warm our bodies, and that there are some waters that will always put out fires; while there are other fires and waters that will not act at all." [32] The ones that do act are termed "energetic" by James, so that once more everything exists on a flat ontological plane of images, with some of them simply more energetic than others. Despite James's earlier complaints that addition is a better model of how the world is formed than subtraction, the way that the sphere of subjectivity is constructed seems to be through the de-energizing of energetic experiences into paler versions of themselves. "This would be the 'evolution' of the psychical from the bosom of the physical, in which the esthetic, moral and otherwise emotional experiences would represent a halfway stage." [36] But "thoughts in the concrete are made of the same stuff as things are." [37] For James, there is no distinction at all between sensual and real. The former are simply less energetic versions of the latter.

The remaining chapters in James's book serve as further development of this radical equation of thoughts and things as explained in the opening thirty pages. Like other empiricists, James favors individually experienced parts over arbitrarily constructed wholes. But what makes his empiricism "radical," he says, is that the relations between separate things must also form part of experience. The empiricism of Berkeley or Hume treats the parts of experience as intrinsically disconnected, and this merely opens the door for rationalists to introduce "trans-experiential agents of unification, substances, intellectual categories and powers, or Selves ...." [43] James fights both of these tendencies by saying that a connection between things does exist, but that it is encountered directly in experience rather than lying somewhere beneath it. James the philosopher echoes James the psychologist in saying that the fundamental fact of reality is "[the] absence of break and [this] sense of continuity in that most intimate of all conjunctive relations."[128] [50] This experience of "one's personal continuum" [50] is the origin of all concepts of continuity and sameness, and hence we can ignore those "over-subtle intellects ... [who] have ended by substituting a lot of static objects of conception for the direct personal experiences." [50] Trans-experiential substances or absolutes are mere fictions compared with these more directly experienced realities.

One of the advantages of this standpoint, James holds, is that it frees us from the idea of a gap between subject and object that needs to be bridged. [52] He famously ridicules this notion as that of a *salto mortale* or perilous leap. [67] Instead, the subject-object conjunction is already given in experience. [53] If I mention Memorial Hall at Harvard, the test of whether I know what I am talking about is whether I can lead you there in person and give some information about the history and use of the building: "that percept was what I *meant* ...." [56] For James as for Husserl, knowledge reaches its fulfillment in the direct presence of the thing to the mind. This fulfillment is not a perilous leap from a mind-pole to an object-pole, but unrolls gradually and continuously in time, as my vague notion of Memorial Hall is replaced by increasingly nearer approaches to it: "Knowledge of sensible realities thus comes to life inside the tissue of experience. It is *made*; and made by relations that unroll themselves in time." [57] For James this is what knowledge is, and it is foolish to expect anything more: "unions by continuous transition are the only ones we know of ...." [59] The supposed mutual otherness of subject and object is a mere illusion. [60] The representations of things in our mind are not epistemological miracles occurring across a fearful gap, but simply result from a process of substitution. [61] The vast majority of our thoughts involve substitutes for nothing actual, and lead only to "wayward fancies, utopias, fictions or mistakes." [64] In these illusions we are all trapped in our individual lives and fail to make contact with one another's thoughts, which intersect only at scattered nuclei of reality. Applying the "pragmatic method" [72] to this question, James asserts that the model of knowledge as self-transcendence would lead to no practical difference from that of the model he has just proposed, and hence the dispute is merely "a quarrel over words." [72] Under both models of knowledge, we have no choice but to move gradually

---

[128] [Here I have corrected a quotation that was garbled when this chapter first appeared in English, in *Bells and Whistles*, p. 51 — G.H.]

and continuously towards immediate perceptual givenness of whatever we wish to know. In this way, "the universe continually grows in quantity by new experiences that graft themselves upon the older mass ...." [90]

Reality for James is primarily a constant flux of experiences. Yet he must also admit that we do not see the world as an unrestricted flux. As he concedes, with typical Jamesian wit: "Only new-born babes, or men in semi-coma from sleep, drugs, illnesses, or blows, may be assumed to have an experience pure in the literal sense of a *that* which is not yet any definite *what* [i.e., a pure experiential flux] ...." [93] These experiences exist entirely in the form of relations, which James (as opposed to F.H. Bradley) treats as *external* relations that are not inscribed in the inherent character of each experience. As we have seen, the fact that something is "conscious" does not mean that it has a different mode of reality from a physical thing, "but rather that it stands in certain determinate relations to other portions of experience extraneous to itself." [123] The pen that stores ink and can be picked up and used to write on paper is the physical pen, while the one that comes and goes in my distracted mind is the perceptual pen. Recall that these two are not different in kind for James, but simply stand in different types of relations to other experiences. But even the physical pen is not an enduring substantial unity through time, but an instantaneous experience that has "successors." When these successors are "energetic," they also earn the right to be called stably existing physical things, [128] whereas the un-energetic successors are not the physical ones. James as a psychologist had made the same point about personal identity through time, which is not that of a durable substance, but only that of later experiences appealing to and building upon earlier ones. But only insofar as the pen is "appropriated" does it become an experience that belongs to me [130], and it is easy to see that a second mind could easily appropriate the same pen in its own way: "a second subsequent experience, collateral and contemporary with the first subsequent one, in which a similar act of appropriation should occur. The two acts would interfere neither with one another nor with the originally pure pen." [131] Whereas "the pen-experience in its original immediacy is not aware of itself [but] simply *is*," [132] the pen in consciousness simply has my being added to it. The pen itself is the one that is intrinsically neither mine nor yours. [133]

As opposed to the usual view of causality as arising from a secret depth in things, James concludes "that real effectual causation as an ultimate nature, as a 'category,' if you like, of reality, is *just what we feel it to be*, just that kind of conjunction which our own activity-series reveals." [185] It would be "healthy" if philosophy were "to leave off grubbing underground" for it [186], and simply "[refuse] to entertain the hypothesis of trans-empirical reality at all." [195] The difference between our idea of an object and the object itself is nothing other than the difference between a less vivid perception and a more vivid one to which it is capable of leading:

> To call my present idea of my dog, for example, cognitive of the real dog means that, as the actual tissue of experience is constituted, the idea is capable of leading into a chain of other experiences on my part that go from next to next and terminate at last in vivid sense-perceptions of a jumping, barking, hairy body. Those *are* the real dog, the dog's full presence, for my common sense. [198]

The last four words of this passage should not be taken as any sort of qualifier. For James, it is not just common sense that equates the real dog with a direct perception of the dog. Much more than this, there is no such thing as the "real" over and above the definitive perceptual experience of a thing. As James puts it a bit later, "a conception is reckoned true by common sense when it can be made to lead to a sensation," [202] and here James treats common sense not as a crusty source of dogma in need of subversion, but as an ally that knows the truth better than overly subtle intellectuals do. Truth should never "consist in a relation between our experiences and something archetypal or trans-experiential." [204]

We should close this summary of radical empiricism with a few choice quotations from the final chapter of James's book, which happens to be written in French (it was read in that language at an international conference in Rome). While none of these passages will be surprising after what we have seen so far, they provide a nice summation of James's philosophy. "I believe that consciousness as we commonly represent it to ourselves, whether as an entity, whether as pure activity, but in any case as fluid, unextended, transparent, empty of all proper content ... I believe, I say, that this consciousness is a pure chimera ...."[129] [222] What we call consciousness is "only a series of intermediate experiences perfectly susceptible of being described in concrete terms."[130] [231] Subject and object are only *functionally*

---

[129] In the French: "*Je crois que la conscience, telle qu'on se la représente communément, soit come entité, soit comme activité pure, mais en tout cas comme fluide, inétendue, diaphane, vide de tout contenu proper ... je crois, dis-je, que cette conscience est une pure chimère ....*"

[130] In the French: "*n'est ... qu'une suite d'expériences intermédiaires parfaitement susceptibles d'être décrites en termes concrets.*"

different, not two utterly opposite terms as in the traditional dualism. They are "made of the same stuff ... which might be called the stuff of experience in general."[131] [233]

3. Problems with Radical Empiricism

Essays in Radical Empiricism is a wonderfully imaginative book, and as beautiful as nearly everything penned by James. Here James the psychologist translates his discovery of the "stream of consciousness" into ontological terms, while James the philosophical innovator is delighted at the chance to eliminate numerous supposed pseudo-problems inherited from the past. Indeed, he seems thrilled by the possible emergence of a great new philosophical era. Nevertheless, I find a certain incoherence in radical empiricism as proposed in this book, and would like to explain why this doctrine should not be adopted. First, there are problems resulting from James's tendency to conflate the distinction between subject and object with that between thought and thing. These differences are by no means the same. For it would be one thing to agree with James that the dog as a perception in my mind is not different in kind from the dog as a thing in the world, so that both are nothing but "experiences" of a different degree of "energy" in each case. James has already told us that there is no dog more real than the dog that is finally encountered in direct face-to-face perception. This claim is already radical enough, in the sense that it verges on frank idealism. Yet it is quite another thing to go even further, and say that there is no difference between I who experience the dog and the series of my experiences of it. James is quick to take this second step while pretending that it is no different from the already dubious step of equating thoughts and things. As he puts it in his French lecture at the close of the book, consciousness is "only a series of intermediate experiences perfectly susceptible of being described in concrete terms." [231] In short, there is no "I" doing the experiencing, but only a series of experiences joined together in an appropriative way and having a similar style. The supposed "I" is really just a bundle of experiences.

The first problem with this claim is that I am in fact something quite different from a bundle of experiences, and for at least two reasons. One is that I can also be experienced by others, even though these others have no

---

[131] In the French: "... *sont faites d'une même étoffe ... que l'on peut nommer, si on veut, l'étoffe de l'expérience en général.*"

direct access whatsoever to my series of experiences. You can read surprise in the movement of my eyebrows and years of forced Gulag labor in the deep creases of my weather-beaten face. But in these cases, the text you are reading is me, not my experiences, which are no more directly accessible to you than yours are to me in return. The other reason why I am not just a bundle of experiences is that I am no more just the things that happen to me than a stone is just the things that happen to it. Rather, certain things happen to us as entities only because *we are* the things that we are. New experiences are possible only because the world is more than how I have experienced it so far, but also because I am more than what the world has seen so far of me. To give a personal example, next week I will visit Morocco for the first time. Note that I am able to do so even though the history of experiences that James would identify with my "self" contains no direct perceptual experiences of Morocco of the sort that James treats as the highest form of both knowledge and reality. Yet there are elements of my self — love of travel, responsiveness to academic duty — that surged forth when summoned, and grasped the fleeting opportunity of Casablanca. The principle through which new experiences emerge does not lie solely on the side of experiences unfolding in a neutral, observer-free space. Instead, there is someone who is undergoing the experiences without being identical to them, and this someone can embrace, reject, and even change the course of whatever happens to unfold in Morocco.

James is also too fond of the *continuum* as his basic model of reality. Despite his concession that only new-born babes and men reduced to semi-coma have anything like pure experience unarticulated into parts, he does tend to view such continua as the primary sort of reality, and treats any landscape carved up into discrete entities as somehow derivative of this primal swirling flux. The problem here is that the supposed continuum of reality is contradicted by James's own views on other topics. When he wonders in his book how two minds can know the same thing, he does not solve the problem with the radical step of saying that all apparently separate minds are part of a primordial world-lump and hence not as different as might be believed. Instead, James takes it for granted that you are one knower and I am another, and even outlines a process by which each of us can appropriate the same landscape or port for ourselves as experiences of our own. And after all, James's extended polemic in the book against Bradley (omitted from the present article for reasons of space) is based on James's view that *external* relations exist — relations into which a thing can enter or not enter without affecting that thing's internal constitution. I can either go to Morocco or cancel the flight one day ahead of time and still be the same person. In short, while James's love of the continuum *within* any given entity's experience might seem partly defensible, it is entirely contradicted by his assumption that there are numerous different zones of experience, numerous different knowers who are in fact distinct from one another and not part of some continuum of knowledge and experience. Many different entities have experiences of their own, and these are communicated only with difficulty. By James's own admission, there is not a single writhing world-soul that simultaneously feels all the pleasures and pains of the cosmos.

But once we see that James is in favor of different zones of experience, of knowers partly cut off from another and drifting through private lives of their own, his erosion of the difference between thought and thing immediately becomes dubious. For if the relations between things are external relations, it is not clear how my direct encounter with the dog can be the same as that dog itself. For if that were the case, the dog would be utterly used up by our encounter, exhaustively deployed in being a perception or experience for me here and now. Yet the dog is clearly *not* the same thing as my experience of the dog, as James fully recognizes when discussing other objects such as candles. The dog residing in my perception cannot eat or reproduce, but at best can only *seem* to do these things without these appearances necessarily having any causal impact. James's assertion that things have causal relations whenever they *seem* to do so, rather than having subterranean causal powers that one must grub for in the depths, is clearly false. The dog in perception is always viewed from a specific angle and distance, while the dog in its own right need not present itself from any particular angle or distance. When combining these observations with the earlier point that I as a series of experiences am not the same thing as the I experienced by others, we will begin to see the impossibility of equating thoughts with things.

In this way it becomes evident that James either rejects or misses both of the cardinal principles of object-oriented philosophy. If James had lived to speak of Heidegger's tool-analysis, for instance, he would probably have said that the breaking of the hammer is something that occurs solely on a plateau where the hammer is *experienced* by someone or something. The realist pretensions of the tool-analysis would then be rejected, and replaced by a sheer phenomenalism of tool-beings. But this claim would be at odds with James's own firm belief in external relations, since the claim would be that reality is nothing more than how it happens to appear to someone or something over time. Yet the hammer breaks, not because a previous experience of the hammer already had the future breakdown inscribed within its heart; instead, what breaks is something in the hammer that was *unexperienced* — a slumbering residue of fragility that had never emerged into the world of experience until now. The hammer was always more than experience took it to be.

So much for James's unjustified rejection of the first axis between real and sensual. But he fails even to notice the second axis found in Husserl's ingenious distinction between objects and their contents. For even *within* the realm of experience, experiences are not equivalent to our experiences of them. Or stated differently, experienced objects are always *less* than what experience takes them to be. The donkeys and zebras trotting across the plain are seen with utter specificity of detail at every instant, yet the animals themselves are not that specific, since they are capable of being encountered in numerous different ways. James is too close to the traditional empiricists in viewing objects as bundles of qualities, and too close to idealism in viewing objects as nothing but their manifestations in the world. At least he avoids the traditional pitfall of idealism through his openness to making experience more global than just a matter for humans and animals.

James is often praised for the so-called "pragmatic method," just as Occam is endlessly praised for his widely misunderstood Razor. The public seems especially fond of methods which allow it to be convinced that other people are merely wasting our time with useless subtleties and non-existent entities. Along these same lines, the pragmatic method tells us that unless a proposed intellectual difference would make some actual difference in the world, then it must be nothing more than a dispute over words. But I would propose that we reverse this into an anti-pragmatic or object-oriented method, and say as follows: unless a given distinction has ontological consequences that might have no effects at all in the practical world, then we are locked in a mere dispute over symptoms, and not yet dealing with the things themselves.

CHAPTER 6
WHITEHEAD & SCHOOLS X, Y, AND Z[132]

Alfred North Whitehead is generally described as a "process philosopher." Little wonder, since his major book is entitled *Process and Reality*, it inspired the so-called "process theology" movement, and kindred phrases such as "process studies" automatically suggest a Whiteheadian influence. The bond between Whitehead and the word "process" is obviously unbreakable, and I will waste no energy attempting to break it. Instead, I want to note an ambiguity in the term that encourages a misleading assessment not only of Whitehead, but of the entire present-day landscape of continental philosophy. Above all, Whitehead has been linked too closely in recent years with the philosophy of Gilles Deleuze.[133] Without engaging in dispute with individual commentators, I would like to suggest that we now suffer from the conflation of two entirely different philosophical schools.

As I see it, one of these schools includes both Whitehead and the present-day French thinker Bruno Latour.[134] We can call this group "School X" to mark the difficulty of inscribing it in either analytic or continental philosophy. After all, the analytics and continentals are both

---

[132] "Whitehead and Schools X, Y, and Z" originally appeared in 2014 in *The Lure of Whitehead*, ed. Nicholas Gaskill & Adam Nocek, pp. 231–248.

[133] See for example Steven Shaviro, *Without Criteria*. And for perhaps the most prominent instance see Isabelle Stengers, *Thinking with Whitehead*. Her subtitle's reference to the Deleuzian phrase "creation of concepts" is already a giveaway that Stengers reads Whitehead through Deleuzian lenses.

[134] For a more complete account of my interpretation of Latour see Graham Harman, *Prince of Networks*.

inclined toward Kantian presuppositions in a manner that Latour and Whitehead brazenly renounce. In the first part of this essay, I will show why Whitehead and Latour should not be linked too closely with a second group of powerful thinkers, including such figures as Henri Bergson, Manuel DeLanda, William James, Gilbert Simondon, and Isabelle Stengers. To distinguish this group from School X, we might whimsically term it "School Y." When these groups are too easily united, with little sense of the friction between them, then we completely miss what ought to be a pivotal debate in present-day continental philosophy. For whereas School X opposes the traditional philosophy of enduring substance with a relational but ultimately punctiform model of entities, School Y opposes substance in the name of an uncensored form of raw, pulsating, nonstop flux-and-flow action in which becoming is continuous and individual states or moments do not really exist. In what follows, I will assess both of these philosophical schools and oppose them from my own preferred position: "School Z," more commonly known as object-oriented philosophy. Whitehead plays a central role in this essay for the following reason. He deserves praise for defending individual entities against the blend-o-rama of becoming that defines today's fashion, but also deserves blame for reducing entities to their relations. This gives Whitehead a compellingly ambiguous status from the standpoint of School Z.

Process, Becoming, and Relation

We should begin by distinguishing between three different notions: *process, becoming,* and *relation*. Unless these terms are treated separately, the nature of the choice now facing continental philosophy will be hopelessly obscured. In the present context, the broadest of the three is surely *process*. Although the phrase "process philosophy" often functions as a proper name referring to Whitehead's own philosophy, we might use it more generally to refer to all recent philosophies that emphasize change over stasis. Rather than viewing the world as made up of enduring substances "which enjoy adventures of change throughout time and space," change is now regarded as primary, and the apparent stasis of enduring things must be explained rather than presupposed.[135] [35] It is true enough that all of the thinkers listed above in both Schools X and Y (Bergson, DeLanda, Deleuze, James,

---

[135] Throughout this chapter, all page numbers in square brackets refer to Alfred North Whitehead, *Process and Reality*.

Latour, Simondon, Stengers, and Whitehead) are philosophers of change. None of them speaks favorably of traditional enduring substance or essence, and all seek a dynamic view of the cosmos in opposition to the supposedly static one of past philosophy.

But not all philosophers of process are philosophers of *becoming*. If "process philosophy" means that underlying substances must be replaced by concrete events, "philosophy of becoming" means that individual entities *per se* are derivative of a more primordial dynamism, thereby reducing individuals to realities of the second rank. Though process and becoming might seem closely related, the former term is actually the broader one: some process philosophers *are not* philosophers of becoming. The two shining examples of this are Whitehead and Latour. For Whitehead, it is by no means true that individuals are derivative of a primordial or virtual indeterminate flux; instead, individuals are the very stuff of reality: "'actual entities' — also termed 'actual occasions' — are the final real things of which the world itself is made up. There is no going behind actual entities to find anything more real. They differ among themselves: God is an actual entity, and so is the most trivial puff of existence in far-off empty space." [18] Later, Whitehead draws an even sharper contrast between this principle of actual entities and the view that everything is in continuous flux:

> the extensive continuity of the physical universe has usually been
> construed to mean that there is a continuity of becoming. But … it
> is easy, by employing Zeno's method, to prove that there can be no
> continuity of becoming. There is a becoming of continuity, but no
> continuity of becoming …. Thus the ultimate metaphysical truth is
> atomism. [35]

We should also remember Whitehead's famous "ontological principle," which means "that actual entities are the only *reasons;* so that to search for a *reason* is to search for one or more actual entities." [24] In other words, everything that happens must be explained by the workings of individuals, and by this alone. There is no "pre-individual" realm in Latour or Whitehead, but a world made up entirely of distinct individuals.[136] This is by no means the case for School Y, in which individuals are derivative in comparison with

---

[136] An exception can be found in Latour's recent writings in his sporadic references to a giant unformatted "plasma" lying beneath all individual things. See Bruno Latour, *Reassembling the Social*, pp. 50, 132, 227, 241, 244, 245, 253. For a discussion of why this plasma is inconsistent with the rest of Latour's philosophy see Harman, *Prince of Networks*, pp. 132–134.

primordial fluxes and wholes, topological structures, attractors, virtualities, and other pre-individuals said to be deeper than fully articulated actors and entities. Latour is entirely Whiteheadian in his tacit embrace of the ontological principle, and Latour's emphasis on real individuals even leads to a candid thesis against the primacy of becoming: "Time is the distant consequences of actors as they each seek to create a *fait accompli* on their own behalf that cannot be reversed. In this way time passes." In other words, "time does not pass. Times are what is at stake between forces."[137] What this means is that time and becoming are not autonomous forces lying somewhere outside or prior to individually determinate entities. Instead of entities being derivative of a primordial flux, time and becoming are produced by individual actors. In this way Latour can even be viewed as a sort of anti-Bergson. The point has become even more obvious with the publication of Latour's new systematic work, *An Inquiry into Modes of Existence,* which includes REP (reproduction) as one of fourteen modes of existence.[138] The reason REP is a basic category for Latour is that nothing continues inertly in existence through any sort of Bergsonian *élan* or *durée.* Instead, each entity is punctiform and passes away in an instant, which entails the need of ontological labor to reproduce it.

This Whiteheadian-Latourian focus on fully determinate individuals would be puzzling to the thinkers I have termed School Y, since none of them places individual entities at the basis of the cosmos. Deleuze tends to treat individuals as sterile efflorescences on the surface of the world, with the deeper "virtual" plane as more vital and less determinate than individuals.[139] Simondon's niche as a metaphysician consists almost entirely in his subordination of fully formed individuals to the *process* of individuation, whereas I will show that Whitehead's use of "process" always goes hand in hand with the absolute supremacy of fully formed (though transient) individuals.[140] James is also a typical School Y figure on the question of individuals. In psychology as in philosophy, James condemns those "over-subtle intellects ... [who] have ended by substituting a lot of static objects of conception for ... direct personal experiences."[141] And then we have Bergson, the granddaddy of them all, for whom individuals are carved out of flux by the needs of human practical action. In *Creative Evolution,*

---

137 Bruno Latour, "Irreductions," p. 165.
138 Bruno Latour, *An Inquiry Into Modes of Existence.*
139 Gilles Deleuze, *Logic of Sense.*
140 Gilbert Simondon, *Individuation in Light of Notions of Form and Information.*
141 William James, *Essays in Radical Empiricism,* p. 50.

Bergson makes the typically Bergsonian statement that "the truth is that we change without ceasing, and that the state itself is nothing but change."[142] And as concerns the status of individual things:

> The distinct outlines which we see in an object, and which give it its individuality, are only the design of a certain *kind* of influence that we might exert on a certain point of space; it is the plan of our eventual actions that is sent back to our eyes, as though by a mirror, when we see the surfaces and edges of things. Suppress this action, and with it consequently those main directions which by perception are traced out for it in the entanglement of the real, and the individuality of the body is re-absorbed in the universal interaction which, without doubt, is reality itself.[143]

The concept of "universal interaction" leads us to the third idea I wished to discuss: *relation*. Philosophies of relation are those that hold that the thing is not an autonomous reality apart from its interactions with other things, but is instead constituted by those interactions. Bergson declares this standpoint in the passage just cited, and even more clearly so in his early masterpiece *Matter and Memory*.[144] James and Simondon are clearly practitioners of a relational ontology, though in the cases of Deleuze and perhaps Stengers, this may or may not be a point of greater controversy. As for the School X of Whitehead and Latour, they serve up what might be the most relational ontologies in the history of Western thought. Latour tells us bluntly in *Pandora's Hope* that the reality of an entity (an "actor," in his terminology) is defined by nothing more than "what other actors are modified, transformed, perturbed, or created by the [actor] that is the focus of attention."[145] In Whitehead's case, we read in similar fashion that "in a sense, every entity pervades the whole world" (28), and further, that "each atom [i.e., each actual entity] is a system of all things." [36] This all sounds a great deal like Leibniz's hyper-relational manifesto in the *Monadology*: "As a result, every body is affected by everything that happens in the universe . . . 'All things conspire,' said Hippocrates."[146] But whereas Leibniz gave us the monads as underlying substances, Latour and Whitehead give us

---

[142] Henri Bergson, *Creative Evolution*, p. 2.

[143] Bergson, *Creative Evolution*, p. 10.

[144] Henri Bergson, *Matter and Memory*.

[145] Bruno Latour, *Pandora's Hope*, p. 122.

[146] G.W. Leibniz, "The Principles of Philosophy, or The Monadology," §62.

monadologies without enduring monads — theories in which individuals are entirely reducible to the conspiracies they weave with other things.

Let me now summarize how all these terms play out for the purposes of this essay. The members of both School X and School Y (unlike, say, Aristotle or Aquinas) are philosophers of *process* rather than static things. But only the School Y philosophers are devoted to *becoming* rather than individuals, since in Whitehead and Latour the reason for everything that happens must be found in individual entities themselves. Moreover, these entities are not just derivative outcroppings of some deeper pre-individual becoming — as we find especially in such figures as Bergson, James, Deleuze, and Simondon. As for *relations,* both School X and School Y prefer relations over things, the former more vehemently than the latter. Since School X and School Y both prefer process over stasis, they seem to present a united front against traditional philosophies of substance. In the present day, they have much momentum in their favor, since the current fashion is to view substance as rigid, static, reactionary, patriarchal, and oppressive, while dynamic fluxes and flows strike the educated public as innovative, liberating, interactive, holistic, and fresh. The roots of this antisubstance reaction can be found in the idealist or empiricist flavor of modern philosophy, which asks what is directly *accessible* in things, rather than what is arbitrarily posited as lying outside direct access; a commitment to *immanence* has become fashionable, while any talk of *transcendence* is taken to be a retrograde mark of intellectual shame. In turn, the tendency to define things in terms of their relations *to us* sometimes mutates, among more speculative thinkers, into the habit of defining them by way of their relations *to each other* as well. In our time, it is widely believed that only a miserable, Scrooge-like curmudgeon would ever defend stasis over process. Yet this nearly unanimous outcry against traditional substance must not overshadow a deeper schism between School X and School Y on the question of becoming. As we have seen, becoming is by no means defended by Whitehead and Latour, who treat individuals as utterly determinate in each instant. Nor must this pair of themes (process and becoming) be confused with that of relation, which will turn out to be altogether separate from the theme of process. At this point a diagram may be helpful. (Exclamation marks refer to especial intensity of commitment.)

As is clear from Figure 1 and the foregoing discussion, School Y affirms all three principles — process, becoming, and relation — as pillars of its ontology. My own position, object-oriented philosophy, rejects all three.[147]

---

[147] For the most concise account available at present see Graham Harman, *The Quadruple Object.*

	Process	Becoming	Relations
School X (Latour, Whitehead)	YES!	NO	YES!
School Y (Bergson, DeLanda, Deleuze, James, Simondon, Stengers	YES!	YES!	YES
School Z (object-oriented philosophy)	NO	NO!	NO!

Figure 1: Though Whitehead's process philosophy has been conflated with Deleuze's philosophy of becoming, the differences between these two schools — and a third school, object-oriented philosophy — can be sharpened by attending to their positions on process, becoming, and relations.

School X is very close to School Y, diverging from it only on the question of becoming. But this divergence has serious implications for present-day continental philosophy, as the remainder of this essay will clarify.

In passing, it should be noted that there are other possibly useful ways of grouping these authors. For example, Latour and Whitehead agree strongly with object-oriented philosophy in treating all relations in the same manner as the human-world relation: the human relation to a window is no different *in kind* from that of raindrops to the window. Some of the School Y figures might also agree on this point, while others would not, but to decide this question would require a more intricate reading of these figures than the present essay can undertake.

I will now give a brief survey of Whitehead's views on the three notions of process, becoming, and relation, and then conclude this survey with a brief discussion of why all three are unsuitable as foundational principles of ontology.

Whitehead and Process

Yes, Whitehead is a philosopher of process.

It would not be unfair to say that Western philosophy has valued the eternal and unchanging, or at least the durable, over the manifold transient processes unfolding in the world. This is clear enough in Plato and his tradition, so devoted to the eternity of forms — the perfect cat, horse, tree, justice, friendship, or other *eidei* that serve as eternal models for all fleeting, mortal entities. It is true, on the other hand, that for Aristotle and many of his followers, substance need not be eternal. (Leibniz is a notable exception.) Yet Aristotelian primary substance is always somewhat durable, enduring as the same thing for many seconds, hours, days, years, or millennia. Even in the phenomenology of Edmund Husserl, which aspires to be so sensitive to the multiple shifting facets of conscious experience, there are intentional objects that endure over time despite being seen in many different "adumbrations." According to Husserl, a blackbird or mailbox can appear to consciousness in countless different ways, but always as the *same* blackbird or mailbox. In all these philosophers, the movement of the world is subordinated to some nucleus of stasis; the adjective and verb are conquered by the noun. In this way, with scattered exceptions (David Hume comes to mind) the Western philosophical tradition through the early nineteenth century shows a marked preference for enduring units that lie beneath the world's surface of transient happenings.

In the late nineteenth century, the tide began to turn. Along with some striking passages in Nietzsche, we find Bergson and James insisting that experience is a ceaseless stream in constant fluctuation.[148] The enduring thing-in-itself, an unchanging subject of change lying beneath all surface fluctuation, is de-emphasized to the point of being abandoned. Throughout the twentieth century, philosophies of substance are widely accused of reactionary archaism and a general opposition to the new. Non-Western cultures are frequently praised for being less beholden to petrified enduring substances and their ostensible counterpart, subject-predicate grammar. One example can be found in Whitehead himself: "the philosophy of organism [i.e., Whitehead's own philosophy] seems to approximate more to some strains of Indian, or Chinese, thought, than to western Asiatic, or European, thought. One side makes process ultimate; the other makes fact ultimate" (7). We find a further well-known example in Benjamin Lee Whorf's praise of Hopi grammar for its superior sense of temporal fluctuation, which in his view makes it better equipped than Western tongues to navigate the mysterious sea of quantum physics.[149] Much of Whitehead's philosophy can be interpreted as belonging to the same recent current of antisubstance sentiment that motivates Bergson and James. For instance, early in *Process and Reality* Whitehead writes as follows: "the philosophy of

[148] Henri Bergson, *Time and Free Will*; William James, *The Principles of Psychology*.
[149] Benjamin Lee Whorf, *Language, Thought, and Reality*.

organism is closely allied to Spinoza's scheme of thought. But it differs by the abandonment of the subject-predicate form of thought .... The result is that ... morphological description is replaced by description of dynamic process." [7] More broadly, Whitehead gives the following condemnation of traditional cosmological speculation:

> the notion of continuous stuff with permanent attributes, enduring
> without differentiation, and retaining its self-identity through any
> stretch of time however small or large, has been fundamental [to
> traditional Western philosophy]. The stuff undergoes change in
> respect to accidental qualities and relations; but it is numerically
> self-identical in its character of one actual entity throughout
> its accidental adventures. The admission of this fundamental
> metaphysical concept has wrecked the various systems of pluralistic
> realism. [78]

He attacks those philosophers who go through the motions of critiquing Aristotle while retaining his traditional subject-predicate grammar. This leads Whitehead to a fairly damning indictment of Aristotle's metaphysics as a whole: "The evil produced by the Aristotelian 'primary substance' is exactly this habit of metaphysical emphasis upon the 'subject-predicate' form of proposition." [30] As Aristotle explains in the *Metaphysics,* the primary substances are individual things that can support different qualities at different times. Socrates can be happy and then sad while remaining Socrates all the while; this is what makes him a substance. By contrast, since happy is always happy and sad is always sad, these terms are never substances. In a grammatical sense, this means that Socrates is a subject while happy and sad are predicates. But Whitehead repeatedly insists that the metaphysics lying behind this grammar is mistaken. As he puts it: "The simple notion of an enduring substance sustaining persistent qualities, either essentially or accidentally, expresses a useful abstract for many purposes of life. But whenever we try to use it as a fundamental statement of the nature of things, it proves itself mistaken." [79] Although Whitehead concedes that there are good pragmatic reasons to speak of enduring substances in everyday language and logic, he holds that "in metaphysics the concept is sheer error." [79] Why sheer error? The reason can be found in Whitehead's personal vision of what an entity is, and that is the topic of the next section. So far, we have seen that Whitehead is undeniably a process philosopher. He does not believe in the primacy of enduring individual things that would serve as the substrate of qualitative surface change. What is primary is change itself.

Whitehead and Becoming

No, Whitehead *is not* a philosopher of becoming.

A philosopher of becoming is one who denies that the world is best understood in terms of individual things or individual instants of time. Instead, the world is a pre-individual field not fully carved up into distinct entities, and time is a continuous duration rather than a series of isolated cinematic frames. We have already seen that neither of these views is affirmed by the School X philosophies of Whitehead or Latour. The Whiteheadian cosmos is governed by the ontological principle, according to which discrete actual entities are the root of all reality. Here we could not be further from Simondon's denunciation of fully formed individuals as the product of philosophical naïveté. Whitehead is not interested in the generation of individuals from a quasi-determinate pre-individual field, but in the generation of individuals *from prior individuals*. The sense of the word "process" in Whitehead is completely different from what it is in Simondon.

Whitehead's world is one of actual entities, which he also calls "actual occasions." The reason for this alternate terminology, "occasion," is the completely instantaneous nature of actual entities: "an actual entity never moves: it is where it is and what it is. In order to emphasize this characteristic by a phrase connecting the notion of 'actual entity' more closely with our ordinary habits of thought, I will also use the term 'actual occasion' in the place of the term 'actual entity.'" [73] Latour proposes the similar principle that each thing happens just once, in one place and one time only.[150] Whitehead's actual entity does not undergo adventures in time and space, because it is completely defined by its specific stance in time and space, its relation to all other things. For this reason the entity can only *perish,* not change: "Actual entities perish, but do not change; they are what they are." [35] Aristotle's primary substances also are what they are, but in Aristotle's case this does not include their exact relational dealings with all other entities, whereas in Whitehead's case it does. His actual entities, like Latour's, are so utterly concrete that they cannot endure the slightest shift in their features without dying instantly. "Actual occasions in their 'formal' constitutions are devoid of all indetermination …. They are complete and

---

[150] Latour, "Irreductions," p. 162.

determinate matter of fact, devoid of all indetermination." [29] Whitehead's technical term for this is "satisfaction."

In short, for all his talk of dynamic process, Whitehead's philosophy is one in which entities are so utterly determinate that they can last only for an instant before perishing and being replaced by other actual entities. If School Y defends a dynamism deeper than any individual entities, the dynamism of School X consists entirely in a chain of such entities stretching across time. Consider the two senses in which Whitehead's philosophy continues the occasionalist tradition in philosophy. Occasionalism began as an early Islamic theological school in Basra, upholding the view that God was not only the sole creator in the universe, but the only legitimate causal agent at all. For this reason, even the mere collision between two inanimate objects must be mediated by God. Moreover, since endurance was viewed as an accident of things, the world was made solely of perishing things and time made solely of disconnected instants, so that a continuous creation of the universe was necessary.[151] These ideas later passed into European philosophy through the French Cartesians, though they lost their prestige during the general Enlightenment onslaught against divinity. Whitehead is perhaps the most candid recent defender of *both* senses of occasionalism: the inability of two entities to interact without the mediation of God, and the disjunctions between separate instants of time.

As for divine intervention in the philosophy of Whitehead, it occurs always and everywhere. When actual entities other than God prehend one another, or relate to one another, they do this always in terms of specific qualities ("eternal objects"). God's role in this process is stated clearly enough: "the things which are temporal arise by their participation in the things which are eternal. The two sets are mediated by a thing which combines the actuality of what is temporal with the timelessness of what is potential. This final entity is the divine element in the world." [40] And as concerns the radical disconnection of temporal instants, this is clear enough from the passages in which Whitehead describes the "perpetual perishing" of actual entities. It is true that Whitehead ascribes to these actual entities an appetite, conatus, or drive that pushes them beyond their current instantaneous being: "Appetition is immediate matter of fact including in itself a principle of unrest." [32] Yet this addition of appetite to actual entities seems utterly

---

[151] For a clear overview of this theme in the history of Islamic philosophy see Majid Fakhry, *Islamic Occasionalism*. A more recent work in German with an even broader theme is Dominik Perler & Ulrich Rudolph, *Occasionalismus*.

gratuitous. In speaking of prehensions, Whitehead writes: "the analysis of an actual entity into 'prehensions' is that mode of analysis which exhibits the most concrete elements in the nature of actual entities." [19] In other words, actual entities are nothing more than their prehensions, and this is what makes them actual *occasions* limited to a specific time and place and unable to undergo adventures outside those exact coordinates. The price one must pay for viewing entities as utterly determined by their specific situation, and hence as nondurable, is that it becomes difficult to see how one such self-contained entity could ever link to the next. It is for this reason that Whitehead posits "appetite" as a sort of bonus property of his self-contained actual entities. In doing so, he risks committing a classic *vis dormitiva* maneuver. Just as Molière's physician claims that opium causes sleep by means of a sleeping faculty, Whitehead's "appetite" — despite his explicit critique of the "faculty psychology" [xiii] — implies that actual entities change by means of a changing faculty. Or rather, since actual entities are excluded from the possibility of change, they are replaced by new entities by means of a faculty-for-being-replaced. In this respect, Whitehead shows himself guilty of the same incoherence that he says can be found in all philosophies after sufficient analysis:

> Incoherence is the arbitrary disconnection of first principles. In modern philosophy Descartes' two kinds of substance, corporeal and mental, illustrate incoherence. There is, in Descartes' philosophy, no reason why there should not be a one-substance world, only corporeal, or a one-substance world, only mental .... The attraction of Spinoza's philosophy lies in its modification of Descartes' position into greater coherence .... The gap in [Spinoza's] system is the arbitrary introduction of the "modes." [6–7]

By the same token, one of the gaps in Whitehead's system is the arbitrary introduction of appetite as a means of shying away from the radical discontinuity in moments of time that would otherwise be required by the absolute concreteness of actual occasions.

But this is not even the main issue. The main issue is that there are vividly occasionalist elements at the center of Whitehead's thought: the role of God as a relational mediator, and the nature of time as composed of disconnected punctiform instants. Latour is indebted to occasionalism in similar fashion, except that he makes no appeal to God as the mediator of all relations and instead treats mediation on a more secular and local level.[152] But what is most striking is how clearly this separates Latour and Whitehead from the figures grouped here under the title School Y. After all, the problems that motivate Whitehead's use of God as a relational mediator, and appetite as a mediator between instants, would be ridiculed by School Y from the outset as false problems. It is merely comical to imagine James or Deleuze positing God as a mediator between entities, and utterly ridiculous to imagine Bergson viewing time as made up of isolated occasions that would need to be bridged by a forward-looking "appetite" in the heart of each occasion.

Whitehead and Relation

Yes, Whitehead is a philosopher of relation.

Along with opposing durable substances that would persist across time, Whitehead even more famously opposes the notion that entities are self-contained. Indeed, Whitehead is one of the foremost champions in Western philosophy of a *relational* metaphysics, in which entities have no reality apart from their interaction with other entities. In this way, the old Western philosophical cosmos of rigid enduring things seems to be replaced by a dynamic universe of process and relation. We have already seen that Whitehead goes so far as to accept a doctrine of *internal* relations, according to which a thing's relations belong to its inner reality. After praising John Locke as a venerable forerunner, Whitehead adds the following objection: "Locke misses one essential doctrine, namely, that the doctrine of internal relations makes it impossible to attribute 'change' to any actual entity. Every actual entity is what it is, and is with its definite status in the universe, determined by its internal relations to other actual entities." [58–59] Stated differently, "the actual entity, in virtue of *what* it is, is also *where* it is. It is somewhere because it is some actual thing with its correlated actual world. This is the direct denial of the Cartesian doctrine, 'an existent thing which requires nothing but itself in order to exist.'" [59]

For Whitehead (and for Latour), the idea that a thing is determined by its relations is a necessary part of the doctrine "of individual actual entities, each with its own self-attainment." [60] Given the commitment of School X to process rather than static substances, we would veer dangerously close

---

[152] For an account of how Latour appeals to local causal mediators, specifically pinpointing Frédéric Joliot as the mediator between politics and neutrons, see Harman, *Prince of Networks*, pp. 73–75.

THE GRAHAM HARMAN READER

to Aristotelian substance if an actual entity were allowed to endure for more than an instant, preserving its reality despite shifting relations and shifting stances in space and time. This explains why School X is so much more vehement about the relationality of the world than School Y, just as the borderlands of a country are often more nationalistic than the capital.

On Behalf of School Z

One purpose of this essay has been to drive a wedge between two types of "process" philosophers, which I have called School X and School Y. Since both agree on dynamic process over stasis, and both roughly agree on a relational ontology (with School X being far more emphatic about relations), their point of disagreement can be found entirely in the theme of *becoming*. This amounts to the question of whether individual entities are the true engine of the world, or merely a sterile byproduct of deeper dynamisms. What we have found is that Whitehead and Latour stand out from the rest in elevating individual entities or actors to the pinnacle of reality, even to the point that such individuals are the root of everything else. The exact opposite is the case for the School Y thinkers, who do not regard actual individuals as the site where everything of importance occurs.

This difference is so glaring, and of such primordial metaphysical importance, that it remains somewhat shocking whenever attempts are made to synthesize Whitehead (and less often, Latour) with the philosophy of Deleuze, however common these attempts may be. Deleuzean philosophy has been in the ascendant since the mid-1990s, and has even become the standard avant-garde weaponry of continental thought. It should also be clear to any observer of the contemporary scene that this blurring of boundaries between X and Y is rarely initiated by the former school. We see few attempts by Latourians to colonize Deleuze for Latourian purposes, nor am I am aware of those who are principally Whiteheadians making such attempts with much frequency. Rather, the movement of conquest always seems to proceed in the opposite direction. Since there are few Jamesians anymore, while today's followers of Bergson, DeLanda, Simondon, and Stengers also tend to be followers of Deleuze, it is really the Deleuzian influence that sets the agenda in mixing Deleuze together with Whitehead in a single "process" stew.

When this happens, we lose what is unique to Whitehead in comparison with School Y. In my view, what is unique are the *gaps* in Whitehead's cosmos that must be bridged. We encountered these gaps when considering the two occasionalist elements in Whitehead's philosophy. First, God is needed to mediate the gap between actual entities (things) and eternal objects (qualities). This might also be described as the gap between the actual and the potential, or the discrete and the continuous. For as Whitehead puts it, "continuity concerns what is potential; whereas actuality is incurably atomic." [61] Note that the gap for Whitehead is not just between actualities and potentialities, but also between actualities and other actualities. After all, they encounter each other only by mediation of the eternal objects, being unable to prehend one another with total accuracy in the manner of which God alone is capable. No such puzzling gaps exist in School Y, which tends to view gaps as false problems left over from the bias of Western intellectual tradition, Indo-European grammar, or the *faiblesse* of common sense. Instead, in School Y there reigns a doctrine of continuity — whether of time (Bergson), the interrelation between things (James), or a pre-individual realm not yet carved into distinct individuals (Simondon). For School Y, it is discontinuity that must be explained rather than continuity.

There is no good reason to accept Whitehead's positing of God as a universal mediator who closes all gaps. I say this not because we must be good post-Enlightenment atheists obliged to ridicule God whenever he is mentioned in public, but because *no* specific entity should be empowered to function as a bridge across all gaps. If actual entities are unable to exhaust others with their mutual prehensions, then it is utterly arbitrary to stipulate that God alone (who is also described by Whitehead as an actual entity) is granted the miraculous ability to prehend other entities to their uttermost depths. Latour avoids this hypocrisy by attempting the first-ever secularized version of indirect causation, though I have argued elsewhere that his solution does not work either.[153] Yet the important point is that they have at least raised the question, which School Y is unable to do. Only a philosophy of actual individuals is capable of seeing that these individuals are individuals only when partly cut off from one another, and that if there are individuals then the world is already not a unified whole in which influence can be transmitted free of charge. Stated simply, either the world is one or it is many. If it is one, then we are in the territory of Parmenides, and there is no way to explain why the many would ever arise from the one. But if the world is many, then communication between this plurality of things poses a problem: they are separate things, there is a gap between them, and communication between one and the other can never be total

---

153 Harman, *Prince of Networks*, pp. 73–75.

and never direct, but requires a mediator.[154] On the question of the one and the many, it might seem as though Whitehead is trying to have it both ways: "The many become one, and are increased by one. In their natures, entities are disjunctively 'many' in process of passage into conjunctive unity. This Category of the Ultimate replaces Aristotle's 'primary substance.'" [21] But the conjunctive unity to which he refers does not ontologically cancel the disjunctive reality of the many, even if it unifies them. Note that Whitehead's Ultimate simply "increases by one" the army of the many, taking its place as a more colossal entity of the same order of being as their own — unlike the one of Anaximander or Parmenides, ontologically different in kind from any multitude.

Second, the utter determinacy of every entity for both Whitehead and Latour means that there is a gap between any entity at time T and the "same" entity at time T^1. Actually, for Whitehead and Latour they are not the same entity at all, but merely have a close resemblance without being one and the same. Just as Whitehead arbitrarily posits "appetite" in the heart of things so as to link one moment with the next, Latour occasionally flirts with the Spinozist conception of *conatus*.[155] But we have seen that this amounts to nothing more than a new version of the *vis dormitiva* ("an entity changes by means of a changing faculty") which is posited to address a built-in drawback of the initial theory. That drawback should be obvious enough: there is no reason to adhere to a theory of internal relations, and hence no reason to view things as so utterly determinate in their relations that they are incapable of adventuring from one moment to the next. Stated differently, this is a point on which School Y is closer to the truth, since this group generally insists on something in reality deeper than any current relational configuration between specific things. We find this above all in Deleuze and DeLanda, since for them the virtual is never fully actualized in specific things.

Nonetheless, it is in Whitehead and Latour that we find a closer approach to the truth, thanks to their sharper sense of gaps and discontinuities. Stated differently, what we must embrace is the occasionalist problems they raise — the first by sharpening the problem, and the second by recognizing it as a dead end. The first problem is the need for a mediator between things, for the simple reason that since things are individual and do not penetrate one

---

[154] See Graham Harman, "On Vicarious Causation."
[155] See the exchange in Bruno Latour, Graham Harman, & Peter Erdélyi, *The Prince and the Wolf,* pp. 106–109.

another to the core, they must meet in some shared third space. It cannot be God, as Whitehead claims, because it is unclear why any specific entity should be able to breach the very ontological laws by which all other entities are constrained. Nor can it be Latour's solution of requiring that Actor A (politics) and Actor B (neutrons) must be mediated by Actor C (Frédéric Joliot-Curie), since the same question will then arise of how C touches either A or B, and in this way the problem is just pushed back another step further. The second problem is the need to determine the link between an entity at time T and at time T¹ without resorting to convenient but empty stipulations such as those of "appetite" or "conatus." But in this case, unlike the first, the problem seems not worth solving, since it should never have arisen at all. Namely, Whitehead's "appetite" appears on the scene only because he himself has imprisoned his actual entities in a single concrete instant, and "appetite" is then pulled from a hat as a means of escape from that instant.

The point is that there was never any need to imprison entities in an instant at all. That would be necessary only if, like Whitehead, one were committed to *attacking* the Aristotelian model of substance that endures through a variety of changes in quality, accident, and relation. Unless there is such an underlying substance existing as a surplus outside the current state of the world, there is no reason why that state would ever change. In other words, if everything were completely determined by its prehensions of all other entities in the world, all entities ought to be thoroughly exhausted by their current relations. They would harbor no residue crying for the right to assert itself beyond the current state of the world; there would be no cause for rebellion or uprising among things. Harman would *internally* contain the determination "sitting on a brown couch typing on a MacBook," and if that is what Harman is, then that is what he is, and he can never be elsewhere. In a world of exhaustive deployment such as that of Whitehead and Latour, we cannot preserve any possibility of transformation with words such as "appetite" or "conatus." Nor are "subjective form" or "subjective aim" any help in escaping relationism. Once the entity has been defined in terms of its prehensions, once any excess of "vacuous actuality" has been mocked, it does no good to stipulate that entities *also* have some magical urge or drive or freedom that saves them from the relationist trap. For if this extrarelational concession has to be made at the end of the argument, then we might ask why it was not simply conceded at the beginning. And if that had been done, then entities could never have been analyzed into their prehensions in the first place, and the old concept of substance would have seemed much more redeemable than Whitehead wished to believe.

What we need, in fact, is a new *antiprocess philosophy*. We need a renewed philosophy of self-contained entities that may not be "static," but whose dynamism must be explained via the ontological principle and the interaction between actual things, rather than presupposed in the gratuitous concept of "appetite." We need entities that are not thoroughly relational but are so much themselves that they cannot automatically communicate with one another, so that their communication is a puzzle to be solved locally. As a name for this alternative school, I propose School Z. With this name we pay passing tribute to Xavier Zubíri the most uncompromising defender of nonrelational entities in post-Heideggerian philosophy.[156] What we need, cutting against the grain of our era, is a philosophy that does not worship process, becoming, or relation.

---

[156] Xavier Zubíri, *On Essence.*

CHAPTER 7

THE FOUR MOST TYPICAL OBJECTIONS TO OOO[157] (FROM *BELLS AND WHISTLES*)

This was a keynote lecture delivered at "OOOIII: The Third Object-Oriented Ontology Symposium," held at the New School in New York on September 15, 2011. In this brief lecture, held before a large and mostly receptive crowd, I tried to answer some of the recurrent objections to the object-oriented approach. It was one of multiple lectures I gave in New York that month, but the only one that took the form of a written text. For some reason I had remembered the Villanova lecture ["The Return to Metaphysics" earlier that year] as being polemical and this one as being mild.[158] But while rereading these texts for publication, I see that the reverse is the case.

Just six weeks ago, I made a blog post entitled "possibly the 4 most typical objections to OOO."[159] Near the end of that post, I wrote as follows: "Maybe a good crisp essay, dealing exclusively with these four objections, would be worth squeezing in during the next few months." This morning's talk is designed as a good crisp *lecture* on those same four complaints about object-oriented ontology. To me they seem indicative of what the *Zeitgeist* wants in philosophy (at least in continental circles) and equally indicative of what OOO is determined to resist and reverse. The four almost automatically predictable wishes of today's continental philosophy avant-garde are as follows:

---

[157] This chapter originally appeared in 2013 in Graham Harman, *Bells and Whistles*, pp. 31–39.
[158] "The Return to Metaphysics" can be found in Harman, *Bells and Whistles*, pp. 8–30.
[159] Graham Harman, "possibly the 4 most typical objections to OOO" (blog post), August 2, 2011.

1 Absolute knowledge, to be obtained either through science or speculative philosophy.
2 Materialism.
3 Hyper-dynamism.
4 Holism.

Like a cruel and devious genie released from an old Egyptian lamp, I not only deny these four wishes, but will offer a ruthless twenty-minute assault on all of them.

We can rephrase each of these four wishes in terms of complaints about the principles of object-oriented ontology, as our critics have already done for us. The first wish, for humans to be able to have absolute knowledge, means that humans must somehow make *direct* contact with reality. This can be expanded into the wider proposition that *all* entities must make direct contact with each other. In other words, the wish goes something like this: "Human knowledge of reality seems to be possible. *Therefore*, such knowledge must be a *direct* contact with reality. More generally, mutual contact and influence between objects seems to be possible. *Therefore*, it must be *direct* contact."

The basic principle of object-oriented philosophy, derived in my own case from Heidegger's tool-analysis, is that objects withdraw from all theoretical and practical contact alike.[160] The science of geology does not exhaust the being of rocks, which always have a surplus of reality deeper than our most complete *knowledge* of rocks; moreover, our practical *use* of rocks at construction sites and in street brawls also does not exhaust them. Yet this is not the result of some sad limitation on human or animal consciousness. Instead, rocks themselves are not fully deployed or exhausted by any of their actions or relations. When a rock smashes a window, these two entities come into contact in only the most minimal fashion, never sounding one another's depths. Direct contact is actually quite impossible. Not only must knowledge be indirect, but causal relations can only be indirect as well. While this may sound strange, it is really just an expanded version of Socrates's defense of *philosophia* (or "love of wisdom") against Meno, who claims with the Sophists that either we already know something or we can never know it at all. This claim might be expanded once more to include the causal realm by saying: "either objects make complete contact or they make no contact at all." Instead, the true situation is that we only make *indirect*

---

[160] Graham Harman, *Tool-Being*.

contact, and I would say the same thing about causal interaction even in the most stupefied reaches of the inanimate realm.

Complaints about this model have come primarily from two groups. The first is the relatively new "scientistic epistemology" wing of continental philosophy.[161] Such people complain about bringing inanimate objects into the picture and constantly assert (not prove, but merely assert) that there must be a difference *in kind* between conscious awareness and sheer causal contact. Here I respond with two points. First, given that such people want to be committed naturalists, it is unclear why they have so much faith in an "ontological catastrophe" that could suddenly have created a mighty power in one kind of natural entity, humans (or perhaps animals more generally), that would allow these creatures to rise above the world and somehow see it "as" it is.[162] Second, I answer that direct knowledge of anything is impossible because to be truly direct, knowledge of a thing would have to be that thing itself. As long as my knowledge of a tree does not actually become a tree, taking root in the soil and bearing fruit, then knowledge about it is obviously not a direct translation without energy loss, because there remains a difference between the tree and knowledge of it. It hardly matters that no one short of Berkeley explicitly *says* that trees and images of trees are the same thing. Rather, the point is that belief in direct knowledge of the world *entails* such a view, and this view is absurd. Finally, such people reply with the crude practical insinuation that if direct knowledge is impossible, then "anything goes," so that all human claims about anything are equally valid. To this I answer that human enlightenment is not primarily a matter of beating up gullible people. If we have succeeded in destroying alchemy and astrology as purported sciences, this has not been on the basis of *direct* knowledge of chemicals and celestial bodies; such knowledge is impossible due to the withdrawal or surplus of entities behind any of their configurations in the mind, and thus no theory of science based on the direct presence of objects or their forms can be correct. The love of science (which I share myself) should not be distorted into a love of the direct presence of reality before the mind — which is not at all necessary for the practice of science, but *is* necessary for the sort of aggressive scientism that glories in knocking others down by adopting a position of self-appointed

---

[161] The reference here is to Ray Brassier and his followers.

[162] The phrase "ontological catastrophe" originated with Slavoj Žižek. See for instance Žižek, *The Ticklish Subject*, p. 31. For a book-length treatment of theme see Joseph Carew, *Ontological Catastrophe*. As for the point about seeing the world "as" it is, the reference is of course to Heidegger's concept of transcendence.

direct epistemological insight. This widespread but regrettable human impulse is purely *unphilosophical*, since it believes it already possesses the key to wisdom and therefore does not need to love it or long for it.

There is also a second group, more sympathetic to OOO, which gets the point about the withdrawal of objects but simply thinks that we push things a bit too far. These people ask: "Why does direct contact with entities have to be impossible? Why can't contact be direct but *partial*?" The motive here seems to be that such people find indirect or vicarious causation too spooky or mystical. But their alternative theory of indirect-but-partial contact cannot work. For one thing, it simply moves the problem elsewhere. Once it is conceded that I am unable to make direct contact with a tree, it is no more possible to make direct contact with its leaves or branches than with the tree as a whole. Nor is it possible to make contact with, let's say, 78% of the tree that is accessible to humans while only dogs and mosquitoes can sense the other 22%. Objects are unities, as Aristotle already knew, and as Leibniz pressed to its logical conclusion. *Direct* contact could only be all or nothing, never partial. What happens instead is indirect contact, whether in the case of human knowledge or sheer inanimate collision.

The second cherished wish of philosophy in our time is materialism. While there are numerous theories that call themselves materialist, what too many of them share is a love of reductionism. The whole point of materialism is its so-called "parsimony," the ability to get rid of the clutter of the world by imposing capital punishment on numerous supposed pseudo-objects. In recent publications I have counter-argued with the following point: if you think individual entities or objects are not worthy of being the fundamental topic of philosophy, there are only two basic ways this case can be made. One is by saying that objects are too shallow to be the truth. "Horses, flowers, and depressive moods are simply constructions of folk ontology, and science will eventually show us that these can be eliminated in favor of tinier particles or deeper mathematical structures or some quasi-unified lump of which reality is genuinely made. The mid-sized horses, flowers, and moods of which you speak are merely vulgar fictions of everyday life, unworthy of philosophical credence." I have called such theories "undermining" philosophies, since they view the mission of philosophy to be demolishing any gullible belief in everyday things. In fact, such people are often a bit shocked and horrified by OOO, because they think we are relapsing into abject naïveté. But a case should be made for naïveté after so many tiresome centuries in which *critique* was always the major professional tool of the intellectual, with the haughty contrarian and the sneer-from-nowhere internet troll being the ultimate decadent outcome of this now exhausted era of critical thinking.[163] The problem with these undermining philosophies is that they are guilty of a dogmatic reductionism, failing to see that mid-sized levels of the world can have their own autonomy, are often partially independent of their tinier constituent pieces, and can affect their own pieces or even generate new ones.

There is also the flip side of materialism, which is generally of a cultural rather than physical sort, and works in reverse. Rather than saying that objects are too shallow to be the truth, they say that objects are *too deep*. "The notion of a unified object enduring through change is a useless fiction. Objects only appear in some social or linguistic context. They are purely relational. Or perhaps they are 'events' that happen very concretely in one time and one place only. There are simply relations, effects, and events, not underlying hidden objects." Beginning in 2009 at the second Speculative Realism workshop in Bristol, I started to call such theories "overmining" philosophies by analogy with the undermining ones.[164] For they reject all talk of hidden depths beneath the human realm, or at least beneath the immanent realm of relational interactions between all beings, such as found in the not-so-anthropocentric philosophies of Whitehead and to some extent Latour. The problem with overmining theories is that they are unable to explain change. If everything that exists were exhaustively deployed in its current state, without surplus or reserve outside their current effects, there would be no reason for anything ever to shift from its current state.

It should also be noted that undermining and overmining theories usually work as a team, reinforcing one another's excesses or covering each other's backs.[165] This began with Parmenides, in his duality between the undermining oneness of Being and the overmining flux of *doxa* or opinion, but is also reflected in contemporary theories such as that of James Ladyman and Don Ross, heroes of continental scientism, who undermine all individual things with deep mathematical structure *and also* claim that real geological and chemical entities exist as so-called "real patterns," though only for human observers: a theory that they incoherently claim is still a form of realism, even though their real individuals exist only in correlation

---

[163] The phrase "sneer from nowhere" was coined — as far as I know — by the late Mark Fisher. See his memorable blog post "Fans, Vampires, Trolls, Masters."

[164] The first use of the pair "overmining" and "undermining" was in my Bristol lecture of April 2009. See Graham Harman, "On the Undermining of Objects."

[165] At the time of this lecture, the term "duomining" had not yet been minted.

with human observers.[166] This is one good example of undermining and overmining at the same time. Another is when so-called "process philosophy" (which holds that objects aren't real because they are just encrustations of a deeper flux) is carelessly mixed with philosophies of relation (which hold that objects aren't real because there are only concrete effects or events, and deeper objects beneath these effects are a useless fiction). This double gesture occurs quite often these days, such as when attempts are made to lump Bergson and Deleuze (who are underminers of objects) together with Whitehead and Latour (who are overminers). Put them together and both extremes are covered, just as in Ladyman/Ross materialism: or as Iago puts it, we have "the beast with two backs."[167] But less flippantly, the defect shared by all these theories is their suspicion of the midsized and the middle-range: unified objects that withdraw from all human access and all environmental effects, knowable only indirectly, and located midway between their tinier components and their external impact on the world.

The third wish of our times is to emphasize flux over stasis. This can be viewed most plausibly as a reaction against eternal identities and their apparently oppressive role in stereotyping and pigeonholing humans into various unappealing social roles. By contrast, flux seems to liberate us from the tyranny of nature. Since I have just discussed the metaphysical "undermining" role of flux, let me address instead the unstated political worry about OOO: the worry that a return to realism means a return to rigid identities after so much work has been done to historicize such identities and reframe them as results of a "performative" process that gives us the freedom to shape our own selves. My first point in response is that too often, realism has been confused with what Heidegger and Derrida call "ontotheology." The critique of ontotheology is a critique of the idea that any specific *kind* of being can stand in for being itself, or that any *particular* being can be an exemplary incarnation of its kind, as for example: "all Dasein is Dasein, but the Ancient Greeks and recent Germans are Dasein to an *exceptional* degree." But OOO completely forbids such privileged incarnations of entities. The fact that my personality and talents have some definite character that exceeds the coding of society and even exceeds my own self-understanding does not mean, first, that anyone has sufficient knowledge of these matters to be able to legislate how I must act on the

---

[166] For a critique of Ladyman & Ross see Graham Harman, "I Am Also of the Opinion That Materialism Must Be Destroyed."
[167] William Shakespeare, *Othello*, Act 1, Scene 1.

basis of this character and these talents. Nor does it mean, second, that they cannot change over time. OOO's position on relatively enduring objects is that they can last through multiple events and relations, not that they have a *permanent* or even *eternal* identity over time. Yet after several decades of vigilantly insisting upon such reservations, for perfectly understandable reasons, in our time we have become too theoretically paranoid about speaking of anything essential behind the play of appearances. For this reason, it is important that we work to rehabilitate the word "essence" as a good classical term for the reality of things deeper than their current effects, without retaining the traditional sense of essence as a permanent and eternal destiny for individuals and peoples upon which direct political obligations and roles can be inscribed.

The fourth wish is that relations rather than self-contained objects should be primary. The metaphysical side of this wish has already been dealt with in my remarks against overmining. To over-emphasize relations at the expense of the *relata* that compose them is to make all change in the world impossible. Aristotle already saw this lucidly in his famous critique of the Megarians in Chapter 3 of *Metaphysics* Book Theta.[168] The Megarians claimed that no one is a house-builder unless they happen to be building a house right now, to which we can object that a sleeping house-builder is still more of a house-builder than some wide-awake bumbler who has no idea how to build. This serves as the launching pad for Aristotle's theory of potentiality, which I refuse on other grounds though some versions of OOO (such as Levi Bryant's) are more sympathetic to it.[169]

And yet again, there is the political side of the question. The political motive for the focus on relations seems to be that any focus on individuals seems to imply excessive emphasis on *human* individuals at the expense of larger *human* collectives. And moreover, relations sound like a dynamic source of social change, whereas individuals sound frozen and static, which might in turn sound like a recipe for social stasis rather than dynamism. To this, I answer that OOO recognizes objects of all different sizes. When we speak of individuals, this does not just mean individual human voters or consumers free to act as they please in the liberal marketplace. The bodily organs of humans are also objects, and political parties, unions, and perhaps even "the global oppressed" *could* be collective objects (not all conceivable objects are real, of course, but that is a different question). Furthermore, the

---

[168] Aristotle, *Metaphysics*.
[169] Levi R. Bryant, *The Democracy of Objects*.

term "objects" is not opposed to "subjects," so it is not such a bad fate to be an object. To be an object does not mean to be physical material without dignity, but simply to be a unified entity irreducible to its component pieces or to its effects on the surrounding environment.

As for the idea that relations are innately politically dynamic, we can make the same response here as we did to the metaphysical point about relations: if people, classes, or societies are nothing but their relations, then they are already everything they ever can be, and have neither the reason nor the ability to change. The true principle of dynamism, in human society as well as inanimate nature, is that real objects always exceed their contexts, always withdraw from our control, and are always filled with surplus and surprise. I cannot close this talk by saying "objects of the world, unite!" because that is precisely what we do not want and cannot achieve. Instead, I would say: "Objects of the world, withdraw!" But even this would be pointless, because it is a *fait accompli*. This is what objects have always done, and it is our task simply to make better use of this fact in our theories and our actions.

PART II
THE FOURFOLD OBJECT

CHAPTER 8

SENSUAL OBJECTS[170] (FROM *THE QUADRUPLE OBJECT*)

Among the greatest philosophical schools of the twentieth century is the phenomenology founded by Husserl and developed by Heidegger. A remarkable paradox lies at the heart of this movement. For although phenomenology calls for a return "to the things themselves," Husserl and Heidegger have both been accused of idealism. And true enough, these thinkers seem to make everything a matter of its accessibility to human beings; an external world beyond humans plays little role in their thinking. And yet there is a certain undeniably realist *flavor* to phenomenology that one cannot find in Berkeley or even Hegel. In Husserl's works we find descriptions of blackbirds, centaurs, and mailboxes. In Heidegger there is much attention to objects such as hammers or jugs, and to everyday scenes at parties and railway platforms. This suggests that the themes of objects and realism do not entirely overlap, since both Husserl and Heidegger are quietly committed to objects despite their lack of full-blown realism.

While Husserl is often dismissed as just another idealist, he is in fact a zoological oddity among philosophers: an *object-oriented* idealist. Although Husserl remains confined to the intentional realm [of consciousness aiming at objects], he also discovers a fascinating rift within that realm: a gulf between objects and their own qualities. The trees and blackbirds we encounter are not detailed presentations before the mind of specific bundles of qualities. Instead, intentional objects have a unified essential

---

[170] This chapter originally appeared in *The Quadruple Object*, pp. 20–34.

core surrounded by a swirling surface of accidents. In Heidegger's case we have a different situation: a genuine taste of the real world lying beyond the intentional sphere. In his tool-analysis we find real hammers and drills withdrawing from direct human access. If Husserl openly gives us intentional objects polarized between their accidents and their essential qualities, Heidegger tacitly gives us this same polarization for *real* objects. This chapter and the next will explain what I mean by "polarity" for each of the two philosophers.

A. Immanent Objectivity

Although phenomenology calls for a return to the things themselves, it paradoxically considers them only insofar as they appear. Since every form of idealism performs this same gesture on behalf of appearance, it might seem unoriginal at first. But we will see that Husserl adds a compelling twist to the problem. It is well known that phenomenology suspends the external world from consideration, refusing to accept any natural or causal theories about things. If I hear a siren in the night, then what I hear is a *siren*, not the transmission of sound waves through space leading to the vibration of my eardrums.[171] All of this remains mere theory, while phenomenology limits us to that which is directly accessible. In *Ideas* I, Husserl goes so far as to exclude all possibility of objects that are unobservable in principle by consciousness, and thus his drift toward idealism is complete.[172] But even within the limits of this idealism, an unexpected attention to *objects* can be found from the start. Husserl's brilliant and charismatic mentor, Franz Brentano, had renovated the medieval doctrine of intentionality. What distinguishes the mental from the physical for Brentano is that mental acts are always directed toward an object. When I judge, there is something judged; when I love, there is something or someone loved. In directing my attention toward this something, I "intend" it. But that which I intend lies within consciousness, not outside it. Existing only on the interior of my experience, it is described by Brentano as "intentional inexistence" or "immanent objectivity." Husserl will push this immanent objectivity beyond Brentano's own understanding of it.

---

[171] Rereading this sentence while editing the present anthology, a police siren in Long Beach goes off in the darkness, as if on cue, at 1 o'clock on Christmas morning 2021.

[172] Edmund Husserl, *Ideas Pertaining to a Pure Phenomenology and to a Phenomenological Philosophy* (Book 1).

By placing any independent natural world outside of philosophy, Husserl pays a terrible price; his bracketing of the natural world is a brutally idealist gesture. In vain do his disciples protest that consciousness is never an isolated entity but always already outside itself through intentional acts of observing, judging, hating, and loving. For in phenomenology these objects have no autonomy from consciousness. Their very existence is already threatened if I shift my attention, fall asleep, or die, and all the more so if all rational beings in the universe were exterminated. A Husserlian might respond to these scenarios by claiming that the *essence* of these objects would endure even after the death of all thinking creatures. But even this response would miss the point: the things would still have no autonomous reality apart from their being the objects of actual or potential observation. They are granted no secret life or inherent causal power, but are "real" only insofar as they might now or someday appear to consciousness. But unless objects are granted reality apart from such appearance, it is pointless to say that humans are always already engaged with things rather than being isolated minds, or that they are passive participants in an event rather than active constitutors of the world. Husserl's intentional realm has nothing real about it, nothing autonomous from an observer.

This problem with Husserl is widely known. His reward for paying such a price can be found in his admirable ability to treat perceptions as genuine realities rather than annihilating them in favor of their physical or neural underpinnings. But this is true of all philosophies that grant some existence to the immanent realm; what makes Husserl unique is the unexpected drama he discovers there. Whereas Brentano focused solely on the immanent life of the mind, some of his students tried to supplement this immanence through reference to an outside world. This occurs most lucidly in the treatise of his Polish student Kazimierz Twardowski, *On the Content and Object of Presentations*.[173] This sparkling little treatise was received by the young Husserl in a spirit of rivalry, with a revealing mixture of admiration and disdain. For Twardowski, a doubling occurs: there is an *object* lying outside the mind and a *content* inside it. Much attention has been paid to Husserl's rejection of this claim. He famously holds that the Berlin intended in consciousness and the Berlin existing in the world are one and the same, and this sentiment paves the way for his increasing idealism over the years.[174] What is less often noticed, though it lies at the

---

[173] Kasimir Twardowski, *On the Content and Object of Presentations*.
[174] Edmund Husserl, "Intentional Objects."

heart of Husserl's breakthrough, is the fact that he does not simply reject Twardowski's distinction between object and content. Instead, he imports it into the heart of the immanent realm itself.

Brentano had said relatively little about objects, and emphasized instead that all conscious acts are rooted in *presentations*. Something must be presented to the mind before it can be judged, hated, or loved. While Twardowski augmented this model by introducing a real object beyond the presentations, Husserl's rejection of such doubling might seem to place him on the side of Brentano. But this is not the case. For in the *Logical Investigations* Husserl openly modifies Brentano's model, saying that consciousness is not formed of presentations, but of *object-giving acts*. And this difference is no trivial subtlety. For in any presentation all qualitative details are on exactly the same footing. All are equally part of the presentation: the lofty ascent of the tree is no more a part of it than the exact position of each individual leaf. In this way consciousness is made up of "bundles of content," and we remain within the bounds of British Empiricism. For Husserl, by contrast, not everything in consciousness is equal. Even while confining us to the immanent sphere of consciousness, he borrows Twardowski's distinction between object and content for use *within* this sphere. Retreating into the phenomenal world like a monk into the desert, what he finds is a previously unsuspected fault line in the world.

B. Adumbrations

Let there be no doubt: the phenomenal world for Husserl is not made up only of specific content, as it is for Brentano and Twardowski. Instead, the Husserlian phenomenal realm is torn apart by a duel between objects and the content through which they are manifest. Recall what happens in any phenomenological analysis. Perhaps Husserl circles a water tower at a distance of one hundred meters, at dusk, in a state of suicidal depression. As he moves along his sad path while observing the tower, it constantly shows different profiles. In each moment he will experience new details, but without the tower becoming a new tower in each instant. Instead, the tower is a unified "intentional object" that remains the same despite being presented through the greatest variety of different perceptions. The tower is always encountered through a specific profile: an *Abschattung* or "adumbration," as Husserl calls them. But these adumbrations are not the same thing as the intentional objects they manifest. If Husserl increases his circuit around the tower to three hundred meters at dawn in a mood of euphoria, it still seems to him like the same tower as yesterday evening. The object always remains the same despite numerous constant changes in its content. But unlike Twardowski's model, in which the object-pole is an anchor lying entirely outside consciousness, for Husserl both the object and content are immanent. It is true that Husserl denies this, but only because he accepts no "transcendent" world that would make phenomena immanent by contrast.

A point worth stressing is that the intentional object is no bundle of adumbrations. We do not grasp a tree or mailbox by seeing it from every possible side — which is physically, mentally, and perhaps even logically impossible. The object is attained not by adding up its possible appearances to us, but by *subtracting* these adumbrations. That dog on the horizon need not have its hind leg raised exactly as it now does, nor does it cease to be the same dog if it stops growling and wags its tail in a spirit of welcome. Intentional objects always appear in more specific fashion than necessary, frosted over with accidental features that can be removed without the object itself changing identity for us. Here already we see Husserl's departure from empiricism. Just as an apple is not the sum total of its red, slippery, cold, hard, and sweet features in any given moment, it is also not the sum total of angles and distances from which it can be perceived. By contrast, Merleau-Ponty relapses into saying that the being of the house is "the house viewed from everywhere," while even Heidegger has little sense of the difference between intentional objects and their qualities.[175]

Despite this difference between the unified object and its myriad qualities, we must avoid the error of thinking that Husserl's intentional object is somehow *concealed* from us. His great heir Heidegger has much to say about the veiling of things, and we will cover this point in detail in the chapters that follow. But by contrast, there is really no concealment for Husserl at all. Husserl's point is not that we only encounter adumbrations of trees, dogs, blackbirds, and mailboxes while the unified objects themselves remain hidden from us; that would be more like Heidegger or even Twardowski. Instead, according to Husserl we encounter the intentional object directly in experience from the start, expending our energy in taking it seriously. In the Husserlian framework, if I observe a distant mailbox from a hilltop under ominous lighting conditions, the mailbox is not "hidden" from me in the Heideggerian manner. Instead it is always present, but merely covered with the gems, glitter, and confetti of extraneous detail. The mailbox is not

---

[175] Maurice Merleau-Ponty, *Phenomenology of Perception*, p. 79.

built up as a bundle of perceptually discrete shapes and colors, or even from tiny pixels of sense experience woven together by habit. Instead, shapes and colors belong from the outset to the unified mailbox. Husserl's breakthrough in philosophy has not been fully assimilated if we neglect his revolutionary distinction within the sensual realm between unified objects and their shifting multitude of features. These features are no less subordinated to their objects than are satellites to the gravity of the earth. For Husserl unlike Brentano, consciousness is not made up of definite presentations, but of object-giving acts. For this reason, any comparison between Husserl and Heidegger on this point is misguided. In Husserl we find that objects are not withdrawn from human access, but are all too heavily adorned with frivolous decorations and surface-effects.

The metaphysics presented in this book lays great stress on several key tensions between objects and their qualities. There turn out to be four such tensions, and we have just met with the first of them. The phenomenal realm is not only an idealist prison cut off from access to the outer world. Rather, it displays a tension between intentional objects and their ever-shifting qualities. But due to the antiseptic sterility of the term "intentional," I propose to speak instead of *sensual* objects as a synonymous phrase. Nor is sterility the only reason for avoiding the phrase "intentional objects." Too much confusion has arisen over this famous term: many analytic philosophers believe that intentional objects are those lying outside human consciousness, even though both Brentano and Husserl mean it in a purely immanent sense.[176] Thus, the phrase "sensual objects" is more effective at conveying that we do not speak here of the real world beyond human access where only real objects belong. In all phenomenal experience, there is a tension between sensual objects and their sensual qualities. The ocean remains the same though its successive waves advance and recede. A Caribbean parrot retains its identity no matter how exactly its wings currently flap, and no matter what curses or threats it now utters in the Spanish language. The phenomenal world is not just an idealist sanctuary from the blows of harsh reality, but an active seismic zone where intentional objects grind slowly against their own qualities.

---

[176] This is the position of John Searle, for instance, in his book *Intentionality*. For a critique of Searle's view see Tim Crane, "Intentional Objects."

C. Eidetic Features

Yet it turns out that Husserl's sensual objects are involved in two tensions or polarizations, not just one. We have already seen a first rift within the phenomenal sphere, which lies between the sensual object and those swirling accidental qualities that encrust its surface like jewels or dust. Yet this cannot be the only polarization in which sensual objects are involved. After all, if we strip away the swirling accidents of an object, what remains is not merely an empty pole of unity. The sensual dog, pine tree, and lighthouse are different objects not just because their shifting accidents are different. By stripping away this surface noise through Husserl's method of eidetic variation, what we attain is not the same featureless unity for every sensual object — a "bare particular," in the terms of analytic philosophy.[177] Instead, we approach what Husserl calls the *eidos* of an object. This second tension is a bit stranger than the first. In one sense the tensions an object undergoes with its own accidents and its own eidetic features are similar, since in both cases the object is not assembled from a bundle of qualities. We cannot construct a mailbox by piling up essential qualities any more than by piling up outward profiles. The object is one; its qualities are many, whether they be accidental or eidetic. Hence in both directions there is a difference between the object and its multitude of traits. Yet there are other respects in which the two tensions are markedly different. For in the first place the object does not need its accidents, which can be shifted nearly at will without affecting the character of the object. Yet the same is obviously not true of its essential features, which the object desperately needs in order to be what it is. And in the second place, the accidental qualities lie directly before us in experience, but the eidetic ones are not. Late in the *Logical Investigations*, Husserl makes it clear that the eidos of an object is incapable of sensual presence; we have access to it only through so-called categorial intuition, such that only the work of the intellect delivers the eidos. But, in fact, there is no reason to assume that the intellect can make reality directly present in a way that the senses cannot. Whether my hands or my mind alert me to the electrical conductivity of copper, neither sensing nor knowing is what conducts electricity through the world. In other words, Husserl is wrong to distinguish between the sensual and the intellectual here; both sensual and categorial intuition are forms of intuition, and to intuit something is not the same as to be it. Hence the eidetic features of any

---

[177] The term "bare particular" seems to have been introduced by the analytic philosopher Gustav Bergmann (of the University of Iowa in my hometown, Iowa City) in his 1967 book *Realism*.

object can never be made present even through the intellect, but can only be approached indirectly by way of allusion, whether in the arts or in the sciences. Copper wires, bicycles, wolves, and triangles all have real qualities, but these genuine traits will never be exhausted by the feeble sketches of them delivered to our hearts and minds. A proton or volcano must have a variety of distinct properties, but these remain just as withdrawn from us as the proton and volcano themselves.

What we have here is the strange case of a sensual object with *real* qualities. For the qualities of its eidos are necessary for it to exist, but are also withdrawn from all access, and "real" is the only possible name for such a feature. Now, we might easily say that the sensual object both has and does not have its accidental features, since the exact profile of a house at dusk is somehow attached to the house without being necessary for it. But somewhat surprisingly, the same is true even of an object's eidetic features. Here too it both has and does not have them, since it is always green, hard, or slippery in its own specific way, and is not built up out of these traits. Just like the accidental qualities, the eidetic qualities are imbued from the start with the reality or style of the object to which they belong.

It should already be clear that Husserl's suspension of the outer world has a positive side no less than a negative one. Though it will be necessary to reject his flattening of reality onto a phenomenal surface, and even to reject his undue exclusion of inanimate entities from the ranks of beings that can encounter phenomena, his sensual realm already raises interesting problems for the metaphysics of objects. In Husserl's hands, sensual objects are no longer two-dimensional apparitions trapped in the human mind: instead, everything from blackbirds, mailboxes, and trees to centaurs, numbers, and wishes becomes the site of two simultaneous polarizations. The sensual object is something less than its sensual qualities, since these superfluous additions can be scraped away without affecting the underlying sensual object. But the sensual object is something less than its real qualities as well, since it deploys these qualities only in a certain specific way. On the one hand, we have the sensual object and its sensual qualities, half-welded together in experience. But on the other hand, to articulate what makes this particular parrot be what it is requires an analysis of real qualities that can only be hinted at allusively or obliquely by the intellect without ever becoming nakedly present.

Terminologically, we can speak of the "encrustation" of qualities on the surface of a sensual object. Any sensual object is always encountered in a more detailed form than necessary: this city skyline need not be glimmering in its exact current way in order to be recognized as this very skyline. But when speaking of the real qualities that a sensual object must possess in order to be what it is, it is not a matter of encrustation, but of what might be called "submergence." The necessary qualities of a sensual object are sunk beneath its surface like the hull of a Venetian galley, invisible to the observer who is dazzled by the flags and emblems covering the ship, or the music played on its deck by captive singers and drummers. Though the hull is submerged, it remains vital for the seaworthiness of the ship. By analogy, the real qualities of the sensual object can only be inferred indirectly rather than witnessed. The sensual object cannot exist without having both sorts of qualities simultaneously. It would not be a sensual object if it did not somehow appear, but would also not be this very sensual object if it did not have the specific eidetic features that make it so. But one important clarification must be made. Husserl speaks of real qualities in generic terms, such that a certain shade of green can be embodied in many different particular objects; the same holds for Whitehead and his "eternal objects," and for most other thinkers who have dealt with the topic of essence. By contrast, qualities as described in this book are always individualized by the object to which they belong. To put it in the terms of analytic philosophy, they are "tropes."[178] But in any case, the sensual object is not merely an idealist illusion, but the site of two crucial polarizations in the cosmos.

D. Summary

As a rule, realist philosophers are satisfied to claim that there is more to things than our representations of them. Consciousness may be filled with manifest images, but these are not primary; instead, these images are generated or produced by realities that are not themselves manifest. In our time, most realists are committed to scientific naturalism, and hold that the natural world has primacy over human images of it. In this way they attack the notion that conscious experience is the starting point of philosophy, and undermine it by grounding philosophy in the deeper natural things that give rise to such experience. But notice that this is merely the undermining flip side of mainstream idealism, which overmines objects by saying that they are nothing more than their manifestation in experience. What typical

---

[178] My version of tropes differs from the original use of the term in ways not developed here. The present-day meaning of "trope" is apparently derived from a pair of 1953 articles by D.C. Wiliams, "On the Elements of Being I" and "On the Elements of Being II."

realists and typical idealists share is a tendency to skip the intermediate level of objects altogether. They say either that there is a basic layer of natural elements that explains all objects, or that objects are nothing more than bundles of traits that are directly manifest to the observer.[179] What makes Husserl so special among idealists is his discovery of objects *within* the phenomenal sphere. Despite being an idealist, he *feels* like a realist to such a degree that his followers often assume there is no more reality to be had than the kind that Husserl already addresses. Husserl is in fact the first *object-oriented* idealist. He knows the painful and seductive labor needed to look beyond the specific traits through which an object is manifest. By contrast, such authors as Berkeley or Fichte pay no attention at all to the duel between mailboxes and their various sparkling and shifting features. Nor is it thinkable that Fichte would ever imagine circling a tree from various distances and angles in different moods. But for Husserl this procedure cannot be avoided: the sensual object cannot be assembled from its current observable features or even its sum total of possible profiles.

At the risk of repetition, it is useful to summarize what we have learned from Husserl. For him the natural world outside the mind is excluded from the starting point of philosophy, since its suppositions are merely theories. We cannot begin by thinking that a mailbox is made of pieces of sheet metal with various chemical properties, or of atoms, quarks, electrons, or strings. By the same token we cannot view either mailboxes or humans as created entities in contrast with a transcendent creator. All we know initially is that objects are phenomena present in consciousness. In our conscious life we intend these objects; as Brentano already knew, perception is perception *of something*, and the same holds true for judgments, wishes, and acts of love and hate. But whereas Brentano claimed that all intentional life is grounded in presentations, Husserl noted that consciousness is not a flatland in which everything is on the same footing. Instead of presentations there are object-giving acts, which means that we must distinguish between sensual objects as unvarying inner cores and all their countless manifestations. The various trees and centaurs encountered in conscious life are simply trees

---

[179] This is effectively Alain Badiou's position in *Logics of Worlds*, pp. 193–230, which treats objects only as an ontological multiple indexed by a specific "world": by which he means a context in which many objects appear together under a specific "transcendental," despite the claim that his notion of "appearing" makes no reference to a human observer. For even if true, this is only true in the same inadequate sense of Husserl's claim that phenomena have "objective validity."

and centaurs, and are not bound up with the superfluity of details through which they are always encountered.

In this way Husserl discovers a tension between object and content *within* the sensual realm — a great fault line that tears phenomena in half from the start. Sensual objects are different from all the sensual accidents through which they appear. But these sensual objects are not empty poles of unity that differ from each other only due to the specific colors, angles, moods, and lighting conditions through which they are manifest. Even if we could strip away all the accidental features of horses, dogs, and chairs, these objects would still differ from each other. Each object has *eidetic* features no less than accidental ones. Normally, we have only a vague sense of the exact character of the dog lying behind the numerous facile encrustations with which it appears. The work of theoretical consciousness is to articulate the features of that dog, to unlock its eidos. Yet we have seen that despite Husserl's belief that adequate intuition into the eidos of a thing is possible, this eidos is made up of *real* qualities. Hence, access to them can only be indirect and allusive, which rules out any direct access to them of either the sensual or the intellectual type. The real qualities of the palm tree do not resemble our lists of these qualities any more than the palm tree itself resembles the one we see. Real qualities withdraw from direct access no less than real objects do. In this way the sensual object serves as the crossroads for two crucial tensions in the cosmos: sensual object vs. its sensual accidents, and sensual object vs. its real qualities. And this intersection is the great discovery of Husserl, ignored by more recent authors who treat him as already passé, or who mistake him for an arid technical maestro.

Nonetheless, Husserl remains an idealist. His objects are incapable of doing anything other than appearing in consciousness. Indeed, without consciousness they are incapable of existing at all: whether that consciousness belongs to me, another thinking being, or at least some *possible* thinking being. Even an object-oriented idealist like Husserl cannot do justice to objects; his objects are of the purely sensual variety, deprived of autonomous reality or action beyond the kingdom of the mind. Now, as a general rule the most dangerous philosophical problems are those that we falsely believe we have already overcome. In such cases the constant thorn in the flesh of an unsolved problem disappears, and one side of a paradox is chosen at the expense of the other, while denying that this has even occurred. And the unfortunate truth is that phenomenology has always been guilty of a sin of this kind. For as much as phenomenology claims to stand somewhere beyond the supposed

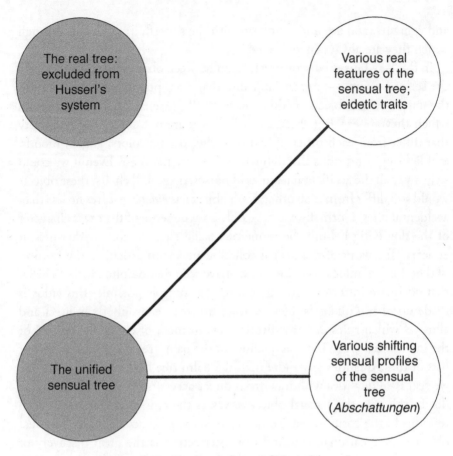

Figure 2: Two Tensions in Sensual Objects (Husserl)

"pseudo-problem" of realism and idealism, it falls squarely on the idealist side of the dispute.

Amidst this paradoxical situation of a philosophy that is both idealist and object-oriented, the music of Martin Heidegger was first heard rising in the distance. His drastic reformation of phenomenology was enough to make him perhaps the greatest philosopher of the twentieth century. There are shortcomings to be found in Heidegger, as in every major thinker. But if there is one problem he does avoid, it is surely Husserl's confinement within the sensual sphere. While it is true that Heidegger leaves *Sein* and *Dasein* in a permanent, mutually dependent couple, this does not entail that being is exhausted by its manifestation to humans. In Heidegger, there are real objects to go along with the sensual ones.

CHAPTER 9

REAL OBJECTS[180] (FROM *THE QUADRUPLE OBJECT*)

In the eyes of many, Heidegger is the major philosopher of the twentieth century; he is certainly the paramount influence on the metaphysics presented in this book. For these reasons he will be the subject of extensive treatment in the coming chapters. So far we have considered Husserl's contribution to our topic. Despite his idealism, Husserl describes a tension that is foreign to most idealists between the sensual objects we encounter and their two kinds of traits: sensual and real. While this insight adds significant conflict and texture to an otherwise misty ideal realm, it still supposes a world in which the reality of objects does not exceed their presence to a conscious observer. For Heidegger the situation is different: if Husserl is a philosopher of presence, then Heidegger is a thinker of absence. His famous tool-analysis in *Being and Time* shows that our usual way of dealing with things is not observing them as present-at-hand (*vorhanden*) in consciousness, but silently relying on them as ready-to-hand (*zuhanden*). Hammers and drills are usually present to us only when they fail. Prior to this they withdraw into a subterranean background, enacting their reality in the cosmos without appearing in the least. Insofar as they recede into the depths, tool-beings tend to coalesce into a *system* of equipment in which it is difficult to distinguish between individual beings. This has the undermining implication that the multiplicity of beings belongs to a derivative level of presence, with priority given to a deeper and unified system of reference.

---

[180] This chapter originally appeared in *The Quadruple Object*, pp. 35–50.

But this is a misunderstanding of Heidegger's discovery, even if it sometimes afflicts Heidegger himself. The tool-analysis does not give us a monistic lump of being, but a landscape where individual objects are withdrawn into private interiors, barely able to relate at all. Contrary to all appearances, Heidegger is an object-oriented thinker no less than Husserl. The key difference is that he replaces Husserl's sensual objects with his own unique model of *real* ones. But these real objects complement sensual objects rather than replace them.

A. The Tool-Analysis

Heidegger radicalizes phenomenology from within. Stirred into action by the writings of Brentano and Husserl, the young Heidegger came to be viewed as the crown prince of phenomenology, and eventually as a traitor to the movement. Husserl's philosophical method is to bracket all consideration of the outside world and focus solely on the phenomena that appear to consciousness. His rebellious heir Heidegger reverses this procedure, drawing our attention to what lies behind all phenomena. He does this not in order to restore scientific naturalism to the throne, but to give us the sense of a reality much weirder than any that science has known. Heidegger's palace revolt against phenomenology is most visible in his famous tool-analysis, first published in *Being and Time*, but already found in his earliest Freiburg lecture course in 1919.[181] The tool-analysis is probably the greatest moment in the philosophy of the past century: a thought experiment comparable in power to Plato's myth of the cave. If Husserl's mission is to suspend all theories of the natural world in favor of a detailed survey of conscious experience, Heidegger's philosophy is a sweeping campaign against presence — whether it be presence to the mind or to anything else. If we pursue this campaign with an intensity that Heidegger never attempted, we soon arrive at the borderlands of a speculative philosophy closed off to the great thinker himself.

Heidegger's tool-analysis is familiar to anyone even loosely acquainted with recent philosophy. At any moment I am conscious of a number of objects lying before me: desk, lamp, computer, telephone. Yet Heidegger notes that most of the things with which we contend are not explicitly present to the mind at all, but have the mode of being of "equipment," or readiness-to-hand. These range from the eyeglasses that I usually fail

---

[181] Martin Heidegger, *Being and Time*; Martin Heidegger, *Towards the Definition of Philosophy*.

to notice, to the beating heart that keeps me alive, to the chair and solid floor that prevent me from toppling to the earth, to the grammatical structures mastered in earliest childhood. Conscious awareness makes up only a tiny portion of our lives. For the most part, objects withdraw into a shadowy subterranean realm that supports our conscious activity while seldom erupting into view. Heidegger also frequently claims that this occluded underground realm is a unified system rather than a collection of autonomous objects: strictly speaking, there is no such thing as "an" equipment, since tools are reciprocally and globally determined by their mutual references. It should also be noted that despite the use of words such as "equipment" and "tool," Heidegger is not describing a limited taxonomy of one specific kind of entity as opposed to others. It is not just an analysis of hammers, drills, knives, and forks, but of everything. For all entities tend to reside in a cryptic background rather than appearing before the mind.

The tool-analysis first occurs in Heidegger's 1919 Freiburg lecture course, with its embarrassing fantasia of a "Senegal Negro" who misinterprets classroom furniture as protection from arrows and slingstones.[182] But the first published appearance of the analysis is found eight years later, beginning with Section 15 of *Being and Time*. Against the claim that the world is filled with objective material things that are later supplemented with values and psychological projections, Heidegger treats tool-being itself as the primordial nature of things: "We shall call those entities which we encounter in concern '*equipment*.'"[183] And while Heidegger claims that we deal with equipment by means of a kind of "sight" (*Sicht*) that he calls "circumspection" (*Umsicht*), this supposed sight does not make the tools visible in the least. For what is most typical of these tools as "ready-to-hand" is as follows: "The ready-to-hand is not grasped thematically at all …. The peculiarity of what is proximally ready-to-hand is that, in its readiness-to-hand, it must, as it were, withdraw in order to be ready-to-hand quite authentically."[184] In short, insofar as the tool is a tool, it is quite invisible. And what makes it invisible is the way that it disappears in favor of some purpose that it serves: "Equipment is essentially something 'in-order-to' …. In the 'in-order-to' as a structure there lies an *assignment* or *reference* of something to something." And furthermore: "Equipment — in accordance with its equipmentality — always is *in terms of* its belonging

---

[182] Heidegger, *Towards the Definition of Philosophy*, pp. 57–59.

[183] Heidegger, *Being and Time*, p. 97.

[184] Heidegger, *Being and Time*, p. 99.

to other equipment: ink-stand, pen, ink, paper, blotting pad, table, lamp, furniture, windows, doors, room."[185] For Heidegger, tools do not exist as isolated entities. Indeed, their very contours are designed with other entities in mind: "A covered railway platform takes account of bad weather; an installation for public lighting takes account of the darkness, or rather of specific changes in the presence or absence of daylight — the 'position of the sun.'"[186] Instead of thinking that extra-mental reality is founded on what appears to consciousness, we must join Heidegger in concluding the opposite, while also agreeing with him that what withdraws from consciousness are not lumps of objective physical matter. Instead, the world in itself is made of realities withdrawing from all conscious access.

Then contra Husserl, the usual manner of things is not to appear as phenomena, but to withdraw into an unnoticed subterranean realm. Heidegger says that we generally notice equipment only when it somehow fails. An earthquake calls my attention to the solid earth on which I rely, just as medical problems alert me to the bodily organs on which I silently depend. But entities need not "break" in the literal sense of the term, as if due to failing bolts, wires, or engines. For there is already a failure of sorts when I simply turn my attention toward entities, reflecting consciously on my bodily organs or the solid floor of my home. Even when I do so, these things themselves are not yet within my grasp. There will always be aspects of these phenomena that elude me; further surprises might always be in store. No matter how hard I work to become conscious of things, environing conditions still remain of which I never become fully aware. When I stare at a river, wolf, government, machine, or army, I do not grasp the whole of their reality. This reality slips from view into a perpetually veiled underworld, leaving me with only the most frivolous simulacra of these entities. In short, the phenomenal reality of things for consciousness does not use up their being. The readiness-to-hand of an entity is not exhaustively deployed in its presence-at-hand.

The implications of the tool-analysis are far weightier than readers of Heidegger usually imagine. This claim will be developed over the next several chapters, but one key point is already clear. We have seen that ready-to-hand and present-at-hand do not give us a taxonomy of different *kinds* of objects; they are not two limited regions of entities among many others. Instead, tool and broken tool make up the whole of Heidegger's universe.

---

[185] Heidegger, *Being and Time*, p. 97.
[186] Heidegger, *Being and Time*, pp. 100–101.

He recognizes these two basic modes of being, and *only* these two: entities withdraw into a silent underground while also exposing themselves to presence. This is certainly true of pitchforks, shovels, knives, tunnels, and bridges, which invisibly perform their labors while also sometimes existing as phenomenal images before the mind. But it is also true of entities not usually regarded as "tools": even colors, shapes, and numbers all have a reality that is not fully exhausted by the exact way in which a thinker considers them. Such entities are locked into a global dualism between ready-to-hand and present-at-hand no less than wooden or metallic hardware are. And despite Heidegger's denials, even human Dasein partakes of both modes of being. For even if Dasein is not "used" in the same way as a rubber hose, it still displays the same two sides as any other entity. Even humans withdraw into a dark reality that is never fully understood, while also being present to observers from the outside.

B. Beyond Theory and Praxis

One typical reading of the tool-analysis is to view it as a form of pragmatism. It is easy to see why this happens. Husserl can be viewed as a philosopher of patient theoretical description of the phenomena, aiming at a best-case scenario of adequate intuition of the essence of things. By contrast, Heidegger has no hope that theory can ever do justice to the things. Theory is secondary for him, and thus might seem to arise only from an unnoticed background of pre-theoretical practices. Instead of granting priority to a lucid conscious observer, Heidegger sees human Dasein as thrown into a context that is taken for granted long before it ever becomes present to the mind. Consciousness is reduced to a tiny corner of reality, while practical handling and coping become central to his model of the world.[187] Invisible praxis is the soil from which all theory emerges. In this way, Heidegger is depicted as a pragmatist. It is often added that John Dewey noticed the same point three decades earlier, and hence (at least in America) Heidegger is sometimes portrayed as just a tardy pragmatist whose tool-analysis teaches us nothing that was not already described by others. If Heidegger has any point of true originality, it is claimed, then this must be found in his tens of thousands of pages of historical writings. As an ontologist, he merely repeats the breakthroughs of pragmatism.

---

[187] "Coping" is one of the leading terms in Hubert Dreyfus, *Being-in-the-World*, and through his influence is found nearly all discussion of Heidegger by analytic philosophers.

Despite my opposition to the pragmatist interpretation of Heidegger, this trend does have certain institutional merits. After all, the Anglo-American world remains dominated by analytic philosophy, an intellectual current in which pragmatism now enjoys great prestige. The abundance of pragmatist interpretations of Heidegger has at least succeeded in shifting his image among analytic philosophers from "unintelligible poet and pompous mystic" to "non-mentalist verificationist anti-realist," or something along those lines. The most prominent analytic reader of Heidegger in America is surely Hubert Dreyfus, but someone more useful for our purposes here is Mark Okrent, whose book *Heidegger's Pragmatism* expresses more open support for the interpretation in question.[188] For Okrent, "being" does not stand alone on the mountaintop of Heideggerian terminology; it is joined there by the term "understanding." As he sees it, "understanding" means practical know-how. For as he describes Heidegger's position: "to understand x (for example, a hammer) is primarily to understand how to do y with x (to hammer) or how to use x (to use x as a hammer)."[189] Yet Okrent also claims that such understanding is ubiquitous, not episodic: understanding occurs *at all times* and *towards everything*. Yet as Okrent realizes, this seems to contradict the evident fact that humans are often perplexed by what they encounter, failing to understand it at all. His remedy for this paradox is to say that what humans ultimately understand are not the hammers, electrons, and dolphins they encounter, but rather *themselves*: "Heidegger doesn't claim that there can be no intention directed toward a thing unless we understand it. Rather, he asserts that one can't intend oneself, and that one can't intend anything else [either] unless one understands oneself."[190] This leads Okrent to a strange position, not rare among pragmatist readers of Heidegger, in which the outside world must be treated pragmatically, but the inner world is accessible to absolute transcendental knowledge *even though* understanding of the outside world is also supposed to be just a variant of self-understanding. The contradiction is glaring, but there is no need to give a full critique of Okrent's book here. I will simply quote his conclusion about Heidegger, since it is so typical of pragmatist interpreters of this philosopher. For just like Richard Rorty, Okrent does not see Heidegger as especially original: "With the possible exception of the emphasis on temporality, the principal doctrines of the early Heidegger

---

[188] Dreyfus, *Being-in-the-World*; Mark Okrent, *Heidegger's Pragmatism*.
[189] Okrent, *Heidegger's Pragmatism*, p. 31.
[190] Okrent, *Heidegger's Pragmatism*, p. 24.

concerning the primarily practical character of intentionality are hardly unique in the twentieth century. A whole series of philosophers, including John Dewey, the late Wittgenstein, and the contemporary American neo-pragmatists …. have made very similar points."[191]

But however popular it may currently be, the pragmatist reading of Heidegger misses the point. For the tool-analysis teaches us something much deeper than the emergence of conscious awareness from the prior unconscious use of things. In the first place, despite the etymology of the terms, it is wrong to identify the ready-to-hand with "practice" and the present-at-hand with "theory." To oppose the arrogant pretensions of theory, the tool-analysis shows us that the being of an apple, hammer, dog, or star is not exhausted by its presence in consciousness. No sensual profile of these things will ever exhaust its full reality, which withdraws into the dusk of a shadowy underworld. But if something hides behind the many profiles of an apple, what hides from our view is not our *use* of the apple, but rather the apple itself. After all, using a thing distorts its reality no less than making theories about it does. If we unconsciously stand on a floor that has not yet broken, this standing relies on just a handful of qualities of the floor: its hardness or sturdiness, for instance. Our use of the floor as "equipment for standing" makes no contact with the abundance of extra qualities that dogs or mosquitoes might be able to detect. In short, both theory *and* practice are equally guilty of reducing things to presence-at-hand. It is true that some things are consciously in mind while others are unconsciously used. Yet the basic opposition in the tool-analysis is not between conscious and unconscious. Instead, the truly important rift lies between the withdrawn reality of any object and the distortion of that object by way of both theory *and* practice. Staring at a hammer does not exhaust its being, but neither does using it.

Yet there is still another way in which the difference between *vorhanden* and *zuhanden* is often misread. We are told that objects in consciousness appear as isolated abstractions, each existing on its own. Supposedly, the tool-analysis shows that entities themselves are not isolated, but belong to a total system in which each thing gains its meaning from its references to the others. Heidegger himself says that there is no such thing as "an" equipment, and this seems to make him an ontologist of relations. It is easy to see why this notion arises. A knife obviously has a very different reality when used in a restaurant kitchen, at a wedding banquet, or in a grisly triple

---

[191] Okrent, *Heidegger's Pragmatism*, pp. 280–281.

homicide. But as convincing as it might sound, this reading of Heidegger misses the point. There is no real opposition between an isolated knife in consciousness and an invisibly used knife that belongs to a system. For whether the knife is seen or used, in both cases it is treated only in relation to something else, not in its own right.

It is certainly true that tools — by which I mean *all* entities — belong to a system. A flock of crows caged in a zoo is less ominous than the same flock hovering over a snowy field, and this in turn is less disturbing than the same group of crows when found in the corridors of a hospital. In this respect, entities seem to exist in reciprocal determination with one another, gaining their significance from neighboring entities, and it is easy to see why some might adopt a holistic view of equipment. But the same problem arises here as with the pragmatist reading of Heidegger. For although we might say that the different parts of a machine refer to and mutually determine one another, this mutual interrelation does not exhaust the reality of these parts. Insofar as tools belong to a system, they are already nothing but caricatures of themselves, reduced to presence-at-hand. And while it might seem that an isolated knife or window in consciousness is viewed in abstract isolation, even these images exist in a system, since they exist only in relation with the person who observes them. In short, both theoretical abstraction and the use of tools are equally guilty of distorting the tools themselves. Insofar as a tool is "used," it is no less present-at-hand than an image in consciousness. But a tool is not "used"; *it is*. And insofar as it is, the tool is not exhausted by its relations with human theory *or* human praxis.

C. Anti-Copernicus

In claiming that praxis distorts the reality of things no less than theory does, we make an important modification to Heidegger's tool-analysis. Given his proclaimed interest in Being itself rather than the various events of human existence, it is a modification he might well accept. Yet we are now on the verge of a more radical modification to which he would never agree. For if the being of things lies veiled behind all theory and practice, this is not due to some precious merit or defect of human Dasein, but to the fact that *all* relations translate or distort that to which they relate: even inanimate relations. When fire burns cotton, it makes contact only with the flammability of this material. Presumably fire does not interact at all with the cotton's odor or color, which are relevant only to creatures equipped with the organs of sense. Though it is true that the fire can change or destroy these properties that lie outside its grasp, it does so indirectly: through the detour of some additional feature of the cotton that color, odor, and fire are all able to touch. The being of the cotton withdraws from the flames, even if it is consumed and destroyed. Cotton-being is concealed not only from phenomenologists and textile workers, but from all entities that come into contact with it. In other words, the withdrawal of objects is not some cognitive trauma that afflicts only humans and a few smart animals, but expresses the permanent inadequacy of any relation at all. If there is no way to make a hammer perfectly present to my thought or action, there is also no way to make cotton present to fire, or glass to raindrops. It cannot be denied that human experience is rather different from inanimate contact, or that it is presumably richer and more complex. But that is not the point. The more relevant issue is whether the difference between human relations with paper and a flame's relation with paper is different in kind or only in degree. And for the purposes of Heidegger's tool-analysis, it turns out to be merely a matter of degree. Although Heidegger tries to establish a pivotal gulf between Being and human Dasein, what he gives us instead is a basic difference between reality and relation.

This cuts against the grain of Kant's Copernican Revolution, which still dominates philosophy in our time. Both Latour and Meillassoux have justly objected to Kant's analogy: whereas Copernicus drove the earth from the center of the cosmos and put it into motion, Kant restores humans to the center in a manner more reminiscent of Ptolemy.[192] If I now use the phrase "Anti-Copernicus," this is directed not at Copernicus the astronomer, but at Kant the self-proclaimed Copernican philosopher. We might ask what is most typical of the Kantian position. It is surely not his theories of space and time or his doctrine of the categories, since few philosophers still adhere to these views, yet Kant continues to dominate mainstream philosophy anyway. It is not the notion of things-in-themselves lying beyond all experience, since his German Idealist heirs abolished this concept with little effect on Kant's stature. No, what is truly characteristic of Kant's position is that the human-world relation takes priority over all others. Even those few who read Kant as a realist who strongly believes in things-in-themselves must still admit that the role of these things for Kant is little more than to haunt human awareness with a specter of its finitude. And more importantly, nowhere does Kant pay serious attention to relations between these things-in-themselves. What is always at stake for him is the relation

---

[192] Bruno Latour, *We Have Never Been Modern*; Quentin Meillassoux, *After Finitude*.

between human subject on one side and world on the other. Today this human-world duopoly is taken for granted and rarely called into question. Heidegger certainly does not question it, and in this respect he remains an unwitting Copernican, forever focused on the relation between Dasein and world, with nothing to say about the interaction of fire and cotton apart from all human observers.

The towering exception in recent philosophy, the greatest of recent Anti-Copernicans, is surely Alfred North Whitehead. This remarkable thinker abolished the Kantian prejudice by saying that all human and non-human entities have equal status insofar as they all *prehend* other things, relating to them in one way or another.[193] For Whitehead, unlike for Heidegger, the human-world coupling has no higher status than the duels between comets and planets, or dust and moonlight. All relations are on exactly the same footing. This does not entail a projection of human properties onto the non-human world, but rather the reverse: what it says is that the crude prehensions made by minerals and dirt are no less relations than are the sophisticated mental activity of humans. Instead of placing souls into sand and stones, we find something sandy or stony in the human soul.

Now, many philosophers claim to be realists despite upholding the Kantian duopoly of human and world. They think that to posit some unarticulated reality beyond experience is enough to escape idealism. Perhaps they are right; perhaps they do deserve the name of realists. But if that is the case, then there is little reason to be excited about realism. Against such claims, we should always observe the following litmus test: no philosophy does justice to the world unless it treats all relations as equally relations, which means as equally translations or distortions. Inanimate collisions must be treated in exactly the same way as human perceptions, even if the latter are obviously more *complicated* forms of relation. As soon as we do this, we have pushed Heidegger in the direction of metaphysics. Though his rejection of the term "metaphysics" is well known, he rejects it only in the form of ontotheology, in which one special kind of entity is viewed as the root of all others, and that is the opposite of my goal. Most importantly, we now have a theory in which rocks withdraw from windows no less than from human theory and praxis. Such a theory surely deserves the name of speculative metaphysics.

---

[193] Alfred North Whitehead, *Process and Reality*.

D. Two Tensions

There are moments when Heidegger tends to treat being as unified and to find multiplicity only in the kingdom of presence, just as we find in the early Levinas.[194] That is to say, there are times when Heidegger equates any talk of multiple beings with talk of mere presence-at-hand. To discuss being itself means to move deeper than the *vorhanden*, and this entails an undermining of all specific beings. At other times, especially from 1949 onward, Heidegger is perfectly willing to allow specific beings to withdraw into shadow and *remain* specific rather than melting into a holistic global tool-system. But our goal is not to learn Heidegger's true opinion: his tool-analysis is a thought experiment, and here as in physics we are bound by the truth of the experiment more than by Heidegger's own personal views on it. What I have tried to show is that if we define an object through its role in a system of interrelations, objects are thereby undermined, reduced to the caricatured image they present to all other things. The only way to do justice to objects is to consider that their reality is free of all relation, deeper than all reciprocity. The object is a dark crystal veiled in a private vacuum: irreducible to its own pieces, and equally irreducible to its outward relations with other things.

In discussing Husserl we spoke of sensual objects. Such objects exist only for another object that encounters them, and are merely encrusted with accidental qualities rather than "hiding" behind them. By contrast, in Heidegger's tools we have *real* objects, which differ from the sensual ones in both respects. First, the real object is autonomous from whatever encounters it. If I close my eyes to sleep or die, the sensual tree is vaporized, while the real tree continues to flourish even if all sentient beings are destroyed along with me. Second, though sensual objects always inhabit experience and are not hidden behind their qualities, real objects must always hide.

But despite these differences, there are important similarities between the two kinds of objects. Both are autonomous units. Both are irreducible to any bundle of traits, since they are able to withstand numerous changes in the qualities that belong to them. And most importantly, both real and sensual objects are polarized with two different kinds of qualities. We saw that a sensual object is encrusted at every moment with purely accidental sensual qualities, while beneath it are submerged the more crucial real features that belong to the eidos. The same two polarities are found in the case of real objects. For, on the one hand, the real hammer emits sensual

---

[194] Emmanuel Levinas, *Existence and Existents*.

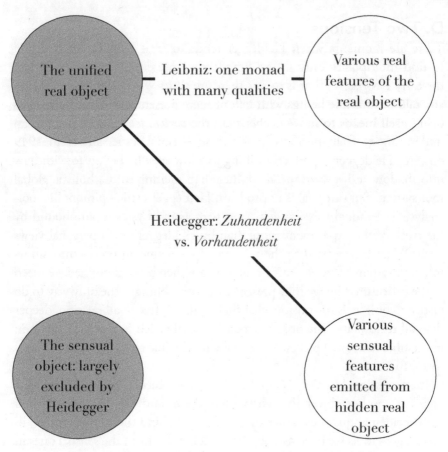

Figure 3: Two Tensions in Real Objects (Heidegger and Leibniz)

qualities into the sphere of presence, despite being withdrawn in its own right. The qualities encountered in experience must somehow emanate from a real object no less than a sensual one, because even though such qualities are obviously attached to a sensual object in any given moment, they are the sole way in which the withdrawn tool-beings become present in consciousness. And on the other hand, the real hammer is not a sheer empty unit, but has a multitude of real qualities of its own. This is clear from some remarks of Leibniz, who observes that even though each monad must be one monad, each also needs a multitude of qualities to be what it is, so as to differ from other monads rather than being interchangeable with them.[195]

This brief survey of Husserl and Heidegger has already given us the basic elements of an object-oriented metaphysics. The two great figures of

---

[195] G.W. Leibniz, "The Principles of Philosophy, or The Monadology," §8, p. 214.

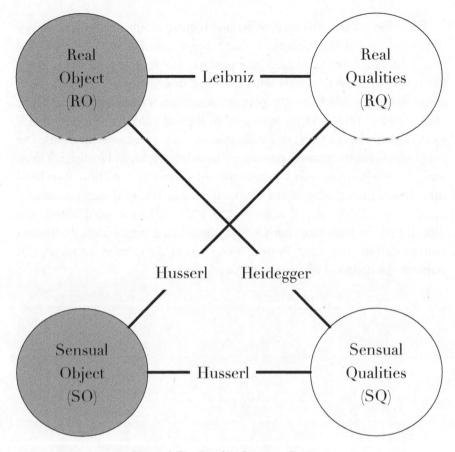

Figure 4: The Fourfold Structure Emerges

phenomenology are united once and for all. While there may be an infinity of objects in the cosmos, they come in only two kinds: the real object that withdraws from all experience, and the sensual object that exists *only in* experience. And along with these we also have two kinds of qualities: the sensual qualities found in experience, and the real ones that Husserl (wrongly) says are accessible intellectually rather than through sensuous intuition. This yields four distinct poles in the universe. Normally, any group of four terms can be paired in six possible permutations — or ten permutations, if we allow for combinations of two of the same kind. But for now we focus only on those pairings that bring together an object-pole and a quality-pole. And of course there are only four such pairs: real object/ real quality, sensual object/sensual quality, real object/sensual quality, and sensual object/real quality. In fact, we have already touched on all four cases, and they provide the major subject matter for the remainder of this book.

The pairing of sensual object with sensual quality is the first great discovery of Husserl, in which sensual objects are fully present, but always surrounded by a mist of accidental features and profiles. His second great discovery is the union of sensual objects with real qualities, since the phenomena in consciousness would be empty poles of unity unless they had some definite character, and this character is formed of the real eidetic qualities that (for him) can only be the target of intellectual and never sensuous intuition. The coupling of real objects with sensual qualities is the topic of Heidegger's tool-analysis, where a concealed subterranean hammer is somehow translated into sensual presence by means of a surface accessible to thought or action. Finally, the pairing of real objects with real qualities is what allows real objects to differ from one another rather than being empty unified substrata with no definite character. By developing this model in more detail, we will arrive at the doorstep of a new kind of philosophy.

CHAPTER 10

THE FUTURE OF CONTINENTAL REALISM: HEIDEGGER'S FOURFOLD[196]

It seems to me that Lee Braver is correct when he argues, in *A Thing of This World* (2007), that continental philosophy has been primarily an *anti-realist* school from the start.[197] We differ only in that Braver heaps praise on this anti-realism, while I view it as an intellectual catastrophe. In any case, an alternative continental philosophy has begun to emerge, in the shape of at least three major realist approaches in continental thought in the twenty-first century:

1 The New Realism led by the Italian ex-relativist Maurizio Ferraris and the prolific German philosopher Markus Gabriel. Given that Ferraris's own realist turn dates as far back as the early 1990s, he may deserve the title of the first blatantly realist philosopher of the recent continental tradition. He also paid a heavy price for this, since it put a permanent strain on his relationship with one-time mentor Gianni Vattimo.
2 The realism of Manuel DeLanda, drawn somewhat counter-intuitively from Deleuze and Guattari, but developed with vigor and passion and

---

[196] "The Future of Continental Realism" originally appeared in 2016 in the journal *Chiasma: A Site For Thought*, pp. 81–98.
[197] Lee Braver, *A Thing of This World*.

unremittingly realist in spirit, emphasizing the realist mandate of recent scientific breakthroughs.

3 The realism of the Speculative Realists (Brassier, Grant, Harman, Meillassoux) gathered at the 2007 workshop at Goldsmiths, University of London.[198] This was a loose confederation of separate realist approaches, and the four original members quickly went their separate ways.[199] Through the influence of these three approaches — and not those of New Materialism, which is a mostly rabid anti-realist movement — realism has finally achieved something like a critical mass in continental philosophy.[200] Far from fading away quietly, it is the subject of more books, articles, and conferences each year.

Thus, it may be a good time to consider possible future developments in continental realism. Given the limited space available for the present article, the best I can hope to do is discuss the possible future of my own preferred continental realism: object-oriented philosophy, or object-oriented ontology (abbreviated OOO, or "Triple O"). Since I cannot assume the reader's prior familiarity with the object-oriented approach, I will begin by explaining its origins in Husserl and Heidegger, before moving on to consider the future prospects of OOO itself.

I. The Tool-Analysis

We begin with Martin Heidegger, the original inspiration for OOO. Heidegger's entire philosophy is contained in the celebrated tool-analysis, first published in his 1927 masterwork *Being and Time*, but found as early as his first university lecture course in 1919.[201] In my view it is the pivotal moment of philosophy in the twentieth century, and it is crucial that we draw the right lessons from it if we ever wish to escape that century.[202] The tool-analysis is best viewed as a response to Husserl, who served Heidegger in the usual double capacity of mentor and rival. Husserl's phenomenology famously "brackets" the natural world, suspending all theories about atoms,

---

[198] Ray Brassier et al., "Speculative Realism."

[199] See also Graham Harman, *Speculative Realism: An Introduction*.

[200] Although Karen Barad (the most systematic of her generation of New Materialists) terms her position "agential realism," it is the exact opposite of realism in the classical sense, since she follows Niels Bohr in contending that thought and reality bootstrap each other into existence rather than pre-existing separately. See Karen Barad, *Meeting the Universe Halfway*.

[201] Martin Heidegger, *Being and Time*; Martin Heidegger, *Towards the Definition of Philosophy*.

[202] Graham Harman, *Tool-Being*.

chemicals, and sound waves, with the aim of focusing on the world as it shows itself to us. When a door slams, I simply hear the door slamming, and this experience contains countless subtle stratifications that patient analysis can eventually uncover. If a scientist counters by saying that the slamming door creates percussive effects in the air, which causes vibrations in the eardrum, which sends signals through the nervous system into my brain, this is just a theory — a derivative mode of understanding, while for Husserl the phenomenal experience of hearing the door slam is primary.

Heidegger's way of deepening this model is both simple and profound. For the most part, things *do not* appear to us as phenomena in consciousness. Most of the things in our environment are hidden from view, silently taken for granted until something happens that makes us notice them. The floor beneath my feet, the oxygen in the air, the neurons in my brain, the English grammar I easily use, generally function with unspoken efficiency unless something goes wrong. This happens often enough: tools do break. When they do, entities reverse from tacit reliability into explicit presence. As a name for such presence, Heidegger chooses the term *Vorhandenheit*, usually rendered in English as "presence-at-hand." As a contrary name for the silent labor of unnoticed things, Heidegger chooses the term *Zuhandenheit*, or "readiness-to-hand." It is important to note that these are not names for two different *kinds* of objects, as if shoes and hammers were always ready-to-hand and colors or numbers always present-at-hand. For in fact, reversals between the two modes constantly occur. The functioning hammer easily breaks, reversing from silent readiness-to-hand into explicit presence-at-hand. But even when this happens, the broken hammer lying before me is not available in sheer, unalloyed presence. Many aspects of the hammer are still taken for granted even when I stare at it explicitly. Conversely, a broken hammer might easily be repaired, returning to its previous unnoticed use: but even then it flashes in the sunlight from time to time, and never fades completely from view.

It is safe to say that presence-at-hand is the sole great enemy of Heidegger's philosophy. His version of the history of philosophy is even somewhat monotonous in accusing all past thinkers of reducing being to presence. Heidegger lists several different ways in which things can be present-at-hand: normal everyday perception, explicit theoretical awareness, and the mournful case of broken tools. What all these experiences have in common is that none of them gives us the *being* of the things. Whether I perceive a hammer, create theories about it, or grieve over its recent malfunction, in all such cases I merely confront the hammer "as" hammer. This explicit awareness of the hammer "as" having such and such characteristics articulates some of its features while inevitably leaving others in shadow. Presence never does justice to a thing's full reality, which withdraws into a depth no awareness can ever exhaust. The hammer "as" hammer always means the hammer *for* someone who considers it. But this is not the same as the hammer in its own right, which no observer can drain to the dregs.

An additional form of presence-at-hand that Heidegger considers is independent physical substance. Science views entities as pieces of objective matter occupying space and time (or shaping them, as in general relativity). Thus, it views entities as a set of objective properties that can be summarized in a theory. This latter form of presence-at-hand, independent physical substance, is the pied piper that so often leads mainstream Heidegger commentators astray. For these interpreters hold that "present-at-hand" for Heidegger means "independent of Dasein." And since reality independent of Dasein obviously spells realism, they conclude that Heidegger's relentless critique of presence-at-hand is also a critique of realism. This leads to the assumption that Dasein's *access* to the world is philosophically paramount, just as it was for Kant and most of his successors. The mistake is understandable, but a mistake nonetheless. To show this, we need only note that when entities are defined as physical matter occupying space-time coordinates, this is just as much a caricature of entities as Husserl's phenomena were. After all, physics is an attempt to see physical things "as" what they are via certain mathematizable properties, even though there always remains a deeper layer in the things that is taken for granted. Whether the as-structure results from phenomenological description, or from physical theorization, in both cases it is derivative of a more primal being of the things. The as-structure is a sort of objectification or distortion: or better yet, a *translation* of entities, rendering them in a present-at-hand language that is never entirely apt. In short, the physical things known to the sciences (and to common sense) are not independent of Dasein at all, but only *seem* to be independent. They result from a purely mathematical projection of nature by Dasein, and this will never be enough to exhaust the depths of the being of things. But this means that presence-at-hand actually refers to the *dependence* of things on Dasein, not their independence. Without some phenomenologist, scientist, or frustrated handyman observing the hammer, it would not be present-at-hand. Presence always means presence *for* someone or something. By contrast, readiness-to-hand refers to absence. This latter point will be refused by most Heidegger commentators, and we will soon consider why.

My initial claim, then, is that Heidegger's presence-at-hand means dependence on Dasein, and readiness-to-hand means the independence of that which withdraws from access. The counterargument is easy to find, since nearly all commentators make it. For them it is the reverse: presence-at-hand means independence, and readiness-to-hand means dependence on Dasein. By countering mainstream Heideggerians on such a fundamental point, am I dismissing them as an unruly mob of hacks and fools? No. They have good reasons for thinking as they do. The main reason is that for Heidegger, there is no such thing as "an" item of equipment in isolation from others. Equipment always forms a total system, the very system that Heidegger calls "world." Hammers gain meaning from the houses they are used to build, houses gain meaning from the climate they are designed to resist, and so forth. Every tool exists "in order to" do something else. And further, all this equipment ultimately gains meaning only from that "for the sake of which" they are used: namely, for the sake of Dasein's own existence. If Dasein were not physically fragile, or not in need of privacy, houses would not be what they are. If Dasein is living in frozen Iowa rather than sweltering Texas, rooftop heaters become too costly for Dasein to afford (which did not prevent my high school in Iowa from installing them). Tools belong to a holistic system that is defined, ultimately, by Dasein itself. This would seem to make an airtight case that readiness-to-hand means "Dasein-dependent," thereby placing my thesis in jeopardy. Yet I will soon demonstrate that my thesis is in no danger at all.

The most widely read Heidegger commentator is surely Hubert Dreyfus. His reading of the tool-analysis is now the standard one, at least among analytic philosophers. Dreyfus sums up the situation as follows: "Heidegger first notes that we do not usually encounter …. 'mere things,' but rather we use the things at hand to get something done. These things he calls 'equipment,' in a broad enough sense to include whatever is useful: tools, materials, clothes, dwellings, etc.'" He continues: "The basic characteristic of equipment is that it is used for something …. An 'item' of equipment is what it is only insofar as it refers to other equipment and so fits in a certain way into an 'equipmental whole.'"[203] And true enough, Heidegger grants us a holistic vision in which all tools fit together in a referential totality, none of them existing in isolation. Dreyfus notes further that "when we are using equipment, it has a tendency to 'disappear.' We are not aware of

---

[203] Hubert Dreyfus, *Being-in-the-World*, p. 62.

it as having any characteristics at all."[204] And "partly as a joke but also in dead seriousness Heidegger adds that this withdrawal or holding itself in is the way equipment is *in itself* …. This is a provocative claim. Traditional philosophers from Plato to Husserl have been led to claim that the use-properties of things, their function as equipment, are interest-relative so precisely *not* in themselves."[205] In this way, Dreyfus lays the groundwork for the standard anti-realist interpretation of the tool-analysis. Tools withdraw from view. They belong to a relational system of purposes. And to say that withdrawal is how entities are "in themselves" must mean that things themselves are relational, despite the views of "traditional philosophers from Plato to Husserl." To counter this reading, it needs to be shown that Dreyfus is wrong to identify withdrawal and relationality. Another telling problem is that Dreyfus repeats the frequent but groundless claim that Heidegger's tool-analysis was anticipated by John Dewey, who "introduced the distinction between knowing-how and knowing that to make just this point …."[206]

To show why it is so wrong to mix Heidegger with Dewey, it simply needs to be observed that the distinction between readiness-to-hand and presence-at-hand is not the same as the difference between pragmatic know-how and explicit theoretical awareness. We begin with the latter point. It certainly seems that Heidegger draws a distinction between our implicit use of tools (*Zuhandenheit*) and our explicit awareness of them (*Vorhandenheit*). But notice that unconscious practice distorts or translates the things of the world no less than conscious theory does. If I suddenly stare at the floor and think about it, I reduce it to present-at-hand features such as color, texture, and hardness, thereby losing the *being* of the floor, which is simply taken for granted. This belongs to the ABC's of Heidegger studies, and is quickly learned by all newcomers to his work. Yet there is also a less obvious lesson that is equally true: my unconscious *use* of the floor does the same. To sit on the floor does not exhaust its being any more than staring at it does. In both cases, the inscrutable withdrawn depth of the floor is reduced to a discrete and limited set of features, even if using the floor can be called "implicit" and staring at it can be called "explicit." Hence, the difference between presence-at-hand and readiness-to-hand is by no means equivalent to that between knowing-how and knowing that. The

---

[204] Drefyus, *Being-in-the-World*, p. 64.
[205] Drefyus, *Being-in-the-World*, p. 65.
[206] Drefyus, *Being-in-the-World*, p. 67.

comparison with Dewey becomes irrelevant — or even hopelessly wrong, given Dewey's remorselessly relational view of the world, since Heidegger's tools are ultimately what *escape* all relation.

Some readers may object that this is a fanciful projection of bizarre non-Heideggerian ideas onto Heidegger's own work. I would answer this objection with two points. Point One: tools are not just efficiently handy for Heidegger, but also *break*. Once the tool is broken, it obviously belongs to the sphere of present-at-hand awareness, as an obtrusive sort of obstacle. But what is it *in the tools* that breaks? It obviously cannot be their current smooth relational functioning: by definition, this is a sleek efficiency already fully assigned to other entities. Hence, whatever breaks in the tool must be something that is not fully inscribed in its current use. In short, the invisible use of a tool does not exhaust its reality any more than the visible properties of a tool do. Point Two: Heidegger uses the as-structure to refer to *both* realms, theory and practice alike. To see a broken hammer is to consider it explicitly "as" a hammer. But for Heidegger, even to use a hammer unconsciously is to use it "as" a hammer, not as a drill or as some vague indeterminate thing. The first kind of "as" is surely more transparent than the second, but it is clear that Heidegger sees tools as always articulated, whether consciously or not. Yet articulation is always a translation or distortion, and never unlocks the full depths of a thing's reality. This leads us to a remarkable observation: insofar as an unconsciously useful tool is relationally assigned to other entities, it is *already a broken tool*. To relate is not to be a tool, but to be *broken*, even if human witnesses do not happen to be looking on. The as-structure governs both theory and praxis, making them ontologically indistinct. To find the tools themselves, we must retreat not just behind theory, but even behind "tools" in the normal pragmatic sense.

From here we can easily see the problem with Dreyfus's other now quite mainstream suggestion: that withdrawal means the same thing as relationality. *Au contraire*. Insofar as the tool is related to other tools, insofar as it belongs to the system of world, it is merely relational rather than withdrawn. An invisible tool that functions smoothly may be withdrawn from Dasein in the sense that we are not "conscious" of it. But it is not withdrawn from Dasein at all in the wider sense, since it is fully determined by a system of references that are enslaved to Dasein's current purposes. To "withdraw" must mean to withdraw from all references, not just from the explicit conscious awareness of humans. Withdrawal is what allows a tool to break eventually, since it holds something in reserve that escapes its current functioning no less than its current presence in consciousness. But this entails that if world is a system of relations, then the world is a system of presence-at-hand. Presence-at-hand means nothing other than relationality: presence for something or someone. The tools themselves are deeper than world, and Heidegger is inconsistent when he identifies tools with world. His famous "ontological difference" between being and beings cannot mean a difference between implicit and explicit, but must be a difference between reality and relation. But this entails that his critique of presence-at-hand gives us realism, not anti-realism.

2. The Thing

Heidegger's realist attitude toward the thing becomes even more apparent in that classic work of his post-war career, "Insight Into What Is." (In what follows I will translate the German text myself rather than using the 2012 Mitchell translation.[207]) The lecture was written down in Heidegger's Black Forest hut in October 1949, and delivered to the Bremen Club on the easily remembered date of December 1. The opening theme of this untranslated lecture is the elimination of distance by modern technology: "All distances in time and space shrivel away …. Yet the hasty elimination of all distances does not bring nearness; for nearness does not consist in a small amount of distance."[208] Here, the central theme of the tool-analysis is alive and well. To bring distant jungles and tribes close to us through television merely brings them close as something present-at-hand. It is a false nearness that reduces them to superficial outer contours. Likewise, our vast temporal distance from the ancient Greeks would only be a false distance, since it overlooks our deep reliance on their concepts of being, and other aspects of Greek Dasein.

But if technology does not give us nearness, then neither does physical science: "It is said that the knowledge of science is compelling. Certainly so. Yet in what sense is it compelling? For our case [it means] that we must renounce the jug filled with wine and replace it with an empty space in which a fluid is extended. Science turns the jug-thing into a nullity, since it does not permit things to be decisive."[209] Here nothing has changed from Heidegger's earlier conception of science, which in his view merely

---

[207] The text of the lecture cycle "Einblick in das was ist" can be found in the German original in Martin Heidegger, *Bremer und Freiburger Vorträge*; and in English in Martin Heidegger, *Bremen and Freiburg Lectures*.

[208] Heidegger, *Bremer und Freiburger Vorträge*, p. 3.

[209] Heidegger, *Bremer und Freiburger Vorträge*, p. 9.

reduces things to a series of objectified properties, thereby shoving the thing itself out of view. Science, like technology, gives us a false nearness to the nature of things by inscribing them in a field of accessible, present-at-hand properties. Thus the thing will not be found in the sciences. And neither will it be found in knowing how a thing was constructed: "The jug is a thing as a container. This container certainly needs to be produced. But its producedness by the potter in no way constitutes what belongs to the jug insofar as it is a jug. The jug is not a container because it was produced, but rather the jug must be produced because it is this container."[210]

What the technological, scientific, and manufacturer's views on the thing all share is their reduction of the thing to its outward features, its *Vorhandenheit*. Heidegger says that what the jug really is can never be experienced through its outward look: its *idea* or *eidos* in the Platonic sense. He asserts that "Plato, who represents the presence of that which is present from the standpoint of its outward look, thought the essence of the thing just as little as Aristotle and all later thinkers."[211] If a new way can be found to understand the thing, this will already put us on an entirely new path of philosophy: "The first step to …. wakefulness is the step back from the merely representative (i.e., explanatory) thinking into commemorative thinking."[212] Such a commemorative thinking would not reduce the jug to its present-at-hand outer contours. For in no way does the thing itself consist in its dependence on humans, despite the Dreyfusian reading of *Being and Time*. Heidegger is quite clear about this: "As a container, the jug is something that stands in itself. The standing-in-itself characterizes the jug as something *independent*. As the independence of something independent, the jug distinguishes itself from an object. Something independent can become an object when we represent it to ourselves, whether in immediate perception or in recollective presentation."[213] If we avoid the aforementioned technological, scientific, and manufacturer's versions of the jug and replace it with the Dreyfusian model of the jug as a useful tool assigned to other tools and to human Dasein, we will still have failed to think the jug itself. Dreyfus (and Dewey) have merely replaced the jug with a pragmatic theory and thereby reduced it to a nullity; they have missed the jug *qua* jug. As already mentioned, Heidegger says in 1949 that "the jug is not a container because it was produced, but rather the jug must be produced because it

---

[210] Heidegger, *Bremer und Freiburger Vorträge*, p. 6.
[211] Heidegger, *Bremer und Freiburger Vorträge*, p. 7.
[212] Heidegger, *Bremer und Freiburger Vorträge*, p. 20.
[213] Heidegger, *Bremer und Freiburger Vorträge*, p. 5.

is this container." He might just as well have added that "the jug is not a container because it is used by Dasein in a referential system, but rather the jug must be used by Dasein in a referential system because it is this container." The jug is real. Like any other real thing, it cannot be replaced by a set of features belonging to its outward look — or its outward *use*, for that matter. The realism of this 1949 lecture cycle is even harder to deny than that of the earlier tool-analysis.

Now, "realism" can admittedly mean any number of different things. Braver's book, the definitive account of continental anti-realism, provides a valuable table including no fewer than *six* possible senses of the term.[214] Two of the six are perhaps the most frequently used: 1. Belief in a mind-independent reality; 2. Belief in a correspondence theory of truth. Heidegger obviously rejects the latter. For him, truth is a matter of *aletheia*: a gradual unveiling or unconcealment that never disposes of shadow, never brings anything forth in total, naked presence. By rejecting correspondence theories of truth in this manner, Heidegger certainly abandons the most common model of truth found among realists. But in no way does this amount to a rejection of realism *tout court*. It is possible to believe in a mind-independent reality while not believing it possible to attain a perfectly lucid grasp of that reality. Indeed, the best proof that such a position is possible is that Heidegger himself maintains it. Braver and others hold that the replacement of correspondence by *aletheia* entails that truth can only be an internal movement within what is already fully accessible to humans. In other words, being is nothing more than the series of historical shapes in which it manifests itself to people; there is no "in itself" hiding behind being's manifestations, but only an emergent process that leads us to yet another manifestation: this is Jacques Derrida's misreading of Heidegger in *Of Grammatology*.[215] This Hegelized version of Heidegger ignores Heidegger's incurable hostility to all attempts to reduce being to presence of any sort. For Heidegger, being is nothing if not *absence*, to such an extent that all comparisons between him and Hegel immediately capsize. It is the same reason that leads Heidegger to attack ontotheology — also known as "the metaphysics of presence," or simply "metaphysics." When ontotheology claims that one kind of entity (say, atoms) is the ultimate constituent to which all others are reducible, Heidegger complains that this

---

[214] Lee Braver, *A Thing of This World*, p. xix.
[215] Jacques Derrida, *Of Grammatology*, pp. 22–23. For a response to Derrida see Graham Harman, "The Well-Wrought Broken Hammer," pp. 195–199.

reduces all beings to a single set of present-at-hand features that characterize their component atoms: mass, position, angular momentum. His position is not that there is no true reality lying behind its manifestations; rather, his position is that this reality can never be adequately described through its present-at-hand features. In short, Heidegger's rejection of ontotheology, of "metaphysics," is merely a rejection of correspondence theories of truth, not of a mind-independent reality.

Yet there is another possible counterargument here, and a reasonably good one. Throughout his career, Heidegger declares that there is no being without Dasein, no Dasein without being, but always a primal correlation or rapport between the two. He finds it nonsensical to ask whether Newton's laws were true or untrue before they were discovered, or to ask what happened in the world before the existence of Dasein. This is the undeniably anti-realist side of Heidegger. But notice that even a permanent being-Dasein correlate does not entail the lack of a mind-independent reality. The fact that being and Dasein always come as a pair does not require that being is fully exhausted in its manifestations to Dasein. Although jugs only exist as jugs for humans, and perhaps for certain dogs and birds, it does not follow that the jug is reducible to its represented features, as Heidegger's jug-analysis makes clear. In similar fashion, the fact that there is no human society without humans or humans without society does not mean that human society is reducible to what humans currently understand about it. Sociology would be an unnecessary discipline if the features of social reality were legible to its members at a glance.[216]

Yet there is a glaring lacuna in Heidegger's thoughts on the jug. As we have seen, he does insist that the jug "as" jug is unattainable by any form of representation; in this respect, he follows Kant's view of the noumena, which lie outside human categories and their determination of phenomena. This is undeniably a form of mind-independent realism, despite repeated attempts to finesse both Kant and Heidegger out of this position. Yet there is also a harmful way, rarely addressed, in which Kant and Heidegger slam the door on a healthy realism. Namely, for both of these thinkers the function of independent reality is simply to exceed human representation, nothing else. The "in itself" is merely a residue unreachable by humans, and does little more than haunt us with dreams or nightmares of our finitude. Phrased more bluntly: what do the things in themselves do *to each other* when humans are not looking? Are there really no relations between these

---

[216] Manuel DeLanda, *A New Philosophy of Society*, p. 1.

things apart from us? Heidegger dismisses the question as nonsense. Kant ignores it, at least in the Critical period. The same holds true for most post-Kantian philosophy, with Alfred North Whitehead providing the most prominent counterinstance.[217] Endless debates erupt between those who believe in a reality apart from humans and those who see this attitude as retrograde and naïve. But both sides tacitly agree on the main point, implicitly assuming that philosophy has nothing to say about the relations between things when no humans are there to see it. This problem is thrown to the natural sciences, which invariably treat it in materialist fashion: one billiard ball smashes another; an iron filing aligns itself with a magnetic field. Yet it ought to be clear, however controversially, that *materialism is not realism*.[218] After all, materialism idealizes its objects by reducing them to a limited number of mathematizable features endorsed by the accidental state of present-day physics. Yet it is not only for us that the jug and wine withdraw from such explicit features, but *in their own right*. It is not the mere accident of my looking at the jug and wine that transforms them from physical masses into strange, withdrawn residues. In other words, withdrawal occurs not just along a single Kantian fault line where human meets world, but crosses the world itself. The wine does not exhaust the jug any more than we humans do. If Heidegger had admitted this additional point, it would necessarily have led him to develop a metaphysics of objects. The withdrawal of things from all access is not some quirky existential/ psychological feature of humans, but infects even the most rudimentary forms of inanimate causation. Veiling and unveiling are ubiquitous: even between billiard balls, even between fire and cotton, and even when humans are not observing, do not yet exist, or exist no longer. Those who do not agree to this principle are in fact committed to a form of idealism, since what they really claim is that a certain assemblage of abstract properties can altogether exhaust a thing's reality.

3. The Fourfold

So far I have avoided mentioning the embarrassing open secret that Heidegger's thing is conceived as a *fourfold* thing. The fourfold, *das Geviert*, was first proclaimed in the same 1949 lecture we have been discussing, aside from a brief initial taste in the habitually overrated *Contributions*

---

[217] Alfred North Whitehead, *Process and Reality*.
[218] Graham Harman, "Realism Without Materialism."

to Philosophy.[219] No major concept of Heidegger has been so ignored as the fourfold. Only in 2015 did Andrew Mitchell publish the first book in English devoted exclusively to this topic, a welcome development despite the considerable flaws of that book.[220] At first taste, the quadruple mirror-play of earth, sky, gods, and mortals seems so precious and obscure that it leaves his admirers either ashamed or confused. But as I see it, the fourfold is Heidegger's crowning discovery. Moreover, the fourfold is not as obscure as it looks, and can even be clarified with such conceptual rigor that it soon appears dryly schematic and sterile. And finally, I hold that earth, sky, gods, and mortals are the necessary horizon of any future continental realism. Here is the sort of passage at which the scoffers understandably scoff: "In the gift of the pouring [from the jug] tarries the onefold of the four. The gift of the pouring is a gift, insofar as it lets earth, sky, gods, and mortals linger. Yet lingering is no longer the mere persistence of something present-at-hand. Lingering appropriates [*ereignet*]. It brings the four into the light of what is their own. From out of its onefold they are confided to one another."[221] My goal in the concluding pages of this article is to replace the reader's mockery with genuine interest.

Fourfold structures, quite common in the history of human thought, are almost always generated by the intersection of two separate dualisms. What we seek here are the specific dualisms that jointly act to produce Heidegger's apparently inscrutable fourfold. The first of these dualisms is so awesomely repetitive throughout his works that at times he seems to have no other ideas at all. I speak of the trademark Heideggerian play of absence and presence, veiling and unveiling, concealing and clearing, withdrawal and as-structure, tool and broken tool, thrownness and projection, past and future, being and beings, and equivalent pairings. The vast majority of Heidegger's thousands of pages can be mastered simply by noting that these oppositions are all *exactly the same.* Things are withdrawn from presence, yet they come partly to presence "as" such and such. The opposed poles of concealing and revealing combine in an ambiguous present, and this is all that Heidegger means by "time": the simultaneous absence and presence of everything. His fourfold structure will emerge as soon as we supplement this solemnly repetitive dualism with another. And this second duality is not hard to find

[219] Martin Heidegger, *Contributions to Philosophy.*
[220] Andrew Mitchell, *The Fourfold.*
[221] Heidegger, *Bremer und Freiburger Vorträge*, p. 12.

in Heidegger: all one needs to do is look, but everyone has been too busy laughing at earth, sky, gods, and mortals to take the trouble to look.

The immediate source of Heidegger's second duality comes from his rather unusual early reading of Husserl. But let's return briefly to Franz Brentano, that seldom-read grandsire of phenomenology, whose interpretation of Aristotle's *De Anima* already provides us with a fourfold structure. Here I cannot improve on the account given by the prominent analytic philosopher Barry Smith: "[For Brentano] we are to imagine two realms, of soul or mind, and of matter .... On both sides we are to distinguish further what we might call *raw* and *developed* forms of the entities populating the realms in question."[222] Though it would not be altogether accurate to say that Heidegger's two basic poles are those of soul and matter, the resemblance is close enough to be interesting: namely, the realm of jugs and hammers themselves is distinct from that of jugs and hammers as they appear explicitly to Dasein. Smith continues:

> The raw form of matter is called *materia prima*. This can become everything corporeal .... In an analogous way, the soul can become everything sensible and intelligible, and does not exist except insofar as it receives the form of something sensible and intelligible. *In each case what gets added is of a formal nature*, and it is the fixed stock of forms or species which informs both the realm of thinking and that of extended (material, corporeal) substance .... *it is forms which mediate between them.*[223]

For Brentano, then, the fourfold model of Aristotle's psychology involves dual realms of soul and matter, both of them crossed by a second distinction between shapeless matter that can become anything, and a stock of forms that can be stamped into that matter. In short, it is a fourfold based on the dualities of soul vs. world and matter vs. form; the duality of matter and form exists in the world, and exists again on a second level in the mind. Whatever criticisms might be made of this model, it is certainly not laughable.

Now jump forward to Husserl, whose connection with Brentano was much more direct than Heideger's own. It is admittedly somewhat harder to find a fourfold structure in Husserl, and for a simple reason. For Husserl, the Aristotle-Brentano-Heidegger "reality itself," as opposed to the realm

---

[222] Barry Smith, *Austrian Philosophy*, p. 36.
[223] Smith, *Austrian Philosophy*, p. 36.

of presence to the mind, is deliberately suspended from consideration. The world itself is bracketed out of the picture, never to return. For this reason Husserl is dismissed in many realist circles as just another idealist, a Johnny-Come-Lately who repeats familiar anti-realist gestures already accomplished more clearly by Descartes, Kant, or Hegel. Yet this assessment of Husserl is disturbingly shallow.[224] While it is true that Husserl suspends reality-in-itself in the name of an immanent phenomenal sphere, a more interesting topic is the duality that occurs for Husserl *within* the phenomenal realm. Consider the following passage from *Logical Investigations* VI:

> The object is not actually given, it is not given wholly and entirely as that which it itself is. It is only given "from the front," only "perspectivally foreshortened and projected," and so on …. On this hinges the possibility of indefinitely many percepts of the same object, all differing in content. If percepts were always the actual, genuine self-presentations of objects that they pretend to be, there could be only a single percept for each object, since its peculiar essence would be exhausted in such self-presentation.[225]

The same point was already made in Husserl's Second Investigation, where he attacked the empiricist doctrine of objects as bundles of qualities. For Husserl, an object *is not* just a bundle of qualities, since that would make each shifting percept an entirely new object, and this is what he most opposes. Similar insights about intentional objects over and above their manifest qualities simply cannot be found in Descartes, Kant, Hegel, or anyone else for that matter. Indeed, the presence of intentional objects is what explains the strangely realist *atmosphere* found in the books of the non-realist Husserl: blackbirds and mailboxes resist our perceptions, unattainable behind their various profiles, masks, and perspectival foreshortenings. The important point for us is that Husserl adds a new kind of duality within the phenomenal realm. For Brentano's Aristotle it was a distinction between the wax-like soul and the forms it takes on. For Husserl, by contrast, it is the difference between intentional objects and the changing costumes they wear from one moment to the next, even while remaining the same

---

[224] Unfortunately, it is also Alain Badiou's misunderstanding when he mistakenly calls Husserl "a great classic, if a little late." Alain Badiou, *Being and Event*, p. 7. For it is hard to imagine a philosopher who, more than Husserl, could not possibly have come any earlier than he did: without Franz Brentano and Kasimir Twardowski, there could have been no Husserl.

[225] Edmund Husserl, *Logical Investigations*, vol. 2, pp. 712, 713.

objects that they were. Yet Husserl has no chance to extend this dualism into the subterranean realm of real things and create a fourfold, since he never accepts such an underground layer of reality.

Heidegger, however, is able to pull it off. His tool-analysis was first presented in the 1919 War Emergency Semester. At the end of that fateful term, Heidegger turns to an unusual interpretation of his teacher's phenomenological method, and speaks of two types of theory (which he even identifies with Husserl's own "generalization" and "formalization" from *Ideas* I).[226] Normally, phenomenological analysis is bound to a step-by-step progression, leading us through increasingly deeper levels of categorial intuition: I see a blurry patch; the blurry patch is brown; brown is a color; color is a kind of perception; perception is a kind of experience; and so forth. Now it might seem that the final step of this passage through many layers would be the category of "something in general." Yet Heidegger oddly mocks this apparently dry and harmless notion.[227] He insists instead that "something in general" can be invoked immediately at any stage of the analysis, unlike all the others. That is to say, categories normally have a layered, onion-like structure. We cannot pass from saying "this is brown" to "this is an experience" without passing through the intervening categorial layers. But for any layer we *can* say "this brown is something in general" or "this experience is something in general." As opposed to the usual "specific bondedness to levels of the steps in the de-living process" (the young Heidegger's term for theory) we have the principle that "everything experienceable at all is a possible something, regardless of its genuine world-character."[228] Stated in less boring terms, everything we experience is both something *specific* and something *at all*. This sounds suspiciously close to the classical rift between essence and existence. But more importantly for us, Heidegger sees this same division as repeated on two levels: that of world, and that of the perception of world. In this way the young Heidegger already gives us his infamous fourfold in germinal form. On the level of world, we have the "pre-worldly something" (something at all) and the "world-laden something" (something specific). On the level of explicit awareness, we have the "formal-logical objective something" (something at all) and the

[226] Martin Heidegger, *Zur Bestimmung der Philosophie*, pp. 109–117; Edmund Husserl, *Ideas: General Introduction to Pure Phenomenology*, pp. 72–74.

[227] Heidegger, *Zur Bestimmung der Philosophie*, p. 113. In this chapter, all translations from this work are my own.

[228] Heidegger, *Zur Bestimmung der Philosophie*. The first passage is from p. 114 and the second from p. 115. Heidegger's emphasis is removed in both cases.

"object-type something" (something specific).[229] To phrase it as an example: if I encounter a pencil, it is both something specific and something at all, and then *outside* our relationship and in-itself the pencil is also something specific and something at all.

In this way, the 1919 Heidegger gives us a rather dull-sounding fourfold in contrast with the all-too-flashy *Geviert* of 1949. The 1949 model is also different in one important respect. Although in 1949 the first dualism still lies between the world itself and our encounter with world, the second axis changes for Heidegger. Instead of being a duel between the existence and essence of every object, it is now a distinction between "world as a whole" and "specific beings," repeated on the veiled level as well as the unveiled one. Earth and gods belong on the level of veiled reality. We know this in the case of "earth" because earth is always a Heideggerian term for that which invisibly withdraws from view. We know it for "gods" because he often tells us that they merely hint without ever coming to presence. "Sky" replaces what was called world in the famous essay on artworks, and this makes it take on the role of visibility against earth's concealment. "Mortals" also belongs on the level of the visible, since he openly associates mortals with the as-structure: only mortals can experience death "as" death. As for the second principle of division, earth and mortals are assigned to "world as a whole," gods and sky to "specific beings." This is somewhat trickier, but I have made a full argument elsewhere and will not repeat it here.[230] In short, the tension between earth and gods can be found in the jug itself, while that between mortals and sky can be found in how the jug is present to us.

Now it seems to me that the young Heidegger's fourfold was better, even if the manner in which it was presented is significantly more boring. But a more intriguing fourfold would be one that Aristotle, Brentano, Husserl, and Heidegger never quite pieced together. Under this model, we would retain Husserl's phenomenal realm, with intentional objects emitting various profiles that shift constantly without changing the underlying intentional unit: the tree remains the same tree even as its colors and shadows change. But unlike with Husserl, we would have the same drama underway in a

---

[229] See the table in my book *Tool-Being*, p. 203. Theodore Kisiel is also alert to the fourfold structure in this important early lecture course. Kisiel's chapter on the course in his *The Genesis of Heidegger's* Being and Time, (Berkeley, CA: University of California Press, 1995) also includes a diagram of these four terms, though without relating them to Heidegger's later *Geviert*, a puzzling oversight given Kisiel's peerless scent for the subtleties of Heidegger's development.
[230] Harman, *Tool-Being*, pp. 190–202.

non-phenomenal reality that he could never accept: *real* objects would also be distinct from their qualities and not just a bundle, in the same way that his intentional objects are not just a bundle of accidental profiles. On both layers of reality (the real and the intentional) we would have a tension between unified things and their plurality of traits. The question would arise of how the four poles of the thing interact, and this is the very question to which Heidegger's fourfold has led us. There can no longer be a question of calling *das Geviert* "absurd." The question, instead, is how to make productive philosophical use of it. And this, I think, is the future of continental realism.

CHAPTER II

THE NEW FOURFOLD[231] (FROM *THE QUADRUPLE OBJECT*)

The obvious danger of a fourfold structure is that it might seem crankish or bizarre, like a New Age doctrine or the creed of a false prophet. [Heidegger's] *Geviert* might lead one to imagine the leader of a cult on some remote Pacific island, with a reformed harlot on one arm and a child bride on the other, all united in worship of the Great Obsidian Cylinder where the four forces of the cosmos are stationed. Yet in the preceding chapters I have tried to show that reflection on the fourfold is inevitable once we acknowledge both the results of Heidegger's potent tool-analysis and Husserl's breakthrough into the duel between a unified sensual object and its multitude of profiles.

Our quadruple enigma arises from the strange autonomy and lack of autonomy of real and sensual objects with respect to their real and sensual traits. In this sense, our problem has a highly classical flavor: the Platonic or Kantian doctrine of a world beyond the senses is fused with an Aristotelian-sounding distinction between the unity of a substance and its plurality of features. We began [earlier in *The Quadruple Object*] with the occasionalist deadlock in which no two objects are able to make contact. Yet this turned out to be just one piece of a larger puzzle in which it is still unclear how an object makes contact even with its own qualities. While it is a serious problem to know how fire touches cotton or human touches world, it is just

---

[231] This chapter originally appeared in *The Quadruple Object*, pp. 95–109.

as hard to know how an apple relates to its own features such as cold, red, hard, sweet, tangy, cheap, and juicy in the first place. In the present chapter I will try to make this model a bit more concrete.

A. Reviewing the Four Poles

We should begin by reviewing briefly the model of Heidegger's fourfold and comparing it with the similar quadruple structure of objects as endorsed by this book. It was noted that every rigorous fourfold structure in the history of philosophy results from the crossing of a pair of dualisms. In Heidegger's case one of those dualities is perfectly clear, since it saturates the whole of his career: the monotonous interplay of shadow and light, veiling and unveiling, concealing and revealing. This challenge to philosophies of presence, this insistence on an obscure subterranean depth that haunts all accessible entities, remains the obvious core of his philosophical trajectory. But Heidegger's second axis of reality is a bit hazier, and shifts during various portions of his career. In 1919, it is the difference between "something at all" and "something specific," a duality placed in the heart of every entity that exists, whether present or absent for conscious view. The broken hammer is both a specific visible entity and also an entity in general, yet the same holds for the hammer-being unleashed in a depth that hides from every gaze. We have seen that in 1949 the fourfold no longer plays out in the heart of every entity. Instead it involves a duel, repeated in the two arenas of the veiled and unveiled, between what Heidegger calls "beings as a whole" and "beings as such": between the world in its totality and the various specific things that populate the concealed and revealed worlds.[232] The terms that merely hint while withdrawing from view are earth and gods; those to which we have access "as" what they are receive the names of mortals and sky. The terms that refer to the unity of the world are earth and mortals, while those that are shattered in advance into a multitude of realities are gods and sky. These four terms cannot be taken literally as a taxonomy of entities, but are four structures of reality in general, found everywhere and at all times: despite Heidegger's romantic tendency to find the quadruple mirroring structure in rustic handiwork while withholding fourfold status from despicable plastic cups and offshore oil rigs.

---

[232] On the distinction between "beings as a whole" and "beings as such" see Martin Heidegger, *Nietzsche*, 2 vols.

The version of the fourfold defended in this book is similar to Heidegger's 1919 model, but shifted in the direction of Husserl's model of intentional or sensual objects. When the young Heidegger says that every entity is both "something at all" and "something specific," the diversity of things is found only in the second of these moments. A hammer, monkey, chimney, watermelon, and star are all "specific" in different ways, but all are "something at all" in exactly the same fashion for Heidegger. In fact, to be "something at all" is a rather boring and formalistic honor that makes any entity interchangeable with the rest, despite Heidegger's occasional nods to Aristotle's principle that being is expressed in many ways. But in the case of Husserl we have seen that this does not happen, and it is Husserl's model that I wish to endorse on this point. For if we consider the phenomenon of a watermelon, we do not find a dull opposition between (a) the melon in all its particularity, and (b) some "being in general" that would belong equally to the melon and to all other things. This is too reminiscent of Hume's bundles of qualities, with the sole difference that "being" is now adopted to serve the role of Hume's unifying bundle. Instead, the duel in question is between the watermelon as an enduring unit and the multitude of profiles that it exhibits at various times. The distinction is not between "something in general" and "specific watermelon" (as the young Heidegger would have it) but between watermelon-object and watermelon-qualities. So far Husserl is right, and should be opposed only in his idealistic claim that this watermelon-object in consciousness is not shadowed by a veiled melon-object inaccessible to every view.

The four poles of the fourfold endorsed by the present book have less poetic names than Heidegger's own. Instead of earth, gods, mortals, and sky, we offer real objects, real qualities, sensual objects, and sensual qualities. The relative lack of poetry in this newest model compared with Heidegger's is due not to some hideous aesthetic preference for "desert landscapes": rather, it is because the drama for us lies not in the poles themselves, but in the tensions between them.[233] Heidegger does refer to a dynamic interrelation of mirroring between the four terms of the fourfold, but never gives names to these tensions or considers them one by one.

The tension between sensual objects and their sensual qualities is the major topic of Husserl's phenomenology. The simplest mailbox or tree remains the same unit for us over a certain period of time, despite the radiation of ever

---

[233] "Desert landscapes" is, of course, a reference to Willard Van Orman Quine, "On What There Is."

new profiles from its surface. Though the deadening habits of common sense strip this event of its mystery, there is something permanently strange about the manner in which an enduring sensual object can appear in countless incarnations depending on the viewer's angle, distance, and mood. Perhaps children still appreciate this strangeness; in adults, strenuous exercises may be needed to recapture the atmosphere of mystery that ought to surround the merest rotation of a wine bottle or the shifting of lights behind a mountain. But Husserl also offers us a second tension in which the sensual object differs not from its shifting accidental facades, but from the plurality of qualities that it truly needs to remain what it is from moment to moment. These can only be called its *real* qualities, since they cannot be stripped from the sensual object without destroying it, and since they are withdrawn from all sensual access, limited to oblique approaches by the intellect or some other faculty. There is a further tension between real objects and their sensual qualities, as found in Heidegger's tool-analysis. The withdrawn or subterranean hammer is a concealed unit, but one that emits sensual qualities into the phenomenal sphere. And finally, these withdrawn real objects are not just unified lumps, but differ from one another insofar as each has its own essential features. The tension between the real thing as a unified thing and its multitude of qualities or notes is not discussed by Husserl or Heidegger, but can be found in the *Monadology* of Leibniz, as well as in the lesser-known works of the twentieth-century Basque Spaniard Xavier Zubíri.[234] Without adopting the Hölderlinian pathos of Heidegger's own terminology, we will still give these four tensions the suggestive names they deserve: *time* (SO-SQ) as in Husserl's adumbrations, *space* (RO-SQ) as in Heidegger's tool-analysis, *essence* (RO-RQ) as in Leibniz's monads, and *eidos* (SO-RQ) as in Husserl's eidetic intuition. Here at last is a fourfold structure that can serve as bedrock for further constructions.

B. Time, Space, Essence, and Eidos
Every thoughtful person occasionally reflects on the nature of time and space, which form the permanent homeland of human action and of everything else. Is time reversible, and can we travel backward and forward through it? Does space have only the three dimensions that we see, or does it contain many more, some of them populated by other life forms? Are time and space absolute and empty containers as they are for Newton, or generated by way

---

[234] G.W. Leibniz, "The Principles of Philosophy, or The Monadology"; Xavier Zubíri, *On Essence*.

of relations as they are for Leibniz? Is it possible to consider time and space as a single four-dimensional space-time, as Minkowski famously asserts?[235] Such questions hold an endless fascination for us. But in all of these cases it is simply assumed that space and time are peerless continua without friend or rival. Kant, for instance, sets them apart and alone in the Transcendental Aesthetic, consigning everything else to the table of categories. But instead of taking the primal status of space and time for granted, it might be asked if both are perhaps derivative of a more basic reality. And if the answer turns out to be yes, then we should also ask whether this more primal dimension might have other offspring than its two most famous children. For this reason it must count as a dramatic development that the metaphysics of objects sketched in this book provides a rare opportunity to reinterpret space and time in terms of something even more basic: the polarization between objects and their qualities.

When we speak of time in the everyday sense, what we are referring to is a remarkable interplay of stability and change. In time, the objects of sense do not seem motionless and fixed, but are displayed as encrusted with shifting features. Nonetheless, experience does not decay in each instant into an untethered kaleidoscope of discontinuous sensations; instead, there seem to be sensual objects of greater or lesser durability. Time is the name for this tension between sensual objects and their sensual qualities. When we speak instead of space, everyone will recall the old quarrel between Leibniz and Clarke over whether space is an absolute container or simply a matter of relations between things.[236] But in fact it is neither: for space is not just the site of relation, but rather of relation *and* non-relation. Sitting at the moment in Cairo, I am not entirely without relation to the Japanese city of Osaka, since in principle I could travel there on any given day. But this relation can never be total, since I do not currently touch the city, and even when I travel to stand in the exact center of Osaka, I will not exhaust its reality. Whatever sensual profile the city displays to me, even if from close range, this profile will differ from the real Osaka that forever withdraws into the shadows of being. This interplay of relation and non-relation is precisely what we mean when we speak of space, and in this respect Heidegger's tool-analysis is actually about space, not about time as he wrongly contends. Space is the tension between concealed real objects and the sensual qualities associated with them.

---

[235] Hermann Minkowski, "Space and Time."
[236] G.W. Leibniz & Samuel Clarke, *Correspondence*.

We now leave time and space and meet with their two neglected sisters, still nameless for the moment. Husserl showed that the sensual realm contains not only a tension between objects and their accidental surface-qualities (which we have now called "time"). For along with this there is another tension between objects and their truly crucial qualities, which are revealed through a process of eidetic variation: we imagine a house from many different viewpoints, stripping away its shifting properties that arise and then vanish. The goal of this method is to approach an inner nucleus of the house, an eidos that makes it what it is for those who perceive it. Husserl is quite clear that these eidetic features can in no way be sensual, insofar as no sense experience can possibly grasp them. Instead, they can only be known through categorial intuition: the work of the intellect and not of the senses. Such intuition points at those vital and never-visible traits that differ from the purely sensual character of the object. And this entails an articulation into parts that is foreign to the sensual object's unity. Here we find Husserl's true kinship with Plato. As opposed to the philosophies of individual substance that place qualities on the surface of the world and view the object as a hidden substratum in the depths, both Plato and Husserl reverse this assumption: putting a multitude of eidetic qualities in the depths while the object unifies them on the surface of the world. This tension between sensual objects and their real hidden qualities is what Husserl calls the *eidos*. And finally there is the fourth and final tension, never accessible to human experience. I refer to the duel, underway in hidden real things, between the unified real object and its multitude of real hidden features. This tension between the real object and its real qualities has always been called its *essence*, though traditional realism lacks Heidegger's remorseless sense that the real is entirely withdrawn from all access. And as a reminder, whereas the traditional model of essence treated real qualities as mobile universals able to be exemplified anywhere, qualities according to the present book are shaped by the object to which they belong, just as the moons of Jupiter are molded by their planetary lord.

In this way the monotonous age-old coupling of time and space is expanded into a new model encompassing four tensions between objects and their qualities: time, space, essence, and eidos. These four terms can be stated in any order; this one is preferred merely because it has the most melodious ring in my ears. We have already determined that the world is apportioned into exactly two kinds of object and two kinds of quality. Their possible pairings lead to precisely these four tensions and no others. The interaction of time, space, essence, and eidos is not the play of four disembodied forces, but of four tensions affecting every object that in some way is. Note that these tensions already encompass both real and fictitious entities, given that sensual objects join real ones as a basic feature of the model. Reductionist, science-worshipping naturalism can never accomplish or even appreciate this feat, since it is in too great a hurry to exterminate all those millions of entities that do not flatter its crude bias in favor of physical things.

C. On Fission and Fusion

Although tensions are always interesting, they sometimes still lead nowhere. The opposed armies of Korea have stared each other down for over fifty years with only minor incidents, and may well do so for another century or more. The same is true of the tensions between the various forms of objects and qualities. In order for something to change in the *status quo*, the bond between object and quality must be dissolved and a new one produced. To use a metaphor from applied physics, we need fission accompanied by fusion. But fission and fusion are the only two options, and they must always go hand in hand, since objects and qualities never exist outside of some existing bond that must be ruptured if another is to emerge. Now, we have just finished naming our four kinds of tension: time, space, essence, and eidos. It will be worthwhile to give a quick preview of what it means when each of these tensions is ruptured or produced.

Time was described as the strife between a sensual object and its numerous sparkling features. Dogs and trees display an excess of carnal detail that shifts in each moment without our viewing them as different objects. This is the very nature of perception, and I will soon claim that primitive perception is found even in the nethermost regions of apparently mindless objects. But of course we do not remain focused forever on a steady landscape of enduring sensual objects; rather, there are intermittent changes in what we confront. This can happen in at least two ways. Perhaps we identify something differently all of a sudden: we find that the tree was in fact a gallows, so that its surface qualities now shift into a far more sinister key. Or perhaps we shift our attention from a sensual object to its neighbors: from a strawberry to its seeds, or perhaps to the strawberry patch as a whole. When this happens there is a momentary breakdown in the former balance between sensual objects and their qualities; the object is briefly exposed as a unified kernel dangling its qualities like marionettes. This event could be called recognition or acknowledgment, but these terms suggest an intricate cognitive process that should perhaps be restricted to more advanced animal entities. What we really need is a term applicable to the primitive psyches of rocks and electrons as well as to humans.[237] I propose the term *confrontation* as sufficiently broad for the task. Wakeful humans confront strawberries and commando raids, a sleeper confronts the bed, and a pebble confronts the asphalt that it strikes as opposed to all the accidental details of that asphalt.

Space was described as the tension between real objects that lie beyond access, and their sensual qualities which exist only when encountered. Whereas sensual objects are conjoined with their qualities in advance, such that fission between the poles is required, the real object is absent from the sensual field; hence, real object and sensual qualities will meet only when *fused*. In such cases the sensual qualities are stripped from their current sensual overlord and appear to orbit a withdrawn *real* object, an invisible sun bending them to its will. The very invisibility of the object makes it impossible to compress the object together with its sensual qualities into a bland purée, as often happens in boring everyday experience. This fusion occurs for example in artworks of every sort, and I would suggest further that Heidegger's "broken tools" also have an aesthetic effect, if not a strictly artistic one. Instead of the direct sort of contact that we have with sensual objects, there is an allusion to the silent object in the depths that becomes vaguely fused with its legion of sensual qualities. As a general term for the fusion of withdrawn real objects with accessible surface qualities, we can use the word *allure*. As I defined the term in my book *Guerrilla Metaphysics*, "allure is a special and intermittent experience in which the intimate bond between a thing's unity and its plurality of [specific qualities] somehow partially disintegrates.[238]

In Husserl's case we noticed that sensual objects not only have accidental surface profiles. They also have an eidos, or qualities crucial for the object to be acknowledged as what it is. These qualities do not press against us like sensual ones. Grasped only by categorial and not sensuous intuition [in Husserl's view], they are never fully present to us. The sensual object has a vague and unified effect on us, not usually articulated into its various eidetic features. It is always fused in advance with its own eidos. Only theoretical labor can disassemble or reverse-engineer the bond between them. The word *theory* can serve as our term for the fission that splits a unified sensual

---

[237] Despite publishing this sentence in my own name over a decade ago, I do not fully embrace panpsychism, since it persists in the same overvaluation of psyche found in modern idealism.
[238] Graham Harman, *Guerrilla Metaphysics*, p. 143.

object from the real qualities it needs in order to be what it is. We will have to decide later whether animals, plants, and airplanes are also capable of theory in some primitive sense. But for now, we can already see that theory is a kind of fission between a sensual object and its multitude of real traits.

Finally, we spoke of essence as the tension between a real object and its real qualities. This relation never enters directly into any experience, since both of its poles are withdrawn from all access. Leibniz was correct in noting the following paradox: to be is to be one, since a real object must be unified; however, a mere unit would be interchangeable with any other, and no two monads would be different; thus, each real object must have a multitude of real traits. What I will now suggest is strange: namely, the object itself does not have its own essential features. We saw already that the real object has no contact with its sensual qualities, and is attached to them only through allure. In similar manner, the real object and its real qualities do not have a pre-existent bond in need of being split. Instead, they must be brought together through *fusion*, by way of some mediating term. This process, strangely akin to the allure of aesthetic experience, can be called causation. There is a precedent for this claim in the masterful treatment of efficient causation by Suárez.[239] For him, direct causal relation between entities is impossible, and things interact only by means of their "accidents," by which he actually means their real qualities.

An even simpler way to look at the four tensions is as follows. The basis of this book are the two kinds of objects and two kinds of qualities, split further into "real" and "sensual" in both cases. What was interesting was the realization that qualities need not marry objects of their own kind. A real object obviously needs real qualities, as Leibniz and some of the Scholastics saw. And a sensual object is always linked with shifting sensual qualities, as Husserl's phenomenology convincingly established. But there were also the two cases of exotic mixture. For real objects are associated with sensual qualities too, as seen from Heidegger's tool-analysis in which the real object hides behind its accessible surface traits. And with equal strangeness, sensual objects were also found to have real qualities, as in Husserl's insight that sensual objects have an eidos made up of genuine real qualities, as opposed to the mere shifting perceptual adumbrations whose qualities are always sensual. In this way we were shocked to discover interbreeding underway between the real and sensual realms, as if metaphysics were a Caribbean

---

[239] Francis Suarez, *On Efficient Causality*.

region where proper relations between objects were corrupted by rum, parrots, and volcanoes.

However, any moral outrage at this mixing of real and sensual bloodlines is beside the point, since it misses the true paradox: the vastly different ways in which real and sensual objects relate to qualities of either kind. Any sensual object is already in contact with its qualities of both kinds. The watermelon or rabid dog we experience is barely distinct either from the flickering shades by which we observe it at each moment (which we called time) or the deeper non-sensual features that the melon or dog cannot lose without ceasing to be recognized as what they are (which we called eidos). Since both of these bonds already exist, their rupture requires a fission of previously linked parts. This may sound unusual enough, but the true paradox is still to come. For let us now consider the *real* melon or dog, withdrawn from the kingdom of experience. We cannot say that these real objects have any inherent bond with their sensual qualities (the distance between them is what we called space), since these are mere appearances for someone or something else. The watermelon itself is completely indifferent to the angle or distance from which it is seen, or the precise degree of gloomy afternoon shadow in which it is shrouded. There are times when these sensual qualities are placed into orbit around the ghostly withdrawn melon (allure), but these occur on a purely *ad hoc* basis, and the melon could hardly care less, even if it were a deeply emotional creature. Thus, it is a form of fusion between previously separate poles rather than a fission of already attached poles.

But an even more paradoxical situation arises when we consider the link between the real object and its real qualities, where a more intimate bond between the two would be expected. Yet here we find that the real object has no closer link with its own real qualities than with the sensual qualities that one would never dream of ascribing to it. Once more, this is an *ad hoc* relation arising only now and then. In other words, the relation between an object and its own real qualities (we called this "essence") is a relation produced by outside entities. This is not the relativist thesis according to which nothing is real, hidden, or essential but is only how it appears to us. Instead, it is a bizarre alternative to relativism in which the real, hidden, and essential do very much exist, but communicate only by way of the unreal, apparent, and inessential. It would be as if mushrooms communicated with their own qualities, not directly or through rhizomal networks, but via radio waves. A real object is real and has a definite character, but its essence is first produced from the outside through causal interactions. Since this would

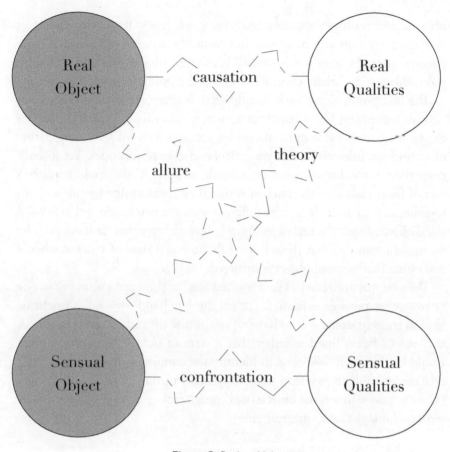

Figure 5: Broken Links

take too long to argue in detail here, I will only observe that this strange result is required by the symmetry of our diagrams, just as certain new particles are predicted by the models of the natural sciences and confirmed only later.

D. On Tension

Yet it is not entirely clear what a tension is, and this needs to be investigated. In the first place, it already turned out that a number of different kinds of relations are possible in the cosmos: ten of them, to be exact. But not all of these relations can really be called tensions, a term that implies simultaneous closeness and separation. For instance, multiple real or sensual qualities can exist in the same object, without this really being a tension in the sense I mean. Likewise, a perceiving agent is a real object in contact with sensual objects, and multiple sensual object are contiguous in the experience of this agent without any of these cases counting as tensions. What all four tensions share in common is that all involve an object-pole and a quality-pole. This section briefly considers some of the implications of this fact.

The first point, as we have already seen, is that two of the tensions can exist in something like a banal form, while the other two cannot. That is to say, a sensual object must always be accompanied by a swirling patina of sensual qualities and a not yet articulated core of real ones. Yet in both cases the tension between the object-pole and the quality-pole requires a sort of fission between the two, in which they are held side by side as both together and separate. It is quite different with the two tensions that involve a real object. Here, the real object is only brought together with qualities by means of fusion, so that there is actually no banal state of tension when a real rather than sensual object is involved.

The next question is why there is a "tension" in these cases rather than one of two other possible extremes. For on the one hand, two poles might be kept so entirely separate as to have no relation at all, and on the other hand, they might be so fused together that a state of utterly banal attachment would be the result. We need to identify the conditions under which both extremes are able to pass into tension, whether through a fission of banality (as is the case with sensual objects) or through fusion of what was previously separate (as is the case with real ones).

CHAPTER 12
REAL QUALITIES[240]

Here I will speak of the distinction between primary and secondary qualities, long viewed with scorn by cutting-edge philosophy, but back at the center of discussion today. John Locke is the most famous theorist of primary and secondary qualities, if not the first.[241] Primary qualities are those that must belong to an entity whether or not they are perceived, while secondary qualities exist only insofar as they are perceived. Roses would continue to reflect the same wavelength of light (primary quality) even if all sentient beings were exterminated, but they could not in any way be experienced as red (secondary quality). The sensation of red requires the interaction between roses and eyes. Thus, roses could not be red if all eyes were destroyed any more than if all roses were destroyed. Nor would the rose have a rosy smell if all noses were annihilated; the smell of a rose requires the existence of noses no less than that of the flowers that are smelled. Locke generalizes the point further:

> What I have said concerning *Colours* and *Smells*, may be understood also of *Tastes* and *Sounds, and other the like sensible Qualities*; which, whatever reality we, by mistake, attribute to them, are in truth nothing in the Objects themselves, but Powers to produce various sensations in us, and *depend on those primary Qualities, viz.* Bulk, Figure, Texture, and Motion of parts; as I have said.[242]

---

[240] "Real Qualities" originally appeared in 2012 as a booklet for a London art exhibition on November 15 entitled "CRISAP/Not for Human Consumption."

[241] John Locke, *An Essay Concerning Human Understanding*.

[242] Locke, *An Essay Concerning Human* Understanding, p. 137.

Nor did this problem die out with seventeenth-century thinkers. One of the most significant books of present-day philosophy opens with the same theme. Quentin Meillassoux writes as follows: "The theory of primary and secondary qualities seems to belong to an irremediably obsolete philosophical past. It is time it was rehabilitated."[243] Meillassoux's proposed rehabilitation of the theory hinges on the following claim:

> all those aspects of objects that can be formulated in mathematical terms can meaningfully be conceived as properties of the object in itself. All those aspects of the object that can give rise to a mathematical thought (to a formula or to digitalization) rather than to a perception or sensation can be meaningfully turned into properties of the thing not only as it is with me, but also as it is without me.[244]

In the brief space remaining, I will make three claims. First, Locke's distinction between primary and secondary qualities must be maintained. Second, Meillassoux is wrong to identify primary qualities with those that can be mathematized. Third, Locke is partially wrong to hold that colors, smells, tastes, and sounds are secondary rather than primary qualities. Let's get right to the point.

There are two possible ways to deny the existence of primary qualities. One is to deny the existence of anything primary at all. In this view, *everything* is secondary: nothing exists except insofar as it is perceived by or related to something else. The second way would be to concede the existence of a primary reality beyond all perception, while still denying that this primary reality possesses anything like "qualities." Let's deal briefly with both of these objections. The first denial is found in most extreme form in George Berkeley's delightfully sarcastic idealist claim that "it is indeed an opinion strangely prevailing amongst men, that houses, mountains, rivers, and in a word all sensible objects, have an existence, natural or real, distinct from their being perceived by the understanding."[245] Here no objects or qualities are primary because, for Berkeley, nothing exists apart from being given to the mind.

---

[243] Quentin Meillassoux, *After Finitude*, p. 1.
[244] Meillassoux, *After Finitude*, p. 3, emph. removed.
[245] George Berkeley, *A Treatise Concerning the Principles of Human Knowledge*, p. 24.

But no such human-centered idealism is required to deny the existence of primary qualities. Bruno Latour, for instance, tries to place all entities (or "actors") on the same footing, granting no privilege to human actors over inanimate ones. But while this differentiates him significantly from Berkeley, it does not prevent Latour from defining entities solely in terms of their effects on other things: "there is no other way to define an actor but through its action, and there is no other way to define an action but by asking what other actors are *modified, transformed, perturbed, or created* by the character that is the focus of attention."[246] What Berkeley and Latour share is the assumption that realities exist *only in relation to other realities*. In this respect they both deny anything "primary" that would exist independently of anything else (other than minds and God, in Berkeley's case). The reason we cannot accept such a claim is that if reality existed only in relation to something else, it would be fully exhausted by that relation. There would be no surplus of reality not currently deployed or expressed in the world here and now, and hence no reason why the current relations between things would ever change.

The second way of denying real qualities would be to agree that objects have a primary reality preceding their relations, while simply denying that this primary reality has anything like qualities. The clearest exponent of such a position is my fellow object-oriented ontologist Levi R. Bryant.[247] In Bryant's philosophy, there is a distinction between the non-relational "virtual proper being" of an object and its "local manifestations," and only the latter can be said to have qualities.[248] Yet it is difficult to see how this restriction of "qualities" to the relational realm is anything more than a terminological decision on Bryant's part. Presumably two dogs, a toothbrush, a skyscraper, and a clown all have different "virtual proper beings," since otherwise these objects would be exactly the same. Bryant does not want to ascribe qualities to these "virtual" entities, but prefers to distinguish them through "what they can do" as opposed to "what they are." But there would be no distinction between what they can do unless there were already a difference in what they are, and I see no reason not to use the term "qualities" to describe the features that differentiate what they are. And obviously, since these qualities precede any relation — insofar as they might generate a large

---

[246] Bruno Latour, *Pandora's Hope*, p. 122.
[247] See for example Bryant's blog post of January 5, 2012, "More on Withdrawn Objects."
[248] See Levi R. Bryant, "The Ontic Principle."

number of possible relations — we must call them primary rather than secondary qualities.

That brings us to Meillassoux's claim that primary qualities are those that can be mathematized. Aside from a recent half-finished attempt in an unpublished Berlin lecture from April 2012, his clearest statements on this topic are perhaps those found in his 2010 interview discussion with me.[249] While conceding that he has not yet demonstrated "the capacity [of mathematics] to describe that which is independent of all thought,"[250] Meillassoux insists that mathematics can do this despite being a human construction. He offers the analogy of archaeological work, in which

> the "constructions" (a complex of winches, sounding lines, scaffolding, spades, brushes, etc.) are not destined to *produce* an object, as in the case of archaeology. On the contrary, they are made with a view to *not* interfering with the object at which they aim: that is to say, excavating the ruins without damaging them, in unearthing them "as is," and not as modified or even destroyed by the impact of the excavation tools.[251]

Yet the problem with mathematizing entities is not that mathematics is a human construction. The problem, instead, is that mathematics claims to present reality *directly* in a way that is utterly foreign to other disciplines. Archaeology never confuses sarcophagi with the winches and pulleys used to lift them. By contrast, mathematics does encourage the belief that its models of things are exact replicas of those things. The mathematical ontologist may well concede that the things have some material substrate in which its mathematizable features inhere. But the nature of this substrate remains untheorized by Meillassoux, who occasionally calls it "dead matter," but then fails to explain the difference between such dead matter and the mathematized version of it that is supposed to yield its primary qualities.

We have now argued as follows: (a) primary qualities must exist, and (b) they cannot be mathematized, which is another way of saying that they cannot be thoroughly known. Belief in a reality outside the mind must not be confused with the belief that this reality can also be *directly known*, as

---

[249] See the "Interview with Quentin Meillassoux" in Graham Harman, *Quentin Meillassoux*, pp. 208–223. The 2012 Berlin lecture referred to above as "unpublished" has since been published as Quentin Meillassoux, "Iteration, Reiteration, Repetition."
[250] Harman, *Quentin Meillassoux*, p. 167.
[251] Harman, *Quentin Meillassoux*, p. 167.

Meillassoux demands. Instead, respect for reality requires a respect for its somewhat inscrutable character, not directly translatable into any form of knowledge, so that it can only be known indirectly, allusively, with a sideways glance. Now, along with speaking of primary and secondary qualities, we must also speak of primary and secondary *objects*. For just as certain qualities belong to a thing without anyone seeing it (primary qualities), while others require the presence of a perceiver (secondary qualities), the same duality can be found in objects themselves. For just as we presume the existence of genuine things apart from the mind and indeed apart from all relation whatsoever, so too there are objects existing only in relation to the mind, such as centaurs and golden mountains.[252] This might also seem to be true of entities such as sounds: a musical tone, after all, seems to exist only for some hearer. We might assume that the "primary" object is merely a physical sound wave, while the musical tone is a merely "secondary" object; as such, only the primary sound wave could have primary qualities, so that the secondary musical tone could only have secondary qualities that exist for some hearer alone, and not in themselves.

Paradoxically enough, the world does not work in such a simplistic fashion. Let's change the terminology of this essay from the more classical "primary" and "secondary" to the related terms more prominent in my previous works: "real" and "sensual." For object-oriented philosophy, real objects are those that withdraw from relation and exist quite apart from any relations in which they might become involved. Sensual objects are those that exist only in relation to some other entity, and they must be distinguished from their sensual qualities, due to Husserl's critique of David Hume's influential "bundle theory" of experienced entities.[253] Hume famously holds that we do not experience a unified object such as a zebra, but only a series of stripes, hairs, eyes, mouths, legs, and tail that seem to move together with such regularity that we form the *habit* of taking all of these together to be a single thing. But Husserl's phenomenology overturns this theory by showing that Hume has it backwards. We do not encounter qualities or parts in isolation, but first encounter the object itself. What we actually encounter is not a dissolute set of partial objects, but the zebra as a whole. This zebra can be viewed from many different angles and distances and still be regarded as the same zebra. This zebra is a *sensual* object rather

---

[252] I have often argued this point in connection with the philosophy of Edmund Husserl. See, for example, Graham Harman, *The Quadruple Object*, pp. 20–34.

[253] David Hume, *A Treatise of Human Nature*.

than a real one, since it is fully present in my consciousness, not withdrawn in the least, unlike the spooky subterranean entities that populate the tool-analysis of Husserl's renegade pupil Martin Heidegger. And this sensual zebra has numerous and ever-shifting sensual qualities, which sparkle across its surface and pass away forever without affecting the integrity of the sensual zebra. Nonetheless, this phantasmal zebra in the mind has other qualities that cannot pass away without consequence. There are certain features that the zebra must always retain, under penalty of my no longer regarding it as the same thing, but instead as a different zebra, a warthog, or perhaps even a wagon, sunbeam, crutch, or puzzle. These real qualities that the zebra needs, in order to remain the very zebra that it is, can be called its *real* qualities. Husserl concedes that these real (or "eidetic") qualities cannot be known through the senses, though he mistakenly assumes that they can be known through direct intuition by the mind, as if the difference between the sensual and the intelligible were some sort of massive rift.

We now have the paradox that a sensual object can have real qualities, or in quasi-Lockean terms, that a secondary object can have primary qualities. This allows for a strange intrusion by sensual, phantasmal, and purely fictional entities into the realm of autonomous reality. Even if we agree with the most hardheaded realists that Popeye, Don Quixote, centaurs, and hallucinations are not real objects in the same manner as neutrons or cliffs made of limestone, Popeye and his cousins must still be acknowledged to have genuine, real qualities. Perhaps this should not come as a surprise, given that by an analogous paradox, real withdrawn objects signal into the realm of perception by means of sensual qualities, in a manner exploited most thoroughly by the arts. Even if the sounds heard by human and animal ears are not as autonomous as waves traveling through air, these sounds immediately generate qualities that are every bit as independent as physical disturbances. The wizard of the techno music mixer who makes a sound scratchy or ghostly, who transposes it into a different key or gives it a different mood, is merely a profiteer reliant upon the durable real qualities of a sensual thing: as if a hallucinated apple had a more-than-imagined color, smell, taste, and even price.

CHAPTER 13

PHYSICAL NATURE AND THE PARADOX OF QUALITIES[254] (FROM *TOWARDS SPECULATIVE REALISM*)

This lecture was given on 21 April, 2006 in Reykjavik, Iceland at the annual meeting of the Nordic Society for Phenomenology. Interesting things were afoot. My reading material on this trip was Quentin Meillassoux's now famous book Après la finitude, which had only recently been published.[255] Ray Brassier, who had invited me to speak at Middlesex University in London the previous year, had recently returned from a visit to Paris, seen the book on sale there, and suggested it was something I might enjoy. From 15–17 April, while in Akureyri on the northern coast of Iceland, I exchanged numerous emails with Brassier about my positive impression of Meillassoux's book, and it was during these discussions that he suggested a group event featuring the three of us and Iain Hamilton Grant. I immediately sent messages of inquiry to both Grant and Meillassoux, and thus was born "the movement," which only received the name "Speculative Realism" the following year. The Iceland lecture itself is interesting for several reasons, but primarily for its link between physical causation and the inner drama of Husserl's intentional objects. The distinction

---

[254] This chapter originally appeared in *Towards Speculative Realism*, pp. 122–139.
[255] Quentin Meillassoux, *Après la finitude*.

it draws between real and intentional objects was received with friendly bewilderment by the largely Husserlian audience that day.

Most schools of present-day philosophy are united in celebrating the death of metaphysics. Phenomenology is no exception. But in the brief paper that follows, I will try to show that Husserl's model of intentional objects is deeply enmeshed in metaphysical themes that cannot be escaped. More than this, it is Husserl who accidentally grants us the resources to revive philosophic concern with physical nature: or more generally with the metaphysics of objects, whether human, animal, angelic, vegetable, plastic, or stone. Furthermore, despite his relative lack of interest in the history of metaphysics and his wish to wipe the slate clean and begin with a newly scientific philosophy, Husserl's intentional objects brush up against classical themes treated by the occasionalist metaphysics dominant at various times among the Arabs and the French. I will begin with Heidegger, pass to Husserl, turn toward some brief remarks on occasionalism in general, and close with a meditation on the inner volcanic structure of objects. The result will be as follows: physical nature must be approached by considering the paradoxical structure of qualities.

1. Real Objects

According to the conventional view, Husserl walled off a space for phenomenology by asking us to ignore the natural reality of objects, focusing instead on how they are given to consciousness. In this way he allowed philosophy to take a distance from the naïveté of science and metaphysics, and built the arena in which rigorous philosophy becomes possible. Heidegger's tool-analysis then showed the limitations of this approach, by showing that objects are used before they are seen. In this way, it is said, Heidegger pointed to a shadowy equipmental background withdrawn from the sphere of lucid awareness. I will in fact endorse this conventional view. But I will also urge that it be radicalized in three different ways. In so doing, we will ironically be led back toward Husserl, who in some ways can teach us more than Heidegger about the relations between one object and another.

First, we need to abandon the persistent yet shallow idea that Heidegger's tool-analysis subordinates theory to praxis. It is true enough that staring at a hammer or making theories about it fails to capture the genuine reality of this hammer as we go about using it. Yes, the hammer is assigned to numerous systems of purposes and finalities, and when we gaze at the hammer theoretically we reduce it to a caricature, ripping it from the world in which it is deeply involved. But this is only half the story. For human praxis turns the tool into a caricature no less than theory does. My grabbing and manipulating of a screwdriver or power drill also fail to grasp the total reality of these objects. My handling of these items can be surprised by their inner reality or be resisted by it just as much as my explicit awareness can. All human relations to objects strip them of their inner depth, revealing only some of their qualities to view. This has only rarely been seen by Heidegger commentators, but was already seen by Bergson and others, who recognized quite early that to use a thing is no more intimate a relation with its depths than to see it. Both approaches to the thing reduce it to a series of superficial profiles far removed from the object in its withering interior activity, which can never be fully exhausted by any human means. That is the first way in which Heidegger's tool-analysis must be radicalized.

The second step will seem strange, though it is also inevitable. Namely, it is not just human relations to objects that cut them down to size by reducing them to outer contours and profiles of their inner reality. Instead, relationality in general does this. It is not some special feature of the human psyche or human deeds that turns a thing into a caricature. This reduction belongs to any relation between any two objects in the universe, no matter what they may be. My perception of fire and cotton fails to use up the total realities of these beings, since they are describable at infinite length in a way that I can never approach. We have seen that the same is true of my use of these objects for practical tasks. But more generally, the fire and cotton also fail to make full contact with *each other* when they touch, despite their uniting in a bond of destruction that takes no heed of the colors and scents that humans or animals may detect emanating from both of them. In other words, objects withdraw from each other and not just from humans. In this respect, human beings are just one more type of object among trillions of others in the cosmos. As I have argued elsewhere and at length, Heidegger's famous distinction between ready-to-hand and present-at-hand is not about a difference between practical handy tools and sparkling lucid perceptions, but entails a more general difference between objects and relations.[256] Presence *means* relationality, nothing more. To consider an object in its being means to consider it in its withdrawal from all forms of presence, whether as something seen, used, or just spatially present among other entities. All objects withdraw from each other, not just

---

[256] Graham Harman, *Tool-Being.*

from humans. This is the second radicalization of Heidegger's tool-analysis. But we now seem to be as distant as possible from phenomenology, since we have descended into the leper colonies of nature and metaphysics that Husserl had urged us to avoid.

And yet, a third radicalization pushes us away from Heidegger and back toward Husserl. For if cotton and fire withdraw from each other no less than from humans, it needs to be asked how they can interact at all. The duel of inanimate entities seems to involve a sort of occasional cause, given the mutual withdrawal of objects that are now turned into concealed dark crystals of reality. What, then, is the real cause that unites them? We cannot say God, as in early Islamic theology and seventeenth-century Europe, since this explains nothing as long as the divine mechanisms are left in darkness. But neither can it be the human mind arbitrarily bundling together discrete qualities into a fictional underlying substance, as is the case for many of the empiricists, since this unjustifiably reduces objects to the way we experience them. And we will soon see that despite his bracketing of the natural world, Husserl does not reduce objects to our experience of objects. Nonetheless, the bracketing does have an effect. I am not among those who contend that Husserl already anticipated the tool-analysis in his own works. For, given that intentional objects have a merely ideal existence devoid of traffic with a real universe of unleashed causal powers, he deserves to be called an idealist, and this title ought to be fairly uncontroversial. By contrast, Heidegger tacitly lays claim to a real cosmos filled with objects in the form of surprising real forces irreducible to any relationality at all. The problem is that Heidegger only allows objects to withdraw from human Dasein, never from each other as well. For this reason, he never reaps the dividends of the weird realism he inaugurates.

2. Intentional Objects

The great breakthrough of phenomenology would have been impossible without suspending natural objects from consideration. It was important to move from a hazy notion of solid billiard balls unleashing forces against each other to a more rigorous foundation in how things actually present themselves to us. The cost of this step was high, since nature and metaphysics were summarily booted from a human-centered realm of conscious acts. This exaggerated view of real objects as something inherently unphilosophical is what opened the door for Heidegger's shadowy, withdrawn tool-beings.

Yet it was never the case that Husserl simply opposed human experience to an unknowable landscape of natural physical solids. For in an obvious sense, Husserl is no empiricist at all. In *Logical Investigations* II we find his marvelous assault on the perceptual theories of Locke, Berkeley, and Hume. The guiding insight of his attack is the same in all of these cases: humans do not intend "experienced contents," as if everything we dealt with lay patent before our eyes. The alternative endorsed by Husserl is that we intend *objects*. These are not the natural objects of the sciences, reducible to physical matter or fields of force; neither are they the unnatural tool-objects of Heidegger, withdrawing into silent subterranean execution. Instead they are the famous "intentional objects," which have no more place in Heidegger than in British Empiricism. For Heidegger, if there are objects, they can only lie in a shadowy depth, not in the midst of perception itself.

Intentional objects are not to be identified with real ones in the least, and for several reasons. For one thing, they are merely ideal and may not exist at all. The real object "fire" scalds, burns, boils, melts, and cracks other real objects, while the intentional object "fire" has a very different function: it merely unifies a shifting set of profiles and surfaces whose various flickerings never affect its underlying ideal unity. Real objects withdraw. But intentional objects do not withdraw, even though they never become entirely visible or utterly fulfilled in perception. The contrast is important. Whereas the real tree forever recedes into its underground reality, untouchable by anything else in the cosmos, the intentional tree is always fully there before us. Although it may taunt us with the endless supply of angles and distances from which it can be viewed, and is never seen in all its profiles simultaneously, there is another sense in which the intentional tree is always completely fulfilled from the start. After all: there it is, the tree, and we are now all thinking about it. What remains unfulfilled is merely its sensuous content, while the tree-object as such is already fully manifest. If we call the real object *withdrawn*, so that too little of its being is present, we might call the intentional object *encrusted*, in the sense that too much of its being is present. For the intentional object is always covered with inessential surface effects that must be scraped away through eidetic variation, so as to move closer toward the more austere essence lying beneath.

Finally, there is the most important difference of all between real and intentional objects. Real objects are sliced apart into private, mutually exclusive vacuums, with none of them ever touching their neighbors. By contrast, there is a sense in which intentional objects pass gradually into one another. Like textile pigments, intentional objects *bleed* into one another.

Or alternatively, like open bottles of wine or linen shirts, they *breathe* into their environment. Although it is true that I am able to distinguish tree, rock, and soil entirely from one another in a single perception, it is nonetheless true that each of these intentional objects is so encrusted with inessential sensuous features that a great deal of labor is required for the phenomenologist to approach their essences.

To repeat, although Husserl seems to begin his philosophy by putting objects out of the picture, he restores them to the throne in the form of intentional objects. It should be noted that this step not only amounts to an attack on the British Empiricists, for whom he never had much sympathy anyway. More than this, it also marks a daring reform of the concepts of his teacher Brentano. In *Logical Investigations* V he modifies Brentano's thesis that all intentionality is based in presentations to say that all are based in "object-giving acts" that are always beyond mere presentation. In another interesting twist, Husserl uses the phrase "nominal acts" as a synonym for object-giving acts. Just as a proper name (for Saul Kripke) continues to point rigidly to a single unitary thing despite all variations in that thing's known attributes, an intentional object rests like the Sphinx amidst the sandstorms of various qualities that rage around its slumbering form.[257]

But here we reach the central problem of this paper: the *paradoxical* structure of qualities. For it is not just that we have intentional objects on one side and sensuous qualities on the other, in a kind of permanent dualism (at least not in the *Logical Investigations*). That would come too close to the neo-Kantian distinction between sensibility and understanding that Husserl openly rejects. Instead, every supposed speck of sensuous or carnal data is already shaped into objective form. There is no red that is not the red of an apple, cherry, wine, or exploding giant star. Any time we try to step back to a point where we might observe purely given colors and shapes, à la the empiricists, we find that Husserl leaves us no room to do so. Everything already points toward intentional objects. There is no pre-given blur of sense data that then gets molded into tangible units. Everything appears in intentional acts, and intentionality is always and only object-giving. Yet intentional objects never appear except by way of some contour or face. What then are these contours and faces? What do the senses actually encounter, given that we do not merely stretch out toward elusive intentional objects, but actually stand somewhere in particular, amidst some buzz or drone in the air, some kaleidoscopic whirl of visual effects? This is

---

[257] Saul Kripke, *Naming and Necessity*.

the paradox of perceptual qualities. At the close of this paper I will suggest that the same paradox lies at the heart of causation as well.

3. Occasional Cause

Despite the different sorts of warnings against metaphysics made by Husserl and Heidegger, we already stand in the midst of it. Heidegger's real objects lead us into metaphysics due to their impossible isolation from each other. If hammers, rocks, and flames withdraw from all other entities, then it needs to be explained why anything happens in the world at all. In this sense, Heidegger faces the same problem as the various Arab and French occasionalists. Occasionalism, well-known as the theory that God intervenes directly at all moments in every grain of dust in the cosmos, even recreating the universe afresh in every instant of time, is generally viewed as a minor historical curio to be pored over by monks and archivists. But in fact, occasionalism is a far broader problem than is usually believed. The key to occasionalism is not the rather dated and arbitrary theology that would have God meddle in everything that occurs. Instead, the key is that things in the world exist only side by side, not bleeding into one another. And this "side by side" is what links the empiricists (even when they are atheists) to full-blown occasionalist theology. As Steven Nadler rightly observes, there is a striking similarity in the arguments of such vastly different figures as the Islamic firebrand al-Ash'ari, the punished anti-Aristotelian Nicolas d'Autrécourt, the devout Catholic Nicolas Malebranche, and the impious David Hume.[258] In all of these philosophies, one object or one quality is unable to link directly to another. Unfortunately, all of them make a single hypocritical exception. For the theologians it is of course God who is able to break the side-by-side principle and let His power link the things. For the empiricists it is the human soul which exerts the hypocritical power by bundling separate qualities into a supposed underlying substratum that probably isn't even there. But hypocrisy is no solution. Instead, we should bite the bullet in each individual case and not look to some magical super-entity to link withdrawn objects together, whether it be almighty God or the almighty human mind. Each individual object must be equipped to touch and jostle others *despite* withdrawing from those others.

Then occasionalism is a philosophy of externality, with things existing side by side without bleeding or breathing into one another. This may

---

[258] Steven Nadler. "'No Necessary Connection.'"

take the form of impotent fire and cotton never interacting without God's intervention, or perhaps it will be expressed instead in the empiricist maxim "relations are external to their terms." But whereas real objects trap us in an occasionalist deadlock in their cryptic mutual withdrawal, intentional objects already bleed and breathe, one phasing into another without difficulty. Furthermore, the intentional object somehow already achieves the godlike effect of blending countless profiles, halos, masks, and veils into a single intentional object, packing numerous qualities into a single essence even as they somehow remain separate qualities. For this reason perhaps the problem of occasional causation can be solved by looking to the field of perception, and then in some way moving back to the zone of real objects. I will now make a brief attempt to do so. The problem is important not only for clarifying Heidegger or Husserl (in however unorthodox a fashion) but also for elucidating numerous central problems of classical metaphysics. For occasional cause, which we can rename *vicarious cause* so as to avoid needless theological overtones, is nothing less than the problem of how things can be both separate and linked. And this problem lies at the root of famous classical oppositions such as the one and the many, identity and difference, and the opposition between substance on the one hand and aggregates, accidents, relations, and qualities on the other.

4. The Volcanic Core of Objects

My thesis, which will sound strange at first, is that everything in the world happens only on the *interior* of objects. Since objects cannot touch one another directly, they must be able to interact only within some sort of vicarious medium that contains each of them. The inside of an object can be viewed as a volcano, kaleidoscope, witch's cauldron, steel mill, or alchemist's flask in which one thing is somehow converted into another. It is not difficult to show why this must be the case. Let's start with the ambiguity lying in intentional acts. Husserl openly admits that our intention of an object is in a certain sense *one*, but in another sense *two*. It is not just as if two entities were sitting side by side; rather, the intentional act forms a union from the start. On the other hand, since the tree or flower and I do not fuse together into some colossal glacier without parts, we must also admit that each of the components of the act still somehow remains separate from the other.

Now, there is no choice but to call this unified act an object in its own right. Not because it is made of atoms or stone or metallic ore; not because it lasts for millions of years; not because it can be picked up and thrown like a ball or a firecracker. No, the intentional object is an object for the same reason as any other object: namely, it is a reality whose full depths can never be exhaustively probed. My intention of a chimney, pirate ship, or avalanche provides endless fuel for *ad nauseam* description by phenomenologists or by Marcel Proust. But since we have spoken of two kinds of objects, it is important to clarify what kind of object the intentional act is. And here, note that the unified intentional act can only be a *real* object, not just an intentional one. My relation to the tree is not something just viewed by others, nor even something just viewed by myself. Instead, I am *actively deployed* in contending with this tree or this mountain right now, even if they turn out to be illusory. The result of this is strange. The intentional object and I both somehow reside in the inner molten core of a *real* object, the total intentional act. This gives new meaning to the old phrase "intentional *in*existence." It is not just that phenomena exist as the contents of a mental sphere. Rather, mental life and its acts are both contained within a larger object in some still undetermined way.

But this is not just a story of human perception. In other words, it is not just the poignantly unique features of human being that place intentionality on the interior of an object. We cannot know exactly what an inanimate object experiences. We cannot be sure whether Leibniz was right to compare the perceptions of a rock to those of a very dizzy human, or whether we should speak of "experience" at all in the inanimate realm. At the moment, it is hard even to imagine a theory able to clarify more precisely the differences between humans, dolphins, pineapples, chairs, and atoms.

However, I would propose that if we look closely at intentionality, the key to it lies not in some special human *cogito* marked by lucid representational awareness. Instead, what is most striking about intentionality is the object-giving encounter. In other words, human alertness stands amidst a swarm of concrete sensual realities. But contra British Empiricism, it encounters objects rather than raw qualities, since qualities never make any sense except as a radiation or odor emanating from intentional objects. This must also hold true for the inanimate realm. For just as raw qualities cannot exist in the human sphere, the world of possibly soulless matter also cannot unfold amidst dots of barely determinate color or heat. One object always encounters another object, albeit never in fully exhaustive form.

To summarize, *every* relation must form an object: one in which its components are somehow pressed against each other, encountering one another in more or less turbulent fashion, even while something links them more stably from above. Whether the converse is also true (namely, whether every object is also composed of relations) is an interesting question indeed, since it involves the problem of whether there can be an infinite regress of objects wrapped in objects sealed in objects frozen in objects, or whether we reach some ultimate atomic point of reality. This problem will have to be dealt with elsewhere.

It should be admitted that there is an asymmetry in the intentional relationship between me and the objects that I witness. But the asymmetry in question is not that of "lucid conscious agent versus stupid block of inanimate matter." Instead, the asymmetry is simply that in this case I am the one doing the intending, and the object may not be encountering me at all: not out of inanimate stupidity, but simply because I may have no effect on it. The point can be seen more clearly if we imagine two people staring at each other. Clearly we have two intentional acts here, not one. If intentionality unfolds on the inside of some object, as claimed earlier, then we will have to speak of two separate objects. But when we intend, note that we cannot be described as the "active" ones, even if it is we who must engage in a frenzy of perceptual arrangements. On the contrary, it is I who am the passive one, since it is I who have been drawn into a new space by the object I encounter.

We have now arrived at the molten inner core of objects as the place where reality unfolds. It is the one site where relations and events might occur, and the only point of reality that is filled with the sparkle of concrete perception rather than withdrawing into cryptic, inscrutable distance. Put differently, Heidegger's *real* objects, the tool-beings that surpass any relation that one might have to them, seem unable to relate to each other at all. Each is trapped in its own private vacuum of reality. And this pushes Heidegger in the direction of occasionalism, since he is left with no way to explain how one thing affects another. By contrast, Husserl's intentional objects, for which there is surprisingly no equivalent in Heidegger's mature phase, do *nothing but* melt and bleed together in consciousness. For the intentional object is all too easily encrusted with sunlight, shadow, and other accidental surface-effects that proclaim its essence without forming part of it. Hence it seems that the field of intentionality is the furnace in which the labors of the world are accomplished. In other words, the solution to the problem of how objects relate is found in the core of objects themselves. The problem that remains to be solved is how one object ever breaks into the core of another. If this did not happen we would be left with nothing but countless private universes, none communicating with any other.

Before moving on, it might be asked what is accomplished by turning toward the interior of objects as the site of reality. The most important result is to have eliminated the idea of a special human transcendence, rising above the world into some windy and starry space from which the things can be seen "as" what they are. Humans do not rise above the world but only burrow ever more deeply into it, digging down toward the heart of things by *fusing* with them. We always stand somewhere.

But even a hermeneutical approach to phenomenology would already claim to know this, conceding that "of course" humans only perceive from amidst certain presuppositions or from a distinct corporeal or historical stance. But this is not enough. For even if we replace the lucid, transcendent *cogito* with a murkier, more cryptic human thrown into its historico-linguistic surroundings, there is still a fixation on a single unique rift or correspondence between human and world. The human/world relation is treated as extra-special, different in kind from the relation of cotton and fire. This is the heritage that must be abandoned. Instead, we should be willing to say that any relation between any two things at all is on the same footing. There are levels of the world, and the human being can only move up or down between them, exploring all the contours of the world that exist with or without our awareness, and not claim to be the single unique fissure across which reality unfolds. Consciousness is no longer special, but just a special case of the relation between part and whole.

But now we approach the conclusion, and it is both difficult and provisional. The initial problem is this: intentionality ought to encounter nothing but objects, since the whole point of *Logical Investigations* II was that the empiricists were wrong to claim there is any surface "given" of experience. Objects are never fully given. But how can they even be *partially* given, since any of the surface qualities by which a thing is manifest should also be an intentional object in its own right? Whenever we try to retreat from the not-fully-presented chair or aluminum can to the sensual data in which it becomes accessible, we find that there is no data. To speak of some raw, dough-like matter that would then be shaped into objects by categorial intuition is to retreat into a distinction between sensibility and understanding that Husserl's Second Investigation aimed to destroy. In short, the problem is how we can experience anything at all. Why do we not hover silently in a black void, cut off from everything and perceiving nothing?

The answer of course is that intentional objects do not withdraw, but are simply *encrusted* with things that do not belong to their essence.

The lingering notion that an intentional tree could in any way be hidden is probably linked to an overly *visual* reading of intentionality: "I only see one side of the tree right now, but there are other sides now invisible to me," as if some massive armada of cubist perspectives could add up to the essence of a thing. In fact, the essence of the thing ought to be discernible without any of these perspectives at all, since they are mere encrustations that have more to do with the light and breeze surrounding the tree than with the intentional tree itself. Intentional objects are never hidden, but simply illuminated with too many lights, salted with too many spices, clothed in too many costumes. They must be stripped progressively bare if we are to know what really belongs to them.

In the intentional field, objects bleed together in ways that muddy the essences of each. Two trees blend together into one at a distance, or transient moonlight gives us false expectations about the color of a distant thing. The goal of eidetic variation (as of most human intelligence) is simply to separate the wheat from the chaff, the essential from the accidental, thereby reversing the mixture or bleeding with which the senses begin. As Merleau-Ponty shows, and already William James, the very movement of our bodies, with its minute adjustments of posture and tiltings of the head and slight squinting or opening of the mouth to hear, is an instrument for approaching the object in just the right way to capture it in its most flattering or revealing light. As James notes, there is a proper distance from which every object ought to be seen: a book would be ridiculous if pressed directly against our faces, or if attempts were made to read it at one hundred meters. The same holds true for all objects at a various range of possible distances. Moreover, Aristotle already observed that *memory* makes this same split for us: we remember the river as an object, not the river with all its shimmering surface distortions, which memory subtracts from the phenomenon as initially presented. In any case, perception and theory try to filter out the accidents of the thing and present it in its essential nature. In this way, perception, theory, and memory all reverse the work of the senses.

But there is a problem. For even if we call certain qualities of an object "essential," they are not yet the thing itself. For each of the thing's qualities are separate from each other, and we do not arrive at the thing by piecing them all together. The thing, beyond all its *essential* qualities, is more like a brooding power or style that lurks beneath the qualities and animates them. It is interesting to recall that Husserl described intentional acts as nominal acts. For this is what proper names do, as seen most recently in

Kripke's school, but as already described by Husserl and even Aristotle. To call out a name ("Paul!"; "Yara!") is not to call out to essential qualities lying beneath all the accidental ones. To say "tree" or "moon" is not to point to any perceptual qualities in particular, since any of these may be falsifiable. When Rimbaud writes: "in the forest there is a clay pit with a nest of white animals," the force of this line does not come from its accurate description of the scene's essential qualities. The poem would not be ruined if the poet were initially mistaken, and the true state of affairs were one of beige animals living in mud. In short, with names we go not just beyond *accidents*, but even beyond *essential* qualities, calling out to some ghostly style inhabiting the world in a never quite definable way. And with this step we seem to move beyond the sphere of intentional objects and toward real ones. Instead of merely reversing the work of the senses, we now seem to be reversing the work of causation itself, since we are pointing to a lonely object in the distance.

For this sort of pointing, let's use the general term "allure," for a thing becomes alluring when it seems to be a ghostly power exceeding any of its lists of properties, one that animates those properties from within by means of some ill-defined demonic energy. Allure splits an object from its qualities. This happens not just in the act of naming, but in countless different cases, all of them carrying a strong emotional charge. We see it in metaphor, in which "man is a wolf" (Max Black's well-known example) seems to split the human from his qualities and replace them with wolf-qualities.[259] We see it in humor, where the comic dupe seems to have no free and easy connection with his face or legs any longer, looking stupid with a giant red nose or while slipping on the ice. We see it in beauty, where the beautiful thing sparkles and recedes, hard to define by any list of specific beautiful qualities. We see it in courage, where people stay true to themselves despite the possibly disastrous impending consequences, and in fierce loyalty, where the commitment to a person or cause remains in place even when all their appealing qualities seem to have vanished. We see it also in embarrassment, where the person no longer seems flawlessly in control of his actions, but awkwardly overexerts himself in trying to row a boat or play a round of golf. Perhaps even more interestingly, we also see it in one type of theory: the kind that Thomas Kuhn called *paradigm-shifting* theory.[260] The reign of a paradigm is not socially constructed mob rule, but simply the

---

[259] See Max Black, "Metaphor."
[260] Thomas Kuhn, *The Structure of Scientific Revolutions*.

THE GRAHAM HARMAN READER

underlying commitment to a specific model of objects that endures in the face of its remaining paradoxes and even many experimental falsifications. This distinguishes it from the sort of theory that simply mops up erroneous views of what is essential and accidental in the world. To shift a paradigm is to create or discover a new object, one that might be identified by certain typical qualities but is certainly never identical with them.

But notice that allure does not just *reverse* the work of causation, by separating a thing from its surroundings. Allure is also a new act of causation, since it brings me into relation with the new object: whether it be Rimbaud's clay-pit metaphor, Deleuze's concept of the virtual, a new style of artwork, or a fascinating new friend. But allure is not just a *kind* of causation: it *is* causation. Not only is it the sole event that brings two objects together, but both causation and allure (unlike normal theory and perception) have a *binary* structure. Different people may disagree over whether the same joke is funny, and some may find it funnier than others do, but ultimately it is either funny or not for me, here and now. Just so, either the fire causes the cotton to burst into flame or it does not. A metaphor either seizes me or it flops completely. Either I am loyal, courageous, or embarrassed at any given moment, or I am not.

In this way, we find a structure at the heart of intentional life that also pertains even to sheer physical causation. Somehow a real object is converted into a merely intentional one, buffered and causally neutralized by being encrusted with various accidents, and ultimately encrusted even with its supposed essential qualities. But sometimes, for reasons that cannot be further explored here, the debris is cleared away and the object is encountered as flickering at a distance, in all its naked allure. In this respect metaphysics may be a branch of aesthetics, and causation merely a form of beauty. In any case, the border is now blurring between ideal or intentional reality and bracketed physical reality. Phenomenology is blurring into metaphysics.

PART III
INDIRECT CAUSATION

CHAPTER 14

TWO FACES OF
MEDIATION[261]

The philosophical school known as Object-Oriented Ontology (OOO), which my colleagues and I have worked for two decades to develop, has always placed special emphasis on the concept of *mediation*. This term suggests that direct relations are to be replaced with indirect ones, that objects A and B make contact only through some object C, and in one sense that is precisely what we mean by it. The technical term is "vicarious causation," and it has a rich backstory in the history of both Islamic and European philosophy in connection with the well-known theme of "occasionalism."[262] Yet there is another, perhaps more familiar sense of mediation that must also be considered. This has to do with the mediation described by media theory, as in Marshall McLuhan's old axiom that "the medium is the message."[263] Here, mediation signifies that the visible content of any medium is overpowered by its silent background conditions: for example, the content of a television show is less important than the basic structural features of the television-medium as opposed to the radio-medium. Having already spoken of vicarious causation in the first sort of case, let's coin the

[261] This article originally appeared in Turkish as Graham Harman, "Dolayımın İki Boyutu," trans. Mustafa Yalçınkaya, *Sabah Ülkesi*, Issue 52, July 1, 2017, pp. 18–23. Its first publication in English was in 2021 in Nicolás Garrera-Tolbert, Jesús Guillermo Ferrer Ortega, & Alexander Schnell, eds., *Phänomenologie und spekulativer Realismus/Phenomenology and Speculative Realism/Phénoménologie et réalisme spéculatif*.

[262] Graham Harman, "On Vicarious Causation."

[263] Marshall McLuhan, *Understanding Media*.

term "ambient causation" for the second. It too has played a role in the long history of philosophy, and not just in recent flashy speculations on the rapidly changing technologies of the present.

Vicarious Causation

The word "occasionalism" refers to philosophies that endorse one or both of the following principles: (1) There is no direct causal relation between any two created entities. Their apparent proximity in space is merely the occasion for God to make something happen. (2) Time does not automatically endure from one moment to the next. Instead, God must continually recreate the cosmos in each instant.

Historians of philosophy in the West generally use the term "occasionalist" to refer to a small circle of post-Cartesian thinkers in seventeenth-century Europe: especially Nicolas Malebranche, Arnold Geulincx, and Géraud de Cordemoy.[264] But the origins of occasionalist philosophy date to much earlier in the Islamic world, in the thought of Abu al-Hasan al-Ash'ari (874–936), a native of Basra. Central to al-Ash'ari's rejection of the more liberal Mu'tazila school — of which he was at one time a member — was his adherence to the notion that all actions are mediated by God, rather than any two entities affecting one another directly. This direct assault on the Aristotelian idea of causation became central to the Ash'arite tradition, as in its most famous adherent, the great Persian thinker al-Ghazali (1058–1111). It is interesting to note that while the Ash'arite school is more associated with "reactionary" theological positions than the earlier, Greek-leaning Mu'tazilite tradition, in some ways Ash'arite occasionalism has had more impact on Western philosophy than any other strain of Islamic thought.[265]

Yet this impact took many centuries to develop. We search in vain for a full-fledged occasionalist school in medieval Christian thought; the great Jesuit philosopher Francisco Suárez notes that while St. Thomas Aquinas (along with Averroës and Albertus Magnus) does refer to the occasionalist position, he does not name anyone in particular who holds it.[266] It is only with the founder of modern philosophy in the West, René Descartes (1596–1650), that occasionalism began to look relevant in a European context. We recall that Descartes held that there are only three kinds of

---

[264] Steven Nadler, *Occasionalism*.
[265] Majid Fakhry, *A History of Islamic Philosophy*.
[266] Francisco Suárez, *On Efficient Causality*, p. 37.

substances in the world: thought (*res cogitans*) and physical matter (*res extensa*) are the two kinds of finite substance, with God the only infinite substance. By positing a radical distinction between thought and matter, Descartes stirred up what has long been known as the "mind-body problem," a mainstay of modern philosophy.[267] The Cartesian solution was to invoke God as the bridge between the two finite substances. Though similar to the much older Ash'arite view, Descartes actually weakens the doctrine by requiring God to act as a bridge only between minds and bodies. There is no body-body problem for Descartes as there was for the Islamic occasionalists, though his French successor Malebranche soon expanded the problem to include the interaction of bodies with bodies.[268] Though many Western historians are finicky about limiting the circle of occasionalists, I would also include G.W. Leibniz (1646–1716) among their number.[269] The case against counting Leibniz as an occasionalist is that, rather than seeing God as intervening in the world in every instant, he holds that God created it just once and programmed a "pre-established harmony" into all the substances (or "monads") in the world. But we should not forget the reason such harmony is needed: for Leibniz, "monads have no windows," meaning that nothing interacts directly with anything else, the most telltale axiom of occasionalist philosophy. Also, it seems to me that we cannot avoid calling the idealist philosopher George Berkeley (1685–1753) an occasionalist.[270] After all, Berkeley held that there are no independent substances, but only images ("ideas") existing in our minds or the mind of God. The fact that everything seems to happen according to causal laws can be attributed to God's production of *apparent* laws of nature in order to shock us once in awhile with miracles, thereby strengthening our religious belief.

In the ensuing centuries, occasionalism came to be treated in the increasingly secular West as an almost laughable doctrine, taken seriously by no one. Nonetheless, it made a surprising if little-noted comeback in the twentieth century. This happened first in the philosophy of the great Englishman Alfred North Whitehead (1861–1947).[271] For Whitehead, all entities "prehend" (relate to) each other. Yet in so doing, they oversimplify or objectify one another. Rather than making direct contact, they prehend each other by way of a limited number of "eternal objects" contained in

---

[267] René Descartes, *Meditations on First Philosophy.*

[268] Nicolas Malebranche, *The Search After Truth.*

[269] G.W. Leibniz, *Selected Philosophical Essays.*

[270] George Berkeley, *A Treatise Concerning the Principles of Human Knowledge.*

[271] Alfred North Whitehead, *Process and Reality.*

God. Whereas God can observe all the diverse colorations of an object, I myself only see it as a particular shade of gray or blue. Variants of this neo-occasionalism can also be found in the works of two of the great philosopher-sociologists in recent European thought. Whitehead's admirer Bruno Latour (b. 1947), despite his strong adherence to the Roman Catholic Church, gives us a secularized version of occasionalism that does not appeal directly to God in the manner of Whitehead. Instead, Latour holds that every interaction has a different local mediator, rather than appealing to God as the mediator for all actions. In his best-developed example, Latour argues that the French physicist Frédéric Joliot-Curie served as the mediator allowing neutrons and politics to be connected for the first time in French history.[272] Another secularized version of occasionalism can be found in the sociological theories of the influential German Niklas Luhmann (1927–1998), who holds that what communicates in society are not individuals, but rather *communications*.[273] In other words, individuals cannot act directly on society, but must act in the form of communications that society already understands, leading to Luhmann's pessimistic assessment of political activism. In turn, he owes these ideas in part to the Chilean immunologists Humberto Maturana (1928–2021) and Francisco Varela (1946–2001), who emphasize the cell's inability to interact directly with the world beyond its outer wall.[274] The cell is concerned only with *homeostasis*, or maintaining a stable inner state.

Ambient Causation

All of the cases mentioned so far concerned the role of a third entity in mediating between two others. Yet I mentioned at the outset that there is a second sense of mediation: namely, the *medium* in which a thing operates or appears. I said that McLuhan's media theory provides a lucid example of this second form of mediation, one that closely resembles the figure/ground dualism of Gestalt psychology. For McLuhan, the surface content of any medium is a historical and psychological distraction. The details of the hundreds of thousands of books we debate are trivial in comparison with the deeper media that make them possible, and in which they appear: alphabetic literacy and Gutenberg's system of movable type.[275] The printing

[272] Bruno Latour, *Pandora's Hope*, Chapter Three.
[273] Niklas Luhmann, *Social Systems*.
[274] Humberto Maturana & Francisco Varela, *Autopoiesis and Cognition*.
[275] Marshall McLuhan, *The Gutenberg Galaxy*.

press and its contemporary descendants are not "vicarious" causes: not third terms that link each book with my mind. Instead, they are "ambient" causes, atmospheric preconditions forgotten amidst the concrete phenomena they make possible. A similar argument was made by the seminal art critic Clement Greenberg, sometimes called the Pope of Modernism, who reduced the pictorial content of painting to what he called "literary anecdote." He defined modern painting in McLuhanesque fashion as art that comes to terms with its medium rather than taking it for granted.[276] In the case of painting, this meant (1) accepting the flatness of the background canvas, and (2) less importantly, a turn from figuration toward abstraction. But perhaps the most important example of ambient causation in the twentieth century can be found in the philosophy of Heidegger. By raising anew the question of the meaning of being, in his 1927 masterwork *Being and Time*, Heidegger calls our attention to the horizon of being that is presupposed by all the numerous particular *beings* with which we are occupied.[277]

But ambient causation did not first appear in the twentieth-century triumvirate of Heidegger, Greenberg, and McLuhan.[278] It appears no later than Aristotle, whose *Rhetoric* is dominated by the pre-McLuhanite thesis that persuasive speech has more to do with unstated "enthymemes" than explicit propositional content.[279] When the Greek orator says simply "this man has been crowned three times with laurel," this is more powerful than spelling it out at length with "this man has been crowned three times with laurel, for he has been an Olympic champion three times," something no ancient Greek needed to be told. St. Thomas Aquinas was no theorist of vicarious or occasional cause, even though his position is sometimes mistaken for occasionalism. For Aquinas God does not recreate the universe in every instant, but merely sustains it. If two electric trains collide in a child's playroom, the occasionalist would say that the trains never actually make contact. But the Thomist position would be a different one: the trains do collide directly, but only because both are enabled to move by electricity (i.e., by God as ambient background cause). This may also be the right place to put Spinoza. Though his view that "God, or nature" is everywhere might

---

[276] Clement Greenberg, *Late Writings*, p. 28.

[277] Martin Heidegger, *Being and Time*.

[278] On the hidden link between McLuhan, Greenberg, and Heidegger see Graham Harman, "The Revenge of the Surface," which was originally published in booklet form in German as *Die Rache der Oberfläche*.

[279] Aristotle, *The Art of Rhetoric*. It is worth noting that McLuhan's early work emerged explicitly from a renewed consideration of rhetoric. See his doctoral dissertation, Marshall Mcluhan, *The Classical Trivium*.

seem to resemble occasionalism, he tells us that God is "the immanent, not the transitive cause" of everything. In other words, God does not intervene in every collision between entities, but is the background that makes all collisions and non-collisions possible.

This brings us to the first two contemporary philosophers in the West. By "contemporary" I mean any philosopher whose views one can defend *literally* in university departments of philosophy without becoming the object of laughter. Though the major seventeenth-century thinkers of continental Europe are widely revered as great figures in the discipline, there is a distinctly non-contemporary feel to the metaphysics of Descartes, Spinoza, and Leibniz, and (in the British Isles) the extreme idealism of Berkeley. It is really with David Hume and Immanuel Kant that we find the emergence of something that feels like present-day Western philosophy.[280] Now, it is well known that Hume thinks nothing can be known of causation beyond the customary conjunction of eating bread and feeling satisfied, or habitually touching a fire and feeling the pain of burning. In this sense, cause and effect exist (as far as we know) only in human experience and not in the outside world. Kant's response to Hume, whom he greatly admired, was to say that cause and effect are categories of the human understanding, so that nothing can be guessed as to whether the unknowable things-in-themselves beyond human experience interact according to causal laws.

In previous publications, I have treated Hume and Kant's manner of dealing with causation as just a deceptive form of occasionalism, one in which the human mind replaces God as the sole locus of all causation. And I still think there is a close relation between the two tendencies. However, the main point of introducing the new term "ambient causation" here is to stress a subtle but real difference between Hume and Kant on one side and the occasionalists on the other. For human experience is not a third entity linking a red billiard ball with the green one it seems to strike, but rather a background medium that defines the character of both balls: a ground for both of these figures.

Emanation

So far we have ignored one of the key places in the history of Western philosophy where mediation can be found: the neo-Platonic theory of

---

[280] David Hume, *An Enquiry Concerning Human Understanding*; Immanuel Kant, *Critique of Pure Reason*.

emanation. When someone is baking a cake, the smell of dates or chocolate emanates from the kitchen as a byproduct; in analogous fashion, each level of being emanates a surplus that establishes a new level of reality lower than the one that preceded it. From the One there is an emanation of the Intellect as the repository of Plato's famous perfect forms. From the Intellect there emanates Soul, the principle of desire. And from Soul there emanates the lowest level, Matter. We might now ask: is emanation an example of vicarious/occasional causation, or of ambient causation? In the case of Plotinus, the answer seems to be the latter.[281] The relations between the various levels are purely vertical and atemporal, and concern only the eternal way in which the lower levels exist only with the higher levels as their deeper background. There is nothing in Plotinus, as far as I recall, about the need for a causal mediator between two entities existing on the same level, such as two objects in physical collision.

Yet the answer is not quite so clear if we look at the great neo-Platonic thinkers of Islam: al-Kindi, al-Farabi, and Ibn Sina (Avicenna). Here the emanations are fleshed out as a series running from the highest level of the heavens downward to the earth, running through the sphere of fixed stars and the planets all the way to the sun and the moon. Now, here too it might seem that it is only a question of an eternal and vertical arrangement of dependence of each sphere on the higher ones. But reference is also made to the *indirect* character of communications received by the Prophets, which entails a horizontal relation between planetary spheres as each passes its message along to the next. Even so, it would be going much too far to refer to al-Kindi, al-Farabi, and Ibn Sina as occasionalists, and entirely out of the question to say this about Ibn Rushd (Averroës), with his famous polemic against al-Ghazali's occasionalist notions about causation.[282] In conclusion, it seems fairly clear that the neo-Platonic theory of emanation is best understood as a theory of ambient rather than vicarious causation.

Conclusion

The foregoing remarks on the history of philosophy and some related fields were not meant solely for historical purposes. The real point of the discussion was to prepare a question about OOO: is it concerned with vicarious causation, ambient causation, or perhaps with both? The answer is

---

[281] Plotinus, *The Enneads*.

[282] al-Ghazali, *The Incoherence of the Philosophers*; Averroës, *The Incoherence of the Incoherence*.

clearly "both." Indeed, it may be the most typical feature of OOO that it is deeply concerned with both (a) the impossibility of direct relation between entities, and (b) the difficult relation between an object and its hidden or withheld ground. Is there another current in the history of philosophy that feels compelled to combine both of these trends? The only name that comes to mind is Aristotle, who was at least dimly aware of both problems, even if he is usually remembered as the champion of direct causation against the occasionalists and of logic and reason against the obscurantists. We have already seen that his *Rhetoric* treats the surface level of communication as not where the real action unfolds. And as for vicarious causation, Aristotle comes very close to this theme when he speaks in the *Metaphysics* about the impossibility of making direct contact with entities by means of language and logic: after all, he tells us, things are always concrete but definitions are made of universals.[283]

Theories of occasional and vicarious causation deal with the mediation needed for any two specific entities to interact. Therefore, it is a variant on what is traditionally called *efficient* causation. The quirk added by occasionalism is that there can be no direct causal contact between any two entities, so that God is the only possible link between them. The new quirk added by Latour is to disallow God as the sole causal mediator: not in the name of belittling religion (Latour is quite religious himself) but simply because the problem cannot be solved by positing one amazing super-entity that is able to make causal links where nothing else is able to do so. However admirably devout such a view may be, it resorts to religious assertion to solve a problem that demands a more secular approach. Thus, Latour holds that the mediator must always be found locally: it is Joliot who first enables politics and neutrons to link together. But the astute reader may have noticed the following problem. If Joliot links politics with neutrons, how is Joliot himself able to link with politics or with neutrons in the first place? Further mediators will be needed at this level, and then mediators between these mediators, and so on to infinity. Latour's proposed solution to the infinite regress is a disappointingly pragmatic one: we simply stop whenever we become bored, or whenever we reach a level of mediation that seems pedantic or irrelevant to our question. But however practical this may be as a research methodology, it fails utterly as metaphysics. OOO is able to solve the problem differently, given its view that there are two and only two kinds of objects: the real and the sensual, which can make direct contact with each

---

[283] Aristotle, *Metaphysics*, p. 145.

other though not with their own kind, just as two opposite poles of magnets easily combine though identical ones will mutually repel.

By contrast, theories of ambient causation concern what is usually called *formal* causation.[284] This is the territory of Heidegger, Greenberg, and McLuhan, all of them bothered by the way that humans are distracted by content and pay little heed to the underlying form that makes the content possible. And how are the form and the content of an object supposed to interact, if the first is hidden and the second is always visible, audible, or tangible? We have seen that for Aristotle this is the province of rhetoric, which uses propositional language to allude to something unstated and perhaps unstateable. But for OOO, it is aesthetics more generally that drives a wedge between the object and its own unnoticed form. By splitting them apart, it calls upon the aesthetic beholder to serve as the mediator between these two dimensions of the objects. The old OOO formula of "aesthetics as first philosophy" requires that both aesthetics and philosophy be reconceived in terms of a theory of media.[285]

---

[284] Marshall McLuhan, *Media and Formal Cause.*
[285] Graham Harman, "Aesthetics as First Philosophy."

CHAPTER 15

TIME, SPACE, ESSENCE, AND EIDOS: A NEW THEORY OF CAUSATION[286]

The title of this article might sound presumptuous or strange. The presumptuous part would stem from the adjective "new." For some people this word implies absolute novelty, a new theory summoned from nowhere like a genie from a bottle. But such pristine newness is neither possible nor desirable. The topic of causation has received considerable treatment from the dawn of philosophy, and the highlights of this story are widely known: Aristotle's four causes, the neo-Platonic doctrine of emanation, the divine intervention found in Islamic and French occasionalism, and Hume's skeptical doubts about causation along with Kant's half-hearted solution. While these well-known theories cannot be considered in depth in what follows, their spirit will be present in what I say.

The *strangeness* of the title, by contrast, would arise from the topic of causality itself. With the exception of Hume's doubts about causal links, the theme of causation has largely vanished from philosophy. Whether necessary causal connections can be established or not, *how* do they work? This is barely spoken of at all. While philosophers remain in perpetual anguish over the single gap between human and world, or the denial of this gap in favor of a primal human-world correlate, causality seems to unfold in

---

[286] This chapter was originally published in the journal *Cosmos and History* in 2010, after first having been delivered as a lecture at the American University of Paris on January 26, 2009.

a place where philosophy no longer enters: the sphere of inanimate physical things. And since the natural sciences already deal with causation with such spectacular success, it may seem rude or unwise for philosophy to intrude on their terrain. In philosophy, we now feel most comfortable when dealing with the limited sphere of human-world interplay. We dare not venture outside, partly through fear that the sciences might strike back and invade philosophy's humanized ghetto, reducing the mind to a brain and all things to narrowly physical interactions.

In this article I call on philosophy to rediscover its global vocation, to speak of the inanimate realm no less than the human-world gap (or non-gap, as some prefer). The way to do this is with an object-oriented metaphysics having a single problem at its core: the tension between objects and relations. The term "object" as I use it means anything that exists. The term "relation" means any interaction between these objects. I hold that such interaction is always a kind of translation or distortion, even at the level of inanimate things. In recent philosophy, the *human* relation with the world has been treated as an extra-special tear in the fabric of the cosmos. The human entity magically transcends the world in unprecedented fashion and becomes the star of philosophy, while inanimate relations are treated as mere boring clockwork: a dull mechanical onslaught where atoms and billiard balls slap each other into submission according to widely known physical laws. Against this assumption, I claim that human beings are objects in precisely the same way as clods of physical matter. In addition, I claim that the relation between fire and cotton is of the same kind as that between fire and the mind. The same universal problem arises in both cases. It is a problem already known to the abandoned occasionalist tradition, which cannot remain abandoned any longer thanks to the contributions of a surprising figure: Martin Heidegger.

I. Heidegger's Occasionalism

The words "Heidegger's occasionalism" were possibly never spoken on earth until this very sentence. That is understandable, since the phrase sounds patently absurd. The occasionalists are remembered for their meddling God who intervenes in every least event in the universe, his continuous creation of a reality that otherwise disintegrates, and the impossibility of direct causal connections between any two substances. None of these topics seems even remotely relevant to Heidegger, since he barely makes room for God at all and dismisses the concept of substance as belonging to the accursed "metaphysics of presence." Obviously, I will not say that Heidegger believes in an interventionist God or continuous creation. But I will contend that he is an occasionalist when it comes to the relations between beings. It is true that he never says anything of the sort, and to make the case requires that we do some violence to Heidegger's self-understanding. But such violence is necessary here.

The point is this: Heidegger inadvertently shows the difficulty of relations of any sort. The heart of his philosophy is the famous tool-analysis, and when read properly this analysis makes a metaphysical case against relationality *per se*. This is the sense in which Heidegger is an occasionalist. Notice that I do not compare him with Hume: I do not say "Heidegger's *empiricism*," a far more ridiculous phrase than "Heidegger's occasionalism." The reason he is no empiricist is that the gap he generates is not between two impressions or ideas, but between any two things. For him these things must be autonomous and inaccessible, and they have every reason to be called *substances* in a slightly new sense of the term.

Everyone is familiar with Heidegger's tool-analysis, so I will keep my summary brief. The phenomenology of Husserl suspends the reality of the world in favor of an exact description of how it appears to consciousness. While there is more to Husserl than this, it is accurate to say that Husserl is unconcerned with the reality of things outside their accessibility to consciousness. In this way, phenomenology is one of the "philosophies of human access" par excellence — even more so than Kant's philosophy, given Husserl's complete lack of interest in the *Ding an Sich*. Husserl's famous motto "to the things themselves" means to the *phenomena* themselves, not the noumena themselves.

Heidegger's tool-analysis has been seen, and rightly so, as a counterpoint to Husserl's extreme form of idealism. As Heidegger notes, we do not usually deal with things as phenomena in consciousness. Instead, we silently rely on them until they malfunction. The hammer is not noticed unless it breaks or is too painful or heavy to hold. We notice the ground only during earthquakes or when stepping on slippery ice. Internal bodily organs are generally noticed only when we are being rushed to the hospital. This is all true enough. But the tool-analysis is usually trivialized into a *pragmatist* reading: Heidegger thinks that all theory emerges from a shadowy background of unnoticed praxis. Once this step is taken, it is easy to claim that Heidegger merely echoes earlier insights of John Dewey. But Heidegger is a philosopher of *being*, not of human praxis, and being for him is not just a meaningless slogan. The question of the meaning of being is often viewed as inscrutably deep and mysterious, and it is rarely noticed that Heidegger gives a provisional *answer* to the question of being, if a largely negative one. Namely, being for Heidegger is that which is not present-at-hand, not *vorhanden*. Among other things, this means that the being of a thing is not identical with its presence in human consciousness.

But the insight goes further than this, and if pushed hard enough it quickly becomes as weird as a ghost story. For when we say that the hammer is not something noticed in consciousness, this means that the hammer we perceive or think of is a mere shadow of its reality. The hammer in its subterranean reality is deeper and richer than the hammer we witness in the phenomenal sphere, which is only a shallow caricature of the hammer executing its own reality. But here comes an important point: human praxis is just as guilty of this caricature as human theory. *To use* the hammer does not give us any more intimate contact with the hammer's reality than *to see* or *to think* about it does. The same sort of translation or distortion occurs in both cases — the hammer is rendered in a foreign tongue distant from the original. Other features of this instrument, which may be of the greatest relevance to mosquitoes, bacteria, angels, or nails, are left untranslated, ignored as if they did not exist. When it comes to distorting the subterranean life of beings, theory and praxis are equally guilty.

In other words, we should not be fooled by etymology and think that theory is about *Vorhandenheit* and praxis about *Zuhandenheit*. For surprisingly enough, both distortions give us nothing but *Vorhandenheit*! Ready-to-hand does not mean "useful" and present-at-hand does not mean "visible." Instead, the ready-to-hand is the reality of the hammer itself apart from any distortion by human access, and the present-at-hand is whatever exists only *in relation* to such access, whether it be lucidly theoretical or unconsciously practical. This reading of *Zuhandenheit* as the lonely isolation of unique things is disputed by most Heideggerians for a simple and understandable reason: namely, Heidegger refers to *Zuhandenheit* as made up of a *system* of things, and states explicitly that it is not a series of individual tools lying around in isolation. But this objection overlooks a very important point: namely, tools only blend together in this system *insofar as they do not break*. Yet the fact that they do break proves they are never fully integrated into the system of purposes in which human Dasein makes use of them. Tools break because they are something a bit more, an excess of reality that no system can ever fully exploit, and which eventually returns to haunt every user. In effect, then, Heidegger's ready-to-hand means "objects" and his present-at-hand means "relations."

But now comes the most surprising step of all: one that bursts the entire framework of post-Kantian philosophy and pushes Heidegger tacitly in the direction of Alfred North Whitehead. For it is not just human theory and praxis that distort the autonomous reality of objects. Humans do not have the unique gift or burden of translating entities into modified terms. Nor is the situation improved if we expand the roster of distorting and translating entities to include the intelligent higher animals. Philosophers must not cry out for dolphins, whales, dogs, monkeys, pigs, and crows to save them, for there is nothing they can do to help. In fact, any relation between any two entities must result in the same type of translation or distortion with which human Dasein treats hammers. Yes, I realize that humans display cognitive powers that only a charlatan would grant to flowers or sand. But these powers are merely a special case of what must be called "relations more generally." The primary dualism in the world is not between matter and mind, but between objects and relations, and most relations will be unrecognizable as anything mental, just as objects turn out not to resemble what is usually called the physical.

In this respect all objects have autonomous reality apart from humans, apart from dolphins, apart from flowers, but also apart from stones. And since each of these hidden objects has a specific reality that distinguishes it from the others, each can be said to have a *form*: not an accidental form stamped in it by an outside entity, but a form in its own right, which the Scholastics and Leibniz call a *substantial* form. But there are at least three ways in which these substances differ from the classical kind. First, they are infinitely withdrawn and cannot be brought into any relation without significant distortion; truth cannot be correspondence, since knowledge is a translation of real things rather than a copy of them. Second, substances do not need to be so-called "natural kinds." It hardly matters that sharks have existed for millions of years, iPhones for just two, and the Obama Administration for less than a year; all can be substances if they have an autonomous reality inexhaustible by any relations, as I hold that they do. And third, while the classical difference between substance and aggregate gives us a world with only two levels, the Heidegger-inspired model of object-oriented philosophy gives us countless levels. A sports car is an autonomous reality compared with all the many uses of it. But the car is also a relational whole built of many parts, none of which the car fully exhausts (as proven by the fact that any of the parts can malfunction). Each of these car parts, in turn, is made of further parts, and I do not doubt that this chain of assemblages stretches to the dankest infinities of Hell and beyond. Kant's Second Antinomy is perhaps not an antinomy, for every entity has a definite qualitative character, and I would claim that to have such a character must mean to be articulated or constructed by pieces. In the classical theory, there was one zone of reality that was always substance and another that was always aggregate. But notice that an aggregate is like a substance when viewed from the outside: as with Latour's "black boxes" or the "assemblages" of DeLanda.

Objects or substantial forms, then, exist in all different sizes. But whatever size they may be, they have a problem relating to one another; here we find Heidegger's link with the abandoned occasionalist tradition. On the one hand, objects withdraw into inscrutable depths. On the other, we know that they somehow relate, or nothing would happen and presence-at-hand would not exist. The impossibility of individual things making contact was first noted not by the French Cartesians, but by the Ash'arite school of Islamic theology in early medieval Iraq. For al-Ash'ari and his followers, the omnipotence of God goes so far that other entities are deprived not just of the power of creation, but of any causal power at all. To use their favorite example, fire does not burn cotton, but is merely the occasion for *God* to burn the cotton. The same holds for all causal relations, not just those between mind and body. This notion was attacked even within Islam, with the critique made by Averroës being surely the most famous. Nonetheless, it is supported by a particular passage in the *Qu'ran*, and makes a good fit with the profound sense of fate and the almighty will of God that is generally even stronger in Islam than in Christianity. While similar passages can be found in the Bible in *I* and *II Corinthians*, it took hundreds of years for the occasionalist spirit to flourish in Europe: until the seventeenth century, when relations became problematic for philosophy as never before.

This began, of course, in France. But it was perhaps foreshadowed in the 1590s in the late Scholastic writings of Francisco Suárez. On the surface, Suárez opposes all occasionalism, which he openly attacks decades before it even appears in Europe. While it is obvious that Suárez is thoroughly schooled in various figures of Arabic-language philosophy — Averroës, Avicenna, Avicebron — he seems unaware of the Ash'arite occasionalists of Iraq. For Suárez says only that

> *there was an old position* which asserted that created things do
> nothing but instead that God effects all things in their presence,
> whereas action is attributed to fire, water, and so on because of the
> appearances and because God has resolved, as it were, to produce

such effects only in the presence of such things. This opinion
is mentioned by Averroës ... by Albertus Magnus ... and by
St. Thomas Aquinas ... *though there is no particular author whom
they cite on its behalf.*[287]

Suárez then digs up a few minor passages from European authors that seem
to point in an occasionalist direction, which he would never have done if
he were familiar with *The Incoherence of the Incoherence* by Averroës, where
al-Ghazali of Baghdad is specifically attacked for occasionalist views. This
scarcity of references is not so important, since Suárez attacks the anonymous
occasionalists anyway. Yet a bit of the occasionalist DNA can be found even
in Suárez's own writings. After all, one of his most famous teachings is the
incommunicability of individuals. He rejects the idea that form stamped
in matter, *materia signata*, is the source of individuation. The work of
individuation belongs to form alone; each thing is a highly specific modal
compound. But this means that no form can shift from one material to
another and still remain what it was: forms are untranslatable, immobilized
in place, incommunicable. Hence Suárez must place especial emphasis on
the old Scholastic principle that things affect one another *through accidents*,
not through some impossible direct contact between substantial forms.
While the occasionalists see God as the glue of the world, and Hume and
Kant grant this honor to the habits or categories of the human mind, Suárez
gives it to the accidents of individual substances. And this is closer to the
true solution than when God or the human mind take all the glory.

Heidegger obviously never meant to be an occasionalist. In fact, it is
fairly clear that Heidegger never meant to abandon the interplay of human
and world that has dominated philosophy since Kant. What is most typical
of Kant, I would say, is that one *type* of relation becomes central to all
philosophy: the duel between human and world. The relation between
raindrops and sand is simply not a topic for Kant or most of his successors,
and is left to the work of meteorologists. From Kant onward, natural science
is granted a total monopoly on such issues, while philosophy cowers in the
slum of human-world interaction, desperately fighting off the incursions
of cognitive science with the mixed emotions of contempt and fear. But
despite Heidegger's apparent willingness to remain in the Kantian fortress,
his tool-analysis takes us much further. There is a *universal* problem in
the relation between any two entities, since they withdraw into concealed

---

[287] Francis Suarez, *On Efficient Causality*, p. 37.

depths, yet they must somehow break out of those depths to engage in the interactions that characterize our world. This cannot be done with the *deus ex machina* of the Malebranchian God, but also not with the *mens ex machina* of Hume's customary conjunction. For Heidegger these would be merely "ontic" solutions, choosing a sole princess entity to be granted all relational power in the cosmos. A more likely solution would resemble that of Suárez, with accidents forming the glue between incommunicable substantial forms. Yet so far we have spoken only of the difference between substance and relation, and have said nothing of substance and accident.

2. The Interior of Objects

Surprisingly enough, this is where Edmund Husserl comes to our assistance. It is well known that Husserl's intellectual father was Franz Brentano, a figure often cited for an idea or two but rarely read in his own right anymore. Yet Brentano's brilliance of argument is astonishing, and his charisma as remarkable as that of Rasputin, a person he physically resembles in certain photographs. Our interest for now is limited to his most famous idea: intentionality, or "intentional inexistence." What typifies mental acts for Brentano is that they contain immanent objects. My wishes, hatreds, and intellectual activity all aim at *objects*, and those objects are contained in the mental sphere. Brentano's great Polish disciple, Kasimir Twardowski, noted the one-sided character of this model. It makes little room for a non-immanent reality: a world outside the mind. Twardowski's early masterpiece *On the Content and Object of Presentations* is still available in English, though at the usual outrageous price of books published by Martinus Nijhoff.[288] The phrase "content *and* object" already gives us the essence of Twardowski's philosophy. Strictly speaking, there are not objects immanent in the mind. Rather, there are objects *outside* the mind and mental contents *inside* the mind. In this way Twardowski establishes two layers of the world, though he also unifies these layers by saying that metaphysics is the science of objects in general: whether these be real physical masses, or mental entities that never escape the immanent sphere.

Twardowski served Edmund Husserl as both an inspiration and a rival. One possible reading of Husserl's early career is that it was nothing but a struggle with Twardowski, his fellow Brentano pupil. Husserl's references to his younger peer are sometimes flattering, sometimes brutal, but always

---

[288] Kasimir Twardowski, *On the Content and Object of Presentations*.

emotionally charged: all signs of a genuine struggle. It is well known that Husserl rejects the Twardowskian split between an object outside consciousness and a content lying within it. When I speak of the city of Berlin, Husserl says, the Berlin of which I speak and Berlin itself are the same thing, not two.[289] While this may sound like a realist philosophy of language, in practice it pushes Husserl increasingly towards idealism as the years go by, since what he really means is that there is no Berlin-in-itself that could not be the correlate of some consciousness. And here is the source of most critiques of Husserl, justified or otherwise. For public attention has been focused almost exclusively on the "idealist" side of Husserl, who seems to lose the real world in a way that Heidegger, natural science, and even Deleuze supposedly avoid. Nor do I say so with a sarcastic tone, since I find this criticism of Husserl to be basically correct. Yet it also misses half the point, since Husserl makes an additional move that may be unprecedented in the history of philosophy. The dispute between Husserl and Twardowski (carried out largely in one direction) may look like a predictable quarrel between one thinker who insists on a world outside the mind and another who denies it. But in fact, Husserl never dropped Twardowski's distinction between object and content: he simply *displaced* it. For even though we never find much of a real world in Husserl, the distinction between object and content remains central for him. But it is now a distinction *within* the mental sphere rather than one that straddles the divide between inside and outside. That is to say, *phenomena themselves* are split into object and content for Husserl.

In a sense this is already familiar from the way his phenomenological descriptions work. Consider the following example: I observe a tree by circling it from many different angles, at different times of day, and in slightly different moods. In each of these cases the tree appears by way of vastly different qualities. Even so, for as long as I take it to be the same tree, I never imagine that it is anything other than a unified thing. The same *eidos* of the tree is present in all these cases, no matter how different the accidental qualities through which it might be manifest. This aspect of Husserl is generally overlooked, simply because no one feels the *need* of an insight on this front. Most philosophers silently assume that the empiricists are right: that an object of perception is nothing but a "bundle of qualities." It is widely assumed that only reactionary fools believe in some reality to objects over and above qualities amassed in a packet. But Husserl teaches

---

[289] Edmund Husserl, "Intentional Objects."

otherwise: in consciousness an object is always manifested through specific content, yet it always *exceeds* that content. Moreover, he does not do this through some sort of hypocritical pointing toward an outside world, for it remains purely immanent. Husserl repeatedly denies such immanence, but only because he does not believe in any *transcendent* world that would render the phenomenal one purely immanent by comparison. But when contrasted with a realist world, Husserl's object/content model is entirely immanent. The unified tree that I witness through all my experience might be a sheer illusion, after all. There is no reason to identify it with a real tree. It is a unified tree-object immanent in consciousness, accompanied by a unified tree-*content* through which it always appears, but which varies in the wildest manner and is never identical with it.

As I see it, this claim is decisive for the phenomenal realm, and the works of Husserl and Merleau-Ponty do much to bolster it. But what if we abandon Husserl's idealism and leave the sphere of consciousness? Is the same duality between object and content found in real objects as is found in intentional ones? If we believe Leibniz (and I usually do) the answer is yes. In Paragraph 2 of the *Monadology*, Leibniz says that the simplicity of the monads "does not prevent a multiplicity of modifications, which must be found together in this same simple substance," and in fact a monad "can be distinguished from another only by its internal qualities."[290] Various Scholastics had said the same thing, and Aristotle, in the *Metaphysics*, already raised the question of whether a substance is the same as its essence. But Husserl was probably the first philosopher to double up *appearance* into an object-pole and a quality-pole, and was surely the first to show how this works concretely in our perceptions of a mailbox, blackbird, tree, or anything else.

Husserl's insight raises new complications for us. Earlier, I spoke of the occasionalist problem of how two *separate* objects relate. But Husserl, and on a different level Leibniz, draws our attention to relations *within* objects. How does a real object relate to its own genuine features, and how does an intentional object relate to its own accidental profiles? And further, when two real objects relate through some occasionalistic third term, are they relating through their object-poles or their quality-poles? Instead of a single kind of relation to worry about, we now have three or maybe four.

But for the moment, let's forget this Husserl/Leibniz fourfold and return to another aspect of Husserl that is too little discussed. I refer to his assertion in the *Logical Investigations* that intentionality is both one and two. The

---

[290] G.W. Leibniz, *Philosophical Essays*, p. 207.

meaning of this statement is simple, yet its implications took me seventeen years to digest after first reading it. Consider once more the perception of a tree, and forget for a moment about the duel between the tree as a tangible content of colors and shapes and the tree as an underlying unit or *eidos* that endures despite all variations in surface content. Focus instead on a simpler aspect of the intention: the relation between me and the tree. On the one hand, the tree and I are distinct. We do not fuse together in instantaneous union; I never confuse myself with the tree. In that sense the intention is made up of two equally primary elements. The object and I are two. But on the other hand the intentional relationship is *one*, since the object and I are together. Five minutes from now, even if the tree is left behind or destroyed, I can still analyze this intentional relationship in memory, and other humans can analyze it at any moment too. In short, the intentional relation has an inherent *reality* that is never exhausted by analyzing it. Husserl does usually claim that direct, perfect intuition into an intention is possible, that pure introspective evidence can be had, and he has come under heavy criticism for this both by Heideggerians and by various recent philosophers of mind. Yet if we simply ignore this part of Husserl's philosophy, nothing much changes. It seems clear enough that the intentional relation between me and the tree has a unified reality that cannot be exhausted by any description or translation of it.

And this real unity is enough to call the relation an *object*. Why would anyone dispute this? For one thing, the relation does not last very long. Goethe once remarked that the most beautiful sunset in the world would still bore anyone after fifteen minutes, and *a fortiori* it is not interesting to stare at a tree for very long. This transience of the relationship seems to be a problem, since we normally think of objects as durable solid things. But recall that there is also nothing durable about most antimatter, or Californium and the other exotic chemical elements lurking near the misty peak of the periodic table, or mayflies which die after minutes or days of adult life, or even the continent of Asia when we look at the long past and future of continental drift. Durability is not a good criterion for objects. For another thing, the intentional relation is produced by a human and does not exist by nature, whereas classical philosophies are usually willing to treat only *natural* things as real objects. But it seems foolish to deny objecthood to such artificial things as a factory or knife, or to genetically engineered tomatoes enhanced with the genes of coniferous trees and pigs. Thus, naturalness is not a good criterion for an object either. And finally, the complaint might be heard that the relation between me and the tree is *not physical*, whereas normally we like objects to be solid material things. But there are plenty of non-physical objects recognized even by those who do not believe in angels or souls: numbers come to mind as one example. In short, the only criterion for a real object is that it be a unified thing with specific qualities, reducible neither to a bundle of qualities nor to its relation to us. And now, notice that the intentional relation between me and the tree meets all these criteria. The relation is *one* thing despite its plurality of parts. It has definite qualities that distinguish it from my grandmother's perception of the tree or from my own perception of a fire. But it is not a bundle of such qualities, nor can any phenomenologist describe it exhaustively: not even if that phenomenologist is called God. If rocks and flowers are objects, then so are intentional relations.

And this leads us to draw a strange but inevitable conclusion, the only kind worth drawing in philosophy. Insofar as intentionality is one, it is a single object. And insofar as intentionality is two, it is two objects: the tree and I. And the only place for these *two* objects to make contact is the interior of the *one* object defined by the intentional relation as a whole. This leads us toward a new theory of causation along several fronts. Heidegger's occasionalism recalled the seventeenth-century lesson that there is something problematic about relations between real objects. In fact, it turned out to be impossible for real objects to make contact, since they will always confront limited caricatures or translations of each other. But the opposite model was found in empiricism: here, the contact has always already occurred, in the form of habit. Hume's doubts are not about whether customary conjunction ever happens (it obviously happens all the time) but only about whether there are hidden secret powers beyond the conjunctions that cause them to occur. These are the two opposite options. It is not so much a contrast between rationalism and empiricism, as Kant believed, since this is merely an epistemological difference as to how the world is *known*. Instead, there is a deeper difference between occasionalism and empiricism. The first model accepts autonomous substances that do not interact, while the second model starts from the interaction and is skeptical about autonomous substance.

But there really are autonomous objects that withdraw from all interaction, just as occasionalists think. I base this on the authority of Heidegger's tool-analysis, which really needs to be read in the way that I have described. But there is also an internal space where interactions occur, just as Hume prefers. Nonetheless, there is one key problem with the occasionalists and three key problems with Hume:

1 The problem with the occasionalists has already been mentioned. For
they solve the problem of the relations between substances only by
invoking God as a magical solution, shielded by the good public repute
of religion (which is merely reversed among intellectuals today). Yet
it is entirely unclear in a *philosophical* context how God can do what
other substances cannot. Hence, this is merely a classic instance of the
"asylum of ignorance."

The three problems with Hume are as follows:

1 First, Heidegger's tool-analysis forces us away from the empiricist stance
toward a theory of concealed real objects. For this reason, Hume's
mens ex machina works no better than the *deus ex machina*, but for a
different reason: it only accounts for half of reality, the half made up of
impressions and ideas rather than the half made of *bona fide* realities.
The fact that such realities are widely unpopular in 2009 means little
to me; shifts of fashion in the history of philosophy are sudden, and
they occur quite often through the return of dead concepts in better-
engineered form.

2 Second, Hume is too focused on the interaction or lack thereof between
impressions or ideas (which I will unify with the single word "images").
But in fact, there is no such interaction. The image of cotton and the
image of fire, or the images of two billiard balls, are merely contiguous,
and always will be. The more important interaction is between *me*
on the one hand, and these images on the other. I am not identical
with what I see, as Hume asserts when he says that I am a bundle of
perceptions. On the contrary, I do not fuse together into these images
as a single thing; I am perfectly aware that I am one thing and the
images are another. Hence, we should change our focus from the
relation between two images to that between observer and image.

3 Third and finally, there is an asymmetry here that Hume is unable
to see, since he does not acknowledge the autonomy of real things.
Namely, although the intentional objects I confront are merely images,
it is the *real* me that is involved in the experience. For it is not some
image of me that sees two billiard balls collide. No, my genuine
life consists in witnessing this collision right now. So although it is
impossible for me as a real object to touch another real object, it is quite
possible for me to touch *intentional* objects, as happens constantly.
This already suggests another initial theorem for the new theory of

causation: all relations occur only between *asymmetrical partners*. A real object withdraws from another real object, and two images merely sit side by side in an experience without touching. But a real object and an image are two kinds of objects that we already *know* can make contact, because that's what experience is: someone or something confronting intentional objects. We may take this, then, as a basic law of causation: two objects in contact must always be of the two different kinds.

There is actually a fourth difference from Hume as well, but it seems best to approach it through a critique of Brentano's position. For when Brentano speaks about intentionality as immanent objectivity, he thinks immanent means "inside the human mind." And there are two problems with this. First, my relation to the intentional object "tree" is not inside *my mind*. Instead, both it and my mind are *inside the relation between me and the tree*. Remember: the tree-image and I are on the interior of some object, and I am not that object. On the contrary, I am simply one of its two components. The unified object is the relation as a whole. Second — and we now enter a strange landscape where Hume and Brentano dare not venture — it is not only humans or sentient animals that do this. If two molecules of iron interact to form a new entity, they too will confront each other on the interior of that larger entity, and moreover will confront each other as translations or caricatures, as Heidegger's occasionalism already showed. In other words, the strange interior space where a real object confronts images need not have a human or a smart animal as one of its ingredients. Sentient creatures are just a more advanced case of a universal drama between any two things. Yes, human cognition is very different from the collision of two grains of salt, but the point is that both are built out of something even more primitive. This is overlooked both by human-centered philosophy and by many forms of panpsychism. Human-centered thinking wants experience to be restricted to humans and possibly a handful of clever dolphins and monkeys. At the opposite extreme, panpsychism wants something like human cognition already tacitly inscribed in grains of dust. But against such extreme panpsychism, human cognition is a very late and highly innovative form of the primitive reactions we are describing; contra human-centered philosophy, it is not different *in kind* from physical collisions.

To summarize, two entities make contact only on the interior of a third, and it is an asymmetrical contact between a real object and an intentional one. Naturally, there are always many intentional objects in any one experience, but all are linked only as experiences of the real perceiver. The intentional trees, horses, chairs, emeralds, and hallucinations that I experience in any one moment are merely contiguous in my experience. In addition, each of these intentional objects is torn in half between its unified reality and its plurality of accidental silhouettes. And the same holds true, as Leibniz notes, at the level of real objects withdrawn from every view. Thus, we have discovered two kinds of relations between a thing and its own qualities (namely, at the real level and the image level) and one or more kinds of relation between real objects and their images as encountered by other objects: whether these others be human, animal, vegetable, plastic, or stone.

3. Objects as Assemblages

If it is true that every relation generates a new object, it seems equally true that every object is pieced together from relations. Though I will insist on the Heideggerian principle of withdrawal, and will also insist that an object is an emergent reality over and above its pieces, it is still the case that an object could not exist in this very moment without *some* pieces. But whenever I say that an object is real apart from all relations with its environment, the following complaint is often made: "objects are obviously dependent on their environment. If I were placed on Saturn or at the bottom of the sea, I would immediately be killed by their hostile conditions. This proves that my environment is a part of who I am." But this is an equivocal use of the word "dependence." Putting me on Saturn would certainly *kill* me, and so would injecting my body beneath the surface of the sea, but neither scenario would change the nature of the person being killed. By contrast, changing my component pieces (if pushed far enough) could change who I am even if the resulting creature survived for thousands of years, or even for eternity. My *success* depends on my environment, as do my partnerships and my physical survival, but my *nature* is not thus dependent. I am the same real object whether I endure on earth for forty more years or perish instantly on Saturn. But I am *not* the same real object if my pieces are shuffled beyond a certain point: a point that can be left undefined in this article.

This gives us an *assemblage* theory of objects. According to this theory, an object is made up of a certain number of components. While it is tempting to call them "smaller" components, this could betray a bias toward the physical realm. For the components are not necessarily smaller: in some sense OPEC or NATO are not physically larger than their component entities, and a friendship or marriage may not be larger than those it unites.

But an object must have components; otherwise it would be purely simple and would have no qualities, as Leibniz noted with his monads. To me this suggests that an infinite regress of compound entities is necessary. And that implies a delightful violation of Kant's Second Antinomy, thereby hinting at a method by which the rest of Kant's Transcendental Dialectic may be undercut as well.

In our time an assemblage theory of entities is already in the air. It can be found in Bruno Latour's model of black boxes opened to reveal their internal components, with those component boxes then opened, and so on to infinity.[291] The theory is worked out with a more candidly realist twist by Manuel DeLanda in his recent book *A New Philosophy of Society*.[292] What constitutes a true new assemblage, as opposed to a random list of words? DeLanda offers some criteria, and I will mention four of the most important. Although the term "assemblage" seems to suggest that an object is "many" while downplaying its unity, there is no question that DeLanda also views his assemblages as unified things. One criterion for a real assemblage, surely the most important, is that a real assemblage has true emergent properties not found in its pieces. Another, which is not openly stated but is tacitly present as the very foundation of DeLanda's realism, is that an assemblage is deeper than any of its effects on its environment. Another interesting criterion offered by DeLanda is "redundant causation," meaning that the assemblage can be created by any number of different causal chains without losing its identity.[293] My blood could be replaced with donated blood, or some of my bones hollowed out and replaced with fiberglass, and I would remain the same object. And finally, an assemblage can have retroactive effects on its parts, or even create new ones. When a city is founded, this may have backwards effects on those who come to inhabit it, and will also generate new institutions and customs that were not initially present.

When we speak of "causation" in relation to an assemblage, we naturally tend to think of its outward effects on other things, whether these be outer entities or its own interior components. The city of Cairo has retroactive effects on its own pieces, such as police officers, and it also casts an economic shadow on Beni Suef, Tanta, Ismailia, and other nearby Egyptian cities,

---

[291] Bruno Latour, *Science in Action*.

[292] Manuel DeLanda, *A New Philosophy of Society*.

[293] As is often the case with DeLanda, his use of the phrase "redundant causation" differs from the mainstream sense of the term used in analytic philosophy. See, for instance, Aimee Thomasson, *Ordinary Objects*.

sparking and inhibiting their growth in specific ways. But all such criteria miss the *primary* meaning of cause: the reality of Cairo itself. Remember that every genuine relation *forms* a new object. To cause is to generate a new relation, and to do this is to create a new object, and objects have what was classically known as *formal cause*. But when we think of causation in daily life, we instead think of the mutual influence of *two* objects on each other, or *efficient cause* in the classical sense. When two fighter planes collide at an air show, we think that their impact caused damage so severe as to lead to the crash and explosion of both. But according to the model just sketched, this is merely a "retroactive effect on its parts" of a larger collision-entity, to which we never pay attention because it lasts so briefly and takes on little or no physical form. But the case of Cairo is perhaps even more convincing. Quite apart from Cairo's effect on its parts or on other cities, Cairo itself is a *reality*, or else it could achieve no effect at all. Its reality is generated by a certain arrangement of its components, but somehow emerges as something over and above those components. It often has many effects on its parts and on other cities, but it does not *need* to have them. It is conceivable, even necessary, that the world is filled with millions of entities that have reality without an effect on anything else, at least for the moment. I find it wrong to hold that a thing is real only when it affects something else. In classical terms, there could be formal causes that have, now or forever, no function as efficient causes.

To repeat, the primary meaning of "cause" is to create a new object. Only secondarily does it mean that an object has an effect on others or retroactive impact on its own parts. If we see one thing influence another, this is merely a retroactive effect of a joint object that unites the two, or once did so. What I want to suggest is that this gives us a new way of reflecting on the principle of sufficient reason. For according to the model just sketched, sufficient reason is less a matter of knowing that the fire necessarily burned the cotton than of knowing that certain pieces arranged in a certain way necessarily *resulted* in the existence of cotton. If this could be shown, then the rules would be the same when fire and cotton combine to produce a joint entity called "burning cotton ball." But if the fire might not burn the cotton the next time under the same circumstances, as Hume holds, then it should also be true that the real components of the cotton arranged in a certain way might give rise next time not to cotton, but to steel or a rabid bat, or a miniature angel dancing in flame. A "mereological" view of causation — objects as parts always generating new objects as wholes — would offer a new angle from which to approach Hume's problem.

4. A Quadruple Cosmology

The model of the world presented here has a finite number of simple features whose interactions may shed light on a number of topics. First, we have numerous objects of all different sizes, in a chain of descending entities that is probably endless: "turtles all the way down," as the old joke puts it. These real objects withdraw from mutual contact, and encounter each other only as translations or caricatures. They somehow come into relation through a vicarious medium, and I have said that this medium can only be the *interior* of some other object: a perceptual space filled with intentional objects rather than real ones. Moreover, the interiors are not just for humans and animals, since *any* entity encounters nothing but caricatures, and the relation to intentional objects must take place almost everywhere, in some ultra-primitive form from which more complicated animal cognition is built. Every relation will also create a new object, and thus a new interior space with still other relations that might one day be generated.

Before clarifying the model further, let me say a word about panpsychism, which seems to be one shocking result of this theory. The accusation is often made that it it is too "anthropomorphic" to put psyche everywhere in the cosmos. But as I see it, this gets things backwards. The point is not to inject tiny human minds backwards into inanimate dirt, but the reverse: to show that what we call minds are simply enhanced versions of the crude contact with intentional objects found in any relation whatever. This sort of theory is usually the province of scientific reductionism, and it simply *assumes* that the root unit of the cosmos is simple physical impact between tiny material atoms. But this is both arbitrary and boring. By pushing Heidegger's respected tool-analysis in an unorthodox direction, I have tried to show that even atomic collisions must involve intentional objects. Imagining what this is like without falsely ascribing human emotional or intellectual features to atoms is difficult, but it could easily become the topic of a philosophical discipline called "speculative psychology," which would try to probe toward what it is like not only to be a *bat*, or my mother, or Martin Heidegger, but also an atom, a grain of dust, an army, the Exxon Corporation, or France.[294]

But in another sense I am merely a *polypsychist*, not a panpsychist. For the panpsychists go too far when they say that *every* object has psyche; there is an option in between, and my theory is the first to make it visible. Namely, I have claimed that absorption with intentional objects occurs only on the

---

[294] The "bat" reference, of course, is to Thomas Nagel's famous article "What is it Like to be a Bat?"

interior of some object, with one of that object's real pieces confronting intentional caricatures of one or more others. But remember, I also claimed that a thing need not enter into relations at all in order to exist! An object is real, in this theory, when it unifies pieces into an emergent reality that has genuine qualities of its own. It does not automatically follow that this new object will have an impact on other objects, whether now or ever. There will always be some turbulent surface of the cosmos that has objects below it but none above. The need for an infinite regress does not also imply an infinite *progress* of objects. In this way, panpsychism is actually overthrown. To be out of relation is not to be *dead*, however, since the "body" of the object is active as long as it is real. The surface of the cosmos is made of objects that are not dead, but sleeping or *dormant* entities, to use the wonderful word that the Anglo-Saxons copied from French long ago. In this sense, for humans to sleep is to rise to the surface of the turbulent sea, which would put dreams in a new and metaphysical perspective, giving us murky glimpses of undersea treasures.

We now return to the model itself. A real object is a unit or monad, which need not be durable, and only needs to unify pieces in order to generate new qualities. These qualities are not the same as the real object itself, and hence it lives in a kind of permanent strife with them, which is precisely what we mean by *essence*. This many-featured essence must be there, Leibniz says, or all monads would be exactly the same, which they are not. This real object hides from every view, and in my opinion (though not Husserl's, we will see) its qualities do as well.

Consider now the sphere of intentional objects. You can forget about panpsychism for a moment, since intentionality is much easier to grasp when thinking of the human-centered version of Brentano, or better yet Husserl. When perceiving a tree, there need not be any such tree at all; it is an intentional object, not a real one. As we saw, the intentional object also exists in strife with qualities, and these qualities can shift at every moment without changing our recognition of the same underlying thing. And these qualities are what we call *accidents*. It is often believed that Husserl's intentional object also hides from view, since we never see every side of it at once. As confessed earlier, I thought this way myself for nearly two decades before seeing the mistake. The intentional tree is *always* there before us whenever we recognize it. We live with the same tree no matter how many accidental profiles, adumbrations, *Abschattungen* we see of it. The intentional tree does not hide: it is there right before us, but forever encrusted with accidents. But in fact, "accidents" is the name for the accidental qualities themselves, not for the tension between them and intentional objects. There is a different and even more famous name for this tension, but I will save it as a surprise for a minute from now.

With four poles in the cosmos (two kinds of objects, and two kinds of qualities) we also have four tensions between those poles. You might think that four terms means *six* unique pairs of relations; the reason it does not is because the tensions must always occur between an object-pole and a quality-pole. There is simply no direct interaction at all between real and intentional objects, or real qualities and accidents; these relations must always be mediated, while the tensions themselves are direct and palpable, and hence they serve as the glue of a lonely occasionalist universe that is desperate for any contact at all.[295] Of the four needed tensions, so far we only have two.

We are now close to the climax, assuming that metaphysics has moments of climax. Husserl claims that phenomenology allows us strip away all the accidents of an object and gain adequate intuitive insight into it. Being a good remote disciple of Heidegger, I happen to disagree with Husserl on this point, but it is not so important. What matters is only my *agreement* with him that an intentional object has two kinds of qualities. A house is encrusted by swirling patterns of lights and my own wild swings of mood. If we were somehow able to subtract all such accidents, even though we cannot, what would be left is not a featureless monadic lump. The house will always have some range of ineffable qualities, some *houseness* that make us keep calling it the same though we never succeed in listing these features. If the swirling lights and moods that encrust the house are called accidents, the *real* features of the house can be called *moments*, and I hold that they are built of the same stuff as the qualities of *real* objects, thereby forming a link or ladder between the two layers of the world. The tension between an intentional object and its real moments is what Husserl calls *eidos*, as opposed to the essence, which is a tension between real objects and their moments.

That leaves only one remaining tension, in some ways the easiest of them all, since it lies at the heart of Heidegger's tool-analysis. A real object recedes from view into a subterranean underworld of being, but is translated for us by means of certain present-at-hand features. There is a tension between a *real* object and its *accidental* manifestations. And this is what we call the object's *relations*, since it refers to what happens when one real object

---

[295] It is no longer my position that real and intentional (i.e., sensual) objects cannot directly interact. Such interaction is what I now call "sincerity." — G.H.

becomes manifest to another. The four tensions have now been exhaustively named, and there can be no others, since there are only two kinds of objects and two kinds of qualities. However, the second as well as the fourth have more familiar but more exciting names that I held back as a surprise.

The second tension was between an intentional tree and its surface-effects, its accidents. But if we speak of enduring units that subsist beneath outward changes, this is exactly what we mean by the experience of *time*.

The fourth tension was between the real tree (if there is such a thing) and the accidental qualities through which it is manifested. It is the tension between objects and relations. But this is precisely what we mean in everyday life by *space*.

Space and time are certainly not empty containers, as Newton and Clarke believed. But neither are they systems of relations generated by objects, as Leibniz believed. Instead, they are the tension of identity-in-difference, the strife between real objects and their accidents (space) or intentional objects and their accidents (time). And since under this model both space and time involve *accidents* as one of their poles, in a sense it is true that both are forms of perception, and Kant was right to say so: though only in a Kantianism extended beyond humans to flowers and inanimate things.

Under this model, time and space are not primordial givens of the cosmos, but are derived from the inherent metaphysical tension between objects and their qualities. In childhood we all start out with a few philosophical questions that differ for each of us. Later we move on to new problems through our reading and our professional training, and the arbitrary childhood starting points can be left behind. But in the present case I have the good fortune of returning to my earliest philosophical question of childhood: not time travel, nor whether space has more dimensions than we can see. But rather, why are time and space always spoken of as two utterly unique pieces of cosmic fabric? Why is no other god ever treated as their equal? Could there be others, with all of them branching from a more basic underlying principle? The answer over thirty years later turned out to be "yes," at least to my own satisfaction. Time and space are derived from the permanent tension between objects and their qualities: but so, we have seen, are essence and eidos. Heidegger's fourfold of earth, sky, gods, and mortals had several problems.[296] But one that has rarely been mentioned is that he used them for names of the four *poles*, when what is more interesting are the seismic fault lines between them. All he did was place them on diagrams

---

[296] Martin Heidegger, "Insight Into What Is."

marked with diagonal lines, without ever naming them: except to speak of mirror-plays, weddings, dances, and songs, all of them interchangeable metaphors not correlated with any of the four specific rifts. But we now have a powerful new fourfold structure of *time, space, essence, and eidos*. It remains to be seen what might follow from this structure.

CHAPTER 16
ASYMMETRICAL CAUSATION: INFLUENCE WITHOUT RECOMPENSE[297]

This is an article on metaphysics, but I have tried to make it both clear and interesting to those with little background in philosophy. The article develops a model of the world that is notably *weird*, and therefore potentially fascinating to everyone, just as ghosts and shipwrecks are universally intriguing. My topic is causation, which I hold to be asymmetrical. Though we generally assume that impact is mutual, and that every action has an equal and opposite reaction, these suppositions arise from a narrowly physical concept of causation. As I see it, there is no such thing as reciprocity; influence is never mutual, but always leads in just one direction. This may sound paradoxical, since it is obvious that two people or cities can shape one another, and that symbiosis seems necessary to explain so much of what happens in biology and elsewhere.[298] I do not deny these facts, and even celebrate them. What I deny is that relation is a reciprocal partnership between two equal terms. Instead, mutual influence would merely be a special case of one-way relation in which two objects happen to relate to one another independently. If fire and cotton affect one another, then this happens only through two parallel and disconnected relations: fire-cotton

---

[297] "Asymmetrical Causation" originally appeared in 2010, in a special issue of *Parallax* edited by Myra Hird.
[298] See Lynn Margulis, *Symbiotic Planet*.

and cotton-fire. This entails that every relation must have one active term and one passive term, without implying that one object is always active and the other always passive. Causation is never reciprocal except by accident; influence is always a free gift, without recompense. While this claim may sound counter-intuitive at first, I will try to show that there are sound reasons for it.

Though causation was one of the great themes of classical philosophy, it is almost entirely missing from recent continental thought. Philosophers in these circles have nothing to say about the interaction of cotton and fire or raindrops and wood; they leave these topics to physics, chemistry, or other natural sciences. Since Kant's "Copernican Revolution" in the 1780s, philosophy has generally dealt with only one kind of relation: the interaction between human and world. As a name for this deep philosophical prejudice of our time, Quentin Meillassoux has coined the helpful term "correlationism," which he introduces as follows:

> the central notion of modern philosophy since Kant seems to be that of *correlation*. By "correlation" we mean the idea according to which we only ever have access to the correlation between thinking and being, and never to either term considered apart from the other. We will henceforth call *correlationism* any current of thought which maintains the unsurpassable character of the correlation so defined. Consequently, it becomes possible to say that every philosophy which disavows naïve realism has become a variant of correlationism.[299]

If there is no access to anything outside the human-world correlate, then philosophy is barred from speaking about object-object relations apart from any human observation or interference. When we speak of the collision of two asteroids, then it is *we* who are speaking of this incident, and hence the human observer reappears as an essential half of a correlational pair. There is nothing for philosophy to say about fire burning cotton, but only about the relation between this event and human access to it. As a result, philosophy has retreated ever more deeply into a tiny human citadel, leaving all non-human things to the natural sciences. And even this final fortress of human cognition has come under siege by neurophysiology.

---

[299] Quentin Meillassoux, *After Finitude*, p. 5.

Now, the correlationist position is more complicated than meets the eye, and actually has two distinct implications that have often been wrongly mixed:

1 Human and world must be the two ingredients in any situation we talk about. It is senseless to discuss the collision of two inanimate stones in its own right, for we can only discuss human *access* to that collision.
2 Human and world exist only insofar as they are mutually correlated, and we cannot speak of any mysterious residue lying beneath their relation without bringing it back into the correlate, precisely because we are speaking of it. Human and world are *exhausted* by their mutual interaction.

This second point, when formulated more broadly, is upheld even by certain non-correlationist philosophies. This broader version would simply be a *relationist* philosophy in which things of any sort are exhausted by their relations with all other things. Though the tyranny of the human-world pair would be suspended, entities would merely become involved in countless correlates with all other things, fully used up by these relations. Wind would be nothing but its effects on all the trees and mountains it touches, and neutrons nothing more than their impact on all the tiny particles with which they make contact. In fact, such a relationist philosophy can already be found in the magnificent writings of Alfred North Whitehead and Bruno Latour.

To repeat, correlationism contains two separate aspects, both of which I condemn. First, it holds that human and world must be the two primal ingredients in any meaningful situation. Second, it claims more subtly that "to be" means "to be in relation" and nothing more. Whitehead is a fascinating figure largely because he makes a daring break with Kantian correlationism on the first point, even while reveling in the just-as-lamentable second one. Speaking of his own system, Whitehead says: "in the main the philosophy of organism is a recurrence to *pre-Kantian* modes of thought."[300] With this step, Whitehead gives us a form of *realism* in which things can relate to each other without human surveillance. Instead of the Kantian model of a single lonely gap between human and world (whether it is deplored, bridged, or even denied), we have a philosophy in which all animate and inanimate relations are placed on the same footing. The human relation to a tree has

---

[300] Alfred North Whitehead, *Process and Reality*, p. xi.

no privilege over the relation of a monkey, tornado, or fire to that tree. The more regrettable step is when Whitehead claims that real entities of every sort are defined by their *relations* to one another ("prehensions"), with no cryptic substance or essence held in reserve. This is stated most clearly by Whitehead's great heir Latour, who says that an entity is nothing more than whatever it "modifies, transforms, perturbs, and creates."[301] But such relationism must be refused just as decisively as the human/world correlate. To develop a theory of causation means accepting Whitehead's realism while rejecting his relationism. Or to say it with less terminology, we need a philosophy in which all objects interact with just as much dignity as human and world, but in which entities retain some autonomy in their relations with other things. It is from these two binding constraints that the theory of asymmetrical causation emerges.

The word "causation" makes us think of two physical entities slamming together, and this immediately suggests that they affect one another mutually: even if the difference in size or power is extreme. Newton taught us that even a paper clip or grain of dust exerts gravitational pull on the sun, and not just the mighty sun on these trivial entities. If a brick breaks a window and not the reverse, we still know that the brick loses speed and gains small cuts and divots while passing through the glass. The physical realm seems entirely symmetrical in this respect, and it is the physical realm that we most associate with causation. To find asymmetrical causation in philosophy we must look first to the neo-Platonic tradition, with its series of "emanations" from higher to lower levels of being. This takes on more tangible form among the neo-Platonists of Islam, such as al-Farabi or Avicenna; for them, each of the planetary spheres emanates the next one in turn, from Saturn on down to the moon. The great Egyptian thinker Plotinus invites us to reascend this ladder of beings through thinking and through ethical devotion to the Good, but he never believes that we humans are capable of causal *impact* on the higher levels of being. Similar complaints are sometimes lodged against the form of vertical causation apparently found in Deleuze, where the virtual seems to affect a sterile layer of actuality and not the reverse. The rejoinder by his fans is usually that the actual *does* have retroactive effects on the virtual, rendering the objection a mere cliché. But this misses the point, since the real problem is not whether actual acts on virtual, but whether actual acts on *actual*. The world is packed full of entities, all of them inherently equal *qua* entities — protons, armies,

---

[301] Bruno Latour, *Pandora's Hope*, p. 122.

zebras, ocean waves — and it is their interactions that must be described. And instead of trying to argue that vertical layers of causation can be made symmetrical, the point is to show that the relations between equally dignified actual beings are always asymmetrical, so that the relation between a zebra and any other entity must always flow in just one direction. But the importance of this theme has not yet been shown.

1. Heidegger and Indirect Causation

The problem of causation, like so much else in our time, is best approached through the most powerful thought experiment of twentieth-century philosophy: the tool-analysis of Martin Heidegger. Over the past decade I have often written about this analysis, and through frequent repetition have learned to explain it quickly.[302] In the phenomenology of Edmund Husserl, all intellectual *theories* about things are to be suspended in favor of a careful description of how they appear to consciousness. The honking of a car horn should not be explained by the mechanics of sound waves and the physiology of the ear, but by a patient analysis of the various subtleties in our experience of hearing the horn. Heidegger, who was once Husserl's star pupil and heir, modifies this thesis in a way that is decisive for the present article. Namely, Heidegger observes that for the most part we do not encounter things as explicit phenomena in consciousness. Most of the time things are ignored, or simply taken for granted. Entities ranging from bodily organs to English grammar to the gravitational pull of the earth are relied upon as a tacit background, and only the minutest fringe of entities stands openly before us in consciousness. Normally, things become visible only when they fail in some way, whether it be pains in the liver or a bus that never arrives.

Heidegger's model depicts a twofold world in which silent underground tools go about performing their deeds, with occasional irruptions into conscious presence. The entities in consciousness are present-at-hand, but these are mere surfaces compared with their subterranean reality, which is veiled forever from any total access; there is an absence rumbling behind every presence. One frequent reading of this analysis is that Heidegger showed that "practice comes before theory," that all conscious life emerges from a shadowy background of tools and tacit social usages. Once this is done, it is often claimed further that Heidegger merely repeats what John Dewey

---

[302] See especially Graham Harman, *Tool-Being*.

had already said some decades earlier. But this relies on a superficial reading of the tool-analysis, which actually goes much deeper than the relation between practice and theory. For although it is true that my perception of a fire is a "present-at-hand" oversimplification of the fire in its shadowy being, the same is equally true of my *use* of the fire. Whether I merely stare at the fire, develop a chemical theory of it, or use it as equipment for arson, cooking, or warfare, in all these cases the reality of the fire is converted into a one-dimensional caricature of its cryptic underground reality. There can be no strong distinction between theory and practice, because theory and practice both reduce entities to their dealings with us, and this contradicts Heidegger's thesis that being withdraws from all presence.

As interesting as this result may be, it is insufficiently daring, for it still remains within the correlational circle that has defined most philosophy since Kant. True enough, Heidegger adds the complication (missed by Meillassoux) that the things are not exhausted by their appearance to us.[303] But all the veiling, withdrawing, sheltering, and concealing in Heidegger's works is a hiddenness *from human Dasein*. There is no discussion in Heidegger of causal relations between non-human things, and in this respect he remains a child of the correlationist era. This need not have been the case. We have already seen that in the wake of the tool-analysis, both theory and practice are equally guilty of distorting or translating the withdrawn reality that they encounter. But the same must be true of *all relations whatsoever*, including those between inanimate things. There may well be something special about human perception, imagination, memory, and cognition in comparison with the reality of rocks and dirt, but it is not our special human psychology that makes us unable to exhaust the reality of the things. When fire burns cotton, it does not matter whether the fire is "conscious" of the cotton in some primitive panpsychist manner; all that matters is that the fire never makes contact with the cotton as a whole, but only with its flammability. The rich reality of cotton-being is never drained dry by the

---

[303] It is only half-true when Meillassoux remarks that for Heidegger, "both terms of the appropriation [in *Ereignis*] are originally constituted through their reciprocal relation…." (*After Finitude*, p. 8.) While it is certainly true that for Heidegger both terms only *exist* through their reciprocal relation, to say that both terms are *constituted* through this relation implies that there is nothing in them that lies outside this relation. This wrongly eliminates the gulf that separates Heidegger from both Husserl and Hegel: there is a definite *realist* dimension to Heidegger's thinking that cannot be found in the other two thinkers. In fact, Heidegger really needs to be called a "correlationist realist," a phrase that Meillassoux would never allow. For Heidegger, human and world exist only as a pair, but without exhausting one another.

fire, any more than by human theories of cotton or human practical use of it. There is a certain unreachable autonomy and dignity in the things.

An obvious problem arises from this para-Heideggerian model of the world, for if it were strictly true, then objects would not be able to affect one another at all. Every object would withdraw into a private vacuous cosmos, never coming into contact with anything else. The quick solution might be offered that things touch "part" of each other even if not the whole, but this would be too easy: strictly speaking, objects do not have parts. An object is a unity that cannot be pieced together through a bundling of qualities, and insofar as a thing *can* be articulated into parts, the relation between these parts and the whole is precisely what needs to be explained. The hammer or the tree in their unified underground reality remain untouchable by all other entities. And yet, things obviously do affect one another in a manner that we still do not understand.

Historically speaking, it was occasionalist philosophy that was most sensitive to this problem. In early medieval Islam and early modern France, it was seen that there was a problem of communication between substances. In Basra and Baghdad, there was concern that granting causal agency to any entity aside from God was an act of blasphemy, and hence God must interfere in every least event. Much later in Paris, there were similar concerns about the ability of entities to interact without divine intervention: mind and body for Descartes, but even body and body for Malebranche. Whatever the merits of occasionalism as a theology, or as a form of day-to-day hope for the faithful, it clearly fails as a philosophy: for it gives no explanation of how God can touch entities when no other entity can do this, and hence a retreat is made to the asylum of ignorance. But more generally, it is a bad strategy to allow *any* one entity or kind of entity to break the rule through which all objects withdraw from one another. Those who ridicule the occasionalist God out of socially acceptable atheism are usually the first to let *humans* function as the site of all relations — whether in Hume's "experience" or Kant's categories. The real point is that there should not be a single pampered entity that globally solves the relational problem. If any entities can interact, then all entities should be capable of it. Withdrawal belongs to objects insofar as they are objects, not insofar as they are non-divine.

Thus, the solution to causality needs to be local. If there is some trick that enables relations to occur, that trick should be available to trees and raindrops as much as to humans, angels, or God. There needs to be some way for objects to relate without relating. This might sound impossible, but analogous situations already exist in other spheres. Consider the case of language. Here we are not just able to say something openly or not say it at all: there is also the third option of *alluding* to it, or saying it without quite saying it. This might sound like a fringe observation of little use to philosophy, if not that Aristotle made abundant use of it in his *Rhetoric*, in his concept of the "enthymeme." One can call someone an Olympic victor without quite saying so, simply by saying that he has been three times crowned with a wreath. Midway between the unspoken fact of an Olympic victory and explicit congratulations lies the *allusion* to it.[304] By analogy, perhaps it is possible that objects interact by way of allusion or allure.

2. Fourfold

If done with just the right touch, it is possible to sketch even the most difficult concepts of metaphysics in a few sentences; the miniature masterpieces of Leibniz are proof of this, though he is seldom emulated. Our paradox at the moment is that objects seem unable to relate, but somehow do. And though we still cannot see how it is possible to relate to real objects, which forever withdraw into shadow, it is obvious that we are always in contact with a sensual realm. Human life is what we know best, and that life is not merely frustrated by hidden entities retreating into shadow. Instead, it is populated at all times by various specific entities — people, buildings, animals — though none of them are present in their genuine being. What we encounter are not real objects, but images, which I have also termed *sensual* objects.[305] It is here that the genius of Edmund Husserl tends to be overlooked. Husserl is often criticized for bracketing the outer world and leaving us confined to an internal zone of phenomena. What is usually forgotten is that Husserl adds a remarkable new complication *within* the phenomenal sphere. For although he rejects any distinction between an object lying outside appearance and a sensory content within it, he brings the object/content dualism *within* the zone of phenomena. In other words, the sensual realm is itself split in two. Whenever we encounter a dog or tree, we observe them from various different angles in varying degrees of light, without the dog or tree being destroyed whenever the tiniest details change. A dog as a sensual object is not a bundle of qualities, but the reverse: its palpable qualities are stained with the hues of a unified dog. This unitary

---

[304] Aristotle, *The Art of Rhetoric*.
[305] See Graham Harman, "On Vicarious Causation."

dog-object of the senses must not be confused with the withdrawn dog in its subterranean reality. For in the first place, there may not be such a thing; I may be hallucinating. Second, even if there is a real dog-object silently performing the labor of its being, the unified dog of the senses is perhaps a grotesque distortion of it. And third, even if the sensual dog I encounter were a near-perfect match for the real one, it still vanishes without a trace whenever I fall asleep or cease paying attention. The difference between the two is clear enough. The real dog withdraws from all access; the sensual dog does not withdraw, but is present as long as I expend my energy in taking it seriously. By contrast, the sensual dog is never "hidden." It is present from the start, and simply encrusted with extraneous detail that can be varied within certain broad limits without changing the underlying thing.

There is already an asymmetry here, insofar as the sensual realm is split into an object-pole and a quality-pole: the tree that remains the same through all its shifting profiles versus these specific profiles themselves. But we also find a gateway to a second kind of asymmetry. After all, the "I" who encounters the various monkeys and candles in experience is a *real* object, while all these monkeys and candles are merely sensual objects. Nor is this merely a deviant feature of human or animal psychology. The same sort of landscape will be present for all objects, including flames and cotton balls (assuming that these are real objects and not mere fictional bulks). We have seen that even inanimate objects cannot encounter other real objects, which withdraw from water and stone as much as they do from us. Inanimate objects must encounter a sensual realm, however primitive, for otherwise they would encounter nothing at all. But they cannot encounter mere disembodied, free-floating qualities, since there is no such thing: qualities always radiate outward from a central object to which they are momentarily enslaved. In short, inanimate objects no less than humans are adrift in a world torn apart between objects and qualities. The important point is that real objects make direct contact with sensual *objects*, not just sensual qualities: the sensual dog or tree do not withdraw from all view, and neither do they hide behind a cloud of ornamental sense-data. Instead, they are always an intimate part of my life. And here we have yet another asymmetry: for not only does a real object pair up only with a sensual one, but I touch the sensual object without its touching me in return. What I see is an image of my friend, but this image does not see me: only my friend herself sees me, or rather an image of me. In both cases the friend-image is merely a passive simulacrum that vanishes from reality as soon as one ceases paying attention, while the real friend is a genuine entity to reckon with. And just as two real objects cannot touch each other, the same is true of two sensual objects. The images of fire and cotton are certainly contiguous in my experience, yet they are linked only insofar as both are part of my experience. I am their constant chaperone or mediator. Given that real cannot touch real, nor sensual touch sensual, it follows that all relations must be between only *two* terms. For if there were more than two, we would have multiple objects of the same kind involved in a relation, which is impossible. Note also that we have here a wonderfully perverse modification of a familiar historical theme. For Descartes there was always a problem with how *opposite* things could come into contact: how could a mind touch a body? For us the problem is the reverse: how could two objects of the *same* kind possibly touch? Real objects mutually withdraw, and sensual ones are incapable of initiating contact at all.

Along with the split between object and quality in the sensual realm, an analogous rift can be found in the heart of *real* objects. The real object is unified, but it also has a plurality of specific traits; otherwise, all objects would be the same. As Leibniz puts it in Paragraphs 12 and 13 of the *Monadology*:

> there must be diversity in that which changes, which produces, so
> to speak, the specification and variety of simple substances. This
> diversity must involve a multitude in the unity or in the simple. For,
> since all natural change is produced by degrees, something changes
> and something remains. As a result, there must be a plurality of
> properties and relations in the simple substance, although it has no
> parts.[306]

Thus we now have two kinds of unified objects (real and sensual), and both are in tension with their plurality of specific traits. This yields a fascinating fourfold model that can serve as a base for further inquiry. In the first place we have four poles: real object, real quality, sensual object, and sensual quality. In this group, there are obviously four permutations of object paired with quality, and we have already discussed two of them. The one described by Leibniz is the tension between the unity of a real thing and the plurality of its traits. The classical name for this is *essence*. In Husserl we saw an analogous tension between an enduring sensual dog and its swirling variety of palpable qualities. The best name for this tension is *time*, since

---

[306] G.W. Leibniz, *Selected Philosophical Essays*, p. 214.

what we mean by the experience of time is "change ... produced by degrees, [in which] something changes and something remains," although here we are speaking of the purely sensual realm. But the third tension could already be seen from Heidegger's tool-analysis: it is the strife between real hammers or drills and their sparkling external qualities. The best name for this third tension is *space*. Space is neither an empty container where events unfold, nor a system of relations between things, but the tension between relation *and* non-relation in things.[307] Tokyo is at a distance insofar as I am not currently there, but not so distant that I am without relation to it. Finally, there is the fourth tension between sensual objects and real qualities. Though this may sound like a forced and mutant coupling summoned only in order to fill the final blank space on a grid, it can already be found in Husserl. If we subtract all the transient shimmerings and qualitative noise from our perception of a dog or tree, what remains is not some empty void or "bare particular," but a specific set of essential features that Husserl knows cannot be encountered in a sensual manner. This is what he calls the *eidos* of an object. It differs from essence insofar as essence belongs to a real object, not just a sensual ("intentional") object. This set of four tensions leads us away from the usual monotonous dual monarchy of time and space toward a broader and more interesting theme: a quartet of time, space, essence, and eidos, all resulting from the tension between a specific asymmetrical pair of object and quality.

But here there is still another kind of asymmetry, for we have *two* distinct species of tensions. In one pair we find object and quality already welded together. For instance, in what I have called "time" there is a sensual dog or tree always appearing in the guise of a specific set of qualities, and it takes some sort of work to produce a *fission* of this bond. Now it seems to me that this labor is performed by what we call perception. Merleau-Ponty is perhaps the strongest author on this theme, showing how our perceptual judgments and even motor movements serve to bring a unified object into focus over and above the accidental traits of its manifestation.[308] Perception is not duped by all the details, but presents the sensual object as more or less constant despite the vast differences in surface ornament from one moment to the next. Perhaps a given mailbox is lovely at dawn and ominous in the

---

[307] In this respect, both sides are wrong in the celebrated debate between Samuel Clarke ("space is an empty container") and Leibniz ("space is a system of relations between entities"). See G.W. Lebiniz & Samuel Clarke, *Correspondence*.

[308] Maurice Merleau-Ponty, *Phenomenology of Perception*. This was first brought to my attention by the wonderful book of Alphonso Lingis, *The Imperative*. Lingis creates a unified field theory of Merleau-Ponty's phenomenology of perception and Levinasian ethics.

night, but in both cases we recognize the same mailbox. Perception creates fission between the sensual object and its sensual traits. An analogous event occurs in what I have called "eidos." Here perception is not enough to do the job, for when I encounter the mailbox as a vaguely durable unit amidst transient alterations, I have not yet articulated the separate crucial or eidetic features that belong to it. This work is performed by a different kind of fission that deserves to be called *theory*. It is the task of theory to piece out the various characteristics that belong to an object of our awareness. The objection might be made that theory deals with real objects and not just "objects in the mind." But recall that the objects of theory are merely formalized and oversimplified versions of whatever real objects exist naked in the wild. Hence it is fair indeed to say that theory is a fission that articulates the *real* qualities of *sensual* objects, whereas perception splits off sensual qualities from sensual objects.

In the other two cases a different sort of "tension" is found, in which the tension does not pre-exist the producing of it. Here it is a matter not of fission, but of *fusion* (to stay with the nuclear metaphor). In the tension that I have called "space," there is a gap between the real hammer that never appears and the plethora of sensual traits through which it is announced. The difference here is that the "object" pole of the tension withdraws and is never present, meaning that the two poles cannot exist together in the flesh. The best that can occur is an *allusion* to the absent hammer. Instead of splitting a pre-existent sensual hammer from its sensual qualities or its crucially important but hidden real notes, we have pre-existent sensual hammer-qualities suddenly fused with an ominous hammer-unit that lies beyond our grasp. Those hammer-qualities now seem like the puppets of an invisible principle exceeding all possible access. There are many different ways in which this can happen: from the surprise of failed equipment, to an artwork's appeal to unspeakable depths, to ethical acts of especial fidelity, to the state of being in love. All these experiences have a strong *prima facie* link through the unusually intense emotions they arouse; insofar as all of them *allude* to an ungraspable veiled object, I would group them under the (surprisingly unrelated) noun *allure*.[309] I covered this term in detail in *Guerrilla Metaphysics*, but there I placed it in what I now consider to have been the wrong place on the gridwork of the world.[310] Allure produces a

---

[309] In the originally published version of this article I wote "related noun," since I had wrongly assumed an etymological link between the two terms.
[310] Graham Harman, *Guerrilla Metaphysics*.

fusion of the previously separate real object and the always accessible sensual qualities.

But the fourth tension remains to be discussed: the one I have called "essence," or the tension between a real object and its real qualities or notes. Since this belongs entirely to the subterranean realm of the real, it is the only one of the four tensions in which direct access plays no part at all. A real object exists as a unit, and cares nothing for its articulation into various essential qualities. Its fusion with these qualities is of relevance only to another object that might use them as a means of navigating into the real object's core. And this is precisely what we mean by *causation*: making contact with a real thing by way of contact with some of its pivotal features, since there is no hope of contacting the object as a whole. While this might sound like science fiction, it is already one of the key ideas in the late Scholastic theory of causation found in Francisco Suárez.[311] For Suárez it is impossible for substantial forms to make contact with one another; hence, they must interact by way of accidents. But the word "accidents" for Suárez does not mean the transient adumbrations of sensual things as described by Husserl; instead, it means "the primary qualities, which, it is obvious, are true and proper accidents."[312] Only by fusing the unified real object with one or more of its articulated real qualities does real causation occur.

We began by discussing four basic poles of the world: real objects, real qualities, sensual objects, sensual qualities. By considering the four possible object-quality permutations, we were led to time, space, essence, and eidos as four basic constituents of the cosmos, rather than the usual case of time and space alone. From this it emerged that there are four separate ways to interfere with object-quality relations, whether by splitting an existing bond or creating a new one across an existing gap: perception and theory on the one hand (fission) and allure and causation on the other (fusion). From all of this we saw that the world is riddled with asymmetries of at least the following sorts: 1. Objects exist in tension between their unity and their plurality of traits; 2. Only objects of the opposite kind can touch, never real-real or sensual-sensual; 3. In any pairing of real and sensual object, the real touches the sensual but never the reverse; 4. A real object is the only bridge between two sensual ones; 5. Despite the fourth point, the bridge between two real objects is not a sensual object, but rather *real qualities*, as seen in the point about Suárez and causation; 6. Two basic

---

[311] Francis Suarez, *On Efficient Causality.*
[312] Suarez, *On Efficient Causality*, p. 102.

tensions (time, eidos) already exist and need to be split for anything to happen, while the other two (space, essence) do not yet exist and need to be produced or fused for anything to happen.

3. Causation

The title of this article is "Asymmetrical Causation." This phrase appears in a different light now that causation has been identified as one of *four* kinds of basic breakdowns in the tensions lying in the heart of the world. Separate inquiries would be needed into the remaining three (allure, theory, and perception) and the question of whether they are symmetrical, asymmetrical, or neither. My aim in these concluding pages is to sketch a few of the basic features of causation, which include several surprising elements.

When we think of causation, we not only think of symmetrical impact between causal agents. We also imagine these agents as autonomous entities that briefly enter into contact and alter each other's properties. Two fighter planes collide in midair, destroying both; Hegel, Hölderlin, and Schelling meet in seminary and change each other's lives forever. But such cases are only variants of a broader form of causation found in the relation between part and whole. Various objects combine to form new objects with emergent properties that do not belong to any of the pieces taken in isolation. When objects become pieces of a more complicated object, they create something that not only exceeds its pieces, but that also retains a certain autonomy from any of the adventures in which it becomes involved. Water is *more* than its atoms of hydrogen and oxygen, but water is also *less* than the highly specific relations in which it enters with humans, rocks, or sand; like any object, it withdraws from such relations. Water cannot be reduced downward to tiny particles, but neither can it be reduced *upward* to its relational effects on other things, as Whitehead and Latour both wrongly hold. Any genuine relation creates a new object. Here we must try to resist our usual prejudice that "object" refers only to durable physical solids. All that "object" really means is a genuine thing with a certain autonomy from its own pieces as well as from its external relations with other things. Every relation forms a new object, and every object is built from relations among its pieces, perhaps regressing to infinity. What is normally described as "causation" is really just the special case of *retroactive* causation, in which a total object has backwards effects on its pieces. Consider once more the midair collision of aircraft. What we have here is not a simple case of two airplane-objects smacking together and changing each other's properties.

Instead, the two form a unified collision-entity, however transient, which then has a backward effect on its pieces. The airplanes unite briefly in a single entity, are retroactively transformed by it, and then separate once more.[313]

In this way, the objects found in a causal relation are pieces of a larger object that may or may not have retroactive effects on those pieces. Now, we encountered earlier the rule that real objects can only touch sensual ones (and can only affect other real objects obliquely by way of the sensual), and this entailed that every relation can have only two terms. For if we imagine a relation involving three or more objects, at least two of them would have to be of the same type, whether real or sensual, and this is impossible. In cases where more than two objects seem to be in relation — the Three Stooges, the fifty states — there will either be a slow accretion of pairs of terms, or a central term that relates independently with each of the others. This might sound like an oversimplification. It might sound naïve to say that the assassination of Franz Ferdinand was the "cause" of World War I, since such a chaotic background of military and diplomatic factors must have been in play. But all these noisy factors can cause nothing unless they are organized first into a single powder keg, a single object for which any possible name would admittedly sound ridiculous: "antebellum Europe," perhaps. But the reader may have noticed that there is an even more interesting way of looking at this principle. Insofar as a relation is composed of two pieces that form a new object, it follows that any object has only two immediate pieces, and I have already hinted that these pieces must be asymmetrical. As in the case of Franz Ferdinand, this might sound like an exaggeration: surely, complicated objects such as a car, human body, or atomic bomb have thousands of pieces. But while this may be true in a physical sense, we have seen that the final stage of assembly must only involve two pieces. One piece is real, and the other merely sensual; one is active, and the other merely passive. From these principles it might even be possible to derive a *practical method* for identifying genuine objects amidst systems of relations and for determining their active and passive constituents. Instead of a bare and counterintuitive abstract principle, we might have a valuable drill or shovel for burrowing into the concrete details of reality.

Another odd fact now emerges. When a real object obliquely touches another by way of a sensual object to form a more complicated total object, the real object is "introjected" onto the interior of the total one. It is easier to

---

[313] This idea was first introduced in Graham Harman, "Time, Space, Essence, and Eidos."

see *that* this is true than to know exactly how and why it occurs. Consider an example. If I cast my gaze upon a tree, we have an interaction of the real me and the merely sensual tree, and this can only occur on the interior of a new and not so durable object: a total entity that might be called me-and-pine. This molten inner core of a larger entity is the place where sentience or the perception of sensual objects occur. And here, at least three things should be noted. 1. I do not perceive insofar as I exist, but only insofar as I am a piece of a larger object composed of me and another thing. The same holds good for any object. This shows the ultimate limits of panpsychism, despite my contention that even corn and bricks encounter sensual objects. An object is real insofar as it has real emergent qualities, not insofar as it relates to something else. The existence of an object requires that pieces be in relation in order to create it, but does not require that it enter into further relations as a piece of something larger. A good analogy for this situation would be as follows: each of us has an unbroken line of successfully reproducing ancestors, but this does not entail that all of us will leave offspring of our own. In similar manner the world must be full of countless real but *sleeping* objects that relate to nothing further, and that hence perceive nothing at all. We are tempted to think that conscious life is intrinsic to who we are, but it turns out to be an accidental feature, since we might exist as real objects while experiencing nothing. We are most ourselves not when conscious, but when asleep. 2. Perception seems to integrate many relations at once, since we perceive many different things simultaneously instead of just one. 3. And again, there is an asymmetry on this interior between the real me and the merely sensual tree. And this leads us to the next point.

Given this basic model of causation, it would be possible to develop a *topology* of relations between objects.[314] The simplest case is a chain, in which an object such as a wagon is composed of pieces, those in turn of their own pieces, and so on presumably to infinity. A slight complication is made if we add retroactive causation to the picture, as when the founding members of a band are transformed by their membership in it. The root form of causation, we have seen, is an asymmetrical link between a real object and another real object grazed only obliquely by way of the sensual realm. Hence another set of complications can be added if we consider two objects as relating to each other simultaneously but independently: I encounter the sensual tree, and the tree may encounter a sensual caricature of me. *Reinforcement* seems like

---

[314] This idea was suggested to me by the system of tetrads in Marshall and Eric McLuhan's *Laws of Media.*

a good name for the situation in which two objects mutually confront one another, and most of the relations that draw our attention (whether human or physical) seem to be of this kind. But rather than always being a case of two objects in close mutual contact, reinforcement may take the form of a longer loop or ring of objects: A makes contact with B, B with C, C with D, and D with A, or any number of such terms. Finally, there is the fact that most objects will not relate to only one object, but will serve as *clusters* of relations with a multitude of other entities. Humans are obviously clusters for instance, since we relate to countless things simultaneously. But I do not form a single super-entity with all the objects to which I relate, since we have seen that an object always has just two pieces. Hence, my relations with numerous different objects remain independent of one another, and I function as a cluster for a number of different relations.

In this article I have tried to give some idea of the numerous asymmetries at work in the structure of objects. There is a basic imbalance between objects and their qualities, and given that there are two kinds of each of these, what resulted was a fourfold system of space, time, essence, and eidos. There is also the more basic asymmetry that a real object only touches a sensual one, and if it touches another real obliquely, the same never happens in return. The most important asymmetry of all still remains on the board: how does a real object cease merely being fascinated by a sensual one, and break through this to make some sort of contact, however oblique, with another real one? Only the answer to this question will give us a clear understanding of the manner in which influence is a pure gift from elsewhere, without recompense.

CHAPTER 17
ON VICARIOUS CAUSATION[315]

This article gives the outlines of a realist metaphysics, despite the continuing unpopularity of both realism and metaphysics in the continental tradition. Instead of the dull realism of mindless atoms and billiard balls that is usually invoked to spoil all the fun in philosophy, I will defend a *weird realism*. This model features a world packed full of ghostly real objects signaling to each other from inscrutable depths, unable to touch one another fully. There is an obvious link here with the tradition known as occasionalism, the first to suggest that direct interaction between entities is impossible. There is another clear link with the related skeptical tradition, which also envisions objects as lying side by side without direct connection, though here the objects in question are human perceptions rather than independent real things. Yet this article abandons the solution of a lone magical super-entity responsible for all relations (whether God for Malebranche and his Iraqi forerunners, or the human mind for skeptics, empiricists, and idealists) in favor of a vicarious causation deployed locally in every portion of the cosmos. While its strangeness may lead to puzzlement more than resistance, vicarious causation is not some autistic moonbeam entering the window of an asylum. Instead, it is both the launching pad for a rigorous post-

---

[315] "On Vicarious Causation," my most widely read article, was originally published in 2007 in the journal *Collapse*. It had previously been solicited for *Radical Philosophy* by Peter Hallward, but was then rejected by the editorial committee of that journal.

Heideggerian philosophy, and a fitting revival of the venerable problem of communication between substances.

The phrase "vicarious causation" consists of two parts, both of them cutting against the grain of present-day philosophy.[316] Causality has rarely been a genuine topic of inquiry since the seventeenth century. The supposed great debate over causation between skeptics and transcendental philosophers is at best a yes-or-no dispute as to whether causal necessity exists, and in practice is just an argument over whether it can be known. What has been lacking is active discussion of the very nature of causality. This is now taken to be obvious: one object exerts force over another and makes it change physical position or some of its features. No one sees any way to speak about the interaction of fire and cotton, since philosophy remains preoccupied with the sole relational gap between humans and the world — even if only to deny such a gap. Inanimate relations have been abandoned to laboratory research, where their metaphysical character is openly dismissed. To revive causation in philosophy means to reject the dominance of Kant's Copernican Revolution and its single lonely rift between people and everything else. Although I will claim that real objects do exist beyond human sensual access to them, this should not be confused with Kant's distinction between phenomena and noumena. Whereas Kant's distinction is something endured by humans alone, I hold that one billiard ball hides from another no less than the ball-in-itself hides from humans. When a hailstorm smashes vineyards or sends waves through a pond, these relations are just as worthy of philosophy as the unceasing dispute over the chasm or non-chasm between being and thought. Neither Kant, nor Hegel, nor their more up-to-date cousins have anything to say about the collision of balls-in-themselves. In the past century, the doctrine of Parmenides that being and thought are the same has been implied by Husserl, stated explicitly by Heidegger, and restated quite emphatically by Badiou. But this equation of being and thought must be rejected, since it leaves us stranded in a human-world coupling that merely reenacts the breakthroughs of yesteryear. Reviving the problem of causation means to break free of the epistemological deadlock and reawaken the metaphysical question of what relation means. Along with causation there is also the "vicarious" part of the phrase, which indicates that relations never directly encounter the autonomous reality of their components. After thousands of years, "substance" is still the best name for such reality. The widespread

---

[316] The term was first introduced in Graham Harman, *Guerrilla Metaphysics*.

resistance to substance is nothing more than revulsion at certain inadequate *models* of substance, and such models can be replaced. Along with substance, the term "objects" will be used to refer to autonomous realities of any kind, with the added advantage that this term also makes room for the temporary and artificial objects too often excluded from the ranks of substance.

Since this article rejects any privilege of human access to the world, and puts the affairs of human consciousness on exactly the same footing as the duel between canaries, microbes, earthquakes, atoms, and tar, it may sound like a defense of scientific naturalism that reduces everything to physical events. But the term "vicarious" is designed to oppose all forms of naturalism, by indicating that we still have no idea how physical relations (or any other kind) are possible in the first place. For as I will contend, objects hide from one another endlessly, and inflict their mutual blows only through some vicar or intermediary. For several centuries, philosophy has been on the defensive against the natural sciences, and now occupies a point of lower social prestige and, surprisingly, narrower subject matter. A brief glance at history shows that this was not always the case. To resume the offensive, we need only reverse the longstanding trends of renouncing all speculation on objects and volunteering for curfew in an ever-tinier ghetto of solely human realities: language, texts, political power. Vicarious causation frees us from such imprisonment by returning us to the heart of the inanimate world, whether natural or artificial. The uniqueness of philosophy is secured, not by walling off a zone of precious human reality that science cannot touch, but by dealing with the same world as the various sciences but in a different manner. In classical terms, we must speculate once more on causation while forbidding its reduction to *efficient* causation. Vicarious causation, of which science so far knows nothing, is closer to what is called *formal* cause. To say that formal cause operates vicariously means that forms do not touch one another directly, but somehow melt, fuse, and decompress in a shared common space from which all are partly absent. My claim is that two entities influence one another only by meeting on the interior of a third, where they exist side by side until something happens that allows them to interact. In this sense, the theory of vicarious causation is a theory of the molten inner core of objects — a sort of plate tectonics of ontology.

1. Two Kinds of Objects
While the phenomenological movement of Husserl and Heidegger did too little to overcome the idealism of the previous cluster of great philosophers,

they and their descendants often show a novel concern with specific, concrete entities. Mailboxes, hammers, cigarettes, and silk garments are at home in phenomenology in a way that was never true for the earlier classic figures of German thought. Even if Husserl and Heidegger remain too attached to human being as the centerpiece of philosophy, both silently raise objects to the starring role, each in a different manner. While Husserl bases his system on intentional or ideal objects (which I will rechristen *sensual* objects) Heidegger restores real objects to philosophy through his famous tool-analysis. It is seldom realized that these two types of objects are both different and complementary. The interplay between real and sensual objects, if taken seriously, provides ontology with a radical new theme.

In the tool-analysis of Heidegger, which fascinates his opponents no less than his allies, we find perhaps the most enduring insight of twentieth-century philosophy. Our primary relationship with objects lies not in perceiving or theorizing about them, but simply in relying on them for some ulterior purpose. This first step is useful enough, but misses the essence of Heidegger's breakthrough, which even he never quite grasps. If we remain at this stage, it might seem that Heidegger merely claims that all theory is grounded in practice, that we need to have an everyday relationship with leopards or acids before staring at them or developing a science of them. But notice that even our practical relation to these objects fails to grasp them fully. The tribesman who dwells with the godlike leopard, or the prisoner who writes secret messages in lemon juice, are no closer to the dark reality of these objects than the scientist who gazes at them. If perception and theory both objectify entities, reducing them to one-sided caricatures of their thundering depths, the same is true of practical manipulation. We distort when we see, and distort when we use. Nor is the sin of caricature a merely human vice. Dogs do not make contact with the full reality of bones, and neither do locusts with cornstalks, viruses with cells, rocks with windows, nor planets with moons. It is not human consciousness that distorts the reality of things, but relationality *per se*. Heidegger's tool-analysis unwittingly gives us the deepest possible account of the classical rift between substance and relation. When something is "present-at-hand," this simply means it is registered through some sort of relation: whether perceptual, theoretical, practical, or purely causal. To be "ready-to-hand" does not mean to be useful in the narrow sense, but to withdraw into subterranean depths that other objects rely on despite never fully probing or sounding them.[317] When objects fail us, we experience a negation of their accessible contours and become aware that the object exceeds all that we grasp of it. This predicament gives rise to the theme of vicarious causation. For if objects withdraw from relations, we may wonder how they make contact at all. Heidegger's tool-analysis opens the gates on a strange new realism in which entities flicker vaguely from the ocean floor: unable to make contact, yet somehow managing to do so anyway.

A different sort of object is the basis for Husserl's philosophy. Despite complicated efforts to save Husserl from charges of idealism, he does confine philosophy to a space of purest ideality. Phenomenology cannot speak of how one object breaks or burns another, since this would deliver the world to the power of scientific explanation, which employs nothing but naturalistic theories. For Husserl, the only rigorous method is to describe how the world is given to consciousness prior to all such theories. Philosophy becomes the study of phenomena, not real objects. But phenomena are objects nonetheless: in a new, ideal sense. For what we experience in perception is not disembodied qualities, as the empiricists hold; instead, we encounter a world broken up into chunks. Trees, mailboxes, airplanes, and skeletons lie spread before us, each of them inducing specific moods and sparkling with various subordinate qualities. Since we are speaking solely of the phenomenal realm, it does not matter if these things are hallucinations; even delusions perform the genuine labor of organizing our perception into discrete zones. Note already that sensual objects have a different fate from real ones. Whereas real zebras and lighthouses withdraw from direct access, their sensual counterparts do not withdraw in the least. For here is a zebra before me. Admittedly, I can view it from an infinite variety of angles and distances, in sadness and exultation, at sunset or amidst driving rain, and none of these moments exhaust all possible perceptions of it. Nonetheless, the zebra is already there for me as a whole in all its partial profiles; I see right through them and look to it as a unified object. Although some specific visual or conceptual profile of the zebra is needed for us to experience it, the unified sensual zebra lies at a deeper level of perception than these transient, mutable images. Each sensual profile is encrusted onto the unified zebra-object like a patina of brine. Whereas real objects withdraw, sensual objects lie directly before us, frosted over with a swirling, superfluous outer shell. But this difference seems to give sensual objects the opposite causal status of

---

[317] For a detailed interpretation of Heidegger's tool-analysis see my first book, Graham Harman, *Tool-Being*.

real ones. Given that real objects never touch directly, their causal relations can only be vicarious. But sensual objects, far from being withdrawn, exist side by side in the same perceptual space from the outset, since we encounter numerous phenomena simultaneously. This presents the contrary problem to vicarious causation: namely, why do all the phenomena not instantly fuse together into a single lump? There must be some unknown principle of blockage between them. If real objects require vicarious causation, sensual objects endure a buffered causation in which their interactions are partly dammed or stunted.

The situation is perplexing, but the general path of this article is already clear. Real objects withdraw into obscure cavernous underworlds, deprived of causal links. Sensual objects, by contrast, are so inclined to interact with their neighbors that we wonder why they fail to do so at every instant. In other words, the only place in the cosmos where interactions occur is the sensual, phenomenal realm. Against philosophies that regard the surface as formal or sterile and grant causal power only to shadowy depths, we must defend the opposite view: discrete, autonomous form lies only in the depths, while dramatic power and interaction float along the surface. All relationships are superficial. For this reason, we must discover how real objects poke through into the phenomenal realm, the only place where one relates to another. The various eruptions of real objects into sensuality lie side by side, buffered from immediate interaction. Something must happen on the sensual plane to allow them to make contact, just as corrosive chemicals lie side by side in a bomb — separated by a thin film eaten away over time, or ruptured by distant signals.

2. A Jigsaw Puzzle

It is well known that Husserl emphasizes the intentionality of consciousness. We are always conscious of *something*, always focused on a particular house, pine tree, beach ball, or star, and indeed on many such objects at once. It is not widely known that Husserl also stumbles across the fateful paradox that intentionality is both one and two. For in a first sense, my encounter with a pine tree is a unified relation; we can speak of the encounter as a whole, and this whole resists exhaustive description. But in another sense, I clearly do not fuse with the tree in a single massive lump; it remains distinct from me in the perception. This gives the strange result that in my intention of the tree, we both inhabit the interior of the total intentional relation. This seemingly dry observation by Husserl has not sparked much interest in his readers.

Even so, if combined with Heidegger's insight into the withdrawal of real objects behind all relations, it provides all the pieces of a new philosophy.

To repeat, the pine tree and I are separate objects residing on the interior of a third: the intention as a whole. But there is a fascinating asymmetry between the members of this trio. We cannot fail to notice that of the two objects living in the core of the third, I am a real object but the pine tree merely a sensual one. The I sincerely absorbed in the things it perceives is not the I as seen by others, but rather the real I, since my life actually consists at this moment in being occupied by these phenomena, not in being a sensual object for the gaze of others or even for myself. By contrast, the real pine tree does not inhabit the intention, since the real tree (assuming there is such a thing) lies outside any relation to it, withdrawing into depths never entered by outsiders. Finally, the intention as a whole must be classed as a real object rather than a sensual one: for even if my intention of the tree is the most depraved hallucination, the intention itself is in fact underway, quite apart from whether it relates to anything outside. To summarize, we have a real intention whose core is inhabited by a real me and a sensual pine tree. In addition, there is also a withdrawn real tree (or something that we mistake for one) lying outside the intention, but able to affect it along avenues still unknown. Finally, the sensual tree never appears in the form of a naked essence, but is always encrusted with various sorts of noise. Elsewhere I have called it "black noise," to emphasize that it is highly structured, not the sort of formless chaos suggested by the "white noise" of television and radio.[318] Black noise initially seems to come in three varieties. First, the sensual tree has pivotal or essential qualities that must always belong to it under penalty of the intentional agent no longer considering it the same thing. Second, the tree has accidental features shimmering along its surface from moment to moment, not affecting our identification of it as one and the same. Finally, the pine tree stands in relation to countless peripheral objects that inhabit the same intention (neighboring trees, mountains, deer, rabbits, clouds of mist).

We should also note five distinct sorts of relations between all these objects:

1 *Containment.* The intention as a whole contains both the real me and the sensual tree.

---

[318] Harman, *Guerrilla Metaphysics*, pp. 183 ff.

2 *Contiguity*. The various sensual objects in an intention lie side by side, not affecting one another. Only sometimes do they fuse or mix. Within certain limits, any sensual object's neighbors can be shuffled and varied without damaging the identity of that object, as when drifting mists do not interfere with my focus on the tree.

3 *Sincerity*. At this very moment I am absorbed or fascinated by the sensual tree, even if my attitude toward it is utterly cynical and manipulative. I do not contain the sensual tree, because this is the role of the unified intention that provides the theater of my sincerity without being identical to it. And I am not merely contiguous with the tree, because it does in fact touch me in such a way as to fill up my life. I expend my energy in taking the tree seriously, whereas the sensual tree cannot return the favor, since it is nothing real.

4 *Connection*. The intention as a whole must arise from a real connection of real objects, albeit an indirect connection. After all, the other possible combinations yield entirely different results. Two sensual objects merely sit side by side. And my sincere absorption with trees or windmills is merely the interior of the intention, not the unified intention itself. Hence, a real object itself is born from the connection of other real objects, through unknown vicarious means.

5 *No relation at all*. This is the usual state of things, as denied only by fanatical holists, those extremists who pass out mirrors like candy to every object that stumbles down the street. Real objects are incapable of direct contact, and indeed many have no effect on one another at all. Even the law of universal gravitation only applies among a narrow class of physical objects, and even then concerns a limited portion of their reality. And in a different case, the sensual tree has no relation to me at all, even though I am sincerely absorbed by it. The oxygen I breathe comes from the real tree, not from my perception of it. The sensual tree is a phantasm surviving only at the core of some intention, and takes up no independent relations even with its contiguous phantoms. They are only related vicariously, through me, insofar as I am sincerely absorbed with both.

The objects populating the world always stand to each other in one of these five relations. In *Guerrilla Metaphysics*, I suggested that causation is always vicarious, asymmetrical, and buffered. "Vicarious" means that objects confront one another only by proxy, through sensual profiles found only on the interior of some other entity. "Asymmetrical" means that the initial confrontation always unfolds between a real object and a sensual one. And "buffered" means that I do not fuse into the tree, nor the tree into its sensual neighbors, since all are held at bay through unknown firewalls sustaining the privacy of each. From the asymmetrical and buffered inner life of an object, vicarious connections arise occasionally (in both senses of the term), giving birth to new objects with their own interior spaces. There is a constant meeting of asymmetrical partners on the interior of some unified object: a real one meeting the sensual vicar or deputy of another. Causation itself occurs when these obstacles are somehow broken or suspended. In seventeenth-century terms, the side-by-side proximity of real and sensual objects is merely the *occasion* for a connection between a real object inside the intention and another real object lying outside it. In this way, shafts or freight tunnels are constructed between objects that otherwise remain quarantined in private vacuums.

We now have five kinds of objects (real intention, real I, real tree, sensual tree, sensual noise) and five different types of relations (containment, contiguity, sincerity, connection, and none). Furthermore, we also have three adjectives for what unfolds inside an object (vicarious, asymmetrical, buffered) and three different kinds of noise surrounding a sensual object (qualities, accidents, relations). While this may not be an exhaustive census of reality, and may eventually need polishing or expansion, it offers a good initial model whose very strictness will help smoke out those elements it might have overlooked. What remains to be seen is how these elements interact, how one type of relation transforms into another, how new real objects paradoxically arise from the interaction between real objects and sensual ones, and even how sensual objects manage to couple and uncouple like spectral rail cars. These sorts of problems are the subject matter of object-oriented philosophy: the inevitable mutant offspring of Husserl's intentional objects and Heidegger's real ones. In turn, these are only the present-day heirs of Hume's contiguous impressions and ideas (Husserl) and the disconnected objects of Malebranche and his Ash'arite predecessors (Heidegger).

The problem of philosophy now resembles a jigsaw puzzle. We have detected the pieces as carefully as possible, and none seem to be blatantly missing. We also have a picture of what the ultimate solution should look like: the world as we know it, with its various objects and interactions. Unlike jigsaw puzzles, this one unfolds in at least three dimensions, ceaselessly changing from moment to moment. But like such puzzles, instead of mimicking the original image, it is riddled with fissures and strategic overlaps that place everything in a new light. Like five-year-olds faced with a massive thousand-piece puzzle, our greatest danger lies in becoming discouraged. But whereas frustrated children angrily throw their pieces to the floor and change activities, we remain trapped in our puzzle from the start, since it is the very enigma of our world. Philosophers can escape it only through insanity, or with the aid of rope or a revolver.

3. Ontology and Metaphysics

Beginners in philosophy often ask the exact difference between ontology and metaphysics. In fact, there is no consistent distinction, since each philosopher redefines these terms to suit individual purposes. For Heidegger, ontology is the account of how being is revealed to humans, while metaphysics remains a term of insult for philosophies that explain all beings in terms of some privileged entity. For Levinas, ontology belongs to the global war between beings, while metaphysics speaks of the infinite otherness that lies beyond such conflict. For my own part, I have generally used these terms interchangeably for a realist position opposed to all human-centered philosophies; at times such flexibility remains useful, as in the opening section of this article. Yet I would also like to propose a more exact difference between them, one not unrelated to their classical distinction. Henceforth, let "ontology" refer to a description of the basic structural features shared by all objects, and let "metaphysics" signify the discussion of the fundamental traits of specific types of entities. In this sense, the aforementioned puzzle-pieces belong solely to ontology, since no object is exempt from their rule. These include the basic opposition between real and sensual objects, the five types of relation between them, and the bondage of sensual objects to their various qualities, accidents, and relations. Time and space also belong to ontology, since even eternal and non-spatial objects elude only the narrowly physical spatio-temporal realm, and by no means escape time and space in a broader sense. The question of universals also seems to be a global theme belonging to ontology as a whole, and there may be others. As for metaphysics, which walls off and analyzes the internal organs of any specific kind of entity, the most obvious possible topics include human being, language, artworks, and even God. Any type of object distinct from others, however hazy the boundaries may be, can become the subject of a metaphysics. There could be a metaphysics of artworks, the psyche, and language, and even of restaurants, mammals, planets, teahouses, and sports leagues. Insofar as philosophy clearly differs from activities such as singing and gambling, there could also be a metaphysics of philosophy itself, unlocking the crucial features of this discipline, whatever its numerous variations and degenerate sophistical forms.

The distinction between ontology and metaphysics is proposed here for a specific reason. Along with real objects, we have also described sensual objects, which exist only on the interior of some intentional whole. Yet intentionality is regarded by almost everyone as a narrowly human feature. If this depiction were correct, sensual objects would be confined to a metaphysics of human perception, with no place in an ontology designed to address plastic and sand dunes no less than humans. This confinement of sensuality to the human kingdom must be refused. Intentionality is not a special human property at all, but an ontological feature of objects in general.[319] For our purposes, intentionality means sincerity. My life is absorbed at any moment with a limited range of thoughts and perceptions. While it is tempting to confuse such absorption with "conscious awareness," we need to focus on the most rudimentary meaning of sincerity: contact between a real object and a sensual one. For instance, I may be sincerely absorbed in contemplating glass marbles arranged on the surface of a table. This is my sincerity at the moment, since I forego other possibilities of greater and lesser import to witness this austere, Zen-like spectacle. But note that the glass marbles themselves are sincerely absorbed in sitting on the table, rather than melting in a furnace or hurtling through a mineshaft. (Though they may not be "marbles" for anyone but humans or playful kittens, we need a nickname for the united object that we draw into our games.) The question for us is not the panpsychist query of whether these marbles have some sort of rudimentary thinking and feeling capacities, but whether they as real objects encounter the table-surface as a sensual one.

The answer is yes. We must ignore the usual connotations of sensuality and fix our gaze on a more primitive layer of the cosmos. It is clear that the marbles must stand somewhere in reality, in contact with certain other entities that stabilize them briefly in one state or another. The entities they confront cannot be real objects, since these withdraw from contact. Nor can the marbles run up against free-floating sensual qualities, for in the sensual realm qualities are always attached to objects. Only one alternative remains: the marbles are sincerely absorbed with sensual objects. This indirect argument becomes more persuasive if we examine the landscape

---

[319] The idea that physical relations also have an intentional structure is a minority view, but by no means my own invention. See for instance George Molnar's fascinating book *Powers*, pp. 60 ff.

inhabited by the marbles, which turns out to share the basic structural features of human intentionality. First, notice that these marbles are perfectly capable of distinguishing between the table and the contiguous *relational* environment, even if not in the panpsychist sense of a primitive judging ability. At present the marbles sit on the table, but are otherwise surrounded by air; hence, this air is contiguous with the tabletop in the life of each marble. But if we now carefully frame the marbles with bookends or melted wax, the table itself remains the same intentional object, unaffected by our eccentric manipulations. Second, the marble confronts the tabletop quite apart from its *accidental* coldness and slickness, though it probably registers these features in some way as well. If we heat the tabletop, or render its surface sticky or granulated by pouring different materials nearby, the table as an intentional object still remains the same. The final question is whether the marbles can make a distinction between the table and its more essential *qualities*, such as its hardness, levelness, solidity, and lack of perforation. Even humans can only make this distinction between objects and their qualities in very special cases; since I will soon describe these cases under the heading of "allure," we should wait to ask whether glass marbles are able to follow suit. What is already evident is that all real objects inhabit a landscape of sensual ones, a playground whose fluctuations enable new real connections to arise. Some of these fluctuations are a mere domestic drama, while others provoke new relations with the outside. But whatever is special about human cognition belongs at a more complicated level of philosophy than these sensual objects, though it must be expressible in terms of them.

Elsewhere I have used the phrase "every relation is itself an object," and still regard this statement as true. But since this article has redefined relations to include containment, sincerity, and contiguity, the slogan must be reworded as follows: "every *connection* is itself an object." The intentional act's containment of me does not make the two of us into a new object, and neither (for the most part) do two or three nearby perceptions of cars make a unified object. But two vicariously linked real objects do form a new object, since they generate a new internal space. When two objects give rise to a new one through vicarious connection, they create a new unified whole that is not only inexhaustible from the outside, but also filled on the inside with a real object sincerely absorbed with sensual ones. And just as every connection is an object, every object is the result of a connection. The history of this connection remains inscribed in its heart, where its components are locked in a sort of kaleidoscopic duel. But connections occur only between two real objects, not any other combination. This entails that my relation to the sensual pine tree is not itself an object, but simply a face-off between two objects of utterly different kinds. Hence, although intentionality seems to be a relation between me and the sensual pine tree, this is merely its interior. The intention itself results only from the unexplained vicarious fusion of me with the real pine tree, or with whatever engenders my deluded belief that I perceive one.

To repeat, my relation with the sensual pine tree is not a full-blown connection, but only a sincerity. This sincerity can indeed be converted into an object, as happens in the analysis of our own intentions or someone else's. When I analyze my relation to the sensual tree, I have converted that relation into an object for the first time. It has become a real object insofar as its exact nature recedes from view, inexhaustible no matter how many analyses I perform. We now face a merely sensual apparition of the original sincere relation, which withdraws from analysis just as hammers withdraw from handling. A second, more tedious observer might now decide to perform an analysis of my analysis, thereby converting it into an object whose nature can never be grasped, and so on to infinity. But note that this is not an infinite regress: all of these objects are not contained infinitely in the situation from the outset, but are sequentially produced *ad nauseam* by an increasingly twisted and pedantic series of analysts. Back in stage one, even my relation to the sensual pine tree is not a real object, but simply a sincere relation of two distinct elements inside a larger one. Unified objects can be molded at will from that clay-like interior. This already shows a way for sincere relations to be converted into real connections. Whether it is the only such way, and whether this method belongs to humans alone, is still unclear.

Another point is in order before passing to the final section. To say that every object is located on the sensual molten core of another object undermines some of the key assumptions of Heidegger. For him, human being partially transcends other beings, rising to glimpse them against a background of nothingness. But the interior of an object leaves no room for transcendence or even distance: a horse seen in a valley several miles away still touches me directly insofar as I witness it. Distance lies not in the sphere of perception, where everything brushes me directly with greater or lesser intensity, but only between the mutually exclusive real objects that lie beyond perception. We do not step beyond anything, but are more like moles tunneling through wind, water, and ideas no less than through speech-acts, texts, anxiety, wonder, and dirt. We do not transcend the world, but only descend or burrow towards its numberless underground cavities — each a sort of kaleidoscope where sensual objects spread their colors and their wings. There is neither finitude nor negativity in the heart of objects. And each case of human mortality is just one tragic event among trillions of others, including the deaths of house pets, insects, stars, civilizations, and poorly managed shops or universities. The Heidegger-Blanchot death cult must be expelled from ontology, and perhaps even from metaphysics.

4. Allure and Causation

Some may find it disturbing to think of the world as made up of vacuum-sealed objects, each with a sparkling phenomenal interior invaded only now and then by neighboring objects. A more likely problem, however, is indifference. There seems to be no need for such a weird vision of reality, since it is easy enough to think of the world as made of brute pieces of inescapable solid matter: "primary qualities" supporting a series of more dashing, volatile human projections. In my view, however, Heidegger has rendered this picture of the world obsolete. Though his tool-analysis aims to describe only the withdrawal of objects behind explicit human awareness, practical activity is equally unable to exhaust the depth of objects, and even causal relations fail to let them encounter one another in full.[320] Finally, even sheer physical presence in space is a concept shaken to the core by the tool-analysis: after all, to occupy a spatial position is to take up relations, and however objects might occupy space, their reality is something deeper. The world is neither a gray matrix of objective elements, nor raw material for a sexy human drama projected onto gravel and sludge. Instead, it is filled with points of reality woven together only loosely: an archipelago of oracles or bombs that explode from concealment only to generate new sequestered temples. The language here is metaphorical because it must be. While analytic philosophy takes pride in never suggesting more than it explicitly states, this procedure does no justice to a world where objects are always more than they literally state. Those who care only to generate arguments almost never generate objects. New objects, however, are the sole and sacred fruit of writers, thinkers, politicians, travelers, lovers, and inventors.

Along with the distinction between real and sensual objects, there were five possible kinds of relations between them: containment, contiguity, sincerity, connection, and none. Our goal is to shed some light on the origin of *connection*, the one relation of the five that seems most troubling

---

[320] See also Harman, *Tool-Being*, throughout.

for a theory of ghostly, receding objects. A connection simply exists or fails to exist; it is a purely binary question. Furthermore, connection must be vicarious, since one purely naked object always recedes from another. An object simply exists, and this existence can never fully be mirrored in the heart of another. What we seek is some fertile soil of relation from which connections surge up into existence: a type of relation able to serve as the engine of change in the cosmos. "Connection" itself cannot provide the solution, since this is precisely what we are trying to explain; if two objects are connected, then the labor we wish to observe is already complete. The option "no relation at all" also fails to help, since if things are unrelated then they will remain so, as long as the intermediary we seek is lacking. "Containment" is of no assistance either. Here too we have a merely binary question: either the sensual pine tree and I are together inside a given intention, or we are not. Finally, "contiguity" does not give us what we need: at best, the shifting play of sensual objects redistributes the boundaries between them, but cannot lead to real changes outside their molten internal homeland. The only remaining option is "sincerity." This must be the site of change in the world. A real object resides in the core of an intention, pressed up against numerous sensual ones. Somehow, it pierces their colored mists and connects with a real object already in the vicinity but buffered from direct contact. If light can be shed on this mechanism, the nature of the other four types of relation may be clarified as well.

It all comes down to the dynamics of sincerity, whether of a human or any other real object. Sincerity contends with sensual objects that are defined by their qualities and shrouded with peripheral accidents and relations. What we seek is the manner in which sincere relation with a sensual object is transformed into direct connection with a real one. The coupling and uncoupling of real and sensual objects is now our central theme. We know that a sensual object is detachable from its accidents and relations. The interesting question is whether it can also be detached from its qualities, which seem to belong to it more intimately. By qualities I mean the essential qualities, without which we would regard an object as no longer the same thing. Remember, there is no hand-wringing crisis of objectivity here, since we are speaking of qualities that belong not to the essence of a real object, but only to the sensual things that command our attention — a realm where we ourselves are the highest judge in the land. Now, it might be imagined that we could liberate the qualities of the marbles by overtly discovering and listing all the crucial features that the marbles cannot do without. This was the great hope of Husserl's method of eidetic variation. But the effect of this procedure is superficial, and does not grasp the sensual marbles in their essence. Notice that even as our analysis of these objects proceeds, we continue to take them seriously as units, even if we brilliantly slice them into thousands of separate features. Even in the case of a sensual object, the essential qualities cannot be stated or analyzed without becoming something like accidents: free-floating traits artificially detached from the sensual object as a whole. Our sincerity is not really concerned with such a list of detached features, as Husserl realizes when he grants privilege to unified sensual objects over their myriad facets. The unity of such objects even indicates that there is just one quality at issue: this marble-essence, this pine-essence. The unified quality of the thing is not noise at all, but is *the sensual object itself*. Concerning Aristotle's question as to whether a thing is identical with its essence, the answer for sensual objects is yes. Although qualities were described as a form of noise earlier in this article, this is true only insofar as they veer off toward the status of accidents, when broken free and itemized separately. But the existence of a unified quality of things means that the sensual realm is already home to a certain "I know not what" that makes the marble a steady focus of my attention. Unlike the followers of Locke, we do not say *je ne sais quoi* in a spirit of gentle mockery, but as a true statement about sensual objects. The sensual thing itself has a unified and basically ineffable effect on us, one that cannot be reduced to any list of traits. But if such listing of traits does not sever a thing from its quality, there may be another way for this to happen. We have also seen that vicarious causation — the enchanted unicorn we seek — requires contact with the essential qualities of a thing without contact with the thing as a whole. In this way, discovery of how the sensual object splits from its quality may be a stepping-stone toward discovering an analogous event among real objects.

The separation between a sensual object and its quality can be termed "allure."[321] This word pinpoints the bewitching emotional effect that often accompanies this event for humans, and also suggests the (surprisingly unrelated) term "allusion," since allure merely alludes to the object without making its inner life directly present.[322] In the sensual realm, we encounter objects encrusted with noisy accidents and relations. We may also be explicitly aware of some of their essential qualities, though any such list

---

[321] See Harman, *Guerrilla Metaphysics*, pp. 142 ff.

[322] The original published version of this article had "related" in place of "(surprisingly unrelated)." As mentioned in an earlier footnote, I only realized later that there seems to be no etymological connection between the two terms.

merely transforms the qualities into something accident-like, and fails to give us the unified bond that makes the sensual thing a single thing. Instead, we need an experience in which the sensual object is severed from its joint unified quality, since this will point for the first time to a real object lying beneath the single quality on the surface. For humans, metaphor is one such experience. When the poet writes "my heart is a furnace," the sensual object known as a heart captures vaguely defined furnace-qualities and draws them haltingly into its orbit. The inability of the heart to fuse easily with furnace-traits (in contrast with literal statements such as "my heart is the strongest muscle in my body") achieves allusion to a ghostly heart-object lying beneath the overly familiar sensual heart of everyday acquaintance. Notice that the inverse metaphor is entirely asymmetrical to the first: "the furnace is a heart" draws cardiac traits into the orbit of a sensual furnace, which is freed from bondage to its usual features and evoked as a sort of hidden furnace-soul, one whose animus now powers rhythmic beating and circulation. Humor does something similar: we can follow Bergson's *Laughter* and note the tension between a comic dupe and the traits he no longer freely adapts to changing circumstances.[323] These qualities are now exposed as a discrete visible shell beneath which the agent haplessly fails to control them. There are countless examples of allure. In instances of beauty, an object is not the sum total of beautiful colors and proportions on its surface, but a kind of soul animating the features from within, leading to vertigo or even hypnosis in the witness. When Heidegger's hammer fails, a concealed hammer-object seems to loom from the darkness, at a distance from its previously familiar traits. In language, names call out to objects deeper than any of their features; in love, the beloved entity has a certain magic hovering beneath the contours and flaws of its accessible surface. The list of possibilities is so vast that they deserve to be categorized in some encyclopedic work of aesthetics. Until now, aesthetics has generally served as the impoverished dancing-girl of philosophy — admired for her charms, but no gentleman would marry her. Yet given the apparently overwhelming scope of allure, aesthetics may deserve a rather vast role in ontology.

Different sensual objects within the same intention are described as contiguous; they do not melt together, but are treated by the intentional agent as distinct, and this agent is the final court of appeal in the sensual realm. This pertains to what has been termed the relations of sensual objects. But accidents are a different case. The surface of a sensual object does not

---

[323] Henri Bergson, *Laughter*.

merely lie side by side with it. Even though we look straight through these accidents to stay fixed on the underlying sensual thing, the accidents are not viewed as separate from that thing, but are encrusted onto it. This frosting over with peripheral qualities comes about in an interesting way. Recall that the sensual tree as a whole is made up of just one quality (the one from which it is severed in allure). But notice that this unified tree-apparition still has parts. If we start taking away branches and leaves, there will come a point at which we no longer regard it as the same tree; the tree is dependent on its parts. Yet these parts are only unified in the tree along one specific path. It never devours them completely, but employs only a limited portion of their reality. What we know as the accidents of the sensual tree are simply the remainder of its parts, the remnant not deployed in the new object. Each of these parts is complicated because it is made up of further parts, and so on to infinity. But however far we advance toward this infinity, we continue to find objects, not raw sense data. It would be wrong to think that we confront a field of color-pixels and then mold them into objective zones. For in the first place, it is arbitrary to think that points of green are more qualitatively basic than a unified tree-quality or branch-quality; all are capable of filling up my sincerity, and all have a specific personal style. And in the second place, even a supposed pixel of green at least takes the spatial form of a dot, and hence is a complicated object in its own right. There are always largest objects in the sensual realm: namely, those that are recognized by sincerity at any moment. But one cannot find a smallest, since there will always be a leftover remainder of parts, and parts of parts, like the endless overtones of notes struck on a piano. These accidents are the only possible source of change, since they alone are the potential bridge between one sensual object and another. For there can be no changes in the sensual object itself, which is always a recognized *fait accompli*; at most, it can be eliminated and replaced by a new one. Accidents alone have the dual status of belonging and not belonging to an object, like streamers on a maypole, or jewels on a hookah. Accidents are tempting hooks protruding from the sensual object, allowing it the chance to connect with others and thereby fuse two into one.

But the relation of part and whole does not occur only in the sensual realm. A real object, too, is formed of parts whose disappearance threatens its very existence. The difference is that the parts of a sensual object are encrusted onto its surface: or rather, certain aspects of those parts are fused to create it, while the remainder of those parts emanates from its surface as noise. By contrast, the parts of a real object are contained on the interior of that object, not plastered onto its outer crust. In both cases, however, there is a vicarious cause enabling the parts to link together. This can be clarified through the historical difference between skepticism and occasionalism, which are complementary in the same manner as encrustation and connection. Hume and Malebranche face opposite versions of the same problem. Although Hume supposedly doubts the possibility of connection, note that for him a connection has actually already occurred: he is never surprised that two billiard balls lie simultaneously in his mind, but doubts only that they have independent force capable of inflicting blows on each other. In this sense, Hume actually begins with connection inside experience and merely doubts any separation outside it. Conversely, Malebranche begins by assuming the existence of separate substances, but doubts that they can occupy a shared space in such a way as to exchange their forces — leading him to posit God's power as the ultimate joint space of all entities. Like Hume, we can regard the intentional agent as the vicarious cause of otherwise separate phenomena. The tree and its mountainous backdrop are indeed distinct, yet they are unified insofar as I am sincerely absorbed with both. But more than this: when the parts of the tree fuse to yield the tree with its single fixed tree-quality, I too am the vicarious cause for the connection of these sensual objects. Even if I merely sit passively, without unduly straining eyes or mind, it is still for me that these parts have combined. Here, a real object (I myself) serves as the vicarious cause for two or more sensual ones. In the inverted case of Malebranche, we cannot accept the pistol shot of the deity as our vicarious cause, since no explanation is given of how God as a real object could touch other real objects; fear of blasphemy is the sole protection for this incomplete doctrine. Instead, just as two sensual objects are vicariously linked by a real one, two real objects must be vicariously linked by a sensual one. I make contact with another object, not through impossible contact with its interior life, but only by brushing its surface in such a manner as to bring its inner life into play. Just as only the opposite poles of magnets make contact, and just as the opposite sexes alone are fertile, it is also the case that two objects of the same type do not directly touch one another. Contiguity between sensual objects is impossible without a real intentional agent, and connection between real ones does not occur except by means of a sensual intermediary.

This entails that all contact must be asymmetrical. However deeply I burrow into the world, I never encounter anything but sensual objects, and neither do real objects ever encounter anything but my own sensual facade. The key to vicarious causation is that two objects must somehow touch without touching. In the case of the sensual realm, this happens when I the intentional agent serve as vicarious cause for the fusion of multiple sensual objects: a fusion that remains only partial, encrusted with residual accidents. But in the case of real objects, the only way to touch a real one without touching it is through allure. Only here do we escape the deadlock of merely rolling about in the perfumes of sensual things, and encounter qualities belonging to a distant signaling thing rather than a carnally present one. The only way to bring real objects into the sensual sphere is to reconfigure sensual objects in such a way that they no longer merely fuse into a new one, as parts into a whole, but rather become animated by allusion to a deeper power lying beyond: a real object. The gravitational field of a real object must somehow invade the existing sensual field. Just as I am the vicarious link between two sensual objects, the alluring tree is the vicarious link between me and the real tree. The exact dynamics of this process deserve a lengthier treatment, but something unusual has already become evident. The separation of a thing from its quality is no longer a local phenomenon of human experience, but instead is the root of all relations between real objects, including causal relations. In other words, allure belongs to ontology as a whole, not to the special metaphysics of animal perception. Relations between all real objects, including mindless chunks of dirt, occur only by means of some form of allusion. But insofar as we have identified allure with an aesthetic effect, this means that aesthetics becomes first philosophy.

CHAPTER 18
OPENING STATEMENT[324]
(FROM *THE PRINCE AND THE WOLF*)

Graham Harman

Maybe first I will address the questions about the title of the book [*Prince of Networks*] and the status of the manuscript. As you may have noticed, the final chapter is missing, and that's not accidental. I deliberately chose to wait until after this event to write the last chapter. Some things you say today could make a contribution to the manuscript, which is already under review by a publisher. But I am still going to make quite a few changes to it.

"King of Networks" was the title of the first paper I ever wrote about Bruno Latour.[325] This was a talk I gave in Chicago almost nine years ago, and one of the audience members said afterwards: "You ought to send the paper to Latour himself. Sometimes you'll be surprised, and these authors will respond."[326] And I did send the lecture to Bruno and received a wonderful response, and thus began our correspondence. But when I tried to use this title for the book manuscript, there were a lot of jokes about the film *King*

[324] Bruno Latour, Graham Harman, & Peter Erdélyi, *The Prince and the Wolf*, is the lightly edited transcript of a debate between Latour and me, held at the London School of Economics on 5 February, 2008. This chapter reprints my opening statement from that event, as found in *The Prince and Wolf*, pp. 23–40.

[325] Graham Harman, "Bruno Latour, King of Networks" lecture delivered on 16 April, 1999 at the Department of Philosophy at DePaul University, Chicago. This lecture was eventually published in 2010 in Graham Harman, *Towards Speculative Realism*, pp. 67–92.

[326] The suggestion was made by Professor Bill Martin of DePaul University.

of New York, and I decided I would rather not deal with any of those jokes when the book was out. And so then it was a choice between "emperor" and "prince," and emperor is simply too polysyllabic. [LAUGHTER] I didn't think Bruno would view prince as a downgrade from king. The word "prince" also hints at Machiavelli's book, and "Prince of Networks" sounds enough like "Prince of Darkness" [LAUGHTER] to be flattering in a backhanded way.[327]

Above all I would like to thank everyone from ANTHEM who made this happen. ANTHEM stands for Actor-Network-Theory-Heidegger Meeting, which is a great acronym. This is a good match for me, because while half of my head belongs to Latour and half belongs to Heidegger and phenomenology, the two usually do not go together. In fact, until I met the members of ANTHEM, some people thought I was unique or quirky in some sense, and it was a pleasure to discover that others are as quirky as I am. Peter [Erdélyi] doesn't know this, but I checked this morning, and since August 2007 we have exchanged a total of 796 emails [LAUGHTER], many of them about this event. That's more than four emails per day. He's one of the few people who likes discussing these things by email as much as I do.

The last preliminary remark I wanted to make is that the date of this conference has a lovely symmetry for me because February of 1988, that's twenty years ago, is when I became a Heideggerian ....

Bruno Latour

Today? This specific day? [LAUGHTER].

Graham Harman

No, I don't remember the specific day. I know it was late February. [LAUGHTER] February of 1998 was when I became a Latourian, and here we are today, ten years after that. And of course I would have been delighted back then if I could have looked ten years into the future and seen what was coming today. Also, I wouldn't trade Bruno Latour's presence here today for Martin Heidegger's. Bruno is a much nicer man. [LAUGHTER] He's much funnier as well as a better interlocutor, I'm sure.

---

[327] Niccolò Machiavelli, *The Prince*.

Since Heidegger lies in the background of this manuscript, we might ask: what draws a Heideggerian to Latour? In my case at least, Heidegger's *weaknesses* are what drew me to Latour, because he does not share those particular weaknesses. Above all, despite my many years of enthusiasm for Heidegger, his tone was always unbearable to me. For me that tone was merely something to be endured: a kind of grim piety, with a sort of oracular heaviness that is found in all of Heidegger's work. I always appreciated the depth of Heidegger, but never appreciated the rhetorical tone. By contrast, as Leslie already mentioned, Bruno is probably the funniest contemporary philosopher. Throughout the margins of all my copies of Bruno's books I have written comments such as "laughing" and "ha-ha." And in fact I was talking to Gerard de Vries in Amsterdam, one of the leading Dutch experts on Latour. I asked de Vries what drew him to Latour's work and he said that Bruno and his friends were the only funny people working in philosophy. [LAUGHTER] Many philosophers were bores and he didn't enjoy spending time with them; Bruno was an exception.

But even more importantly than the question of tone, there was the fact that Bruno's philosophy is almost the only one of the past century that takes individual objects seriously. Individual objects play a role in his philosophy. In Heidegger that isn't the case because individual objects are dismissed as merely "ontic." What is real is the depth behind the present-at-hand configurations of objects. In Husserl you do find individual things. But they are just phenomena in consciousness, and they don't really do anything. In other contemporary philosophies you'll find that the role of the object is minimized: objects don't play any significant role. One of my favorite moments when we brought Bruno to Egypt in 2003 was his lecture on how the price of apricots in Paris is determined, which I cannot imagine Heidegger or most others attempting as a philosophical topic.

So, what *are* individual things for Bruno Latour? We need to look at "Irreductions", one of his most underread books, which is often hidden from view because it's not a book in its own right, but a large appendix to his book on Pasteur.[328] And when I first contacted Bruno about the *Prince of Networks* project three or four years ago and told him what I had in mind, he said that any discussion of his philosophy must begin with "Irreductions". To my surprise, he said it has never been reviewed once, even now. And though *Prince of Networks* cannot really be called an "authorized" book, because I think he disagrees with much of it, the structure of the manuscript

---

[328] Bruno Latour, *The Pasteurization of France*.

243

was determined by Bruno Latour himself. He is the one who first made me seriously consider that *Irreductions* should provide the impetus for the entire book. And it now is, which is Bruno's own fault. And as stated in my manuscript, there are probably four major concepts in *Irreductions*.

First there is *irreduction* itself, which he presents with his wonderful "Paul on the road to Damascus" anecdote. I'm referring to the sudden revelation he had when he was 24 or 25 years old, and as he tells us he was driving his van on the road between Dijon and Gray and had to pull to the side of the road. He actually went back and found his diary entry from the time and typed it up for me. It was a very dramatic moment, when he decided that what most theories shares in common is a desire to reduce things to something else. Most theories take some primary reality that explains the others and then use that to explain the rest. Latour decided to reject this notion at a young age. And by the way, this also makes him the ally of Heidegger's critique of ontotheology: the notion that any particular *kind* of being can explain being itself. So there's one link between Latour and Heidegger.

Second, we have *actors*, probably the most important concept of his philosophy. Actors are obviously different from traditional substances, the most famous version of objects in the history of philosophy. Actors come in all sizes. The London School of Economics can be an actor, and so can an atom or a piece of paper. Latour is not distinguishing between substance and aggregates the way that Leibniz did, where a circle of men holding hands cannot possibly be a substance because it is merely an aggregate of many individuals. For Latour every individual is already an aggregate to begin with. We heard this again in his nice lecture last night on Gabriel Tarde. So it cannot be said that an actor is simple; it can be of any size. It doesn't have to endure: in fact, actors do not endure for him at all, but it certainly doesn't matter that they're not eternal, though classical substances were usually supposed to be eternal. Also, the difference for Latour between real and unreal is not important. Harry Potter can be an actor just as much as a pillar of granite. Anything that has an effect on other things is an actor, and hence there's no difference between physical and non-physical actors. Each actor is a black box containing other actors *ad infinitum*, and all actors are equally real.

But the third point, *alliances*, tells us that if all actors are equally real, not all are equally strong. The fact that an actor is real does not mean that it is just as convincing as the others. Latour is not a relativist: anything does not go. Some actors are very weak; not much proof can be mustered on their behalf, not many allies rush to their aid. But some actors are very strong, because other allies recognize them as real, respond to them, and alter their trajectories to adapt to them.

And finally we have *translation*, the idea that one thing can never be fully translated into another place or time. There is always going to be information loss, or energy loss. You have to pay a price when translating something from one place to another. This is especially wonderful in his brilliant alternative model of truth, which I don't think we've ever seen before from any philosopher. Usually there are disputes between the "correspondence" version of truth where the mind is copying the world, and the "coherence" view of truth where what matters is that your views are consistent with each other. But what we find in Bruno Latour, in *Pandora's Hope*, is an "industrial" model of truth, one of my favorite notions in his work. In order to move the oil trapped in the geological seams of Saudi Arabia to the gas tank in France, you're not "copying" the oil, and neither is it just coherence.[329] I mean, there is a real thing there that has to be translated at each stage. I'm afraid I don't even know all of these stages, but you have to refine it into petrol somehow (I don't know how that happens), then put it on a ship and take it to Europe, and finally it has to be sold to the customer and be put into the gas tank. And if you think of truth as this sort of process, it opens new possibilities for philosophy.

The other thing about actors for Latour is that there is no hidden essence or potential in them. You cannot say that the actors have some hidden inner kernel which is more important than their accidental crust. Actors contain *all* of their features. An actor simply is what it is, which means that an actor contains all of its qualities, or contains all of its relations with other actors. There is nothing hiding behind those qualities and relations. An actor is wholly deployed in the world in every second. There's no cryptic reservoir hiding behind what the thing is doing here and now, what qualities it has here and now. The reality of the actor is its way of perturbing, transforming, and jostling other things.

Now, here's the paradox. And by paradox I don't mean contradiction: I don't mean "Gotcha!" A philosophy is real only when it contains a central paradox. Who was it who said that paradox is the mark of truth? I think it was Count Yorck as quoted by Heidegger in *Being and Time*.[330] And Aristotle even says that substance is that which can have different qualities

---

[329] Bruno Latour, *Pandora's Hope*.
[330] Martin Heidegger, *Being and Time*, p. 454.

at different times. So, something is more substantial the more it is capable of paradoxical properties. On the one hand, Latour is clearly a philosopher of relations. His whole philosophy is about relations: the way that things interact, the way they form networks, alliances, and relations. And yet, since everything happens in one time and one place only, and every actor is utterly concrete, this means that actors are completely cut off from each other as well. Everything is completely cut off in its own self, and as we will see in a moment, it can't possibly endure from one instant to the next because it's so utterly concrete that even the smallest change essentially makes it a new actor: unless some other actor does work to establish that the change wasn't important and it's actually still the same thing. But another actor is required to do that. Nothing endures; everything is in a state of perpetual perishing. It's a lot like Whitehead, and also a lot like the occasionalists, and I'll come to that point shortly. Actually, I'm going to it right now: I didn't realize it was my next notecard.

There's a growing tendency to hear people speak of a school of "process philosophy," and you'll sometimes hear Whitehead, Bergson, Deleuze, and Latour grouped together. And I can see why, because what all of those names have in common is that they don't accept the traditional models of substance. That's true. However, it's also a bit sloppy to put those names together, for a reason that becomes pretty obvious if you look at the underpinnings of their philosophies. You have to put Bruno Latour with Whitehead, if you're going to group names together, because what matters for Latour and Whitehead are individual actors in individual instants. There is no flux, no becoming, and no *élan vital* as separate realities for Latour and Whitehead. For them, time is produced by actors. Time is a result, not a starting point. It's not an independent force. Individual actors for Bruno create time by doing something irreversible. The example he gave at dinner last night: Fermat's Last Theorem.[331] For many centuries nothing happened, and now it is solved. A cut has been made, something irreversible has happened, time has been created by an actor. Whitehead even emphasizes this point with his terminology. He talks about actual entities, but he also calls them "actual occasions," because an actual entity is frozen in an instant. Once it is altered, it's not really the same thing anymore. You can try to find enduring entities in Whitehead at the higher level of societies. But when you talk about actual entities, they are always perishing. In a famous and wonderful

---

[331] Fermat's Last Theorem, whose existence was alluded to by Pierre de Fermat in a marginal note from around 1637, was finally proven in 1993 by the British mathematician Andrew Wiles.

phrase, Whitehead tells us that actual entities do not undergo adventures in space and time. They exist in one place and time only, just as for Bruno.

Let me go back and say a little about the history of occasionalism, because it's a neglected but extremely important movement in the history of philosophy, and I think it is one that still dominates us. (I'm going to write something about this later.) Occasionalism goes back to Islamic philosophy. When people think of occasionalism in philosophy, they usually think of France in the seventeenth century, but it actually goes back to Islamic theology. We find it fairly early in the so-called Ash'arite School, which for theological motives did not want to grant the ability to act to created substances. Only Allah could have the power of creation, and even to cause anything to happen at all. They were so extreme that even to give fire the power to burn cotton was for them a kind of blasphemous presumption. And this is why God had to be introduced as a mediator. God is the mediator for all interactions. And this to me is the key contribution of Islamic philosophy. Every so often we see an attempt to revive Islamic philosophy, and certain texts are retranslated or commented upon. But too often this gets stuck in the rut of just saying: "well, we are indebted to the Arabs for keeping Aristotle alive," or something like that. But the main contribution of Islam is that occasionalism entered the very heart of Western philosophy. It took it awhile to get to the West. Notice that for Aristotle and his tradition, causation itself isn't really a *problem*; there are no gaps between things. I mean, he has the four causes — final, formal, efficient, material — but it's not really a problem for Aristotle that one thing can touch another. It took a theological motive to ask how one thing can touch another at all. And the answer was that this is impossible: God must be the mediator.

For Descartes, the motivation is different. His motive is that you have two different kinds of substances, the mind and the body. The only way for the mind to cause the body to move would be for God to serve as the mediator between them. But that's less interesting than the Muslim position on occasionalism, because it's less universal. But the wider Islamic version of occasionalism was brought back by Cordemoy and Malebranche, for whom the interaction between *bodies* is already a problem again. That's because they brought back the theory of atoms, which Descartes rejected. And for them the interaction of physical atoms requires God's mediation as well. And I would go so far as to say that the term "occasionalism" is used far too restrictively. Sometimes historians get touchy about this. They want to restrict it only to Malebranche and a few others, and don't even want to include Descartes. I would call most of the seventeenth-century figures occasionalists, including Leibniz, Spinoza, Berkeley. And I think it's fairly clearly the dominant trend in seventeenth-century metaphysics. Of course no one takes occasionalism seriously anymore. It seems like a very dated theology, and it's fun for undergraduates to refute it in introductory classes. The exception of course is Whitehead, who takes pride in starting *Process and Reality* by saying: "Let's forget about Kant and go back to the seventeenth century." And then he is able to walk freely among all these philosophies, and take occasionalism seriously.

But what is not laughed at today is skepticism, and Kant has a solution to skepticism. Skepticism is in many ways still the horizon of contemporary philosophy and so it's taken seriously, at least in the back of almost everyone's mind. And if you think about it, skepticism is really just an upside-down version of occasionalism. You've got the same problem in both cases: how can one thing necessarily connect with another? In a way these two are just the inverse of one another, and here it is interesting to note that Hume was a great fan of Malebranche, and was deeply inspired by him. In occasionalism the problem is that you have individual substances, you know these substances can exist. But how can they touch? It would be blasphemous to allow them to touch, so it must be God who's allowing them to do so. God comes in as the solution to link substances. In a way, what you have with Hume is that you're simply starting with the relations: things are already related by habit and custom. I already do link these impressions together. The problem is how we know that they can exist independently of such links. How can we know that they have independent powers outside of my habitual linking of them? We can't. So in a way the human mind, or habit, or custom are simply playing the role for Hume that God plays for all the occasionalists. So people can laugh at occasionalism all they want, but most contemporary philosophy is simply adopting the converse solution. So they shouldn't be laughing. Instead, they should be trying to reform their own opposing position.

Now, the problem with both of these theories is that they share the same flaw. Both start off by problematizing relation, specifically causal relation. There's a problem of how two things can relate to each other. And both positions cheat. They both solve the problem falsely by imagining one privileged super-entity that solves the problem. For the occasionalists nothing can touch, but God is an exception. For Hume nothing can touch, but they're already linked in the human mind by habit, so it doesn't matter. So in a sense both are shying away from the abyss: the problem of how two things interact at all. And so I would say that most post-Kantian philosophy is simply an upside-down occasionalism, insofar as it's restricting itself to human access to things and not talking about the interaction of things themselves. Whitehead is of course the permanent exception to most of the rules of post-Kantian philosophy. He begins *Process and Reality* by simply saying "Let's go back to the seventeenth century; philosophy has gone downhill since Kant."[332] And how do things communicate for Whitehead? Things are actual entities and they are fully defined by their relations to other things, which he calls *prehensions*. But how do they prehend each other? Well, they prehend each other through the eternal objects, which can roughly be described as Platonic forms. Things oversimplify each other when they prehend each other through these ... universal qualities, you could call them. And these universal qualities have to be somewhere. Where are they? For Whitehead they are in God. So it's the same solution, the old occasionalist solution. And it is very refreshing compared to most recent philosophy, but still has the same problem of bringing in a sort of magical solution at the end.

And I happen to think that this is the greatness of Latour as a metaphysician. I think he has made a real breakthrough in being the first person to problematize relations and not employ one of these magical last-ditch solutions. He's not from the Kantian tradition and so he doesn't put everything in the human mind. He doesn't follow Whitehead in utilizing God to serve this particular causal role in his philosophy. Latour's philosophy is a kind of secular occasionalism, and we've never seen that before. It's a philosophy where you have to ask how things interact on a local level without appealing to some all powerful super-entity that's hidden somewhere from us. He does not flee from the problem of translation, but makes it the central theme of his philosophy.

All relation for Latour requires a mediator. Any two things *can* be linked, but only if something links them. In perhaps his most wonderful example, politics and neutrons can be linked, but only if Joliot in France links them: only if he's able to convince the French government that neutrons are part of a good defense policy, and only if he is able to convince neutrons to participate by designing experiments in the right way to give the sorts of results that are plausible enough to make a working bomb. It's not God who links politics and neutrons, and it's not the human mind that links them.

---

[332] Alfred North Whitehead, *Process and Reality*. (The words in quotation marks are a paraphrase, not a direct quotation.)

It's Joliot. And every actor is a kind of Joliot. Any entity can link any two other entities, and so a local occasionalism must be possible.[333]

We know that Bruno Latour is a philosopher of actors and networks. We can rewrite this to say that he is a philosopher of objects and relations (those are the terms I prefer to use). His actors are objects of all sizes; they can be either real or unreal in physical terms; they are black boxes that you can open to find many more actors hidden within them; and every actor has effects on other entities. And as for relations, we know from Latour's philosophy that their link is only occasional: they need a third term or mediator, something that links them. And for these reasons I will always be a Latourian, no matter how much he might not like certain parts of the second half of my book. I will always have this Latourian base in my philosophy because Heidegger doesn't give me any of these things. Heidegger pays no real attention to objects at all, and Latour's kind of relation isn't really found in Heidegger, since human *Dasein* is the one doing all the relating. And furthermore, Latour has launched a style of philosophy (secular occasionalism) that's completely unavailable elsewhere. You're not going to find it even in Whitehead, because there's always an appeal to the eternal objects and to God. Whitehead is not going to look the problem of relations squarely in the face. And of course Bruno does this with a wit and liveliness that are well worth emulating, just as Heidegger's tone is worth avoiding.

And I will now select four of the things I said in the second half of the book that I think need to be worked on to make the philosophy of objects and relations feasible. One of them is that given that any two actors can only be linked through a mediator, there's the possible problem of an infinite regress. If Joliot is required to link neutrons and politics, what links Joliot and neutrons, and what links Joliot and politics? Well, you could say that Joliot's eyeballs link him with the neutrons, or that his training in physics links him with the neutrons, and you could say that that's not so interesting, so we don't have to consider it. Yes, if you are simply trying to give an analysis of Joliot's life, you could say that for all practical purposes it's not very interesting to know what lies between Joliot and politics or neutrons, and so we can avoid the question. But in metaphysical terms, there is a problem here. You have to explain how any two things can be linked. And for this reason there must be a space where direct contact is

---

[333] Latour, *Pandora's Hope.*

possible without mediation. We need to discover what that space is where links are possible.

Okay, points 2 and 3 come from my phenomenological background, which Bruno Latour does not share. One of them is that my Heideggerian side makes me resist the idea that objects can be made up of relations. This is an unorthodox reading of Heidegger, of course. But the way I read Heidegger's tool-analysis ... Let me summarize this quickly because maybe not everyone here is familiar with Heidegger. I think I have maybe a few more minutes? Okay.

Heidegger's tool-analysis is meant as a critique of Husserl, who was Heidegger's great teacher. Husserl's goal can roughly be described as protecting philosophy from the growing advance of the natural sciences. Philosophy in the late 1800s was in danger of becoming experimental psychology. And Husserl's way of preventing this from happening was to say that all these physical theories are just theories. If you hear a door slam, you can invent a theory about vibrations going through the air and coming into your ear and vibrating your eardrum and sending chemical signals up the nervous system, but we don't really have any direct access to that. Those theories are grounded in my *experience* of the door slamming. So what we should do instead is simply describe what it's like to hear the door slam: what I'm actually hearing, what I'm inferring, and what the different layers of sound are to which I might not normally be paying attention. This is what phenomenological description is about, and it's often accused of becoming a kind of psychology in its own right, and to some extent it does verge on psychology.

Heidegger's attack on this position was simply to say that our normal interaction with things is not phenomenal, not as images in consciousness. We take things for granted; we use them; we rely on things. Our consciousness is a very small percentage of our interaction with things at any moment. You're using the floor now to support you; you're using the oxygen in the room to breathe; you're using your bodily organs to keep you alive. And most of the time you're not thinking about these things unless they break. And so Heidegger's famous tool analysis in *Being and Time* talks about the "disturbance of reference" when things malfunction or fail in some way, and come to our attention in a way that they didn't before. They emerge from shadow into light. And they don't actually have to break for this happen. You can do this with theoretical consciousness. You can do this simply by talking about something or noticing something. All these different ways show that for Heidegger there's something hidden behind all of our theories or our seeing; there's a deeper layer.

251

Now, it is sometimes said that this means that "practice comes before theory for Heidegger; Heidegger is a pragmatist." No, this is not true, because notice that even our practical use of things does not exhaust them. By sitting on the chair you're also not coming into contact with all the properties of the chair. The chair has many different qualities that your sitting in it does not exhaust any more than your looking at the chair does. There are tiny electro-magnetic vibrations coming off the chair that certain insects might be able to perceive though you cannot, and they're completely irrelevant to us as humans. But the chair seems to have an infinity of these qualities that no other entity will ever unlock. And then you have to take a third step (and I got this from Whitehead actually, even before I knew Bruno's work) and see that things do this to each other as well. Things are oversimplifying each other just as much as we do. It's not a special property of human consciousness to distort the world. Entities will distort each other *ipso facto* by the mere fact that they relate. For fire to burn cotton, which is the favorite Islamic example discussed in all those ancient texts, fire does not need to react to most of the properties of the cotton: its smell and its color are irrelevant to the fire. The fire is going to burn the cotton based on flammable properties, whatever those are.

And so the object is deeper than any possible relations to it. If you say that an object is reducible to its relations with other things, which I know Bruno believes, I think a couple of other problems arise. One problem is that I don't think you can explain change. And this is something Aristotle says against the Megarians in the *Metaphysics*. Like Bruno, I'm also opposed to "potentiality," but I think there has to be something outside of a thing's relations. If a thing is nothing other than its current relations, then why would it ever change those relations? If I am completely exhausted by my current state of relations to all of the entities in the world, then there's nothing hidden in reserve, nothing cryptic, nothing that would later unfold and give me the chance to have new relations to things. So in a way this position doesn't do justice to my future. And in a way it can't even explain my present, because we can imagine a counterfactual situation in which other people would be sitting in this room who aren't currently here, who would be seeing me from different angles and having different reactions to me than any of you do. And they would still be reacting *to me*, not to your relations to me. So there is something here that is really *me* that these people are all encountering. I'm not just the sum total of the way that I relate to all of you right now.

Okay, so that's the second point I wanted to make, and I only have two more. The other thing that Bruno does in his philosophy is that he identifies an object with its qualities: not just with its relations but also with its qualities. In his view you cannot say that an object is different from its qualities. Whereas for Husserl (and here's my phenomenological background coming in) I would say that Husserl's primary insight is the distinction between a thing and its qualities. These days people often dismiss Husserl: he's just an idealist, he's taking us back to Descartes and Kant. It's not quite that simple. Yes, Husserl was an idealist; yes, he does suspend the real world from consideration. But notice that when you're reading Husserl, it *feels* like realism. There's a definite taste of realism in your mouth when you're reading Husserl, even though he's an idealist. Now why is that? It's because Husserl is talking about objects. They're simply not real objects that have independent force; they're called intentional objects. To take a famous example, Husserl spent a whole semester having his students analyze a mailbox. You cannot imagine Fichte or Hegel spending a whole semester having their students analyze a mailbox; it would make no sense for them. An object has no opacity and no resistance for these German idealists. It's simply one transient moment of the dialectic and then it's gone; you're already removed to some higher structure. For Husserl, individual objects already have a kind of potency and weight, an obscurity for Husserl: even though they're not real, and are present only in the human mind. If you circle a building, you keep thinking of it as the same building even though you're seeing utterly different qualities in each instant, which means that there is a distinction between the building and the qualities through which it is manifested. Those qualities are almost accidental; you just need to be seeing *some* qualities of the building in order to be able to see it. But you can keep circling the building and it stays the same. It remains identical, even if it's not real: even if it's the Tooth Fairy that you're circling in your mind, the same thing happens.

Now this is important, because this is Husserl's challenge to the entire tradition of British Empiricism, whose position is often very much taken for granted: the idea that a thing is nothing more than a bundle of qualities. There's nothing called a thing that's independent of those. Locke says it; Hume says it. There's a tradition of mockery of the "I know not what." When they say "I know not what," it's with a sarcastic tone, since supposedly all that we really know are the qualities. But for Husserl, the objects come first. And for one of his followers, Merleau-Ponty, there are no qualities independent of the thing. If you're looking at ink, a shirt, a flag, the black is different in each of those cases even if it is technically the same shade of black, because it's now impregnated with the underlying object, which is never fully present to you. And on this point Bruno sides with the British Empiricists.

There's also a whole debate in the philosophy of language, which has been very central for analytic philosophy. On one side you have Russell and Frege, who uphold the traditional view that a person's name is simply an abbreviation for all the qualities we know about them. And on the opposite side there is Kripke, who says, "No, with a name you're pointing at something that's deeper than the qualities."[334] Why? Because I can discover that all the qualities I thought I knew about somebody, all the properties I thought I knew about you, were false. What I will say if that happens is, "Oh, I was wrong about everything I thought I knew about you." I'm not going to say, "You're a different person." It doesn't matter that the qualities change. I'm still pointing at the same thing: a "rigid designator," he calls it. And you have that in Husserl too, because you're pointing at the same intentional object no matter how the qualities change.

And so to repeat, my first point is that there's an infinite regress of mediators, and that's a problem with Latour's theories of relations. The second and third points were problems with the theory of the actor, possible problems with the theories of actors. Maybe a thing is not the same as its relations, and maybe a thing is not the same as its qualities. And the fourth problem is that, despite Bruno's wonderful career-long assault on Kant, which I cheer every step of the way, we still have not brought back the problems that Kant threw out of philosophy. All of the cosmological problems that were supposedly eliminated forever in the Transcendental Dialectic, all those traditional metaphysical problems are not back with us. Whitehead picks up on a few of them, Latour picks up on a few of them. Kant thinks it's impossible to know whether or not there's an infinite regress of wholes and parts; Latour tells us there's an infinite regress. You might read him as merely saying that "for all practical purposes" we never know where the last black box is. But I think that if you follow his logic, you have to say the black boxes never stop opening. And so in a way he is asserting a *metaphysical* claim that there is no final atom that will be an unopenable box. And so I would think we also need to be a little more ambitious about going right at the cyclops eye of Kant in trying to save all of these problems that were cancelled in the second half of *the Critique of Pure Reason*. And we see a few people trying this now from various different angles. In Meillassoux's

[334] Saul Kripke, *Naming and Necessity*.

book we see an attempt to tackle some of these cancelled Kantian problems as well, and he's coming from a totally different angle than mine.[335]

So, what I've tried to do in this opening summary is talk about what I consider to be the key concepts of Latour's metaphysics, the key things that I appreciate about it, and also some reservations that I have that stem mostly from my Heidegger/Husserl background. And I know some of his reactions to these points, because we've had a few email exchanges. But perhaps he would like to spell out some of his reactions today.

Edgar Whitley
Thank you, Graham.

[APPLAUSE]

---

[335] Quentin Meillassoux, *After Finitude*.

PART IV

AESTHETICS AS FIRST PHILOSOPHY

CHAPTER 19

GREENBERG, DUCHAMP, AND THE NEXT AVANT-GARDE[336]

In Marcel Duchamp and Clement Greenberg we have two of the pivotal figures in the twentieth-century arts. Yet they seem to stand in complete opposition, so that the reputation of Duchamp rises as that of Greenberg falls, and vice versa. Greenberg is viewed as the champion of formalism, of artworks sealed off from their socio-political surroundings and even from the private intentions of the artist. He even held that Duchamp was simply "not a good artist," and that his devotees (including the highly regarded Joseph Beuys) were "also not especially good artists."[337] Through the early 1960s, Greenberg's critical views marched step-by-step with the progressive advance of the artistic avant-garde, the eclipse of Paris by New York, and the triumph first of Jackson Pollock and then of the so-called "post-painterly abstraction" of such figures as Kenneth Noland and Jules Olitski. Since that time, both Greenberg and his preferred styles have fallen into disfavor, while in the words of one observer "the reputation and work of Marcel Duchamp ... [have] surpassed those of Picasso in the eyes of art historians, artists, and Duchamp's admirers alike."[338]

---

[336] This chapter originally appeared in *Speculations* V (2014), pp. 251–274.
[337] Clement Greenberg, *Late Writings*, p. 221.
[338] Gavin Parkinson, *The Duchamp Book*, p. 6.

Over the past decade, there has been a growing sense that Greenberg is becoming readable once again, while Duchamp's legacy is perhaps on the verge of becoming overexploited. My hope is that by re-examining Greenberg's complaints about Duchamp, by weighing the strengths and weaknesses of those complaints, we might gain a fresh sense of what avenues might still be open to art criticism and perhaps to the arts themselves.

1. Greenberg's Critique of Duchamp

From the dawn of his career in 1939 through May 1968, Clement Greenberg published a total of 333 essays, articles, and reviews. As far as I can determine, all of this written output contains just two references to Marcel Duchamp. In January 1943 there is a passing reference to some pieces by Duchamp in Peggy Guggenheim's new gallery, which Greenberg felt were unsuccessfully displayed.[339] Almost a quarter century later, in April 1967, Greenberg tells us that minimalism commits itself to the third dimension because this is where art intersects with non-art, and credits Duchamp and the Dadaists with this discovery.[340]

But beginning with Greenberg's lecture in Sydney in May 1968, which was published the following year, Duchamp becomes more central for him. Though the references become only slightly more numerous, they become more vehemently negative, as well as more central to Greenberg's defense of his own aesthetic views. The tables had turned. Greenberg was now an intellectual exile rather than a king, while Duchamp had been retroactively anointed as the heroic forerunner of more recent artistic trends. Let's look briefly at each of these references, so as to prepare for a more general discussion.

In the Sydney lecture of May 1968, Duchamp is criticized twice for attempting to transcend the untranscendable difference in quality between good art and bad art. The first instance condemns not just Duchamp, but a large portion of the art of 1968:

> Things that purport to be art do not function, do not exist, as art
> until they are experienced through taste. Until then they exist only
> as empirical phenomena, as aesthetically arbitrary objects or facts.
> These, precisely, are what a lot of contemporary art gets taken for,

---

[339] Clement Greenberg, *The Collected Essays and Criticism, Volume 1*, p. 141.
[340] Clement Greenberg, *The Collected Essays and Criticism, Volume 4*, p. 253.

and what any artist wants their works to be taken for — in the hope, periodically renewed since Marcel Duchamp first acted on it fifty-odd years ago, that by dint of evading the reach of taste while yet remaining in the context of art, certain kinds of contrivances will achieve unique existence and value. So far this hope has proved illusory.[341]

Later in the Sydney lecture, Greenberg expands on this notion.[342] No art person, he says, had ever questioned the difference between high-quality and low-quality art until the emergence of the "popular" avant-garde, by which he means Dada and Duchamp. The inherent difficulty of high artistic taste and production was replaced by the difficulty of accepting an ostensibly non-artistic phenomenon as an artwork. Greenberg offers a sarcastic list of real or imagined pseudo-artworks produced by the Duchampian popular avant-garde:

The idea of the difficult is evoked by a row of boxes, by a mere rod, by a pile of litter, by projects for Cyclopean landscape architecture, by the plan for a trench dug in a straight line for hundreds of miles, by a half-open door, by the cross-section of a mountain, by stating imaginary relations between real points in real places, by a blank wall, and so forth.[343]

Greenberg concludes: "In this context the Milky Way might be offered as a work of art too. The trouble with the Milky Way, however, is that, as *art*, it is banal."[344] In the 1968 Sydney lecture, then, Duchamp is presented as someone who evades questions of aesthetic quality and replaces them with the claim that any arbitrarily designated object can be an artwork. This interpretation of Duchamp is not surprising and not inaccurate.

In Greenberg's 1971 essay "Counter-Avant-Garde," the critique of Duchamp becomes harsher and more intricate. In Western art, Greenberg says, there had always been a small number of innovators who also led the way in terms of aesthetic quality. Beginning in the 1860s, there was increasing distance between advanced art and official taste. Advanced art began to challenge that taste to such an extent as to cause a certain degree

---

[341] Clement Greenberg, *The Collected Essays and Criticism, Volume 4*, p. 293.
[342] Clement Greenberg, *The Collected Essays and Criticism, Volume 4*, pp. 301–303.
[343] Clement Greenberg, *The Collected Essays and Criticism, Volume 4*, p. 302.
[344] Clement Greenberg, *The Collected Essays and Criticism, Volume 4*, p. 303.

of shock: important new art actually became *scandalous* with Manet, the impressionists, Cézanne, the Fauves, and cubism. In each case the scandal wore off after some time, though the underlying aesthetic challenge of the avant-garde remained. But the challenge and the scandal came to be mistaken for one another. With the Italian futurists, "innovation and advancedness began to look more and more like ... categorical means to artistic significance apart from aesthetic quality."[345] With Duchamp, this avant-gardeness was replaced by a full blown avant-garde*ism*. As Greenberg sees it, "in a few short years after 1912, [Duchamp] laid down the precedents for everything that advanced-advanced art has done in the fifty-odd years since .... [He] locked advanced-advanced art into what has amounted to hardly more than elaborations, variations on, and recapitulations of his original ideas."[346] These are strong words, given the almost total absence of Duchamp from Greenberg's writings until the critic was almost sixty years old.

And what was the core of Duchamp's vision, now credited by Greenberg with setting the agenda for advanced-advanced art as of 1971? That agenda is as follows:

> the shocking, the scandalizing, the mystifying and confounding, became embraced as ends in themselves and no longer regretted as initial side effects of artistic newness that would wear off with familiarity. Now these side effects were to be built in. The first bewildered reaction to innovative art was to be the sole and appropriate one.[347]

More than this, the shock and scandal in question were no longer aesthetic, as had been the case with great avant-garde art, but came solely from the extra-aesthetic realm: "Duchamp's first readymades, his bicycle wheel, his bottle rack, and later on his urinal, were not at all new in configuration; they startled when first seen only because they were presented in a fine-art context, which is a purely cultural and social, not an aesthetic or artistic context."[348] The point became to violate not the aesthetic standards of the recent avant-garde in order to create progress in taste, but to violate social decorum.

---

[345] Greenberg, *Late Writings*, p. 6.
[346] Greenberg, *Late Writings*, p. 7.
[347] Greenberg, *Late Writings*, p. 7.
[348] Greenberg, *Late Writings*, p. 12.

There are a few other points to consider. Duchamp always took pride in an art that appealed to the mind rather than the eye, against what he dismissively called "retinal art."[349] But for Greenberg, this excess of *thinking* is precisely the death of art. In other words, avant-gardism of Duchamp's type involves too much conscious choice. The artist performs a series of easy cognitive stunts that fail to outrun their conception; the artist is no longer surprised by what the artwork discovers: "Conscious volition, deliberateness, plays a principal part in avant-gardist art: that is, resorting to ingenuity instead of inspiration, contrivance instead of creation, 'fancy' instead of 'imagination'; in effect, to the known rather than the unknown."[350] The new becomes a consciously available set of external gestures rather than the object of unremitting struggle. As a result, "the exceptional enterprise of artistic innovation, by being converted into an affair of standardized categories, of a set of 'looks,' is put within reach of uninspired calculation."[351] Yet aesthetics ought to be a matter of surprise rather than of shock, of a difficult grappling with something slightly beyond our grasp rather than the transparent mastery of a clever subversive concept. As Greenberg later put it, mathematical demonstrations become boring when repeated, and so too do the "demonstrations" of Duchamp as to the arbitrariness of what counts as an art object. By contrast, "that's not the way it is with more substantial art, good and bad: that kind of art you have to experience over and over again in order to keep on *knowing* it."[352]

A related notion is that avant-gardism thinks it can overturn the entire history of art with a single transgressive gesture, whereas for Greenberg art advances by mastering the best art of the past (especially the immediately preceding generation) and adapting it in some relevant way:

> Maybe the most constant topic of avant-gardist rhetoric is the claim made with each new phase of avant-garde, or seeming avant-garde, art that the past is now being finally closed out and a radical mutation in the nature of art is taking place after which art will no longer behave as it has heretofore.[353]

---

[349] Parkinson, *The Duchamp Book*, p. 6.
[350] Greenberg, *Late Writings*, p. 7.
[351] Greenberg, *Late Writings*, p. 8.
[352] Greenberg, *Late Writings*, p. 82.
[353] Greenberg, *Late Writings*, p. 9.

Attempts to shock and overturn art from the outside have replaced challenges to taste from within the established tradition. But for Greenberg, surprise must always occur inside a given context: "new and surprising ways of satisfying in art have always been connected closely with immediately previous ways .... There have been no great vaults 'forward,' no innovations out of the blue, no ruptures of continuity in the high art of the past – nor have any such been witnessed in our day."[354] As he would claim five years later in his Bennington Seminars, "Duchamp had hardly grasped what real cubism was about"[355] – namely, the flattening-out of the picture plane as opposed to the deepening illusion of pictorial depth since the Italian Renaissance. For Greenberg this is evident from the rather traditional perspectival elements in Duchamp's own quasi-cubist painting efforts before he gave up painting and turned to the bicycle wheel and other readymades. Instead, Greenberg holds, Duchamp mistakenly believed that the force of cubism lay in its difficulty and shock value.

This leads us to the final and perhaps most important aspect of Greenberg's anti-Duchampian views. Though it might seem surprising at first, Greenberg is adamant in treating both Duchamp and surrealism as forms of "academic art." There are two kinds of academic artist, Greenberg holds. The first is able to recognize the new avant-garde trends of the present day but follows them in a watered-down, nonthreatening form. Greenberg offers the example of Paul Albert Besnard, whose vulgarized if imaginative variant of impressionism in the 1880s "outsold Sisley and Pissarro, to their grief, and became better known too, in the short term."[356] The second kind, far more common, "is one who is puzzled [by the new trends], and who therefore orients his art to expectations formed by an earlier phase of art."[357] Duchamp was a half-hearted early devotee of Cézanne and the Fauves, but was simply unable to grasp the new aesthetic standards generated by cubism, and misinterpreted that movement as nothing more than a shock and a scandal to previous standards rather than as a style of its own with inherent aesthetic merit. For this reason, Greenberg holds, Duchamp can be taken seriously as an interesting cultural figure, but not as an artist *per se*.[358] Dada, surrealism, pop art, and minimalism mark a gradual relaxing of

---

[354] Greenberg, *Late Writings*, p. 15.
[355] Greenberg, *Late Writings*, p. 81.
[356] Clement Greenberg, *Homemade Esthetics*, p. 87.
[357] Greenberg, *Late Writings*, p. 15.
[358] Greenberg, *Late Writings*, pp. 153–154.

aesthetic standards, with everything boiling down to how severely one can shock previous expectations as to what counts as art.

But we have not yet heard Greenberg's most powerful definition of academic art, from another important Sydney lecture, this one given in 1979:

> Academicization isn't a matter of academics — there were academies long before academicization and before the nineteenth century. Academicism consists in *the tendency to take the medium of an art too much for granted*. It results in blurring: words become imprecise, color gets muffled, the physical sources of sound become too much dissembled.[359]

Up through the 1920s and even 1930s, academic art tended to be blatantly academic, defended by official academies and conventional taste while disdained by a relatively small modernist elite. But Greenberg holds that with surrealism, the heir of Dada, we see a form of academic art that is cannily disguised as cutting-edge modernism.

As early as his pioneering essay "Avant-Garde and Kitsch" in 1939, Greenberg wrote that "Picasso, Braque, Mondrian, Miró, Kandinsky, Brancusi, even Klee, Matisse, and Cézanne derive their chief inspiration from the medium they work in,"[360] but added in a dismissive footnote that "the chief concern of a painter like Dalí is to represent the processes and concepts of his consciousness, not the processes of his medium."[361] For all the scandal value of Dalí's flaming giraffes and skinny-legged towering elephants, his art is focused on shocking literary content, and in Greenberg's view we have reached a stage in the history of visual art in which literary content is just a non-artistic distraction. In this respect, surrealism and Dada are simply two sides of the same academic coin. Surrealism takes its medium too much for granted by replacing drawing room portraits with wild fantasies of hallucinogenic entities. Meanwhile, Dada takes its medium too much for granted by giving up on the project of transforming it from within, and challenging it only with shocking gestures from the outside.

---

[359] Greenberg, *Late Writings*, p. 28, emph. added.
[360] Greenberg, *The Collected Essays and Criticism, Volume 1*, p. 9.
[361] Greenberg, *The Collected Essays and Criticism, Volume 1*, p. 9, n. 2.

There are other details to Greenberg's critique of Duchamp, other scathing and witty remarks, but we have already encountered the core principles of this critique, of which there are perhaps six:

1 Duchamp rejects quality as an aesthetic standard.
2 He treats the shock value of advanced art not as an unfortunate side effect that wears off over time, but as the central purpose of art.
3 He shocks established standards not by internal aesthetic means, but by transgressing everyday social decorum: displaying urinals, breasts, or the spread-out naked body of a murdered woman in a fine art context that will be predictably horrified by such gestures.
4 He privileges thinking in art, turning artworks into transparent concepts to an excessive degree.
5 He overestimates the radical break his work makes with the past.
6 Though he thinks himself to be the pinnacle of artist advancement, Duchamp is actually an academic artist who takes the medium of art too much for granted, despairs of being able to innovate from within, and is thus led into a sort of juvenile sabotage through shocking affronts to the art gallery context.

This six-point list is perhaps more interesting if we reverse it into Greenberg's own positive artistic program:

1 Art is always a matter of high and low aesthetic quality.
2 Shock value is merely a temporary symptom of advanced art, never its central purpose.
3 Important art is characterized by aesthetic challenge rather than extra-aesthetic shock.
4 Art is a matter of taste rather than of thought, and taste must always struggle to refine and improve itself in contact with the art object.
5 Important art builds on the past rather than breaking radically with it.
6 Art should not be academic, meaning that it should not take its medium for granted. This final principle entails that art reflects a constant struggle to reinvent its form.

Stated differently, art avoids academicism when its content manages to *reflect* or *embody* the possibilities of its medium, rather than presenting content as an isolated figure whose ground or medium can be taken for granted. This is why Greenberg increasingly celebrated painting that announced the flatness of canvas, why cubism was for him the greatest school of art in the twentieth century, and why he experienced such rapture over synthetic cubist collage as a way of negotiating the dangers of cubism's possible two-dimensional deadlock.[362] The content of cubism, for Greenberg, reflected and mastered the highest possibilities of its medium at that point in history. In other words, despite his concern with the flatness of the canvas, there is a sense in which Greenberg is primarily interested in *depth*: in making the invisible deep conditions of any medium somehow visible in the content of the art itself.

2. Non-Relational Philosophy

This links Greenberg closely with two key figures in the twentieth-century humanities. One is the Canadian media theorist Marshall McLuhan, famous for his statements that "the medium is the message" and that "the content or message of any particular medium has about as much importance as the stenciling on the casing of an atomic bomb."[363] In other words, we waste our time when we argue about the good or bad content of television shows, since the real work is done by the invisible changes in the structure of consciousness brought about by television regardless of what high- or low-quality content it might possess. If we translate Greenberg into McLuhanian terms, then "the content of any painting has about as much importance as the stenciling on the casing of an atomic bomb." All political activism in art, all literary anecdote and inspirational messaging, fades before the purely formal consideration of how the medium itself is made to shine forth in the content.

But perhaps an even more important link is with Martin Heidegger, the heavyweight champion of twentieth-century philosophy, who in my view is still unmatched by any figure since. Is not Heidegger's entire philosophical breakthrough a premonition of what McLuhan and Greenberg formulated much later? The phenomenology of Edmund Husserl asked us to suspend judgment about any hidden reasons in nature for things to happen as they do, and to focus instead on the patient description of phenomena in consciousness, in all their subtlety. (There is more to Husserl than this, but this is enough for our current purposes.) Heidegger's great breakthrough

---

[362] Greenberg, *The Collected Essays and Criticism, Volume 4*, pp. 61–66.
[363] The longer quotation comes from the famous 1969 *Playboy* interview also contained in Marshall McLuhan, *Essential McLuhan*, pp. 222–260.

came when he first noted that usually we *do not* encounter entities as present in consciousness. This is already an artificial special case that occurs most often in the *breakdown* of entities. As long as your heart and lungs are healthy and working effectively, as long as the highway is not buckled by earthquakes, as long as the hammer and screwdriver are working in your hands rather than shattering into tiny pieces, they tend not to be noticed. While phenomena in the mind are *present* or *present-at-hand*, entities themselves are *ready-to-hand* for Heidegger, remaining invisible as they work toward various purposes.

Even this standard way of reading Heidegger turns out to be too superficial. He is not just giving us a difference between conscious perception and theory on the one hand and unconscious practical action on the other. Notice that even praxis reduces things to figures, since my use of a chair or hammer reduces it, oversimplifies it by interacting with only a small number of its vast range of qualities. The lesson from Heidegger is not that conscious awareness is the site of figure and unconscious praxis is the site of ground. Instead, the hidden ground is the thing itself, which is reduced, caricatured, or distorted by *any* relation we might have with it, whether theoretical or practical. And moreover, this is not just a special fact about human beings, but is typical even of inanimate relations. But for the moment there is no need to defend an unorthodox reading of Heidegger, since even the most orthodox reading already makes the point we need: what is visibly present in the world appears only against a hidden background from which it draws nourishment. In this sense, Heidegger's critique of presence in the history of philosophy can be viewed as another critique of "academic art" as consisting in the tendency to take the medium of an art too much for granted, to recall Greenberg's powerful definition. In similar fashion, "academic philosophy" for Heidegger would be the kind that treats being as something that can be exhausted in some form of *presence*.

Yet there is a funny thing about this celebration of the deep background medium in Heidegger, McLuhan, and Greenberg. In all three cases, the depth turns out to be utterly sterile, incapable of generating anything new. Let's start with the clearest case, that of McLuhan. For him, the dominant medium in any situation is so deeply buried that there is no way to address it in direct cognitive terms. But not only can we not look at the medium directly – since any attempt to explain the effects of television or the internet will always fall short of the awesome depths of these media – the medium itself cannot even change without some impetus from the outside. As far as I am aware, McLuhan only allows for two ways that media can change. There is reversal through overheating, or retrieval through the work of artists.[364] Reversal occurs when, for example, the speed and convenience of cars reverses into the slowness and inconvenience of traffic jams. Notice that this is not because cars themselves have changed, but only because their apparently superficial features (such as their shiny metallic bulk) became unmanageable due to the vast quantitative increase in the number of cars. What causes one medium to flip into another is not the deep aspect of a medium, but its more secondary and frivolous features.

As for retrieval, this happens for McLuhan when some current cliché or obsolete medium is given new life and made credible again.[365] When vinyl LP records go from obsolete technology outstripped by compact discs to the newly revered medium of connoisseurs who despise the cold and sterile sound of CDs, we have a case of retrieval. But primarily, McLuhan thinks this is the work of *artists*. It is artists who transform banal visible figures by situating them in some sort of enlivening background medium that breathes new life into them. The crucial point for us here is as follows. For McLuhan, background media are more important than any of their content. Yet precisely because these media are *so* deep, *so* inaccessible to conscious contact, they are incapable of transformation. Such transformation can occur only at the most superficial layer of media: whether it be their peripheral features in the case of overheating and reversal, or the level of dead surface content in the case of the artist who retrieves some past medium as the content of a new one.

In Heidegger's philosophy the same point also holds, whatever the appearances to the contrary. There are admittedly some passages in Heidegger, especially in the later writings, when he treats humans as if we could only passively await the sending of new epochs of being. But in fact, the implicit problem faced by Heidegger is that since his objects withdraw so deeply from one another, they are unable to make contact precisely *because* they are deep. If they make contact, it is only through their most superficial outer layer. If I am injured by a hammer or virus, it is not because they assault the very core of my personality, but only because they exploit minor features of my being: such as a sensitive thumb or a few accidental cuts in the skin. Heidegger's depth is so deep that everything must happen on the surface, though he does not realize this as clearly as McLuhan.

---

[364] See Marshall & Eric McLuhan, *Laws of Media*.
[365] On retrieval see Marshall McLuhan & Wilfred Watson, *From Cliché to Archetype*.

Even Greenberg admits that the content of painting is not unimportant. At times he calls it the site of inspiration: Picasso's painting is not just about a relation between the image and the flat picture surface of the canvas, but also about a guitar or horse or the face of a woman. Yet this remains merely a placeholder in Greenberg's writing; he concedes the point without developing further what the role of sheer content might be in art. His primary concern remains the way that the content of the medium reflects its very structure: famously, in his case, the flatness of the picture plane. And though Greenberg freely admitted that this was a transient historical constraint not binding for all eras, he wrote so little about non-modern art that we can only guess the principles he would have used to distinguish good from bad Renaissance perspectival painting, or good from bad twenty-first-century installation art.

3. Art and Relations

It is well known that Greenberg was an opinionated man, capable of swift and harsh judgments; for this reason it can be tempting to dismiss him as cranky and arrogant, his views not worth taking seriously. But this would be a mistake. Greenberg's dismissal of artists we might happen to like is based on his adoption of certain principles underlying contemporary art, and it is better to reflect on and possibly challenge those principles than to condemn Greenberg for being their messenger.

There was no more vehement defender of modernism than Greenberg, who viewed the modern not as a break with the past, but as an attempt to maintain the *quality* of the past by preventing its degeneration into a series of mechanically repeated academic gestures. His definition of the academic, we have seen, is "art that takes its medium too much for granted," and we have linked this claim with certain insights in the media theory of McLuhan and the philosophy of Heidegger. If academic art is the kind that takes its medium too much for granted, we can understand why Greenberg objected to Dalí and other surrealists as academic. There seems to be no innovation as to medium in the case of surrealist painting. Indeed, Greenberg thinks the surrealists deliberately retained the realist and perspectival conventions of academic painting in order to keep everyone's focus on the startling *content* of their works. Though it may seem difficult to call Dalí an "academic artist" with a straight face, the charge is understandable if we accept Greenberg's definition of the term.

But with Duchamp, it seems more difficult to use this designation. We have seen that Greenberg actually makes six separate critiques of Duchamp, with academicism being only one of them. The others were Duchamp's apparent rejection of quality as a standard, his overestimation of the value of shock in art, his tendency to shock not through aesthetic means but through breaches of social expectation, his overreliance on transparent concepts rather than the uncertainty of aesthetic struggle and surprise, and finally his excessive claims of breaking radically with the past. But let us focus on the "academicism" charge. Dalí can easily (if controversially) be treated as an academic artist simply on the basis of Greenberg's definition of the term: academic art as insufficiently aware of its medium. In Duchamp's case a more oblique argument is needed, given that Duchamp is widely considered the shining example of someone who challenges our expectations of what an artistic medium should be.

Greenberg's point seems to be that Duchamp was so deeply academic in outlook (to judge from his insufficiently brilliant early efforts at fauvism and cubism) that he became frustrated by his limitations and misinterpreted cubism primarily as a brazen shock to societal expectations. He then tried to outdo even the cubists in this respect by exhibiting the most banal objects as if they were artworks: a bicycle wheel, a bottle rack, a urinal. In other words, Greenberg's point seems to be that for Duchamp the sole choice is between academic art and provocative gestures, and Duchamp wrongly thought he was following Picasso and all other modernists in pursuing a dazzling career of provocative gestures. This explains Greenberg's other complaints about Duchamp as well. For once art is conceived merely as a shocking gesture, then quality as a standard of measurement no longer matters. New and provocative concepts of what might count as an artwork replace patient aesthetic struggle within a set of plausible ground rules. And finally, by putting ever more ironic quotation marks around the artistic enterprise than anyone before him, Duchamp might easily think of himself as making the most radical break with the history of art.

Surrealism and Dada will forever be linked in the history of art, and the two movements do share some overlapping membership, the use of humorous or incongruous titles for their works, and the deployment of irreverent public personalities. But from a Greenbergian standpoint they actually work in contrary directions, like two scientists performing experiments with opposite controls. Dalí adopts the already banal conventions of three-dimensional illusionistic oil painting, all the better to let the strangeness of the content shine through. Duchamp works in reverse, choosing the most utterly banal content, all the better to shock our expectations about what might count as an artistic medium. If the two artists had not performed these respective controls, the result would have been massive confusion. Imagine that Dalí had painted his classics *The Ghost of Vermeer of Delft Which Can Also Be Used as a Table* and *Gala and "The Angelus" of Millet Preceding the Imminent Arrival of the Conic Anamorphoses*, not in what Greenberg calls academic illusionistic style, but broken up into planes in the manner of high analytic cubism.

Such a chaos of innovation would surprise the viewer from too many directions at once. It is hardly an accident that Picasso and Braque chose such simple subject matter for their cubist masterpieces — *Violin and Candlestick, Fruit Dish and Glass, Portrait of Daniel-Henry Kahnweiler* — since these banal themes allow undivided attention to innovations in technique. Likewise, Duchamp's readymades would have tangled things too badly if he had chosen to display not simple and recognizable everyday objects, but more complicated, esoteric, or ambiguous things. In any case, we can conclude from this that neither Dalí nor Duchamp can plausibly be treated as an academic artist. Dalí does not "take his medium for granted," but *deliberately suspends* innovation of medium in order to open up innovation of subject matter. Meanwhile Duchamp, at least in his readymade pieces, neither takes his medium for granted nor suspends innovation of it, but innovates his media to such a degree that Greenberg can view them only as shocks to fine art decorum, as in his followers' use of

> a row of boxes … a mere rod … a pile of litter … projects for Cyclopean landscape architecture … the plan for a trench dug in a straight line for hundreds of miles … a half-open door … the cross-section of a mountain … stating imaginary relations between real points in real places … a blank wall, and so forth.[366]

Such strategies can reach the point of academic banality as much as any other, and perhaps the arts in 2013 have long since reached that point. But there is no reason to assume that no distinctions of quality are possible within the medium-stretching genre of recent art, that such art really flouts gradations in quality in any sweeping sense, or that it exists solely to provide shocks to social decorum. We should also consider Greenberg's uneven track

---

[366] Greenberg, *The Collected Essays and Criticism, Volume 4*, p. 302.

record as a predictor of greatness. For while he deserves much credit for his early defense of Jackson Pollock, it is by no means clear that history will join him in preferring Gottlieb, Morris, Noland, and Olitski to surrealism, Duchamp, Warhol, and Beuys. In fact, the opposite now seems more likely.

A Greenberg foe might say that he simply uses the term "academic" for anything that he happens not to like. But this would not be quite fair, since Greenberg's critical vocabulary is more versatile than that. For instance, another famous target of Greenberg's harshness is Wassily Kandinsky. A month after the Russian artist's December 1944 death in liberated Paris, Greenberg offered a dismissal of his career that was cold and brazen, but also rather fascinating. It would be difficult to describe a late-blooming innovator like Kandinsky as an "academic artist," and Greenberg does not try to do so. Instead, he classifies Kandinsky as a "provincial" artist. His obituary review opens as follows:

> There are two sorts of provincialism in art. The exponent of one is
> the artist, academic or otherwise, who works in an outmoded style
> or in a vein disregarded by the metropolitan center — Paris, Rome,
> or Athens. The other sort of provincialism is that of the artist —
> generally from an outlying country — who in all earnest and
> admiration devotes himself to the style being currently developed
> in the metropolitan center, yet fails in one way or another really to
> understand what it is about …. The Russian, Wassily Kandinsky,
> [was a provincial of this latter sort].[367]

For Greenberg, the provincial Kandinsky was no naïve simpleton, but a quick-witted observer of advanced art:

> Like many a newcomer to a situation, seeing it from the outside
> and thus more completely, Kandinsky was very quick to perceive
> one of the most basic implications of the revolution cubism had
> effected in Western painting. Pictorial art was at last able to free itself
> completely from the object — the eidetic image — and take for its
> sole positive matter the sensuous facts of its own medium, reducing
> itself to a question … of non-figurative shapes and colors. Painting

---

[367] Clement Greenberg, *The Collected Essays and Criticism, Volume 2*, pp. 3–4.

would become like music, an art contained in its own form and thus capable of infinitely more variety than before.[368]

But in this way, Kandinsky repeats Duchamp's supposed error of thinking he can make a clean break with the history of art. Greenberg makes other objections that seem even more decisive for his verdict on Kandinsky, who in his view "for a relatively short time was a great painter," namely in his earlier period.[369] Greenberg's biggest complaint is that Kandinsky was too focused on the *abstraction* of cubism while missing a more important aspect of that style. As he puts it in the same obituary review:

> [Kandinsky] rejected what to my mind is a prior and perhaps even more essential achievement of avant-garde art than its deliverance of painting from representation: its recapture of the literal realization of the physical limitations and conditions of the medium and of the positive advantages to be gained from the exploitation of these very limitations.[370]

Although it might seem as if Kandinsky is fully aware of the flatness of the picture surface, "he came to conceive of the picture ... as an aggregate of discrete shapes; the color, size, and spacing of these he related so insensitively to the space surrounding them ... that this [space] remained inactive and meaningless; the sense of a continuous surface was lost, and the space became pocked with 'holes.'"[371] Aside from this purely technical shortcoming, Greenberg sees one clear sign of relapse by Kandinsky into academic art: for, "having begun by accepting the absolute flatness of the picture surface, Kandinsky would go on to allude to illusionistic depth by a use of color, line, and perspective that were plastically irrelevant .... Academic reminiscences crept into [Kandinsky's paintings] at almost every point other than that of what they 'represented.'"[372]

In another accusation of insensitivity to medium, Greenberg complains that "the consistency of [Kandinsky's] paint surface and the geometrical exactness of his line seem more appropriate to stone or metal than to the

---

[368] Greenberg, *The Collected Essays and Criticism, Volume 2*, p. 4.
[369] Greenberg, *The Collected Essays and Criticism, Volume 2*, p. 6.
[370] Greenberg, *The Collected Essays and Criticism, Volume 2*, p. 5.
[371] Greenberg, *The Collected Essays and Criticism, Volume 2*, p. 5.
[372] Greenberg, *The Collected Essays and Criticism, Volume 2*, p. 5.

porous fabric of canvas."[373] Finally, his supposed failure to master what the avant-garde was really all about led Kandinsky to become an insecure and eclectic stylist. As Greenberg puts it, "the stylistic and thematic ingredients of Kandinsky's later work are as diverse as the colors of Joseph's coat: peasant, ancient, and Oriental art, much Klee, some Picasso, surrealist protoplasma, maps, blueprints, musical notation, etc., etc."[374] From all of this, Greenberg concludes with a few concessions and a single crowning damnation: "[Kandinsky] was and will remain a large and revolutionary phenomenon — he must be taken into account always; yet he stays apart from the main stream and in the last analysis remains a provincial. The example of his work is dangerous to younger painters."[375]

But Greenberg's description of the dangers of Kandinsky seems to hinge too much on a single debatable point. He cautions that Kandinsky's exact line would be more appropriate for stone or metal than canvas, yet he immediately concedes that the same is true of Mondrian, whom Greenberg regards as a truly great artist despite that stony-metallic exact line. He also tries to warn us that "academic reminiscences" creep into Kandinsky, which should mean that Kandinsky has a lingering tendency to take his medium for granted. But even if this turned out to be sweepingly true for the whole of Kandinsky's work, it would not follow that it *must* be true for any art that adopts the abstractions of cubism while downplaying its relation to the flatness of the medium. Revolutions are often fuelled when heirs adopt only one portion of their forerunners' legacies while refusing the others. As Greenberg himself repeatedly admits, there is not just one way to make great art, and what succeeds in one era will fail in others, precisely because the same techniques are fresh at one moment and banal in the next. He even makes the surprising admission that Duchamp was right to be "wild" early on as a way of escaping the "cubist vise," which suggests Greenberg's firm awareness that even the greatest styles can become suffocating prisons.

Just like the Renaissance-era growth of perspectival illusionist painting, the reverse movement towards painting that exploits the *limitations* of the flat canvas can reach a point of decadent banality. Were Duchamp, surrealism, and Kandinsky truly *relapses* from cubism in the way that Greenberg claims? Or were they not instead more like probes seeking a new planet, quite apart from the question of whether they succeeded in finding it? Nonetheless,

---

[373] Greenberg, *The Collected Essays and Criticism, Volume 2*, p. 5.
[374] Greenberg, *The Collected Essays and Criticism, Volume 2*, p. 5.
[375] Greenberg, *The Collected Essays and Criticism, Volume 2*, p. 6.

it is dangerous to call Greenberg old-fashioned, as many of his opponents do. His keen intelligence deserves more than that, as does his literary brilliance. Due to his work as a critic and his spiritual guidance of the shift in avant-garde art from Paris to New York, Greenberg is no doubt one of the half-dozen or so most important intellectual figures the United States has produced. Moreover, *everyone* becomes old-fashioned someday, and those who dance on Greenberg's tomb will eventually be danced upon in turn, viewed as outdated in their own right.

What will it look like when this happens? Let us assume for the sake of argument that surrealism produces no further avant-garde revolution, since its basic principles have been thoroughly explored. The same holds for abstraction, a known quantity for just as long, even if its lifespan was longer. Duchamp's wager of continually questioning what counts as art may have a few years of life left in it, and hence we are still prepared to be impressed by "a row of boxes … a mere rod … a pile of litter … projects for Cyclopean landscape architecture … the plan for a trench dug in a straight line for hundreds of miles … a half-open door … the cross-section of a mountain … stating imaginary relations between real points in real places … a blank wall, and so forth." But this too will eventually become old and tired, if it is not already so, and something different will need to awaken to surprise us.

What will this new thing be? We have already considered the "academicism" of Duchamp and surrealism, and the "provincialism" of Kandinsky, and have stipulated a future in which all are spent forces along with Greenberg's School of Flatness. What else is left? It could be many things, but so far we have only encountered one other possibility in the course of our discussions: the *first* kind of provincialism, different from Kandinsky's second kind. To refresh our memories, Kandinsky's sort of provincialism was said to be "that of the artist — generally from an outlying country — who in all earnest and admiration devotes himself to the style being currently developed in the metropolitan center, yet fails in one way or another really to understand what it is about."[376] The other kind of provincialism, which we have not yet discussed, is that of "the artist, academic or otherwise, who works in an outmoded style or in a vein disregarded by the metropolitan center."[377]

At first it might sound as if this sort of artist cannot be a candidate for cutting-edge status, since the word "outmoded" suggests otherwise. But Greenberg already gives us an example of one such "outmoded" artist

---

[376] Greenberg, *The Collected Essays and Criticism, Volume 2*, pp. 3–4.
[377] Greenberg, *The Collected Essays and Criticism, Volume 2*, pp. 3–4.

working in a vein disregarded by the metropolitan center, and indeed one of the greatest artists: Paul Cézanne, whom he considers in a beautiful 1951 essay entitled "Cézanne and the Unity of Modern Painting."[378] The opening claim of that essay is that the apparent eclecticism of avant-garde art in 1951 is merely an appearance. Great figures do not exhaustively accomplish what they aim to achieve, and always leave behind a tangle of loose threads for their successors to tie together. Greenberg views the late nineteenth century, and Cézanne in particular, as the origin of these threads. Even as great a movement as cubism, like all later phases in every revolutionary era (the German Idealists were prodigies compared with the slow-moving Kant, their master) was able to speedily benefit from the untied threads of Cézanne:

> Picasso's and Braque's Cubism, and Léger's, completed what Cézanne had begun, by their successes divesting his means of whatever had remained problematical about them and finding them their most appropriate ends. These means they took from Cézanne practically ready-made, and were able to adapt them to their purposes after only a relatively few trial exercises.[379]

But the truly interesting topic of Greenberg's essay on Cézanne is the opposite one: not Cézanne as the far-seeing grandfather of later trends, but as the struggling admirer of the classical painters before him. It is the story of the artist who does not simply extrapolate from the threads of his immediate forerunners, but who attempts to bring back something important that recent revolutions had prematurely left behind. So it was with Cézanne and the Impressionists. As Greenberg unforgettably puts it:

> [Cézanne] was making the first — and last — pondered effort to save the intrinsic principle of the Western tradition of painting: its concern with an ample and literal rendition of the illusion of the third dimension. He had noted the Impressionists' inadvertent silting up of pictorial depth. And it is because he tried so hard to re-excavate that depth without abandoning Impressionist color, and because his attempt, while vain, was so profoundly conceived, that it became the turning point it did …. Like Manet and with almost as little appetite

---

[378] Clement Greenberg, *The Collected Essays and Criticism, Volume 3*, pp. 82–91.
[379] Clement Greenberg, *The Collected Essays and Criticism, Volume 3*, p. 90.

for the role of revolutionary, he changed the course of art out of the very effort to return it by new paths to its old ways.[380]

The danger faced by all modernizers is that of robotic extrapolation. They assume that the previous revolution performed innovation X, and therefore the next revolution must perform double-X or triple-X. For instance, since the Enlightenment advanced by denouncing superstition and defending reason, the next phase of history requires a redoubled campaign of utter persecution against all "irrational" people, and so forth. Extrapolation has its historical moments, and those lucky enough to live in such moments can complete their work rapidly at a young age based on struggling prior mentors, as did Picasso and Braque in their analytic cubist period. Others must struggle slowly like Cézanne (or Kant) to find the new principle of an age, painstakingly retrieving the old while not abandoning what is new, and perhaps dangling dozens of loose threads that others in the following generation can tie together as they please. If we follow Greenberg in treating art since 1960 as the reign of Neo-Dada, then what is most valuable in the past that this period sacrificed and left behind? What outmoded provincial might emerge as the Cézanne of the coming era?

---

[380] Clement Greenberg, *The Collected Essays and Criticism, Volume 3*, pp. 83–84.

CHAPTER 20

MATERIALISM IS NOT THE SOLUTION: ON MATTER, FORM, AND MIMESIS[381]

Object-oriented philosophy is often included on lists of recent materialist theories. Let me begin by decisively rejecting the term "materialism," which I view as one of the most damaging philosophical temptations of our time. Nonetheless, the people who call object-oriented philosophy a form of materialism are not fools. There is a reason why they see a close proximity between my approach and that of other nearby authors who sympathize with materialism, whereas no one has ever called object-oriented philosophy "Hegelianism" or "Marxism," for instance. For this reason, I will begin by considering the defense of materialism offered by Jane Bennett. That will take us only partway to the goal, since I want to say something about aesthetics. My rejection of materialism is made in favor of something that might be called "formalism." But formalism already has a long and contested history in literature, architecture, and the visual arts. I will try to show that the kind of formalism I advocate has little to do with the familiar sort. In fact, I will try to show that formalism (in the usual sense of the term) and materialism (in every sense of the term) are two faces of the same error. Lastly, I will try to revive a term that is even older and more discredited in the arts than formalism is: namely, *mimesis*, or the idea that art is primarily

---

[381] This chapter originally appeared in the *Nordic Journal of Aesthetics*, No. 47 (2014), pp. 94–110.

an imitation of the world. My claim here is that art *is* mimesis, but in the theatrical sense of method acting, rather than the productive sense of fabricating imitations.[382] The artist imitates not by producing copies of external things, but by *becoming* external things.

1. Materialism

The word "form" has several opposites. We speak of form vs. matter, but also of form vs. content and form vs. function. "Matter" is not as versatile, and almost always appears in opposition to form. Whereas form must have some kind of shape — usually a visible one — matter is that which escapes this shape and resists taking on definite contours. This might happen in one of two different ways. Matter can either be some ultimate term into which all derivative shapes break down, as when we say that all physical things are composed of the elements in chemistry's periodic table. But beyond this, matter can also be that which lies in the depth as absolutely formless, an amorphous reservoir more primordial than any definite thing.

This ambiguity defines the two basic types of pre-Socratic philosophy, as Aristotle already noted in the *Metaphysics*. All pre-Socratic philosophy can be described as materialism of one of the two sorts just distinguished. Either it tries to identify some privileged physical element from which everything else is built (air, water, air/earth/fire/water combined, or atoms), or it chooses instead to defend a formless *apeiron* from which all of these elements provisionally emerge. Even today, we find two basic kinds of materialism, both of them deriving from pre-Socratic philosophy. First, there is the materialism beloved by the Marxist and physicalist traditions, in which ultimate material elements are the root of everything and higher-level entities are merely secondary mystifications that partake of the real only insofar as they emerge from the ultimate material substrate. This kind of materialism owes everything to the ancient line of Thales, Anaximenes, Empedocles, and Democritus. It generally has a *critical* flavor, and thus was preferred by the figures of past and present-day Enlightenment standpoints: even tables, trees, and the brain must be eliminated in favor of the ultimate elements, to say nothing of angels, gods, and folk psychologies.

But second, there is the materialism of the *apeiron*, for which even the physical entities of science are not deep enough since they already have too

---

[382] See Konstantin Stanislavski, *An Actor's Work*, though Stanislavski himself refers to an acting "system" rather than a "method."

much particular structure to deserve being called the bottom layer of the cosmos. This brand of materialism inherits the line of Anaximander and Anaxagoras, usually with a bit of Heraclitean flux-loving thrown into the mix. The cosmos is not inherently made of tiny physical pieces, but is an amorphous or hemi-morphous whole from which individual pieces arise only as transient local intensities. The world is pre-individual in character, and is made up primarily of fluxes and flows and becomings. The world is basically a continuum, and all attempts to break it into local districts are inherently provisional and relative. This type of materialism is usually not critical in flavor, but tends to be holistic and affirmative. All things are interconnected; emotions and social practices are no less real than the particles which themselves are nothing but a fleeting manifestation of a cosmic whole.

Both standpoints have their merits, but object-oriented philosophy firmly rejects them. Against the two kinds of materialism, object-oriented philosophy insists on the rights of *form*, as that which has structure at every level of scale, and which cannot be reduced either downward to a privileged layer of triumphalistic physical being, or upward to a cosmic holism that treats differences as merely continuous gradients in an uninterrupted, quivering flux. The cat and the table may not be eternal, yet they withstand environmental fluctuation nonetheless, and can gain and lose certain attributes or shift their relations to all other things, while only sometimes being infiltrated or destroyed. The world is made neither of physical ultimates nor of a whole, but of *objects*, and what most typifies objects is that they always have structure or form. Against Heidegger's veneration for the pre-Socratics, we must say that the task of philosophy begins only when it becomes distinct from the tasks of physics and of cosmic holism (which are surprisingly similar): namely, only when philosophy ends the worship of matter and begins to account for the problem of form. This occurs in distinct ways in Plato and Aristotle, who remain the foundational giants of our discipline and are still the two greatest philosophers of the West.

What is ultimately wrong with the two materialist standpoints, which I often call strategies for "undermining" the object? Their shared defect is their inability to account for true *emergence* at levels other than the most basic one. Consider a body of water such as Lake Michigan. It may be difficult to specify in geological terms exactly when this lake was formed and when it will have changed so much as to turn into something else completely. But let's suspend that problem for a moment. There is a certain stability to Lake Michigan despite the fact that its population of water molecules is never quite the same. Evaporation occurs constantly. Water splashes ashore with the waves and some of it is lost for good, and the coastline alters slightly. Tourists sometimes pour unwanted drinking water over the side of a boat, augmenting the lake with what used to be the consumer's Evian or Dasani. Some rivers flow directly into the lake. And of course, somewhere on the lake it may be raining. While it may never be clear precisely where the lake begins and ends, it would be purely arbitrary to claim that the lake is identical with its exact population of water molecules at the moment. The lake has lake-effects not found in individual droplets of water, and might have an endless number of other effects that it does not currently have. The lake has a robust character that withstands the arrival or departure of its individual droplets. The lake has a structure different from the structure of other things. In short, the lake is a form. The scientistic lake would treat it nominalistically as just a nickname for a series of varying collections of water that have enough family resemblances over time that we can call it "Lake Michigan" in a loose sense, and only in a loose one. Meanwhile, the holistic position would treat it as just a zone of relative lakeness, one that is basically continuous with neighboring lakes and with the shore. What both materialisms miss is the way in which the lake cuts itself off from its neighbors and its own causal components, allowing a certain degree of entry and exit to all the forces of the non-lake, but remaining a form that endures for some time even if not eternally. The lake endures until other entities actually do the *significant and not inevitable work* of destroying or changing it.

Object-oriented philosophy treats objects as forms that do not automatically dissolve back into that from which they came. By contrast, materialism is a reductionism that falls short of the true task of philosophy: the study of the elusive *forms* which are never identical either to that of which they are made or the ways in which they are described or known. The form of the object is that which hides midway between its material substrate and its concrete manifestation at any given moment in any given context. Forms are hidden in the floorboards of the world, and cannot be known by replacing them with something that seems to be known already: whether it be their constituent material or their effects. In this sense, materialism is a strictly *anti-philosophical* position, and that is why I have written elsewhere that materialism must be destroyed.[383] Many of the calls for "materialism"

---

[383] Graham Harman, "I Am Also of the Opinion That Materialism Must Be Destroyed." See also Graham Harman, "Realism Without Materialism."

today are calls to resume the Enlightenment legacy of *critique*, in the sense of the debunking of superstition and a critique (made from the Left) of existing social institutions. But while this tradition has much to be proud of, it is unclear that we can or should extrapolate it into the future, given the intellectual weakness of the materialism whose banner it waves. The work of debunking and of revolution may need to be transformed in view of new intellectual circumstances, rather than merely extended, or else it risks turning into a moralistic revival movement.

We can only expect that this call for a non-materialist philosophy will be attacked by its outright enemies, who have much to lose if the project succeeds. But what about the intellectual friends and neighbors of object-oriented philosophy, who continue to call for materialism as a way to address object-oriented defects? As promised, I will speak here of Jane Bennett, who among other things is an unusually powerful writer. I have written elsewhere about her wonderful book *Vibrant Matter*.[384] Here I will deal instead with Bennett's response to me and Timothy Morton in the pages of *New Literary History*, where Morton and I had proposed different object-oriented theories of literary criticism.[385] Bennett shows a clear understanding of what object-oriented philosophy is all about, with its attempt to reverse the recent fashion of "networks, negotiations, relations, interactions, and dynamic fluctuations."[386] When I call it a "prejudice" to favor these terms, Bennett wants me to acknowledge an equal degree of prejudice on my part in favor of objects. And that leads her to proclaim, quite rightly, that a theory ought to be able to deal with both of these extremes. As she puts it:

> But perhaps there is no need to choose between objects or their relations. Since everyday, earthly experience routinely identifies some effects as coming from individual objects and some from larger systems (or, better put, from individuations within material configurations and from the complex assemblages in which they participate), why not aim for a theory that toggles between both kinds or magnitudes of "unit"?[387]

---

[384] Jane Bennett, *Vibrant Matter*; Graham Harman, "Autonomous Objects."
[385] See Jane Bennett, "Systems and Things," written in response to Graham Harman, "The Well-Wrought Broken Hammer" and Timothy Morton, "An Object-Oriented Defense of Poetry."
[386] Bennett, "Systems and Things," p. 226, citing from Harman, "The Well-Wrought Broken Hammer," p. 187.
[387] Bennett, "Systems and Things," p. 227.

Compromise always sounds reasonable. Yet Bennett explains her proposal in terms that quickly return objects to a secondary status. As she has it, the broader compromise position "would then understand 'objects' to be those swirls of matter, energy, and incipience that hold themselves together long enough to vie with the strivings of other objects, including the indeterminate momentum of the throbbing whole."[388] Notice that far from making a peace offering to object-oriented philosophy, Bennett simply reasserts the privilege of a "throbbing whole" that we already encountered, in germ, in the pre-Socratic *apeiron*. The main innovation is that Bennett does not just speak of a whole, but also describes it as "throbbing." One online dictionary defines the word "throb," accurately enough, as meaning "to beat or sound with a strong, regular rhythm; [to] pulsate steadily."[389] This word is obviously Bennett's attempt to avoid the specter of *stasis* that arises whenever we think of the world as a unified whole rather than carved into discrete and competing districts. That is to say, Bennett wants it both ways. The world is a whole, but also a whole that is somehow injected with a principle of motion and local differentiation. The world needs fluctuation in local intensities in order to avoid a purely motionless *apeiron*. She also holds that there is a place for objects in this throbbing whole. Objects, we have seen, would be "those swirls of matter, energy, and incipience that hold themselves together long enough to vie with the strivings of other objects, including the indeterminate momentum of the throbbing whole."[390] Bennett's cosmos is a throbbing matter-energy (form is not mentioned) containing local "swirls" that sometimes last long enough to be identified (by *people*, it seems) as having a sort of fleeting identity. In order to attain a balanced perspective, we would have "to make both objects and relations the periodic focus of theoretical attention."

This might seem to recall the famous, evenhanded particle/wave duality of light in modern physics. The difference is that if we translate Bennett's views into physical terms, she would treat photons (light particles) as nothing but swirls emerging from a more primordial throbbing wave. In short, she allows for no duality at all, except insofar as people sometimes take swirls to be durable. In echoing the object-oriented dualism between objects and relations, Bennett never explicitly clarifies how relations fit into the picture of the throbbing whole, but given that the word "whole"

---

[388] Bennett, "Systems and Things," p. 227.
[389] Oxford Dictionaries, http://oxforddictionaries.com/definition/english/throb, last accessed on October 5, 2013.
[390] Bennett, "Systems and Things," p. 227.

suggests a pre-established link between all that resides in its embrace, it seems disingenuous for Bennett to suggest that she merely wants a balanced assessment of the two. It is clear enough which term is the dominant one for Bennett and which is the dominated. Though adopting the role of a diplomat, Bennett has already shown her anti-object-oriented cards.

Bennett adds that she "finds ... attempts to do justice both to systems and things, to acknowledge the stubborn reality of individuation and the essentially distributive quality of their affectivity or capacity to produce effects, to remain philosophically and (especially) politically productive."[391] But where is the supposed imbalance in my own approach? She continues:

> Harman rejects the very framing of the issue as things-operating-in-systems, in favor of an object-oriented picture in which aloof objects are positioned as the sole locus of all the acting. And yet ... Harman, against that object-prejudice, finds himself theorizing a kind of relation — "communication" — between objects. He tries to insulate this object-to-object encounter from depictions that also locate activity in the relationships themselves or at the systemic level of operation, but I do not think that this parsing attempt succeeds.[392]

With the words "and yet," Bennett suggests that I work at cross-purposes in first insisting on the aloofness of objects and then also, perhaps against my will, referring to a kind of communication between them. But this twofold fate of objects as both communicating and non-communicating is the *whole point* of object-oriented philosophy, which is designed precisely to create a "balance" between objects and relations that no theory of swirls and throbbing wholes can ever give us. The point is not that relations are either non-existent or secondary. The point is that relations are neither automatic nor easy, as the theory of a pre-existent unifying whole would suggest. Humans are not affected by every tiniest thing that happens in their vicinity, just as tectonic plates do not constantly generate major earthquakes and volcanoes do not constantly erupt. Things are not *always* affected by each other, are not *always* in relation to each other. The claim that all stasis can be reduced to an imperceptible motion simply adopts motion as the principle of the world without *earning* the right to say so. And despite what Bennett says, objects for me are by no means the sole locus of all the acting,

---

[391] Bennett, "Systems and Things," p. 228.
[392] Bennett, "Systems and Things," p. 228.

since objects, insofar as they are aloof, *do not act at all*: they simply exist, too non-relational to engage in any activity whatsoever. Their relations with other objects are a very special case, and demand an explanation that cannot seriously be provided if we assume that they are always already related in the embrace of a cosmic matter-energy.

2. Formalism

I have explained why we must reject materialism, whether it defends one privileged type of entity at the expense of others dismissed as immaterial, or whether it champions a deeper pulsating whole from which all specific entities are held to emerge. Further, I have claimed that both types of materialism are essentially pre-Socratic in origin, and therefore (contra Heidegger) belong to a still immature phase in the history of philosophy when it did not yet struggle with the crucial status of form. Reality consists of objects of all different scales, complicit in the production of other objects, which can never be identified either with the smaller objects that compose them or the larger objects that they compose. Relation and interference occur, but remain somewhat rare. Not everything that happens is relevant to everything else. All things do not reflect all other things as if in a mirror; there are firewalls between things breached only occasionally and with difficulty. What is admirable in materialism is its sense that any visible situation contains a deeper surplus able to subvert or surprise it. Yet this surplus is never shapeless; it always has form. And no one level of form can be considered more real than another. This is why we must defend formalism over materialism: not (as in most formalism) because there is no excess beneath the forms that are given, but because *the excess is itself always formed*. Here is the problem with Heidegger's view of the artwork as strife between world and earth, since the earth that juts through in the Heideggerian artwork has too much of Bennett's throbbing whole about it.[393] Earth is not formed, but acts only to subvert any given form, just as his Being is too often hinted to be a One in opposition to the many beings, rather than treated as a plurality of hidden faces of the many individual beings.

Having defended form against matter, I would now like to defend it against function and content as well. The duel of form and function is most familiar in architecture, where functionalist architecture embeds the art of

---

[393] Martin Heidegger, "The Origin of the Work of Art."

building in a system of wider social needs, while formalist architecture rejects this task and occupies itself with the self-contained character of visible form. The architect Patrik Schumacher rejects both extremes in the following way:

> Architectural discourse is organized around the lead-distinction of *form* versus *function*. Architecture, like all design disciplines, hinges upon this distinction. That architecture always has to address both terms of this distinction has been asserted over and over again by many architects and architectural theorists. Whenever one term of the distinction seems to be in danger of being neglected, vehement reminders are issued .... There are countless instances of this theoretical steering effort against the twin evils of a one-sided Formalism and one-sided Functionalism. The perennial Formalism-Functionalism controversy is itself the clearest evidence for the thesis proposed here that the distinction between form and function is the lead-distinction of architecture/design and thus a fundamental, permanent communication structure of [architecture].[394]

While Schumacher, like Bennett, strives to balance two concerns, there is a sense in which form and function are not distinct at all.

Note that functional concerns treat architecture in its relation to external needs, such as the features of housing or schooling or government that a building must serve, so that the building is dissolved into ulterior purposes. But note as well that even form is relational, since it is always a form *for* designers and observers. Form in Schumacher's sense is still not the building itself, but merely its outward look. Whether we consider the building as existing for a client with practical needs, or for an avant-garde architectural public, in both cases the building is overdetermined by its relations. The building itself remains unacknowledged as a source of surprise or resistance to both its formal and functional concerns.

This is reminiscent of the usual reading of Heidegger's famous tool-analysis.[395] As is well known, Heidegger distinguishes between the present-at-hand and the ready-to-hand. To perceive an object is to perceive its form or outward look (Schumacher's "formal"); to use an object is to let it function in relation to all other objects in a referential whole (Schumacher's "functional"). The hammer has a definite visual look, yet this look emerges

---

[394] Patrik Schumacher, *The Autopoiesis of Architecture*, vol. 1, p. 207.
[395] For a full account of Heidegger's tool-analysis see Graham Harman, *Tool-Being*.

only rarely, in cases of breakdown; the rest of the time, the hammer functions smoothly in relation to a whole system of other things. This often yields the interpretation that Heidegger shows us that praxis comes before theory, or (in architectural terms that he never uses) function before form. Heidegger argues further that the visible hammer seems to be independent, while the functional hammer belongs to a systematic whole. Yet as I have often argued, this cannot be the case. The hammer's true independence comes not from the fact that it is sometimes seen as an isolated thing, but from the fact that it can *break*. And insofar as the hammer can break, this makes it a surplus not contained in the holism of systematic functions any more than the kingdom of visible form. Insofar as we see the hammer, it exists in relation to us; insofar as the hammer is engaged in relation with nails, boards, and construction projects, it exists in relation to these other things. But the fact that the hammer can break shows that it is deeply *non*-relational, that it resists being appropriated by us and by other equipment. What is this real hammer lying in the depths, beneath our perceptions and beneath all invisible function? This real hammer is also a form, since it has structure and qualities that distinguish it from all other things, but a form that exists regardless of any contact with us or anything else. It is not unlike what the medievals and Leibniz called "substantial form." This deeper formalism of objects simultaneously refutes materialism, functionalism, and formalism (in the derivative sense of outward visual look).

Let's speak now of the opposition between form and content. This will prove to be the most important of the three, since form and content turn out to be a more ambiguous pair than the others. And here we will make use of the great Canadian media theorist Marshall McLuhan, perhaps the most explicit champion of form against content. When McLuhan speaks of media, he is speaking of the hidden background condition of any medium that makes its content irrelevant.[396] It is foolish to speak of the difference between good and bad radio shows, since what is really at stake are the features of radio itself: which differ from those of newspapers or television, and which structure our consciousness differently regardless of how we judge the content of individual programs. The content of any medium, McLuhan once provocatively remarked, is no more relevant than the graffiti on an atomic bomb.[397] The medium itself is the deep, the unnoticed, and the decisive. Gutenberg's press is of greater significance in changing ratios of

---

[396] Marshall McLuhan, *Understanding Media*; Marshall & Eric McLuhan, *Laws of Media*.
[397] Marshall McLuhan, "The Playboy Interview."

human perception than any Bible or other book that came from it.[398] Like Francis Bacon (one of his heroes) McLuhan thinks that objects are not what their surface properties tell us, since "every body contains in itself many forms of natures united together in a concrete state, [and] the result is that they severally crush, depress, break, and enthrall one another, and thus the individual forms are obscured."[399]

It seems at first that for McLuhan, depth is everything and surface is a mere distraction. In this respect he obviously resembles Heidegger, whose contempt for the surface of beings is no less vivid than McLuhan's own. For Heidegger, any surface configuration of the world is merely "ontic," whereas the real is that which is veiled, concealed, sheltered, harbored, or withdrawn. But along with McLuhan and Heidegger, we should add a third dark knight of depth against surface: Clement Greenberg.[400] At first it might sound counterintuitive to call Greenberg a theorist of depth. After all, it was he who defended the flatness of painting and denounced the post-Renaissance tradition of three-dimensional illusionism as a spent force, as the very embodiment of "academic art" in his time. Yet the point is not so much that the flat canvas is *flat*, but the fact that it is a *medium* deeper than any possible content. For Greenberg, pictorial content degenerates into "literary anecdote" unless it somehow incorporates a reference to the flatness of the painting. Consider his rejection of Salvador Dalí as just another academic painter, since for all the bizarreness of his content he uses the same now-discredited techniques of post-Renaissance illusionism that we find in full-blown academic painting.[401] Or even more surprisngly, consider his rejection of Kandinsky, who in Greenberg's view misunderstands the essence of cubism as abstraction rather than as flatness, and thus gives us circles and triangles floating in empty space in a way that indulges what Greenberg calls "academic reminiscence," or even "provincialism."[402] For Greenberg, the canvas medium is the depth hiding behind any surface content, which is obliged to incorporate that depth in some way for any painting that wishes to be avant-garde rather than academic.

Yet all intellectual theories of depth have the inherent problem that there is not much for us to say about a depth beneath all access. Some such

---

[398] Marshall McLuhan, *The Gutenberg Galaxy*.

[399] Francis Bacon, *The New Organon*, Book 2, p. 24.

[400] See Graham Harman, "The Revenge of the Surface." This is an English translation, by the author, of the German booklet *Die Rache der Oberfläche*.

[401] Clement Greenberg, *The Collected Essays and Criticism, Volume 1*, p. 9, n. 2.

[402] Clement Greenberg, *The Collected Essays and Criticism, Volume 2*, pp. 3–4.

theories, including Heidegger's, have the additional problem that we cannot gain access to this minimal depth in the first place. By belittling content at the expense of form, Heidegger, McLuhan, and Greenberg seem to give little role to content other than to be mocked by its deeper condition. Nonetheless, all three of these authors are aware of this problem to some extent, and all are forced to give way to what we might call "the revenge of the surface."[403] Heidegger, after all, is less a theorist of being than of human Dasein's striving towards this being. Being needs us, he says, in order to come to presence in manifold ways through the unfolding of the history of being. Perhaps more importantly, though Heidegger did not quite see this, his theory of the withdrawal of all beings makes causal relation itself into a problem. If we push his theory of tools beyond its initial holism, we are not only led to a hammer-in-itself and nail-in-itself outside the tool-system. We also need to ask how a hammer could ever hit a nail in the first place, if they are both too deep to engage in mutual contact. If tool-beings exist only at an ultimate depth for Heidegger, then their relations can only occur on the most superficial surface of the world. Whereas Gilles Deleuze tends to view surfaces as loci of sterile effects, for Heidegger there is the paradoxical fact that events must unfold entirely on the surface.

In Greenberg's case, it cannot just be a question of an artist's reflexive awareness that there is a flat canvas medium behind the content of a painting. This insight is quickly mastered, but not all masterpieces of modern painting do it in precisely the same way. Displaying a plain white canvas is not the best artwork imaginable, since even for Greenberg the aesthetic challenge of such a work would not be very rich. What is crucial for Greenberg is the way the content of the painting assimilates background flatness and embeds it *within* the content, which thereby rises above the literary anecdote of academic painting that takes an illusionistic three-dimensional tradition for granted. There are still at least two problems here: and they are historical problems, despite Greenberg's admission that flatness is binding only for a limited era of art. The first points backward in time. Since Greenberg concedes that incorporation of the flat background is the principle of advanced art only in his own time, by what criteria shall we judge pre-modern painting? It is noteworthy that while Greenberg occasionally passes judgments on the older Florentines and Venetians and Spaniards, these topics occupy a relatively minimal part of his written output, and often seem free-floating or unconnected with his general theory of painting.

---

[403] See Graham Harman, "The Revenge of the Surface."

Do Raphael or Velázquez exceed their lesser contemporaries through better incorporation of the conditions of the background medium, or is it not for some other reason? The second problem points forward in time. Doesn't the principle of hinting internally at the background medium eventually grow as stale as every other? Is it not the case that abstraction itself eventually turned into academicism, despite Greenberg's definition of academic art as "art that is unaware of its medium"? Unless we wish to read the history of art after Pollock, Noland, and Olitski as a prolonged decadence with no end in sight, art needs a different guiding principle than flatness. Artists themselves have known this for half a century.

In the case of McLuhan, the revenge of the surface is even more obtrusive. For all his talk of the inaccessibility of the background medium, these media do nothing but silently dominate us. Their very depth makes them unable to communicate with us or with each other, just like Heidegger's tool-beings. The only two ways in which McLuhan allows media to change are both surface-events. The first is what he calls the reversal of the overheated medium, when the quantitative increase or overdevelopment of a given medium overloads the world with information, leading to a sudden flip of the medium into something that looks like the opposite. Cars begin as a speedy convenience and tool of freedom, but eventually turn into urban clutter: increasing our travel time, the pollution of our breath, and effectively enslaving us to a network of parking ramps, banks, and insurance companies. Note that all these effects are *side-effects*, emanating not from the inherent functional shape of the car itself, but from its accidental surface features such as price, exhaust, and metallic bulk. The second way media change is through what McLuhan calls retrieval. We are surrounded with the dead media of yesteryear, but McLuhan grants artists the special power to revive these dead clichés by bringing them into relation with the living background of our own time, thus making the dead things credible again. In this sense artists are "the antennae of our race," not because they glimpse the hidden background of the world in superhuman fashion, but because they turn the dead forms of the past into creatures of the background.[404]

But not only does the formerly despised surface become our fresh gateway into the dark and rumbling underworld. More than this, we discover that the depth is not something *distinct* from the things, but is directly incarnated in them. Think again of Heidegger's "earth," which supposedly juts forth in every artwork. The problem is that earth tends to be just as monistic as his

---

[404] McLuhan appears to have borrowed this phrase from Ezra Pound, *Literary Essays*, p. 58.

conception of Being. Just as Being is always the same no matter in what plurality of beings it chooses to manifest itself, earth is the same earth in every artwork. Or maybe not, you say? Maybe Heidegger realizes that the earthy red of a painting is different from the earthy gold leaf of another, just as it differs from the earthy marble of a sculpture? But in that case he has already conceded the central point: that the earth is many rather than one, and that the depths are already formed.

Think too of McLuhan. Unless we accept that only media *revolutions* show any skill, and such that all radio and television programs would be equally stupid in their ignorance of the background, then we have to conclude that McLuhan would allow for more and less successful programs, with the more successful ones shaping their content in a way that better reflects the inherent conditions of the medium. McLuhan seems to know this, since he reports that Kennedy defeated Nixon in their debate among television viewers, while those listening on radio tended to favor Nixon: a sign that Kennedy-content was a better match for one medium and Nixon-content for another.[405] Or consider McLuhan's related assertion that Hitler could never have risen to power in the age of television, a medium in which his shrill proclamations would have been ridiculous to the masses rather than energizing.

Greenberg must make the same concession. The background incorporated by all the aspects of a modern painting cannot just be a single canvas *apeiron* like that of the pre-Socratics, since then the flat canvas would jut forth in the same way in each image. All elements of all paintings would be interchangeable stand-ins for each other, as long as each performed the sole task of hinting knowingly at the background behind them. Instead, each painting, each artwork, must generate its own background. More than this, each part of each artwork must have its own background, so that we do not fall into the untenable holism of claiming that an artwork is a well-oiled machine in which each part is thoroughly determined by all the rest. If this were the case, then any modification of any artwork, however trivial, would result in the production of a completely new artwork. It would be art as a "bundle of qualities," to use David Hume's famous and regrettable phrase.

In short, the relation between figure and ground cannot be the relation between many and one. Each figure embodies its *own* ground, and embodies it concretely. In the terms of ancient philosophy, this is analogous to a shift from Aristotle to Plato. One of the clearest but least convincing aspects

---

[405] McLuhan, *Understanding Media*, p. 329.

of Alain Badiou's *Logics of Worlds* is his basically Platonic conception of art.[406] Art, of course, is one of Badiou's four "truth procedures," which he tells us have been the same four since at least Ancient Greece. The others are politics, love, and science (though the latter is inexplicably replaced in *Logics of Worlds* by the easier case of mathematics). Badiou is concerned to secure the objectivity or even eternity of these truth procedures. Romantic love, especially of the heterosexual sort, is freed from all historicizing and is described as a recurrently enacted truth. Politics is guided at all points in history by the "communist invariant." Mathematics, the easiest case of the four, bears witness to truths about prime numbers that weigh heavily on every subject, irrespective of historical time or place. This leads him to a rather unconvincing account of art, one that Greenberg would have dismissed as a reversion to academicism. Badiou's example of an artistic invariant is that both Picasso and prehistoric cave painters painted horses, and that the same "horseness" is at work in both cases. There is an invariant form of the horse across thousands of years. Although Badiou seemingly allows art to deal with a plurality of backgrounds (since there are many other things one might paint besides horses) to say that both cave painters and Picasso are painting the same thing is a needlessly literal reading of both, and mainly serves the Platonizing function of creating a forced analogy between art and mathematics, the love of Badiou's life. It would be closer to the truth if we said that prehistoric art gives us one horse and Picasso gives us another. Each painted horse is a different horse, just as for Aristotle there is no perfect eternal horse-form, but simply many individual horses. But what is the individual aesthetic horse behind the pigments through it which it is suggested? Or more generally, what is the relation between the form and the content of any given thing?

3. Mimesis

One of the central concepts of object-oriented philosophy is the notion of objects as withdrawn from access so that only their sensual qualities are accessible. This already gives us something that Heidegger's position cannot, since it zeroes in on Being as *plural* rather than as a semi-amorphous *apeiron*, as the great German philosopher unfortunately does. Heidegger already oversimplifies a broader situation, since the tension between concealed objects and their tangible qualities is just one instance of tension

---

[406] Alain Badiou, *Logics of Worlds*.

between objects and their qualities. Under the object-oriented model, there are actually two kinds of objects (the real and the sensual) and two kinds of qualities (the real and the sensual again).[407] Each type of object is bonded to each type of quality, yielding a fourfold of real objects, real qualities, sensual objects, and sensual qualities, with time, space, essence, and eidos as the four possible permutations in the group. I mention this only to indicate the scope of the problem, since only one of the four is relevant to us here: the tension between real objects and sensual qualities, which can be identified with space, and whose breakdown can be called *allure*.[408]

The theory goes as follows. Whereas in everyday perception we tend to identify a tree or an apple with its series of manifest qualities, there are special cases in which the tree, apple, or anything else suddenly seems to stand at a distance from these qualities. Metaphor is a good example. If we say "Churchill is like Roosevelt," there is no metaphorical effect, since the two compared items have such an obvious historical similarity that the resemblance creates no friction. But if we follow Ortega's example and say "a cypress is like a flame," this metaphor (in the special case of a simile) does not have a banal effect unless we are inattentive, or unless we have read the poem many times before and have now lost interest.[409] Though cypress and flame do have a vaguely similar shape, this similarity seems so accidental that their marriage seems far less possible than that of Churchill and Roosevelt. What happens, according to Ortega's analysis, is that the palpable flame-qualities seem to cluster around the cypress as the tree's own properties. Yet it is not the easily accessible cypress of perception, since this tree already has banal qualities of its own. Instead, the cypress in the metaphor is like the hammer following its Heideggerian breakdown: our attention is drawn to it, yet it is still a withdrawn enigma inaccessible to us, incommensurable with any possible relation we might have to it.

The problem arises as to how, if this cypress is withdrawn, it could ever participate in the metaphor. Is the metaphor nothing but a set of accessible flame-qualities supplemented by the cypress tree as an absent void? In a sense yes, but this is only one side of the situation. The flame-qualities cannot be attached to the sensual cypress that we see and talk about, because then it would simply be a failed comparison: we know that the cypress tree shares few if any important qualities with flames. But qualities never exist without

---

[407] See Graham Harman, *The Quadruple Object*.

[408] For a discussion of allure see Graham Harman, *Guerrilla Metaphysics*.

[409] José Ortega y Gasset, "An Essay in Esthetics by Way of a Preface."

an object, and if these flame-qualities cannot belong to any object of sense, then they can only belong to a *real* object. Yet we have seen that the real cypress (like all others) is inherently withdrawn, which means that it cannot touch anything else: not even poetic flame-qualities. And this seems to leave us at a dead end.

But there is one alternative, which I mention with reluctance since it took me years to begin to accept. When speaking of cypress and flame, the real objects to which these words refer are both withdrawn, stationed beyond all possible direct access, including even access of the causal kind. Only one real object is present on the scene, fully involved in the situation rather than withdrawn: and that object is *each of us* as readers of the poem (the author is also a reader). Since we cannot hope to bind sensual flame-qualities to an absent real cypress, we must concede the strange result that each of us is the real object to which the flame-qualities become attached. Stated differently, each of us as readers (unless we are bored, unmoved, or distracted) *becomes* the cypress tree, just as method actors are supposed to become the tree or rock they are assigned to portray.

This is the surprising sense in which we must defend the long-abandoned concept of *mimesis*: not that art is about producing imitation things that copy natural things, but that it imitates in the sense that actors imitate rocks, trees, Jim Morrison, or Nixon. The role of being a tree is transferred from the tree to us, with the difference that we ourselves are now trees with flame-qualities that orbit us impossibly like demonic moons. This model would shed light on Aristotle's interesting remark that the poet must be nearly insane, crying when writing a tragedy and enraged when presenting the wrath of Achilles. In this way, it seems that the form of any aesthetic content must be found in the *involvement* of the spectator of that content. One implication of this has been in the air of our culture for awhile: an end to irony, self-reflexivity, distance, and the placing of everything in quotation marks. Just as the notion of critique as tearing things down with a sneer from nowhere should be replaced by the critique of wine and food critics and their deep personal investment in their topics, sincerity may need to return to places in art from where it has long been exiled. The literary critic Harold Bloom once paraphrased Oscar Wilde as having said that "all bad poetry is sincere," and perhaps one could try to extend this remark to the arts in general.[410] And while on the very same page he claims that Wilde was "right about everything," it is a small step from being right about everything

---

[410] Harold Bloom, *The Western Canon*, p. 16.

to being *wrong* about everything. What if Wilde's remark were valuable precisely because it finds the truth through negating it? What if it were the case that all *good* art is sincere, in the sense that it provokes our investment by placing us inside the scene, letting us step in as understudies for the real object, forcing us to play the part of the cypress enslaving the qualities of the flame? If this were the case, then all art would be a branch of the performing arts. Form defeats content, not because content must refer to its background medium, but because aesthetic participants themselves provide the aesthetic medium, by standing in for the cypress and stone that cannot attend in person.

CHAPTER 21

LOVECRAFT AND PHILOSOPHY[411] (FROM *WEIRD REALISM*)

The Problem with Paraphrase

When one of our friends speaks ill of another, the effect is usually painful. The situation is different when the two friends in question are both admired authors: here, the dispute is often fascinating. One of my favorite literary critics is Edmund Wilson, but Wilson does not share my admiration for the fiction of H.P. Lovecraft. His dismissive assessment begins as follows:

> I regret that, after examining these books, I am no more enthusiastic than before. The principal feature of Lovecraft's work is an elaborate concocted myth ... [which] assumes a race of outlandish gods and grotesque prehistoric peoples who are always playing tricks with time and space and breaking through into the contemporary world, usually somewhere in Massachusetts.[412]

Like a sharp college quarterback mocking the Dungeons & Dragons games of his less popular hallmates, Wilson continues:

---

[411] This chapter is a trimmed-down version of Part One of *Weird Realism: Lovecraft and Philosophy*, published in 2012. Included here are pp. 7–27 & pp. 33–49 from the original. The three sections omitted for reasons of space are "A Writer of Gaps and Horror" (pp. 2–6), "The Phenomenological Gap" (p. 28–32), and "Style and Content" (pp. 50–52).

[412] Edmund Wilson, *Literary Essays and Reviews of the 1930s and 1940s*, p. 700.

["At the Mountains of Madness" concerns] semi-invisible polypous monsters that uttered a shrill whistling sound and blasted their enemies with terrific winds. Such creatures would look very well on the covers of the pulp magazines, but they do not make good adult reading. And the truth is that these stories were hackwork contributed to such publications as *Weird Tales* and *Amazing Stories*, where, in my opinion, they ought to have been left.[413]

If Wilson were alive today, he would be appalled to find his long-desired Library of America series tainted by the shared presence of Lovecraft.[414] Yet there is a problem with Wilson's approach, since the unchallenged classics of world literature can also be reduced to literal absurdity in the same way as Lovecraft. Consider what a severe critic might say about *Moby-Dick*:

The hero of the book is a bipolar one-legged skipper who cruises the world from Nantucket with a team of multi-ethnic harpooners. The climax comes when a scary, evil white whale (the object of their hunt) swims around the ship so fast that everyone is sucked into a whirlpool — everyone except the narrator, that is, who somehow survives to tell the tale. When reflecting on such inanity, I marvel once more at the puerile enthusiasm of Melville's admirers.

Even Dante might be converted to the ludicrous in similar fashion:

The plot of the work is visibly cracked. An Italian poet, age thirty-five, is lost in a forest. He is sad and confused and pursued by several ravenous African animals. At this point he happens to run into the ghost of Virgil, in whose company he enters a cave issuing into Hell. There, they meet scores of demons and observe a drooling Satan chewing the heads of three historic villains. They then descend Satan's body and climb a giant mountain in the Pacific Ocean where people are forced to push boulders as punishment for minor sins. Virgil is then suddenly replaced by the dead sweetheart of the Italian poet's childhood years. The Italian and his late muse (we are not

---

[413] Wilson, *Literary Essays and Reviews of the 1930s and 1940s* pp. 701–2.

[414] Wilson would be no happier about the inclusion of "pulp" detective writers Raymond Chandler and Dashiell Hammett, whose writing he also disdains. See Wilson's contemptuous 1945 essay on detective fiction, "Who Cares Who Killed Roger Ackroyd?" in Wilson, *Literary Essays and Reviews of the 1930s and 1940s*, pp. 677–683.

told whether she carries a lollipop or a teddy bear) magically fly past all the planets and finally see Jesus and God. And appropriately so, I might add: for if this is the future of poetry, then only these Divine Persons can save us.

Any literature, even the greatest, is easily belittled by such a method. The mere fact that a work of art can be literalized in this manner is no evidence against its quality. Wilson gets away with it in Lovecraft's case only due to the continuing low social status of science fiction and horror compared with mainstream naturalistic fiction, whereas no critic would be allowed to offer such rude handling to Melville or Dante. But there are only good and bad works of art, not inherently good and bad *genres* of art. As Clement Greenberg puts it: "One cannot validly be for or against any particular body of art *in toto*. One can only be for good or superior art as against bad or inferior art. One is not for Chinese, or Western, or representational art as a whole, but only for what is good in it."[415] By the same token, one cannot be for or against all naturalistic novels, science fiction, horror, Westerns, romance novels, or even comic books, but must learn to distinguish the good from the bad in each of these genres: which is not to say that all genres are equally filled with treasure at all moments in history. Lovecraft, Chandler, and Hammett emerged from the social slums of pulp. Even Batman and Robin may find their Tolstoy in the twenty-fourth century, once their Metropolis (our New York) is reduced to nostalgic vine-covered ruins. Wilson cannot refute Lovecraft's value with mocking phrases such as "invisible whistling octopus,"[416] for there is no inherent reason why such a creature could not inhabit the greatest story of all time, just as the poem about a middle-aged Italian and his dead sweetheart flying to God is possibly the greatest ever written.

The present book will have much to say about the sort of literalizing attempted by Wilson. Let's use "paraphrase" as our technical term for the attempt to give literal form to any statement, artwork, or anything else. The problem with paraphrase has long been noted by literary critics: by twentieth-century "New Critic" Cleanth Brooks,[417] for example, whose line of reasoning we will consider near the end of [*Weird Realism*]. What Wilson misses is that Lovecraft's major gift as a writer is that he deliberately and

---

[415] Clement Greenberg, *The Collected Essays and Criticism, Volume 4: Modernism with a Vengeance, 1957–1969*, p. 118.

[416] Wilson, *Literary Essays and Reviews of the 1930s and 1940s*, p. 702.

[417] Cleanth Brooks, *The Well Wrought Urn*, especially Chapter 11, "The Heresy of Paraphrase."

skillfully *obstructs* all attempts to paraphrase him. No other writer gives us monsters and cities so difficult to describe that he can only hint at their anomalies. Not even Edgar Allan Poe gives us such hesitant narrators, wavering uncertainly as to whether their coming words can do justice to the unspeakable reality they confront. Against Wilson's blunt assertion that "Lovecraft was not a good writer," I would call him one of the greatest of the twentieth century.[418] The greatness of Lovecraft even pertains to more than the literary world, since it brushes against several of the most crucial philosophical themes of our time.

The Inherent Stupidity of All Content

The problem with paraphrase is explained with typical humor by Slavoj Žižek while teasing the *Shakespeare Made Easy* series of editor Alan Durband. As Žižek informs us, "Durband tries to formulate directly, in everyday locution, (what he considers to be) the thought expressed in Shakespeare's metaphoric idiom — 'To be or not to be, that is the question' becomes something like: 'What's bothering me now is: Shall I kill myself or not?'"[419] Žižek asks us to consider a similar exercise for the poems of Hölderlin, which are treated so piously by Heidegger. Hölderlin's oracular lines *Wo aber Gefahr ist, wächst das Rettende auch* ("But where the danger is, the saving power also grows") is transformed grotesquely into this: "When you're in deep trouble, don't despair too quickly, look around carefully, the solution may be just around the corner."[420] Žižek then drops the theme in favor of a long series of dirty jokes, but by then he has already established the same complaint made against Wilson in the previous chapter: literal paraphrase can turn anything into banality.

Žižek takes up a related topic elsewhere, in his commentary on Schelling's *Ages of the World*. The passage in question concerns "the inherent stupidity of proverbs," and is too wonderful not to quote in full:

Let us engage in a mental experiment by way of trying to construct proverbial wisdom out of the relationship between terrestrial life, its pleasures, and its Beyond. If one says "Forget about the afterlife, about the Elsewhere, seize the day, enjoy life fully here and now,

[418] Wilson, *Literary Essays and Reviews of the 1930s and 1940s*, p. 701.
[419] Slavoj Žižek, *The Parallax View*, p. 11.
[420] Žižek, *The Parallax View*, p. 12.

it's the only life you've got!" it sounds deep. If one says exactly the opposite ("Do not get trapped in the illusory and vain pleasures of earthly life; money, power, and passions are all destined to vanish into thin air — think about eternity!"), it also sounds deep. If one combines the two sides ("Bring eternity into your everyday life, live your life on this earth as if it is already permeated by Eternity!"), we get another profound thought. Needless to say, the same goes for its inversion: "Do not try in vain to bring together eternity and your terrestrial life, accept humbly that you are forever split between Heaven and Earth!" If, finally, one simply gets perplexed by all these reversals and claims: "Life is an enigma, do not try to penetrate its secrets, accept the beauty of its unfathomable mystery!" the result is no less profound than its reversal: "Do not allow yourself to be distracted by false mysteries that just dissimulate the fact that, ultimately, life is very simple — it is what it is, it is simply here without reason and rhyme!" Needless to add that, by uniting mystery and simplicity, one again obtains a wisdom: "The ultimate, unfathomable mystery of life resides in its very simplicity, in the simple fact that there is life."[421]

Beyond the entertainment value of this passage, it may be one of the most important things Žižek has ever written, and deserves to be taken seriously. While the annoying reversibility of proverbs provides a convenient target for his comical analysis, the problem is not limited to proverbs, but extends across the entire field of literal statement. Indeed, we might speak of the inherent stupidity of all *content*, a more threatening result than the limited assault on proverbial wisdom. Žižek overlooks this broader problem because his remarks are guided by the Lacanian theme of "the Master." As he puts it: "This tautological imbecility [of proverbs] points towards the fact that a Master is excluded from the economy of symbolic exchange .... For the master, there is no 'tit for tat' ... when we give something to the Master, we do not expect anything in return ...."[422] Stated more simply, the imagined Master who utters each proverb does so in a lordly manner apparently immune to counterargument. But once we consider the actual verbal content of a proverb, devoid of the Master's tacit backing, all proverbs sound equally arbitrary and stupid.

---

[421] Slavoj Žižek/F.W.J. Schelling, *The Abyss of Freedom/Ages of the World*, pp. 71–72.
[422] Žižek, in Žižek/Schelling, *The Abyss of Freedom/Ages of the World*, p. 72.

It might be assumed that we can settle the issue in each case by giving *reasons* for why one proverb is more accurate than its opposite. Unfortunately, all reasons are doomed to the same fate as the initial proverbs themselves. Consider the following argument between a miser and a spendthrift. The miser cites the proverb "a penny saved is a penny earned" while the spendthrift counters with "penny wise, pound foolish." In an effort to resolve their dispute, they both give reasons for their preference. The miser explains patiently that in the long term, cutting needless losses actually accrues more wealth than an increase in annual income; the spendthrift objects that aggressive investment opens up more profit opportunities than penny-pinching cost savings does. The intellectual deadlock remains, with neither able to gain ground on the other. In the next stage of the dispute, both speakers produce statistical evidence and cite various star economists in defense of their views, but the evidence on both sides looks equally good and no progress is made. In the ensuing stage, both combatants hire vast teams of researchers to support their positions with crushing reams of data. The miser and the spendthrift are now locked into what is essentially an endless version of *Shakespeare Made Easy*: turning their initial proverbs into a series of ever more detailed statements, none of them directly and immediately convincing. Neither of them claims to be the Master as in the first, proverbial stage; both realize that they need to give evidence for their claims, yet both fail to establish those claims decisively. The point is not that the miser and the spendthrift are "equally correct." When it comes to a specific question of public policy, one of them may be far more right than the other. The point is that no *literal* unpacking of their claims can ever settle the argument, since each remains an arbitrary Master for as long as they attempt to call upon literal, explicit evidence. There may be an underlying true answer to the question, assuming that the dispute is properly formulated, but it can never become directly present in the form of explicit content that is inherently correct in the way that a lightning flash is inherently bright.[423]

---

[423] It is useful to compare ostensibly similar examples of dispute in books by Bruno Latour and Quentin Meillassoux. On pp. 64–67 of Latour's *Science in Action* we have a potentially endless argument between a scientist and a dissenter. On pp. 55–59 of Meillassoux's *After Finitude* the argument is between a dogmatic theist and an equally dogmatic atheist. In Latour's pragmatic strategy, the quarrel terminates only when someone gives up. In Meillassoux's speculative approach, it ends when the speculative philosopher comes along and provides the correct answer that transcends both of the dogmatic ones. My own approach lies midway between those of Latour and Meillassoux: one of the two proverbs may turn out to be truer than the other (unlike for Latour) but the matter is not to be decided by directly accessible literal proof (unlike for

The same holds true for any dispute between philosophical theses. For example, to argue between "the ultimate reality is flux" and "the ultimate reality is the stasis beneath the apparent flux" risks stumbling into Žižek's bottomless duel of opposing proverbs. It is true that in different historical periods one of these alternatives is generally the cutting edge while the other is the epitome of academic tedium, just as three-dimensional illusionistic painting was fresh as the dawn in Renaissance Italy but crushingly academic in cubist Paris. There is no reason to think that any philosophical statement has an inherently closer relationship with reality than its opposite, since *reality is not made of statements*. Just as Aristotle defined substance as that which can support opposite qualities at different times, there is a sense in which reality can support different truths at different times. That is to say, an absolutism of reality may be coupled with a relativism of truth. Žižek's comical translation of Hölderlin's poem turns out to be stupid *not* because the original poem is stupid, and *not* because the translation misunderstands Hölderlin's advice, but because all content is inevitably stupid. And content is stupid because *reality itself is not a content*. But this requires further explanation.

The Background of Being

The most important moment in twentieth-century philosophy came in 1927, when Heidegger raised the question of the meaning of being. While the question might sound so pompously obscure as to be fruitless, Heidegger makes genuine progress in addressing it. What we learn from all of Heidegger's thinking is the insufficiency of presence, or presence-at-hand (*Vorhandenheit*). From the age of twenty-nine onward, Heidegger transformed the phenomenology of his teacher Husserl, who tried to preserve philosophy from the encroachments of natural science by insisting that all theories must be grounded in evidence presented directly to the mind. Heidegger's counter-claim is that most of our interaction with things *is not* with things as presented to the mind, but rather with items silently taken for granted or relied upon. Entities such as chairs, floors, streets, bodily organs, and the grammatical rules of our native language are generally ignored as long as they function smoothly. It is usually only

---

Meillassoux). There are many truths and there is one reality, but their relationship must remain oblique rather than direct. The whole of the present book is based on this notion of a purely oblique access to a genuine reality, which Lovecraft grasps better than any other writer of fiction.

their malfunction that allows us to notice them at all. This is the theme of Heidegger's famous tool-analysis, found in his 1919 Freiburg lectures[424] but first published eight years later in *Being and Time*.[425] I have written about this analysis frequently,[426] and in effect my own intellectual career has been nothing more than an attempt to radicalize its consequences.

As is often the case in intellectual history, the tool-analysis can be pushed further than Heidegger himself ever attempted. Most of his readers hold that the analysis establishes a priority of unconscious praxis over conscious theory, so that explicit theoretical awareness emerges from a shadowy background of tacit everyday "coping." What this reading misses is that coping with things distorts them no less than theorizing about them does. To sit in a chair does not exhaust its reality any more than visual observation of the chair ever does. Human theory and human praxis are both prone to surprises from sudden eruptions of unknown properties from the chair-being of the chair, which recedes into the darkness beyond all human access. Pushing things another step further, it must be seen that the same holds for inanimate entities, since the chair and floor distort one another no less than humans distort the chair.

Here we see the reason for the inherent stupidity of all content, as resulted from Žižek's attack on proverbs. No literal statement is congruent with reality itself, just as no handling of a tool is the same thing as that tool in the plenitude of its reality. Or as Alfred North Whitehead puts it: "It is merely credulous to accept verbal phrases as adequate expressions of propositions."[427] The meaning of being might even be defined as *untranslatability*. Language (and everything else) is obliged to become an art of allusion or indirect speech, a metaphorical bond with a reality that cannot possibly be made present. Realism does not mean that we are able to state correct propositions about the real world. Instead, it means that reality is too real to be translated without remainder into any sentence, perception, practical action, or anything else. To worship the content of propositions is to be a *dogmatist*. The dogmatist is one who cannot judge the quality of anyone else's thoughts other than to agree or disagree with them. If someone says "materialism is true" and the dogmatist agrees, then the dogmatist salutes this person as a brother no matter how shoddy their reasoning, and the dogmatist equally denounces the one who says

---

[424] Martin Heidegger, *Towards the Definition of Philosophy*, pp. 56–58.
[425] Martin Heidegger, *Being and Time*.
[426] For the most elaborate version see Graham Harman, *Tool-Being*.
[427] Alfred North Whitehead, *Process and Reality*, p. 11.

"materialism is false," no matter how fresh and insightful the basis for this statement may be. The dogmatist holds that truth is legible on the surface of the world, so that correct and incorrect statements — someday formalized and determinable by a machine — is the arena where truth is uncovered.

Yet this is precisely what Kant renders impossible with his split between appearances and things-in-themselves. As Kant sees it, the problem with dogmatic philosophy is not that it believes in the things-in-themselves (Kant himself believes in them). Instead, the problem is that the dogmatist wishes to make the things-in-themselves accessible through discursive statements. In this way Žižek's assault on proverbs should be viewed as the jesting younger cousin of Kant's famous antinomies, in which positive propositions about various metaphysical issues are placed side by side on the page and shown to be equally arbitrary. Yet the mistake made by Kant, and even more so by his German Idealist successors, is to hold that the relation of appearance to the in-itself is an all-or-nothing affair: that since the things-in-themselves can never be made present, we are either limited to discussions of the conditions of human experience (Kant) or obliged to annihilate the very notion of things-in-themselves by noting that this very notion is an accessible appearance in the mind (German Idealism). What few have realized is that both attitudes abandon the mission of *philosophia*: a love of wisdom by humans who both have and do not have the truth at all times. The inability to make the things-in-themselves directly present does not forbid us from having *indirect* access to them. The inherent stupidity of all content does not mean the inherent impossibility of all knowledge, since knowledge need not be discursive. The absent thing-in-itself can have gravitational effects on the internal content of knowledge, just as H.P. Lovecraft can allude to the physical form of his monster Cthulhu even while canceling the literal terms of the description. Instead of representational realism, Lovecraft works in the idiom of a *weird realism* that inspired the title of this book.

Additional historical and contemporary support can be found for this approach. Despite the condemnation of rhetoric by Socrates and Plato, Aristotle saw fit to teach his students rhetoric for half of the school day. This was not a concession to the regrettable corruption of our unavoidable fellow humans, but stems from the fact that rhetoric is the essential art of the background behind any explicit statement. Rhetoric is dominated by the *enthymeme*, a proposition that need not be stated since it is already known to one's audience. If we say [in early 2012 that] "Obama will be in the White House two years from now," no contemporary reader of this book needs an explanation that this means that Barack Obama will be re-elected in 2012 as President of the United States, whose official residence is called the White House. These further inferences can be taken for granted, just as most of the tool-beings in our vicinity are taken for granted, as shown by Heidegger. Rhetoric is the art of the background, and if philosophy is not the science of the background, then I do not know what it is. Aristotle pursues similar insights in the *Poetics*. Derrida is simply wrong to claim that Aristotle wishes to enslave all figurative meanings to a single literal meaning for each word.[428] For what Aristotle defends is not literal meaning, but the rather different notion of a univocal *being* for each thing. He is by no means a defender of literal paraphrase, as seen from his admiring tributes to poets and his view that metaphor is the greatest of all human gifts.[429]

In more recent times, the media theorist Marshall McLuhan is the unacknowledged master of rhetoric and the secrets it conceals from literal visibility. This happens through the background medium: for McLuhan, all arguments over the good and bad content of television programs miss the fact that the medium of television itself alters our behavior and lifestyle regardless of the content it depicts. This is why for McLuhan "the medium is the message," whereas the usual assumption is that "the content is the message." This view takes on its most extreme form in McLuhan's famous *Playboy* interview, when he says that "the content or message of any particular medium has about as much importance as the stenciling on the casing of an atomic bomb."[430] In important late work conducted jointly with his son Eric, McLuhan frames this idea in terms of the Classical Trivium as a defense of rhetoric and grammar as opposed to the dialectic of explicit surface content.[431] While the dogmatist is a dialectician in this classical sense, the artist and the lover of wisdom are rhetoricians. This is not from some devious desire to seduce the unwary, but from recognition that the background is where the action is.

We have already noted several instances of failed awareness of the tacit background of one's actions or utterances. In perception and action we fail to exhaust the deeper reality of the things with which we are engaged. In German Idealist philosophy it is held that there is no more to things or thoughts than their ultimate accessibility to reason. In dogmatic assertions

---

[428] Jacques Derrida, "White Mythology." For a discussion of this point, see Graham Harman, *Guerrilla* Metaphysics, pp. 110–116.
[429] Aristotle, *Poetics*.
[430] From Marshall McLuhan, "The Playboy Interview."
[431] Published posthumously as Marshall & Eric McLuhan, *Laws of Media*.

it is assumed, contra Whitehead, that verbal propositions can in principle exhaust whatever they describe. These phenomena are strikingly similar to *academic art* as defined and denounced by the great art critic Greenberg. In his 1979 Sydney lecture "Modern and Postmodern," he stated it as follows: "Academicism consists in the tendency to take the medium of an art too much for granted."[432] McLuhan would be pleased by these words. The point is neither to take the medium for granted (like academic art), nor to believe falsely that the medium can be made purely explicit (like dogmatic philosophy), but to generate content that has an oblique or allusive relation with the background medium that is effective nonetheless.

Along with academic art, Greenberg speaks frequently of its trashy younger sister *Kitsch*, the lowbrow imitation that offers a tasteless execution of high art's hard-earned technique.[433] One obvious form of *Kitsch* in literature would be pulp. Here too the background medium is largely taken for granted. If you wish to submit a story to a pulp Western magazine, simply throw in a dozen cowboys, a few gunfights, a rodeo, a love interest, some cattle rustling, and other stock elements of the genre. Pulp detective writing will surely include a hard-boiled hero and a number of criminal villains, with occasional murders sprinkled in along the way. Pulp horror and science fiction will consist of the arbitrary postulation of new monsters and planets, each equipped with amazing qualitative features designed to stun the reader with their novel *content*, while accepting the banality of the established framework. There is even a kind of pulp philosophy, in which the rational materialist hero (generally a first-person narrator) slays hordes of irrational alchemists, astrologers, witch doctors, and Christians. The dogmatist is a pulp philosopher. Although I am unaware of any comments by Greenberg on the writings of Lovecraft, it is easy to imagine him reacting in much the same way as Edmund Wilson: "And the truth is that these stories were hackwork contributed to such publications as *Weird Tales* and *Amazing Stories*, where, in my opinion, they ought to have been left."[434]

But if we define pulp as fiction unaware of its medium, there is a problem with any dismissal of Lovecraft as a pulp writer: namely, Lovecraft was *by no means* unaware of his medium. The most frequently cited essay by Lovecraft is probably his "Supernatural Horror in Literature," a detailed survey of the genre that earned surprising praise from Edmund Wilson as "a really able

---

[432] Clement Greenberg, "Modern and Postmodern."

[433] Greenberg, "Avant-Garde and Kitsch."

[434] Wilson, *Literary Essays and Reviews of the 1930s and 1940s*, pp. 701–2.

piece of work."[435] But of greater interest for us here is Lovecraft's biting four-page essay "Some Notes on Interplanetary Fiction."[436] In this essay Lovecraft speaks in Wilson-like tones of the horrible quality of most work in this genre: "Insincerity, conventionality, triteness, artificiality, false emotion, and puerile extravagance reign triumphant throughout this overcrowded genre, so that none but its rarest products [which includes the novels of H.G. Wells] can possibly claim a truly adult status."[437] Most such stories contain "hackneyed artificial characters and stupid conventional events and situations … [that are] a product of weary mass mechanics," and are filled with "stock scientists, villainous assistants, invincible heroes, and lovely scientist's-daughter heroines of the usual trash of this sort."[438] And in a final wonderful litany, Lovecraft denounces further clichés of the genre such as "worship of the travelers as deities," "participation in the affairs of pseudo-human kingdoms," "weddings with beautiful anthropomorphic princesses," "stereotyped Armageddons with ray-guns and space-ships," "court intrigues and jealous magicians," and even "peril from hairy ape-men of the polar caps."[439] All these examples should establish that Lovecraft is perhaps an even more acerbic critic of pulp literature than Wilson himself, and that as an author he is fully aware of the minefields of banality that one must scrupulously avoid.

And yet, Lovecraft pivots in a direction that Wilson never attempted: "The present commentator does not believe that the idea of space-travel and other worlds is inherently unsuited to literary use."[440] There is one essential fallacy that leads interplanetary writers into the mire of pulp banality, and "this fallacy is the notion that any account of impossible, improbable, or inconceivable phenomena can be successfully presented as a commonplace narrative of objective acts and conventional emotions in the ordinary tone and manner of popular romance."[441] As he explains, two paragraphs later: "Over and above everything else should tower the stark, outrageous monstrosity of the one chosen departure from Nature."[442] There follows the most important passage in the essay:

---

[435] H.P. Lovecraft, *Collected Essays. Volume 2: Literary Criticism*, pp. 82–135; Wilson, *Literary Essays and Reviews of the 1930s and 1940s*, p. 702.

[436] Lovecraft, *Collected Essays. Volume 2: Literary Criticism*, pp. 178–182.

[437] Lovecraft, *Collected Essays. Volume 2: Literary Criticism*, p. 178.

[438] Lovecraft, *Collected Essays. Volume 2: Literary Criticism*, pp. 179, 180.

[439] Lovecraft, *Collected Essays. Volume 2: Literary Criticism*, p. 181.

[440] Lovecraft, *Collected Essays. Volume 2: Literary Criticism*, p. 178.

[441] Lovecraft, *Collected Essays. Volume 2: Literary Criticism*, p. 178.

[442] Lovecraft, *Collected Essays. Volume 2: Literary Criticism*, p. 179.

The characters should react to it as real people would react to such a thing if it were suddenly to confront them in daily life; displaying the almost soul-shattering amazement which anyone would naturally display instead of the mild, tame, quickly-passed-over emotions prescribed by cheap popular convention. Even when the wonder is one to which the characters are assumed to be used, the sense of awe, marvel, and strangeness which the reader would feel in the presence of such a thing must somehow be suggested by the author.[443]

In other words, the mere *content* of alternative worlds is not enough to be credible. If Zartran the half-alien hero slays the enemy on distant ice-planet Orthumak with an argon-based neuron degenerator, then marries the princess inside a volcano while wearing heat-resistant triple neonoid fabrics, and if all this is stated as a matter-of-fact event, what we have is nothing but a cheap novelty of "unprecedented content." Ten thousand rival pulp writers can then try to invent even more unprecedented species and weapons and chemicals and incidents. The clichés cannot be eliminated by simple variation: replacing the stock mad scientist with a sane and goodhearted dog-man scientist, and dropping all weddings in favor of heroes who reproduce with gelatinous spores, would not address the deeper cliché at work. Namely, the real banality of interplanetary fiction is the idea that simple novelty of content is enough to produce genuine innovation. What Lovecraft argues instead is surprisingly similar to Greenberg's vision for modern art: the content of an artwork should display some skillful relation with the background conditions of the genre. To innovate in science fiction, we cannot simply replace New York and Tokyo with exotically named extra-galactic capitals, which is merely trading a familiar content for a bizarre but comparable one (Greenberg's critique of surrealism is similar). Instead, we must show the everyday banality of New York and Tokyo undercut from within, by subverting the background conditions assumed by the existence of any city at all. Rather than inventing a monster with an arbitrary number of tentacles and dangerous sucker-mouths and telepathic brains, we must suggest that no such list of arbitrary weird properties is enough to do the trick. There must be some deeper and more malevolent principle at work in our monsters that escapes all such definition. That is the manner by which Lovecraft escapes all pulp, all *Kitsch*, and all academic art: by systematically

---

[443] Lovecraft, *Collected Essays. Volume 2: Literary Criticism*, p. 179.

debilitating the role of content, to the greater glory of the background enthymeme. The medium is the message.

Not Unfaithful to the Spirit of the Thing

A dogmatic acquaintance of mine once objected to the Lovecraftian monster Cthulhu on the grounds that "a dragon with an octopus head is not scary." But that is not exactly how Cthulhu is described. Lovecraft's first description of a Cthulhu idol runs as follows: "If I say that my somewhat extravagant imagination yielded simultaneous pictures of an octopus, a dragon, and a human caricature, *I shall not be unfaithful to the spirit of the thing* ... but it was the *general outline* of the whole which made it most shockingly frightful ...."[444] [169] The fact that the T-shirts and fantasy paintings of the world depict Cthulhu straightforwardly as a dragon with an octopus head is not Lovecraft's fault. If he had written "I looked at the idol and saw a horrifying monster that was part dragon, part octopus, and part human caricature," then we would simply be in the realm of pulp. But capitalizing on the indirect character of literature as opposed to painting or cinema, Lovecraft *hints* at an octopoidal dragon while also suspending that literal depiction in three separate ways: (1) he downplays it as merely the result of his own "extravagant imagination"; (2) he evasively terms his description "not unfaithful to the spirit of the thing" rather than as dead-on correct; (3) he asks us to ignore the surface properties of dragon and octopus mixed with human and to focus instead on the fearsome "general outline of the whole," suggesting that this outline is something over and above a literal combination of these elements. Any seasoned reader of Lovecraft knows that this sort of de-literalizing gesture is not an isolated incident in his stories, but is perhaps his major stylistic trait as a writer. This is what I have called the "vertical" or allusive aspect of Lovecraft's style: the gap he produces between an ungraspable thing and the vaguely relevant descriptions that the narrator is able to attempt.

A different sort of example is found in "The Dunwich Horror," when the three professors observe the decaying corpse of Wilbur Whateley on the Miskatonic University Library floor: "It would be trite and not wholly accurate to say that no human pen could describe it, but one may properly say that it could not be vividly visualized by anyone whose ideas of aspect and contour are too closely bound up with the common life-forms of this planet

---

[444] In this chapter all page numbers in square brackets refer to H.P. Lovecraft, *Tales*.

and the known three dimensions." [389] So far, we have a "vertical" gap resembling the one found in the description of the Cthulhu idol, and this is the sort of case where I am now willing to concede a "noumenal" element in Lovecraft's style. The sentence above could have been ruined if Lovecraft had adopted either of the extreme alternatives. If he had simply said that "no human pen can describe it," we would have one of the cheapest tricks of bad pulp writing and shallow thinking. If he had tried instead to shock us with monstrous detailed descriptions alone, we would also have veered toward pulp. Instead, we find a disclaimer that neutralizes the cliché by calling it "trite and not wholly accurate," but which then delves into a descriptive effort that is nearly impossible to visualize in literal terms anyway: "Above the waist it was semi-anthropomorphic; though its chest ... had the leathery, reticulated hide of a crocodile or alligator. The back was piebald with yellow and black, and dimly suggested the squamous covering of certain snakes. Below the waist, though, it was the worst; for here all human resemblance left off and sheer fantasy began ...." [389] Here we have something different: a "horizontal" weirdness that I would not call allusive but "cubist," for lack of a better term. The power of language is no longer enfeebled by an impossibly deep and distant reality. Instead, language is overloaded by a gluttonous excess of surfaces, planes, and aspects of the thing. Again there is reason to be impressed with Lovecraft's technique. The explicitly described image is difficult enough to visualize, but becomes all the more so when this elusive description is further qualified as "dimly suggestive" of a snake and its "squamous" covering, a word that even educated readers will probably need to look up in the dictionary. And then comes the crowning transition, telling us that while all of this might have been intelligible enough, what comes next will enter the realm of sheer fantasy.

Let's take another example of the "horizontal" kind, this time shifting from biology to architecture: another field where Lovecraft excels at obstructed description. In "At the Mountains of Madness," Professor Dyer and his party are flying across Antarctica toward the campsite of Professor Lake's party, which they will soon discover to be completely annihilated. En route they witness what Dyer terms a "polar mirage," though it later turns out to have been the disturbing reflection of an actual hidden city. Dyer describes it as follows: "The effect was that of a Cyclopean city of no architecture known to man or to human imagination, with vast aggregations of night-black masonry embodying monstrous perversions of geometrical laws and attaining the most grotesque extremes of sinister bizarrerie." [508] Edmund Wilson would dismiss such descriptions as of low literary quality, but here we must disagree, for the simple reason that the passage is highly effective. "Vast aggregations of night-black masonry" is a perfectly suggestive and frightening phrase, if somewhat hard to visualize accurately. The phrase "monstrous perversions of known geometrical law" would be impossible to film or paint, but has a powerful effect on the reader, who can sense the darkness of any place where such perversions are permitted to exist. The final element, "the most grotesque extremes of sinister bizarrerie" might be dubious in isolation, but here it bears no weight other than summing up Dyer's personal anguish after the real literary work is already completed in the first two elements. It is the rhetorical cherry on the sundae, but the sundae itself was purchased through the labors of night-black masonry and perversions of geometrical law.

This is the stylistic world of H.P. Lovecraft, a world in which real objects are locked in impossible tension with (1) the crippled descriptive powers of language, and (2) visible objects in unbearable seismic torsion with their own qualities. An account such as Wilson's, which immediately advances to a literalizing mockery of the *content* of the stories, overlooks Lovecraft's primary trait as a writer, a gift that Lovecraft (contra Wilson) shares intimately with Poe.[445] Normally we feel no gap at all between the world and our descriptions of it. But Lovecraft unlocks a world dominated by just such a gap, and this makes him the very embodiment of an *anti-pulp* writer. And this is the grain of truth in the descriptions of Lovecraft as a Kantian writer of "noumenal" horror. It is true that this description becomes dangerous if it leads us to overlook Lovecraft's materialist and utterly non-noumenal side. As Houellebecq puts it: "What is Great Cthulhu? An arrangement of electrons, like us."[446] But if Houellebecq's statement is true in the negative sense that Lovecraft's monsters are not spirits or souls, they are also not just electrons, any more than Kant's things-in-themselves are made of electrons or any other particle of matter. And this is the side of the truth that must be preserved from the Kantian reading.

A Lovecraftian Ontography

As mentioned, the German poet Hölderlin has been the dominant literary hero of recent continental philosophy. This is largely Heidegger's doing, since it was he who repeatedly gave lecture courses on Hölderlin's hymns

---

[445] Edgar Allan Poe, *Poetry and Tales*.
[446] Michel Houellebecq, *H.P. Lovecraft*, p. 32.

and treated him as a figure of staggering significance for philosophy. What makes Hölderlin so great in Heidegger's eyes? The philosopher addresses this question openly at the beginning of his essay "Hölderlin and the Essence of Poetry":

> Why choose *Hölderlin's* work if our purpose is to show the essence of poetry? Why not Homer or Sophocles, why not Virgil or Dante, why not Shakespeare or Goethe? Surely the essence of poetry has come to rich expression in the works of these poets, more so indeed than in Hölderlin's creation, which broke off so prematurely and so abruptly. That may be so. And yet I choose Hölderlin, and him alone ... because Hölderlin's poetry is sustained by his whole poetic mission: to make poems solely about the essence of poetry. Hölderlin is for us in a preeminent sense *the poet's poet*. And for that reason he forces a decision upon us.[447]

A similar question might be asked in connection with Lovecraft. If we are looking for philosophical depth in a writer of fiction, then why not Cervantes or Tolstoy, Joyce or Melville, George Eliot or Dostoevsky? Why not even Poe, who is Lovecraft's thoroughly canonized literary ancestor? Our answer is similar to Heidegger's response on the question of Hölderlin, but with the following twist. I am not making the Heideggerian claim that Lovecraft writes stories about the essence of writing stories, but that he writes stories about the essence of *philosophy*. Lovecraft is the model writer of ontography, with its multiple polarizations in the heart of real and sensual objects. Therefore, as I wrote in a 2008 article on Lovecraft: "In symbolic terms, Great Cthulhu should replace Minerva as the patron spirit of philosophers, and the Miskatonic must dwarf the Rhine and the Ister as our river of choice. Since Heidegger's treatment of Hölderlin resulted mostly in pious, dreary readings, philosophy needs a new literary hero."[448]

We have already discussed Lovecraft's tendency to undercut his own statements, a primary method by which he escapes a pulp literature unaware of its own background conditions. We have also seen that he does this in more than one way. At times Lovecraft does this by splitting off a thing as a dark, brooding unit in distinction from its palpable qualities. This happens for instance when the sailor Parker is bizarrely "swallowed up by

---

[447] Martin Heidegger, *Elucidations of Hölderlin's Poetry*, p. 52.
[448] Harman, "On the Horror of Phenomenology," p. 338.

an angle of masonry … which was acute, but behaved as if it were obtuse." [194] As a general rule, anytime we run across a passage in Lovecraft that is *literally* impossible to visualize, we are dealing with this first kind of tension between a real object and its sensual qualities, so reminiscent of Heidegger's tool-analysis. At other times, there is the "cubist" tension between sensual or non-hidden objects and their sensual qualities, which pile up in disturbing profusion. Another good example is found in "The Shadow Over Innsmouth" when the narrator first encounters the repulsive local bus driver, who is undoubtedly one of Innsmouth's many fish-frog-human hybrids: "This, I reflected, must be the Joe Sargent mentioned by the ticket-agent; and *even before I noticed any details* there spread over me *a wave of spontaneous aversion that could be neither checked nor explained.*" [597; emph. added] While this portion might seem like a vertical allusion to depths of reality lying far beneath all language, it is followed with a detailed list of the various problematic features of Sargent's physical appearance, much like Husserl or Picasso analyzing the multi-faceted surfaces of a blackbird that is *not* withdrawn from all experience, but simply encrusted with a multitude of sensual planes.

Another good example occurs in Lovecraft's description of the witch's familiar known as Brown Jenkin: "Witnesses said it had long hair and the shape of a rat, but that its sharp-toothed bearded face was evilly human while its paws were like tiny human hands …. Its voice was a kind of loathsome titter, and it could speak all languages." [658] Although Brown Jenkin is not unvisualizable in the way that an acute-obtuse angle is, the little monster hardly qualifies as an empiricist "bundle of qualities" due to the unsettling range of traits it unifies. Indeed, Brown Jenkin might even be read as a *parody* of Hume's empiricism, in which we sense that beyond its mass of qualities, there must be some vile underlying unit holding all these grisly features together. An additional case occurs in "At the Mountains of Madness" in connection with the distant city distorted via polar mirage:

> There were truncated cones, sometimes terraced or fluted,
> surmounted by tall cylindrical shafts here and there bulbously
> enlarged and often capped with tiers of thinnish scalloped discs;
> and strange, beetling, table-like constructions suggesting piles of
> multitudinous rectangular slabs or circular plates or five-pointed stars
> with each one overlapping the one beneath. There were composite
> cones and pyramids either alone or surmounting cylinders or cubes

or flatter truncated cones and pyramids, and occasional needle-like
spires in curious clusters of five. [508–509]

No other figure in world literature is able to make such outbursts work so
effectively. Here as with cubist painting, there is a clean separation between
the multiple facets the thing displays to the outer world, and whatever
organizing principle is able to hold together all these monstrous features.

There is also the second Husserlian case, in which a sensual object is in
tension with its real qualities. While far rarer in Lovecraft than in Husserl,
it occurs in his stories whenever scientists enter the scene and have trouble
classifying the features of a given object despite all their analytic labor. We
return to "The Dreams in the Witch House," where the object retrieved by
Gilman from a supposed dream baffles a scientific expert:

> One of the small radiating arms was broken off and subjected to
> analysis, and the results are still talked about in college circles.
> Professor Ellery found platinum, iron, and tellurium in the strange
> alloy; but mixed with these were at least three other apparent
> elements of high atomic weight which chemistry was powerless
> to classify. Not only did they fail to correspond with any known
> element, but they did not even fit the vacant places reserved for
> probable elements in the periodic system. [677]

The fact that we are not dealing here with any mysterious withdrawn
object, but with a perfectly accessible one whose *features* are withdrawn
from scrutiny, is emphasized by Lovecraft's witty touch of stating that there
is still a public museum exhibit in Arkham devoted to the object. A similar
incident already occurs in "The Colour Out of Space," when fragments
of the meteorite are tested but lead science to a dead end, despite the use
of state-of-the-art glass beakers, silicon, borax bead tests, anvils, and oxy-
hydrogen blowpipes. [344]

That leaves us with the fourth tension between a real object and its real
qualities. Such moments are most evident in Lovecraft's fiction whenever
there is talk of outermost regions of the cosmos ruled by deities or forces
so bizarre that an empty proper name is used to designate something for
which no tangible qualities are available. For instance, in "The Dreams in
the Witch House," we read that Gilman "must … go with them all to the
throne of Azathoth at the centre of ultimate chaos … to the throne of Chaos
where the thin flutes pipe mindlessly …. [He] had seen the name 'Azathoth'

in the *Necronomicon* and knew it stood for a primal evil too horrible for description." [664] Here the final phrase lets us know that we are dealing with a real or undescribable object, while the thin and mindless flutes are sufficiently inconceivable that we can interpret them as dark allusions to real properties of the throne of Chaos rather than literal descriptions of what one would experience there in person.

On Ruination

A college classmate of mine once asked a witty faculty member to explain the philosophy of Richard Rorty. The response: "Basically, you debunk everything, and what you're left with is pragmatism and American democracy." Here we have yet another version of critique through literalizing. But even if it is open to dispute whether this is a fair summary of Rorty's intellectual career, the remark is so potentially devastating that his caliber as a thinker must frankly be measured by the extent to which his work is able to escape it.

We also find that *jokes* are highly vulnerable to literalizing, which almost always ruins them. Consider the following simple joke, rated as the favorite of the Belgian populace in a survey some years ago (the favorites of other nations were far worse): "There are three kinds of people — those who can count, and those who can't." This mildly humorous remark can be ruined in at least two different ways. One way is to transform it into this: "There are *two* kinds of people — those who can count, and those who can't." Here we have a banal classification, not a joke. Another way is to spell out the joke in excessive detail: "There are three kinds of people — those who can count and those who can't. And the funny thing is, the person telling the joke obviously can't count properly! Did you notice that he said three kinds of people but only gave two options? The joke is on him!" This feature is one that jokes share with magic tricks: among the international fraternity of magicians we find the credo that the secrets to tricks must never be shared with outsiders. In similar fashion, scantily clad bodies are usually more tantalizing than completely naked ones: a nudist colony filled with frank sex talk would not be more arousing than the everyday world of clothed innuendo.

But there are other ways besides literalization to ruin statements, jokes, magic tricks, eros, or anything else. Let's consider a well-written passage from Nietzsche, who might be the greatest literary stylist in the history of philosophy (his chief competition is Plato). Writing of Shakespeare in *Ecce*

Homo, Nietzsche exclaims: "What must a man have suffered to have such need of being a buffoon!"[449] Here we have a fine sampling of Nietzsche: crisp, concise, and delightfully paradoxical. But imagine that Nietzsche were a boring literalizer who did not know where to stop. In that case he might have written as follows: "What must a man have suffered to have such need of being a buffoon! For although we might expect the contents of Shakespeare's writing to be a direct reflection of his personality, modern psychology teaches the contrary. For in fact, what people write is often the *opposite* of what they are feeling inside. In Shakespeare's case, the clowning in his comedies may be an effort to counterbalance painful personal experience with an outward show of good cheer." Unless this person is a schoolteacher making things plain for children, he is the bane of social conversation, tediously spelling out points that are already clear to everyone. He is the equivalent of Žižek's trite reducer of Hölderlin: "the solution may be just around the corner."

But to be allusive is not the sole aim of a writer, and transforming allusion into literal statement is not the only way to ruin a brilliant remark. Along with the bore just described, we can add other personae capable of leading Nietzsche's remark into ruin.

- The Simpleton: "How happy Shakespeare must have been that he played the buffoon so often!" (Here the twist of paradox is destroyed in favor of a facile correspondence between an author's life and work.)
- The Moralistic Resenter: "What must a man have suffered to have such need of being a buffoon! And I must say I find it a bit pathetic that Shakespeare is so needy and always clowns around to try to make us like him." (Nietzsche's cool distance and non-judgmental appreciation of human pathos is extinguished in a cesspool of private bitterness.)
- The Waffler: "What must a man have suffered to have such need of being a buffoon! At least I'm pretty sure about that. The other possibility is that he was actually happy. I could go either way on this one." (Here we lose Nietzsche's gallant decisiveness.)
- The Self-Absorbed: "What must a man have suffered to have such need of being a buffoon! But I'm not like that at all. Personally, I take a balanced approach to life and don't feel the need to overcompensate." (Nietzsche's vigorous interest in the outer world gives way to a petty, low-budget narcissism.)

---

[449] Friedrich Nietzsche, *Ecce Homo & The Antichrist*, p. 30.

- The Down-Home Cornball: "Whenever he has those comical scenes, I ain't fooled. I know Ole Billy's got somethin' stickin' in his craw!" (Here we completely lose the aristocratic elegance of Nietzsche's style.)
- The Clutterer: "What people like Shakespeare, Molière, Aristophanes, Plautus, Menander, Juvenal, and Brecht must have suffered to have such need of being buffoons!" (No longer is Shakespeare addressed as one solitary figure by another. Instead, we have a confusing general proposition about a long list of comic authors.)
- The Pedant: "Shakespeare's plays exhibit instantiations of a ludic affect that, as it were, bespeak an inversion of his 'true' state of mind. Much work has been done in this area, but a full consideration lies beyond the scope of this essay. See Johnson 1994a, Miner & Shaltgrover et al., 1997." (This character combines aspects of both the Waffler and the original Literalizing Bore.)

By Karl Popper's famous principle, a theory is scientific only if it can be falsified. I would go further and say not only that a statement is effective only when it can be ruined, but that the statement is of higher quality the more *ways* it can be ruined.[450] After all, the fact that a statement *can* be ruined means that this has not already occurred. It also means that we can use possible ruinations, and sometimes possible *improvements*, as a method of analyzing the effects of a literary statement. Part Two of [*Weird Realism*] will often make use of this method.

A Lonely and Curious Country

Fissures between objects and their qualities are not always as explicit as in the cases where Lovecraft deliberately paralyzes his own powers of language. Simple metaphorical effects can also do this, without taking on truly Lovecraftian proportions. As I argued in *Guerrilla Metaphysics* when discussing the closely related theories of Max Black and José Ortega y Gasset, metaphor succeeds by transferring sensual qualities from a sensual object to a real one: in Black's rather bland example "man is a wolf," wolf-qualities are stripped from their usual alliance with a sensual wolf and placed in servitude to a vague and withdrawn human-object, which both attracts

---

[450] Karl Popper, *Conjectures and Refutations*.

and repels its new wolf-qualities.[451] Turning to an especially metaphorical passage from Lovecraft, there is the case when Cthulhu temporarily explodes after collision with a ship: "There was a bursting as of an exploding bladder, a slushy nastiness as of a cloven sunfish, a stench as of a thousand opened graves, and a sound that the chronicler would not put on paper." [195] The final clause is the crowning horror. It falsely implies that putting the sound on paper would be of help in the first place, and thereby ascribes to the chronicler an impossible capacity to explain the sound if only he so chose. The dual attraction and repulsion between object and quality also occurs in the figure known as catachresis. Consider Lovecraft's phrase "great Cthulhu slid greasily into the water," [195] in which it is not immediately clear how a sliding movement into water could have a "greasy" consistency. Yet the reasonable liquid similarity between water and grease makes the combination disturbingly feasible, much like the two minutely different shades of brown found in the jacket and tie of a chic young architect.

But we should also consider cases of good writing that are not actually metaphorical. Since I have referred already to Greenberg, one of the finest prose stylists of the twentieth century, let's consider a sample from his 1941 memorial essay on Paul Klee: "In spite of Klee's own aspirations [his art] pretends to no statements in the grand style; it concentrates itself within a relatively small area, which it refines and elaborates. It moves in an intimate atmosphere, among friends and acquaintances. It belongs to Berne, Basel, Zurich, old-fashioned Munich, a region of bright, alert small cities ...."[452] Here there are no Lovecraftian self-erasures in the face of indescribable withdrawn entities, and no toying with masses of unmanageable qualities to create a flickering spirit or "general outline" of Switzerland imperfectly manifest in its individual cities. Instead, the writing is good simply because Greenberg says something relevant and fresh about Klee's milieu, evokes the warmth of limited circles of friendship (in contrast with Picasso's frenzied cosmopolitan circles), and mentally pinpoints a region on the map by citing four well-known cities where the spirit in question is embodied: provincial, yet bright and alert. Without creating any explicit fissures in the heart of objects, Greenberg retrieves relevant objects from the shadows of indifference, and makes them the target of our awareness in a plausible way.

---

[451] Harman, *Guerrilla Metaphysics*, pp. 102–110, 116–124; Max Black, "Metaphor"; José Ortega y Gasset, "An Essay in Esthetics by Way of a Preface."

[452] Greenberg, *The Collected Essays and Criticism, Vol. 1: Perceptions and Judgments, 1939–1944*, p. 66.

This point is worth raising because Lovecraft is fully capable of such writing as well. I know few better passages of English prose than the opening two pages of "The Dunwich Horror," which begins as follows: "When a traveller in north central Massachusetts takes the wrong fork at the junction of the Aylesbury pike just beyond Dean's Corners he comes upon a lonely and curious country." [370] In stylistic terms this is hardly Lovecraft *shtick*, since it lacks any indescribable substrata or vast agglomerations of contradictory qualities, or even favorite adjectives along the lines of "eldritch" or "abominable" or "monstrous" (words of the sort that Wilson is so quick to condemn). Instead, Lovecraft begins with a subtly menacing tone that succeeds in stirring up a serious and slightly worried mood in the reader. The traveler has taken the wrong fork in the road; the terrain is lonely and curious; Dean's Corners and Aylesbury are invoked with a note of geographic authority, though both places seem to be inventions of Lovecraft himself. The passage goes on to offer more of the same: "The ground gets higher, and the brier-bordered stone walls press closer and closer against the ruts of the dusty, curving road. The trees of the frequent forest belts seem too large …." [370]

Not all art explicitly produces gaps in the heart of objects in the way that Lovecraft so often does. But it must produce something like *sincerity*; we must be truly fascinated by whatever is placed before us. Lovecraft's abominable crevices between objects and qualities can do this, but so can a joke, a simple story well told, or the quiet rhythm of a passage that brings objects before us as somehow relevant to our concerns. By "sincerity" I do not mean that artworks need be prudish or morally upright, simply that they need to be engrossing. The brother Jason in Faulkner's *The Sound and the Fury* is one of the most repugnant cynics in world literature, yet he fascinates us for precisely this reason.[453] The same holds for Sade's criminal libertine friends in the *120 Days of Sodom* and Sartre's joyless Roquentin in *Nausea*.[454] Sincerity means that a character or object is truly wrapped up in being what it is, and it becomes of interest to us for precisely this reason. If in our normal dealings with the world we use things hazily as bland instruments of our will, a thing is marked by sincerity when it seems to exhibit a genuine inner life of its own. Yet in this way a certain gap is still created between the thing and its accessibility, and hence Lovecraft's

---

[453] William Faulkner, *The Sound and the Fury*.
[454] Marquis de Sade, *120 Days of Sodom*; Jean-Paul Sartre, *Nausea*.

unease before indescribable objects displays the aesthetic rift in its most explicit form.

Comic and Tragic Intentionality

The medieval term "intentionality" was revived by Franz Brentano in his 1874 philosophical classic, *Psychology from an Empirical Standpoint*.[455] It quickly became a pillar of the writings of his students, Husserl among them. Readers from outside professional philosophy should not think that the word has anything to do with "intentions" in the sense of what someone hopes to accomplish with their actions. Instead, intentionality in the philosophical sense means that mental acts (unlike physical acts, Brentano says) are always aimed at some object. To wish is to wish for something; to love or hate is to love or hate something or someone; to make a judgment is to judge about some particular thing. Contrary to the mistaken view of many who footnote Brentano and Husserl, these intentional objects are not something that we point at *outside* the mind, but exist *inside* the mind as purely immanent features of experience. We can hate or doubt imaginary objects, for instance. But even though the intentionality of consciousness is not enough to escape idealism, there is no experience from which intentional objects are missing.[456]

In this way intentionality works as an "adhesive" term, gluing together subject and object as permanent correlates of one another. But in addition to its adhesive function, intentionality also has a "selective" one. For my intentions not only show that I am bonded to the world rather than being a free-floating disembodied consciousness, they also show what is "at issue" for me in my life. To some extent we are what we intend, and the same holds true for authors. In Hemingway's world we find that bullfights, military actions, hunting, and the seduction of beautiful nurses fall within the range of likely and frequent events; in Lovecraft, of course, such incidents are unthinkable. When reading Lovecraft we often encounter apparently human voices with disturbing undertones of buzzing, slopping, or vibration, while nothing of the sort could happen in Jane Austen. Austen's provincial English courtships and inheritance battles are absent in turn from the literary world of Kafka, whose dithering obscurities of legal process would be unthinkable in a novel

---

[455] Franz Brentano, *Psychology from an Empirical Standpoint*.
[456] The already classic discussion of how the human-world correlate does not escape idealism is Quentin Meillassoux, *After Finitude*, especially pp. 5 ff.

written by Sade. In similar fashion, we might allow for a flexible range of possible surprising things to occur in a book of philosophy, but would be truly startled if a treatise on metaphysics also contained the report of a horse race or a pornographic centerfold. In this sense, along with speaking of intentionality as a general feature of all conscious experience, we can also speak of *specific* intentionalities as defining the world of any individual or of any literary work.

Strictly speaking, there are two distinct kinds of intentionality. One is the first-hand sort that we ourselves have at any given moment. The other is the second-hand intentionality that we observe at work in some other person or animal or inanimate object (Bergson showed the latter to be possible in his book on laughter), or in ourselves when we reflect on our status as conscious agents or as characters cutting a figure in the world when viewed by others.[457] For example, the stories of Lovecraft often ask us to consider certain ominous landscapes that barely lie within the realms of the describable, monstrous creatures that half-emerge into tangible form, various respectable universities and their faculty members, and so forth. Yet we also encounter the *reactions* to all these things by the narrators of his stories, who in his great tales are usually first-person participants in the events described.[458] The reason for making this point is that even as great a critic as Wilson conflates the two levels, when he disdains Lovecraft's stylistic talents in the following way:

> One of Lovecraft's worst faults is his incessant effort to work up
> the expectation of the reader by sprinkling his stories with such
> adjectives as "horrible," "terrible," "frightful," "awesome," "eerie,"
> "weird," "forbidden," "unhallowed," "unholy," "blasphemous,"
> "hellish," and "infernal." Surely one of the primary rules for writing
> an effective tale of horror is never to use any of these words ....[459]

True enough, it is generally a good rule of writing and of thinking not to let our adjectives do the work for us. But in this case Wilson is off the mark.

---

[457] Henri Bergson, *Laughter*.
[458] Of the eight stories serving as the focus of Part Two below, only "The Dunwich Horror" and "The Dreams in the Witch House" use an omniscient third-person narrator. In the other six, the narrator is more or less personally involved in the events being described, as is generally the case in Poe as well. "The Colour Out of Space" presents the special situation of a first-person narrator relating events from decades ago, of which he himself was told by an aged eyewitness of the time.
[459] Wilson, *Literary Essays and Reviews of the 1930s and 1940s*, pp. 701–702.

In Lovecraft such adjectives rarely serve as feeble primary instruments for bullying a reader into terror, as Wilson implies. Instead, Lovecraft sprinkles them onto an already completed description, as an enhancing spice that reflects the mental turmoil of the narrator rather than shaping our own direct grasp of the scene. Consider the following description of the strange written characters on the base of the Cthulhu idol found in Louisiana: "They, like the subject and material, belonged to something horribly remote and distinct from mankind as we know it; something frightfully suggestive of old and unhallowed cycles of life in which our world and our concepts have no part." [176] Contra Wilson this is not bad writing, despite the occurrence of "horribly," "frightfully," and "unhallowed." For the heavy lifting is done not by these adjectives themselves, but by the previous description of the idol and the troubled puzzlement of the archaeologists who provide only minimal help to Inspector Legrasse. The adjectives condemned by Wilson are merely ratifications and amplifications of things we have already been led to believe by Lovecraft's skilled artisanship.

That is a first division of intentionality, then: the difference between the primary interest we take in whatever we experience at the moment, and a secondary interest that we observe in other intentional agents. But we should also recognize a second division between "comic" and "tragic" intentionality, which Aristotle defines in terms to be taken in all seriousness: "Comedy aims at representing men as worse, Tragedy as better than in actual life."[460] This definition can be adopted without reserve, as long as we are clear about what "better" and "worse" mean here. People can be better or worse than we are in any number of respects: social rank, wealth, intelligence, ethical probity, athletic skill, or beauty. But high status in any of these areas cannot protect those who hold it from becoming comical at times, nor does low status exclude the occurrence of tragedy. Often enough we can mock the foibles of the Kennedy Family or Miss Universe, however superior to us they may be in wealth, public position, or physical attractiveness. Conversely we find that slaves, fools, and the poor can rank among the greatest heroes of a tragic literature fit to make dictators and millionaires weep. Ultimately, the only thing that can be meant by "better" and "worse" people here is whether they are better or worse in terms of the things they invest their energy in taking seriously. The tragic figure is involved with objects and incidents that command our respect or interest, while the comic figure has invested

---

[460] Aristotle, *Poetics*, p. 14.

attention in things we regard as ridiculous: ranging from red rubber clown noses to absurd addictions and compulsions.

This brings us to another famous classical remark about comedy and tragedy. At the end of Plato's *Symposium* [223D], Socrates is overheard making an argument about the two: "Socrates was trying to prove to [Agathon and Aristophanes] that authors should be able to write both comedy and tragedy: the skillful tragic dramatist should also be a comic poet."[461] Quite aside from the evidence of figures such as Shakespeare who clearly mastered both, it is easy to see that the comic and the tragic exist in such close proximity as to easily flip into one another. If Mombo the Clown falls dead with cardiac arrest while making balloon animals for children at the mall, we have a sudden reversal from the comic into the tragic. Likewise, if the victim of marital infidelity is merely Harlequin in a *commedia dell'arte* skit, or if the destroyer of Tokyo is an unconvincing reptilian monster rather than genuine firebombs, even cuckolding and mass death can become objects of wholesome laughter.

More interesting than these examples, however, would be a deliberate and controlled combination of the comic and the tragic *simultaneously*. And this is something that Lovecraft does quite well, with the tragic element usually coming from the horrors he depicts for us, and the comic side stemming from the laughably genteel or prudish response of the Lovecraftian hero to incidents we know to be worse than he suspects. For instance, as the narrator winds down his conversation with the drunkard Zadok at the docks of Innsmouth, we read as follows: *"Iä! Iä! Cthulhu fhtagn! Ph'nglui mglw'nafh Cthulhu R'lyeh wgah-nagl fhtagn* — Old Zadok was fast lapsing into stark raving ...." [622] But this is no mere alcoholic outburst, and we the readers know it so well that the narrator thereby becomes a comical figure despite the impending danger of which he is so deeply unaware. A few pages later, with Zadok's terrible story now complete, the narrator's fright does not prevent him from saying "later I might sift the tale and extract some nucleus of historic allegory," [625] thereby giving a laughably effete and academic response to a cosmic horror that we the readers know to be unfolding. The effect is both comic and tragic simultaneously. This is a regular feature of Lovecraft as a writer that should not be forgotten in what follows.

---

[461] Plato, *Symposium*, p. 77.

CHAPTER 22

THE WELL-WROUGHT BROKEN HAMMER: OBJECT-ORIENTED LITERARY CRITICISM[462]

For nearly a decade I have been publishing on the theme of object-oriented philosophy, which can be treated as part of a wider movement known as speculative realism.[463] Both trends have rapidly gained influence in fields outside academic philosophy, with especial resonance so far in the fine arts, architectural theory, and medieval studies. For this reason I am often asked to present my views on various topics lying outside my usual professional sphere: How should political activism be done in the wake of speculative realism? What new directions should be taken by contemporary art as a result of object-oriented philosophy? My instinctive reaction in the face of such questions is to feel a certain reluctance. It is my view that philosophy should not be the handmaid of any other discipline, whether it be theology, leftist politics or brain science. But by the same token, I also believe that other disciplines should not be subordinated to philosophy. Nor is there much point

---

[462] This chapter is Copyright © 2012 *New Literary History*, The University of Virginia. The article first appeared in *New Literary History* 43.2, Spring, 2012, pp. 183–203.

[463] The original published version of my philosophical position can be found in Graham Harman, *Tool-Being*. A more compact and up-to-date account can be found in Graham Harman, *The Quadruple Object*. The final chapter of the latter book contains a history and overview of the Speculative Realism movement.

in proclaiming in advance that all boundaries are artificial while throwing everything into a blender. The various districts of human knowledge have relative disciplinary autonomy due to their differing objects and the varying sorts of expertise required to practice them competently. The transgression of these boundaries should not be constant and rampant and decreed as a global principle, but can only be be justified by its effectiveness in individual cases. Hence my reluctance to preach to those who deal in materials different from my own. Often it is better to let ourselves be surprised by what others do with our work, rather than command those adaptations like a bossy partygoer selecting the music in all other homes.

Nonetheless, as long as someone is asking, it would be either rude or lazy to sit by in silence. Lately there have been numerous requests for my views on object-oriented philosophy in relation to the arts, and the same is increasingly true of literary theory as well. Thus I will try to shed some light on how the most recent philosophical trends might contribute to literary theory. In what follows I will begin with a brief summary of those trends, and then show how object-oriented philosophy differs from three prominent currents in twentieth-century literary theory: New Criticism, New Historicism, and Deconstruction. In closing I will try to sketch what an object-oriented criticism might look like.

I. Speculative Realism

"Speculative Realism" was the name of a one-day workshop at Goldsmiths College, University of London on April 27, 2007.[464] It thereafter became the name of a loose philosophical movement opposed to trends that have dominated continental philosophy from its inception. The central problem at stake is none other than realism: does a real world exist independently of human access, or not? Since the era of Immanuel Kant, it has often been held that the question is invalid, since we cannot think of world without humans nor of humans without world, but only of a primordial *correlation* between the two. This type of philosophy was dubbed "correlationism" by the French philosopher Quentin Meillassoux (b. 1967), whose 2006 book *After Finitude* provided speculative realism with this useful name for its mortal enemy.[465] The speculative realists are of course *realists*, given their defense of a mind-independent reality. But they are also *speculative*, in

---

[464] For a transcript of the event, see Ray Brassier er al., "Speculative Realism."
[465] Quentin Meillassoux, *After Finitude*.

the sense that they do not wish to establish a commonsense middle-aged realism of objective atoms and billiard balls located outside the human mind. Instead, the speculative realists have all pursued a model of reality as something far *weirder* than realists had ever guessed. It is no accident that the only shared intellectual hero among the original members of the group was the horror and science fiction writer H.P. Lovecraft.

What prevented speculative realism from becoming a cohesive philosophical movement was the vast range of options available within its rather general founding principles: realism plus unorthodox speculation. Iain Hamilton Grant followed paths established by the philosophers F.W.J. Schelling and Gilles Deleuze in defending a productive nature-force that meets with retarding obstacles and only thereby generates individual objects.[466] Others adopted a more predictable strategy of scientistic nihilism that increasingly identifies with the most anti-philosophical strains of neuroscience.[467] But there is also the instructive contrast between Meillassoux's philosophy and my own. While speculative realism is often presented as an enemy of Kant's so-called "Copernican Revolution" in philosophy, the relation with Kant is more complicated than this, and even points to a key internal fissure within speculative realism itself. Oversimplifying somewhat, we can say that there are two basic principles underlying the Kantian Revolution in philosophy.

1 Kant distinguishes between phenomena and noumena. The things-in-themselves lie beyond all possibility of human access, given that all experience is confined to the twelve categories and the pure intuitions of space and time. Human beings are finite; absolute knowledge is unavailable to them. The things-in-themselves can be thought but never known.

2 For Kant, the human-world relation is philosophically privileged. From the standpoint of Kantian philosophy, the relation between two colliding physical masses is something best left to the natural sciences, while the relation between human and world is where the genuine problems of philosophy unfold.

---

[466] Iain Hamilton Grant, *Philosophies of Nature After Schelling*.

[467] I refer primarily to original Speculative Realism member Ray Brassier, who has since distanced himself from the group with such violent rhetoric that he can no longer plausibly be named in connection with its activities. Cf. "I am a nihilist because I still believe in truth," Ray Brassier interviewed by Marcin Rychter, *Kronos*, March 4, 2011. http://www.kronos.org.pl/index.php?23151,896

Now, whereas Meillassoux rejects 1 and affirms 2, my own position affirms 1 and rejects 2. That is to say, Meillassoux rejects Kantian finitude in favor of absolute human knowledge, while I reject absolute knowledge and retain Kantian finitude, though broadening this finitude beyond the human realm to include all relations in the cosmos, including inanimate ones.

The correlationist argument says that we cannot think a reality outside thought, for in so doing we instantly convert it into a thought. We remain trapped in the correlational circle, and must remain there if we wish to remain rationalists. The only easy way out of the circle, Meillassoux claims, is through a "rhetoric of the Rich Elsewhere."[468] This rhetoric simply complains that the correlationist argument is boring and prevents us from exploring the world in all its rich empirical detail. It merely *refuses* the correlationist argument without *refuting* it. Instead of such a refusal, Meillassoux initially *accepts* the correlationist argument. He tries to work his way through the circle and provide a new proof of the existence of things-in-themselves that would persist even after the death of all humans. For Meillassoux, what belongs to things-in-themselves are those aspects of them that can be mathematized.[469] But this heavily Badiouian mathematical element in Meillassoux's work has not been endorsed by most others in the speculative realist camp, which remains loosely affiliated around the critique of correlationism. While Meillassoux tries to move beyond Kant by attacking Kantian finitude, he tacitly endorses Kant's privileging of the human-world relation as the root of all other relations. But this decision can also be reversed, so that Kantian finitude is retained, but also expanded well beyond the realm of human-world interaction. In this way, even the duel between colliding billiard balls or between raindrops and tin roofs would be haunted by the inaccessibility of the thing-in-itself. The name of this position is object-oriented philosophy.

II. Object-Oriented Philosophy

Whereas Meillassoux's philosophy emerges from dialogue with Alain Badiou and German Idealism, the object-oriented philosophy to which I and others subscribe can be seen as an attempt, within the broader framework of speculative realism, to come to terms with phenomenology

---

[468] This phrase comes from Meillassoux's portion of the Goldsmiths transcript referred to above, Brassier et al., "Speculative Realism," p. 423.

[469] For a detailed account of the difference between my philosophical position and Meillassoux's, cf. Graham Harman, *Quentin Meillassoux*.

and its radicalization at the hands of Heidegger.[470] Phenomenology was launched in 1900–01 by Edmund Husserl's landmark *Logical Investigations*. In a climate where the natural sciences were on the rise and philosophy seemed in danger of being replaced by experimental psychology, Husserl insisted instead on a patient description of the phenomena as they appear to us. For example, any scientific theory of color in terms of the wavelength of light must be grounded in our prior immediate experience of color: in a description of how red or blue appear to us, and how they affect our motor reactions and our moods. Phenomenology must also include the description of non-existent objects, given that centaurs and unicorns can appear before my mind no less than masses of genuine granite. But Husserl also noted that the intentional objects before my mind are not "bundles of qualities," as British Empiricism held. I can view a blackbird or mountain from numerous different angles, thereby changing their manifest qualities, yet the blackbird and mountain still remain the same things despite these shifting profiles. In this way, there is strife within the phenomenal realm between objects and their shifting qualities. The phenomenological method aims to strip away the inessential qualities of things, and to gain an insight into what is really essential about any given intentional object — what it truly needs in order to be what it is.

Heidegger radicalized phenomenology by noting that most of our contact with entities *does not* occur in the manner of having them present before the mind. Quite the contrary. When using a hammer, for instance, I am focused on the building project currently underway, and am probably taking the hammer for granted. Unless the hammer is too heavy or too slippery, or unless it breaks, I tend not to notice it at all. The fact that the hammer can break proves it is deeper than my understanding of it. This has led many to read Heidegger's famous tool-analysis in "pragmatist" terms, which implies that all theory is grounded in a tacit practical background. The problem with this interpretation is that praxis does not use up the reality of things any more than theory does. Staring at a hammer does not exhaust its depths, but neither does wielding that hammer on a construction site or a battlefield. Both theory and praxis are distortions of the hammer in its subterranean reality. Object-oriented philosophy pushes this another step further by saying that objects distort one another even in sheer causal

---

interaction. The raindrops or breezes that strike the hammer may not be "conscious" of it in human fashion, yet such entities fail to exhaust the reality of the hammer to no less a degree than human praxis or theory.

Heidegger's own distinction between "objects" and "things" is irrelevant for our purposes; we can use the single term "object," simply because that was the term used by phenomenology when it first revived the philosophical theme of individual things. Husserl's intentional objects (or "sensual" objects, as I prefer) do not hide from the mind at all. They are always present before us, and are simply encrusted with accidental surface features that must be stripped away to discover the object's essence. This includes all the objects of our theoretical and practical experience. Sensual objects are in strife with their swirling sensual qualities. By contrast, Heidegger's tools always remain hidden from the mind, just like Kant's things-in-themselves. In Heidegger's terminology, they "withdraw" (*sich entziehen*) from all access: they remain veiled, concealed, or hidden. But real objects must also have individual features, since otherwise all things would be interchangeable. Hence the strife between objects and their qualities is repeated in the depths of the world as well. In Husserl's philosophy there is a further hybrid strife between sensual objects and their *real* qualities; it need not be discussed in this article, though I hold that this is the root of all theoretical activity in all domains. Of more importance to us here is the fourth conflict, between *real* objects and their *sensual* qualities. For this is precisely what happens when Heideggger's hammer breaks. The broken hammer alludes to the inscrutable reality of hammer-being lying behind the accessible theoretical, practical, or perceptual qualities of the hammer. The reason for calling this relation one of "allusion" is that it can only hint at the reality of the hammer without ever making it directly present to the mind. I call this structure *allure*, and quite aside from the question of broken hammers, I contend that this is the key phenomenon of all the arts, literature included.[471] Allure alludes to entities as they are, quite apart from any relations with or effects upon other entities in the world.

This deeply *non-relational* conception of the reality of things is the heart of object-oriented philosophy. To some readers it will immediately sound deeply reactionary. After all, most recent advances in the humanities pride themselves on having abandoned the notion of stale autonomous substances or individual human subjects in favor of networks, negotiations, relations, interactions, and dynamic fluctuations. This has been the guiding

---

[471] Graham Harman, *Guerrilla Metaphysics.*

theme of our time. But the wager of object-oriented philosophy is that this programmatic movement towards holistic interaction is an idea once but no longer liberating, and that the real discoveries now lie on the other side of the yard. The problem with individual substances was never that they were autonomous or individual, but that they were wrongly conceived as eternal, unchanging, simple, or directly accessible by certain privileged observers. By contrast, the objects of object-oriented philosophy are mortal, ever-changing, built from swarms of subcomponents, and accessible only through oblique allusion. This is not the oft-lamented "naïve realism" of oppressive and benighted patriarchs, but a *weird* realism in which real individual objects resist all forms of causal or cognitive mastery.

III. The New Criticism

We have seen that for object-oriented philosophy, there is a series of tensions between objects and their qualities. Real objects withdraw from all human access and even from causal interaction with each other. This does not mean that objects engage in no relations (for of course they do), but only that such relations are a problem to be solved rather than a starting-point to be decreed, and furthermore that these relations must always be indirect or vicarious rather than direct. No object relates with others without caricature, distortion, or energy loss; knowledge of a tree is never a tree, nor do two colliding asteroids exhaust one another's properties through this contact. At first glance, this model of objects might seem to step backward into a retrograde intellectual past. According to one familiar narrative cited above, philosophers used to be naïve realists who believed in real things outside their social or linguistic contexts; these things were ascribed timeless essences that were not politically innocent, since they subjugated various groups by pigeonholing each of them as oriental, feminine, pre-Enlightenment, or some other such tag. According to this view, we have luckily come to realize that essences must be replaced with events and performances, that the notion of a reality that is not a reality *for someone* is dubious, that flux is prior to stasis, that things must be seen as differences rather than solid units and as complex feedback networks rather than integers. I will deal with these prejudices as this article progresses.

For the moment, we should simply consider what might seem to be obvious similarities between the relationless concept of objects just presented and the New Criticism's long unfashionable model of poems as encapsulated machines cut off from all social and material context.

In "The Heresy of Paraphrase," surely the most famous chapter of his book *The Well Wrought Urn*, Cleanth Brooks says that a poem cannot be paraphrased. What this strictly means is that the poem cannot be rephrased as a series of literal propositions, yet it can also be taken to mean (as Brooks argues elsewhere) that poems cannot be reduced to the series of social influences or biographical facts that gave rise to them. The poem is an integral unit irreducible either to its ancestors or its heirs, not constituted by its relations in any decisive way. This might seem to have dismal political consequences, since the poem as a closed-off unit seems to lead to an aesthetic elitism supporting a privileged caste of white ruling-class men and their arbitrarily selected literary canon. I will consider the political side of the question in the next section, when discussing the New Historicism. Here I only want to show that Brooks is by no means true to the non-relational view of poems that he seems to propose.

The object-oriented side of Brooks can be found in his hostility to paraphrase. A poem cannot be translated into literal prose statement: "all such formulations lead away from the center of the poem — not toward it …."[472] Any attempt to summarize the literal meaning of a poem inevitably becomes a long-winded effort, filled with qualifications and even metaphors, a lengthy detour that comes more and more to resemble the original poem itself. The poem is not a "prose-sense decorated by sensuous imagery."[473] Only weak poets use facile ornament to spice up literal content, and any literal idea drawn from a poem can be nothing better than an abstraction.[474] It is unavoidable for critics and students to make prose statements about poems, but these statements must not be taken as the equivalent of the poem itself.[475] Hence Brooks's focus on "irony" and "paradox" in poems, since ironic or paradoxical content is two-faced and thus cannot be translated into any literal meaning at all.[476] The poem differs from any literal expression of its content just as the hammer itself differs from any broken, perceived, or cognized hammer. It is not just that the poem or hammer usually acts as an unnoticed background that can then be focused on explicitly from time to time. Instead, the literal rendition of the poem is *never* the poem itself, which must exceed all interpretation in the form of a hidden surplus.

---

[472] Cleanth Brooks, *The Well Wrought Urn*, p. 199.

[473] Brooks, *The Well Wrought Urn*, p. 204.

[474] Brooks, *The Well Wrought Urn*, pp. 205, 213–214.

[475] Brooks, *The Well Wrought Urn*, p. 206.

[476] Brooks, *The Well Wrought Urn*, pp. 209, 210.

So far, all is well. But there are two key points where we must dissent. The first is that Brooks is guilty of what I have sometimes called the Taxonomic Fallacy, which consists in the assumption that any ontological distinction must be embodied in specific *kinds* of entities. Namely, we can accept Brooks's claim of an absolute gulf between literalized prose sense and the non-prose sense that it paraphrases or translates. Yet *it does not follow* that there should be a division of labor in which poetry has all the non-prose sense while other disciplines have all the literal sense. And this is precisely what Brooks holds. By literalizing a poetic statement, he tells us, "we bring [it] into an unreal competition with science or philosophy or theology," as if these disciplines, unlike poetry, had direct rather than allusive contact with their objects.[477] Object-oriented philosophy says otherwise. The failure of paraphrase is not monopolized by the arts, but haunts *all* human dealings with the world, and even the relations between inanimate entities within that world. As Brooks puts it later, "the terms of science are abstract symbols which do not change under the pressure of the context. They are pure (or aspire to be pure) denotations ...."[478] But regardless of aspiration, the irreducibility of reality to literal presence applies as much to the sciences as it does to poetry, as is demonstrated by (among other things) scientific theory changing over time. By treating poetry as a special case, Brooks wrongly concedes the claims of much "science or philosophy or theology" to deliver prose truth incarnate, and also needlessly shields poetry from the literal surface dimension that it also possesses. The literal and the non-literal cannot be apportioned between separate zones of reality, but are two distinct sides of every point in the cosmos. Thus the attempt of the New Critics to treat literature as a *uniquely* privileged zone standing outside the rest of space-time must indeed be rejected: not because everything has reality only within this cosmic network, but because everything stands partially outside it just as poems do.

Yet there is another complaint to be made against Brooks, which concerns the *reason* he gives for why poetry is supposedly so special. In one sense it is obviously true that he views the poem as existing in pristine isolation from the rest of the cosmos. Yet once we have entered the gates of the poem, nothing is autonomous at all: instead, we inhabit a holistic wonderland in which everything is defined solely by its interrelations with everything else. For whereas "a scientific [proposition] can stand alone,"

---

[477] Brooks, *The Well Wrought Urn*, p. 201.
[478] Brooks, *The Well Wrought Urn*, p. 210.

a poem is defined instead by "the primacy of the pattern."[479] A poem is a *structure*: "a structure of meanings, evaluations, and interpretations; and the principle of unity which informs it seems to be one of balancing and harmonizing connotations, attitudes, and meanings."[480] Stated differently, "the relation of each item to the whole context is crucial …."[481] Yet this is clearly false. To make a slight change in two lines of the Fool might not alter the general effect of *King Lear*, nor would it likely make much difference to the characterizations of Regan or Kent. To add a few chapters' worth of adventures to *Don Quixote* might increase or decrease our enjoyment of the book, yet it would possibly just reinforce rather than renovate our previous sense of Sancho and the Don. In everyday life, changing my shirt at the last minute before boarding the bus certainly affects "the total context" of the bus ride, yet it would not have any discernible effect on the bus or most of the passengers riding it, indifferent as they are to my fashion mediocrity. What is truly interesting about "contexts" is not that they utterly define every entity to the core, but that they open a space where *certain* interactions and effects can take place and not others. There is no reason to descend the slippery slope and posit a general relational ontology in which all things are utterly defined by even the most trivial aspects of their context. Here as in the case of Heidegger's hammer, if all objects were completely determined by the structure or context in which they resided, there is no reason why anything would ever change, since a thing would be nothing more than its current context. For any change to be possible, objects must be an excess or surplus outside their current range of relations, vulnerable to some of those relations but insensible to others: just as a hammer is shattered by walls and heavy weights but not by the laughter of an infant. The New Criticism gets it wrong twice: first by making the artwork a *special* non-literal thing, and second by turning its interior into a relational wildfire in which all individual elements are consumed.

IV. The New Historicism

Since it is well known (and often lamented) that the New Critics were primarily well-off white gentlemen, we are not unprepared for the following report by Stephen Greenblatt from his student days at Yale:

---

[479] Brooks, *The Well Wrought Urn*, pp. 207, 194.
[480] Brooks, *The Well Wrought Urn*, p. 195.
[481] Brooks, *The Well Wrought Urn*, p. 207.

I was only mildly interested in the formalist agenda that dominated graduate instruction and was epitomized by the imposing figure of William K. Wimsatt .... I would go in the late afternoon to the Elizabethan club — all male, a black servant in a starched white jacket, cucumber sandwiches, and tea — and listen to Wimsatt at the great round table hold forth like Doctor Johnson on poetry and aesthetics.[482]

This passage is not just a cringe-inducing anecdote about Wimsatt and his environment, but also a tacit intellectual claim. Namely, it makes the familiar implication that all "formalism" tends towards socio-political blindness, as an aestheticism exploiting the marginal servitude of subaltern actors. This suggestion is reinforced by the praise on the next page for Leftist critic Raymond Williams for asking such "non-formalist" questions as "who controlled access to the printing press, who owned the land and the factories, whose voices were being repressed as well as represented in literary texts, what social strategies were being served by the aesthetic values we constructed ...."[483] Surely we should all prefer the critic who champions the oppressed over the dominant fat cat of an all-male club, attended by Black servants and nibbling on cucumber sandwiches while holding forth like Doctor Johnson.

The question, however, is whether this proves that a relational ontology is better than one in which objects are autonomous from their contexts, as Greenblatt's remarks seem to imply. On the contrary, I hold that this is one of the most deeply rooted intellectual biases of our time. In the current landscape, the notion of autonomous substances seems to evoke a world of stagnant subjugation, while the dynamism of relational and materialist ontologies seem to open up a vast panorama of political and intellectual breakthrough. Here we need only note that the historical prejudice used to be quite the opposite. At the time of the French Revolution, for instance, it was the arch-conservative Edmund Burke who defended socially constructed rights, while the ultra-radical Jacobins defended the natural autonomy of human nature from its current social conditions.[484] No doubt the day will come again when the political Left and Right will reverse direction on questions of nature and culture once more. We must not commit the

---

[482] Stephen Greenblatt, *Learning to Curse*, p. 1.
[483] Greenblatt, *Learning to Curse*, p. 2.
[484] Edmund Burke, *Revolutionary Writings*.

Taxonomic Fallacy by holding that relations are always liberating and non-relational realities always reactionary.

Brooks was able to turn the world of the poem into a holistic machine at the cost of making it an *inner* world, famously cut off from the biographical, social, and economic conditions in which the poem was produced. The New Historicism is less hypocritical, turning *everything* into an interrelated cosmos of influences. As stated in one of its best-known manifestoes, the New Historicism has "struck down the doctrine of noninterference that forbade humanists to intrude on questions of politics, power, indeed on all matters that deeply affect people's practical lives ...."[485] All disciplinary boundaries have been dissolved, since the New Historicism "brackets together literature, ethnography, art history, and other disciplines and sciences hard and soft," a list that seems to exclude nothing.[486] We are told that "literary and non-literary 'texts' circulate inseparably," and are asked to "admire the sheer intricacy and unavoidability of exchanges between culture and power."[487] Empty formalism is combated "by pulling historical considerations to the center stage of literary analysis."[488] We will bring together "metaphors, ceremonies, dances, emblems, items of clothing, popular stories ...." and all will be "circulation, negotiation, exchange ...."[489] Amidst this general blend of all disciplines and practices, this fiesta of interactivity, we will realize "that autonomous self and text are mere holograms, effects that intersecting institutions produce; that selves and texts are defined by their relations to hostile others ... and disciplinary power ...."[490] Somewhat paradoxically, despite this advocacy of a firestorm of holistic interaction between all things, it is the *opponents* of the New Historicism who are accused of "[constructing] a holistic master story of large-scale structural elements directing a whole society," when what they should really do instead is "to perform a differential analysis of the local conflicts engendered in individual authors and local discourses."[491]

But it is difficult to see how "local" conflicts and discourses could exist at all in light of the ontology just outlined, built of furious interactivity, with academic disciplinary walls immediately broken down along with the

---

[485] H. Aram Veeser, "Introduction," in H. Aram Veeser, ed., *The New Historicism*.
[486] Veeser, "Introduction," p. xi.
[487] Veeser, "Introduction," p. xi.
[488] Veeser, "Introduction," p. xi.
[489] Veeser, "Introduction," pp. xii, xiv.
[490] Veeser, "Introduction," p. xii.
[491] Veeser, "Introduction," p. xiii.

distinction between literary and non-literary texts. My purpose is not to identify contradictions for the sake of scoring easy points. Instead, I simply want to note that both philosophical and political problems arise when individual selves and texts are described as holograms, as the relational effects of hostile others and disciplinary power. First, despite Veeser's passing nod to the hard sciences and the rampant talk of "materiality" in the New Historicism (and other Foucault-inspired trends) there are few traces of non-human entities amidst all this discussion of mutually conditioning forces. What we find instead is a historicism of the human subject as shaped by various disciplinary practices. But while the New Historicism is interested in "the manifold ways culture and society affect each other," the phrase "culture and society" does not encompass an especially diverse range of entities.[492] For the world also contains parakeets, silver, limestone, coral reefs, solar flares, and moons, none of them easy to classify as "culture" or "society," and all of them interacting with *each other* whether humans discuss it or not. As Bill Brown accurately puts it when trying to distinguish his own "Thing Theory" from the work of New Historicists:

> However much I shared the new historicist "desire to make contact
> with the 'real,'" I wanted the end result to read like a grittier,
> materialist phenomenology of everyday life, a result that might
> somehow arrest language's wish, as described by Michel Serres, that the
> "whole world … derive from language." Where other critics had faith
> in "discourse" or in the "social text" as the analytical grid on which to
> reconfigure our knowledge about the present and the past, I wanted to
> turn attention to things — the objects that are materialized from and
> in the physical world that is, or had been, at hand.[493]

The problem that Thing Theory seems to share with the New Historicism lies in the assumption that "the real" has no other function than to accompany the human agent and mold or disrupt it from time to time. If the real has an inner struggle of its own quite apart from the human encounter with it, this is apparently not something in which we are expected to take much interest, and Thing Theory shows symptoms of a correlationism in which the human-world duet is always central. But at least Brown allows for some recalcitrance in material things, however human-centered the

---

[492] Veeser, "Introduction," p. xii.
[493] Bill Brown, *A Sense of Things*, p. 3.

notion of recalcitrance always remains.[494] For the New Historicism, even this sense of recalcitrance is weaker. We read, for instance, that "everyone's sexual identity, not just Rosalind's, remains in ceaseless upheaval, [and] *our society rewards* those who choose one gender or another."[495] Rather than being recalcitrant in opposition to our wishes, gender is depicted here as a mutable, indeterminate lump shaped at will by societal reward systems. And given the general New Historicist attitude towards fixed essences and boundaries, this seems not to be a special point limited to sexual identity, but a generally negative hypothesis about identity in general, heavily flavored with Bourdieuian sociology: everything is in flux, but *society rewards* those who gullibly believe in fixed identities.

The political problem here is that a consistently relational ontology would only lead to a perpetual ratification of the status quo. For if humans are merely the effect of a ceaseless upheaval of discursive practices, if they are merely holograms, then it is difficult to see why any situation at all should count as oppression: after all, the current residents of a dictatorial state would only count as holograms produced by intersecting institutions and disciplinary practices. It is difficult to see why these holographic citizens would have any inherent right to exist outside the institutions and practices that produced them, which perhaps ought to be honored as parents instead. One suspects that the hostility of the New Historicism to *fixed* identities leads the movement to an unjustified suspicion even of *instantaneous* identities. For example, even if we assume it to be true that everyone's gender identity is in ceaseless upheaval, and that even the identity of a rock is in ceaseless upheaval as well, it does not follow that in this particular moment neither we humans nor rocks have any identity at all. It may be that fifteen different observers and institutions all make different inferences or classifications about this identity simultaneously, but all this really proves is that none of them is capable of fathoming what that identity currently is. What you are may mutate; it may shift through countless upheavals over the course of years, months, or fleeting hours. It does not follow from this that you are everything and nothing simultaneously. You are perhaps a human in a state of upheaval over your gender identity, but you are not at the same time also a trireme, a wall, a butterfly, a non-butterfly, and a human *devoid* of any upheaval in gender identity. If this critique sounds like the sort of vulgar realism too often thrown at postmodern theories, I would answer that not

---

[494] Cf. Jane Bennett, *Vibrant Matter*, esp. pp. 1, 3, 9, 35, 61.
[495] Veeser, "Introduction," p. xiv.

all realism is vulgar. We must not let adjectives such as "vulgar" and "naïve" do our thinking for us.

The strictly philosophical problem with this boundary-free holism is one that we already encountered earlier. Namely, relational ontology is incapable of thinking adequately about the concept of "locality" on which the New Historicism also prides itself. A completely interconnected cosmos would have no individual location at all: everything would affect everything else, and all things would be mutually and utterly near. I would be sitting in Cairo and Sydney at the same time, just as some early Islamic theologians held that God could allow us to sit simultaneously in Baghdad and Mecca. For there to be location, there must also be individuality, however ephemeral and mutable it may be. If Japanese cities are in constant upheaval in terms of their identity, they are nonetheless in Japan and not in Brazil. In short, contextuality is not universal. Shakespeare is molded by some aspects of his era while completely unaffected by others, and his own character is partly responsible for which aspects are assimilated and which are screened from view. Indeed, Shakespeare as a writer is a *style*: a style that among other things would enable us to distinguish between authentic and inauthentic plays under his name. Falstaff is an individual character who guides Shakespeare's decisions as to which scenes work and fail to work, and who silently resists or embraces the new lines placed in his mouth. In turn, the economy of London and the disciplinary practices of kings and bureaucrats do not just dissolve into Shakespeare's plays, but retain an autonomous character and also influence and fail to influence playwrights, moths, the diffraction of moonlight, and the parabolic movement of stones.

Here is another way to put it. Cleanth Brooks severed literary texts from the world but turned their interiors into contextual houses of mirrors where everything reflects everything else. By contrast, the New Historicism tacitly dissolves literary works into a house of mirrors that is now ubiquitous and is held to define the whole of reality. Object-oriented philosophy, however, simply rejects the house of mirrors. Objects may change rapidly; they may be perceived differently by different observers; they remain opaque to all the efforts of knowledge to master them. But the very condition of all change, perspectivism, and opacity is that objects have a *definite character* that can change, be perceived, and resist. This holds not only for literary works, but also for scientific, philosophical, and theological propositions. It holds equally well for genders, prisons, clinics, zebras, and volcanoes. All literary and non-literary objects are partially opaque to their contexts, and inflict their blows on one another from behind shields and screens that can never entirely be breached.

V. Deconstruction

We now turn to deconstruction and Jacques Derrida, who, along with Michel Foucault, is probably the most influential continental philosopher of the past half-century. What Derrida shares with object-oriented thought is the conviction that Heidegger changed the state of the art in our discipline, and that further progress requires coming to terms with what Heidegger saw. Nonetheless, the two standpoints draw precisely the opposite conclusions. As object-oriented philosophy sees it, Heidegger showed that being withdraws behind any form of presence. Not only does theoretical comportment fail to exhaust the being of things, but so does practical activity, and so too does sheer inanimate contact. Object-oriented philosophy is a frank *realism* which views objects or things as genuine realities deeper than any of the relations in which they might become involved. This realism is what *prevents* the sin of ontotheology or metaphysics of presence, since objects are so deeply and inexhaustibly real that no form of access can ever do them justice. Any attempt to translate this reality into masterable knowledge for logocentric purposes will fail, precisely because being is *deeper* than every logos.

Derrida takes the opposite tack. He does call for "the undermining of an ontology which, in its innermost course, has determined the meaning of being as presence."[496] But far from agreeing that presence is overcome by the absence of a withdrawn real being, Derrida treats this notion as the heart of the problem. As he reads the evidence, "Heidegger's insistence on noting that being is produced as history only through the logos, and is nothing outside of it, the difference between being and the entity — all this clearly indicates that fundamentally nothing escapes the movement of the signifier, and that, in the last instance, the difference between signified and signifier *is nothing*."[497] The question of being "does not amount to hypostatizing a transcendental signified ...."[498] For this reason, Derrida takes pleasure in speaking of threats to substantiality and what he calls "the metaphysics of the proper."[499] He does not try to escape presence by pointing to a withdrawn

---

[496] Jacques Derrida, *Of Grammatology*, p. 71.
[497] Derrida, *Of Grammatology*, pp. 22–23.
[498] Derrida, *Of Grammatology*, p. 23.
[499] Derrida, *Of Grammatology*, p. 26.

absent reality, since this could result only in a "naïve objectivism."[500] For even if an object were absent from us, it would still be present *to itself*, which is exactly what Derrida holds to be impossible: "The so-called 'thing itself' is always already a *representamen* shielded from the simplicity of intuitive evidence. The *representamen* functions only by giving rise to an *interpretant* that itself becomes a sign and so on to infinity."[501] Although Derrida sometimes speaks of "concealment," it is a concealment "always on the move" in an infinite chain of signifiers, not a self-identical reality sheltered in cosmic depths beneath all relation, as is the case for object-oriented philosophy.[502] Concealment for Derrida is merely a constant lateral shifting and sliding from whatever might seem to be given at any moment, rather than a hidden oracle buried beneath the temple of the world. "The literal [*propre*] meaning does not exist, its 'appearance' is a necessary function — and must be analyzed as such — in the system of differences and metaphors."[503] And furthermore, "the thing itself is a collection of things or a chain of differences ...."[504] To ignore this point, to treat the thing as something real existing outside the chain of differences, amounts in Derrida's eyes to "logocentric repression."[505] By contrast, object-oriented philosophy insists that *only* the relationless depth of objects, incommensurable with any signs, is capable of combating the logocentrism that thinks it can make reality directly present to the mind. Despite what Derrida thinks, the problem is not self-presence, otherwise known as "identity." Instead, the problem is the assumption that such self-presence can be converted adequately into a form of presence for something else.

The thing is a *representamen*, whose property "is to be itself and another, to be produced as a structure of reference, to be separated from itself."[506] This observation speaks to the core of who Derrida is as a thinker. The thing is not simply itself, but *différance*, "an economic concept designating the production of differing/deferring."[507] The world is a "play," and "in this play of representation, the point of origin becomes ungraspable. There are things like reflecting pools, and images, an infinite reference from one to the other,

---

[500] Derrida, *Of Grammatology*, p. 61.
[501] Derrida, *Of Grammatology*, p. 49.
[502] Derrida, *Of Grammatology*, p. 49.
[503] Derrida, *Of Grammatology*, p. 89.
[504] Derrida, *Of Grammatology*, p. 90.
[505] Derrida, *Of Grammatology*, p. 51.
[506] Derrida, *Of Grammatology*, pp. 49–50.
[507] Derrida, *Of Grammatology*, p. 23.

but no longer a source, a spring. There is no longer a simple origin"[508] in this "game of the world."[509] The movement of difference is "arche-writing," a play or game in which, instead of the supposedly derivative or parasitic character of writing as subordinate to living speech, the tables are turned so that "non-presentation or de-presentation is as 'originary' as presentation."[510] It is the "trace," which "was never constituted except reciprocally by a nonorigin … [and] thus becomes the origin of the origin … [and] if all begins with the trace, there is above all no originary trace."[511] We hear of the trace that it "must be thought before the entity" and is where "the other" is announced, though this other is occluded not because it is deep, but simply because it is always elsewhere.[512] Amidst all this shifting and meandering without any naïvely objective underpinning of real things, Derrida finds a key ally in the American philosopher Charles Sanders Peirce, who "goes very far in the direction that I have called the de-construction of the transcendental signified," by which Derrida means a de-construction of so-called naïve realism.[513] We never reach the end of the chain of signs: "From the moment there is meaning, there are nothing but signs."[514] And as even Husserl fails to notice, "the thing itself is a sign."[515] In short, Derridean deconstruction is an uncompromising *anti-realism*, despite the strange and growing fashion of calling him a realist.[516]

The central error of Derrida's position lies in his tendency to conflate ontotheology with simple realism. That is to say, Derrida assumes that any belief in a reality outside the play of signs automatically entails the view that this reality can also *be made present to us* apart from the play of signs. In other words, he thinks that all ontological realism automatically entails an epistemological realism according to which direct access to the world is possible. This confounding of two different registers is seen even more clearly in Derrida's celebrated "White Mythology" essay, where he draws the mistaken conclusion that Aristotle's insistence on the law of identity, or

---

508 Derrida, *Of Grammatology*, p. 36.
509 Derrida, *Of Grammatology*, p. 50; emph. removed.
510 Derrida, *Of Grammatology*, p. 62.
511 Derrida, *Of Grammatology*, p. 61.
512 Derrida, *Of Grammatology*, p. 47.
513 Derrida, *Of Grammatology*, p. 49.
514 Derrida, *Of Grammatology*, p. 50.
515 Derrida, *Of Grammatology*, p. 49; emph. removed.
516 See for example Michael Marder, "Différance of the 'Real.'" For a thorough counter-explanation of why Derrida is every bit as anti-realist as he seems, see Lee Braver's account in Chapter 8 of the already classic *A Thing of This World*.

a proper *being* for individual substances, also implies that every word must have a proper, literal *meaning* — despite Aristotle's high praise for metaphor throughout the *Poetics*, and despite his insistence in the *Metaphysics* that substances can never be defined in language.[517] Because of Derrida's understandable fear that genuine things-in-themselves would overpower the play of signs by becoming directly visible to us in logocentric fashion, he also takes the needless step of holding that things-in-themselves cannot *exist* in proper, literal form, even if this were to occur in an absent depth on the underside of all signification. In Heideggerian terms, Derrida would say that there is no withdrawn self-identical hammer apart from all the entanglement of its references. There is only a hammer on the surface of the world, immersed in the play or game of the world, marked with traces of otherness so that the hammer is not one identical thing, but a collection of things or chain of differences.

The reason this conception fails, stodgy though it may sound, is precisely on the grounds already noted by Aristotle in his criticisms of Anaxagoras. If nothing has identity and everything is merely a chain of differences, then everything will be everything else. The same thing will be a battleship, a wall, and a human, so that there will be no specific locations or entities of any sort within the world. But if each thing is a *specific* set of differences, as could only be the case, then it would have to be this specific set of differences and no other. Whatever the constant upheaval of play, trace, writing, and dissemination in which I am lodged, at the end of the day I am myself rather than Charlie Chaplin, Queen Elizabeth, a cat, or a stone. The only way to prevent the universe from turning into a holistic blend-o-rama in which everything melts into a perfectly interrelated lump is to concede from the start that there are individual, self-identical sectors or entities in the cosmos, and that this self-identity (however transient) requires that things be irreducible to their relations. Only this absolute untranslatability of things into their relations can explain the failure of logocentrism to legislate the proper forms of the visible world. Only here do we grasp why its edicts must always fall short of the things themselves, which can only be known obliquely. Much like Brooks, Derrida makes the mistake of concluding that relationality (here the play or game of signifiers) is what makes literal paraphrase impossible, when the opposite is true. Only because the thing is *deeper* than its interactions are they unable to do it justice. The fact that

---

[517] Jacques Derrida, "White Mythology." My account of Derrida's misinterpretation of Aristotle on metaphor can be found in Harman, *Guerrilla Metaphysics*, pp. 110–116.

models of autonomy and depth have been under fire in recent decades tells us more about the character of those now past decades than about the mission of thinking in the years to come.

VI. Concluding Remarks

The rejection of literary texts as isolated individual things can proceed in two different directions. As Charles Altieri sums it up when speaking of "materialist" literary studies: "At one pole the text dissolves into its readings and the applications people make of those readings. At the other pole the text dissolves into its cultural elements — the practices, the active ideologies, and the webs of interest that are largely responsible for the author's sense of the possible significance of what he or she writes."[518] This dual tactic is not only found in cultural studies, but is also the basic double maneuver of philosophy in our time. Everyone wants to demolish the object, as if it were some naïve remainder that no philosopher could allow on earth unchallenged. On one side the object dissolves downward into its physical subcomponents, so that what we call a "table" is just a set of subatomic particles or an underlying mathematical structure. This strategy can be called *undermining*. On the other side the object can be dissolved upward into its effects on human consciousness, so that what we call a "table" is nothing in its own right, but only a functional table-effect for someone or a table-event for other entities. By analogy, I have called this strategy "overmining."[519]

Just as humans do not dissolve into their parents or children but have a certain autonomy from both, so a rock is neither downwardly reducible to quarks and electrons nor upwardly reducible to stoning the Interior Ministry. The rock has rock-properties not found in its tiny inner components, and also has rock-properties that are not exhausted by its uses. The rock is not affected when a few of its protons are destroyed by cosmic rays, and by the same token it is never exhaustively deployed in its current use or in all possible uses. The rock does not exist because it can be used, but can be used because it exists. If this severing of a thing from its surroundings above and below can be called "formalism," this is not because the rock is just a form in our minds, but because it is a real form *outside* our minds. It is what the

---

[518] Charles Altieri, "The Sensuous Dimension of Literary Experience: An Alternative to Materialist Theory," http://socrates.berkeley.edu/~altieri/manuscripts/Sensuous.html

[519] For a detailed explanation of the terms "overmining" and "undermining" see Graham Harman, *The Quadruple Object*.

medieval philosophers called a *substantial form*: the reality of an individual object over and above its matter, and under and beneath its apprehension by the mind.

Given that the modern revolutions in physics and philosophy began (with Descartes, for example) by ridiculing the substantial forms, there should be no surprise if it proves difficult to retrain our minds to look for objects in between the various sets of relations. Leibniz made serious efforts in this direction, but his metaphysics of windowless monads was perhaps too outlandish to become a mainstream theory. The object is "unparaphrasable," or indissoluble into its components or its neighbors. But this does not entail, as Altieri's remarks might imply, that the alternative is a criticism focused on "idealizations about coherent meanings or guesses about authorial intentions ...."[520] As we have seen, the autonomy and integrity of the object in no way implies the autonomy and integrity of our *access* to the object. The literary text runs deeper than any coherent meaning, and outruns the intentions of author and reader alike.

This brings us to the question of object-oriented method. What is most characteristic of intellectual methods is that they are always two-faced, opening up new approaches while also reversing into petrified dogma. This is why the work of theorization must always be on the move. We always want to identify "the next big thing" not for the sake of social capital and a with-it image, but because any theoretical *content* eventually reaches a point where it is no longer liberating. The Marxist idea that there is economics and all the rest is ideology was once a fresh approach to the human sciences, but eventually became petulant, robotic, and blind. Freud's model of dreams as wish fulfillments gave closure to an otherwise impenetrable subject, and thereby shed light on the entire field of culture, while also tending to veer toward petrified dogma. All of these methods provide key flashes of insight at crucial moments in intellectual history and individual biography, yet over time they have become empty clichés that spare us the necessity of thinking. From time to time something new is needed to awaken us from various dogmatic slumbers. Properly pursued, the search for "the next big thing" is not a form of hip posturing or capitalist commodification, but of hope.

Allow me, then, to speak of my hopes. What object-oriented philosophy hopes to offer is not a method, but a *counter*-method. Instead of dissolving a text upward into its readings or downward into its cultural elements, we should focus specifically on how it resists such dissolution. For the sake of

---

[520] Charles Altieri, "The Sensuous Dimension of Literary Experience."

time, let's focus here on resistance in the downward direction. All efforts to embed works exhaustively in their context are doomed to failure for some fairly obvious reasons, though one usually avoids stating them because they are often associated with people whose motives are viewed with suspicion. One of those obvious reasons is that to some extent, the social conditions under which authors produced *The Epic of Gilgamesh* or *Frankenstein* are not entirely relevant to these works themselves. For one thing, these works travel well across space and time — and generally the better the work, the better it travels. If literary canons have been dominated by white European males, then this may be cause for shaking up the canons and reassessing our standards of quality, not for dissolving all works equally into social products of their inherently equal eras. We are all at our best not when conditioned by what happens around us, but when an inner voice summons us to take a courageous stand, walk in a different direction, or do the most outstanding work of our lifetimes. The same social era produced Jackson Pollock, Patricia Highsmith, Frank Sinatra, and President Truman, but to ascribe them all to this era vastly understates the widely different temperaments and talents on this list. The call for "the death of the author" needs to be complemented by a new call for "the death of the culture." Rather than emphasize the social conditions that gave rise to any given work, we ought to do the contrary, and look at how works reverse or shape what might have been expected in their time and place, or at how some withstand the earthquakes of the centuries much better than others. To call someone "a product of their time and place" is never a compliment; neither should it be a compliment when aimed at a literary work.

This is something that the New Critics largely got right. Social and biographical factors should not be excluded from the picture. But they are always chosen selectively even by materialists, for the simple reason that we are never affected by *all* aspects of our surroundings. "Everything is connected" is one of those methods that has long since entered its decadence, and must be abandoned. What is more interesting is why *certain* things are connected rather than others. We must be fully aware of non-connections in any consideration of cultural influence on literature.

What the New Critics *did not* get right, as argued above, is their view of the text as a holistic machine in which all elements have mutual influence. Here we have the same dogmatic relationism upheld by the materialists, but simply relocated to the interior of the text. If Keats's "beauty is truth, truth beauty" can only adequately be read as the outcome of the earlier part of the poem, this is not true of the *whole* of the earlier portions, Cleanth Brooks notwithstanding.[521] We can add alternate spellings or even misspellings to scattered words earlier in the text, without changing the feeling of the climax. We can change punctuation slightly, and even change the exact words of a certain number of lines before "beauty is truth, truth beauty" begins to take on different overtones. In short, we cannot identify the literary work with the exact current form it happens to have. And while many of the literary methods recommended by object-oriented criticism might already exist, here I would like to propose one that has probably never been tried on as vast a scale as I would recommend. Namely, the critic might try to show how each text resists internal holism by attempting various *modifications* of these texts and seeing what happens. Instead of just writing about *Moby-Dick*, why not try shortening it to various degrees in order to discover the point at which it ceases to sound like *Moby-Dick*? Why not imagine it lengthened even further, or told by a third-person narrator rather than by Ishmael, or involving a cruise in the opposite direction around the globe? Why not consider a scenario under which *Pride and Prejudice* would be set in upscale Parisian neighborhoods rather than rural England? Could such a text plausibly still be *Pride and Prejudice*? Why not imagine that a letter by Shelley was actually written by Nietzsche, and consider the resulting consequences and *lack* of consequences?[522]

In contrast to the endless recent exhortations to "Contextualize, contextualize, contextualize!" all the preceding suggestions involve ways of decontextualizing works, whether through examining how they absorb and resist their conditions of production, or by showing that they are to some extent autonomous even from their own properties. *Moby-Dick* differs from its own exact length and modifiable plot details; it is a certain *je ne sais quoi*, or substance, able to survive certain modifications and not others. By showing how the literary object *cannot* be fully identified with its surroundings or even its manifest properties, criticism will show us the same tension between objects and their sensual traits displayed in the tool-analysis of Heidegger. It will reveal the nature of the well-wrought broken hammer, and it will reveal further that not all broken hammers are equally well-wrought.

---

[521] John Keats, *The Complete Poems of John Keats*, p. 322.
[522] Thanks to Rita Felski for noting that this is precisely what is attempted in Pierre Bayard, *Et si les oeuvres changeaient d'auteur?*

PART V
ETHICS AND
THE POLITICS OF THINGS

CHAPTER 23

ETHICS (FROM *DANTE'S BROKEN HAMMER*)

The philosophy of Immanuel Kant (1724–1804) is pivotal for the modern disciplines of ethics, aesthetics, and metaphysics, which serve as the topics of his Second, Third, and First Critiques respectively. I will use the term "formalism" to describe Kant's position in each of these fields, drawing on his own explicit view that ethics should be viewed in "formal" rather than "material" terms. As we will see, this makes Kant the exact opposite of Dante, who provides valuable resources for overcoming the limitations of formalism in all branches of philosophy.

Though Kant made his authorial debut as early as 1749, it was not until 1781 that the publication of his mature Critical Philosophy began. From that point forward it took him less than a decade to revolutionize Western thought with the series of major works just mentioned. His trio of monumental books appeared in the following order:

- *Critique of Pure Reason* (1781, revised second edition in 1787)
- *Critique of Practical Reason* (1788)
- *Critique of Judgment* (1790)

From this same decade we also have more accessible versions of the first two Critiques: *Prolegomena to any Future Metaphysics* in 1783, just two years after the First Critique; and the anticipatory *Groundwork of the Metaphysics of Morals* in 1785, three years prior to its counterpart, the Second Critique.

I will move Kant's metaphysics to the end of our discussion for the same reason that the *Inferno* was saved until last [earlier in *Dante's Broken Hammer*]: such is its intellectual charisma that it too easily overshadows its companions.

We begin, therefore, with the topic of ethics. Much of Dante's allure as a poet comes from the colorful variety of sins and punishments that he depicts, along with the diverse human characters who embody them. If Kant had somehow tried his hand at writing a *Divine Comedy*, the result would probably have been rather boring. This is not because of the notorious terminological density of his writing; the young Kant was in fact a gifted prose stylist. The problem, instead, is that Kant's ethical theory does not consist, like Dante's, of a multitude of specific moral rules whose violation leads to retribution by God in the afterworld. This is no accident, since Kantian ethics is meant to *exclude* any motivation by reward or punishment. Though the principles of this ethical system are widely known, it will be useful to summarize them briefly here.

a. Formalism in Ethics

Midway through the *Groundwork of the Metaphysics of Morals*, Kant gives an especially concise definition of ethical formalism: "Practical principles are *formal* if they subtract from all subjective ends, whereas they are *material* if they have put these, and consequently certain incentives, at their basis."[523] [36] This strikes at the heart of the matter, since the entire point of Kantian ethics is to exclude the material as not properly ethical. Any given talent or purpose can be twisted to evil ends, as long as a *good will* is absent:

> Understanding, wit, judgment, and the like, whatever such *talents* of mind may be called, or courage, resolution, and perseverance in one's plans, as qualities of *temperament*, are undoubtedly good and desirable for many purposes, but they can also be extremely evil and harmful if the will which is to make use of these gifts of nature ... is not good. [7]

Professors of ethics often refer to Kant's doctrine as "non-consequentialist," meaning that ethics does not hinge on the good or bad results of our

---

[523] Until further notice, all page numbers in square brackets refer to Kant, *Groundwork of the Metaphysics of Morals*.

actions, which often arise from factors beyond our control. A good will is thus "to be valued incomparably higher than all that could merely be brought about by it in favor of some inclination and indeed, if you will, of the sum of all inclinations." [8] If we imagine the worst-case scenario of a perfectly ethical human who is made to endure the sufferings of Job, whose actions were based purely on a good will though they all somehow led to disaster for herself and for others, we should admire this person more than a calculating, self-interested individual whose actions lead indirectly to numerous public benefits. In the case of the highly ethical person who fails to achieve good results, the good will, "like a jewel ... would still shine by itself." [8] Herein lies the strength of all formalism in philosophy, whether in ethics or elsewhere: by highlighting the independence and integrity of something apart from its surroundings, it prevents it from being smeared into its relations with other things. In ethics, formalism protects us from overvaluing mere success. In aesthetics, it preserves the artwork from being reduced to its biographical origins or its usefulness as propaganda for the favored political views of the moment. In metaphysics, it guards each thing from confusion with other things, ensuring the distinction between relations and their individual terms. Formalism lets each thing shine like a jewel, regardless of its more or less favorable surroundings. Since later there will be much to say about the downside of formalism, it is worthwhile that we not lose sight of its merits.

Two more quick examples will help clarify the sort of ethical vision that Kant has in mind. One is the imagined case of a merchant who does the right things for possibly the wrong reasons:

> It certainly conforms with duty that a shopkeeper not overcharge an inexperienced customer, and where there is a good deal of trade a prudent merchant does not overcharge but keeps a fixed general price for everyone, so that a child can buy from him as well as everyone else. People are thus served *honestly*; but this is not nearly enough for us to believe that the merchant acted in this way from duty and basic principles of honesty; his advantage required it .... Thus the action was done neither from duty nor from immediate inclination but merely for purposes of self-interest. [11]

This is informative but not very surprising, since one would imagine that many philosophers would offer scant praise to this self-interested shopkeeper. A more startling example of Kant's theory comes when he ranks a warm-hearted philanthropist who takes joy in helping others as ethically *lower* than a cold and joyless Samaritan who simply follows duty to the letter:

if nature had put little sympathy in the heart of this or that man; if (in other respects an honest man) he is by temperament cold and indifferent to the sufferings of others … would he not still find within himself a source from which to give himself a far higher worth than what a mere good-natured temperament might have? By all means! It is just then that the worth of character comes out, which is moral and incomparably the highest, namely that he is beneficent not from inclination but from duty. [12]

In a related example, Kant sees little moral value in our usual avoidance of suicide, since in most cases this arises directly from self-interest. But by contrast, "if an unfortunate man … wishes for death and yet preserves his life without loving it, not from inclination or fear but from duty, then his maxim has moral content." [11] For Kant, the problem with self-interest is not that it is inherently narcissistic or wicked, but that it is too "material" and insufficiently "formal":

For, the will stands between its *a priori* principle, which is formal, and its *a posteriori* incentive, which is material, as at a crossroads; and since it must still be determined by something, it must be determined by the formal principle of volition as such when an action is done from duty, where every material principle has been withdrawn from it. [13]

Kant admits the impossibility of actually *identifying* a specific case in which someone acted purely from duty, since we cannot look into another person's head to learn the true motivations for their deeds. But even if we could do so, it would hardly help, since even in cases of intense introspection we cannot be sure of our own motivations. Kant puts this lucidly:

It is indeed sometimes the case that with the keenest self-examination we find nothing besides the moral ground of duty that could have been powerful enough to move us to this or that good action and to so great a sacrifice; but from this it cannot be inferred with certainty that no covert impulse of self-love, under the mere pretense of that idea, was not actually the real determining cause of the will; for we like to falsely attribute to ourselves a nobler motive .... [19]

Though the basic principle of Kantian ethics should already be clear, a few more steps will make us familiar with the accompanying features and terminology of his ethical theory. For one thing, Kant holds that his ethics of duty applies not just to human beings, but to "all *rational beings as such*," [20] though no examples of rational non-humans are given. He clearly does not include God under the heading of non-human rational beings, and apparently not even Christ or the angels, since "no imperatives hold for the *divine* will and in general for a *holy* will: the 'ought' is out of place here, because [in such cases] volition is necessarily in accord with the will." [25] Instead, we can speak of imperatives only in cases of "the subjective imperfection of the will of this or that rational being, for example, of the human will." [25] Imperatives come in two basic kinds, with Kant himself the inventor of the second. The familiar sort of imperative is *hypothetical*: we act in such and such a way in order to achieve a certain aim. If you wish to be elected President of the United States, and are eligible for this goal as a natural-born citizen, there are a number of imperatives that come to mind. One must avoid scandalous actions whenever possible, and certainly must not commit a felony. It is important to achieve intermediate positions first: significant service in the Senate will be helpful, but being elected as Governor of a state tends to be even more so. One ought to pay attention to one's style of dress, improve in the areas of speech and debate, and spend a good deal of time mastering questions of policy. But obviously, none of this matters if your life aspirations do not include the Presidency. The same holds for most imperatives, such as remaining on good terms with your superiors if you wish to keep a job to feed your family, or behaving in a charming and honorable way when courting a beloved person. The same holds for most of the familiar maxims of life wisdom, such as listening more than speaking, or saving rather than squandering. However prudent such hypothetical imperatives may be, they clearly have no place in the foundations of Kantian ethics, since they have value only in terms of some desired aim. What Kant needs instead is an imperative absolutely binding on all rational beings, regardless of their personal goals:

There is one imperative that, without being based upon and having as its condition any other purpose to be attained by certain conduct, commands this conduct immediately. This imperative is categorical. It has to do not with the matter of the action and what is to result from it, but with the form and the principle from which the action itself follows; and the essentially good in the action consists in the disposition, let the result be what it may. This imperative may be called the imperative of morality. [27]

Kant speaks here in the singular because there is not a wide variety of categorical imperatives; this would require that we consider a multitude of different ethical topics, and for Kant such a multitude could only be material (that is, dealing with specific objects) rather than formal. His conclusion results in one of the most famous sentences in the history of Western philosophy: "There is, therefore, only a single categorical imperative and it is this: *act only in accordance with that maxim through which you can at the same time will that it become a universal law.*" [31] Though Kant is often skeptical as to the value of examples, he immediately gives us four brief "case studies" that show the categorical imperative at work. The first concerns a person racked with despair who is considering suicide. The maxim that would guide the decision to take one's own life is expressed as follows: "from self-love I make it my principle to shorten my life when its longer duration threatens more troubles than it promises agreeableness." [32] Kant rejects this maxim outright, since "a nature whose law it would be to destroy life itself by means of the same feeling whose destination is to impel toward the furtherance of life would contradict itself." [32] But the supposed contradiction here may not seem compelling, and thus Kant's second example may give a clearer case of the categorical imperative. In this case, a person is badly in need of money. He knows that whatever he borrows he will not be able to repay, yet he considers making a false promise to repay the loan if this is needed to escape his dire financial predicament. The maxim of such an action would say roughly that whenever necessary, I will make promises regardless of my ability to fulfill them. But this could of course never be a universal law, since if that were the case, "no one would believe what was promised him but would laugh at all such expressions as vain pretenses." [32] The very possibility of receiving loans through promises of repayment would immediately be undercut if people as a rule made false promises in such a situation. [32] Let's skip ahead for now to Kant's fourth example, which is almost comical in the situation it describes. In this case, a person for whom things are going well while he sees that others (whom he could very well help) have to contend with great hardships, thinks: "what is it to me? Let each be as happy as heaven wills or as he can make himself; I shall take nothing from him nor even envy him; only I do not care to contribute anything to his welfare or his assistance in need!" [33]

The contradiction that Kant sees here is that "many cases could occur in which one would need the love and sympathy of others and in which, by such a law of nature arisen from his own will, he would rob himself of all hope of the assistance he wishes for himself." [33] I have saved Kant's third example for last, since it is somewhat different in flavor from the others. One thing that many readers find lacking in Kant's categorical imperative is the sense it can give of a drab ethical uniformity, with the same actions binding on all humans at all times. But the third example opens the door somewhat to the cultivation of unique individual qualities. It concerns a person who has an unspecified talent that "by means of cultivation could make him a human being useful for all sorts of purposes." [32] Yet he prefers to become a pleasure-seeking idler: "like the South Sea Islanders," [32] as Kant rather callously puts it. Perhaps he should simply "let his talents rust and be concerned with devoting his life merely to idleness, amusement, procreation — in a word, to enjoyment." [33] The supposed contradiction in making such a decision is that "as a rational being he necessarily wills that all the capacities in him be developed, since they serve him and are given to him for all sorts of possible purposes." [33]

Just two other formulations are needed to give a relatively complete overview of Kantian ethics. The first is also famous: "*So act that you use humanity, whether in your own person or in the person of any other, always at the same time as an end, never merely as a means.*" [38] People are not things, but are deserving of *respect*, and hence should not be treated as merely the means to an end. Just as the person contemplating suicide treats their own life as merely a means to an agreeable existence, cases such as "assaults on the freedom and property of others" [38] reduce others to a means to one's own aggrandizement or enrichment. Human society should be a kingdom of ends, "a systematic union of various rational beings through common laws." [41] In this kingdom, everything has either a price or a dignity, with price being appropriate for goods that serve human needs, and dignity belonging only to rational beings themselves. [42]

The second formulation, more technical though just as important, is Kant's terminological distinction between the *autonomy* and *heteronomy* of the will. Nothing here is surprising: "Autonomy of the will is the property of the will by which it is a law to itself (independently of any property of the objects of volition)." [47] All of the objects of ethical activity must be excluded, at the risk of leading us into the not strictly ethical realm of *heteronomy*: "If the will seeks the law that is to determine it *anywhere else* than in the fitness of its maxims for its own giving of universal law — consequently if, in going beyond itself, it seeks this law in the property of any of its objects — *heteronomy* results." [47] If the heteronomous will avoids lying in order to preserve its good reputation, the autonomous will avoids lying for no other reason than obedience to the categorical imperative. "The latter must therefore abstract from all objects to this extent: that they have no *influence* at all on the will ...." [48]

If judged by the standards of Kantian ethics, Dante's *Divine Comedy* would fare rather poorly.[524] The whole of the *Comedy* looks like a heteronomous ethics governed by a merely hypothetical imperative: act in such a way that you will not be punished eternally in Hell. And this presupposes further that one is not only religious, but a fully-fledged Roman Catholic, since there is not much hope for pagans or most Jews in Dante's cosmos — to say nothing of Muslims, whose Prophet is subjected to gruesome eternal torment. There is not even a trace of the categorical imperative in Dante, who simply urges obedience to the almighty will of God. In ethical terms, the *Divine Comedy* seems to demand a simple yes-or-no decision, either affirming Dante's Catholic vision or bracketing that vision and merely enjoying the *Comedy* as literature. Yet there is another way of looking at it. First of all, a good number of Dante's ethical principles will be acceptable even to secularized minds. To avoid such sins as pride, envy, and wrath will seem like sage counsel even to those who accept no concept of "sin." But perhaps more importantly, the sheer ethical color of Dante's world makes his vision of ethics inherently more *interesting* than Kant's.

I mentioned earlier that a *Divine Comedy* written by Kant sounds like a rather boring prospect, even if we imagine a younger Kant at the peak of his literary skill. Would Kant's *Inferno* merely contain a single pit of boiling tar for all those who do not obey the categorical imperative? Would his *Purgatorio* be home to shopkeepers who were honest only from fear of

---

[524] Dante Alighieri, *The Divine Comedy*.

losing their reputations, and to "South Sea Islanders" and other wastrels? Would the saints of his *Paradiso* include the flinty man-without-warmth who helped others only from a sense of duty? My objection is not facetious. The relative lack of color in Kantian ethics results from a deliberate decision on Kant's part to exclude anything "material" or object-related from the sphere of genuine ethics, and this is what leaves him with a single formal imperative, irrevocably binding on all rational beings. Obviously, Kant has very good reasons for doing so, since he needs to avoid an ethics of success or of hypothetical imperatives. But our recognition that Kant has admirable motives in excluding everything material from ethics should not prevent us from noting that the result is rather gray when compared with Dante's often carnivalesque afterworld. I will soon suggest that this is not the inevitable price of a philosophically rigorous ethics, but that it arises from Kant's mixing together two different meanings of autonomy, which for our own part we can easily separate. But before introducing this claim, we should consider the views of that continental European thinker who showed the most boldness in challenging Kantian ethics: the rambunctious German philosopher Max Scheler.

b. Ordo Amoris

Scheler (1874–1928) is well remembered for his loose but fruitful affiliation with the phenomenological movement, and for his authorship of the weighty book *Formalism in Ethics and Non-Formal Ethics of Values*. More than this, he was the most engrossing philosophical personality of his era, comparable to Slavoj Žižek in our own day. Scheler's personal life was rocked by erotic scandals that landed him in tabloids and damaged his career. His warmly assertive personality often intimidated colleagues, including figures as important as Husserl and Heidegger. An omnivorous learner and ceaseless innovator, Scheler died early from what some have claimed was an inability to shut off his thoughts and fall asleep, though the *Stanford Encyclopedia* speaks less romantically of "a series of heart attacks most likely due to the 60–80 cigarettes he smoked each day."[525] Heidegger famously interrupted his Freiburg Lecture Course on the *Metaphysical Foundations of Logic* to give an impromptu obituary for Scheler. As he put it there: "Max Scheler was, aside from the sheer scale and quality of his productivity, the strongest philosophical force in modern Germany, nay, in contemporary Europe and

---

[525] Zachary Davis & Anthony Steinbock, "Max Scheler."

even in contemporary philosophy as such."[526] Yet Heidegger also recognized something daemonic in the man:

> one recognizes here — something which of course only a few could directly experience in day-and-night-long conversations with him — an obsession with philosophy, which he himself was unable to master and after which he had to follow, something which in the brokenness of contemporary existence often drove him to powerlessness and despair.[527]

Hans-Georg Gadamer adds more detail to Heidegger's account. In Gadamer's depiction, listening to Scheler was "like being drawn along, a nearly satanic sense of being possessed that led the speaker on to a true *furioso* of thought."[528] An even more striking anecdote runs as follows:

> Max Scheler was characterized by an enormous intellectual gluttony. He swept up whatever could nourish him, and he possessed a power of penetration that everywhere pushed through to the essential. The story is told that his reading so devoured him that whenever he met a colleague he would compel his participation simply by ripping pages out of whatever book he was reading and pressing them into the hands of his astonished companion.[529]

It is hard to imagine a personality more different from that of the dry and cautious Immanuel Kant, and it is hardly surprising that Scheler tried to counter Kantian ethics with one based on an implacable love of the things in the world.

Scheler's *Ethics*, as his great book is usually known, was completed by 1913, though the latter parts of the work were not published until three years later. It is probably the most ambitious attempt by any author to strike a lethal blow against ethical formalism. For Scheler, ethics is not primarily a question of formal maxims, but of highly concrete *values*, and these values are often binding on *specific* individuals rather than on rational beings in general. However, it should be noted that there is nothing "pre-Kantian" about his *Ethics*: Scheler holds that Kant made a decisive step forward in

---

[526] Martin Heidegger, *Metaphysical Foundations of Logic*, p. 50.
[527] Heidegger, *Metaphysical Foundations of Logic*, p. 51.
[528] Hans-Georg Gadamer, *Philosophical Apprenticeships*, p. 29.
[529] Gadamer, *Philosophical Apprenticeships*, p. 33.

critiquing any ethics of "goods and purposes" that would place the value of an ethical act outside that act itself.[530] [5] In his own words: "It would be a great error, in my judgment, to maintain that any of the post-Kantian versions of non-formal ethics have refuted the Kantian doctrine." (5) He adds that he admires "the greatness, strength, and terseness of Kant's work." [6] Nonetheless,

> this Kantian colossus of steel and bronze ... bars us from any true insight into the place of values in man's life. As long as Kant's terrifyingly sublime formula, with its emptiness, remains valid as the only evidential result of all philosophical ethics, we are robbed of the clear vision of the fullness of the moral world and its qualities .... [6]

Since we lack the space here for a full consideration of Scheler's own six-hundred-page colossus, we will focus instead on a brilliant unfinished essay from his literary remains entitled "Ordo Amoris."[531] This essay gives us the nectar of Scheler's critique of Kantian ethics, and establishes obvious points in common with Dante's own ethics of love.

Born into an Orthodox Jewish family in Munich, Scheler later became Roman Catholic, and traces of this new religion can be found everywhere in his work. One of his chief influences is the great Catholic thinker Blaise Pascal, whose "logic of the heart" is one of the pillars of Scheler's outlook. The influence of St. Augustine is also not hard to find. God is often described, without irony, as the ultimate source of meaning in human life. That life is defined primarily by love, to such an extent that Scheler defines the human as *ens amans* or the loving being, as opposed to a thinking or willing being. [110–111] For all of these reasons, it is striking that Scheler does not mention Dante in his major works, though the great Italian poet would seem to be a strong natural ally. I would venture to guess that Dante is simply too pre-Kantian for Scheler, who seeks to radicalize the imperative from within, rather than harking back to a time when Kantian ethics did not yet exist. Nonetheless, a summary of "Ordo Amoris" reveals obvious links between Scheler's theory of love and Dante's.

---

[530] Until further notice, all page numbers in square brackets refer to Scheler, *Formalism in Ethics and Non-Formal Ethics of Values*.
[531] From here through the remainder of the chapter, all page references in square brackets refer to Max Scheler, "Ordo Amoris."

Scheler is clear that his Latin phrase *ordo amoris* has both a normative meaning and a descriptive one. All human thought and activity depends "on the play of [the] movement of my heart." [98] There is an objectively correct order of values, and some objects are worthier of love than others:

> It follows that any sort of rightness or falseness or perversity in my life and activity are determined by whether there is an objectively correct order of these stirrings of my love and hate, my inclination and disinclination, my many-sided interest in the things of this world. [98]

Modern philosophy tends to view our knowledge of the outer world as capable of strict scientific determination, while holding in parallel that ethical and aesthetic values belong to an inner "psychological" sphere governed by arbitrary assertions of personal taste. Scheler has no patience for such a view, which he ascribes to a "general slovenliness in matters of feeling" [118, emph. removed] in conjunction with a "ridiculous ultraseriousness and comical busyness over those things which our wits can technically master." [118] There is in fact an objective order of values that reaches its peak in the love of the divine, of a "One all-knowing and all-willing God, [who] is the personal center of the world as a cosmos and as a whole." [110]

The normative *ordo amoris*, therefore, points to a global standard of love to which everyone must aspire if life is to gain its full meaning: God as the ultimate object of love, just as in Dante's great poem. Yet Scheler also gives *ordo amoris* a descriptive meaning, in which each person and collective is governed by a typical rank-ordering of loves, each of which we should appreciate for its uniqueness.

> Whether I am investigating the innermost essence of an individual, a historical era, a family, a people, a nation, or any other sociohistorical group, I will know and understand it most profoundly when I have discerned the system of its concrete value-assessments and value-preference, whatever organization the system has. [98–99]

We must seek "the basic ethical formula" by which any person or people is guided. [99] Even more concisely, "*whoever has the* ordo amoris *of a man has the man himself.* He has for the man as a moral subject what the crystallization formula is for a crystal." [100] As a more familiar synonym for *ordo amoris*, Scheler also employs the term *ethos*. [99]

The philosophical biologist Jakob von Uexküll famously describes the environment of each animal as determining what it is able or unable to see.[532] Scheler views the *ordo amoris* of an individual or collective as functioning in much the same way: "Nothing in nature which is independent of man can confront him and have an effect on him even as a stimulus, of whatever kind or degree, without the cooperation of his *ordo amoris*." [100] Indeed, we cannot even detect certain values if they are inconsistent with our ethos: "What [the human being] actually notices, what he observes or leaves unnoticed and unobserved, is determined by this attraction and repulsion; these already determine the material of *possible* noticing and observing." [101] The highly amorous Scheler makes sure to give the example of "the sexual types which especially attract or repel us." [133] But whatever kind of value may be in question, the most important way that Scheler differs from Kant is found in his diversion of ethics outward, away from the self. For even if what we notice is determined by our *ordo amoris*, we cannot detach that order from our involvement with things, despite Kant's attempt to expunge non-human things almost entirely from ethics. In Scheler's words: "attraction and repulsion are felt to come from things, not from the self … and are themselves governed and circumscribed by potentially effective attitudes of interest and love, expressed as readiness for being affected." [101]

Another notably non-Kantian element in Scheler's ethics is his commitment to a doctrine of the singularity of individual fate. We saw earlier that Kant left the door open for individual duties, in his example of the man who was deciding between developing his unique talents or giving himself over to a life of selfish and empty pleasure. But whereas Kant merely left that door slightly ajar, Scheler blows it wide open, and even uses it as one of the central passageways of his ethical theory. As he puts it:

> when we survey a man's whole life or a long sequence of years and events, we may indeed feel that each single event is completely accidental, yet their connection, however unforeseeable every part of the whole was before it transpired, reflects exactly that which we must consider the core of the person concerned. [102]

In a clear attack on Kant, Scheler adds that "the unique content of individual destiny … is peculiar to each man alone. There is no positive, circumscribed

---

[532] Jakob von Uexküll, *A Foray Into the Worlds of Animals and Humans*.

image of it, still less a formulatable law." [107] Each of us has a "calling" or vocation, which in some respects lies outside us rather than within. For one thing, we cannot always recognize our own vocation: "it can very well be that another knows my individual destiny more adequately than I do myself." [104] And even if we know our true calling, we might fail to live up to it: "The subject can deceive himself about this, he can (freely) fail to achieve it, or he can recognize and actualize it." [104] There can also be poignant conflicts between a person's *destiny* and his or her *fate*, as seen most clearly in cases when someone is simply in the wrong environment to actualize their destiny:

> A tragic relation exists where we see men, even whole peoples, whose fate itself forces them to act against their destiny, where we see men who do not "fit in," not only with the contingent and momentary content of their milieu, but with the very *structure* of that milieu. This is what forces them always to select a new milieu with an analogous structure. [108]

Moreover, we are not only responsible for actualizing our own private destiny, since "the individual shares the responsibility for the comprehension and realization of each man's destiny." [105] A related notion is that none of us starts life with an ethical clean slate, since along with individual blame accrued by our own actions, there is also "ancestrally and communally assumed guilt." [116] As an American I inherit a certain degree of guilt over the fate of native populations and the long and cruel West African slave trade, though neither I nor my family members directly harmed any Native American, and though my great-great-grandfather Harman was shot three times while fighting with General Grant against the slave-holding Confederacy.

Quite aside from the failure to grasp or attain our vocation, there are also cases described as a "confusion" of *ordo amoris*. [103] "Loving can be characterized as correct or false only because a man's actual inclinations and acts of love can be in harmony with or oppose the rank-ordering of what is worthy of love." [111] For instance, there are cases of outright ethical delusion in which we become obsessed with some finite good, in which someone "is enchained by an impulse drive; or better, that function of the drive by which love is aroused and its object held within limits is perverted into one which enchants and *represses*." [114] Scheler describes this phenomenon with the familiar word *infatuation*. While the absolute form of infatuation turns a finite good into an idol, there is also a relative form that arises from the excesses of one's own character, in which someone "in accordance with the actual structure of loving peculiar to him and with the fashion in which he prefers one value over another, transgresses against the objective rank-ordering of what is worthy of love." [115]

I have already mentioned the important role of God in Scheler's ethics. As he sees it, God is needed even to understand one's own individual destiny. For such destiny "is a matter of insight," [106] and this insight requires "genuine *self-love*, or love for one's own salvation, which is fundamentally different from all forms of self-love." [106] The spirituality of this noble form of self-love stems from the fact that "we see ourselves *as if* through the eyes of God himself, and this means, first, that we see ourselves quite objectively, and second, that we see ourselves as part of the entire universe," [107] which Scheler means not in the sense of holism — each of us retains his or her own individual destiny, after all — but in the sense of a maximum attachment to the things of the world rather than an aloof self-distancing from them. By seeing ourselves as if through the eyes of God, we can begin to chip away like sculptors at our inessential features: "The self-shaping, creative hammers of self-correction, self-education, of remorse and mortification strike away all the parts of us which project beyond that form which is conveyed to us by this image of ourselves before and in God." [107] Scheler compares this self-shaping to negative theology, which in his view does not merely negate, but helps to show that the encounter with our destiny "is not so much a positive shaping as a pushing aside, a mortification, a 'curing' of 'false tendencies'...." [108]

Against "the fetishists of modern science," [119] Scheler joins Pascal in always insisting on the special logic of the heart: "The Middle Ages still knew a *cultivation of the heart* as an autonomous concern, completely independent of the cultivation of understanding." [119] In this respect, ethical life gives us access to dimensions of reality that are "*simply not present* for an attitude of pure thought." [122] But it does not follow that the heart is always right, "for the heart can love and hate blindly or insightfully, no differently than we can judge blindly or insightfully [by means of reason]." [117, emph. removed] Scheler's ideas about love lead him in addition to a new conception of hate. In disagreement with the old saw that those who cannot hate are also incapable of love, Scheler leaves room for hate in his ethical vision, while nonetheless seeing it as derivative of love. As he puts it: "it always holds true that the act of *hate*, the antithesis of love, or the emotional negation of value and existence, is the result of some *incorrect* or *confused* love." [125] Hate and love are opposites, in the sense that we cannot love and hate the same thing at the same time and in the same respect. But this should not be taken to imply that hate and love are equals: "*Our heart is primarily destined to love*, not to hate. Hate is only a reaction against a love which is in some way false." [126] When a value we rate highly seems eclipsed by a different and less worthy object of someone's love, this is what drives us to hate. This explains why sometimes little preparation is needed in order to feel hatred, as when "a thing awakens hatred the first time it is given [or] a man is hated as soon as he appears." [125] In short, "hate is always and everywhere a *rebellion of our heart and spirit against a violation of* ordo amoris." [127]

In some sense, the difference between the respective ethical theories of Kant and Scheler seems to follow from the disparity between these two vastly different human characters. It is just as hard to imagine the cautious and punctual Kant writing an ethics of love as it is to envision the scandalous Scheler composing a dry treatise on ethical duty. But the core of the difference between their theories can best be described as follows. For Kant, we reach the true ethical state by abstracting from all objects of our interest; for Scheler, it is a matter of enthusiastically increasing our attachments to more and more things. As he puts it:

> In our account love [is] thus always the primal act by which a being, without ceasing to be this one delimited being, abandons itself, in order to share and participate in another being as an *ens intentionale* [what Husserl would call an "intentional object" — G.H.]. This participation is such that the two in no way become real parts of one another. [110]

Whereas Kant preaches detachment from the material, Scheler urges a heightened attachment, as when he recommends an "*increased depth of absorption* in the growing fullness of one object." To summarize, "we live with the *entire fullness of our spirit* chiefly among *things*; we live in the *world*." [113] This is not the sort of formula one would expect to find in Kant, and the vanishing nullity of things in Kantian ethics is often quite disappointing after a tour through Dante's or Scheler's worlds, filled as they are with strong personalities absorbed and passionate in their relations with various things.

c. Two Senses of Autonomy

Perhaps the most central feature of modern philosophy is its tendency to declare a deep *ontological* rift between thought on one side and everything else on the other, which takes the form of a taxonomy. Humans are not treated as just exceptionally interesting and flexible beings, as is carbon in organic chemistry: the star element of the discipline without being granted an entire new chemistry of its own. Instead, human thought is treated as so utterly different in kind from everything else that it receives a special ontological category, encompassing fifty percent of the structure of the universe. To modern philosophers, it hardly seems to matter that grouping all the trillions of non-human entities under a single lump term like "the world" or "extension" is a terrible oversimplification of a vast catalog of cosmic non-human entities, including such samples as dragonflies, positrons, spy satellites, melons, bridges, and neutron stars. The obvious differences among all these entities are treated as mere local permutations in a single "non-human" category, while human thought is seen as so taxonomically special, so unprecedented in its ability to tear a hole in the fabric of the universe, that it deserves a segregated niche of its own. This is the position still defended by the line in modern philosophy that runs from Jacques Lacan, through Žižek and Alain Badiou, on up to Quentin Meillassoux in the younger generation. This group of thinkers is so appalled by the specter of a "panpsychist" theory that grants thought to many or all entities that it prefers to accept the drawbacks of holding that human thought is a sudden rupture with all else that has ever existed. Thus Žižek imagines the birth of the human subject through a bizarre "ontological catastrophe," and Meillassoux through an inexplicable "irruption *ex nihilo*" devoid of any physical reason.

One of the most glaring symptoms of this shaky outlook is the difficulty modern philosophy has always had with animals, since the rigid distinction between thought (apparently too much for animals) and matter (apparently too little for them) gives no obvious insight into non-human creatures. René Descartes takes the most extreme position on this issue by treating animals as soulless machines, a position as implausible as it is inhumane.[533] Heidegger, in his popular 1929/30 Freiburg Lecture Course, tries to ascribe "world-poverty" to animals, by contrast with the "worldlessness" of stones and the "world-forming" of humans. But despite some interesting citations of Uexküll's work, Heidegger never sheds much light on what

---

[533] René Descartes, *Discourse on Method*, Part Five.

world-poverty is.[534] By contrast with these failed efforts to take animals seriously, Kant's silence on the topic is almost a welcome relief. In Uexküll and later authors, one finds more satisfying attempts to consider animals on their own terms. And more recently, books such as Michael Marder's *Plant-Thinking* (2013) and Eduardo Kohn's *How Forests Think* (2013) have brought philosophy into the vegetable kingdom in a way that would have made Kant rather uncomfortable.[535]

It is even possible to ask about the reach of Kant's ethics beyond the realm of animals and plants. In 1997, Alphonso Lingis published *The Imperative*, one of the most important books ever to emerge from the American continental philosophy scene, and a work showing important features in common with Scheler. Lingis accepts Kant's notion of the ethical imperative, but extends it in at least two important ways. First, Lingis draws on his work as a translator of Maurice Merleau-Ponty to argue for an imperative structure at work even in pre-ethical human perception. When observing objects, we try to find the proper angle and distance from which to see them in the way that they ought to be seen. It is rare that our head is perfectly upright, and hence rare that we actually *see* the objects in a room as vertically aligned. Nonetheless, we correct for the ways in which perception is askew, and manage to see objects in what we regard as the "proper" manner, pressed in that direction by a perceptual imperative. Second, Lingis contends that ethical imperatives can be found in many situations where we are not chiefly interacting with other rational beings. He finds it ethically *wrong* if someone remains indoors in an air-conditioned room with the television on during a beautiful spring evening as an electrical storm approaches from afar. It is wrong as well if someone enters a temple in Kyoto during snowfall while wearing headphones and listening to vulgar popular music. There is something ethically repulsive about chugging down expensive wine rather than savoring it, and so too it is *ethically* repellent to eat gourmet chocolates at the same time as generic cola and corn chips. Here as with Scheler, non-human objects are brought back into the ethical sphere. And here even more than with Scheler, it is easy to imagine what an orthodox Kantian would say to Lingis: "Rational beings are ends in themselves, but the same is not true of electrical storms, wine, or chocolate. While it may admittedly be wasteful to miss a beautiful evening or to squander expensive foods, no one's feelings are hurt in such situations, and no rational being is disrespected." Here the

---

[534] Martin Heidegger, *Fundamental Concepts of Metaphysics*.
[535] Michael Marder, *Plant-Thinking*; Eduardo Kohn, *How Forests Think*.

disciple enforces Kant's view that ethics is a realm that ought to be purified of non-human things, left only to the formal imperative at work in my own mind as well as the formal dignity of other humans.

But there is a genuine problem with formalist ethics, one that is better avoided by Scheler, Lingis, Dante, and others than by Kant. This problem arises from Kant conflating two entirely different senses of autonomy. First, we can agree with Kant — as even Scheler does — that ethical formalism might seem like the only way to avoid an ethics of success. Any action performed in order to gain something else, whether it be a promotion, a spouse, public honor, or the avoidance of Hell, cannot count as more than a well-played practical measure. The ethical must be self-contained, an end in itself, or it is merely a means to some other thing. The formalist move in aesthetics works in precisely the same way. Against all attempts to treat the artwork merely in terms of its historical context or socio-political impact, the formalist critic of art or literature asks us to focus on the internal aesthetic qualities of the work itself. We will see later that the formalist approach has as much downside in aesthetics as it does in ethics, but this should not prevent us from seeing the genuine formalist achievement in both areas. After all, any domain is quickly lost to view if we let it bleed holistically into everything else. Art will turn into political propaganda, and architecture is devoured by a worried ecology of the carbon footprint.[536] Ethics will become a mere path to an existent or non-existent Heaven, and philosophy, like art, will be reduced to the handmaid of smug political pamphlets. In all of these cases, the formalist option allows us to focus on the *autonomy* of any discipline from extraneous concerns that belong to neighboring disciplines. At the present time this is really the only way to protect specific disciplines from the overly *moralistic* spirit that has taken over politics, the social sciences, philosophy, art, and ecology.

Yet Kant mixes this sort of autonomy with another, less justifiable one, though it stems directly from the spirit of modern philosophy. With this second sense of autonomy, Kant means the *taxonomical purification* of humans from non-humans. As Bruno Latour has shown, such purification of the world into two distinct zones — a mechanistic world of nature on one side, and a free world of human thought on the other — is the very essence of modernism.[537] The heart of the problem is as follows. Though I am willing to concede the formalist point that ethics should be an

---

[536] See David Ruy, "Returning to (Strange) Objects."
[537] Bruno Latour, *We Have Never Been Modern*.

autonomous realm freed from heteronomous ulterior concerns, *it does not follow* that this requires purifying ethics from anything non-human. That is to say, why does Kant automatically identify non-human (i.e., "material") beings with the ethics of ulterior purposes that he opposes? Why is the "rational being" considered the basic ethical unit, even though it is difficult to imagine any ethical life at all for a mere thinking mind floating in empty space? We should hold instead, with Scheler and Dante, that *love* is the basic ethical unit: love in the sense of a union between the human and some other human or non-human object. What is truly autonomous in ethical life is not a rational being subtracted from all traces of a world, but rather an ethical relation of love between one entity and another that does not exist for any heteronomous purpose but as an *end in itself*, despite Kant's efforts to restrict this category to humans. In this way, we preserve the best aspect of formalism (autonomy) while avoiding the worst (human exclusivity). This allows us to re-open ethics to the colorful pageant of the world, rather than remaining imprisoned in "Kant's terrifyingly sublime formula, with its emptiness."[538]

If we refer to the ethics of Dante and Scheler as *amorous*, we find that amorous ethics is partly formalist and partly nonformalist. The formalist aspect comes from the fact that every entity in the world commands a greater or lesser degree of love from any one of us, and we can comply with such commands or fail to do so through our own confusion, perversity, or infatuation with something less worthy. The non-formalist part comes from the fact that if we purify rational beings of all traces of the world, there can be no trace of love, and we are asked to admire such grotesque figures as Kant's cold-hearted Samaritan who helps others purely out of duty, without passion or enthusiasm. To repeat, the basic ethical unit is not a worldless rational being, but a *compound amorous being* made up of a loving entity and its beloved entity.

What amorous ethics restores is not only the world and its multitude of lovable things, but also the uniqueness of individual ethical destiny. Whereas the cold-hearted duty monger is held out by Kant as a model of what humans could be if purified of all inclinations, Scheler and Dante open up vast galleries of individual imperatives. To give a personal example, as a philosopher I have already published two books on Latour, and am currently

---

[538] Scheler, *Formalism in Ethics and Non-Formal Ethics of Values*, p. 6.

preparing a third.[539] This can hardly be called a categorical imperative binding on all rational beings — or even on all philosophers, since Latour is still widely viewed as merely a social scientist. But for someone like me, a philosopher who happens to think that Latour is the most important philosopher alive today, there is indeed a personal imperative to bring his work to the notice of others in my field. If I had failed to write these books it would not merely have been an act of laziness, but an outright ethical failure to give something important its due. It is likely that no one else was in a good position to write what I have written about Latour, and hence the imperative and the mission were in this case purely my own. It is no exaggeration to say that failing to write these books would have left scars on my conscience as deep as if I had failed to stamp out a cigarette in Yosemite National Park.

Or consider a more prominent example: Dante's love for Beatrice. It is difficult to make a Kantian maxim out of this highly unusual love: "You must remain loyal to a deceased beloved even if you have only spoken with her once, she married someone else, you married someone else too, and the beloved has now been dead for many years." Written in the form of a categorical imperative, this love is both absurd and unethical. But Dante would not be Dante without his loyalty to this particular beloved, and Beatrice seems to agree when she scolds him for certain lapses in fidelity. To summarize, ethics is not about rational beings in abstraction from the world, but about the bonds between an amorous agent and its beloved objects in the world. Ethics consists not of binding universal maxims that hold for all rational beings, or at best is such only in universal prohibitions against assault, rape, murder, and the like. Rather, it is a specific local chemical that arises from the bond between one particular amorous agent and one particular object of its love. Though imperatives are autonomous in the sense of having no ulterior purpose, they are very much immersed in the world, and very much belong to an individual destiny rather than to rational beings in general.

In closing, let's return to a point made at the outset. The concept of intentionality is usually used an "adhesive" concept that claims to surpass the modern dualism of subject and object, though earlier I agreed with Meillassoux and [Tom] Sparrow that it fails to do so.[540] But intentionality

---

[539] Graham Harman, *Prince of Networks*; Graham Harman, *Bruno Latour: Reassembling the Political*. The third, not yet published, is Graham Harman, *Prince of Modes*.

[540] The latter reference is to Tom Sparrow, *The End of Phenomenology*.

also functions ethically as a "selective" term. I follow one life-path rather than another, writing books on Latour (who is important to me) rather than François Laruelle (who is not). My nephew Erem Kesgin, a pilot for Turkish Airlines, lives in a world of airplanes, airports, takeoffs, landings, simulator exams, and weather reports followed attentively on an iPad: a fascinating life that is nonetheless completely different from my own. The life of an atheist is not that of a Christian or a Muslim; the life of a fourteenth-century person like Dante is not that of a robot war commander in the globally heated wasteland of the twenty-second. To point to the "selective" aspect of intentionality is to say that we are not only occupied with objects, but always occupied sincerely with *specific* objects that define who we are: our characteristic ethos or *ordo amoris*.

CHAPTER 24

ALPHONSO LINGIS ON THE IMPERATIVES IN THINGS[541] (FROM *TOWARDS SPECULATIVE REALISM*)

In October 1997, Alphonso Lingis visited the Department of Philosophy at DePaul University in Chicago, where I was then a doctoral student. Lingis had been my advisor as I earned a Master's Degree in Philosophy at Penn State during 1990–91. On 11 October, a roundtable discussion was held, with several DePaul faculty members and graduate students presenting short papers in response to his work. The following was my contribution to that event, from which I was initially excluded by a powerful enemy on the faculty. In conceptual terms, this paper gives an early hint of the full-blown realism that first emerged two months later. While Lingis had argued that inanimate objects have an ethical force over us no less than humans do, I extended this claim to say that objects encounter imperatives in their own right, rather than merely providing humans with them.

It has often been noted that our encounter with other human beings displays a twofold character. In the first instance the other is a limited, specific object of the world. To this extent, his or her personality, body-type, and temperament can be considered as the net product of physical and chemical forces, easily reducible to a series of causal mechanisms. While the most extreme version of this materialism is generally held in low regard today,

---

[541] "Alphonso Lingis on the Imperatives in Things" was originally published in *Towards Speculative Realism*, pp. 14–21.

it can still be an interesting experiment to push this view as far as possible. Behind our most compelling thoughts, then, we imagine enzymal secretions giving rise to various brain-states. Behind our most flamboyant individual passions, we detect concealed hereditary cravings just now breaking into full bloom, or the first traces of a culture or family in a state of gradual decay. This can be done not only for our character traits, but for every last event that befalls us. The most devastating strokes of bad luck often result from trivial miscalculations; at the same time, a cynic might easily trace the rise of every friendship back to some concealed motive of utility. The ability to explain all human phenomena in terms of some indefinite set of underlying causes might be called the "depth perception" of the other.

But there is also what we might term the "surface sensitivity" toward human beings. In the words of Lingis: "the other is also *other*. To recognize the other as other is to sense the imperative weighing on his or her thought. It is to sense its imperative force …."[542] Not merely a product of a limitless chain of causal forces, the other is absorbed in some task, acts in accordance with the imperative summons lying before her mind, expends her energy in taking something seriously. The same is true for us too, since even the most hardened egotist would never imagine that he alone is exempt from the conditions of physical reality, free from the sphere of natural laws that work upon all objects equally. The person is marked, then, by two separate currents: the person is an object reversing into an other, or an earthly force doubling up into a face. The imperative that calls me obliges me to understand the causes and grounds that unleash their energies within the world. Still, the other interrupts that movement, posits a law that commands me with an irreducible force. Amidst the realm of nature or thought, the other represents a sort of intruder.…

To see the other as other, even to see myself as an autonomous agent, is to stand before an actual imperative, a sincere finality in the world that cannot be identical with the history that gave birth to it. We see the other as ordered not by biochemical laws and cultural codings, but by a task. Pierrot builds a wagon or juggles no matter whether Harlequin convinced him to do so, and no matter whether wine or fever makes him do it. The human actor is always locked in some stance toward the objects surrounding him; he is immersed in this sincerity, a behavioral candor that does not escape our notice, and that weighs on us with equal force. He is not, as Lingis puts it, a simple phosphorescent image streaking across our consciousness:

---

[542] Alphonso Lingis, *The Community of Those Who Have Nothing in Common*, p. 25.

"To recognize the other, Kant says, is to recognize the imperative for law that rules in the other. To recognize the other is to respect the other."[543] The human agent, whether self or other, has already doubled up into a surface. In this way the whole of the human realm is shown to consist of two basic principles: the other regarded as the nexus of conditioning forces and energies, and the other as *sincere* or as occupied with the world that surrounds her.

We can proceed further, since this sincerity of the world contains several distinct strands. We have already spoken of the upsurge of a face of the other from the subterranean causal layers that sustain him, the emergence into the daylight of the other's commanding imperative. This imperative is present in both the hero and the mediocrity; it is present whether she be constructing some kind of unusual device or enjoying the simple pleasure of eating fruits. The face is always a face, whatever the nobility or pettiness of what drives the other on through the years.

At the same time, the face is never just a brute fact. It casts shadows and haloes, compels us to confront it with this or that attitude, seducing us in this or that way: "The things are not only structures with closed contours that lend themselves to manipulation and whose consistency constrains us. They lure and threaten us, support and obstruct us, sustain and debilitate us, direct and calm us. They enrapture us with their sensuous substances and also with their luminous surfaces and their phosphorescent facades, their halos, their radiance and their resonances."[544] Luring and threatening us, laying claim to our energies in some particular way, the face is an *idol*. We began by seeing that the other reversed from a natural object, a sort of puppet under unceasing causal coercion, into a vulnerable actor in the world. But we now find that this sincerity is split in half as well. For on the one hand it is the absolute fact of our being seduced by the faces of the world; on the other, it is the specific realm of lures and threats posed by those faces, the full spectrum of blessings and curses unleashed into the world by this face that also takes the shape of an idol.

The other is both face and idol. But there is still another possibility, ever present along with the first two. The idol also becomes a *fetish*, a mask no longer drifting across the world like an independent power, but now used to manipulate or enslave. In the author's example:

---

[543] Lingis, *The Community of Those Who Have Nothing in Common*, p. 23.
[544] Lingis, *The Community of Those Who Have Nothing in Common*, p. 42.

The professor who enters the classroom the first day has been preceded by the legend or myth of himself which the students now see materializing before their eyes. They adjust practically to the level of his voice and to the arena of his movements; he knows they are looking at the personage and fits his person into it as he enters the room. He will use this professorial mask to intimidate them .... When in the classroom he slouches over his papers and stifles a yawn, he is not simply shrinking back into a bare anatomy moved by fatigue, he is agitating his masks disdainfully or ironically.[545]

And again, "A fetish is used to obtain something one needs or wants; it is put forth in the service of one's fears or one's cupidity. The idol is noble; the fetish is servile."[546]

The imperative face, then, is by the same stroke both idol and fetish, and this is true in all instances. The pedant in the example just cited can modulate or oscillate his own self-generated caricature as much as he pleases, extending his personal dominance to a formidable degree. But even behind this jaded mask, the idol of a human face transmits its law through the air and commands a genuine response from us. Likewise, even the idolized face of a saint or a hero does not escape the inevitable fetishization of itself; human nature is too duplicitous for this. If seduction is an event, it is also always to some degree a tool used to fascinate, conquer, or even pillage the other. For this reason, the phenomena entitled "idol" and "fetish" are not so much distinct kinds of masks as they are inverse dimensions of a single inescapable fate: the fate of the image in its power over reality.

So far we have been discussing several distinct aspects of the imperative face of the other. To repeat, this imperative arises by way of a reversal in which the other as an object subjected to a crushing network of earthly laws and determinations reverses into the other as an autonomous commander, by virtue of the task he confronts us with. This is the point at which Lingis takes a step that never occurs even to Levinas: the structure of the imperative, it is claimed, lies even in the things themselves. As Lingis puts it, the corporeal element *of objects* doubles into an interior motor schema and an outward aspect, a duplication that no longer belongs to the human being alone: "When I look at the sequoias I do not focus on them by circumscribing their outlines; the width of their towering trunks and the

---

[545] Lingis, *The Community of Those Who Have Nothing in Common*, pp. 42–43.
[546] Lingis, *The Community of Those Who Have Nothing in Common*, p. 45.

shape of their sparse leaves drifting in the fog appear as the surfacing into visibility of an inner channel of upward thrust."[547] If this description is to be believed (and we believe it wholeheartedly) then even the sequoia, that mass of semi-aware organic material, presents a face to those who encounter it.

To speak of an "inner channel of upward thrust" in the tree itself is not a metaphor, or at least not primarily a metaphor. For what we see before us in the forest is not a large patch of brown color, nor even the settled datum of a tree-object onto which we could graft personifying tendencies. Instead, amidst the elemental chaos of the forest and its iridescent gloom and its infernal insect chants, we encounter something like a tree-effect. Amidst the primitive confusion of the terrestrial landscape, we run across something with the "style" of a tree. It doesn't have that apple look, that corncob feel, or that soybean air about it; rather, we sense that familiar sequoia thickness and grandeur. In this way the sequoia itself becomes idolized; the tree doubles up into an idol. And like any idol, it cannot protect itself from the role of a fetish. We can see this more easily in the author's own example of a pen, which he insists we do not encounter as a black cylindrical object, but rather as "the condensation of a somber power." This idol-worship of the pen as an ominous force gives way just as quickly to its simple appropriation for everyday tasks, picked up and used in a facile way by those no longer attuned to its "inner channel of horizontal thrust."

It is in this connection that the reader of these essays on the imperative encounters a remarkably fresh approach to the problem of technology. Historians of the tool have long noted that equipment externalizes human organs.[548] The hammer prolongs the length and power of the human forearm, the telescope one-ups the eyeball, while internal combustion vehicles render obsolete the long-distance function of the legs. Given what has just been said about idol and fetish, we could say that all of these devices somehow de-fetishize the object, displace its usefulness and manipulability onto some external point, leaving behind the original object as a useless but gorgeous flower, as an orchid: "Orchids are plants with atrophied trunks and limbs, parasitically clinging to the rising trunks that shut out the sun, flowering their huge showy sex organs, awaiting the bees for their orgasmic unions."[549]

For this reason, perhaps far from stripping objects down into calculable reservoirs of fuel, the progress of technology is leading us toward a

---

[547] Alphonso Lingis, *Foreign Bodies*, p. 17.
[548] See for instance Marshall McLuhan, *Understanding Media*.
[549] Lingis, *Foreign Bodies*, p. 32.

completely de-fetishized world, a landscape of imperative simulacra, a planet populated with orchid-like residues, phantom objects devoid of any serviceability. Lingis imagines the final stage of this process in a passage of ominous beauty: "Can we imagine at some future date the faculty of memory, reason, and decision disconnecting from the computers which it now serves, ceasing to be but an organ-for-apprehending, and, swollen with its own wonders, becoming an organ-to-be-apprehended, an orchid rising from the visceral and cerebral depths of the cybernetic forest with its own power, rising into the sun?"[550] For us at least, much of the appeal of this unique passage lies in the fact that it reads like anything but a warning.

The object is an imperative, radiating over us like a black sun, holding us in its orbit, demanding our attention, insisting that we reorganize our lives along its shifting axes. The object is a force, and thus our valuation of it is a gift of force, and nothing like a recognition at all. This fact leads the reader toward a series of remarks on language. The phrase "how beautiful you are!" does not communicate information, but bows to your beauty or at least pretends to bow, expressing either your own seductive force or my own deceit.[551] These evaluative terms also become especially clear, as the author indicates, in the speech of children: "bad fire," "dangerous street."[552] To respond to these objects populating the earth, and to the elemental medium that supports them, is to enter into the seductive chant of insects, the realm of solar expenditure and vegetative sexualities: "Life's blessing extends over a universe of riddles and dreadful accidents."

The servile are those who face others with their faces closed off from the world, who substitute for the vulnerability of their surface the indomitable power of a fetish. But "the idol glows with its own light."[553] That is to say, "the face refracts a double of itself, made of warmth and light, which speaks, not messages addressed to other orders, but vitalizing and ennobling …. We expose our carnal substance to the grandeur of the oceans and the celestial terror of electrical storms …. mantras with which an idol crystallizes."

We would like to end this summary with a question. We have seen that the other is at work, devoted to her task, and that this task commands us. Our question is whether this command really arises only within the narrow confines of human representation. The upward thrust of the sequoia commanded me to see it as an object, as a durable "sequoia style" amidst the

[550] Lingis, *Foreign Bodies*, p. 44.
[551] Lingis, *The Community of Those Who Have Nothing in Common*, p. 49.
[552] Lingis, *The Community of Those Who Have Nothing in Common*, p. 50.
[553] Lingis, *The Community of Those Who Have Nothing in Common*, p. 45.

scrambled hysteria of contradictory forest objects. But is it just that reality commands me to see this tree for what it is? Or does this giant tree itself, cutting across the ether, turning toward the sun, sucking juice from the soil, not already live in the domain of the imperative? Given the vast scope of this new interpretation of the imperative, it would be hard to deny this structure to wolves and dolphins, to the zebras racing across the savanna and the ravens playing pranks with clotheslines. Even the more widely despised organisms, the ones we all join in destroying (moths, beetles, microbes) must then be governed by an imperative as well.

And ultimately, this must be true even of inanimate matter itself: would it be necessary to reinterpret causality itself as a form of the imperative in things? A possible key to answering this question can be found in other passages from Lingis's *Foreign Bodies*, with which we will bring this summary to a close. The first runs as follows: "The things have to not exhibit all their sides and qualities, have to compress them behind the faces they turn to us, have to tilt back their sides in depth and not occupy all the field with their relative bigness, because they have to coexist in a field with one another and that field has to coexist with the fields of the other possible things."[554] Making room for one another in this way, objects contest each other, seduce each other, empower or annihilate each other. Commanding one another by way of the reality of their forces, the objects exist as imperatives. Like fish hunting food or dogs playing with balls, it is possible that gravel and tar, cloth and magnesium wage war against one another, compress one another into submission, command *respect* from one another.

The second passage runs as follows: "… as [the body] rows across waters it becomes for itself something seen by the lake and the distant shore; as it grapples with the rocks it takes on mass and weight …. But in letting loose its hold on things, letting its gaze get caught up in the monocular images, reflections, refractions, will-o'-the-wisps, our body dematerializes itself and metamorphoses into the drifting shape of a Chinese lantern among them."[555] A lantern among Aztec, eagle, sphinx, cobra, quetzal bird.

---

[554] Lingis, *Foreign Bodies*, p. 18.
[555] Lingis, *Foreign Bodies*, p. 24.

CHAPTER 25

REALISM WITHOUT HOBBES AND SCHMITT: ASSESSING THE LATOURIAN OPTION[556]

1. Two Senses of Realism

This article will argue for political realism in a sense very different from the usual one of cold, hard *Realpolitik*. To do so, I will argue that Bruno Latour's recent writings on climate politics resonate in important ways with the concerns of Object-Oriented Ontology (OOO).[557] "Realism," of course, is one of many important theoretical terms that can mean different things depending on the field in which it is used. Yet it is one of the few such terms that can also mean *opposite* things in different contexts; thus it goes beyond the common scenario of the incalculable polysemia of a word. For there are in fact just two basic meanings of "real," depending on what we take to be its most important contrary term.

In a first sense, "real" means the opposite of "imaginary." When we tell someone to wake up and get back to reality, shaking them out of "unrealistic" thinking, we are trying to alert them to unpleasant brute facts that they need to take into account. They are thirty-nine years old and still living with their parents; their alcohol or gambling problem is out of control; they are working a dead-end job, still hoping pathetically that their rock band

---

[556] "Realism Without Hobbes and Schmitt" was originally published in 2020 in Dominik Finkelde & Paul Livingston, eds., *Idealism, Realism, and Relativism*.
[557] See Graham Harman, *Object-Oriented Ontology*.

strikes it rich. Such warnings, of course, also occur on the geopolitical rather than the personal level, as when anti-Brexit citizens of the United Kingdom argue that there will no longer be a reliable insulin supply after departure from the European Union; or when someone floats the unpleasant prospect that India, with its billion citizens, might be uninhabitable within decades due to global warming. Admittedly, it is not always obvious who has the best handle on reality in any given case. To give one recent example, most educated Americans thought it impossible that the lifelong con artist Donald Trump could be nominated by the Republican Party for President, and once he was, we were sure that he would take that Party down in flames in ludicrous defeat. In that instance, of course, the joke was on us: a painful jest from which the United States has not yet recovered. In any case, we know the type of political realism that emerges from this sense of the term: it belittles naïvely idealistic motivations in global affairs in favor of a cool calculation of stability and national interest. Like nearly any political standpoint, this one has its golden moments, though at times it can seem alarmist in retrospect. Consider the following passage by the thoughtful conservative philosopher Eric Voegelin concerning the aftermath of the Second World War:

> If a war has a purpose at all, it is the restoration of a balance of forces and not the aggravation of disturbance; it is the reduction of the unbalancing excess of force, not the destruction of force to the point of creating a new unbalancing power vacuum. Instead the [liberal] politicians have put the Soviet army on the Elbe, surrendered China to the Communists, at the same time demilitarized Germany and Japan, and in addition demobilized our own [American] army ....
> [I]t is perhaps not sufficiently realized that never before in the history of mankind has a world power used a victory deliberately for the purpose of creating a power vacuum to its own disadvantage.[558]

The same has often been said of the more recent American wars in Afghanistan and Iraq, which created two separate power vacuums on the borders of Iran despite many American military theorists viewing the latter country as the real long-term threat.

From this sort of realist standpoint, since the world is filled with frail humans rather than angels, we should not expect the earth to be a paradise,

---

[558] Eric Voegelin, *The New Science of Politics*, p. 172.

but must steel ourselves against the grim unchanging truths of human nature. As Voegelin further laments: "practically every great political thinker who recognized the structure of reality, from Machiavelli to the present, has been branded as an immoralist by [liberal] intellectuals ...."[559] We might call this attitude Cold Shower Realism, since it is always deployed in an effort to scold someone's daydreaming failure to be in contact with the way the world really is rather than how they wish it to be. Its usual political target is the naïve idealist who too quickly assumes that ours could be a world of peace and justice if everyone would just put aside their petty differences and dethrone the corrupt corporate and military interests that manufacture conflict for their own benefit. Against these purportedly sweet but gullible Pollyannas, the Cold Shower Realist insists on recognizing the way things really are.

Yet there is a second and opposite sense of "realism." It is one that does not take facts on the ground to be the ultimate reality, but merely a superficial and transient appearance, or even an immoral or untruthful one. Here the target of criticism is not the gullible dreamer, but the one who is *too* focused on mere present-day realities. The critic driven by this second sense of realism calls our attention to deeper underlying realities, beyond the sphere of contemporary fact, that the Cold Shower Realist fails to take into account. One example occurs when some on the Israeli Left argue that demographic realities require a different national security approach than the continued deployment of crushing military superiority, which is likely to prove less feasible under the population conditions of several decades from now. Here again, this sort of realist is not always right: we recall the grim but inaccurate predictions about the Y2K computer bug causing global chaos on the first day of the year 2000, and similar if lesser worries about the introduction of the Euro in 2002. In any case, this is a second and different form of realism, one that looks beyond appearances toward the supposedly deeper factors in a situation not currently registered in its balance of forces, either because they have not yet emerged or because by nature they can never fully emerge. We thus call this version the Realism of Depth, since it is fixed on something deeper than the actual, whether it be optimistic or pessimistic in spirit.

Cold Shower Realism is the sort we generally find proclaimed in artistic movements and manifestoes. Literary realism wants to replace romantic and heroic narratives with detailed, sometimes disgusting portraits of the

---

[559] Voegelin, *The New Science of Politics*, p. 170.

way things supposedly really are. Émile Zola does this so comprehensively that Nietzsche famously describes his writing as a "delight in stinking."[560] Upton Sinclair's *The Jungle* gave such a repellent portrait of the American meat-packing industry that new regulations were demanded and finally imposed.[561] Realist painters did something similar, giving us de-idealized portraits of lower-class suffering and the undistinguished grind of peasant life; Michael Fried's book *Courbet's Realism* shows us some of the technical aspects that this shift entailed.[562] By contrast, the Realism of Depth turns its back on what seems to be the reality of present experience and digs for something beyond what meets the eye. Plato seeks the otherworldly perfect forms of which the imperfect entities of everyday life are pale copies or gloomy shadows. Likewise, Platonist mathematicians — who make up a majority in their field — consider mathematical objects to have a real existence over and above their instantiation in practical life or in our minds. Among current realist philosophies, OOO is distinguished by its insistence that objects are real not only "outside the mind," but outside any relation with other objects whatsoever. In this way, OOO finds reality in a place that no fact on the ground can ever possibly express.[563]

When it comes to politics, we have already had a glance at Voegelin's balance-of-power version of realism. More generally, when speaking of realism in international relations theory, we are speaking of a Cold Shower Realism stripped of all rosy delusions, as in the work of Hans Morgenthau, academic mentor of Henry Kissinger.[564] Political realists are seen as hard-headed strategists who focus on what is genuinely possible rather than on ideal conditions and optimistic scenarios. This is why political realism is so frequently found in the company of geographical determinism: "England has no eternal allies or enemies, but only eternal interests," as Palmerston's words are often simplified, since the United Kingdom is a relatively safe island nation historically focused on obstructing whichever continental power — usually France or Germany, but sometimes Russia — has had the upper hand at any given time.[565] The United States is essentially an island naval power like England, due to the comparative weakness of its

[560] Friedrich Nietzsche, *Twilight of the Idols*, p. 51.
[561] Upton Sinclair, *The Jungle*.
[562] Michael Fried, *Courbet's Realism*.
[563] Graham Harman, *The Quadruple Object*.
[564] Hans Morgenthau, *Politics Among Nations*.
[565] Henry Temple, 3rd Viscount of Palmerston, "Treaty of Adrianople — Charges Against Viscount Palmerston."

land neighbors Canada and Mexico throughout American history. Under conditions of rising Canadian or Mexican militancy, American strategy would probably veer more towards a continental European balance of power policy rather than its familiar long-term swings between isolation and intervention, both of them tinged with a specific form of morality known as "American exceptionalism." Strategic and geographic conditions are seen to change slowly when contrasted with the ongoing human pageant of shifting political incident and changing individual leaders. American governments of whatever political party will likely continue to support Israel, South Korea, and the United Kingdom, and will usually oppose both Russia and whichever East Asian country is strongest: currently China, though recently enough it was Japan.

Obviously, a great deal of modern political theory has not been realist at all, even in those cases when it calls itself "materialist." Although modern political discussions tend to revolve around the polarity between Left and Right that arose during the French Revolution, I have argued elsewhere that there is a more important distinction cutting across these two: namely, that between what I have called Truth Politics and Power Politics.[566] The former group thinks itself to be already aware of the ideal political form, which is prevented from coming into existence only by one or more unfortunate factors: usually class conflict or more general corruption in government or society. The most obvious examples of this attitude in the modern period are found on the Left, with Rousseau and Marx coming immediately to mind.[567] But we find Truth Politicians on the Right as well, as when the late Straussian philosopher Stanley Rosen writes that for Nietzsche (though more for Rosen himself) "there cannot be a radically unique creation .... The fundamental task is one of rank-ordering [human] types that have always occurred and will always exist."[568] We also find countless Truth Politicians in the pre-modern era, with Plato and al-Farabi being among the most prominent modelers of ideal cities, however literally or not they may have been intended.[569] By contrast, Power Politics amounts to the claim that there is no transcendent truth governing the political sphere, so that the only political truth is the immanent struggle for power itself; to the victor go the spoils. Prominent in this group are such figures as Machiavelli, Hobbes, and

---

[566] Graham Harman, *Bruno Latour: Reassembling the Political*.
[567] Jean-Jacques Rousseau, *Discourse on the Origin of Inequality*; Karl Marx, *Capital*, vol. 1.
[568] Stanley Rosen, *The Mask of Enlightenment*, p. 5.
[569] Plato, *Republic*; Abu Nasr al-Farabi, *On the Perfect State*.

Schmitt.[570] But we will see that there is an important difference between Hobbes and Schmitt, and that neither figure gives us the sort of political realism we need.

Finally, I would also mention two authors who have an interesting relation to these Power Politicians without quite belonging to their group. The first is the aforementioned Voegelin, a Christian thinker who is more deeply committed to transcendence than any of the Machiavelli/Hobbes/Schmitt trio (including Schmitt, also a Christian) but who adds that transcendence should be restricted to spiritual and intellectual life, given the danger of all attempts to "immanentize the eschaton" in the political sphere.[571] The second exceptional author, not often read as a political philosopher, is Bruno Latour. His ontology, widely implemented in the social sciences as Actor-Network Theory (ANT), is committed to the sheer immanence of actors entering and exiting from networks, consisting in nothing more than the sum total of their actions, with no unexpressed surplus in things beyond what they actually do.[572] For this reason, it should come as no surprise that the young Latour sings the praises of such remorseless political theorists of immanence as Machiavelli and Hobbes.[573] In *We Have Never Been Modern*, Latour describes the Hobbesian stance nicely:

> Civil wars will rage as long as there exist supernatural entities that citizens feel they have a right to petition when they are persecuted by the authorities of this lower world. The loyalty of the old medieval society — to God and King — is no longer possible if all people can petition God directly, or designate their own King. Hobbes wanted to wipe the slate clean of all appeals to entities higher than civil authority.[574]

Yet his previous approval of this immanent standpoint is abandoned in the very same work: for here Latour finds his mature voice in a surprising *attack* on Hobbes, with the claim that immanent political force is no less subject to deconstruction than scientific truth. Less than a decade later, Latour already insists — against the Hobbesian doctrine he once adored — on the need

---

[570] Niccolò Machiavelli, *The Prince*; Thomas Hobbes, *Leviathan*; Carl Schmitt, *The Concept of the Political*.
[571] Voegelin, *The New Science of Politics*, p. 121.
[572] Bruno Latour, *Reassembling the Social*.
[573] Michel Callon & Bruno Latour, "Unscrewing the Big Leviathan."
[574] Bruno Latour, *We Have Never Been Modern*, p. 19.

for the *polis* to detect those entities that transcend it.[575] This includes both the work of scientists in discovering new things, and that of the moralists in championing those people who have previously been excluded: two classes of humans feared by Hobbes as disturbers of civil peace. Latour eventually comes to agree with John Dewey that far from being a purely immanent affair, politics involves coming to temporary consensus about issues that are never fully clear to anyone: a liberal attitude toward compromise combined with a metaphysical doubt about the very possibility of transparent political knowledge.[576] This residual lack of clarity in issues of political dispute opens a window beyond immanence like nothing else in Latour's philosophy, and puts him somewhere beyond the reach of Power Politics, while also separating him from Truth Politicians who think they can grasp the very essence of political matters. Yet Latour also belongs outside the usual Left-Right polarity, in which both sides are largely defined by their view of human nature as either inherently good or evil, respectively. Evidence for this can be found in the uniquely pivotal role Latour grants in his political theory to non-human objects, which act as important stabilizers in the political realm.[577] This is another issue to be considered below.

In any case, the meaning of this article's title is as follows. There is something to be said for the differing Cold Shower Realisms of Hobbes and Schmitt, which help to dispel the excessive idealism found in many forms of contemporary political theory. Yet the excessive immanence of their realism gives it too much the aspect of a mere struggle for survival *hic et nunc*, and makes a poor fit with the metaphysical realism advocated by OOO. In what follows, a first section will be devoted to Hobbes and Schmitt, as well as an important contrast drawn between their positions by the conservative political philosopher Leo Strauss on behalf of knowledge or truth. A second section will consider the benefits of Latour's own unorthodox realism in politics, laying stress on his recent work *Down to Earth*, in which climate politics is plausibly defined as our new collective horizon.[578]

2. Schmitt and Hobbes

Latour once stated for the record, in London, that it "is a common thing in political philosophy, that reactionary thinkers are more interesting than

---

[575] Bruno Latour, *Politics of Nature*.

[576] John Dewey, *The Public and its Problems*; Bruno Latour, *An Inquiry Into Modes of Existence*.

[577] S.S. Strum & Bruno Latour, "Redefining the Social Link."

[578] Bruno Latour, *Down to Earth*.

the progressive ones ... in that you learn more about politics from people like Machiavelli and Schmitt than from Rousseau."[579] Although Latour does not specify the source of this maxim, it seems probable that it was the apparently sinister Nazi-supporter Schmitt. Though it is common for Leftists to admire Schmitt's conception of politics as existential struggle — against the "bourgeois" liberal preference for individual economic and intellectual freedom within a relatively de-politicized sphere — Latour is the rare liberal who often looks to Schmitt as a political North Star. While this passing salute to "reactionaries" may seem to mark a reversion by Latour to the Hobbesian stance of his early career, there is a crucial difference between Schmitt and Hobbes, one that colors Latour's own recent political writings. Let's begin with Schmitt, even though he is later than Hobbes chronologically.

Schmitt opens Section 7 of his 1932 work *The Concept of the Political* with a statement that sounds a great deal like Latour's London formula. There we read as follows: "One could test all theories of state and political ideas according to their anthropology and thereby classify these as to whether they consciously or unconsciously presuppose man to be by nature evil or by nature good ... [by their] answer to the question whether man is a dangerous being or not, a risky or a harmless creature."[580] There are at least three separate things going on in this brief statement. First, Schmitt declares himself to be one of what Latour calls the "reactionaries," in opposition to liberals who think that mutual economic interest, abstract humane principles, and theoretical debate should ultimately be enough to bring humanity together. There is little surprise here, and no one familiar with the spirit of Schmitt's writings would expect otherwise. Second, Schmitt does not divide the world into morally good and evil individuals, but rather sees every *collective* as potentially dangerous to every other: as a possible existential threat to a given people's own way of life. Here again, liberals are Schmitt's target, given their tendency to wage war only in the name of abstract causes such as human rights: as in the case of the Allied Powers in World War I, who saw it as a war for democracy and the right of self-determination, as a "war to end all wars." Schmitt objects that this sort of war on principle tends to dehumanize one's enemies, depicting them as monsters and justifying their outright annihilation rather than mere defeat. Third — and here is Schmitt's Cold Shower Realist moment — there is his

[579] Bruno Latour, Graham Harman, & Peter Erdélyi, *The Prince and the Wolf*, p. 96.
[580] Schmitt, *The Concepts of the Political*, p. 58.

famous principle that "the specific political distinction to which political actions and motives can be reduced is that between friend and enemy."[581]

Only the sovereign — defined here as the state — can determine the enemy, who is understood in an existential sense as one who seeks to destroy our way of life. No moral principle can surmount this fundamental distinction between friend and enemy, and thus the political marks the summit of human existence, given that physical death at the hands of the enemy is the ultimate concrete possibility for each of us. As for the Christian injunction to love one's enemies, Schmitt flatly denies its relevance to the political sphere: "Never in the thousand-year struggle between Christians and Moslems did it occur to a Christian to surrender rather than defend Europe out of love toward the Saracens or Turks."[582] Even the tolerance defended by Locke is not liberal enough to include Muslims, and though liberal tolerance today is far broader in scope than Locke's early modern version, no Western liberal of our time would accept living under the self-described Caliphate of ISIS or the Kim regime in North Korea.[583] Instead, liberals would immediately embrace death-struggle with these entities if they were to threaten us directly, and would simply moralize the struggle into one of good versus evil. On this same note, it is well known that the United States has difficulty waging conflict without demonizing the leaders of its enemies, even while insisting to the world that it does not hate the German, Japanese, Russian, Vietnamese, Afghani, or Iraqi people *per se*.

Though Schmitt cannot receive the full treatment he deserves here, a few additional words are in order. He is well aware that existential struggle with the enemy can also occur *within* a given polity rather than between two separate states, as in cases of civil war, and even considers the possibility of a global class war of the sort envisaged by Marx. For this reason, Slavoj Žižek is unfair with his Marxist complaint that Schmitt "already displaces the *inherent* antagonism constitutive of the political on to the *external* relationship between Us and Them," which means rather than focusing as one should on the class struggle.[584] Schmitt's formula tying politics above all to the threat of death is not aimed — as in the case of Hobbes — at the death of autonomous individuals, but at that of the group. Thus, "[i]n case of need, the political entity must demand the sacrifice of life. Such a demand is in no way justified by the individualism of liberal thought .... For the

---

[581] Schmitt, *The Concept of the Political*, p. 26.
[582] Schmitt, *The Concept of the Political*, p. 29.
[583] John Locke, *A Letter Concerning Toleration*.
[584] Slavoj Žižek, "Carl Schmitt in the Age of Post-Politics," p. 27.

individual as such there is no enemy with whom he must enter into a life-and-death struggle if he personally does not want to do so."[585] Finally, the formula of existential threat is "realist" in the sense that it points to what lies radically outside one's polity or faction, in a thoroughly "non-immanent" sense. The sort of realism that impresses Schmitt is the kind found in those clear-headed thinkers who have been able to recognize the enemy concretely. He cites examples: "the fanatical hatred of Napoleon felt by the German barons Stein and Kleist ... Lenin's annihilating sentences against bourgeois and western capitalism. All these are surpassed by Cromwell's enmity towards papist Spain." At the opposite pole of such clarity, "the incapacity or unwillingness to make this distinction [between friend and enemy] is a symptom of the political end," as with the naïve French and Russian aristocracies who romanticized the very social classes who were about to destroy them.[586] In Schmitt's eyes, such struggle for survival is the sole place where the political can be found; any fantasies about a future benevolent world government have nothing to do with our present concrete existence.

In his staunch opposition to liberal idealism, Schmitt certainly qualifies as a Cold Shower Realist. The question is whether he remains in this position, or whether he also attempts a further step into what I have called a Realism of Depth, a position from which — we will see — Strauss criticizes his work. Schmitt tends to see struggle between peoples as a matter of survival rather than principles, the latter serving mostly to provide hypocritically idealistic cover for an existential death match with the enemy beyond good and evil. If Thrasymachus in Plato's *Republic* views justice cynically as "the advantage of the stronger," Schmitt sees justice as beside the point, and treats struggle as the attempt to ensure the survival of one's own people as a whole.[587] Yet it is not difficult to imagine a situation in which citizens of one nation decide that justice is on the side of their enemy in a particular conflict, on the basis of transcendent principles of the sort that Schmitt excludes via his doctrine of war as existential struggle; widespread American opposition to the war in Vietnam is one obvious example. Is Schmitt's immanent focus on the survival of a people enough to count as political realism in more than the unapologetic Cold Shower sense? Whether or not one is persuaded by the essentials of Schmitt's doctrine, it seems clear that he cannot pass

---

[585] Schmitt, *The Concept of the Political*, p. 71.
[586] Schmitt, *The Concept of the Political*, p. 68.
[587] Plato, *Republic* 338c.

the realist test, since the enemy counts as nothing more than a traumatic Other that must be repulsed at all costs. It is somewhat reminiscent of "the Real" in the psychoanalysis of Jacques Lacan, which does not have an autonomous existence apart from the symbolic and imaginary orders, but functions only as an immanent impasse or breakdown in these orders.[588] Although the trauma for Schmitt usually comes from the outside rather than from within one's own national or social group, he strips us of the ability to come to terms with what lies beyond except through defeating it; he also silently consolidates the human realm as an immanent sphere constituted by the darkness of human nature and closed off to non-human entities. Lacan — much like the German idealist philosopher J.G. Fichte — is a "traumatist" without being a realist, and I would say the same about Schmitt.[589]

Let's turn briefly to another of Latour's reactionaries, Thomas Hobbes, who seems at first glance to have much in common with Schmitt. The possibility of violent death is the foundation of Hobbes's political philosophy as well. It is not only the weak who must fear death in the state of nature, since "as to the strength of body, the weakest has strength enough to kill the strongest, either by secret machination, or by confederacy with others, that are in the same danger with himself."[590] Following Thucydides (whom he translated) Hobbes identifies three causes of war among humans: the love of gain, the fear of loss, and the desire for reputation.[591] All these motives are sufficiently intense that "during the time men live without a common power to keep them all in awe, they are in that condition which is called war; and such a war, as is of every man, against every man."[592] War leaves no room for cultivation of the earth, for commerce and industry, or for arts and letters, leading to a situation of "continual fear, and danger of violent death; and the life of man [is] solitary, poor, nasty, brutish, and short."[593] There can be no relevant conception of justice in this bellicose state of nature, given that "[f]orce, and fraud, are in war the two cardinal virtues."[594]

Justice exists only on the interior of a society already established, and to attain such a peaceful condition requires that certain sacrifices be made. For "as long as the natural right of every man to every thing endureth, there can

---

[588] Jacques Lacan, *Écrits*.
[589] J.G. Fichte, *The Science of Knowledge*.
[590] Hobbes, *Leviathan*, p. 82.
[591] Thucydides, *The Peloponnesian War*.
[592] Hobbes, *Leviathan*, p. 84.
[593] Hobbes, *Leviathan*, p. 84.
[594] Hobbes, *Leviathan*, p. 85.

be no security to any man (how strong or wise however he be) of living out the time which nature ordinarily alloweth every man to live."[595] And thus it is required "that a man be willing, when others are too … to lay down [the] right to all things; and be contented with so much liberty against other men, as he would allow other men against himself."[596] Hence "there must be some coercive power, to compel men equally to the performance of their covenants, by the terror of some punishment, greater than the benefit they expect by the breach of their covenant …."[597] This power, the commonwealth or "great Leviathan," emerges when everyone renounces their natural right to self-rule, so that the sovereign "hath the use of so much power and strength conferred on him, that by terror thereof, he is enabled to conform to the wills of them all, to peace at home, and mutual aid to their enemies abroad."[598] The natural right of individuals to preserve themselves from harm is retained as long as no else is harmed, but any appeal to a transcendent outside is excluded. Note that it is not only religious transcendence that Hobbes finds threatening, but the transcendence claimed by scientific truth as well, as recounted in an important book by Steven Shapin and Simon Schaffer on the rivalry between Hobbes and the chemist Robert Boyle.[599]

This quick summary of the respective standpoints of Schmitt and Hobbes has already revealed important similarities between the two. Above all, both have a pessimistic assessment of human nature. Both are preoccupied with the danger of sudden death, and end up defending authoritarian systems of government as a bulwark against this danger. Beyond this, Schmitt and Hobbes alike want peace at home while permitting the most rampant violence in conflicts between nations, as if the state of nature were still in force when it comes to foreign affairs. Yet there are crucial differences as well. Despite his negative view of human nature, Hobbes can plausibly be called the founder of liberalism, due to his exclusive delegation of politics to the sovereign and the creation of an internal space of peace.[600] By contrast, Schmitt is an explicit anti-liberal, someone who apparently *wants* humans to face up seriously to the existential danger at the root of human life, rather than remaining safely engaged in a peaceful zone of cultural and economic development. There is also Hobbes's liberal stress on the individual right

---

[595] Hobbes, *Leviathan*, p. 87.
[596] Hobbes, *Leviathan*, p. 87, emph. removed.
[597] Hobbes, *Leviathan*, pp. 95–96.
[598] Hobbes, *Leviathan*, p. 114.
[599] Steven Shapin & Simon Schaffer, *Leviathan and the Air-Pump*.
[600] Leo Strauss, "Notes on Carl Schmitt."

to self-preservation and the *voluntary* character of military service, whereas Schmitt's group-oriented stance emphasizes the sovereign right to demand the sacrifice of individual life.

But where do Schmitt and Hobbes stand on the realist question, the topic of the present article? We know, at the very least, that realism in politics as in philosophy requires dealings with an outside rather than enclosure in one's own immanent sphere. And here Strauss finds both thinkers the same in their lack of focus on *truth*, the ultimate access to what lies beyond immanence. As Strauss puts it:

> whereas the liberal respects and tolerates all "*honest*" convictions, so long as they merely acknowledge the legal order, *peace*, as sacrosanct, he who affirms the political as such respects and tolerates all "*serious*" convictions, that is, all decisions oriented to the real possibility of *war*. Thus [Schmitt's] affirmation of the political as such proves to be a liberalism with the opposite polarity.[601]

The way out of this dilemma, for Strauss, is to seek the outside in the form of political *knowledge*: "the life-and-death quarrel: the political — the grouping into friends and enemies — owes its legitimation to the seriousness of the question of what is right."[602] Schmitt remains a kind of Thrasymachus as long as he makes no search for truth beyond the arbitrariness of the sovereign decision. This is why Schmitt is often called a "decisionist," and a link could easily be established with Heidegger's principle of resoluteness, in which firm commitment to any life decision is more important than the specific content of any such decision.[603] We now have what looks like a continuum running from least to most realist positions among the authors we have mentioned, as follows:

Less Realist
- Liberal idealism. Too optimistic about human nature and wrongly committed to the idea of humans as indefinitely improvable.
- Hobbesian liberalism. Walls off the citizenry from direct contact with the perilous state of nature, but (unlike liberal idealism) is at least clear-headed about the dire character of human nature.

---

[601] Strauss, "Notes on Carl Schmitt," p. 120.
[602] Strauss, "Notes on Carl Schmitt," p. 118.
[603] Martin Heidegger, *Being and Time*, p. 278.

- Lacan and Fichte. More open to our direct contact with the Real than Hobbes, but only in the form of an immanent breakdown or resistance of the Real to our efforts.
- Schmitt. Open to direct contact with a reality that is not just immanent, but transcends us in the shape of a dangerous foreign element that might cost us our lives. This is the enemy.
- Voegelin. Transcendent truth may be attainable in spiritual and intellectual matters, but not in the political sphere.
- Strauss. It is possible to make direct contact with a reality that can in principle be known, in the form of true political content.

More Realist

Yet it seems to me that Strauss is not a political realist any more than are Hobbes or Schmitt. It is true that philosophical realism often implies not only that something exists "outside the mind," but also that this outside can be known. This is the sort of realism defended, for instance, by my New Realist friends Maurizio Ferraris and Markus Gabriel, who are opposed, above all else, to relativism.[604] Yet the idea that one can have knowledge of the real implies the non-Socratic claim that beyond *philosophia* (or love of wisdom) we can directly attain *sophia* (or wisdom itself). Reality is what it is, and to translate it into knowable terms will always require a good degree of distortion or simplification; the form of a thing cannot be neatly extracted from the matter in which it inheres and transported into our brains without alteration. A form cannot be moved from one place to another without transformation, whether we are speaking of knowledge or mere causal interaction between mindless things. For this reason I would be inclined to move Strauss further back on our realist list, perhaps even midway between the liberal idealist and Hobbes. Any attempt to make contact with reality will have to find some way to acknowledge not only that it is autonomous from us, but also that we cannot know exactly what it is. A realist politics, one that does justice to reality rather than simply indulging in our theoretical fantasies about reality, must somehow incorporate our ultimate uncertainty as to the nature of things. On this note I turn to that paradoxical and misunderstood thinker, Latour.

---

[604] Maurizio Ferraris, *Manifesto of New Realism*; Markus Gabriel, *Fields of Sense*.

3. Latour's Object-Oriented Politics

As mentioned, Latour has built a philosophy that might look as immanent as Hobbes's own. His ANT strips the world of transcendence to the point that an actor (meaning any entity at all) is defined solely in terms of what it does. There are no properties in things that remain currently unexpressed; an actor exhausts its being in every instant, and becomes something different in succeeding instants when it does something new.[605] This in itself sounds anti-realist, since it grants nothing outside the sum total of actions *hic et nunc*. Latour has the additional anti-realist tendency — occasionally but not often avoided — of behaving as if any network of actors needs to be registered ultimately by a human observer. In his most extreme moments this leads him to make openly shocking claims, as in his argument that the Egyptian Pharaoh Ramses II cannot have died of tuberculosis, since that disease had not yet been discovered in ancient Egypt.[606] There is also his somewhat ironic use of the term "realism" in the opening pages of *Pandora's Hope*, in the same manner often employed by anti-realists to deflate the challenge posed by the term "realism" altogether.[607]

Nonetheless, there are at least two places in Latour's philosophy where he opens himself to a form of transcendence so robust that Hobbes could only have scowled in response. The first comes in his important but neglected rejection of materialism, on the grounds that materialists always assume that they know what "matter" is, thereby reducing it to a limited number of abstract properties.[608] Here Latour is actually more Socratic than Socrates's admirer Strauss, given Latour's awareness that the nature of matter must remain to some extent a mystery in view of our inability to reach a "right" definition of it. The second comes in Latour's political theory, where knowledge and technocratic expertise are downplayed to the point of irrelevance, and we are led to something like Dewey's model of a deliberative provisional consensus between various stakeholders.

Yet an even more important realist moment in Latour comes from his awareness of the role of inanimate objects, in politics as elsewhere. It is not a question of granting political rights to rocks, shadows, and pipelines, but of recognizing the way in which debates over the goodness or badness of human nature are somehow beside the point. After all, what separates human from baboon society is primarily the great number of objects we

---

[605] Graham Harman, *Prince of Networks*.
[606] Bruno Latour, "On the Partial Existence of Existing *and* Non-Existing Objects."
[607] Bruno Latour, *Pandora's Hope*.
[608] Bruno Latour, "Can We Get Our Materialism Back, Please?"

humans deploy to differentiate our identities and roles: contracts, proper names, titles, money, wedding rings, identification cards, brick walls, eyeglasses, trains, and the like.[609] Failed states are often the result of material rather than human failure, as Peer Schouten has demonstrated in the case of present-day Congo.[610] While this commitment to non-human agents has always been a hallmark of Latour's political philosophy, it has attained new urgency in connection with global warming: a problem that Hobbes, Schmitt, and Strauss alike would have difficulty handling from their existing standpoints, oriented as they are by the specific features of human nature.

In his Edinburgh Gifford Lectures, eventually published in book form as *Facing Gaia*, Latour seems to make a Schmittian gesture, proposing that global warming deniers be treated as the "enemy" in a manner no longer worthy of rational debate.[611] Yet his more recently published booklet *Down to Earth* shows more of a turn from Schmitt back to Dewey, as interpreted by Noortje Marres.[612] The Deweyan element of Latour's realism, one that is missing from Hobbes, Schmitt, and Strauss alike, is his ongoing search for a form of transcendence-without-knowledge that would properly characterize the political sphere. Modernization, Latour's career-long enemy, is marked by the attempt to *purify* two taxonomically distinct realms from one another: the human and the non-human, the cultural and the natural, the humanities or social sciences and the hard sciences, truth and politics. His alternative is to point to the proliferation in our world of hybrids that cannot always be neatly classified as belonging to one of these two zones alone: the ozone hole is both an artifact of human behavior and a portion of the earth itself.[613] As we saw when Latour denied the existence of tuberculosis prior to its registration by human science, he often tarnishes this insight by claiming that *every* actor in the world is a mixture of human and non-human associations, a claim that fails as soon as we consider entities in distant galaxies or pre-human eras of the earth; to deny their existence apart from humans would be a form of rank idealism, as Meillassoux argues with his concept of the "ancestral."[614]

Nonetheless, Latour provides us with two powerful tools for moving beyond the political immanence and political humanness of moderns

609 Strum & Latour, "Redefining the Social Link."
610 Peer Schouten, "The Materiality of State Failure."
611 Bruno Latour, *Facing Gaia*, pp. 220–254.
612 Bruno Latour, *Down to Earth*; Noortje Marres, "No Issue, No Public."
613 Latour, *We Have Never Been Modern*.
614 Quentin Meillassoux, *After Finitude*.

like Hobbes and Schmitt, without laying claim to a political knowledge that Socratic *philosophia* is always prepared to debunk. The first tool is his insistence that politics always remains shrouded in our ultimate ignorance, which is precisely why technocrats cannot save us. Our inability to make *direct* proofs of global warming in the manner of modern science is a powerful index of this fact, and is the main reason that Latour had recourse to Schmitt when lecturing on Gaia. Donald Trump's escapist effort to deny the existence of global warming, and the brewing migration crisis closely linked with it, is parasitical on our inability to *know* global warming in the same way we can know the mass of an electron.[615] While it may seem easy to deny the political element of subatomic physics, it is much more difficult to produce knowledge about the climate without a political assembly of the scientists and governments who can design (or "engender," as Latour prefers) a world in which humans are fruitfully interwoven with their environment rather than merely modernizing it beyond any plausible resource base. We can no longer be modernizing globalists, but Trumpian escapist anti-realism shows us by way of contrast the sort of realists we need to be: *terrestrials*, or those who must find a way to live in common with fish, birds, ice, CO_2, methane, and our former Schmittian national enemies. In Latour's own words, "[a] territory ... is not limited to a single type of agent. It encompasses the entire set of animate beings — far away or nearby — whose presence has been determined — by investigation, by experience, by habit, by culture — to be indispensable to the survival of the terrestrial."[616] If the enemy is no longer a foreign people, but a Gaia that may heat up by 7° C in a century, political immanence is a luxury we can no longer afford. The outside environment will need to be woven into the *polis* as it has never been before, whether in political practice or the books of political theorists.

But this immediately brings us to the second new tool provided by Latour: the need to construct a political theory that takes into account not just "the entire set of animate beings," but numerous inanimate ones as well. In this sense, Latour has to push even beyond James Lovelock, who was primarily interested in Gaia as an environment produced and maintained by living things rather than simply a stable backdrop for them.[617] If modern philosophy always foundered on the problem of animals, not knowing whether to place them closer to *res cogitans* or *res extensa* and

---

[615] See also Graham Harman, "Latour's Interpretation of Donald Trump."
[616] Latour, *Down to Earth*, pp. 95–96.
[617] James Lovelock, *The Ages of Gaia*; Latour, *Down to Earth*, p. 76.

unable to develop a plausible alternative, modern thinkers have failed as well to describe the inanimate world, but have simply abandoned it to the natural sciences. Yet a successful climate politics will have to embrace the inanimate as a political actor intimately intertwined with human politics, rather than as dead matter invested with accurately measurable properties. When Latour insists on the need for all things to be made terrestrial rather than global, it is not only Trump who provides the negative impetus, but Hobbes, Schmitt, and Strauss as well.

CHAPTER 26

CONCERNING THE COVID-19 EVENT[618]

Of the numerous recent articles on the COVID-19 pandemic written by prominent philosophers, the one by Alain Badiou stands out for its spirit of pragmatic restraint.[619] The reader is surprised to find Badiou, the revolutionary Maoist, taking the side of managerial democratic centrism against radical pretensions as to the impact of the virus. He even defends "the unfortunate [French President Emmanuel] Macron, who is simply doing … his job as head of state" and disdains those who "make a hue and cry about the founding event of an unprecedented revolution." If we were to make an informed guess at the author of such phrases, the normally fire-breathing Badiou is one of the last people who would come to mind. Later in the article, he makes an additional effort to downplay the novelty of our current situation:

> What's more, the true name of the ongoing epidemic should
> suggest that in a sense we are dealing with "nothing new under the
> contemporary sun." This true name is SARS 2, that is "Severe Acute
> Respiratory Syndrome 2," a name that signals the "second time"
> of this identification, after the SARS 1 epidemic, which spread
> around the world in Spring 2003 …. It is clear then that the current

[618] "Concerning the COVID-19 Event" was originally published in *Philosophy Today*, 64:4 (Fall 2020).
[619] Alain Badiou, "On the Epidemic Situation."

epidemic is by no means the emergence of something radically new or unprecedented.

Here he is not so convincing. The reference to 2003, of course, is to the SARS epidemic that killed nearly 800 people in China, Hong Kong, Taiwan, Singapore, and Canada. But tragic and worrisome though it was, the SARS-1 scare cannot sustain even loose comparison with the current pestilence. COVID-19 has spread to every country on earth, and by the time these words are published will have killed more than one million people worldwide, with over 200,000 dead in the United States alone. The novel coronavirus has caused enormous upheaval in the education, health, hospitality, and travel sectors, and has further polarized an already sharply divided American polity. To claim that COVID-19 is nothing new under the sun — do not take Badiou's scare quotes seriously — simply because a related coronavirus already appeared in 2003 is a bit like saying that the atomic bomb in Hiroshima was nothing new, given that firebombings had already occurred in Coventry, Hamburg, Dresden, and Tokyo.

The reason for this disagreement, of course, is that Badiou is rather demanding in his standards for what counts as an event.[620] His amorous events go well beyond both legal matrimony and sexual passion, requiring a total change in one's mode of being, no matter the consequences. As for the art-event, nothing will do in twentieth-century music but high atonal serialism, and one senses that even in that group only Anton Webern is rigorous enough to please Badiou. Mainstream musical fashion is summarily dismissed: "Today, the music-world is negatively defined. The classical subject and its romantic avatars are entirely saturated, and it is not the plurality of 'musics' — folklore, classicism, pop, exoticism, jazz and baroque reaction all in the same festive bag — which will be able to resuscitate them."[621] Even Igor Stravinsky is held at arm's length. Perhaps most emblematically, Badiou permits no political event unless it somehow partakes of "the communist invariant," which he means in a most uncompromising sense that includes both Mao's Cultural Revolution and ancient Chinese Legalism.[622] This is one problem with Badiou's dismissal of the evental character of COVID-19. He creates such a dualism between mediocre "situations" and consummate revolutionary upheaval that no room is left for meso-events that cut deeply

---

[620] Alain Badiou, *Being and Event*.
[621] Alain Badiou, *Logics of* Worlds, p. 89.
[622] Badiou, *Logic of Worlds*, p. 78, Table 1.2.

into history without redeeming the oppressed masses and doling out suitable doses of revolutionary terror. The American Revolution certainly would not fit the bill, and neither would the Roman destruction of Carthage, the appearance of Viking longboats, or perhaps even the invention of the printing press. Thus we can see that COVID-19 is in good company among all those phenomena excluded from Badiouian eventhood.

Another issue is well worth noting, though it may seem to be of lesser relevance to the present article. It has not gone unnoticed that there is a pronounced idealist streak to Badiou's philosophy, not even among the two Speculative Realists who have been intellectually closest to that philosophy. Ray Brassier laments as follows: "[for Badiou] the Big Bang, the Cambrian explosion, and the death of the sun remain mere hiccups in the way of the world, in which he has little or no interest."[623] Quentin Meillassoux makes the following concession: "there is in [Badiou's *Logics of Worlds*] no example of purely 'natural' events, radically foreign to every human intervention, to every subjective intervention in general. For example, there is in Badiou no description of the evolutionary emergence of species in terms of events — no evental Darwinism."[624] The reason this aspect of Badiou seems less relevant here is that we are interested in the 2019 emergence of the novel coronavirus not so much as a realist virological event occurring outside human awareness, but are concerned with the human disease resulting from it. Nonetheless, for Badiou there is no event without some degree of human fidelity to it, and while this marks an important extension of the tradition he valuably terms "anti-philosophical," there will be a need to give the event a certain minimal autonomy from the subject even when the event in question — such as the current pandemic — requires human involvement.[625]

Let's begin with this second point, the minimal autonomy of events from the human subject. It is rarely noticed that human beings can have two different roles with respect to any event, and only sometimes play both roles simultaneously. In one sense, we are the *beholders* of events, as when Michael Fried speaks of an eighteenth-century French painting as deliberately fending off its beholder by depicting the figures in these

---

[623] Ray Brassier, *Nihil Unbound*, p. 114. For further discussion see Graham Harman, *Speculative Realism: An Introduction*, Chapter 1.

[624] Quentin Meillassoux, "Decision and Undecidability of the Event in *Being and Event* I and II," p. 27. For further discussion see Graham Harman, *Quentin Meillassoux: Philosophy in the Making*, pp. 121–122.

[625] For one example see Alain Badiou, *Lacan: Anti-Philosophy* 3.

paintings as intensely absorbed in whatever it is they are doing.[626] In another sense we can be the *ingredients* of an event without necessarily beholding it. To speak of Fried again, he is well aware that the anti-theatrical detachment of pictorial figures from their beholder is a "supreme fiction," given that there is no painting without someone to look at it, even if it only be artists themselves. A simpler way to make the point is to say that events can occur without anyone knowing it, contra Badiou's assertion that a faithful political subject must be well aware that what is happening marks a dramatic rupture of the situation. Now, I fully agree with Brassier and Meillassoux that recent continental philosophy has had too little to say about events lying entirely outside the sphere of givenness to human beings, and that Badiou remains largely confined to this anti-realist dogma. But even if we limit ourselves to considering events like COVID-19, which by definition *require* a human ingredient, it is still necessary to stress the gap between what an event is doing to humans and what they consciously ratify about it. For Badiou, those who experience an event without full fidelity to it are actually not experiencing that event at all; in a sense, there is not even an event without someone's loyalty to it. Here I will make the opposite claim: the more transparently an event seems to be understood, the less likely that it is really an event. A certain degree of bafflement generally falls on those who have just been brushed by an event. One thinks of Ernest Rutherford's shock at the deflection of particles from a previously unsuspected atomic nucleus, or even of Georg Cantor — one of Badiou's own heroes — with his "I see it, but I don't believe it" after his discovery of transfinite numbers. A genuine event in the human sphere must be characterized by a certain gap between human participation in it and human understanding of it. While the gap may not be permanent, is seven or eight years of struggle to understand an event too much to ask? With respect to COVID-19, while the new virus was quickly identified, we are still far from understanding the exact nature of this disease and the ways in which it will likely transform the recent civilization we knew through the end of 2019.

Let's turn in closing to the aforementioned weakness of Badiou's theory in dealing with events that fall short of radical upheaval. Manuel DeLanda is fond of opposing both the micro-reduction of society to its smallest actors and the macro-reduction of society to sweeping structural explanations, so as to focus instead on the meso-level of society, including such weighty if

---

[626] Michael Fried, *Absorption and Theatricality*. For a critical appreciation of Fried's theory of absorption and theatricality see Graham Harman, *Art and Objects*.

non-ultimate forces as sub-national institutions.[627] Consider such entities as the United States Federal Reserve Bank, Harvard University, or the Dutch East India Company (VOC for short); in fact, I have written an entire book on the VOC.[628] It is likely that COVID-19 itself will turn out to be one of these meso-institutions in human society, lingering as a serious seasonal illness, and thereby triggering phenomena that may have happened anyway, though less quickly and decisively. There may be a possible end to in-person university curricula, for instance, or perhaps to physical money due to the now obvious downside of its well-established filthiness. Trends of this sort will be too minimal to interest a self-proclaimed "militant" like Badiou; those impressed by the magnitude of such large but sub-revolutionary changes will look to the militant like mediocrities too easily impressed by moving the furniture around even as Capital continues to rot our souls and pillage our planet. Militants will look down on the meso-theorists with a certain degree of scorn, secure in their moral and intellectual superiority. But is this really because they are militants, too uncompromising to accept half-measures? Or is it not instead because they are philosophical *idealists*, overestimating the power of the human mind to make a clean sweep not only of the sum total of human history (this is the part that bothers conservatives), but also of the sum total of social objects to whose functions and interactions our intellects are never quite equal. The fact that COVID-19 will not cause political revolution does not make it just another mediocre happening that changes nothing. Instead, like all important events, it will probably shuffle the arrangements of six or eight key human institutions, while all the attention goes to the two or three it destroys and the three or four it creates. The philosophical problem with militants is not their militancy, but their idealism.

---

[627] Manuel DeLanda, *A New Philosophy of Society*.
[628] Graham Harman, *Immaterialism*.

CHAPTER 27

MALABOU'S POLITICAL CRITIQUE OF SPECULATIVE REALISM[629]

The French philosopher Catherine Malabou has been near the cutting edge of the continental tradition for several decades. Initially one of the most promising figures to emerge from the circle of Jacques Derrida, she quickly staked out her own intellectual terrain with books ranging from a powerful interpretation of Hegel to a novel account of "neuroplasticity" that treats the mind as neither a hard-wired mechanism nor a disembodied spirit untethered from all material constraint.[630] Malabou has also shown a willingness — rare among thinkers of her stature — to engage seriously with the efforts of younger authors, including those from outside the Francophone world. A fine example is her memorable collaboration with Adrian Johnston in *Self and Emotional Life*.[631] In 2014, she also engaged with the work of Quentin Meillassoux in a stimulating piece entitled "Can We Relinquish the Transcendental?"[632] More recently, Malabou has published an article in French entitled "Le vide politique du réalisme contemporain" ("The Political

---

[629] "Malabou's Political Critique of Speculative Realism" originally appeared in 2021 in the journal *Open Philosophy*.

[630] Catherine Malabou, *The Future of Hegel*; Catherine Malabou, *What Should We Do With Our Brain?*

[631] Adrian Johnston & Catherine Malabou, *Self and Emotional Life*.

[632] Catherine Malabou, "Can We Relinquish the Transcendental?"

Void of Contemporary Realism," hereafter "The Political Void").[633] This recent article is my topic, though I limit myself to considering the political friction it expresses with Speculative Realism. In one respect, Malabou is deeply alarmed by the political consequences of acknowledging a world-in-itself free of human subjects, and this divides her from Speculative Realism and its various models of a reality apart from us. Yet the disagreement itself is less important than what it illuminates: the fact that there are political consequences whenever an ontology takes one sort of relation to be more primary than others. Insofar as every philosophy highlights certain kinds of relations in the world while minimizing or outright forbidding others, every philosophy faces a landscape of pre-verbal political options. I can hardly put it better than the anonymous Reviewer #1 of the present article: "The form of the relation influences the contour of a political process."

By now it is generally known that Speculative Realism was launched in April 2007 at an event of the same name at Goldsmiths, University of London.[634] Organized and moderated by Alberto Toscano, the event featured four speakers appearing in alphabetical order: Ray Brassier, Iain Hamilton Grant, myself, and Quentin Meillassoux. In "The Political Void" Malabou briefly considers my ideas, then Brassier's, then Meillassoux's, confronting us with an anticipatory political challenge drawn in large part from the founder of structuralist Marxism, Louis Althusser.[635] Despite Grant's absence from Malabou's article, one is generally struck by her diligence in dealing with the Speculative Realists. With respect to my own work, Malabou zeroes in on two relatively obscure pieces that manage to encapsulate my philosophical position nicely: an article entitled "The Future of Continental Realism," and a book chapter called "The Four Most Typical Objections to OOO," with the latter abbreviation referring to Object-Oriented Ontology.[636] In Brassier's case Malabou goes even further afield, digging up his little-known doctoral thesis from the University of Warwick (*Alien Theory*) which she pairs with his more widely read article "Concepts and Objects."[637] Meillassoux is covered — less surprisingly — by way of *After Finitude*, which remains his major publication to date.[638]

---

[633] Catherine Malabou, "Le vide politique du réalisme contemporain." All English translations from this article are the author's own, and all page references in parentheses refer to it.

[634] Ray Brassier et al., "Speculative Realism."

[635] Louis Althusser, "Le courant souterrain du matérialisme de la rencontre."

[636] Graham Harman, "The Future of Continental Realism"; Graham Harman, "The Four Most Typical Objections to OOO." Both are contained in the present volume as well.

[637] Ray Brassier, *Alien Theory*; Ray Brassier, "Concepts and Objects."

[638] Quentin Meillassoux, *After Finitude*.

Malabou on Speculative Realism

In Malabou's account, the Speculative Realists — though she acknowledges the rapid collapse of the group as a collective project — are united by two shared principles. The first seems uncontroversial enough: their shared rejection of what Meillassoux calls "correlationism," the view that we can never know thought without the world or the world without thought, but only the primordial relation between the two. For Meillassoux this notion begins with David Hume and Immanuel Kant, but extends throughout most of the tradition that follows: whether in the dialectical philosophy of G.W.F. Hegel, the phenomenology of Edmund Husserl, or the *Sein-Dasein* correlate of Martin Heidegger.[639] If pre-Humean philosophy argued over who had the best model of substance, since Hume there has mostly been strife over who best conceives the structure of the thought-world correlate. For the Speculative Realists, correlationism is a lamentable development that ought to be opposed, and the respective thinkers of this current each pursues a different way of discussing the world as it is apart from thought. In a tradition as anti-realist in spirit as continental philosophy, this effort has provoked much resistance. Malabou expresses her own reservations as follows:

> But whereas the realist affirms that the real only exists in de-correlated form, the materialist asks: what becomes of this subject once it is revoked? Does it purely and simply disappear from the real? Or is it only sutured, to adopt a term from [the Lacanian] Jacques-Alain Miller? Foreclosed but still visible despite being cut off?[640] [486]

A clarification is already in order, given that my position on this point differs somewhat from those of Brassier and Meillassoux. As a rule, I have gladly enlisted in the fight against correlationism, and have been perfectly willing to adopt Meillassoux's term as more concise and memorable than

---

[639] Quentin Meillassoux, "Iteration, Reiteration, Repetition"; G.W.F. Hegel, *Phenomenology of Spirit*; Edmund Husserl, *Logcal Investigations*; Martin Heidegger, *Being and Time*.

[640] From here through the rest of the chapter, all page references in square brackets are to Malabou, "Le vide politique du réalisme contemporain." Malabou's mention of Jacques-Alain Miller concerns his 1966 article "La Suture." "*Mais là ou le réaliste affirme que le réel n'existe que décorrelée, le matérialiste demande : que devient le sujet une fois congédié ? Disparaît-il purement et simplement de la scène du réel ? Ou n'est-il, pour reprendre un terme de Jacques-Alain Miller, que « suturé » ? Forclos mais encore visible dans sa coupure ?*"

my own "philosophy of access."[641] Nonetheless, Niki Young has published a convincing article in an earlier volume of this journal, arguing powerfully that I should maintain a distinction between the two terms.[642] For whereas Meillassoux is concerned primarily with the epistemological issue of how to subtract the thinking subject to get at the mathematized primary qualities of things themselves, my own attack on human access is ontological in flavor.

The reason is that I am not especially bothered by finitude, that great demon with which Meillassoux wrestles, but rather with "onto-taxonomy": the typically modern view that there are basically two different kinds of realities: (1) human thought, and (2) everything else.[643] Young, again, has further developed the critique of onto-taxonomy in a separate article.[644] What makes this worth mentioning is that Malabou's critique that for Speculative Realism "the real only exists in de-correlated form" [486] is less to the point when it comes to my position than those of Brassier and Meillassoux.[645] For while Meillassoux actively seeks an "ancestral" or "diachronic" realm in which the subject is either not yet or no longer present, and Brassier is occupied with the nullity of human representation given the eventual extinction of our species, I retain the thought-world correlate as a hybrid entity, no less real than either thought or the world in isolation. This has perhaps been clearest in my critique of traditional aesthetic formalism in Kant's *Critique of Judgment* and the early work of the art historian Michael Fried, who resemble Meillassoux in their efforts to subtract the "theatrical" human from the scene.[646] Stated more simply, I am less interested in "de-correlating" reality by subtracting the subject than in showing that even obvious correlates — such as the human-artwork relation — are themselves indissoluble units that cannot be reduced to a mere correlation of their human and non-human parts. For example, an individual beholder's encounter with Picasso's *Les demoiselles d'Avignon* is itself an impenetrable real object, just like the beholder or the painting taken in isolation. This has led some critics to complain — wrongly, it turns out — that I never manage to escape correlationism in the first place.

---

[641] Graham Harman, "The Current State of Speculative Realism"; Graham Harman, *Speculative Realism: An Introduction.*

[642] Niki Young, "On Correlationism and the Philosophy of (Human) Access."

[643] Graham Harman, *Dante's Broken Hammer*; Graham Harman, "The Only Exit from Modern Philosophy."

[644] Niki Young, "Only Two Peas in a Pod."

[645] "*le réel n'existe que décorrelée.*"

[646] Graham Harman, *Art and Objects*; Immanuel Kant, *Critique of Judgment*; Michael Fried, "Art and Objecthood"; Michael Fried, *Absorption and Theatricality.*

That critique would only be relevant if we presuppose, with Meillassoux, that the root problem with correlation is its finitude. By contrast, I find fault with the correlate not for being finite, but for retaining as its sole principal ingredients a "thought" term and a "world" term. The point is not to eliminate finitude, but to show that not all relations consist of a thought-world pair, as Alfred North Whitehead did in the 1920s without having much of an effect.[647]

When it comes to Malabou's second generalization about Speculative Realism, the tables are turned, since here she ascribes a position to the group as a whole that is actually found in my work alone. Namely: "All of the 'new realists' insist for example — but what an example! — on the fact that realism is not a materialism."[648] [486] This gets an important point right that is missed by many of my readers: the fact that object-oriented thought has nothing to do with materialism at all.[649] That is to say, the objects of OOO belong to the basically Aristotelian tradition of "substantial forms" that extends through the medieval period up to and including the thought of G.W. Leibniz. In more recent centuries, "form" is usually treated as something coming from the side of the subject, while "matter" is associated with objects themselves. OOO refuses this tradition, treating objects (including those objects known as "subjects") as consisting of nothing but an endless regress of forms. With the notable exception of Levi Bryant, OOO generally treats matter as a useless and deceptive concept designed to allow for an impossible passage of forms from their material substrate into the mind in undistorted fashion: as when Meillassoux holds that mathematics can give us direct insight into the very structure of things.[650] Malabou is certainly right about OOO's hostility to matter, but wrong in her evident assumption that the other Speculative Realists share this hostility. Brassier remains deeply involved with a variant of scientific materialism, despite Malabou's intriguing reference to his dissertation's concept of a "materialism without matter." Grant, unmentioned in her article, can be read as a materialist in the rather different manner of F.W.J. Schelling and Gilles Deleuze.[651] And while Malabou is perfectly correct about Meillassoux's

---

[647] Alfred North Whitehead, *Process and Reality*.

[648] "*Tous les « réalistes nouveaux » insistent par example — mais quel example! — sur le fait que le réalisme n'est pas un materialisme.*"

[649] Graham Harman, "I Am Also of the Opinion that Materialism Must Be Destroyed"; Graham Harman, "Materialism Is Not the Solution"; Graham Harman, "Realism Without Materialism."

[650] Levi R. Bryant, *Onto-Cartography*.

[651] Iain Hamilton Grant, *Philosophies of Nature After Schelling*.

hostility to the usual sense of materialism, given its allegiance to mechanical necessity over the pure contingency he demands, he proudly regards himself as a speculative materialist even more than a speculative realist.[652] [489–491]

Thus, when Malabou proclaims herself to be a "post-realist materialist," this puts her more at odds with my position than those of the other three Speculative Realists, since I am the reverse: a "post-materialist realist." [486] Furthermore, her lament that Speculative Realism advocates "[a] brutal eclipse of the subject" [486] does not apply univocally to all the authors in this tradition.[653] For as already seen, OOO retains the human subject as an ingredient in many real objects, such as artworks and socio-political arrangements. Meillassoux upholds not only a rationalist model in which the subject is able to access reality directly, but also a quasi-Christian soteriology in which only the justice of the virtual God can surmount the grandeur of human thought.[654] And while Brassier openly regards humans as a measly and transient cosmic species, he at least takes humans to be a species uniquely able to conceptualize its doom through admirable scientific procedures. Finally, for Grant, although the subject is no longer anything special, it is still an intimate part of nature's grand drama of production, since thoughts are "products" no less than the creations of nature itself are products.

Materialism and Contingency

Having briefly summarized the views of the Speculative Realists, Malabou goes on to explain her own objections to realism and the nature of her type of materialism. She begins by summarizing Meillassoux's rejection of traditional materialism in the name of an absolute contingency of the laws of nature. [490–491] Her first complaint is that the old materialism is not really what Meillassoux thinks it is. At least since Marx, Malabou argues, "materialism has left the state of nature … it is no longer concerned solely with the movement of atoms or the problem of physical necessity, but also weaves both of these intimately together with political and social necessity."[655] [491] This leads her to lament in passing that "the question of economic laws is not raised by any of the 'realists,' as if they were unworthy of the interest shown to physical laws

---

[652] See Quentin Meillassoux, "Iteration, Reiteration, Repetition."

[653] "[un] éclipse brutale du sujet."

[654] Quentin Meillassoux, "Appendix: Excerpts from L'Inexistence divine."

[655] "le matérialisme est sorti de l'état de nature … il n'est plus seulement concerné par le mouvement des atomes ou le problème de la nécessité physique mais bien aussi, tenant les deux dans un tissage serré, par celui de la nécessité politique et sociale."

alone."[656] [491–492] This is reminiscent of Slavoj Žižek's complaint, against the opposite sort of threat, concerning "[t]he 'pure politics' of Alain Badiou, Jacques Rancière, and Étienne Balibar, more Jacobin than Marxist, [which] shares with its great opponent, Anglo-Saxon Cultural Studies and their focus on struggles for recognition, the degradation of the sphere of economy."[657] [55] The point is worth mentioning insofar as both Žižek and Malabou appeal to economic reality, then ultimate deny it any place to exist in their radical conceptions of politics as a kind of retroactive subjective positing of reality. For Žižek, economics is wielded as a reality principle against idealist neo-Jacobins who think politics plays out mostly on the side of the human will; for Malabou, economics is to be deployed as a human principle against the Speculative Realists' purported obsession with inanimate things. Yet both eventually betray economics through their joint turn to a subjective politics of the void. In Žižek this happens through his fondness for the subject's ability to retroactively posit its own conditions in radical freedom, rather than passing through a series of historical underpinnings: "every dialectical passage or reversal is a passage in which the new figure emerges *ex nihilo* and retroactively posits or creates its necessity."[658] Having effectively eliminated anything that might pre-exist the positings of a subject, Žižek no longer has much to differentiate him from the neo-Jacobin voluntarists in the political sphere: among other problems, no clear place remains for the economic reality on which he had insisted. As for Malabou, once she as well turns — we will see — to a radically potent political subject, economics can no longer be classed as a human force belonging on her side of the argument, but looks now like a recalcitrant force allied with the inanimate world that humans can never master. In other words, once one commits to a political subject that radically posits its decisions out of thin air, economics is left behind as a species of realism: after all, it would not be economics if we could arbitrarily decree our own economic environment rather than already finding ourselves in one.

In any case, if Malabou sees no room for economics in Speculative Realism, she is probably getting this sense mostly from Brassier and Meillassoux. For it is certainly true that for this pair of rationalists, the laws of nature are of interest primarily because they contain no human ingredient, since economic or historical laws could never have quite the same pristine status

---

[656] *"la question des lois de l'économie n'est évoquée par aucun des « réalistes », comme si n'étaient dignes d'intérêt que les seules lois physiques."*
[657] Slavoj Žižek, *The Parallax View*. See also Graham Harman, "Žižek's Parallax."
[658] Slavoj Žižek, *Less Than Nothing*, p. 231.

as those uncovered by physics. In a sense, both interpret the fight against correlationism too literally: as if economics were inherently "idealist" merely because it involves humans rather than inanimate things alone. Meillassoux thinks that realism shows its best face only twice: before humans existed, and after they are gone. For Brassier's part, he is famously contemptuous of the humanities and social sciences by contrast with the natural sciences. But my own position is more like Manuel DeLanda's, in which realism is attained not by getting rid of the humans in any situation, but by treating reality as an excess beyond human thought even in cases when humans are there on the scene.[659] For example, OOO has a realist conception of commodities without needing to contest Marx's argument that they are always socially produced: the point is that the reality of objects is never fully expressed in their commodity-form, just as electrons and quarks remain a real surplus deeper than any of their theoretical or experimental effects.[660]

But let's return to Malabou's point about nature and culture and see where it leads. Contemporary materialism, she holds, has already reconceived contingency in its own manner, one that — unlike Meillassoux's doctrine — does not limit itself to nature alone. Like Marx, with his dual awareness of the laws of nature and of society, the new sort of materialist contingency recognizes both of these two great spheres of reality. Malabou assigns the credit for this broader notion of contingency to Althusser, which in 1982 he termed a contingency of "encounter" (rencontre).[661] As Malabou puts it: "It is, in fact, this philosopheme of the encounter that enables, first, the articulation of nature and politics, and second, the emergence of a new question of the subject characterized as the remnant of this encounter."[662] [492] From Meillassoux's standpoint this would no doubt sound like just another "correlation" of the natural and the political, but let's play along and listen to Malabou for now.

As Malabou sees it, the great virtue of Althusser's strange new materialism is that it "begins with nothing" (commence par rien).[663] We could actually say that it has three noteworthy aspects in particular: (1) it has no traffic with anything that determines thought, including any supposed anteriority

---

[659] See the opening pages of Manuel DeLanda, A New Philosophy of Society.

[660] For a first object-oriented approach to Karl Marx, Capital see Graham Harman, "Object-Oriented Ontology and Commodity Fetishism."

[661] See Althusser, "Le courant souterrain du matérialisme de la rencontre."

[662] "C'est en effet ce philosophème de la rencontre qui permet premièrement l'articulation de la nature et de la politique, et deuxièmement l'émergence d'une nouvelle question du sujet compris comme résidu de la rencontre."

[663] Althusser, "Le courant souterrain du matérialisme de la rencontre," p. 561.

of sense as found in phenomenology; (2) it holds that things crystallize through their relations rather than beforehand; (3) it proclaims the absoluteness of contingency, not quite in Meillassoux's sense — since subjects are implicated here as well — but in the sense that all things take shape unpredictably and without teleological aim. The formation of a thing actualizes no prior possibility, but comes about for the first time through the encounter between distinct elements. In Malabou's words: "Althusser rejects the long dominant version of materialism according to which 'everything is accomplished in advance, the structure precedes its elements and reproduces them so as to reproduce the structure.'"[664] [493] How far we have come from the structuralist position of Althusser's prime!

There are two points worth noting here. The first is that this position closely resembles the one defended more than two decades later in *Meeting the Universe Halfway* by Karen Barad, who is less a correlationist than an outright idealist, despite her hedging use of the term "agential realism."[665] For Barad as for Althusser — and who would have guessed at such a pairing? — "nature" and "thought" do not pre-exist one another; instead, each of these terms bootstraps the other into existence. In Barad's case this is inspired by her deep admiration for the quantum-theoretical speculations of Niels Bohr, while Althusser cites no scientific referent in particular. The second point concerns Bryant's suspicion toward all humanized forms of materialism, of which Althusser's position is clearly one. As Bryant memorably puts it in *Onto-Cartography*: "materialism has become a *terme d'art* which has little to do with anything material. Materialism has come to mean simply that something is historical, socially constructed, involves cultural practices, and is contingent .... We wonder where the materialism in materialism is."[666] This raises a fairly obvious question: given that any materialism of the 1982 Althusser variety dispenses with nearly all of the properties traditionally ascribed to matter, including the attribute of pre-existing human thought, why call it materialism at all? Here I speculate that the word retains its appeal mostly due to the long critical and emancipatory legacy of "materialism" in Western history. But it is questionable whether this suffices to justify "materialism" as a name for

---

[664] "*Althusser rejette la version du matérialisme, longtemps prédominante, selon laquelle « tout et accompli d'avance, la structure précède ses éléments et les reproduit pour reproduire la structure ».*" The portion cited from Althusser is taken from his article "Le courant souterrain du matérialisme de la rencontre," p. 574.

[665] Karen Barad, *Meeting the Universe Halfway.*

[666] Levi R. Bryant, *Onto-Cartography*, p. 2.

a theory that recognizes nothing resembling what we usually think of as matter. This is why I prefer Malabou's franker statement of the doctrine: "Here, everything procedes from 'an ontological and political void.' A void which is precisely the place of politics."[667] [493]

Malabou's commitment to the void is clearly no jest, since it enables the entirety of her argument and motivates her preference in political allies. "The subject," she says, "is that which only appears when things begin to lack." [493][668] Although Malabou appreciates Brassier's sense of the proximity between reality and the void, she faults him for not deriving the subject itself from this same void. By recommending that we do so, she comes into close proximity with another great thinker of the Real as void, Jacques Lacan. As Malabou tells us:

> The "dis-universe," that is to say the abyssal disappearance of things produced by their very being, is what liberates subjectivity that speaks. The subject is the result (and not the premise) of a stalling of the world .... The subject of the correlation certainly thinks itself as a "before," an a priori, but this anteriority is only the shadow of this subject which always comes after, once the cliff of the real crumbles onto itself.[669] [493–494]

Such materialism no longer pretends to address a material outer world independent of the subject. Instead, it proceeds in the Lacanian mode: refashioning the real as a trauma, and remodeling objects into projections of desire.

Politics of the Void

If one were to accept this strange materialism without realism, what might be the political consequences? This question occupies the last three or four pages of Malabou's article, and the results are every bit as surprising as the ontology she proposes. For it turns out that Althusser rereads no

---

[667] "Ici, tout précède d' « une vide, ontologique et philosophique ». Un vide qui est précisément le lieu du politique."
[668] "Le sujet est ce qui ne peut apparaître que là où les choses viennent manquer."
[669] "Le « désunivers », c'est-à-dire la disparition abyssale des choses produite par leur être même, est ce qui libère la subjectivité parlante. Le sujet est le résultat (et non la prémisse) d'un décrochage du monde .... Le sujet de la corrélation se pense certes comme un « avant », un a priori, mais cette antériorité n'est que l'ombre de ce sujet qui vient toujours après, lorsque la falaise du réel s'est effondrée sur elle-même."

less a figure than Jean-Jacques Rousseau in terms of the void. Malabou reports that for Althusser's Rousseau, "the subject takes form ... only when things are lacking."[670] [494] Even the social contract, that pivotal concept of Rousseau's career, is said to emerge *ex nihilo* through the sheer resolve of the community. Althusser demonstrates that "the birth of politics coincides with the desertification of the earth, provoked by the finger of God: in other words by nothing, with neither origin nor reason, which opens the possibility of the symbolic — that is to say, of the concept, of thought. Even the concept of the universal can only emerge from the dis-universe."[671] [494] By apparent contrast with the Speculative Realists, Malabou asserts that "the real *is not only* the relation of things among themselves, of things in themselves, outside all subjective synthesis. The real *also* delivers, in withdrawing, this empty place where the subject takes form." [495; emph. added] I have added italics to this sentence to indicate those places where Malabou understates her position considerably. It is not just that she thinks the void where the subject arises is "also" there "along with" relations between things themselves. Quite the contrary: the void alone is there, and she seems to leave no place for things themselves at all. Obviously, this is a rather radical position on the status of the world, one that we have also encountered in the works of Žižek, another ally rightly cited by Malabou in her article. What bothers me about this notion of reality as posited by a subject in the void is not its departure from common sense, but its heavy debt to a Lacanian dismissal of autonomous entities that has never struck me as sufficiently motivated.[672] For while it is understandable that a psychoanalyst would wish to focus on things as they appear to the human subject, Lacan goes considerably beyond a psychoanalytic stance, upholding and inspiring "materialisms" that require the effective vaporization of any world beyond the subject. And as utterly daring as this may seem, it is too dependent both on Kant's assumption that all relations are thought-world relations, and on Hegel's collapse of thought and world alike into an immanent plane where nothing is inaccessible for long.

But let's ask more concretely what sort of politics might emerge from such a void. It should go without saying that in his 1982 article, "Althusser engages materialism in a direction that is no longer Marxist." [495] Indeed.

---

[670] "*le sujet ne prend forme, en effet, que là où les choses manquent.*"

[671] "*la naissance de la politique coïncidait avec la désertification de la terre, provoquée par le doigt de Dieu, autrement dit par rien, sans origine ni raison, qui ouvre la possibilité du symbolique : c'est-à-dire du sens, du concept, de la pensée. Aussi le concept d'universel ne peut-il émerger que du désunivers.*"

[672] See especially Jacques Lacan, *The Object Relation: The Seminar of Jacques Lacan, Book IV.*

What could Marx possibly do with a materialism where both nature and economics are generated *ex nihilo* through an "encounter" between two terms that did not even pre-exist their meeting? Here Malabou turns to another of the allies enlisted in her article, Jacques Rancière. In Rancière's own words, a community "is borne by no historic necessity, and bears none in turn."[673] This is what he calls a community on the edge of an "anarchic void." Malabou completes the thought on her own: "For my part, I call anarchist (and not simply anarchic) the contingent withdrawal of the real from which the subject emerges. Materialism becomes anarchist when it no longer has any more need of a 'prince,' that is to say of an arche, in order to think its originary contingence."[674] [496]

In closing, Malabou reflects on the possible political failings of her allies and opponents. Althusser's materialism is not enough, since he remains committed to the notion of a "prince," a dominant subject. [496] As for the Speculative Realists, she has this to say:

> Contemporary "realism" was not born at just any moment, and ought not to be satisfied with the political neutrality that it has systematically adopted to this day. It is important to note that it appeared at the same time as a planetary awareness manifested in increasingly visible fashion, by the awakening of collective initiative, autonomous experimentation, and the appearance of a new social coherence everywhere in the world. Realism is inscribed in the anarchist turn of contemporary materialism.[675] [497]

This could be read in several different ways, and it is not clear that any of them strike the mark. For in one sense, it is not really true that the Speculative Realists have remained politically neutral while obsessing over the things themselves as studied by science. In my 2010 interview with

---

[673] Malabou, "Le vide politique du réalisme contemporain," p. 495; "*n'est portée par aucune nécéssité historique et n'en porte aucune.*"

[674] "*Pour ma part, j'appelle anarchiste, et non simplement anarchique, le retrait contingent du réel d'où émerge le sujet. Le matérialisme devient anarchiste lorsqu'il* n'a plus besoin de « prince », c'est-à-dire d'archè, *pour penser sa contingence originaire.*"

[675] "*Le « réalisme » contemporain n'est pas né à n'importe quel moment et ne doit donc pas se satisfaire de la neutralité politique qu'il a systématiquement affichée jusqu'à ce jour. Il est important de voir qu'il est apparu en même temps qu'une prise de conscience planétaire qui se manifeste de façon de plus en plus visible par l'éveil de l'initiative collective, l'expérimentation autonome et l'apparition de nouvelles cohérences sociales partout dans le monde. Le réalisme s'inscrit dans le tournant anarchiste du matérialisme contemporain.*"

Meillassoux, for instance, he commented as follows: "I am very hostile to neo-liberalism, which has turned the contemporary world (and the work world in particular) into a nightmare of rare intensity, one with which the politics of [Nicolas] Sarkozy is utterly impregnated." He goes on to describe this type of capitalism as a "moral and intellectual madness, which the crisis of 2008 was apparently insufficient to bring down."[676] Brassier's political comments have been somewhat more sparse, arising mostly in the context of denouncing Bruno Latour as a "neo-liberal" while making faint calls in his own voice for "revolution."[677] One could perhaps lodge the complaint that Speculative Realists fiddle with pure ontology as the world burns around them, but Malabou herself is also more thinker than activist, and thus it is unlikely that this is her point.

What she does seem to mean is that Speculative Realism has a political problem in its effort to account for independent reality at all. The view developed in her article is that it is only in the anarchic void that the freedom of the human subject truly emerges. More than this, she implies that a great planetary awakening is underway, one characterized by spontaneous collective invention rather than any slavish limitation in the face of a non-existent "reality in itself." It is also noteworthy that she praises "the awakening of collective initiative, autonomous experimentation, and the appearance of a new social coherence," but says nothing about the most glaring political problem of our time: the ongoing collapse of the climate. As if to drive this point home, Malabou's final page offers further maxims in a human-centered spirit. For instance: "[t]here is no real without a subject," [497] a phrase that haunts her unconvincing efforts later on the page to seem even-handed.[678] For nowhere does Malabou say, equivalently, that there is no real without an object. And this is where OOO may pose a stronger challenge to Malabou's politics than do the other brands of Speculative Realism. In *Bruno Latour: Reassembling the Political*, I made the case that there are two and only two central problems with modern political theory, and both are still present at the heart of Malabou's stance.[679] The first is an obsession with what humans are like in the state of nature: with the Right of Machiavelli, Hobbes, and Schmitt convinced that humans are dangerous animals who ultimately respond only to force,

---

[676] Meillassoux, "Interview with Quentin Meillassoux (August 2010)," in Harman, *Quentin Meillassoux: Philosophy in the Making*, p. 173.

[677] Brassier, "Concepts and Objects," p. 53.

[678] "*Il n'y a pas de réel sans sujet.*"

[679] Graham Harman, *Bruno Latour: Reassembling the Political*.

and the Rousseau-Marx Left defending the opposite view that humans are naturally good but corrupted by society and its competitive systems.[680] We can escape this endless Right/Left deadlock simply by noting that human nature is partly beside the point: the political world is massively stabilized by non-human entities that encourage and restrict action and thought in different ways. When Latour accompanies the primatologist Shirley Strum in her observation of baboons, they make careful note of this role of inanimate objects.[681] In no way are these objects generated in "encounter" with a speaking subject. Although in some sense Malabou shares Latour's interest in the interface where humans meet non-humans, she seems to imagine that this encounter is generated as if *ex nihilo*, which hardly does justice to the material and political constraint posed by things. It seems far less plausible to treat today's political awakening — if indeed there is one — as a voluntaristic resolve in the face of the void, and more likely that such an awakening would be incited by the breakdown of an especially important non-human thing: the climate itself. What launched today's youthful "anti-extinction" movement was surely not a pure inner, subjective drama. Instead, it was the realization that the subject is now threatened by some very non-subjective things: carbon dioxide, methane, micro-plastics. To respond to the revenge of Gaia by calling for anarchic liberation of the subject from pre-existent reality seems like a dubious strategy. Lacan was a thinker of many gifts, but he is one of the last people I would phone for advice on global warming, and the same holds for Althusser.

The second political lesson to be drawn from Latour follows closely from the first. That is to say, modern political theory likes to imagine there is something called political knowledge: whether it be knowledge of human nature, or of the best way to organize societies if only people were not so stupid (the Right) or not so greedy (the Left). One of the little-noticed strengths of Latour's position is his awareness that the political truth never really becomes visible. What we have in its place is experimentation leading to brief consensus and provisional ostracism of those forces with which we currently cannot co-exist.[682] This need for a makeshift assembly of political solutions would make little sense if the only political actor were a human subject hovering in a void. It is — or

---

[680] Graham Harman, "Realism Without Hobbes and Schmitt."
[681] S.S. Strum & Bruno Latour, "Redefining the Social Link."
[682] Bruno Latour, *Politics of Nature*.

MALABOU'S POLITICAL CRITIQUE OF SPECULATIVE REALISM

should be — a commonplace that political life is defined largely by constraints: economic, geographical, demographic, and historical. While a case can certainly be made for not accepting our current interpretation of these factors as ironclad destiny, it seems a strange position to hold that nothing holds us back but our own failures of imagination.

Two Points in Conclusion

Before leaving the reader in peace, I would like to add one final remark about Malabou, and another about the current predicament of radical political theories more generally. We have seen that Malabou seems rather warm to the notion of a pure politics of the subject, one compatible with certain ideas of Lacan, Rancière, the 1982 Althusser, and the 2012 Žižek (as partly opposed to the 2005 version). Whatever constraints the political subject might face in principle, they count for little by contrast with the *ex nihilo* positings of anarchic heroes. What makes this so strange, coming from Malabou, is that it was she who did so much to free us from the dualism in philosophy of mind between rigid physical determinism on one side and a de-physicalized *cogito* on the other. With her notion of plasticity, Malabou put forth a more sophisticated model in which the brain can be shaped decisively by training, but only within limits. Unlike most continental thinkers, in their vague background disdain for the sciences, Malabou was willing to take brain injuries seriously, and to speak of the lasting effects of emotional trauma on the human psyche. Here was a theoretical space where significant interaction between brains and cultures was not just made possible, but was required by the very terms of her theory. Why, then, does Malabou not offer us a comparable theory of political plasticity? This would be a theory in which economic, geographical, demographic, and historical constraints were not easily outstripped by anarchic dreams, but one in which such constraints might be molded or reformed within certain limits while still respecting their force and legitimacy. But that would require a willingness to push back on the default political stance of continental theory at the moment, which takes pretty much any event as grounds for the utterly orgasmic overthrow of all that has existed heretofore. Humans do not exist in a void, insofar as humans are not "subjects" in the neo-Jacobin sense, but just unusually complex and fascinating objects that exist in a political space with other such objects. This is why Latour's attempt to model politics after ecology seems like a better start than the claim that subjects make "anarchic" (and why not "monarchic"?) decrees in the midst of a cosmic vacuum.[683]

This brings us back to what is actually the central issue brushed against by this article: the consequences of deciding which kinds of relations are politically primary. It is perfectly clear that for Malabou, the only relation worth asking about politically is the one where subject meets world. This is true not only of Malabou and of the recent allies she enlists, but of modern political theory as a whole. There is a defined human political sphere, and outside the walls there lies nature, the enemy, or Death, master us of all. Earlier I mentioned the "onto-taxonomical" character of modern philosophy, referring to its assumption that there are two and only two basic kinds of entities: (1) the human subject, and (2) everything else. The political theory offered by Malabou in "The Political Void" is clearly onto-taxonomical in this way. All that matters is settling the relative strength of the human side and the non-human side — to say that "the subject is not the same as the human" would merely muddy the waters — and categorizing the various ways in which they meet. We might also decide whether the subject is good or evil by nature and calibrate our actions accordingly, which is precisely what the Right and Left have been doing for centuries. The problem with making all politics orbit a single human/non-human relation is that it grants the subject a full fifty percent of every situation. Co-owners of every relation in the cosmos, we humans feel free to dissolve whatever we find, since we own half of everything in sight — and perhaps own everything, if we really are floating in a void and positing all the rest *ex nihilo*, or determining it as the retroactive effect of a "count."[684]

The reason the future of politics is ecological, rather than revolutionary or anarchic, is that the point where human meets world is not the only point where politics appears, or even the primary one. Nor do we find such a primary point at the site where humans meet capital. Consider the dependence of humans on the relations between swamps and methane, sulfur dioxide and ozone, or bees, herbicides, and cellular telephone towers. Here we are not always the masters; still less are we princes. It took a great deal of nerve for the 1982 Althusser to assert that he was dethroning all princes at the very moment of making the subject the prince of all politics.

[683] Bruno Latour, *Facing Gaia*.
[684] Badiou, *Being and Event*.

CHAPTER 28

OBJECT-ORIENTED ONTOLOGY AND COMMODITY FETISHISM[685]

Object-oriented ontology (abbreviated OOO, and pronounced "Triple O") has become the most interdisciplinary of the four different strains of Speculative Realist philosophy, with an especially large following in architecture and the arts.[686] By and large, OOO has not been greeted as warmly on the political Left as elsewhere.[687] To some extent this cold reception is inevitable, since OOO — at least in my version of the theory — is suspicious of the established Left's claim to the continuing status of an intellectual and moral vanguard for our time. Now, there is certainly no reason to abandon the Left's general commitment to equality, education, access to medicine, as well as the redress of structural economic grievance, a general opposition to racism and misogyny, and its spirit of horror at the re-emergence of slavery, white nationalism, the massacre of tribes by miners, and other nightmares we hoped had been left far behind. While the cautious streak of the conservative may sometimes provide a useful check on our confidence in the ability to set everything right, conservatism habitually

---

[685] "Object-Oriented Ontology and Commodity Fetishism" originally appeared in 2017 in the Polish journal *Eidos*.

[686] Graham Harman, *Object-Oriented Ontology*; Ray Brassier et al., "Speculative Realism."

[687] Technically, OOO refers loosely to four separate position, including those of Ian Bogost, Levi R. Bryant, and Timothy Morton along with my own, though Bryant has distanced himself somewhat from the term. In this article, I speak only for myself.

understates the heavy component of *history* that flows through human veins. As for political liberalism, though it strikes me as the most prudent course available, it is admittedly built on the edge of a crater where justice is too quickly sacrificed to Hobbesian order, and where the economic freedom of the liberal is too often enabled by the exploitation of the foreigner.

Given that I refuse to ignore the list of monsters in liberalism's closet, then why not just wave the flag of the Left? The heart of the problem, as I see it, is that the modern Left arose during the heyday of philosophical idealism, and shares the two primary vices of that stage of philosophy: (1) its mistaken claim to a non-existent *knowledge* of reality, in this case political reality; (2) its relative failure to account for the political role of *non-human entities*. A third issue, one less directly connected to idealist philosophy, is the frequent failure of the Left to note the difference between politics and morality: not morality in general, but *egalitarian* morality specifically, as if injustice and exploitation were the sole political problems. There is also a fourth and more local issue, which is that in my own personal and professional milieu, endorsing Leftist slogans in print or in person brings such immediate social rewards that we ought to distrust it for that reason alone. I am not suggesting that we join the ranks of the contrarians: an annoying species who simply find a different social reward in the false superiority of one-upmanship. What I am suggesting is that we not forget to push back — as Francis Bacon insisted with his four types of idols — against the inherent exaggeration of any idea that is taken to be obviously true in the circles where each of us travels.[688] In present-day continental philosophy circles, at least, the supposedly inevitable political truth is not the widely detested "neo-liberalism," but some form of Leftism. The topic is a large one, but I will limit myself here to a single task: responding to the accusations that OOO indulges in a form of "commodity fetishism", as described by Marx in the opening chapter of *Capital*.

Commodity Fetishism

OOO promotes a return of philosophy to individual things, not just apart from their relations to human beings, but apart from their relations *to each other* as well. This has aroused some criticism from those who regard OOO-inspired thingism as a degeneration into the historical period preceding

---

[688] Francis Bacon, *The New Organon*.

the heavily relational ontologies of Hegel and Marx. The politest and most coherent case of this critique I have found was penned by Wesley Phillips:

> Schelling and Hegel did away with the distinction between subjective activity on the one side and objective passivity on the other a long time ago. The recent return to "thinghood" emerged with Harman's account of "equipment." Harman thus reproduced Heidegger's (neo-Kantian) blindness to the alternative, more radical attack upon thingism presented in German idealism and, subsequently, in historical materialism. In fact, speculative realism remains closer to "mainstream" continental philosophy than it would like to think. Without any historical materialism, Harman's "universal theory of entities" falls back into a thing-ism of its own: the theoretical pluralisation of entities now precedes their practical pluralisation (for Marx, "congealed labour"). Why, then, the return to things themselves? Is it an unwittingly masochistic fetishisation of commodity fetishism ...?[689]

This brief passage is rich in accusations, even in the sphere of personal psychology ("unwitting masochism"). But the heart of the matter is Phillips's dual claim that OOO suffers from the "neo-Kantian" blindness to the great step forward in philosophy made by Schelling and Hegel, and a "fetishistic" blindness to Marx's discovery that things are actually congealed labor. A pair of blindnesses, then, not just one.

Since the focus of the present article is closer to Marx than to German Idealism, I can only address the "neo-Kantian" point quickly. The central idea of Kantian philosophy is also its least popular element today: the thing-in-itself existing beyond all human access, which can be thought but not known. We cannot know the noumena, but only the phenomena.[690] German Idealism's manner of dealing with Kant is to eliminate the thing-in-itself as a fruitless residue of pre-Kantian dogmatic philosophy. Pedantic objections may be made about the need to distinguish between Fichte, Schelling and Hegel, but there is no need to incorporate such differences here, since OOO fully upholds Kant's basic conception of the thing-in-itself, while no German Idealist does so. From their point of view,

---

[689] Wesley Phillips, "The Future of Speculation?" p. 298.
[690] Immanuel Kant, *Critique of Pure Reason.* For a more accessible account of his thought, see Immanuel Kant, *Prolegomena to Any Future Metaphysics.*

to think something outside thought is already to think it, and therefore the noumena are inherently contradictory; to know a limit requires that we also know what is beyond that limit; we cannot claim that the noumena "cause" the phenomena, since the concept of cause is applicable only to phenomena; and so forth. By discounting the noumenal status of the noumena and transforming them into a special case of the phenomena, we supposedly reach a more radical position than Kant himself — not to mention more radical than Heidegger, who is then treated as a mere *neo-* in comparison with Kant.

Unfortunately, I cannot join Phillips in assessing his own position as "more radical" than OOO, since he merely repeats well-known arguments from the eighteenth and nineteenth centuries, and even seems unaware of the primary difference between OOO and Kant: our claim that objects are noumenal not just for us, but for each other as well. Any critique of OOO that fails to mention this difference has not just missed the target, but has failed to see the target at all. Even as Phillips and his comrades-in-argument claim to overcome Kant's inbuilt limitation when it comes to the thing-in-itself, they nonetheless adopt the more deeply rooted error of Kantian philosophy: the assumption that we cannot speak of any relation that does not include humans as one of its elements. We cannot talk about thunder-in-itself, but only about how thunder manifests to humans under the conditions of space, time, and the twelve categories of understanding, or whatever we take to be the post-Kantian equivalent of these. We cannot think of how fire-in-itself affects cotton-in-itself, but only about how this relation might be mathematized according to the principles made accessible by the conditions of human understanding. We cannot speak of rice in its own right, but only of rice as a place where *human* labor is consolidated. Once we realize that OOO's chief virtue consists in its avoidance of this anthropocentric treadmill, we immediately have new tools at our disposal for examining what is living and dead in Schelling, Hegel, Marx, and other heroes of the anti-object club (recall that by "object," we mean noumena that are noumenal for each other too, and not just for us). For while it is true that organic chemicals must contain carbon, and true that such chemicals are of great importance, no one would dream of saying that *all* chemicals must be organic. And likewise, though human beings may prove to be necessary ingredients of politics, art, and love, we would never say that *all* relations must involve a human being as one of its terms. To give just one example, the unseen collision of two comets in the distant Oort Cloud is clearly not a case of "congealed human labor," and we will therefore realize that it is hard to see how the Marxist theory of commodities can say anything against philosophical realism.

Marx's thoughts on commodity fetishism are not difficult to find, since *Capital* opens on this very topic. Chapter 1, entitled "The Commodity," gives us a roughly forty-page analysis of the several different kinds of value before concluding on the fetishist theme. Since Marx holds that commodities — defined as useful goods subjected to exchange — are "congealed quantities of homogeneous [human] labor," [135–136] they are inherently social products whose value arises from social relations rather than existing prior to those relations. The "fetishist" misses this point, and mistakenly believes that commodities gain their value directly from nature. Two representative quotes will serve to solidify the point. Here is the first: "the commodity reflects the social characteristics of men's own labour as objective characteristics of the products of labour themselves, as the socio-natural properties of things …. In the same way, the impression made by a thing on the optic nerve is perceived not as a subjective excitation of that nerve but as the objective form of a thing outside the eye." [164–165] This is how Marx defines fetishism, and like all forms of anthropomorphism, it is said to transfer what belongs to the human side of the equation onto things, in this case resulting in the false naturalization of value. Marx's famously barbed wit makes him capable of stating the point in even harsher terms, which he soon proceeds to do:

> It is nothing but the definite social relations between men themselves
> which assumes [in commodity fetishism] the form of a relation
> between things. In order, therefore, to find any analogy we must take
> flight into the misty realms of religion. There the products of the
> human brain appear as autonomous figures endowed with a life of
> their own, which enter into relations both with each other and with
> the human race. [165]

From here it seems a brief step for the anti-fetishists to dismiss OOO, which would appear to enter "the misty realms of religion" when it speaks of objects themselves outside of any relation.

The fatal flaw in this view should be obvious: for Marx's theory of commodity fetishism is a theory of *value*, not of *reality*. Even if we accept the Marxist claim that the value of cotton must be deciphered through a social analysis of the labor that made it an item of exchange, it does not follow that cotton only *exists* in the social context of labor. There are numerous passages which make it clear that Marx by no means intends an anti-realist ontology of this sort — the sort that we find in a radical idealist (even if self-styled "materialist") thinker such as Karen Barad.[691] The Anti-Fetishist case against OOO entails the bizarre implication not only that commodities are congealed human labor — as Marx himself held — but that *everything* is, and that therefore *everything* is congealed human labor. Yet this is clearly not what Marx means, as we learn in a series of passages near the beginning of the chapter. For instance: "A thing can be a use-value without being a value. This is the case, whenever its utility to man is not mediated through labour. Air, virgin soil, natural meadows, unplanted forests, etc. fall into this category." [131] *A fortiori*, we could say that things *without* use-value do not have the socially congealed value of commodities, such as exotic planets far beyond the limits of humanity's ability to travel.

Yet for Marx, the realm of non-commodities goes even further than this. It also includes the goods we produce for private sustenance: "A thing can be useful, and a product of human labour, without being a commodity. He who satisfies his own need with the product of his own labour admittedly creates use-values, but not commodities. In order to produce the latter, he must not only produce use-values, but use-values for others, social use-values." [131] Friedrich Engels adds in a note to his friend's *magnum opus* that even goods produced for others do not automatically count as commodities: "The medieval peasant produced a corn-rent for the feudal lord and a corn-tithe for the priest; but neither the corn-rent nor the corn-tithe became commodities simply by being produced for others," [131] since in these cases there was no question of exchange. Marx himself adds for good measure that "labour is socially divided in the primitive Indian community, although the products do not thereby become commodities. Or, to take an example nearer home, labour is systematically divided in every factory, but the workers do not bring about this division by exchanging their individual products." [132] Thus we see that, far from being a universal ontological category, "congealed human labor" for Marx does not even describe the totality of conditions found on a factory floor. Let this suffice to show that OOO's discussion of objects outside all relations in no way contravenes the Marxist principle that commodities have no *value* outside the social relations through which they were produced. Since there are no OOO writings on economic value as of 2017, it can safely be called intellectually neutral on this question.

---

[691] Karen Barad, *Meeting the Universe Halfway*.

But the anti-fetishist will not give up so easily, and may now try a modified, "weak" version of its criticism of OOO. For even if Marx concedes that many things exist in their own right without being commodities, he nonetheless detects the commodity at work in most of *human* existence. Thus, we can imagine the anti-fetishist speaking as follows: "OOO may have a point about the independent existence of planets, rocks, unknown species of fish, primitive barter economies, and so forth. We concede the existence of these things beyond the scope of congealed human labor. But insofar as OOO aspires to be not just an ontology of inanimate things, but also of human society, it seems ill-equipped to discuss social entities that do not 'withdraw' from relations with humans, and which are even *constituted* by these very relations. What sense would it make to speak, in OOO fashion, of a non-relational economy, a non-relational money, or non-relational textile mills?" There are two separate problems with this new anti-fetishist argument against OOO. The first is its philosophical clumsiness, and the second is the fact that Marx himself would disagree yet again.

The philosophical clumsiness consists in conflating two different sorts of relation or non-relation that humans can have with things. In the first sense, humans can be or fail to be *ingredients* of things. And here there is an obvious difference between something human-made like coats, and something non-human-made like unused minerals on a distant planet. When it comes to coats, OOO agrees with Marx — and even the anti-fetishists who criticize us — on the point that human social production created not only the value of these coats, but their very existence. Without human labor, there would be no coats in the world; we are happy to concede this rather commonsensical point. Human beings are *ingredients* in the production of coats in a way that we are not ingredients in the production of stones on distant planets where no human has ever trod.

Yet when considered in a second sense, one that is far more important for OOO, the coat and the alien minerals have precisely the same status. For no matter how they were produced, whether with or without human labor, both the coat and the minerals are now independent realities in the world that cannot be reduced to the human understanding of them, or even to the mere human use of them. Manuel DeLanda makes this point lucidly in the first pages of his book *A New Philosophy of Society*, when fending off charges that his wish to understand society apart from humans is meaningless insofar as humans are obviously a necessary ingredient of society. DeLanda's response, a model for all such cases, is that even though humans are a necessary precondition for human society, it does not follow that such society is reducible to what we know about it or to how we make use of society pre-theoretically. In short, it is perfectly plausible for OOO to speak about a non-relational economy, non-relational money, and non-relational textile mills. We do not dispute the obvious point that each of these things was constituted by relations, since the same is true even of gold (composed of atoms) and mountain ranges (composed of mountains). We simply note that just because every object has a relational backstory that tells us how it came to exist, it does not follow that this now-existent object is nothing more than its current relations with its neighboring entities.

And here once again, perhaps surprisingly to some, Marx turns out to agree with OOO. For if commodities were determined purely by their relations, then they would be equivalent to their *price*: though this is the view not of Marx, but of the "bourgeois" economists he habitually derides. When it comes to matters of value, Marx is more of a realist than these bourgeoisie, since he contends that the value of a commodity is not determined through the contingencies of the marketplace, but by how much abstract human labor is congealed in a particular object. As Marx puts it, in his typical scathing tone:

> Our analysis has shown that the form of value, that is, the
> expression of the value of a commodity, arises from the nature of
> the commodity-value, *as opposed to value and its magnitude arising*
> *from their mode of expression as exchange-value.* This second view is
> the delusion both of the Mercantilists ... and their antipodes, the
> modern bagmen of free trade .... For [the free traders] ... there
> exists neither value, nor magnitude of value, anywhere except in its
> expression by means of the exchange relation, that is, in the daily list
> of prices on the Stock Exchange. [152–153; emph. added]

And even more simply, "the properties of a thing do not arise from its relations to other things, they are, on the contrary, merely activated by such relations," [149] which sounds like something taken straight from a OOO manifesto rather than from Marx. From all this it should be clear that Marx's analysis of the commodity form, and of the fetishism that misses the social component of commodities, does not conflict with OOO's insistence on the non-relational reality of objects. Since this was the main intended argument of this article, we now conclude with two closely related side-issues.

Fetishism and Formalism

It is interesting to ask about the relation between Marx's critique of "fetishism" and Kant's embrace of "formalism," the source of the latter's greatest strengths and weaknesses alike.[692] It comes down to a question of whether we recognize the possibility of compound objects made up of both human and non-human elements, which Bruno Latour has helpfully termed "hybrids." For example, the ozone hole over Antarctica is to some degree the unfortunate byproduct of human labor, but is also a part of environing nature.[693] Does Marx recognize the existence of such hybrids? A case could be made either way. In one respect, we have just heard Marx say that "the properties of a thing do not arise from its relations to other things, they are, on the contrary, merely activated by such relations." But in another respect, the commodity qua commodity abstracts from all of its properties as a concrete thing, and is considered *purely* in terms of the quantity of socially necessary labor that was needed to produce it.

As for Kant, it is obvious that he *cannot* recognize hybrids, given that the whole of his philosophy proceeds according to a rigid taxonomical split between just two kinds of entities: (a) rational beings, a.k.a. humans, and (b) everything else. In his ethical theory, for example, Kant's chief negative motivation is to avoid any ethics that seeks to obtain rewards and escape punishments in this life and the next, or any ethics whose purpose is to let me sleep with a clean conscience at night, or to gain a reputation for upstanding behavior in my community. Ethical acts must be performed for their own sake, out of duty to the categorical imperative. Though Kant obviously makes no use of a Marxist terminology that did not exist during his lifetime, we could imagine Kant critiquing the "fetishism" of those who want to place ethical value in the things rather than in a purely human action regardless of consequences. This opens up Kant to the famous critique of Max Scheler, who admires Kant's rejection of all ethical theories revolving around reward and punishment, and effectively takes the basic unit of ethics not to be I myself as a duty-bound rational creature, but rather the compound entity formed of I myself as a being who loves and the objects of my love.[694] While no Scheler has emerged so far to make a similar

---

[692] For a more detailed analysis of formalism see Graham Harman, *Dante's Broken Hammer*.

[693] Bruno Latour, *We Have Never Been Modern*.

[694] Max Scheler, *Formalism in Ethics and Non-Formal Ethics of Values*; Max Scheler, "Ordo Amoris."

critique of Kant's theory of art, the same issue is found here as well.[695] Kant's admirable goal is to grasp the autonomy of art from any personal preference or merely agreeable sensations in the contemplation of art, and to secure the objectivity of taste against the rampant horde of individual opinions. Yet in doing so he locates both the beautiful and the sublime entirely within the human sphere: not in the artwork, but simply in the transcendental faculty of judgment that all humans share. When some of his followers reverse this relation and find all the aesthetic action on the side of the artwork rather than the human mind, they merely join Kant in ignoring the possibility that the basic aesthetic unit is a hybrid object made up of both human and work.[696] Formalism assumes that the human and the non-human must never be mixed in one and the same object; whether Marx's critique of fetishism assumes the same, or opposes it directly, remains for now an open question.

Marx and Heidegger

Finally, it is worth attempting a brief sketch of the relation between Marx and Martin Heidegger, given that the latter is a key influence on OOO. Though the two are clear political opposites (the original Marxist paired with a Nazi) it is interesting that they begin their respective major works with what sound like strikingly similar themes. Marx begins *Capital* with a discussion of the difference between what he calls use-value and exchange-value: "The usefulness of a thing makes it a use-value …. Use-values are only realized in use or in consumption. They constitute the material content of wealth, whatever its social form may be …. [By contrast,] exchange-value appears first of all as the quantitative relation, the proportion, in which use-values of one kind exchange for use-values of another kind." [126] Heidegger gives us, near the beginning of *Being and Time*, a famous distinction between readiness-to-hand (*Zuhandenheit*) and presence-at-hand (*Vorhandenheit*). The former obviously sounds a lot like "use-value," and presence-at-hand — which encompasses such diverse forms as perception, scientific theorization, broken equipment, interpretation, and the mere occupation of a spatio-temporal position — shares with Marx's exchange-value the reference to

---

[695] Immanuel Kant, *Critique of Judgment*. [Eventually, I grew convinced that Michael Fried does provide such a critique of Kant's theory of art, despite his considerable reluctance in doing so — G.H.]

[696] Clement Greenberg, *Homemade Esthetics*; Michael Fried, *Art and Objecthood*.

"quantity." Yet there is actually not an easy overlap between these two pairs of terms, and it is worth noting their points of difference here.

The first evident difference is that Marx apparently *starts* from individuals (various use-values) and *ends up* with a vast social system (the exchangeability of all commodities through money), while Heidegger apparently *starts* from a vast system of equipment (all ready-to-hand entities refer to each other) and *ends up* with a number of isolated present-at-hand entities (individuals broken off from the giant tool-system). But as I have often argued in print, this interpretation of Heidegger — which also appears to be his own self-interpretation — does not work.[697] For even though Heidegger wants to claim that ready-to-hand entities are all dissolved into a holistic tool-system while present-at-hand beings are merely derivative individuals, the opposite would be closer to the truth. When it comes to present-at-hand entities, such as images in my mind or utensils on a table, it should be clear that such entities are *utterly relational*: after all, to be present-at-hand is always to be present *to something*, whether to me or to anything else. As for the tool-beings silently and invisibly at work in the total system of equipment, it is too often forgotten that for Heidegger tools *break*. And there would be no possibility of anything breaking if it were really as sleekly assigned to the holistic tool-system as Heidegger claims. Rather, the function of an object in the tool-system is already an abstraction. If the roof of a factory collapses, or a fuel truck explodes, this proves the very opposite of holism: it proves, namely, that these objects had a dangerous reality that was ignored for as long as these objects functioned innocuously in a co-operative system. Yet even if we conclude, against Heidegger's own wishes, that present-at-hand entities are inherently relational, they are still not relational in the sense of Marx's exchange-value. The latter requires *social* exchange: we cannot trade with ourselves, nor even with others who have produced the same thing we ourselves have, since two corn-farmers would probably never meet to trade corn. As a result, the Marxist concept of exchange-value has profound social implications that are nowhere to be seen in Heideggerian *Vorhandenheit*, which can be found even in the most solitary cases of idle daydreamers and Robinson Crusoes.

A final point to be noted is that Heidegger remains Kantian in a way that Marx simply does not — though unlike many others, including Wesley Phillips, I think this works to Heidegger's advantage. In the notion of an object withdrawing from any relational access, it is hard not to hear the

---

[697] Graham Harman, *Tool-Being*.

overtones of Kant's *Ding an sich*, the thing-in-itself that can be thought but never known. The following passage, taken from late in Heidegger's famous book on Kant, is too often ignored:

> What is the significance of the struggle initiated in German Idealism against the "thing in itself" except a growing forgetfulness of what Kant had won, namely, the knowledge that the intrinsic possibility and necessity of metaphysics … are, at bottom, sustained and maintained by the original development and searching study of the problem of finitude?[698]

As for Marx, though he concedes more independent existence to virgin waters and forests than we find in the rather non-object-oriented Hegel, there is never the sense of a mysterious residue in things that lies beyond all approachability by human thought. If something is not a commodity, one gets the sense that Marx would qualify that statement by saying: not *yet* a commodity. Nonetheless, one simply cannot claim — in the manner of a number of critics of OOO — that Marx's theory of commodity fetishism requires a philosophical anti-realism in which nothing has any reality apart from human contact with it.

---

[698] Martin Heidegger, *Kant and the Problem of Metaphysics*, pp. 252–253.

PART VI

EPISTEMOLOGY, MIND, AND SCIENCE

CHAPTER 29

I AM ALSO OF THE OPINION THAT MATERIALISM MUST BE DESTROYED[699]

1. Introduction

This article refers to two kinds of materialism that have grown increasingly popular in recent philosophy. One kind is usually motivated by scientific realism; the other, somewhat paradoxically, often draws on German Idealist currents. In what follows I will describe in detail a lucid example of the first kind of materialism (that of James Ladyman and Don Ross) and speak briefly about its deep similarity with the apparently opposite kind. I will then urge that both be rejected, and propose an alternative. These two senses of "materialism" might seem different from a positive use of the word that may be more familiar to readers of this journal. In this positive sense of the term, materialism refers to a standpoint that breaks down the tired dualism of subject and object, allowing these two poles to interpenetrate and mutually constitute one another. Michel Foucault (see especially his *Discipline and Punish*) is usually regarded as one of the heroes of this brand of materialism.[700] Yet Foucault is not among my own intellectual heroes, precisely because "human subject" and "world" remain the two dominant poles of his universe, even if they are now glued together rather than left

---

[699] "I Am Also of the Opinion That Materialism Must Be Destroyed" originally appeared in 2010 in the journal *Environment and Planning D: Society and Space*. But it was originally given as a lecture at a conference at the University of Dundee, Scotland on March 27, 2010.

[700] Michel Foucault, *Discipline and Punish*.

in lonely Cartesian solitude. A truly multipolar cosmos requires that the human being be treated as just one kind of entity among trillions of others, not as a full half of a dual monarchy: a mere Habsburg Metaphysics.

In 1999 I coined the whimsical phrase "object-oriented philosophy" to describe my own multipolar model of the world; the phrase caught on and I am now happily married to it.[701] Object-oriented philosophy is based on two central ideas. First, there is the aforementioned principle that all relations are on equal footing. While philosophy since Immanuel Kant's 1781 masterwork *Critique of Pure Reason* has been obsessed with the single gap between human and world, whether to assert, dissolve, or finesse that gap, Alfred North Whitehead in the 1920s invited us into a non-Kantian world where the relation between prisons and human subjects is of no higher status than that between the various bricks in a prison, or between prison rats and the cosmic rays annihilating protons in their brains.[702] The human-world relation is of obvious interest to humans, but it cannot serve as the foundation for philosophy. But second, we must avoid Whitehead's tendency to *reduce* the entities of the world to their interrelations. While this may feel like a breath of fresh air in comparison with the rigid old theories of substance, it makes a bad fit with reality. For it fails both in explaining how change could ever occur, and also in accounting for counterfactual cases such as the arrival of other relations.[703] Whitehead's vision of all entities on equal footing must therefore be supplemented with Heidegger's insight into the withdrawal of entities from their relations, and indeed from any sort of presence at all.[704] The world is filled with a vast array of objects receding from mutual contact into strange private vacuums, but somehow making contact through indirect or vicarious means.[705] This is the vision of object-oriented philosophy, which has already had an effect throughout the arts and humanities, and was officially launched as the "Object-Oriented Ontology" movement (OOO) in Atlanta in April 2010.[706]

Now, much of the present article consists of a critical overview of the Ladyman and Ross book *Every Thing Must Go*, a remorseless work of analytic scientism that might seem far removed from my own philosophical

---

[701] See Graham Harman, *Towards Speculative Realism*, pp. 93–104.
[702] Immanuel Kant, *Critique of Pure Reason*; Alfred North Whitehead, *Process and Reality*.
[703] Graham Harman, *Prince of Networks*, pp. 130–132.
[704] Graham Harman, *Tool-Being*.
[705] Graham Harman, "On Vicarious Causation."
[706] Ian Bogost, "Object-Oriented Ontology Symposium."

concerns.[707] Yet Ladyman and Ross are relevant here for both systematic reasons and contingent ones. The systematic reason is as follows. Although Ladyman and Ross are perhaps the most *anti*-object-oriented philosophers one could imagine (just look at their title: *Every Thing Must Go*), their exact "evil twin" inversion of my own position points to our shared preoccupation with the status of individual things. The contingent reason has to do with the continued splintering of the Speculative Realist movement into competing subgroups. In 2006, I joined with Ray Brassier (it was his idea initially) in founding Speculative Realism, which held its first public event the following year at Goldsmiths College in London. There we were joined on stage by our comrades Iain Hamilton Grant and Quentin Meillassoux.[708] In this way, four philosophies were briefly united that have surprisingly little in common beyond a shared rejection of what our sole French member brilliantly terms "correlationism": the philosophical view that we can neither think human without world nor world without human, but only the primal correlation or rapport between the two.[709] Among other drawbacks, correlationism prides itself on the novel approach of *uniting* human and world, though in so doing it merely cements the post-Kantian dogma that human and world are the two basic elements of reality (see my earlier remarks on Foucault).

Yet the four philosophies of Speculative Realism have vastly different approaches to overcoming correlationism. Elsewhere I have contrasted my object-oriented philosophy with the ideas of both Grant and Meillassoux.[710] Brassier's position differs notably from the others in his commitment to science-minded eliminationism, which leads him to express outright contempt for the works of figures central to my own position such as Edmund Husserl and especially Bruno Latour.[711] Brassier's attitude must be addressed in due course, since the contrast between our positions is perhaps the most glaring and hence the most interesting in all of Speculative Realism. Yet he remains a moving target: I and others have detected a shift in his thinking since *Nihil Unbound*, which makes that book an inconvenient subject of engagement as we await a full public account of his new position. But from various remarks by Brassier in correspondence, and from the proclamations

---

[707] James Ladyman & Don Ross, *Every Thing Must Go*.
[708] Ray Brassier et al., "Speculative Realism."
[709] Quentin Meillassoux, *After Finitude*, p. 5.
[710] Graham Harman, "On the Undermining of Objects"; Harman, *Prince of Networks*, pp. 26–31.
[711] Ray Brassier, *Nihil Unbound*, pp. 26–31; Ray Brassier, "Concepts and Objects."

of his disciples on the staff of the journal *Collapse*, it is clear that Ladyman and Ross have infiltrated Brassier's position to a considerable degree and served as a rallying point for his faction. This, then, is the contingent reason for my focus on Ladyman and Ross: their 2007 book seems to be a clear and accurate guide to the leanings of the scientistic wing of Speculative Realism, of which Brassier remains the undisputed guru, and which I frankly regard as an unhealthy turn in the movement.

2. Two Forms of Materialism

"I Am Also of the Opinion That Materialism Must Be Destroyed." The historical reference of my title is well known. Before the destruction of Roman archenemy Carthage in 146 B.C., Cato the Elder acquired the habit of ending speeches on just about any topic with the phrase: "I am also of the opinion that Carthage must be destroyed," famously shortened in Latin to *Carthago delenda est*. But my related phrase "materialism must be destroyed" is meant as a provocation for thinking, not as a literal call for eradication. In the first place, to destroy one's opponents in philosophy is usually not a wise aspiration, even on those rare occasions when it is possible. For there is generally a grain of truth in the positions we dislike that cannot be eliminated. Furthermore, the word "materialism" has been used promiscuously for so many theories that to destroy it might mean to destroy every philosophical position that exists. And finally, the attempted destruction might also strike the thrower in boomerang fashion. Consider the most recent book of Jane Bennett, whose philosophical views have often been described as similar to my own.[712] Bennett uses "materialism" in a way that could easily apply both to object-oriented philosophy and to the closely related writings of Latour. Bennett takes materialism to be a suitable name for any philosophy that dissolves the usual strict opposition between free human subjects and inert material slabs. Naturally, I am all in favor of this dissolution; I simply doubt that "materialism" is the best name for it.

In one sense, terminology is always somewhat arbitrary, and we should be free to coin and use it as we wish. But as a general rule, it seems best to avoid confusion by grounding terms in their tradition of historical use. What links Bennett's position most closely with Latour's and my own is that she opposes reduction as a general philosophical method: music and governments cannot be reduced to carbon, oxygen, metal, or some

---

[712] Jane Bennett, *Vibrant Matter*.

deeper alternative structure. Instead, all human and nonhuman things of every scale are placed on the same footing. By contrast with this position, materialism throughout the ages has generally been reductive, and its victim of choice has been midsized everyday objects. One form of materialism tears these objects down to reveal their deeper physical foundations, as if mocking them from below. Another rejects the reality of these objects for precisely the opposite reason, denying them any depth beneath the way they are given to us, as if jeering from above. Given the apparent opposition of these two strategies, it is remarkable that *both* are often denoted with the term "materialism." Although I used to wonder why the second was called materialism at all, I now think there is good reason to accept this dual usage. For the two positions share much in common, are beginning to form a strong unspoken alliance, and are even on the brink of dominating continental philosophy in our time.

The first great upsurge of materialism in the West can be found in pre-Socratic philosophy.[713] Whatever their rich diversity, the pre-Socratics can easily be divided into two basic groups. The first chooses some specific physical material to be the underlying root of things: whether it be air, water, fire, four elements together, or atoms. But the second views these materials as too specific to serve as the bedrock of the cosmos, and gives us instead a boundless *apeiron* deeper than any physical element. All are agreed in showing little respect for the famous "midsized everyday objects," which they reduce to a more primitive basis. Only two of the pre-Socratics deviate slightly on this point. Pythagoras does so by making number the ground of everything, and Anaxagoras by retaining midsized objects in minuscule form as the *homoiomereiai*: everywhere, the world is laced with tiny horses, sharks, and trees. But notice that even these two thinkers hold that there was once a shapeless *apeiron* later destroyed to make way for their new elements of choice. Thus, the original meaning of materialism is that all compound and non-physical things can be reduced to a simpler physical basis. It need not be hard red billiard balls: a churning, shapeless *apeiron* will do, and there are other alternatives as well. In any case, this form of materialism seeks to eliminate all composite and immaterial beings, unmasking them as the gullible reveries of an unphilosophical populace. Such materialism has a proud history of debunking superstition, has often done service for human enlightenment, and I reject it without ridiculing it.

---

[713] A nice introduction is Eduard Zeller, *Outlines of the History of Greek Philosophy*.

But another form of materialism is with us today, in some respects the opposite of the first. It emerges from the German Idealist tradition that it wants to turn upside-down, though in my view without escaping it. I speak of *dialectical* materialism, a theory of social relations rather than of tiny components deeper than all relation. Familiar everyday things are not so much illusions, but vulgar fetishes granted a false independent identity. As Leon Trotsky wrote in 1939:

> Vulgar thought operates with such concepts as capitalism, morals, freedom, workers' state, etc. as fixed abstractions, presuming that capitalism is equal to capitalism, morals is equal to morals, etc. Dialectical thinking analyses all things and phenomena in their continuous change, while determining in the material conditions of those changes that critical limit beyond which 'A' ceases to be 'A,' a workers' state ceases to be a workers' state.[714]

These relations among "all things and phenomena in their continuous change" are not withdrawn into some dusky underworld of things in themselves, but are concealed from us only by "ideology," which will eventually be eliminated. This type of materialism is obviously more compatible than the first with Slavoj Žižek's otherwise shocking statement that "the true formula of materialism is not that there is some noumenal reality beyond our distorting perception of it. The only consistent materialist position is that the world does not exist ...."[715] It is found as well in the "speculative materialism" of Meillassoux, who freely admits his debt to Marx. Meillassoux's principle of "ancestrality" has been widely misunderstood: even by me, at first. Meillassoux is not a classical realist any more than are Žižek or Alain Badiou. Although none of these authors want to be called idealists, they are realists even less. Despite Meillassoux's valuable critique of correlationism, he has stated clearly in print that he thinks correlationism is basically right: we cannot *think* an unthought X without immediately turning it into an *X that is thought*. The correlational circle cannot be escaped, but only radicalized from within.[716] This is materialism repackaged in immanent form, with nothing lying beyond its possible accessibility to

---

[714] Leon Trotsky, "ABC of Materialist Dialectics," p. 357.
[715] Slavoj Žižek & Glyn Daly, *Conversations with Žižek*, p. 97.
[716] See Meillassoux's remarks in Brassier et al., "Speculative Realism," pp. 408–435.

thought. There is no need for a material stratum deeper than all access, since access itself *is* the material stratum; the rest is mystification.[717]

In what follows it will be useful to have shorthand names for both of these doctrines. But experience has taught me that to assign them existing names such as "scientific realism" or "dialectical materialism" merely stirs up distracting controversy. After all, dialectical materialism also claims to be scientific, and many scientific realists are understandably touchy about being lumped together with positivists. And finally, to attack the replacement of metaphysics by science is often mistaken for an attack on science itself, and the indifference to science by the past century of continental philosophy is too regrettable to deserve even a hint of endorsement. For this reason I will adopt a more drolly neutral set of terms, and speak instead of Ground Floor Materialism and First Floor Materialism (following the European rather than the American system of numbering).

The apartment where I live in Cairo is located in a classy older building on Brazil Street, in the leafy neighborhood of Zamalek. On the Ground Floor of the building one finds a powerful national bank, perhaps the hidden basis of economic activity in the neighborhood. Let this bank serve as a mascot for the sort of materialism that seeks to eliminate hypocrisy, alchemy, deities, and folk concepts, and instead trace everything back to its real underpinnings. Meanwhile, the First Floor is home to no businesses but only people, myself included. Each residence is equipped with a stunning terrace that overlooks the street and provides a clear view of everything that happens. And yet the most fascinating part of the building is neither the Ground Floor nor the First Floor. Conveniently enough for this allegory, there is also a partly concealed *mezzanine* level. This cryptic intermediate zone is home to perhaps the finest art dealer in the city: the Zamalek Art Gallery. A humble sign in the entryway alerts the public that the gallery exists, but otherwise there is nothing to announce its presence beyond fame and rumor. By the terms of this analogy, materialism can be described as a philosophy that either goes to the bank, sits on a scenic terrace and gazes at the world, or even does both on the same visit. What it misses in each case is the concealed art gallery lying directly between those two activities. But take note: I am not saying that objects are hermaphrodites transgressing the boundary between a pure physical world on one side and a pure subjective sphere on the other; this view cannot be maintained after reading even

---

[717] Yet Meillassoux also relies heavily on the notion of "dead matter" in a more clasically materialist sense. See Quentin Meillassoux, "Iteration, Reiteration, Repetition."

thirty or forty pages of Bruno Latour.[718] Instead, my position is that both the bank and the terrace are art galleries as well: with trillions of others stretching to the ninth floor and beyond, and infinite galleries burrowing deep into the earth. There is no Ground Floor, no First Floor, and hence no unification of the two. It's galleries all the way down.

3. The Ground Floor Materialism of Ladyman and Ross

In recent writings I have made a number of challenges to First Floor Materialism. These can be found in the long final chapter of *Prince of Networks,* and an additional statement on the matter will be found in my forthcoming book on Meillassoux.[719] At times I have also written on Ground Floor Materialism, though it might be claimed that my attacks on the undermining of objects have been more effective against the pre-Socratic physicalist forms of materialism than against the more cutting-edge varieties available today. For this reason I will speak about Ground Floor Materialism in connection with the remarkably acerbic book of Ladyman and Ross. It is true that the authors show some indifference toward the term "materialism," and that they openly deny the existence of any ground floor of the world. Nonetheless, they still meet the prime criterion for Ground Floor Materialism insofar as they undercut the everyday world of familiar objects with what they call "structure." They are materialists through their dismissive attitude toward individual objects. And they live on the ground floor insofar as they undermine objects rather than "overmining" them. That is to say, Ladyman and Ross obviously do not make the correlationist argument that everything is trapped in the circle of thought, since their whole point is to claim that knowledge makes contact with a reality lying *outside* thought. To deny this would defeat the whole purpose of a science-based metaphysics like their own. Structural Realism, the philosophical current to which they belong, was launched precisely in order to account for how scientific contact with the real is preserved despite changes in scientific theory over time. Even if many past objects of scientific knowledge (phlogiston, partless atoms, the planet Vulcan) have vanished under the onslaught of scientific progress, Structural Realism claims that a certain amount of mathematical structure has been preserved throughout such changes.

---

[718] Bruno Latour, *We Have Never Been Modern.*
[719] Graham Harman, *Quentin Meillassoux: Philosophy in the Making.*

Their book *Every Thing Must Go* is worth considering for several reasons. First, Ladyman and Ross seem to have written as vehement a work of *anti*-object-oriented philosophy as one could imagine, while also endorsing many claims that have a familiar ring for readers of object-oriented thought. This gives the book a paradoxical flavor. At first they seem rather aggressive in their dismissal of both objects and the related topic of causation. Nonetheless, they also claim to replace sterile desert landscapes with a "rainforest" (their term) of what, following Daniel Dennett, they call "real patterns" descending endlessly without limit.[720] Ladyman and Ross also tacitly oppose the correlationist argument in the name of realism, as I do more explicitly. A second reason for choosing this book is that, despite its 300-page length and vast supply of footnotes and technical terms, *Every Thing Must Go* proposes a relatively simple metaphysical position. A longer treatment of the book would be worthwhile, yet it is still possible to give an accurate description of its contents as briefly as one describes the shape and position of France on a globe. Third and finally, Ladyman has recently joined Thomas Metzinger, Paul Churchland, Wilfrid Sellars, François Laruelle, and sometimes Alain Badiou on the list of heroes of the scientific nihilist wing of Speculative Realism, just as Latour, Whitehead, Xavier Zubíri, Marshall McLuhan, and Alphonso Lingis are the frequent heroes of the object-oriented splinter of the movement.

"We admire science," say Ladyman and Ross, "to the point of frank scientism."[721] [61] In this way they accept "scientism" in the same manner that other insulted groups once adopted "impressionist," "fauvist," or "queer," former terms of abuse now embraced by their targets as proud slogans. Their scientism leads them to make unusually harsh remarks about some of their colleagues, which they justify by saying that they care too much about philosophy to speak anything less than the painful truth. [vii] More specifically, they hold that "analytic metaphysics ... fails to qualify as part of the enlightened pursuit of objective truth, and should be discontinued," and mock it throughout the book as a form of "neo-Scholasticism." [vii] It may safely be assumed that they also do not view *continental* metaphysics as part of the enlightened pursuit of objective truth; this still-tiny subfield is probably not even on their radar. While Ladyman and Ross do describe their own work as metaphysics, they are

---

[720] Daniel Dennett, "Real Patterns."
[721] For the remainder of this chapter, all page references in square brackets refer to Ladyman & Ross, *Every Thing Must Go*.

prepared to denounce any "armchair" metaphysics not based on or inspired by the natural sciences. But in a surprising pragmatist twist reminiscent of Latour himself, they hold that the standards of best current scientific knowledge are determined by institutions, down to and including grant proposal committees.

"No scientist," they say, "has any reason to be interested in most of the conversation that now goes on under the rubric of metaphysics," and for them the indifference of scientists counts as damnation. [26] They denounce "esoteric debates about substance, universals, identity, time, properties, and so on, which make little or no reference to science, and worse, which seem to presuppose that science must be irrelevant to their resolution. [For these] are based on prioritizing armchair intuitions about the nature of the universe over scientific discoveries." [10] Such armchair intuitions are rejected for reasons already endorsed by devotees of Wilfrid Sellars and Paul Churchland: namely, "what people find intuitive is not innate, but is rather a developmental and educational achievement …. we should expect developmental and cultural variation in what is taken to be intuitive, and this is just what we find." [10] In this connection they cite the pop relativist example that Americans tend to blame crimes on individual people and Chinese on circumstance. In their view, science *outstrips* intuition: "no one's intuitions, in advance of the relevant science, told them that white light would turn out to have compound structure, that combustion primarily involves something being taken up rather than given off, that birds are the only living descendants of dinosaurs, or that Australia is presently on its way to a collision with Alaska." [11–12] For this reason, science trumps armchair metaphysics: "Special Relativity ought to dictate the metaphysics of time, quantum physics the metaphysics of substance, and chemistry and evolutionary biology the metaphysics of natural kinds." [9] Their scientism is frank indeed.

But the sciences are not a democracy for Ladyman and Ross; there is a queen in their kingdom. One of the pillars of the book is what the authors call the PPC, or "Primacy of Physics Constraint." They formulate this principle as follows: "Special science hypotheses that conflict with fundamental physics, should be rejected for that reason alone. Fundamental physical hypotheses [by contrast] are not symmetrically hostages to the conclusions of the special sciences." [44] But while endorsing naturalism, they reject the physicalism that views the world by way of "a physics of objects, collisions, and forces," which they sometimes ridicule as "the philosophy of A-level chemistry." [44] They even name names, finding examples of this amateurish science in such prominent "neo-Scholastic" thinkers as Jaegwon Kim and David Lewis.

Ladyman and Ross view the task of metaphysics as the unification of physics with the special sciences. As they put it, "we should surely have our metaphysics informed by our best physics ..." though here the phrase "informed by" turns out to be a euphemism for "utterly dominated by." [149] And since forces, things, and essences "find no representations in mathematical physical theory," we are entitled to say that they do not exist. [247] The authors have no sympathy for the metaphysics of individual entities: "naturalists should not believe in 'material objects'.... [These] are not what physics (or any other science) studies; they are pure philosophical inventions." [302] The wish for an ontology of individuals amounts to "the demand that the mind-independent world be imaginable in terms of the categories of the world of experience." [132] Objects are merely pragmatic devices used to orient oneself in the world. As they put it: "There are no things. Structure is all there is." [130] Objects merely belong to the world of the "manifest image." [158] They are the product of human psychology and of "the parochial demands on our cognition during our evolution ..." [155] as well as, they bitingly add, "an education in the classical texts of the metaphysical tradition." [158] Reality is not a sum of concrete particulars. After dismissing objects and causation as folk products, they are biting once more with their mock concession that "folk metaphysics generally makes for better poetry than scientific metaphysics." [297]

Hence, Ladyman and Ross would seem to be the anti-object-oriented thinkers par excellence. This impression is initially heightened when they apparently gear up to attack the theory of emergent levels of the world. Knowing the authors' scientism and their celebration of physics as Queen of the Cosmos, the reader might well assume that they view all large- and medium-scale entities as illusory byproducts of a micro-layer of reality. But somewhat surprisingly, this is not what happens in the book. Unlike many whose temperament and worldview they share, Ladyman and Ross *support* the idea that emergent properties are unexplainable, unpredictable, and irreducible to what came before. Whereas many critics of emergentism are annoyed that it gives midsized entities *too much* autonomy from their component pieces, these authors accuse it of granting *too little*. With admirable strangeness, they simply do not think that gold atoms, gold molecules, chunks of gold, and display cases filled with gold jewelry have any sort of causal or compositional relationship at all. The reasons for this will be clarified shortly. But the point is that rather than denying that an individual is something over and above its components, they deny that individuals are discrete units engaged in compositional layering at all. In short, if they dislike the theory of levels of the world, this is not for the usual reason that their world has only one level, but rather because the levels of Ladyman and Ross have no mutual influence at all. In their view, to say otherwise would merely amount to a folk poetry of cohesive individual things engaged in causal relations.

With this we begin to see what an unusual metaphysics Ladyman and Ross serve up for the reader, one so different from more familiar versions of scientism. First, although physics is said to have asymmetrical priority over the special sciences, these sciences are granted independence nonetheless: there are specifically geological and chemical facts about reality, and according to the authors there are even facts about traffic jams. Despite their complaints about poetry, they indulge at one point in their own quasi-poetic "Latour Litany" (Ian Bogost's term for the long lists of concrete things favored by object-oriented philosophers). Just listen to this example: "[The sciences] do not …. lead a whole parade of special-science objects into metaphysical purgatory. Prices, neurons, peptides, gold, and Napoleon are all real patterns, existing in the same sense as quarks, bosons, and the weak [nuclear] force." [300] This passage might easily have come from one of Latour's books, or one of my own for that matter. The authors even boast that they make room for a rainforest of realities: a breath of fresh air in comparison with the usual appeals to Occam's Razor and Quine's desert landscapes. The world is swarming with real patterns, some undiscovered and some of them literally impossible to discover. It follows that an infinite number of still unknown sciences lie in our future, each dedicated to types of patterns still unknown. And this is perhaps the most surprising aspect of their book. At first their scientistic program and generally abrasive tone make Ladyman and Ross seem like aggressive, annihilating bullies of the stereotypical sort: roaming the streets in their leather Structural Realist jackets on a Friday night, roughing up poets and neo-Scholastics with switchblades and brass knuckles. But now their "rainforest" approach, their world of non-interlocking and scale-dependent objects, makes them look as inflationary as an all-you-can-eat buffet hosted by Alexius Meinong. This latter remark is simply a playful exaggeration, of course, since much is still eliminated in the model of Ladyman and Ross. But the point is that their jungle of patterns, each cut off from genuine causal or mereological links with its neighbors, sounds a great deal like the occasionalist dream of a pluralist landscape of independent realities in need of a deeper force to link them. But there are at least three key differences between Ontic Structural Realism and Object-Oriented Philosophy, and these differences show why Ladyman and Ross are materialists and I am not. The first is that they are quite strict about distinguishing real patterns from mere "folk" patterns that can be eliminated by the usual procedures of scientism: and for them, unsurprisingly, the folk patterns include sensory qualia. The second difference is their denial of any genuine composition or causation in the world. The third difference is that their ultimate reality is "structure," which has nothing at all to do with individual things, but which so closely resembles the Kantian *noumenon* that they are forced to spend several paragraphs denying it. Let's take a brief look at this strangely imaginative brand of rainforest scientism.

If the physics of the past featured genuine tiny objects such as chemicals and atoms, Ladyman and Ross are concerned only with the most up-to-date quantum theory. And in this theory they find no objects and no causation of the traditional sort. Let's not argue with this claim, which they rightly admit to be controversial. [191] Instead, let's focus on their concession that the special sciences (all sciences other than physics) *do* deal with such matters. "The following worry now arises," they concede. "It is easier to give up on self-subsistent individuals in physics than it is in the special sciences because the latter, but not the former, express many (or most) crucial generalizations in terms of transmission of causal influence from one (relatively) encapsulated system to another." [191] Instead of being made up of objects and causes, they say, reality is structure. Yet they also say that "to be is to be a real pattern." [226] Or as they put it earlier, "the tentative metaphysical hypothesis of this book .... is that the real patterns criterion of reality is the last word in ontology, and there is nothing more to the existence of a structure than what it takes for it to be a real pattern." [178] That they call this hypothesis "tentative" is a bit misleading, since they push it aggressively as the centerpiece of their book. It is tentative only in the sense of supposedly being open to empirical falsification, though it is difficult to see what experimental test could possibly pull off such a feat.

Reference is made to John Conway's Game of Life (made famous by Martin Gardner), in which black squares on a grid follow simple rules of generation and decay.[722] As is well known, these simple rules often generate elaborate patterns that have an enduring reality over and above their component squares: so-called "gliders" move across the screen, and there is

---

[722] The game was made famous by Martin Gardner's 1970 article in *Scientific American*, "Mathematical Games."

even an elaborate "glider gun" pattern that shoots out new gliders endlessly. Ladyman and Ross defend the reality of the large-scale patterns in the Game of Life, invoking Dennett's view that the scale-level description of these shapes is more efficient than the bit-map description. For them this is enough to let gliders, eaters, and shooters count as real patterns. They also accuse "conservative metaphysicians" of denying reality to anything other than the individual dots in the game, although mainstream materialism is surely just as guilty of this. Shifting to more serious domains, they also claim that the genius of Charles Darwin in biology and Charles Lyell in geology lay in recognizing "scale ascendance" in their respective fields. That is to say, they recognized the existence of patterns that are not found in the tinier elements of any situation; each layer of the world is thus granted a certain autonomy. For example, natural selection in evolution is invisible at the level of individuals, but becomes easily visible at the level of populations. Nor can the mountain ranges and fault lines of geology be found in the individual pebbles of which they are composed. But as already stated, Ladyman and Ross want to increase this autonomy exponentially to the point that patterns are not causally composed of smaller patterns at all. They even claim that emergence in the compositional sense violates the second law of thermodynamics, a claim best left for another occasion. [215]

But if "to be is to be a real pattern," then we should ask what a real pattern is and how it differs from those supposed gullible fictions known as objects. The first thing to note is that, despite the adjective "real," these real patterns are treated largely in pragmatic terms. This is not your father's hardcore scientism: Ladyman and Ross often express their admiration for pragmatism in the book. To take an example, Napoleon is not an individual for these authors, but a real pattern. What this means is that "observers tracking him in 1801 could get lots of highly useful leverage projecting the pattern forward to 1805; so (sure enough) Napoleon is a real pattern." [229] Providing "useful leverage for observers" edges toward becoming a key criterion of reality itself. By contrast, "the object named by 'my left nostril and the capital of Namibia and Miles Davis's last trumpet solo' is not a real pattern, because identification of it supports no generalizations not supported by identification of the three conjuncts considered separately." [231] The authors assure us that "no observer ever has access to the complete extent of a real pattern," [241] and that *this* is what forces us to be pragmatic about real patterns. The reason we never have such access is not due to some sort of Heideggerian withdrawal into cryptic, veiled reality, but rather because a certain amount of information must always be inaccessible to observers: the exact number of hairs on Napoleon's head at Waterloo is now irrecoverable information, as are events so distant that no human will ever be able to observe them. Deprived in this manner of the total reality of things, we must pragmatically focus on "core" properties that allow us to "very reliably predict" that our attention "is still tracking the same real pattern through any given operation of observation (and reasoning)." [241] We make do with individuals, which for Ladyman and Ross are "only epistemological bookkeeping devices." [240] This is said to be true already for animals no less than for humans. If individual things are "constructs built for second-order tracking of real patterns .... [they] are not necessarily *linguistic* constructions, since some non-human animals .... almost certainly cognitively construct them." However, they add, "all questions about the relationship between real patterns and the individuals that feature in special sciences concern individuals constructed by people." [242] But as for real patterns, there are "real patterns all the way down." [228]

To repeat, everything that exists is a real pattern. But they come in two kinds: representational and extra-representational. The latter are those that are not "second-order" with respect to any other real pattern. And as the authors say, "the overwhelming majority of real patterns that people talk directly about are .... representational." Restated in Kantian terminology, "this is the not-very-exciting idea but true point at the heart of the exciting but false idea that people think only about 'phenomena' while what really exist are 'noumena.'" For as they put it, "people *can* think and communicate about extra-representational real patterns but don't usually try to; scientists often try and *succeed* in so thinking and communicating ...." [243] The real can be known, but only through formalization rather than natural language. When discussing the famous example of Eddington's two tables — the table encountered practically and the material table of physics — their interesting twist on the problem is that the *scientific* table is the one that does not exist. And they are proud of how their metaphysics is able to handle this case:

> It is an advantage of our view that it makes it possible to understand how both the scientific image and the common-sense image can capture real patterns. The everyday table is probably a real pattern. Strictly speaking there is no scientific table at all because there is no single candidate aggregate of real microscopic patterns that is best suited to be the reductive base of the everyday table. [253]

Moreover, "we deny that everyday or special science real patterns must be mereological compositions of physical real patterns ...." [253] And finally, the only difference between physics and the special sciences is "that fundamental physics discovers something of a kind that special sciences don't; and we call this kind of something a universal real pattern." [283]

Too much exposition easily becomes dull. But before putting an end to the current dose of it, we need to touch on the thoroughly *relational* character of this new scientism. For after defending the role of institutions in establishing scientific truth, and speaking in praise of networks, Ladyman and Ross have a *third* Latourian moment when they identify their metaphysics as a form of relationism. Real patterns not only do not exist as autonomous causal agents: they do not exist independently of their context at all. This theme recurs throughout the book. The authors approvingly cite Mauro Dorato as saying that "entities postulated by physical theories are to be regarded as a web of relations, not presupposing substance-like entities or 'hangers' in which they inhere," as well as Cassirer's words (as Leibniz spins in his grave) that they are "a definite aggregate of relations and [consist] in this aggregate." [245] It's relations all the way down. [152] Classical metaphysics believes in the principle of the Identity of Indiscernibles and treats every pound sterling as unique. But mathematics and quantum theory do not, insofar as the relational properties of both pounds are the same: and it is these disciplines we must follow, rather than "neo-Scholastic" metaphysics. Most vividly of all, Ladyman and Ross call it "beguiling nonsense" for a naturalist to think that things can be transported to "radically new environments in space and time" while remaining the same thing, since "nothing in contemporary science motivates the picture." Here, whether they like it or not, they have both Latour and Whitehead on their side as they try to close the deal with the following thought experiment:

> Take giant pandas to Saturn, or 6000 [million years ago] backwards in their light-cone. It's easy to *think about*, isn't it? But organisms are unusually strongly cohesive real patterns, unlike many real patterns studied by scientists. Now imagine taking the market in airlines risk derivatives to Saturn or 6000 [million years ago] back ago in its light cone. That was a bit harder even to imagine, wasn't it? [294]

And finally, it should be added that the authors have little use for causation, though they agree that the special sciences need it as a "heuristic device" for discovering real patterns. On the one hand, they call it "[a folk idea] that has caused no end of confusion in metaphysics." [246] They ridicule causation with the nickname of "microbangings," and take the following position instead: "Because we think fundamental physics describes .... real patterns, we believe there are universal laws. [But we] do not believe they are about causal factors." [289] For them it is wrong to believe in microbangings for the simple reason that, even if the analytic metaphysics of 2007 believes in them, the physics of 2007 does not: "[the] question is for fundamental physics to settle, and it *now* speaks against them." [289; emph. added] But despite all this, they oppose Bertrand Russell's attempt to eliminate causation from the sciences altogether. [270] For as they put it, "though physics doesn't require the metaphysician to work causation into the structural fabric, it is harder to avoid this while maintaining a realist attitude toward the special sciences." [159] Generally, they prefer to replace the word "causal" with the phrase "information-carrying," [221] though this issue must be left for another time.

4. Disconnected Turtles, All the Way Down

The surprising brand of materialism proposed by Ladyman and Ross is one that they happily describe as "turtles all the way down," though with an unusual twist: the turtles are not standing on one another's backs, or even connected at all. Different turtles, different real patterns, are simply found at different scales without being supported by or composed of others. But there is an obvious tension between the pragmatic scale-dependence of these patterns and the claim that they are real. In fact, the patterns are "real" only in the minimalist sense that they are not mere patterns in the mind that can be eliminated by being compressed into more efficient descriptions. If we stumble into the real pattern known as a table, it blocks our progress or injures us, which proves its mind-independence. Let's ignore for now that the ambiguous status of causation in the book ought to make it difficult for the table to do any such thing, and ask instead why there are supposed to be real patterns *in the plural*. If the world is structure, and if structure is a relational whole broken into discrete patterns only at the specific scales occupied by human or animal observers, then there is a problem with knowing how patterns can exist in the plural, and with the related issue of why there are different scales in the first place. If my friends and I and my pack of wild dogs and their fleas all witness the world at different scales, this means that there are discrete observers and perspectives in the world. And if there are discrete realities of this sort, then there must already be individuals, whether or not they are the enduring things of traditional substance-theory.

There are two options here, and both face insuperable difficulties. The first option is that structure in its own right is already broken up into diverse patterns and scales. But in this case it would have individual (or at least "pre-individual") zones, and there would be no reason not to use the term "things" for the various humans, monkeys, and zebras observing patterns at various scales, as long as our definition of "thing" is broad enough. The second option is that structure itself *does not* have discrete zones, with the result that specific patterns must emerge for the first time only when paired with the observers who confront them. This carries the additional difficulty that the observers themselves would also have to surge into existence from an incompletely differentiated structure. But even if we think there is no difficulty with a real pattern and its observer emerging simultaneously, it is unclear why a global relational structure would ever generate discrete scales of observers and observed at all.

Yet there is an even more basic problem with this model of the world, which is that Ladyman and Ross never fully clarify the relation between patterns, structure, and mathematics that lies at the heart of their metaphysics. Recall that they insist on real patterns ("real turtles") all the way down. But they also say there is structure all the way down. And this leads to one of several surprisingly tough questions aimed at Ladyman by *Collapse* in their 2009 interview of him. Namely: "what exactly is it which [your philosophy] affirms to be ontologicially fundamental when it insists that "structure" is all that there is? Is it mathematical structure itself, or is it those 'extra representational real patterns' which mathematical structures are taken to represent?[723] Ladyman responds with refreshing candor: "this question gets to the heart of the matter and I must confess that I am not sure what the answer to it is."[724] The reason for his uncertainty is not that he accidentally froze up with anxiety during the interview; in fact, he and Ross are already quite candid on this topic in their book. There they say that physical structure is in fact physical, not just mathematical. But what exactly makes it physical rather than mathematical? Their reply: "That is a question we refuse to answer." [158] A strange response from such hardcore rationalists! But at least they attempt a justification for their remarkable

[723] James Ladyman, "Who's Afraid of Scientism?" pp. 165–166.
[724] Ladyman, "Who's Afraid of Scientism?" p. 166.

answer: "The 'world-structure' just is and exists independently of us and we represent it mathematico-physically by our theories." [158]

In passing, they bluntly concede that this sounds Kantian. For it now sounds as if structure were nothing more than a noumenal physical realm that can never be approached, although they are absolutely sure (as Kant was not) that it contains no individuals. After all, they are convinced in advance that individuals are merely the folk product of the manifest image. They see no more reason to be "agnostic" about the possible existence of objects than about "two-headed gerbils that sing the blues." [131] And obviously they *cannot* endorse such a Kantian model of unknowable noumena: for this would defeat the very purpose of structural realism, whose whole *raison d'être* is to assert that even obsolete scientific theories have some sort of mathematical contact with the real that can survive the very downfall of these theories. During four paragraphs of damage control late in the book, they ask as follows: "since we can only represent the real patterns in question in terms of mathematical relationships, in what sense are the patterns 'real' other [than] that in which, according to Kant, noumena are real?" [299] They answer with something that is no better than table pounding: "our differences from Kant are profound. Unlike Kant, we *insist* that science can discover fundamental structures of reality that are in no way constructions of our own cognitive dispositions." [300; emph. added]

And here we find the deadlock not just of this single book by Ladyman and Ross, but of materialism as a whole, which they are simply more candid than others in revealing. Namely, there is an irresolvable tension between realism and verificationism, two principles that the authors want to embrace simultaneously. In fact, they are quite proud of having combined them in what they see as an original fashion, as is clear from the closing paragraph of the book:

> We thus conclude that what we defend in this book, having assumed
> naturalism, are verificationism and realism. Since these two things
> have generally been thought to be incompatible, it is no wonder
> that a significant logical space in the metaphysics of science has gone
> unexplored, and some conundra have seemed insurmountable. [310]

But far from being new, I would suggest that the attempt to combine the real (as in realism) with an accessibility of the real (as in verificationism) in one and the same philosophy is the key feature of materialism as defined at the outset of this article. At the outset, Ladyman and Ross want a real that is physical rather than mathematical: even though they "refuse to say" what that difference would mean, or sometimes "confess" that they are not sure. When it is observed that this sounds like nothing more than the inaccessible Kantian noumenon, they change tack and assert: no, because our knowledge is of reality itself and not just of structures imposed by the human mind. For despite being verificationists, they insist that they are not *positivists*, and that there is in fact a real world outside our representation of it. But we have seen that this never allows them to attain anything more than a weak sense of realism.

In the end, it becomes impossible to determine whether Ladyman and Ross are Ground Floor or First Floor Materialists. From one side they look more like neo-Fichteans (or First Floor) than neo-Kantians (Ground Floor) when they edge toward the notion that the real is what can be mathematized, despite the watery caveat that some information is irretrievably disconnected from us (the number of Napoleon's hairs, the interior of black holes). But from another angle, when they shy away from the consequences of this mathematization of the universe and its markedly anti-realist implications, they veer toward Kant and posit a noumenal physical structure beneath the mathematical one: all while refusing (not just forgetting, but *refusing*) even to say in what the difference consists. Thus, the world of Ladyman and Ross is made up of two zones that mutually implode into one another. The first is the luminous mathematical district of the known and the knowable, dominated by the greatness of Science. Such knowledge may never be final, but it does always have some significant contact with the real thanks to a mathematical core that endures into next-generation scientific theories. But this cannot be the whole story, or we would have a purely mathematized universe, resulting in either Berkeleyan Idealism or Neo-Pythagorean Mathematism. Thus, I conclude that the reason Ladyman and Ross posit a non-mathematical real is to add bulk and *gravitas* to what would otherwise be unmitigated mathematical idealism. In short, the world of Ladyman and Ross offers only two basic ingredients: (a) real physical structure, and (b) human or animal observers who stand at a specific scale and thereby encounter mathematical structure in the local form of representational real patterns. There can be no possibility of individual things lying outside this human-world or animal-world pair, because such things are supposedly just "epistemological bookkeeping devices" for those who encounter them. Everything boils down to a correlation between physical structure-in-itself and mathematical structure-for-living-creatures, even though the mathematical is also granted partial contact with the physical. In short, this purportedly realist philosophy of science quickly reverses into a form of *correlationism*: a term that we normally do not associate with scientific naturalism, to say the least. It should no longer be a surprise, as it once surprised me, that so many philosophies of directly correlationist lineage also call themselves "materialist," with Žižek, Badiou, and Meillassoux all being outstanding examples of this trend. It is true that these three figures are not strictly correlationists in Meillassoux's sense, given that correlationism as he describes it is a skeptical/agnostic position marked by finitude, whereas Žižek, Badiou, and Meillassoux all belong to a post-finite landscape moved by the spirit of the absolute. Nonetheless, all are correlationists in the wider sense allowed by Meillassoux himself. For in fact he admits to finding it quite compelling that to think something outside the circle of thought thereby converts it into a thought. Hence we cannot escape the correlational circle of thought and world. Philosophy must proceed as an "inside job," with no reference to relations between inanimate things apart from human access to such relations.

Now, Ladyman and Ross are sufficiently proud in their realism that they would never openly accept the correlationist argument. Yet in practice, their metaphysics turns out to be indistinguishable from the view that "to think an unthought X is to turn it into an X that is thought," and which always tries to avoid charges of idealism by appealing to some excess beyond what is currently formalized: Žižek's real-traumatic kernel, Badiou's inconsistent multiplicity, Meillassoux's virtuality.[725] The Ladyman/Ross version of this excess is the physical structure lying beyond mathematics, which they openly refuse to describe. As for correlationism, I leave it to another occasion to say more about how the Žižek/Badiou/Meillassoux First Floor Materialism also implodes into the Ground Floor; my task in this article was to depict the converse movement. But what both positions share is their combination of a lucid sphere of human intellection with a largely formless physical remainder as their supposed "realist" component. Meanwhile, both skip the level of individual objects altogether. Stated in a simpler phrase, what materialism really means is this: *idealism with a realist alibi*.

As for Ladyman and Ross, how could these authors be led to such an impasse that they either refuse to reveal (or confess their ignorance about) the central distinction of their own philosophy, in which real patterns of different scale magically appear to specific people and animals who this

---

[725] See Slavoj Žižek, *Tarrying With the Negative*; Alain Badiou, *Being and Event*; Quentin Meillassoux, "Potentiality and Virtuality."

philosophy grants no room to exist in the first place? The answer is obvious: it is their specific brand of *scientism* that leads them to this juncture. The more general point of their scientism is that metaphysics should be based on or at least inspired by science, and limit itself to attempts to unify the various branches of science at any given moment in history. Their more specific point is that quantum theory does not allow for individual things, and hence metaphysics must disqualify them too. The latter point is easily disposed of by noting that this is by no means the universal interpretation of quantum theory; if experimental results have not yet disproven the metaphysics of Ladyman and Ross, its aforementioned "armchair" contradictions certainly do. But as concerns the more general point: *why* exactly is it the mission of philosophy to limp along after the science of its time? It is not clear why philosophers must prematurely unify their own speculations on space, time, and substance with those of a quantum theory and relativity that are not yet unified with each other. In fact, there is little evidence that scientists even want philosophers to limp along after them. Despite the strange claim of Ladyman and Ross that a certain suggestion by philosopher of biology David Hull was "one of the *rare* cases of philosophy influencing science," [296; emph. added] it is well known that Albert Einstein profited greatly from his studies of Kant and Ernst Mach, as did Niels Bohr from reading Søren Kierkegaard. The relativity of time and space was first proposed by G.W. Leibniz — perhaps from a miserable armchair — and certainly not from a laboratory. A related moment occurs in the *Collapse* interview, when Ladyman is asked about physicist Carlo Rovelli's statement that

> if a new synthesis is to be reached, I believe that philosophical thinking will be once more one of its ingredients .... As a physicist involved in this effort, I wish that philosophers who are interested in the scientific conceptions of the world would not confine themselves to commenting [on] and polishing the present fragmentary physical theories, but would take the risk of trying to look *ahead*.[726]

In response, Ladyman fires back with the weakest answer in his otherwise skillful interview. He says that: "some philosophers have the capacity to work at the cutting edge of physics or theoretical biology, and have done so and of course should continue to do so." [183] But this simply dodges the point. Rovelli was not asking philosophers to work at the cutting

---

[726] Ladyman, "Who's Afraid of Scientism?" p. 182.

edge of these sciences, but to work *beyond* the cutting edge. Yet this is a possibility of which Ladyman cannot even conceive, since he assumes that any metaphysics operating independently of present-day science is merely armchair philosophy. Let's also not forget that the word "armchair" is no argument. It is a clever verbal weapon, useful for scoring debating points. But in intellectual terms it is really no better than if I were to refer to the Ladyman/Ross position as "Bunsen Burner Realism," another clever insult with which I could score debating points in turn. Moreover, their claim that philosophical *intuitions* are invalid since what is taken to be intuitive changes historically and geographically is a red herring, since it relies on the ambiguous meaning of *a priori* as both "prior to experience" and "necessary." For instance, the fact that Heidegger's tool-analysis might not seem intuitively plausible to the great Chinese philosophers of 2750 A.D. does not entail that his concept of readiness-to-hand must be subjected to empirical testing today. There is plenty of *a priori* work to be done in philosophy, and plenty of rigor to be found in a war of competing *a priori* intuitions. The problem with the philosophy of Ladyman and Ross stems less from any failure to unify the scientific facts of the present day than from their insufficiently imaginative *a priori* deliberations.

And here I have my own specific *a priori* reflection to offer, one that was neither conceived nor written in an armchair. We have seen that Ladyman and Ross are not sure whether extra-representational real patterns are made of the same mathematical stuff as knowledge, or whether they exist in some other physical fashion whose difference from the mathematical they remain unable (or unwilling) to specify. In either case they are sure that real patterns are not *individuals*, but part of a relational or contextual structure. For them nothing makes sense when taken out of context: certainly not airlines risk derivatives markets, but ultimately not even pandas. A pattern, for these authors, is a bundle of relations no less than a bundle of qualities. The reasonable objection that there can be no relations without relata is quickly dismissed by the authors as an old-fashioned gimmick, in the eye-rolling spirit of "here we go again." And yet they must tacitly concede that our knowledge of specific subject matter is never exhaustive at any given moment; science changes and advances. After all, this difference between representational and extra-representational real patterns is the key to their whole position, since this alone enables them to maintain realism against an idealism that would hold that whatever science thinks at any given moment is always true. Our knowledge of the planet Neptune is surely incomplete, and hence our current mathematization of that planet is at best a translation of the real pattern Neptune itself, even if it were granted that certain mathematical aspects of our current translation will survive into any future understanding of it. In short, the real pattern Neptune is something more than our or anyone else's *relation* to it. This means that they already accept a distinction between relation and relata at at least one level. But as soon as representation is taken out of the picture and we move to the realm beyond representation, we supposedly find that Neptune belongs to a giant relational structure rather than being a discrete individual. In other words, although Neptune cannot be dissolved into observers' current relations with it, Neptune itself is supposedly dissolved into the relational structure of the world, having no status as an individual except when viewed by an observer from a specific scale. In this way, representation is granted an almost magical power to create distortions by making a unified relational structure falsely discrete. But this supposition reawakens the mystery of how a continuum of relational structure without individual zones would differ from the monism of a whole-without-parts. There is the further mystery of why such structure would fragment into specific pieces for an observing entity, and the related riddle of why such an observer would be distinct enough from the rest of the structure to occupy a specific scale to begin with.

Moreover, the clearest example offered by Ladyman and Ross in defense of relationism does not accomplish its intended labor. I refer to their claim that the market for airlines risk derivatives cannot be imagined as situated six billion years earlier in its light-cone, given how dependent this market is on its relational context. But this claim is based on a typically ambiguous use of the word "relational," one that is quite often found in such arguments. After all, to move this market six billion years backward in time would amount to moving it to a place where the earth itself does not exist: much less airlines, the insurance industry, and a populace willing to invest in exotic financial instruments. Obviously, no one would claim that the derivatives market could exist under those conditions. But neither would anyone claim that the *panda* could be moved back six billion years ago if its body parts were left in the present. In other words, the thought experiment is only fair if an entity is subtracted from its "foreign" relations with other things. The fact that individuals are all dependent on the "domestic" relations of their own pieces is a different problem. Namely, the fact that I cannot exist if all my internal organs are removed does not entail that I am not the same person when removed from Cairo or Dundee.

If we try a less radical experiment, and simply imagine the panda and the derivatives market on a day-to-day basis in our own time, we can see that their context is *constantly* shifting without the panda or the market thereby being destroyed or changed. New investors appear who purchase and discard shares in the market; the pandas' supply of bamboo waxes and wanes; governments rise and fall; the weather changes; hairs fall from the head of Wellington's descendants; babies are born and elderly sages perish. All these occurrences are certainly part of the "context" of both the panda and the derivatives market, yet it would be purely arbitrary to say that each of these changes automatically alters the panda and the market. Assuming that the market is as real as the panda, as the Ladyman/Ross rainforest certainly allows, both must be robust enough to endure at least a limited number of external shocks, or they would not differ from anything else in the first place. The wider philosophical point is this: there is not just a difference between Neptune and our current scientific knowledge of Neptune; there is also a difference between Neptune and its context. Uranus and Pluto do not drink Neptune to the bottom of the glass any more than we do.

5. In Conclusion

This article has described two key problems with the philosophy of Ladyman and Ross. First, it allows for no genuine plurality in its model of the real. Second, its concept of reality is insufficiently deep. Let's take these points briefly in order. Perhaps every reader is easily persuaded that the ancient Greek *apeiron* model of the real is hopelessly abstract. If the world itself were really just a monolithic lump, it is impossible to see why there would be myriad separate phenomena for an observer, especially since that observer should already have melted into the lump along with the rest of the cosmos. And this is precisely why no one openly embraces the *apeiron* as a model of the real anymore, with the possible exception of the brave young Emmanuel Levinas in *Existence and Existents*. Instead, we now meet with more sophisticated models of a real world without full-blown individuals. These models invariably try to have it both ways, blending the continuous with the discrete by means of initial fiat alone. Consider Gilbert Simondon's "pre-individual," (which displays both aspects at once) or Manuel DeLanda's own Deleuzean references to a "heterogeneous yet continuous" realm.[727] Consider too the "structure" of Ladyman and Ross, which is a totally relational structure but one that is also supposedly blessed

---

[727] Gilbert Simondon, *Individuation in Light of Notions of Form and Information*; Manuel DeLanda, *Intensive Science and Virtual Philosophy*.

with a *multitude* of real patterns. The problem is that there is genuine strife between the continuous and the discrete, and it cannot be resolved simply by positing a magical underground kingdom where cake is both eaten and preserved. It is instead a genuine paradox, as seen from the tortuous labors of Aristotle's *Physics* and *Metaphysics* on up to today's quest for the elusive quantum gravity. The underworld is either made of chunks or it is a continuum. Any philosophy must account for both of these aspects of the world in some way, but not by programming both into the game in advance. We must work our way up to a resolution of this problem, not claim that the puzzle is an easily dismissed "pseudo-problem." And since all will agree that the idea of a monolithic world-lump magically reversing into a plurality of appearances is incoherent, this leaves us with the sole remaining option that the world in itself is many. Contra Ladyman and Ross, the world swarms with individuals. And since it would be strange to hold that these individuals meet up only in our minds, we need to reopen the theme of causation between inanimate things as a key philosophical topic for our time. Objects are not a gullible fetish resulting from a sad, reactionary obsession with the manifest image. Instead, individuals are needed in philosophy due to the futility of all other options.

My second major complaint about Ground Floor Materialism (applicable also to the First Floor kind) is that its sense of the real is insufficiently deep. When the real is made commensurable with knowledge of the real, it survives merely as a phantom, an alibi consisting of just one memorized line: "I am not an idealist." It is the table on which we bang our knee, proving itself to be more than a dream. It is the physical structure that differs from mathematics in ways that cannot be revealed or even discussed. It is the formerly excluded multiple erupting to shake up the boring state of the situation, as for Badiou. It is the traumatic-real kernel leaving us wounded and in search of the spear that smote us, as for Žižek. None of these are sufficient models of the real, not only because they grant it no plurality, but because they leave it too commensurate with our *knowledge* of it even when it comes from the outside.

Let's imagine that we were able to gain exhaustive knowledge of all properties of a tree (which I hold to be impossible, but never mind that for the moment). It should go without saying that even such knowledge *would not itself be a tree*. Our knowledge would not grow roots or bear fruit or shed leaves, at least not in a literal sense. Even in the case of God, the exhaustive knowledge of a tree and creation of a tree would have to be two separate acts. Now, it has sometimes been objected to this point that it is a straw man. After all, who confuses knowledge of a tree with an actual tree? The answer, of course, is that *no one* does, since no one could openly identify a thing with knowledge of it and still keep a straight face. But the point is not that people defend this view openly, which they do not. Instead, the point is that many people uphold a model of the real that *entails* that knowledge of a tree and a real tree would be one and the same, and hence their views are refuted by *reductio ad absurdum*. Namely, if someone holds that there is an isomorphic relationship between knowledge and reality such that reality can be fully mathematized, then it also follows that a perfect mathematical model of a thing should be able to step into the world and do the labor of that thing. But this is absurd. Every model we form of a thing is an oversimplification: a *translation*, to use Latour's terminology. And if even the exhaustive, godlike knowledge of a tree does not add up to a real tree, the point is all the more evident in our lesser everyday sorts of knowledge. The real object is invariably withdrawn from all access. It is unified and hence we cannot even say that it is known with 78% or 83% accuracy, since we cannot even have *partial* knowledge of a thing that is one.[728] For in the strict sense, insofar as an object is one, it has no parts.[729] But just as our encounter with objects can only be a kind of translation, the same holds of the relations of objects among each other: as they cut, break, burn, and melt each other according to the same rules by which human scientists, mystics, carpenters, and clowns turn objects into caricatures.

In short, materialism must collapse into object-oriented philosophy, and this holds for *both* families of materialism. Although Object-Oriented Ontology (or OOO) remains a minority camp even within Speculative Realism, let alone continental philosophy or philosophy plain and simple, there is no good alternative to the OOO model of a real world deeper than all access, broken in advance into individuals, each withdrawing from the other no less than they withdraw from us, accessible through allusion rather than direct contact, and perhaps approachable only with a good deal of the "poetry" to which some concede no cognitive value at all.[730] It is a philosophy in which to be *does not* mean "to be a real pattern," but to be something more like a unicorn roaming across bridges and lunar craters, unable to make contact with anything else that exists.

---

[728] See Graham Harman, "On Vicarious Causation."

[729] See G.W. Leibniz, "Monadology, *or* Principles of Philosophy."

[730] Harman, "On Vicarious Causation."

The slogan that we cannot think an unthought X without turning it into something thought still has tremendous prestige in contemporary philosophy, and is vehemently defended by many of our best thinkers both young and old. And yet I must oppose it, not least because I find it historically troubling. In asserting that what is thought is thereby converted entirely into thought, and that what lies outside thought must always remain unthinkable, the correlationist rejects the etymological sense of the word *philosophia* as that which both has and does not have wisdom and therefore *loves* it. In short, the correlationist unwittingly embraces Meno's Paradox: whatever we have we already have, and whatever we do not have we can never obtain. At the risk of sounding pious and saccharine, in the debate between Meno and Socrates I will always choose Socrates. Philosophy remains the *love* of a wisdom that is never attainable: it is neither a wisdom about thought nor a wisdom about nature nor a wisdom about what can be mathematized. And although it is no longer controversial to say that philosophy should not be the handmaid of theology, we should beware lest it become the handmaid of physics, mathematics, sociology, or politics instead. Philosophy is the handmaid of nothing: for it is not wisdom, and must not serve anything that claims to be wisdom. And furthermore, I am also of the opinion that materialism must be destroyed.

CHAPTER 30

ZERO-PERSON AND THE PSYCHE[731]

This article addresses several closely linked issues: the mind-body problem, the relation between first-person and third-person descriptions, and panpsychism. Every approach to consciousness has its own way of addressing each of these questions, and the lines of battle are now firmly drawn and widely known. But while all three issues should be of great interest to any thinking person, I contend that each marks an artificial restriction on a broader underlying problem.

First, the mind-body problem is one small part of a more basic *body-body* problem, as found in the abandoned occasionalist tradition. On this point I will make two claims: (a) The occasionalist problem of interaction between any two entities has not been overcome, but was merely inverted by Hume and Kant without solving the problem. (b) Natural science also does not solve the problem of body-body interaction, but flourishes only by ignoring it. To hold that bodies interact by slamming together in space or responding to fields is to adopt a narrowly commonsense view of what interaction means. Thus, the inadequacy of materialism arises *not* from its inability to explain a special pampered entity called consciousness, but because it cannot even balance its accounts in the physical realm. That is to say, it ignores the problem of how relations arise between any two beings, and merely treats interaction as successfully calculable. One of its worthy

---

[731] "Zero-Person and the Psyche" was first published in 2009 in David Skrbina, ed., *Mind That Abides: Panpsychism in the New Millennium*.

goals in doing so is to draw mental facts back into the same sphere as physical ones, in a Galilean effort to unify the supposedly separate worlds of mind and body. This makes it an appealing alternative to dualism. Unfortunately, materialism leaves the nature of relations between bodies in obscurity. In this sense, it is less a metaphysics than a police action, offering a fairly bleak vision of the harmony that will ensue once the final obscurantist holdouts are crushed. Hence, the position defended in this article can be called "physicalist" only if the term "physical" is expanded far beyond the scope of the usual scientific conception of matter.

Second, there is something missing from the picture when we divide the world between first- and third-person descriptions. What is missing is not the second-person, which can easily be dissolved into the third-person, but rather what I will call the *zero-person* stance (the ordinal "zeroth" is too awkward in English), referring to the "essence" or intrinsic nature of an entity apart from any access we might have to it. The problem shared by first- and third-person descriptions is obvious: namely, both are *descriptions*. Against any ontology in which things are reducible to a listing of attributes, I hold that the being of things is never commensurate with descriptions of any sort. Objects, in a broad sense including trees, protons, animals, cinder blocks, nations, humans, and fictional characters, are never exhausted by any possible manifestation. Hence, objects must be granted a zero-person reality that can only be *translated* into descriptive terms of the first- or third-person kind. Here we have yet another variant of the forgotten occasionalist problem, since human consciousness is stripped of its purported ability to exhaust apples and stars with third-person descriptions, and even of its purported ability to drink its own self dry by means of direct first-person awareness.

Third, there is need to replace the word "panpsychism" with a more accurate term, even if the initial options are somewhat awkward. The one I will propose here is "endopsychism," though I reserve the right to replace it with a more mellifluous one in the future. Franz Brentano presaged the phenomenological movement by reviving the medieval term "intentionality," in the sense of "immanent objectivity."[732] All consciousness contains objects within itself as the focus of its acts. Now, Brentano was no panpsychist, and allowed only the usual limited range of entities to have consciousness. But this article contends that there is a universal interplay between: (a) objects in their concealed zero-person reality, and (b) the distorted first-person *or*

---

[732] Franz Brentano, *Psychology From an Empirical Standpoint*.

third-person way in which these objects are encountered. This might seem to lead to a panpsychist version of Brentano, in which *all* entities (not just humans) have an inner psychic life focused on immanent objects.[733] Yet there is a slight problem with calling it panpsychism. I hold that Brentano is right to describe as consciousness in terms of immanent objectivity, and also right that all consciousness must be occupied with such immanent objects. But *in what* are the immanent objects contained? Brentano simply assumes that they are contained in me the conscious agent, but this will turn out to be false. Both I the conscious agent and the immanent objects I confront are contained on the interior of a higher object, not on the interior of me. And this slight, strange modification alters the sense of the "pan-" in panpsychism. "To be conscious" means *to be in the interior of a larger entity,* but "to exist" means only *to have an interior,* not to be conscious. In other words, there may be numerous entities that house others without residing in turn on the interior of higher entities, just as water at the surface of the ocean only has neighbors below it, and none above. But if psychism means to exist on the interior of a higher entity, and if there are entities that contain without themselves being contained, then the turbulent "surface" of the cosmos at any given moment has no psychic life at all, even if all other entities do. In that case, innumerable "inanimate" objects would turn out to have a primitive psyche, yet we would still fall short of a fully panpsychist vision.

The Body-Body Problem

One of the chief philosophical riddles of modern times is the mind-body problem, most familiar from the writings of René Descartes. How can two substances as different as mind and body ever interact? And how might a physical world of blind causal impact give rise to an apparent inner world of perceptions? While countless solutions have been proposed, there is a more basic opposition between those who accept that there is a mind-body problem in the first place and those who do not. The latter group finds its purest form in the *eliminativist* position, which goes so far as to deny

---

[733] David Skrbina was the first to propose that I bite the panpsychist bullet. He writes as follows, referring to my interpretation of Heidegger in *Tool-Being*: "Harman adds that 'the as-structure of human Dasein turns out to be just a special case of relationality in general. We ourselves are no more and no less perspectival than are rocks, paper, and scissors.' Yet Harman resists casting this interpretation in a panpsychist light …. Yet this raises the question of the relationship (if any) between 'psychic relations' and relationality in general." David Skrbina, *Panpsychism in the West,* pp. 181–182.

that there is anything like inner experience or a self at all. This position is often described as the denial that there are *qualia*, immediate experiences that would be fundamentally different from the senseless impact of real physical things. It is generally countered by the insistence that experienced qualities are more real than anything else we know, and that such experience is irreducible to the blind interactions described by the sciences.[734] In short, there are those who accept the mind-body problem as a true conundrum, and those who wish to dissolve it by reducing the entire world to a question of bodies. A few scattered visionaries might still try the opposite reduction, turning everything into a kind of mental experience. But in our time they are vastly outnumbered by the legion of scientific materialists, who greatly exceed their rivals in self-confidence and institutional prestige.

Yet all of these groups share the assumption that no *body-body* problem exists. After all, the sciences already work in a body-body idiom, and apparently with great success. Descartes proposed that the realm of *res extensa* functions solely through physical displacement, rejecting the substantial forms and occult qualities of the earlier physics. In this way the superhighway to mechanistic theories of nature was built, and it has handled most serious intellectual traffic ever since. While the quantum theory may add certain complications to the mechanistic view of nature, it does not alter the basic model of physical entities slamming together in space or interacting with fields. There remain certain problems of calculation, of statistical inference, and of deducing the exact laws by which physical entities affect one another. But the basic features of causation are taken for granted, and have assumed an air of self-evidence that makes materialism the default intellectual position of our time. Anyone trying to deviate from this model will feel ceaselessly pulled upon by the claims of scientific mechanism. As a result, philosophy has been forced into a defensive posture: either worshipping the sciences and merely supplying commentary, or upholding the rights of a special inner sphere that the mutual impact of bodies cannot fully explain.

Since Kant, this situation has reached the point that philosophy now deals almost exclusively with the single relational drama between humans and world. It makes no difference whether we see an unbridgeable gap between these two realms (Kant), or claim instead that they are fused together from the start (Hegel, phenomenology, pragmatism). Whether the relation between humans and world is an irrevocable divorce or a harmonious marriage, all philosophical energy is focused on this single

---

[734] For a fine example see Galen Strawson, "Realistic Monism."

point of relation. Most will admit that there must be relations between fire and cotton or comets and planets, no less than between humans and world. But these inanimate duels are generally excluded from philosophy's subject matter, unless they are inscribed in some sort of manifestation to humans. Such relations are simply left to the natural sciences. But if philosophy is to reclaim the universal subject matter that it was born to address, it cannot continue to leave the vast majority of relations outside its mandate. We need to reawaken a body-body problem ignored by the sciences, rather than defend the mind-body problem as the final citadel beleaguered by eliminativists streaming from Mordor.

The body-body problem is not unknown to philosophy, and was most prominent under the now ridiculed name of "occasionalism." Cordemoy and Malebranche expanded the Cartesian mind-body problem into a generalized problem of communication between all entities. Similar arguments had long been made in Islamic philosophy, from al-Ash'ari in Basra through al-Ghazali in Baghdad. The latter's motives were theological, stemming from the apparent blasphemy of granting any causal power to entities other than Allah. Hence, God became the sole medium enabling relations to occur. In today's Western intellectual climate, divine intervention is no longer a defensible explanation of causality; occasionalism has become a dusty footnote to history, mocked as superfluous even by undergraduates. It is sometimes remembered that such figures as Spinoza, Leibniz, and Berkeley also deprived individual entities of direct causal power and made them take detours through God. But this never amounts to anything more than an argument for the "great historical importance" of occasionalism, not for its relevance to us today. And while Spinoza, Leibniz, and Berkeley are still respected, their literal disciples are few. The reason is simple: Hume and Kant have established the horizon for acceptable versions of mainstream philosophy. Anything prior to Hume will usually look like dogmatic metaphysics of the old-fashioned variety.

Yet the occasionalist problem is not only relevant today: it even forms the enduring backbone of modern philosophy. It is little noted that Hume's position is merely an inverted form of occasionalism. The free-thinking Hume admired the writings of the arch-Catholic Malebranche because of their shared objection to the idea that causal relations can be directly observed. What we see are conjunctions and contiguities, not the workings of actual causal powers. Recall that for occasionalists what was doubted was never the existence of individual substances, but only their ability to come into relation, which required that God be invoked as the global relational medium. But for Hume the situation was merely the opposite: the relations were already present in the form of custom or habit, and what was denied was that real causal powers could be known to exist outside the conjunctions we observe. From here it is a short distance to Kant, for whom cause and effect become human categories that never escape the bounds of experience.[735] What is common to all these positions is a model in which one special entity does what others cannot: for occasionalism, nothing creates links but God; for Hume and Kant, nothing creates links but human experience. Both groups raise the profound problem of how interaction is possible, but solve it hastily with either a *deus ex machina* or *mens ex machina*. And while it is all too easy for enlightened Western philosophers to chuckle at the notion of a hidden almighty divine cause, they merely defend the socially acceptable underbelly of the problem: letting the human mind serve as an equally almighty universal glue. In both cases, the metaphysics of the world is only allowed to play out in a *single* kind of entity. And while materialism manages to escape this deadlock and regain the full plurality of animate and inanimate relations, this comes at the cost of denying their highly problematic character.

Hume pleads ignorance as to whether there are real causal relations between real things, and Kant pleads even greater ignorance by turning cause and effect into human categories inapplicable to the things-in-themselves. However, today's philosophical mood is not really this skeptical in practice. Our *Zeitgeist* assumes that once we leave the sphere of human reality, interaction between bodies takes place without difficulty, so that the sciences can continue with their successful research projects, unhindered by philosophers. Materialists are granted their point about bodies, and merely denied access (by many) to the mysterious fortress of the mind. And here I must object. Admittedly, the divine solution of occasionalism solves nothing; its best weapon is a mere piety toward forbidden things that now holds little force in a Western context. Nonetheless, I still believe occasionalism is closer to the truth than the various positions inspired by Hume and Kant, in whose shadow all non-materialists continue to dwell. Stranger still, I became convinced of this point by an unlikely figure, one

---

[735] Everyone notes the difficulty with Kant saying that the noumena "cause" the phenomena even though cause is supposed to be a merely phenomenal category. What is almost never discussed is the question of causal relations *between noumena*. In fact, rejection of this topic is the secret shared assumption of most post-Kantian philosophy. Materialism "solves" the problem only by denying that inanimate entities are noumenal, thereby claiming that everything in the world is phenomenal, describable by qualities observed in the third person.

who appears to scorn all metaphysical speculation beyond the bounds of human existence: Martin Heidegger.

In the famous tool-analysis (whose appearance in 1919 predates the publication of *Being and Time* by eight years), Heidegger breaks with his mentor Edmund Husserl.[736] For Husserl, philosophy proceeds by bracketing the existence of any external world and setting up shop in a world of phenomena. I will say more about Husserl's virtues a bit later, but Heidegger's critique hits home. For as Heidegger observes, we do not normally encounter things by staring at them or describing them; this is an artificial special case forming a small portion of our lives. Most of our environment is silently relied upon until it malfunctions. The field of phenomena is a thin film or surface in comparison with all those entities whose silent performance we take for granted: bodily organs, chemical structures, habits, linguistic abilities, floors and furniture. Insofar as these things function, they tend to remain unnoticed, withdrawn into shadow. Under the usual reading of the tool-analysis, we have a contrast between explicit theory (Husserl) and implicit practice (Heidegger), with Heidegger's view having the upper hand. This leads W. Teed Rockwell, among others, to identify Heidegger's theory with an earlier insight by John Dewey.[737] More specifically, Rockwell credits both Heidegger and Dewey with seeing that when I use the hammer, the hammer and I are one.[738]

This is a misreading, however widespread it may be. The point of Heidegger's analysis is not that Dasein and the hammer are one, but that they are fundamentally *not* one: their apparent unity is a merely temporary illusion. The reason the hammer can sometimes malfunction is because it is not reducible to Dasein's current use of it, and in fact holds many surprises in store. The point of the tool-analysis is not that praxis is richer than theory: the point is that the hammer itself is richer than both praxis *and* theory. To stare at a hammer is to reduce it to a limited set of surface-properties, but to

---

[736] See Graham Harman, *Tool-Being*, Chapter One. The reference to 1919 is to Martin Heidegger, *Towards the Definition of Philosophy*.

[737] W. Teed Rockwell, *Neither Brain Nor Ghost*. On page 189, Rockwell says that Dewey made Heidegger's distinction between readiness-to-hand and presence-at-hand "thirty years earlier." On page 180 he states as follows: "I think it is important to give credit where it is due. It was Dewey, not Heidegger, who first said that the problems of modern epistemology arise from assuming that one can have Dasein without Being-in-the-world, although he said it in less technical language ...." But this rather typical claim rests on a trivialization of what Heidegger's tool-analysis actually achieves.

[738] Rockwell, *Neither Brain Nor Ghost*, p. 146: "Insofar as we are at home in the world, and what we encounter is ready-to-hand, we *are* the world."

use the hammer creates a similar caricature of its genuine being. Otherwise, there could be no such thing as a "broken hammer": the hammer would be entirely used up by its relation to practical Dasein. On the contrary, praxis is no better than theory at exhausting the reality of things, and this fact gives the tool-analysis a surprisingly *realist* force. This interpretation might seem at odds with Heidegger's apparently Kantian outlook, in which human Dasein stands at the center of reality and even Newton's laws are said to be neither true nor untrue before they were formulated by Newton. Yet the realist strand of Heidegger's thinking haunts such anti-realist readings, as seen especially in the famous 1949 essay on "The Thing."[739]

But we have not yet gone far enough, and must take an additional step that Heidegger himself never took. If we say that both theory and praxis fail to exhaust the reality of things, this makes it sound as though only human intervention turns things into caricatures, making Dasein a unique instrument of distortion in the cosmos. A human who looks at a rock or uses it to smash other objects would be responsible for converting the rock's reality into a present-at-hand image of this reality, but a rock slamming into another rock would supposedly do no such thing. Yet this view cannot be maintained. Each of the rocks has countless qualities in its own right; obviously, most of these do not come into play in any given collision. Hence, one rock smashing another will encounter nothing but a distorted rock, a "straw man" rock, just as would be the case for human theoretical or practical agents. If anything, one rock is likely to reduce the other even more obtusely than would relatively flexible and open-minded human beings. Relations *per se* are always a *translating* force, always giving us something a bit different from that to which they relate.

The real problem is not the opposition between things and human access to them, as the models of Descartes, Hume, and Kant all suggest. Instead, the problem is the opposition between any two entities at all. The single pampered modern rift between human and world (whether stubbornly retained or heroically bridged) gives way to trillions of rifts between all beings in the cosmos. There is a universal body-body problem, and the mind-body problem is only one of its tiny subsets, though admittedly one of special interest to those who have minds. Heidegger never saw quite this far: even his most realist moment (in 1949) in which a jug stands in itself apart from all human access, usage, science, or production, tells us only that

---

[739] Martin Heidegger, "The Thing."

the jug itself hides *from human Dasein*, never from other things.[740] Having scoured the whole of Heidegger's *Gesamtausgabe* as of 2008, I can assure the reader that he never offers a single example of two inanimate things smacking together without Dasein conducting surveillance on them. In this way, Heidegger remains within the Kantian Dual Monarchy of human and world. His assertion that they always come as a pair, via the unified term "being-in-the-world," simply mends the rift without replacing it. Human and world are always the two terms that are linked. It is never a matter of "bridging the gap" between wind and tree, or offering a primal correlation of hailstones and corn. Yet Heidegger could and should have taken this further step. The tool-analysis provides immediate incentive to revive the occasionalist body-body problem, and this time without theological baggage. No relation to a thing can exhaust it, whether it be theory, praxis, or blind causal interaction. No external model of a thing can drain it to the dregs, and this is true not only of our conscious experience, but also of such lowly entities as dust and wheat. But though I propose to revive the problem of occasional causation, I do not wish to revive this precise *term*, which remains too freighted with theological baggage. Hence, I have often suggested "vicarious causation" as a suitable phrase.[741] Any two entities must interact vicariously, by way of a third. And just as importantly, *any* entity can serve as such an intermediary, not just God or the human mind.

Here, someone might ask how we can know that there are objects above and beyond their phenomenal accessibility. We cannot respond simply by appealing to the authority of Kant, who famously finds it absurd that there could be appearances without anything that appears. This argument by Kant is not highly esteemed by today's readers; indeed, it is often seen as a naïve maneuver subject to easy rebuttal, and as marked by the flavor of a dated, traditional style of reasoning. This is also how it was viewed by his prestigious successors, the German Idealists. By making the supposed difference between appearance and reality internal to appearance itself, it is easy to produce an idealist philosophy that dispenses with the supposed phantom of the *Ding an sich*. Furthermore, those who do accept something outside appearance can make a different sort of objection: even if a real world is there, why not view it as a single unified lump that is broken into pieces only by mind? This already happens in pre-Socratic philosophy with Parmenides and Anaxagoras. It even happens in more recent cases, such

---

[740] Martin Heidegger, "Insight Into That Which Is."
[741] Graham Harman, "On Vicarious Causation."

as the lucid treatise *Existence and Existents* by Emmanuel Levinas, whom I regard as Heidegger's greatest interpreter.[742] For Levinas, being itself is a rumbling *il y a* ("there is") without parts, which is then *hypostatized* into parts by the human observer.

Nonetheless, these positions merely disagree as to whether the number of realities-in-themselves is zero (idealism) or one (Parmenides, Anaxagoras, Levinas). Both agree that there is no plurality of things apart from human access. Despite their obvious differences, both positions claim that *specific* realities are entirely exhausted by their relation to us, with nothing lying in reserve. Hence, they endorse a permanent correlation between human and non-human reality, with neither existing apart from the other. Quentin Meillassoux describes all such views with the marvelous term "correlationism."[743] For the correlationist, there is no human without world and no world without human, but only a primal correlation or rapport between the two. In other words, both humans and world are fully deployed in their mutual relationship. As a variant of this position, we could point to a less human-centered version that might be called "relationism," as found most lucidly in the works of Alfred North Whitehead and Bruno Latour. Relationist philosophies do not agree that a human must be involved in every relation, but still insist that things are the sum total of their relations to all other things, and nothing more.

This gives us three possible stances against the plurality of hidden things-in-themselves (personified nicely by Fichte, Levinas, and Whitehead). These positions all face the same two difficulties. All agree that individual trees are exhausted by being *given* as trees, with Whitehead in particular simply adding the complication that trees are not only given to humans. But let's imagine a counterexample in which other perceivers are added to the situation. New observers now enter the scene and perceive the tree, each in his, her, or its own way. Now, what these observers will be perceiving in each case is *the tree*, not the earlier observers' *perceptions* of the tree. This counterfactual case gives a first reason why a thing cannot be exhausted by the current perceptions or prehensions that other things have of it. The second reason has to do with change. If all entities in the world were fully determined by their current relations with everything else, their reality would already be

---

[742] Emmanuel Levinas, *Existence and Existents*.

[743] Quentin Meillassoux, *After Finitude*. However, Meillassoux does not *reject* correlationism so much as attempt to radicalize it into an absolute knowledge that the laws of nature must be contingent. See his remarks on this point in Ray Brassier et al., "Speculative Realism," pp. 408–435.

fully deployed. There would be no principle of dynamism in the world if nothing in the things were withheld from current expression, no surplus of reality outside all current states of affairs. For this reason Merleau-Ponty misses the point when he states, with a false revolutionary air, that a house is not a house viewed from nowhere but a house viewed from *everywhere*.[744] On the contrary, a house is simply not a set of outer perspectives on it by other things, no matter how many such perspectives we might tally up.

This brings us to the sole feasible alternative: the world is home to a vast number of objects and there is a communication problem between all of them, since all partly withdraw from their manifestations to other things. Instead of the lonely, pampered mind-body problem with its special elitist features, we now have a universal body-body problem between all entities. The body-body problems trumps the Hume-Kant view by stripping monopoly rights from the human-world gap and introducing a global rift between all things. It trumps materialism by insisting that there really is a communication problem between entities. It trumps the standard occasionalist view by saying that God is not a sufficient answer, since God ought to have the same relational problems as every other entity. It even trumps today's chic philosophies of "the virtual" by denying that individuals exist only at the surface of the world, and by rejecting the shell game of claiming both that the virtual is pre-individual *and* that it is made up of different pre-individuated zones. This really amounts to saying "the virtual is both one and many, and hence there is no communication problem." But this merely posits a solution by fiat while solving nothing.

To summarize, I recommend a fresh embrace of the body-body problem, of the view that objects have individual character (a.k.a., "substantial forms") prior to any relations. All objects must solve the communication problem in precisely the same way, with no special diplomatic immunity for God or the human mind. As a consequence, we no longer need to defend the lonely stockade of the *cogito* against the materialist Golden Horde, since the materialists do not even get bodies right.

First-Person, Third-Person, and Zero-Person

The mind-body problem is often equated with the need to reconcile first-person and third-person descriptions. The difficulty is that first- and third-person descriptions are both *descriptions*, and a body is no more a

---

[744] Maurice Merleau-Ponty, *Phenomenology of Perception*, p. 79.

sum of descriptions than a mind is. A body exists. It cannot be exhausted by the sum total of things we say about it, because these statements would not be able to step in for the thing and do what it does, or be what it is. Nor can a body be exhausted by any set of relations, no matter how large. For this reason I will coin the adjective "zero-person" to refer to the reality of any entity apart from its interactions with other entities of any kind. This changes the nature of the problem. Instead of trying to bridge the gap between two kinds of descriptions, we now have a gap between description and reality.

Note that the first- and third-person standpoints are essentially the same thing. There are no third-person views without some entity doing the viewing; conversely, it is unthinkable that there could be a pure stream of first-person experience without something dancing before us in the third person, even if it were nothing but imagined sparks of light, or vague and rambling urges. A body is never equivalent to what can be said or noticed of it in the third person, nor is mind the same as what is noticed of it in the first person: both mind and body occupy the zero-person stance, quite apart from any experience of them. The gap that needs to be explained lies not between an external third-person and an internal first-person experience, but between the reality of mind or body, and the access to them by whatever might encounter them.

Now, a possible synonym for "zero-person" would be *essence*. While essence is viewed with suspicion in much recent philosophy, there is nothing mystical or naïvely traditional about it. Something has an essence simply because it is what it is. To describe a thing's essence seems possible to some extent, but no set of descriptions will be able to replace it. For instance, a perfect list of all the properties of a house, and of all possible relations that other entities might have with it, do not yet add up to a house. Georg Cantor's insights into transfinite numbers even suggest that we cannot have a total set of all properties of the house, which strengthens the hand of the zero-person stance all the more. Nor is the house reducible to its potential to affect other entities: a thing may be known or detected through its causal power over other things, but is not identical with those powers. This immediately revives the classical problem of which things really have an essence, and which are mere aggregates of smaller real things — a problem that cannot be solved in the present article, though I will address it briefly below.

Obviously enough, most approaches to consciousness do not make use of the global duality I have proposed between zero-person reality and descriptions of whatever sort. They overlook this theme thanks to assumptions that can easily be refuted, and by paying attention to disputes (such as first-person vs. third-person) that ought to be repackaged in more fundamental terms. As an example of some of these problems, I propose to examine some of the basic theses found in one widely known work in the field: *The Conscious Mind* by David Chalmers.[745] Regardless of the reader's views on Chalmers, he provides a useful foil for the zero-person stance, since his ontology is not only quite different from the kind I propose, but also makes a strikingly close approach to the universal opposition between objects and relations that I wish to defend.

The core of his argument can be found in the distinction he draws between "logical supervenience" and "natural supervenience." For Chalmers, almost everything is logically supervenient on the physical. [71] For a higher-level fact to supervene logically on a lower-level one means that there is really nothing more to it than was already included in the lower level.

> In general, when B-properties supervene logically on A-properties, we can say that the A-facts *entail* the B-facts, where one fact entails another if it is logically impossible for the first to hold without the second .... In a sense, when logical supervenience holds, *all there is* to the B-facts being as they are is that the A-facts are as they are. [36]

Logical supervenience goes hand-in-hand with reducibility:

> for almost every natural phenomenon above the level of microscopic physics, there seems in principle to exist a *reductive explanation*, that is an explanation wholly in terms of simpler entities. In these cases, when we give an appropriate account of lower-level processes, an explanation of the higher-level processes falls out. [42]

He does add a caveat:

> [But] a reductive explanation of a phenomenon need not require a *reduction* of that phenomenon .... In a certain sense, phenomena that can be realized in many different physical substrates — learning, for example — might not be reducible in that we cannot *identify*

---

[745] David Chalmers, *The Conscious Mind*. In this chapter, all page references in square brackets refer to this book.

learning with any specific lower-level phenomenon. But this multiple realizability does not stand in the way of reductively *explaining* any instance of learning in terms of lower-level phenomena. [43]

This proviso turns out to be irrelevant for us, since for Chalmers learning has a purely "functional" sense. While the different possible physical substrates of learning make it impossible to *identify* learning with specific lower-level constituents, learning can still be reduced in the other direction. Namely, many different substrates of "learning" can amount to the same thing because of their similar effects. Chalmers holds that *almost everything* in the world can be reductively explained. He cites the example of biological phenomena such as reproduction, adaptation, and even life itself. "Once we have told the lower-level story in enough detail, any sense of fundamental mystery goes away: the phenomena that needed to be explained have been explained." [42] And "a reductive explanation is a *mystery-removing* explanation" [48] that turns a mystery into a mere *puzzle*.[746] Chalmers does concede that a reductive explanation is not always illuminating: to reduce the great 2004 tsunami to molecular motions is possible in principle, but would not be pitched at the right level to be very helpful.

But for Chalmers, consciousness is a special case. It is not reducible as physical phenomena generally are, and this makes it a rare and genuine mystery: "the existence of conscious experience seems to be a *new* feature .... It is not something that one would have predicted from [the lower-level features] alone." [4] And "if logical supervenience fails (as I will argue it does for consciousness), then *any* kind of reductive explanation fails, even if we are very generous about what counts as explanation." [50] Yet along with logical supervenience, there is also *natural* supervenience. For instance:

> [T]he pressure exerted by one mole of a gas systematically depends on its temperature and volume according to the law $pV=KT$, where K is a constant .... [However,] this supervenience is weaker than logical supervenience. It is *logically* possible that a mole of gas with

[746] Chalmers's use of the word "puzzle" immediately brings to mind Thomas Kuhn's famous idea of puzzle-solving "normal science" in *The Structure of Scientific Revolutions*. Yet the difference between their respective views of "puzzles" is itself illuminating. For Kuhn, puzzle-solving science is opposed to paradigm-shifting scientific revolutions, so that puzzles can give way to paradigm shifts at any time and in any field of study. But for Chalmers, puzzle-solving has permanent methodological rights over almost the whole of the cosmos, with only a few fixed areas (consciousness, causal laws) retaining a certain autonomy and mystery. It should be obvious that Kuhn's vision of science is more dynamic than that of Chalmers.

a given temperature and volume might have a different pressure; imagine a world in which the gas constant K is larger or smaller, for example. Rather, it is just a fact about *nature* that there is this correlation. [36]

Borrowing an image from Saul Kripke, Chalmers [40] quips that once God created the universe with its microphysical facts, all the logically supervenient facts came automatically as a free lunch, but that God had to do further work to create naturally supervenient (and hence "mysterious") facts such as consciousness and causal laws.

When Chalmers says that almost everything in the universe is logically supervenient on the physical, he means that almost everything can be reduced to either its "structural" or its "functional" properties. For him, a mid-sized object such as a table has no autonomous reality, but only a structure and a function. In structural terms, a table needs to "have a flat top and be supported by legs." But such terms as "flat top" and "legs" are obviously rather crude, parochial examples of structure. A flat top is flat only for entities of a relatively large size, while bacteria encounter the tabletop as a landscape cratered with pores. Most of our loose examples of "structural" properties turn out to be purely functional. Hence, when Chalmers says that "structural properties are clearly entailed by microphysical facts," what he means is that microphysical facts are the only real structure the physical world has. In other words, the ultimate structure of a thing comes from the basic particles of which it is composed. This claim is more perplexing than it might seem. After all, Chalmers has no better idea than the rest of us what these fundamental particles might be (fifty-year-old quarks and century-old electrons are merely the limit of current physics), nor does he give any reason for holding that such ultimates must exist in the first place. Elsewhere in the book, Chalmers is openly critical of those who hope to explain consciousness through the possible future achievements of physics, yet he shows the same faith in physics here, reducing almost everything to functions other than the "microphysical" structural facts in which he straightforwardly believes.

In functional terms, the fact that something is a table means that people use it to support various objects. For Chalmers as for most others, the functional means the *relational*; the ability of the table to support objects, just like its flat surface and possession of legs, is something real only for the other beings that encounter it. Objects pass the buck of reality down to their tiniest microcomponents; the table has no features in its own right *qua* table, but is merely a functional figment produced from the outside. Its structure comes from beneath (basic particles), and its function comes from above (those who use it). The table is thus reducible in two separate directions, and once this happens there nothing is left. Other than a few briefly described exceptions that need not concern us here (such as "indexicality") Chalmers ends up with a rather sparse ontology: "almost every phenomenon is reductively explainable [i.e., expressible in terms of structure or function] …. except for conscious experience …. along with the rock-bottom microphysical facts and laws, which have to be taken as fundamental."[747] Generally speaking, he holds that everything real is either a physical particle or law (both describable in the third-person), or it is conscious experience (describable only by first-person qualitative "feels"). Although he later ascribes consciousness to such offbeat entities as a thermostat, this merely widens the number of beings permitted to have mind, and does nothing to expand Chalmers's basic roster of ontological personae. Other than particles, laws, and consciousness, nothing has reality in its own right. My claim, by contrast, is that the cosmos is riddled with autonomous entities at every level, and that they are reducible neither to microphysical structure nor to functional/relational use. But Chalmers anticipates my objection:

> A frequent response is that conscious experience is not alone …. and that all sorts of properties fail to supervene logically on the physical. It is suggested that such diverse properties as tablehood, life, and economic prosperity have no *logical* relationship to facts about atoms, electromagnetic fields, and so on. [71]

He responds to the objection as follows:

> on a careful analysis, I think it is not hard to see that this is wrong, and that the high-level facts in question are …. logically supervenient on the physical insofar as they are facts at all. Conscious experience is almost unique in its failure to supervene logically. [71]

---

[747] Since Chalmers holds that consciousness and causal laws are the only two genuine realities in the cosmos aside from brute basic particles, he muses further that "it is not unnatural to speculate that these two [logically] nonsupervenient kinds, consciousness and causation, may have a close metaphysical relation." (86) This has consequences that will concern us a bit later.

Chalmers concludes that "the relationship between consciousness and physical facts is different *in kind* from the standard relationship between high-level and low-level facts." [71; emph. added] His ten-page analysis of the issue hinges entirely on a point already discussed: "most high-level concepts are not primitive, unanalyzable notions .... [insofar as] their intensions can be seen to specify *functional* or *structural* properties." [81; emph. added]

Two names that Chalmers uses to describe his own position are "naturalistic dualism" and "nonreductive functionalism." These phrases mean the same thing. Naturalistic dualism is dualistic because it does not allow consciousness to be reduced to the physical, but at the same time it is "naturalistic because it posits that everything is a consequence of a network of basic properties and laws, and because it is compatible with all the results of contemporary science." [128] Nonreductive functionalism likewise points to the dual sense of a consciousness that arises from the physical while still being something fundamentally new. Chalmers's brand of functionalism denies "that the playing of some functional role is all there is to consciousness, or all there is to be explained. Rather, it is a nonreductive account, one that gives functional criteria *for when consciousness arises*." [229; emph. modified] Standard reductive functionalism holds that something is conscious when it *behaves* in conscious terms, displaying all the outward symptoms and effects that one expects of a conscious being, and for reductive functionalism there is nothing more to be explained than this. But this runs afoul of Chalmers's favorite thought-experiment of the *zombie*: a being identical to me in all physical and behavioral respects, but lacking any conscious experience. [94–99] Reductive functionalism effectively treats us as zombies reducible to our outward functions. By contrast, Chalmers holds that consciousness is different from all its outward manifestations, though without being independent of the physical conditions through which it arises. It is dependent on the physical ("naturally supervenient") without being reducible to it ("logically supervenient").

In the course of developing this position, Chalmers argues against numerous opposing views. But there are two alternative positions that he treats with an especial degree of respect. One is panpsychism: "we ought to take the possibility of some sort of panpsychism seriously: there seem to be no knockdown arguments against the view ...." [299] His relationship with panpsychism, as it is for so many of us, is a sort of unconsummated flirtation, though Chalmers is more open to consummation here than most. Yet even if he were to accept panpsychism, it would not threaten his dualism, since it would merely allow thermostats and other strange entities to join humans, monkeys, and dolphins on the side of conscious beings. While this would be no small gamble in the current intellectual climate, the basic dualist picture would remain. Hence, the more threatening rival that shadows Chalmers is a speculative metaphysics of hidden protophenomenal essences. That is to say, dualism might be challenged with the following point:

> to claim that the zombie world is *physically identical* to ours is to misdescribe it .... [Namely,] the zombie world *seems* physically identical [despite] being physically different .... there are properties essential to the physical constitution of the world that are not accessible to physical investigation. [134–135]

Chalmers notes that this latter position echoes the neutral monist views of Bertrand Russell in *The Analysis of Matter*, which Chalmers glosses as saying that "physical theory only characterizes its basic entities *relationally*, in terms of their causal and other relations to entities. [Even] basic particles .... are largely characterized in terms of their propensity to interact with other particles."[748] [153] For instance:

> reference to the proton is fixed as the thing that causes interactions of a certain kind, that combines in certain ways with other entities, and so on; but what is the thing doing the causing and the relating? As Russell notes, *this is a matter about which physical theory is silent*. [153]

While Chalmers is correct that this position would still be much closer to dualism than to materialism, [136] it would completely change the terms of the duality. Instead of a difference between first-person qualitative feels and third-person descriptions of physical matter, there would be a difference between nonrelational protophenomena and their relational manifestations. Both first-person and third-person descriptions would have to fall on the latter side of such a rift, since we do not exhaust our own reality in introspection any more than a proton is exhausted by our description of it, or even by its interactions with other particles when no one is looking. We also need to ask why only tiny particles should be granted a cryptic

---

[748] Bertrand Russell, *The Analysis of Matter*, as summarized in the words of Chalmers.

protophenomenal reality, rather than extending this gift to bulkier objects as well. In other words, why should *physical* structure always be reducible to its microphysical basis, as Chalmers assumes?

A bit more can be said about this. What Chalmers envisions is a theory of consciousness that will give us "psychophysical laws" irreducible to more basic physical ones. These laws will have a certain "brute" aspect that describes the workings of any sort of mind in our universe. If this bruteness of the psychophysical realm sounds disappointing, Chalmers reminds us that it is no different in the case of physical laws themselves:

> the theories that physics gives us of matter, of motion, or of space
> and time. Physical theories do not derive the existence of these
> features from anything more basic, but they still give us substantial,
> detailed accounts of these features and of how they interrelate ....
> They do this by giving a simple, powerful set of *laws* involving the
> various features .... [213]

More generally, "in science, we never get something for nothing: something, somewhere, must always be taken for granted .... So be it. That is the price of constructing a theory." What is interesting here is the claim that we are left with nothing to talk about but *laws*. Laws express relations between entities. Notice that for Chalmers there could be no such thing as "laws of tables," since these could be re-expressed either as structural accounts of how a table is an aggregate built up out of miniature physical particles, or functional laws of how the table can be used by people and cats. This would not be the case for such realities as consciousness, matter, motion, space, and time. These must be taken for granted because they are real entities, "part of the basic furniture of the universe," unlike non-basic furniture such as wooden or plastic tables.

One point of tension is as follows: while Chalmers usually regards only physical particles, consciousness, and laws as basic furniture, there are two occasions when he uses the discoveries of James Clerk Maxwell as analogies for the absolute novelty of consciousness. Chalmers recounts that after numerous failed attempts to explain electromagnetic phenomena in traditional mechanical terms,

> features such as *electromagnetic charge and electromagnetic forces*
> had to be taken as fundamental, and Maxwell introduced new
> fundamental electromagnetic laws .... *In the same way*, to explain

consciousness, the features and laws of physical theory are not
enough. [127; emph. added]

The oddity here is that electromagnetic charge and force are admitted
as new sorts of objects with the same degree of surprising novelty as
consciousness itself, irreducible to more basic physical mechanisms. To me
at least, this seems to open the floodgates and allow for novel objects on
countless different layers of the universe. Chemistry and geology also have
brute laws pertaining to the sorts of entities with which these sciences are
concerned: laws that "could not have been predicted" just by knowing all
the facts about quarks and electrons. Chalmers would probably counter
that chemical and geological entities can still be reduced, in principle, to
lower-level physical explanations based on microparticles. But the problem
here is that electromagnetism can itself be reduced to an "electroweak"
force, following the Nobel Prize-winning work of Sheldon Glashow, Abdus
Salam, and Steven Weinberg. Pushing even further, some future theory
may well unify the electroweak and strong nuclear forces with gravity, as
expressions of an even more fundamental layer of reality. And beyond this,
the philosopher Kasimir Twardowski imagined a general metaphysics of
objects to which both material and imaginary objects could be reduced.[749]
Hence it is unclear why Maxwell's electromagnetic realities receive a special
status not granted to other non-basic, non-mechanical entities.

My purpose is not to attack Chalmers's understanding of science, which
is evidently solid throughout the book. Rather, I simply wonder why he
conflates "autonomous" with "physically fundamental." Gravity remains a
relatively brute fact in our own time, and is also an autonomous subject
matter with its own laws and its own basic entities (including masses, and
also — since Einstein — including curvatures of space-time as well). But
the brutality and the autonomy of gravity *are not the same thing*, since the
former would disappear with a future scientific revolution, while the latter
may or may not disappear in such a case. Geology would not be considered
a "brute" realm for Chalmers any more than a table, since both would be
reducible to a tinier microphysics: yet both geology and the world of tables
have their own autonomous entities and laws, even if they are larger-scale
ones than in nuclear physics. And though Chalmers is committed to the
dubious idea that a given subject matter must be "fundamental" in order
to be filled with its own autonomous personae, he makes a bad gamble by

---

[749] Kasimir Twardowski, *On the Content and Object of Presentations.*

citing such examples of "fundamental" realities as mass, space, time, force, and charge. Quite obviously, the fundamental character of these realities is as open to further reduction and unification as the formerly basic proton was once we learned it was made of quarks. Demanding that a thing be "rock-bottom" in order to be real is too heavy a price for any ontology to pay. The world of Chalmers is disturbingly devoid of layers, giving us a physical model in which everything of greater than microscopic size is dismissed as a crude functional metaphor. This eventually creates severe problems for his version of dualism.

But let's return to the theme of nonreductive functionalism, where all these issues come to a head. Despite his objections to materialism, Chalmers remains committed to naturalism: consciousness may be mysterious, but it is not a spooky property that comes from nowhere, as if entirely unrelated to matter. And neither does it arise from some currently unknown *physical* X-factor. Rather,

> a natural suggestion is that consciousness arises in virtue of the
> *functional organization* of the brain. On this view, the chemical
> and indeed the quantum substrate of the brain is irrelevant to the
> production of consciousness. What counts is the brain's *abstract
> causal organization* .... (247; emph. added)

Since the specific physical substrate of consciousness is irrelevant, all kinds of strange media might give rise to consciousness if their abstract causal organization were of the right kind. Among other things, this leads Chalmers to defend strong artificial intelligence, which might come as a surprise given his public image as a holistic, anti-materialist bohemian. Without a trace of irony, Chalmers openly holds that "the organization of our brain might be simulated by the people of China," [251] with every Chinese citizen using radio links to mimic the functioning of neurons. If it sounds bizarre that such a rickety arrangement might lead to consciousness, Chalmers counters that "it is equally intuitively implausible that a *brain* should give rise to experience!" He faintly implies that Searle's famous "Chinese Room" might be conscious, [314] and openly entertains the notion that a thermostat might be as well, though he admits it would probably not be capable of thought or self-consciousness. [293–297]

This model bears directly on both of the neighboring theses that stalk Chalmers through his book: (a) panpsychism, and (b) the metaphysics of hidden essences. This becomes especially clear in his idea of consciousness as an information-processing system. Borrowing Gregory Bateson's slogan that "information is a difference that makes a difference," [281] Chalmers gives an intriguing account of information as *abstraction*.[750] When light strikes our eyes and activates cells in the retina,

> three varieties of cones abstract out information according to the amount of light present in various overlapping wavelength ranges. Immediately, many distinctions present in the original light wave are lost .... The system cannot report 'This patch is saturated with 500- to 600-nanometer reflections,' as all access to the original wavelengths is gone. Similarly, it cannot report about the neural structure, 'There's a 50-hertz spiking frequency now,' as it has no direct access to neural structures. The system has access only to the location in information space. [289–290]

This leads to an interesting conclusion: "it is information that plays the key role. It is *because the system has access only to information states* that the various judgments of brute 'qualities' are formed." [292; emph. added] Information is described as having a "double aspect," since both phenomenal and physical realities can be seen in informational terms. This is true not only for the phenomenal realm of vision and other such abstractions. It is also true in the physical realm, thanks to Chalmers's interpretation of Claude Shannon as saying that "information is always a *transmittable* state."[751] [282; emph. added] While he admits that this principle is merely implicit in Shannon's work, it seems convincing enough that transmitted information about physical states will always amount to a *translation*, and that translation is always a kind of abstraction or distortion. Hence, both the physical and phenomenal realms can be described in informational terms, and this obviously suggests a powerful means of linking them.

In fact, "we find information everywhere we find causation. We find causation everywhere, so we find information everywhere. But surely we do not find experience everywhere?" [293] We now arrive at Chalmers's well-known panpsychist moment. Though he considers the possibility that only certain *kinds* of information might yield experience, this sounds like an artificial shield against panpsychism, and Chalmers does not shy away from entertaining a more dramatic option. Since information is ubiquitous,

---

[750] See Gregory Bateson, *Steps to an Ecology of Mind*.
[751] See Claude E. Shannon, *The Mathematical Theory of Communication*.

it may follow that "experience is ubiquitous too." Among the many virtues of panpsychism, one is that

> if experience is truly a fundamental property, it seems natural for it to be widespread …. It would be odd for a fundamental property to be instantiated for the first time only relatively late in the history of the universe, and even then only in occasional complex systems. [297]

Perhaps the most worrisome problem with panpsychism, for Chalmers, is what is often termed "the combination problem." In his own words,

> the central reason why the term [panpsychism] is misleading …. is that it suggests a view in which the experiences in simple systems such as atoms are fundamental, and in which complex experiences are somehow the sum of much simpler experiences. [And] while this is one way things could go …. complex experiences may be more autonomous than this suggests. [299]

It is interesting to note that Chalmers (along with most panpsychists) is not worried about any combination problem in the *physical* realm. He never finds it troubling that complex physical objects could somehow be the sum of much simpler ones, since he actually believes that macro-entities such as tables do not really exist except as a crude sort of functional identity for those who encounter them. The combination problem supposedly arises only in the realm of consciousness, and "the *informational* view suggests a picture on which complex experiences are determined more holistically than this." Let's return, then, to the informational view.

Chalmers warns us that he is now venturing into "speculative metaphysics, but [this] is probably unavoidable in coming to terms with the ontology of consciousness." [302] The metaphysics in question resembles Russell's neutral monist view that both the mental and the physical arise from a more fundamental reality. After all, "physics tells us nothing about what mass *is*, or what charge *is*: it simply tells us the range of different values that these features can take on, and it tells us their effects on other features." For scientific purposes, "specific states of mass or charge might as well be pure information states …." Chalmers spends two pages entertaining the possibility that information is the *only* thing that exists — a pure informational flux without anything concealed behind it. Yet he finally concludes that this picture does justice neither to bodies nor to phenomenal experience. [303–304] For there is a certain "intrinsic" character to experience, which does not immediately pass into further abstract information for some further purpose; it is simply *there*, absorbing our attention. And as for the physical realm, a model of pure information with nothing behind it might give the impression that "[such a] world is too lacking in substance to *be* a world .... one might find it plausible [instead] that every concrete difference in the world must be grounded: that is, that it must be a difference *in* something." [304]

And this is where Chalmers feels close to Russell. If the informational model falls short of the intrinsic character of both phenomena *and* bodies, then perhaps some hidden intrinsic X can unify the dualism of Chalmers's model. Yet his own take on the problem tends to privilege the phenomenal side, about whose intrinsic quality he is much more convinced; his vague hunch that the physical realm might have some intrinsic character is overshadowed by his utter certainty that this is true of phenomenal experience. This leads him to suspect that everything in the world comes down to what is *phenomenally* intrinsic. As Chalmers sums up his proposal, "every time a feature such as mass and charge is realized, there is an intrinsic property behind it: a phenomenal or protophenomenal property, or a *microphenomenal* property for short." [305] This gives him a double-aspect ontology, "or as a slogan: Experience is information from the inside; physics is information from the outside." [305]

His worry about this model, yet again, is the so-called combination problem. For "our conscious experience does not seem to be any sort of sum of microphenomenal properties corresponding to the fundamental features in our brain .... Our experience seems much more holistic than that, and much more homogeneous than any simple sum would be." [306] One approach to this problem, he admits, would be to expand the double-aspect ontology from the level of basic particles into the macroscopic sphere. But here Chalmers runs aground on an old prejudice: his disbelief in macroscopic *physical* entities that would be irreducible to basic particles. The problem, he holds, is as follows:

> once we have fundamental physical features realized in phenomenal
> information spaces, then macroscopic information seems to be
> grounded already: the differences that make a difference here are
> now grounded in microscopic physical features, which are themselves
> grounded in microphenomenology. [306]

In short, there is no room in Chalmers's ontology for intermediate physical objects. In physical terms there are only microparticles, while in mental terms there are both tiny and large minds, with a nagging difficulty in linking these two sizes of mind together. Chalmers is perfectly happy to view a table as nothing but a swarm of tiny particles, but finds it harder to picture our consciousness as a swarm of tiny minds.

Yet the problem of how to build macro minds out of tiny minds is not even Chalmers's greatest concern. What he seems to fear most is the classic difficulty of mind becoming a useless epiphenomenon, a frivolous film on the surface of a causally closed universe. Earlier in the book he admitted briefly that "the biggest worry about [my] view is that it implies a certain irrelevance of phenomenal properties in explaining behavior, and may lead to epiphenomenalism ...." [165] And even earlier,

> if consciousness is merely naturally supervenient on the physical, then it seems to lack causal efficacy .... This implies that there is no room for a nonphysical consciousness to do any independent causal work. It seems to be a mere epiphenomenon hanging off the engine of physical causation, but making no difference in the physical world. [150]

This problem will be considered below.

To summarize, the two main problems that Chalmers acknowledges with his model are the combination problem and epiphenomenalism. The major problem he fails to acknowledge is his strangely asymmetrical treatment of body and mind, which grants no macroscopic-sized entities in the physical case but is plagued with an odd tension between tiny- and large-sized minds. There is also the perplexing issue of why Chalmers is fixated on the difference between bodies and minds at all. If the entities of physics are described in purely informational terms, and if phenomenal experience is also filled with nothing but abstract information, then it seems fairly clear that Chalmers is discussing the wrong dualism. He should drop the idea that there are two basic classes called bodies and minds, and replace it with a dualism of *intrinsic realities* and *the information transmitted about them*. Objects would be zero-person intrinsic realities that simply go about being whatever they are, prior to any informational abstraction by other entities. But for objects to become *accessible* to other objects means that they must be reduced to abstractions, translated into informational holograms that do not do full justice to their reality. And this is all the dualism we need. Minds and bodies are both objects, not two fundamentally different pieces of furniture in the universe. An electron both is what it is, and is also information making a difference to other realities, though in pitifully abstracted form. The same is true of a conscious mind: I am what I am, but all introspection comes up woefully short of exhausting what it is to be me. In a sense, eliminativists are right when they argue that first-person description is no different from the third-person kind.[752] Both are descriptions, and hence both are purely informational. My consciousness is not equivalent to my first-person "feel" of it, because my self-understanding is never adequate at any given moment.

Combination and Epiphenomenon

The reason I have spent so much time on Chalmers is because his mistakes strike so close to the truth. Already, I have argued that his traditional distinction between bodies and minds needs to be replaced by one between objects and relations; furthermore, I have contended that he is wrong to reduce macroscopic *bodies* to lower-level structures and higher-level functions, since consciousness is not unique in being irreducible to its component parts.

Chalmers portrays himself as a former materialist who was finally forced to admit that consciousness must be irreducible to matter. Yet the most striking point is that even though Chalmers is no longer a materialist about consciousness, he remains a materialist about everything else. Now, the main problem with materialism was already noted by Chalmers: it is a purely *relationist* model of the world. As Russell observed, scientific matter is defined only by its relational effects on other things, never in its own right. But since these effects are always measurable in mathematical terms, this makes materialism a form of *idealism*, not of realism.[753] And though Chalmers might seem like a hardnosed realist, given his loyalty to the supposed microparticles of physics, he is an idealist about all physical things any larger than that. Chalmersian physics exists only at the micro-level, while Chalmersian consciousness exists both at the micro-level of basic particles and (somehow) at the macro-level of complex living beings. For him it is largely a matter of adding conscious tiny particles to the known list of conscious humans, dogs, and mice, with nothing in between. This makes

---

[752] See for instance Paul Churchland's lucid early work *Scientific Realism and the Plasticity of Mind*, p. 97.

[753] See Bruno Latour, "Can We Get Our Materialism Back, Please?"

his proposal of conscious thermostats especially refreshing, since it begins to populate the intermediate zone of the world for the first time in the book. However, if every conscious state is associated with a physical state, this immediately suggests that the *physical* thermostat should also be a real entity over and above the quarks of which it is made, just as the *conscious* thermostat is something over and above its microphenomenal components. Yet Chalmers's instinctive materialism in physical questions prevents him from taking this step.

We must proceed further into speculative metaphysics than Chalmers himself. Recall his proposed final slogan: "Experience is information from the inside; physics is information from the outside." The difficulty lies in seeing how there could be any such thing as information from the *inside*. Chalmers extends Shannon's theory to say that all perceptual and physical information is an abstraction from some more complicated reality, filtering out all access to 50-hertz spiking frequencies and other causal entities. In this respect, both experience and physics are concerned with *outside* views on information. Therefore, I ask: why preserve the dualism between experience and bodies? Why not just unify them as forms of information straightaway? The reason stems from Chalmers's lingering sense that only phenomenal experience is intrinsic. Since he holds that the physical is always reducible, but the phenomenal never is, the phenomenal must count as something intrinsically real. Even physical microparticles turn out to be purely relational for Chalmers, due to Russell's point about the purely relational character of the physical. Thus, the only way for Chalmers to prevent the reduction of the world to a sheer causal flux, the only way to give it some sort of intrinsic reality, is to double up relational microparticles with intrinsically real microminds. But whatever the gains of such a model, it is certainly not neutral monism. Instead, it is a dualism of two *types* of entity, with minds playing the intrinsic role and bodies the relational role.

But if any genuine dualism arises from Chalmers's reflections, it lies between information and whatever it informs us about. Phenomenal experience can only be called "intrinsic" on the basis of an ambiguity. To begin with, I will agree with Chalmers against eliminativism that phenomenal experience is a brute *factum*: here it is right now, I am having such experience as I write these words. But introspection can never grasp this experience as a whole. Introspection, just like the relational descriptions of physics, gives us information viewed from without — it is a more or less noisy translation of whatever this information is *about*. Consciousness is intrinsic not because it is *experienced*, but because it *is*, and my experience of myself can only be an informational abstraction no less than physics is. Moreover, in this sense even bodies are intrinsic: no list of features of an electron can replace that electron, and this means that the electron too is an intrinsic, autonomous object. We do not need to add a micro-mind to the electron *just for the sake of making the electron intrinsic*; if there are grounds for panpsychism, they are not to be found here. This means once again that the difference between first-person and third-person is superficial, even nonexistent. Electrons exceed my information about them, and my conscious reality exceeds my own informational "feels" about it. The key opposition is not between mind and body, but between objects and relations, as the occasionalists already knew. The difference is not between first-person and third-person, but between zero-person and any-other-person.

But it is not only we humans who encounter other entities as information; the same holds for non-human entities in their encounters with each other. In terms of Russell's remark, it is not just that *science* only gives us protons and electrons in relational terms, but that protons and electrons only encounter *each other* that way as well. It is not just human consciousness that translates reality into information; relationality in general must do this. This is the true root for any form of panpsychism. You and I encounter nothing but information, and so do protons, electrons, candles, and dogs. It does not follow from this that all of these entities are *nothing but* information, since this would eliminate any intrinsic features from the cosmos, and Chalmers is right to see problems with all such attempts. Protons and electrons are intrinsically *objects*, irreducible to any causal information they might generate, and so are human beings. Shifting terminology slightly, the real dualism in question is one between objects and images. Objects are real, but withdraw permanently from any adequate relational access, just as in the occasionalist model. And given that real objects withdraw from interaction, it cannot be real objects that interact. They only interact *vicariously* in some shared medium where they are somehow able to meet. It should be clear by now that this shared vicarious medium of objects must be purely informational, since information is the only common currency that all objects share. Objects collide only indirectly, by means of the images they present as information. Yet there must be some way for this to lead to effects on real objects themselves, or else causal relations would never occur.

An obvious question arises as to where information is located. Strangely enough, the only possible answer is that images of objects are found *on the interiors of other objects*. As bizarre as this might sound, it is already the basic principle of Brentano, the forefather of phenomenology.

Brentano's discussion of the difference between the mental and the physical is well-known:

> Every mental phenomenon is characterized by what the Scholastics of the Middle Ages called the intentional (or mental) inexistence of an object .... or immanent objectivity. Every mental phenomenon includes something as object within itself, although they do not all do so in the same way. In presentation something is presented, in judgment something is affirmed or denied, in love loved, in hate hated, in desire desired and so on.[754]

This intentional inexistence (meaning "existence inside") is characteristic exclusively of mental phenomena. No physical phenomenon exhibits anything like it. We can, therefore, define mental phenomena by saying that they are those phenomena which contain an object intentionally within themselves. In fact, such inexistence is the one portion of Brentano's doctrine that I wish to retain. Information or images, which we might also term "intentional objects" in the manner of Husserl, are contained in another object, giving them the status of immanent objectivity. This contrasts with the withdrawn, never-immanent objectivity of real objects. Intentional objects are not autonomous, but exist only on the interiors of real ones.

Two other aspects of Brentano's theory must be rejected. First, we should refuse his implication that there is no intentionality in the physical realm. We have already suggested that information, translation, relation, or image do not just belong to mind in the narrow sense of advanced conscious beings, but characterize any relation at all. Electrons, just like humans, encounter mere informational images of atomic nuclei, and do not deal with these nuclei in naked presence any more than we do. This is the sense in which electrons have intentional experience, however primitive it may be. Second, even if intentional objects exist at the core of some other object, there is no reason to claim that this other object is *I myself*. In fact, my perception of the tree is not on the inside of me, but on the interior of a strange new object: my *relation* with the tree. Too often, the term "object" is restricted to durable physical solids, and for this reason it might seem odd to describe my relation with the tree as an object. But the problem disappears if we redefine an object as anything that has intrinsic reality apart from the information that someone or something might have

---

[754] Franz Brentano, *Psychology From an Empirical Standpoint*, pp. 88–89.

THE GRAHAM HARMAN READER

about it. And my relation with the tree clearly meets this standard. The relation clearly occurs, or there would be no perception; yet this relation is also not exhausted by my consciousness of it, since I can make mistakes in describing my perception, and painstaking phenomenological work is needed to attain even partial success. Just as little can some outside observer exhaust my relation to the tree, perhaps by describing it in the functional terms of experimental psychology. Hence, the relation between me and tree meets the criteria for an object. And it is this object, not me, whose interior contains my perception of the tree. It should be noted in passing that there is a strange asymmetry here. While the tree-image or tree-information is what appears in-existently in the perception, I myself am present as a *real* object rather than a merely intentional one, since I really am experiencing the image. Thus, the interior of an object contains the proximity of a real object with an intentional object. This means that if the tree manages to relate to me as well, this would generate a reciprocal but non-identical object in which the real tree brushes against the phenomenal version of me. But this is a theme for another occasion.

To change perception from something immanent in me to something generated by my *relations* with other things is reminiscent of W. Teed Rockwell's best arguments in *Neither Brain Nor Ghost*. His central idea in this book is the impossibility of localizing consciousness in the brain. Rockwell first contends that mind must be extended into the nervous system as a whole, but he eventually brings the entire surrounding world into the drama of consciousness:

> When we inquire into the world, we discover the system whose natural parts are the body, the brain, and the world. But we have no reason to assume that the brain can produce experience without the other two, any more than the lung can perform its proper function without oxygen.[755]

And here I agree. But while it is admirable that Rockwell brings relations into the picture, he indulges in the pragmatist excess of *reducing* things to their relational contours:

> we experience, not sense data that remind us of objects, but *the objects themselves* in a world with which we interact: tables and chairs

---

[755] W. Teed Rockwell, *Neither Brain Nor Ghost*, p. 101.

in which we sit, and people with whom we have relationships, people whose likeability and cruelty or beauty is every bit as predicable to them as is their height or weight.

This passage denies the model that I advocate of information as a more-or-less faulty translation of intrinsic objects. For Rockwell, the things themselves simply *are* the information we have about them. What bothers Rockwell most is "the idea that we start from experience that exists only in our minds, and from this infer the existence of a universe of dead clockwork." But here he mixes two distinct issues. Realism about the external world in no way entails a universe of dead clockwork. Rockwell clings to the relationist view that there is no cryptic reality behind how things are accessed. But his pragmatist views need not be opposed with a dead-clockwork version of realism: *au contraire*, the "dead clockwork" of physics means a purely *relational* system of things dealing with each other as simplified abstractions. Hence, Rockwell's pragmatist relationism ironically puts him in the same camp as the relationism of the clockwork materialism he purports to detest. Furthermore, his insistence that a person's cruelty or beauty are just as real as their height or weight is both revealing and irrelevant. For why does Rockwell assume that height and weight are dull clockwork realities existing in a gray outer world, while cruelty or beauty must be exhausted by their manifestation to us? Beyond any *information* I have about a person's cruelty or beauty are the cruelty or beauty themselves, summoning me to explore their flickering depths. Although we should honor Rockwell's sensitivity to the fact that perception is produced by relations rather than by a simple brain-thing, there is no reason to endorse his pragmatist relationism, which also leads him to miss the surprisingly *realist* lesson of Heidegger's tool-analysis: tools that hide behind any informational or relational profile.

We should make a final point concerning the various different *levels* of the world. We have seen that Chalmers largely rejects such levels. He offers a one-layered physical world of tiny things, and an apparently two-layered mental world in which tiny microminds combine at some point into full-blown macrominds. Yet we should no longer speak of a misleading dualism of minds and bodies. The real duality is between real objects and their interiors: volcanic regions riddled with intentional objects. Now, there is no reason to assume that objects are found only at Chalmers's own levels of microparticles and two sizes of minds, with everything else reducible to structure or function. Objects emerge at countless different levels. This is argued for instance by Manuel DeLanda, who proposes a wonderful model of a world consisting of *assemblages*: real units made up of subpersonal components.[756] In this way, he populates Chalmers's empty macro-sized wasteland with countless genuine entities. As DeLanda puts it, "the terms 'micro' and 'macro' should not be associated with two fixed levels of scale but used to denote the concrete parts and the resulting emergent whole *at any given spatial scale*." An emergent whole "must be shown to emerge from the interaction between *subpersonal components*." [32] DeLanda even offers some criteria for what makes a real assemblage. He names at least four characteristics of new emergent realities, none of them permitted by Chalmers's less stratified vision:

1 Obviously, the emergent whole must have emergent properties not possessed by its parts. Here we should not be hasty in assuming that emergent *physical* processes can easily be reduced to lower-level physical ones.[757] If "no one could have predicted" the emergence of consciousness from the brain, it is equally true that "no one could have predicted" inert gases and rare earths just by knowing about protons, and "no one could have predicted" the basic forms of government just from knowing about human beings. There are effects of surprise and novelty at every possible level, not just at a single magical gap between microparticles and consciousness.

2 The whole can have retroactive effects on its parts.[758] This is easier to see in the case of large social objects such as fraternities and armies, but it holds at lower levels as well.

3 Emergent wholes are characterized by "redundant causation," in the sense that many of their parts can be removed or replaced with no impact at all on the whole.[759] For example, even if it is true that the atoms in the human body are completely replaced every seven years or so, this is not grounds for claiming that the body is no longer the same body.

---

[756] Manuel DeLanda, *A New Philosophy of Society*.

[757] The contrary assumption is shared even by Galen Strawson, who agrees with Chalmers that phenomena such as liquidity and convection cells do not pose the same sort of mystery as consciousness. Strawson writes: "In both these cases we move in a small set of conceptually homogeneous shape-size-mass-charge-number-position-motion-involving physics notions with no sense of puzzlement." Strawson, "Realistic Monism," p. 13. Like Chalmers's own model, this grants materialism the right to run rampant over all of reality *except* consciousness.

[758] DeLanda, *A New Philosophy of Society*, p. 34. DeLanda credits this point to Roy Bhaskar, *A Realist Theory of Science*.

[759] DeLanda, *A New Philosophy of Society*, p. 37.

4   Emergent wholes often create *new* parts. As DeLanda puts it,

> while some parts may pre-exist the whole, others may be generated
> by the maintenance processes of an already existing whole: while
> cities are composed of populations of interpersonal networks and
> organizations, it is simply not the case that these populations had to
> be there prior to the emergence of a city. In fact, most networks and
> organizations come into being as parts of already existing cities.[760]

This too is clearer in the case of large social entities, but holds for smaller objects as well.

In short, there is far more drama underway at each level of objects than Chalmers is willing to grant. To assemble a new object also means to assemble a new interior to that object, and hence a new information space. Instead of Chalmers's two-story building of physical and phenomenal, DeLanda suggests a palace of infinite stories. Every object is a capsule or container hiding its own interior. The world is made of autonomous ascending and descending levels of bubbles: vacuum-sealed spaces of information that nothing can penetrate, as if the world were a nested set of black holes.

This model may seem strange, but it has the immediate benefit of dissolving Chalmers's two biggest problems. First, consciousness is no longer a sterile epiphenomenon irrelevant to causation. Quite the opposite: an informational space that houses intentional objects is now the *only possible site* of causation, since real objects withdraw from each other to such a degree that they are never able to touch. Instead of an epiphenomenon, consciousness is now an *infraphenomenon* in the heart of an object, confronting images in their intentional inexistence or immanent objectivity. Second, the notorious combination problem is transformed into something more like the occasionalist problem. It is no longer a question of billions of microminds being packed together in a single mid-sized macromind. Instead, there are new assemblages of objects at each level, whose abstracting tendencies *cut them off* from most of the reality existing below. Just as cones in the retina abstract from most visual information, any macro-sized object will not have a chance of accessing most of the information possessed by its increasingly tiny sub-components. The world is filled with levels and way stations, and information does not smoothly cascade from one level to the next. The world is made of chunks, and each chunk translates information

---

[760]   DeLanda, *A New Philosophy of Society*, p. 39.

into a new language. A table is not locally composed of trillions of particles, but is made of only four or five pieces, isolated from most of what goes on deep below. Likewise, the conscious experience on the interior of an object arises from the relation between a small number of locally relevant objects, not from the trillions of tiny minds that swarm beneath the radar. Thus, we no longer have a combination problem of the sort that plagues Chalmers. But we do have a new problem, as any philosophy must. Namely, the problem is how immanent relations in the interior of an object ever puncture that immanence so as to affect *real objects*, instead of just making contact with pure images. This problem defines a lengthy research program, and cannot be discussed further here. Instead, I will close with a brief reflection on whether the model just described also amounts to panpsychism.

Panpsychism and Endopsychism

Among other activities, David Skrbina often acts as a ruthless Minority Whip in the field of panpsychist studies. He frequently wonders aloud why certain authors walk the edge of the panpsychist pool while refusing to dive in. Instead of clear consideration of the panpsychist option, "one [usually] finds a mushy middle ground in which philosophers fail to clearly articulate their views one way or the other."[761] In the specific case of Chalmers:

> If [John] Searle has one valid point [in his response to Chalmers],
> it is that Chalmers is unwilling to follow through explicitly on the
> consequences of his own theory: information is postulated to have a
> phenomenal aspect, and [since] information is everywhere, then so is
> experience.[762]

Concerning my own case, Skrbina once sent me an email containing the following sentence: "I know you have been dancing around this whole [panpsychist] issue for awhile …."[763] Fair enough. Here is a good example of my previous dancing:

> [It is] invalid to draw [panpsychist] conclusions, and to conclude
> that because humans and rocks both enter into relations, rocks must

---

[761] Skrbina, *Panpsychism in the West*, p. 7.
[762] Skrbina, *Panpsychism in the West*, pp. 242–243.
[763] David Skrbina, personal communication, June 27, 2007.

already have human cognitive powers in germinal form .... If we shift to the case of glass .... the [panpsychist] is like someone who says that everything in the world is equally glass, though perhaps in a "weaker" form than windows. What is lacking is the most sensible alternative, which is to say that human knowledge, just like glass, backbones, reptiles, music, and mushrooms, arises at a certain point in the history of the universe, but without necessarily forming some sort of root metaphysical dualism in the world. I see no convincing reason to regard human knowledge as of such pivotal importance in the universe.[764]

There are two problems with this passage from my recent past. The first is that it takes panpsychism in too narrow a sense. Skrbina's book frequently observes that there is "a sort of panpsychist hierarchy of terminology, ranging from the most human-like to the most universal."[765] His examples of various aspects that one might include in a panpsychist theory include self-consciousness, cognition, thought, consciousness, sense, awareness, sentience, emotion, experience, mind, mental state, what-it-is-like, qualia, nous, and psyche. The theory of universal relations between objects sketched above clearly belongs somewhere on this list, though it remains unclear exactly where.

The second problem with the passage is its insufficient candor in admitting to the key dualism in question. If we speak of a universe where all objects withdraw equally from one another, then this is neutral monism insofar as everything is an object, and radical pluralism insofar as there are countless objects. But in another sense it is admittedly a form of frank dualism, given its basic split between hidden real objects and accessible images housed on the interior of objects. While it may be true that the *human* mind is of no more ontological importance than glass, something like mind is still present everywhere, and this is surely not true of glass. In the duality of objects and relations, there is something distinctly mind-like about the "relations" side. On the whole, I am now more inclined to embrace the term "panpsychism" than before, since the obligation I feel of placing all relations between entities on the same footing puts me closer to the panpsychist position than to either materialism or the usual human-world couplet.

---

[764] Graham Harman, *Guerrilla Metaphysics*, pp. 83–84.
[765] Skrbina, *Panpsychism in the West*, p. 18.

If one thing seems to unify the mentality of all entities, from specks of dust, to bats, to humans, to demigods, it is what Chalmers describes as the experience of information. And if we are committed to reality having some sort of intrinsic character (as I am), then this entails some sort of sub-informational reality that can be presented only in translated form. It seems obvious that a genuine realist standpoint would need to focus on the tension between these two realms: realities vs. their informational profiles for other realities. But this would still miss something important, since it would overlook any stratification *within* the informational sphere. And here a surprising contribution is made by Husserl, whose human-centric phenomenology otherwise seems like such a poor match for panpsychist themes.

Husserl is rightly viewed as an idealist who brackets all consideration of the natural world and lets philosophy unfold only in the conscious sphere. But there is more to Husserl than this. Unlike most idealists, Husserl gives us an ideal realm that contains both intentional objects *and* the accidental ways in which they happen to appear (a.k.a. "adumbrations"). This challenges the usual model of conscious experience, which holds that experience encounters a certain content of specific qualities. In the famous *Logical Investigations*, Husserl challenges the mainstream standpoint of British Empiricism, which holds that experience is always of "experienced contents": that our supposed experience of a unified apple or horse result from a supplementary bundling of numerous discrete qualities.[766] For Husserl, and for the entire phenomenological tradition he inaugurates, what we experience are intentional *objects* rather than free-floating pointillistic sensations held together through the force of habit. He even makes a similar criticism of his honored teacher Brentano. Whereas Brentano had held that "[intentions] are either presentations or founded upon presentations,"[767] Husserl counters that "every intention is either an *objectifying act* or has its basis in such an act."[768]

Now, what is the difference between a presentation and an objectifying act? A presentation consists of highly specific informational content, in which everything in our field of experience has a determinate color, position, surface glitter, and a specific distance and angle from the observer. All parts of the presentation are equally real *qua* presentation. Yet things are

---

[766] Edmund Husserl, *Logical Investigations*, 2 vols.

[767] Husserl, *Logical Investigations*, vol. 2, p. 556. Emphasis modified.

[768] Husserl, *Logical Investigations*, vol. 2, p. 648. Emphasis added.

different if we consider experience as made up of objectifying acts. In this case, I look straight through the outer costume of things and intend objects as *essential units*. When circling a tree or a warehouse the presentation changes constantly, but the objectifying act itself does not. I intend the same *object* through all my motions, even though the *presentation* changes constantly. This all comes to a head in the famous *Logical Investigations* VI, where Husserl speaks of how the object "is only given 'from the front,' only 'perspectivally foreshortened and projected' etc."[769] And moreover:

> whether I look at this book from above or below, from inside or
> outside, I always see *this book*. It is always one and the same thing,
> and that not merely in some purely physical sense [which plays
> no role in Husserl's philosophy — G.H.], but in the view of our
> percepts themselves. If individual properties dominate variably at
> each step, the thing itself, as a perceived unity, is not in essence set up
> by some over-reaching act, founded upon these separate percepts.[770]

In other words, we no longer have just a distinction between real objects and their informational simulacra, with the latter forming the straightforward topic of experience. Instead, Husserl's philosophy gives us a permanent duel *within* the informational realm: a duel between intentional objects and the swirling surface-effects through which they are announced. In short, experience for Husserl is quantized into chunks, each of them encrusted with an ever-shifting patina of accidents.

Now, even panpsychists will surely accept that at least *some* features of human mentality are not found in whatever microminds might populate the world. High-level thinking capacity, color vision, language, emotional life, and the ability to dream are among the numerous mental gifts that we would not expect to find very far down the chain of mental beings. But what about Husserl's object-oriented model of intentionality? When considering the duality between intentional objects and their shifting surface-effects, it might be asked whether this is the sort of primitive mentality that belongs to all real beings, or whether it has all the special human complexity that we find in the ability to learn languages and make mathematical discoveries. The question is not whether all objects experience information generated by other, concealed real objects, since that point is already granted by the

---

[769] Husserl, *Logical Investigations*, vol. 2, p. 712.
[770] Husserl, *Logical Investigations*, vol. 2, p. 789.

model developed so far. Instead, the question is whether even the most primitive sort of experience must encounter immanent objects in the intentional realm, rather than splotches of isolated qualities. My suspicion is that intentional objects are a primitive phenomenon found in all experience, and do not first arise in higher forms of consciousness. If this is so, then even the most rudimentary inanimate experience is torn by a rift between unified intentional objects and their shifting accidental profiles. And this suggests that greater mental complexity must arise from improved articulation of this very rift. Is it not the case that the apparently superior achievements of animals compared with stones are a matter of creating and distinguishing new *objects*? Physical organs ranging from ears to eyes to brains allow for greater fragmentation of experience into ever finer-grained chunks or zones. The discovery of mathematical objects adds even non-tangible realities to the field of human mentality. Complex human societies are able to preserve even dead persons in the form of historical records, while our fixed names, identification numbers, and career résumés help turn us from interchangeable others into highly articulated specific objects. What makes one mind more complex than others is probably its greater ability to discover, generate, and maintain a greater number of autonomous objects, and in turn this is what makes the social mind more powerful than any of our individual minds.

If this is true, if all interaction between entities involves an encounter with intentional objects, does this give us panpsychism? Almost, but not quite. The truth is subtler and stranger than this. Namely, although there is psychic experience on the inside of every object, that experience is not being had by the object itself. Hence, although every object has an interior, it is not necessarily the case that every object will enter into relations with others, and hence have experience of immanent objectivity on the inside of another. Earlier I claimed (against Brentano, and to some extent with Rockwell) that experience is not something internal to me, but internal to my *relation* with a tree, horse, apple, or whatever I perceive. If all experience occurs on the inside of an object, that object is never I myself, but a composite object formed of me and that to which I relate. Within that interior, I experience an informational image of the tree, and it may well encounter an image of me as well (though that would take place on the inside of a different object, if a closely related one). But consider the status of the larger object formed of me and the tree, or the parallel object formed of the tree and me. It need not be the case that such a larger object enters into relation with anything else. It certainly has an interior, because that is where my experience occurs right now. And to have an interior is enough to make it real, since that is all it means to be an object: to have a genuine internal reality not exhausted by any outside view. But the interior of that larger object is experienced only by one or more of its *pieces*, not by the larger object itself. No object experiences *its own* interior, just as I myself do not: I experience the interior of my relations with the things I perceive, not the interior of myself. It is nearly certain that there are many objects that have a genuine reality but that still enter into no further relations. Such objects would be genuine inhabitants of the world, despite not entering into relation with anything else. Hence they would be real, but without experience. Instead of a full-blown *pan*-psychism, then, we would have to content ourselves with an *endo*-psychism, in which entities might be real while encountering nothing at all. Many real objects might be doomed to perpetual sleep.

In closing, let's review what this article has tried to show. First, the traditional mind-body problem was replaced by the occasionalist model of a body-body problem. Second, the supposed difference between first- and third-person descriptions was shown to be a false duality, since both kinds of description belong on the same side of the fence when contrasted with the zero-person intrinsic nature of things. And finally, it was suggested that while there is experience or immanent objectivity on the inside of every object, what does the experiencing is not the whole object itself (my relation with a tree), but only one of its components (in this case, I myself). This opposes Brentano's claim that perception occurs on the inside of the perceiver, and veers toward Rockwell's view that consciousness is a relational sort of reality. It follows that even if all entities *contain* experience, not all entities *have* experience. Hence panpsychism is not strictly true, even if there are exponentially many more minds than is usually believed.

CHAPTER 31

ON PROGRESSIVE AND DEGENERATING RESEARCH PROGRAMS WITH RESPECT TO PHILOSOPHY[771]

The Hungarian-born philosopher Imre Lakatos (1922–1974), who reached the peak of his fame at the London School of Economics, had a career as influential as it was brief. Fortunately, his works are not difficult to come by: especially his book *Proofs and Refutations*, and the two volumes of his collected philosophical papers available since 1978.[772] As stimulating as Lakatos's philosophy of science has proven to be, with its insight into the difference between "progressive" and "degenerating" research programs, he is not entirely clear as to how to apply these ideas to philosophical rather than scientific programs. This article will explore the outlines of how we might go about doing so. In an effort to reach the largest possible readership, I will assume no prior familiarity with Lakatos whatsoever. Those who already know his work are therefore asked to be patient as we first review the ABC's of his methodology of scientific research programs. Later, I will proceed to make more controversial claims.

---

[771] "On Progressive and Degenerating Research Programs With Respect to Philosophy" first appeared in 2019 (in English) in *Revista Portuguesa de Filosofia* 75.4, pp. 2067–2102.

[772] Imre Lakatos, *Proofs and* Refutations; Imre Lakatos, *The Methodology of Scientific Research Programs*; Imre Lakatos, *Mathematics, Science, and Epistemology*.

Although Lakatos is famous for his work on both science and mathematics, it is the former that concerns us here. His philosophy of science boils down to the following two basic ideas:

1 Popperian falsificationism in science, however dramatic an improvement over its predecessors, is incorrect on a decisive point. There are no "crucial experiments" that falsify a scientific theory once and for all, since every such theory is always surrounded by a cloud of anomalies. Science is less about individual propositions than about broader *research programs*, which are sometimes defended for decades despite mountains of contradictory evidence. Newton's theory was not abandoned due to being "falsified" as Popper would claim, since hundreds of anomalies had accrued from the start. It was only with A.S. Eddington's startling confirmation of General Relativity in the solar eclipse of May 29, 1919, by measuring that starlight was bent by the sun at double the amount predicted by Newtonian theory, that Einsteinian General Relativity was shown to be more progressive than Newtonian universal gravitation.

2 This might seem to put Lakatos closer to Thomas Kuhn than to Popper, since Kuhn's model of "paradigm shifts" does provide an account of why scientists stick with already refuted theories. Lakatos's "research programs" are nonetheless not the same thing as paradigms, since according to Kuhn — as Lakatos reads him (wrongly, in my view) — the latter shift for no rational reason, but are sociological phenomena resembling "religious conversions." While all research programs are confronted by numerous falsifications, Lakatos draws a key distinction between "progressive" and "degenerating" ones. What characterizes progressive research programs is that they are able to predict new and unforeseen facts, whereas degenerating programs tend to explain already established facts in their own new terminology. As another example, Einsteinian General Relativity was able to explain the precession of the perihelion of Mercury in a way that Newton's theory simply could not. If we imagine a hypothetical Newtonian who responded to Einstein by saying "Newtonian gravitational theory works for all planets other than Mercury," we would have a good (even comical) instance of a "degenerating problemshift," since Newton's theory now preserves itself only by *saying less* than it previously did.[773]

---

[773] Lakatos, *Mathematics, Science, and Epistemology*, p. 171.

More detailed accounts of the emergence of Lakatos's theory of science are easy enough to find in the literature.[774] This article wishes to determine the potential philosophical use of the two points just listed. There are widely contested and differing views about whether philosophy is continuous with science, or whether the two are fundamentally different in kind. Quine and Sellars are good representatives of the first view, while Heidegger and Badiou (who regards science but not philosophy to be a "truth procedure") are emblematic of the second.[775] I begin with a pair of limited questions, corresponding to the two points above. Namely:

1 To what extent can a philosophy be considered a "research program"?
2 Does the opposition between "progressive" and "degenerating" research programs make sense in a philosophical as well as a scientific context? And if so, then what modifications are needed — if any — when shifting from one case to the other?

A. Is There a Philosophical Research Program?

Lakatos is fulsome in his praise of Karl Popper, whom he identifies as the chief influence on his own mature work:

> Popper's ideas represent the most important development in the philosophy of the twentieth century …. Personally, my debt to him is immeasurable: more than anyone else, he changed my life. I was nearly forty when I got into the magnetic field of his intellect. His philosophy helped me to make a final break with the Hegelian outlook which I had held for nearly twenty years. And, more important, it provided me with an immensely fertile range of problems, indeed with a veritable research program.[776]

The praise is obviously sincere, even if the critical pages that follow (in "Popper on Demarcation and Induction") led to a rupture between the two. The heart of Popper's theory of science, of course, is his notion of "falsifiability."[777] Any theory, whether inside or outside science, can point

---

[774] Alan Musgrave & Charles Pigden, "Imre Lakatos."
[775] Quine, "Two Dogmas of Empiricism"; Sellars, "Philosophy and the Scientific Image of Man"; Heidegger, *What is Called Thinking?*; Badiou, *Being and Event*.
[776] Lakatos, *The Methodology of Scientific Research Programs*, p. 139.
[777] Karl Popper, *Conjectures and Refutations*.

to confirming evidence in its favor. But to be truly scientific, a theory must be willing to risk possible refutation. As Lakatos summarizes his mentor's view: "A theory is 'scientific' if one is prepared to specify in advance a crucial experiment (or observation) which can falsify it, and it is pseudoscientific if one refuses to specify such a 'potential falsifier.'"[778] Marxism and psychoanalysis are two theories famously accused by Popper of being unfalsifiable and therefore "pseudoscientific."[779]

Although Lakatos admires the falsifiablity criterion as an important philosophical breakthrough, it does not satisfy him. Far from being a rare event, refuting evidence (no less than confirming evidence) surrounds any theory at all times: "Each research program, at every moment of its existence, has unsolved problems and undigested anomalies. All theories, in this sense, are born refuted and die refuted."[780] If Popper were right, it would simply be *irrational* to adhere to any theory already contradicted by empirical evidence: meaning any theory at all. And yet, "Popper ignores the remarkable tenacity of scientific theories. Scientists have thick skins. They do not abandon a theory merely because facts contradict it. They normally either invent some rescue hypothesis to explain what they then call a mere anomaly, or ... they ignore it, and direct their attention to other problems."[781] Moreover, although Popper's outlook suggests that the history of science should consist of numerous "crucial experiments" that falsify previous theories, Lakatos argues that such experiments are merely the stuff of mythology: "History of science, of course, is full of accounts of how crucial experiments allegedly killed theories. But such accounts are fabricated long after the theory had been abandoned."[782]

We should now ask how the tenacity of scientists in the face of refuting evidence can be explained. As mentioned, one explanation is offered by Kuhn in *The Structure of Scientific Revolutions.*[783] For Kuhn, there is a sharp distinction between (a) everyday "normal science" which focuses on solving discrete narrow puzzles within an already established framework, and (b) rare "paradigm shifts" in which the basic assumptions of a science are shaken to the core, such as the advent of Copernican astronomy or — more

---

[778] Lakatos, *The Methodology of Scientific Research Programs*, p. 3.
[779] Popper, *Conjectures and Refutations*, pp. 46–47.
[780] Lakatos, *The Methodology of Scientific Research Programs*, p. 5.
[781] Lakatos, *The Methodology of Scientific Research Programs*, pp. 3–4.
[782] Lakatos, *The Methodology of Scientific Research Programs*, p. 4. See also Lakatos, *Mathematics, Science, and* Epistemology, pp. 211–215.
[783] Kuhn, *The Structure of Scientific Revolutions.*

recently — relativity and quantum theory. But Lakatos is bothered by the same concerns that trouble so many of Kuhn's critics:

> Do we have to capitulate and agree [with Kuhn] that a scientific revolution is just an irrational change in commitment, that it is a religious conversion? ... But if Kuhn is right, then there is no explicit demarcation between science and pseudoscience, no distinction between scientific progress and intellectual decay, there is no objective standard of intellectual honesty. But what criteria can he then offer to demarcate scientific progress from intellectual degeneration?[784]

Thus, while Kuhnian "paradigms" do a better job than Popper of explaining why scientists cling to already falsified theories, Lakatos objects that Kuhnian paradigms are still nothing more than irrational social products. In any case, Lakatos remains a "rationalist" by replacing the "irrational" paradigm with his concept of the research program. As he tells us: "the typical descriptive unit of great scientific achievements is not an isolated hypothesis but rather a research program."[785] Such programs have a complex structure consisting of three identifiably different layers:

> Newtonian science, for instance, is not simply a set of four conjectures — the three laws of mechanics and the law of gravitation. These four laws constitute only the "hard core" of the Newtonian program. But this hard core is tenaciously protected from refutation by a vast "protective belt" of auxiliary hypotheses. And, even more importantly, the research program also has a "heuristic," that is, a powerful problem-solving machinery, which, with the help of sophisticated mathematical techniques, digests anomalies and even turns them into positive evidence.[786]

A research program can survive any number of anomalies and outright failures as long as it remains basically "progressive" rather than "degenerating," terms defined in the next section. Although the phenomenal success of the Newtonian research program leads us to imagine him in retrospect as an

---

[784] Lakatos, *The Methodology of Scientific Research Programs*, p. 4.
[785] Lakatos, *The Methodology of Scientific Research Programs*, p. 4.
[786] Lakatos, *The Methodology of Scientific Research Programs*, p. 4.

invincible hero of science, Lakatos gives us (in his article "Newton's Effect on Scientific Standards") a more nuanced portrayal of a Newton beleaguered by Cartesian rivals, plagued with internal doubts, and indulging in rhetorical tricks to protect his theory.[787] Many readers have been persuaded to accept this ambiguous version of a purportedly rationalist model of science: which is what Lakatos repeatedly calls it, mostly in opposition to the scientific "anarchism" of his friend Paul Feyerabend.[788] In the wake of Popperian falsificationism, it has become easier to accept that science has no unshakeable foundations, that everything is on the table for possible refutation at any moment. It has even become easier to abandon the idea of science as a cumulative process in which proven facts serve as the support for additional facts proven later. What is more surprising is Lakatos's claim that the same holds true for mathematics, often viewed as the foundational and cumulative discipline *par excellence*.[789]

But for now we leave mathematics aside in order to turn to philosophy. To what extent can philosophy be treated as a "research program" rather than as a set of true and false statements? As luck would have it, there is a close analogy between Lakatos's theory of science and Alfred North Whitehead's theory of philosophy. As Whitehead famously states: "It has been remarked that a system of philosophy is never refuted; it is only abandoned."[790] Just as Lakatos rejects Popper's notion of "crucial experiments," Whitehead seems dismissive in advance of what analytic philosophers like to call "knockdown arguments": as if some particular logical insight could lay waste to entire systems of philosophy, consigning those who defend them to the hell of irrationality. The reason, Whitehead holds, is that the detection of logical mistakes is only a small part of how a philosophy is weakened. As he puts it: "logical contradictions ... are the most gratuitous of errors; and usually they are trivial. Thus, after criticism, [philosophical] systems do not exhibit mere illogicalities. They suffer from inadequacy and incoherence."[791]

Just as Lakatos expresses opposition to the idea of a mathematics grounded in indubitable axioms, so too Whitehead — despite his admiration for Spinoza, and his own mathematical prowess — rejects the idea of philosophy conducted *more geometrico*: "Under the influence of mathematics, deduction has been foisted upon philosophy as its standard method, instead of taking

[787] Lakatos, *The Methodology of Scientific Research Programs*, 193–222.
[788] Paul Feyerabend, *Against Method*; Paul Feyerabend, *Farewell to Reason*.
[789] Lakatos, *Proofs and Refutations*.
[790] Whitehead, *Process and Reality*, p. 6.
[791] Whitehead, *Process and Reality*, p. 6.

its true place as an essential auxiliary mode of verification whereby to test the scope of generalities."[792] This is not as obvious as it sounds. Even today, Quentin Meillassoux's philosophy begins with the axiomatic assumption that we must accept the argument of the "correlationist circle": that we cannot think something outside thought without turning it into a thought, thereby renewing the German Idealist critique of Kant.[793] Even those who would not say this as bluntly as Meillassoux tacitly rely on the axiom that only the transcendental standpoint makes valid philosophy possible. On the post-Kantian landscape, philosophy cannot discuss the interaction of two inanimate objects, but only describe how this interaction appears to the human mind; as a corollary, scientists are granted a monopoly on discussing inanimate interaction. Lakatos's maxim that every theory is born refuted and dies refuted finds a parallel in Whitehead, who writes as follows: "if we consider any scheme of philosophic categories as one complex assertion, and apply to it the logician's alternative, true or false, the answer must be that the scheme is false."[794] As we will see, Lakatos also insists on a principle of lenience for new research programs, which need time to develop before being judged too severely. This principle resonates with Whitehead as well: "while a philosophical system retains any charm of novelty, it enjoys a plenary indulgence for its failures in coherence. But after a system has acquired orthodoxy, and is taught with authority, it receives a sharper criticism. Its denials and its incoherences are found intolerable, and a reaction sets in."[795] Finally, the same spirit of fallibilism found in Lakatos can also be found in Whitehead who has this to say on the matter: "There remains the final reflection, how shallow, puny, and imperfect are efforts to sound the depth of nature in things. In philosophical discussion, the merest hint of dogmatic certainty as to finality of statement is an exhibition of folly."[796]

But most important for Whitehead are the demands that philosophy aim at both adequacy and coherence. He gives more examples of the latter virtue, or at least of the vice that inverts it. In his own words: "Incoherence is the arbitrary disconnection of first principles. In modern philosophy, Descartes's two kinds of [finite] substance, corporeal and mental, illustrate incoherence. There is, in Descartes's philosophy, no reason why there should not be a one-substance world, only corporeal, or a one-substance world,

---

[792] Whitehead, *Process and Reality*, p. 10.
[793] Quentin Meillassoux, in Ray Brassier et al., "Speculative Realism," pp. 408–449.
[794] Whitehead, *Process and Reality*, p. 8.
[795] Whitehead, *Process and Reality*, p. 6.
[796] Whitehead, *Process and Reality*, p. xiv.

only mental."[797] The example is a good one, even if one could quibble — as I would — as to whether this is fair to Descartes. Whitehead has less to tell us about inadequacy, and settles for the following account of how an inadequate philosophy works: "Failure to include some obvious elements of experience in the scope of [one's] system is [wrongly] met by boldly denying the facts."[798] Although Whitehead gives no example of such failure, we find one again in Descartes. His restriction of mental substance to full-blown human cognition entails that animals cannot be placed anywhere else than mechanical physical extension, so that their screams of pain indicate nothing of importance.[799] While it may be impossible to "disprove" this claim to a committed Cartesian, it clashes so badly with our daily experience of animals that most observers will take it to be inadequate.

B. Are There Progressive and Degenerating Research Programs in Philosophy?

We have now established a degree of overlap between the views of Lakatos and those of Whitehead. This helps us see it as at least *feasible* to treat philosophies as research programs, by which I mean that they are not instantly refuted by any piece of counter-evidence. But Lakatos has a specific method for judging research programs in science, and some such method will also be needed for philosophies if we wish to consider them as research programs; Whitehead's requirements of coherence and adequacy are only a start.

We have seen that Lakatos distinguishes between "progressive" and "degenerating" research programs. How can we distinguish between them? One method that *cannot* be used is Popper's criterion of falsification, as Lakatos shows with the following examples: "When Newton published his *Principia*, it was common knowledge that it could not properly explain even the motion of the moon; in fact, lunar motion refuted Newton. [Walter] Kaufmann, a distinguished physicist, refuted Einstein's relativity theory in the very year it was published."[800] If research programs are always already falsified, then how can one of them be any better than the others? It is here that Lakatos, Popper's one-time disciple, takes what looks like a paradoxically anti-Popperian turn: returning from falsification back in the direction of

---

[797] Whitehead, *Process and Reality*, p. 6.
[798] Whitehead, *Process and Reality*, p. 6.
[799] Descartes, *Discourse on Method*, Part Five.
[800] Lakatos, *The Methodology of Scientific Research Programs*, p. 5.

verification, an older criterion in the philosophy of science that Popper had consciously attacked. In Lakatos's words: "all the research programs I admire have one characteristic in common. They all predict novel facts, facts which had been either undreamt of, or have indeed been contradicted by previous or rival programs."[801] Some of the most spectacular examples come from the world of Newtonian physics: the dramatic confirmation of Edmund Halley's prediction as to when and where his eponymous comet would return long after his death, or John Couch Adams foretelling the existence and location of the planet Neptune with the aid of Newtonian theory. Another example, mentioned above, is the way that General Relativity explains the precession of the perihelion of Mercury in a way that Newton's theory could not. At first this case may look trickier, since this deviant fact about Mercury was known long before the development of Einstein's theory. But if we accept Elie Zahar's amendment to Lakatos (aired in their co-authored article "Why did Copernicus's Research Program Supersede Ptolemy's?"), the fact that Einstein was not specifically *trying* to explain the perihelion of Mercury allows it to count as novel evidence in the theory's favor.[802]

In the world of continental philosophy, there have already been at least two polemical uses of Lakatos's distinction between "progressive" and "degenerating," both of them directed against my own philosophy. The more recent can be found in one of Ray Brassier's numerous attacks on object-oriented ontology (OOO). As he puts it, in his acerbic postscript to Peter Wolfendale's own lengthy book against me: "Wolfendale's autopsy for [Graham] Harman's Speculative Realism brand embodies everything that the [2007] 'Speculative Realism' workshop seemed to promise: the breakout from a terminally sclerotic Continental tradition epitomized by a motley of what Lakatos called 'degenerating research programs.'"[803] Taken in isolation this might be read as mere invective, since it is not yet clear what Brassier regards as "degenerating" about the continental tradition: at least not if he means it in Lakatos's precise sense of the term. Yet there are important clues in the next paragraph, where Brassier asserts that continental philosophy "equates representation with repression, objectivity with oppression, and naturalism with scientism."[804] From this we surmise that Brassier identifies "progressive" philosophy with a commitment to representation, objectivity,

---

[801] Lakatos, *The Methodology of Scientific Research Programs*, p. 5.
[802] Lakatos, *The Methodology of Scientific Research Programs*, p. 192.
[803] Brassier, "Postscript: Speculative Autopsy," p. 421.
[804] Brassier, "Postscript: Speculative Autopsy," p. 421.

and naturalism, and "degenerating" philosophy with the opposite investments. To what extent does this get Lakatos right?

Although Brassier does not tell us exactly what he means by representation, objectivity, and naturalism, his use of these terms is not especially difficult to grasp. Let's take them in reverse order. Although *The Stanford Encyclopedia of Philosophy* tells us rightly that "the term 'naturalism' has no very precise meaning in contemporary philosophy," it helpfully adds that one early group of naturalists "aimed to ally philosophy more closely with science. They urged that reality is exhausted by nature, containing nothing 'supernatural,' and that the scientific method should be used to investigate all areas of reality, including the 'human spirit.'"[805] Those familiar with Brassier's work more generally will recognize him in this definition of naturalism, even if his own version of the doctrine is considerably more intense, given the nihilistic consequences he draws from it.[806] It would also be fair to say that for Brassier, "the scientific method should be used to investigate all areas of reality, including the 'human spirit.'" As for "objectivity," let's take this to mean the notion that truth can be obtained from a neutral standpoint not colored by the views of the one who happens to claim possession of it, a view that can also plausibly be ascribed to Brassier. It is with the final case, "representation," that one misses a definition most acutely, since this term can have different and sometimes even opposite meanings. In one sense, "representation" often refers to the view that truth *is not* directly attainable, but only by way of a mediating representation, as in the philosophies of Locke or Kant.[807] While there is something of this in Brassier as well, given his conviction of an irremediable gap between reality and any of our perspectives on it (including scientific ones) this is a point where he actually *agrees* with OOO; hence, the polemical flavor of his passage suggests he has something else in mind. We know from other sources that what most bothers Brassier about OOO is its claim that the human representation of the world is no different *in kind* from any animal or vegetable representation, or even from inanimate causal interaction.[808] Hence, I infer that Brassier's endorsement of "representation" amounts to the assertion that thought is something radically different in kind from everything else. It is effectively praise for Descartes's theory of two distinct finite substances, with allowances

---

[805] David Papineau, "Naturalism."
[806] Brassier, *Nihil Unbound*. See also Graham Harman, *Speculative Realism: An Introduction*, pp. 7–52.
[807] John Locke, *An Essay Concerning Human Understanding*; Kant, *Critique of Pure Reason*.
[808] Brassier, "Deleveling."

made for Brassier's otherwise physicalist conception of mind, so foreign to Descartes himself.[809]

All this having been said, to what extent is Brassier right to imply that a "progressive" theory must be committed to naturalism, objectivity, and representation? We first consider the possibility that the answer may be different depending on whether science or philosophy is in question. Let's start with science, where Brassier might be assumed to have an easier case: for what could sound more scientific than calls for naturalism, objectivity, and representation? Now, Lakatos makes no mention of these three terms when giving criteria for the two basic kinds of scientific research programs, but this in itself means nothing, since perhaps Brassier is trying to illuminate the more implicit underpinnings of Lakatos's theory. Starting with naturalism, it does seem like a good bet that a scientific theory cannot be progressive if it admits "supernatural" principles, since these tend to be invoked in a purely *ad hoc* way, and only after natural explanations have failed. Even so, it is not always clear what is "natural" and what is "supernatural" in science, since great steps forward in science often amount to redrawing the border between the two. For Einstein — he of the speed of light as the greatest possible velocity — any theory of gravity that allows for instantaneous action at a distance could only sound supernatural, which is precisely why he was driven to a decade-long search for General Relativity. This was not so for Newton, who *did* include action at a distance in his own landmark theory of gravity: even if he never really "believed" it, as Lakatos notes.[810] But it was not only prior to Einstein that action at a distance could be portrayed as natural rather than supernatural: we need look no further than J.S. Bell's famous 1964 theorem, the bane of Einstein's "hidden variables" admirers such as David Bohm.[811] So, is action at a distance a "supernatural" conception as Einstein thought, or a perfectly "natural" one as Bell's Theorem suggests, just as Newton's theory of gravitation once did? It is impossible to say in advance: for as Lakatos is so fond of saying, there is no "instant rationality."

So much for naturalism as an infallible criterion. Unfortunately for Brassier, objectivity and representation have an even weaker claim to inherent progressiveness than naturalism does. We begin with "objectivity." While there are numerous ways to interpret quantum theory, the independence

---

[809] Descartes, *Meditations on First Philosophy*.

[810] Lakatos, *The Methodology of Scientific Research Programs*, p. 1.

[811] J.S. Bell, "On the Einstein Podolsky Rosen Paradox"; David Bohm, *Wholeness and the Implicate Order*.

of measurement from the measurer is, to say the least, severely challenged by both Werner Heisenberg and Niels Bohr, each in his own fashion. Unless Brassier wishes to make the startling claim that the Copenhagen Interpretation of quantum theory was "degenerating" from the outset, it seems clear that progressive science is not intrinsically incompatible with the view that scientific objectivity in the classical sense is no longer possible. As for "representation," which I identified with Brassier's view that thought is something radically different in kind from everything else, it is not clear that this should be taken as a *sine qua non* of progressive science either. We cannot exclude some continuity between human thought and the possible experience of objects such as thermostats, as David Chalmers proposes.[812] Current evidence to this effect may well be lacking, though there is hardly greater evidence for a radical leap in nature across a gaping chasm with apes, dolphins, houseflies, and trees on one side and humans alone on the other. Weigh the evidence as you will: there is nothing *a priori* more progressive about treating human thought as radically different from all that came before *or* as the reverse. Neither thesis is an infallible truth demanded as a precondition of forming a rational research program: rather, their competing claims must be settled from within a battle between rival programs. Lakatos tells us to judge research programs as progressive or degenerating in terms of whether or not they are able to predict surprising facts rather than simply explaining things *ex post facto*. Viewed in this light, there is no way to determine beforehand whether it is more fertile to see humans as continuous with pre-human nature or as a radical departure from it: just as there is no *a priori* reason to prefer either action at a distance or its rejection. Less open-minded than Lakatos himself, Brassier predictably jumps the gun by labeling his own favored research program (naturalist, objectivist, and representationalist) as progressive, and that of his opponents as degenerating.

This being the case with respect to science, we might also note how much worse his reading of Lakatos fares in the case of philosophy. If "degenerating" really meant "non-naturalist," this would entail that any resurgence of core hypotheses from such key philosophical figures as Plato, Plotinus, St. Augustine, Spinoza, Leibniz, Hegel, Nietzsche, Bergson, Husserl, or Heidegger would automatically result in a degenerating problemshift. As for "objectivity" in Brassier's sense, it is hard to find it in Kant, Hegel, Nietzsche, or many others, though it is far from clear that these thinkers are dead dogs.

---

[812] David Chalmers, *The Conscious Mind*.

As for "representation," if we take this to mean a strong gap between human thought and everything else, we need only mention Leibniz, Bergson, and Nietzsche as counter-instances along with Whitehead. Of course, Brassier could always retort that the past progressiveness of such philosophers — assuming he were to concede that point — does not make them progressive today. And true enough, the fact that Newton's theory of gravitation was once progressive did not prevent it from becoming a degenerating program once it was superseded by the program of General Relativity. In similar fashion, it is hard to imagine that a philosopher today could *literally* defend neo-Platonic emanation or Leibnizian pre-established harmony without wholesale changes to the structure of such theories. But the point is that we *cannot really know* what might count as progressive in the future, whether in science or philosophy: action at a distance returned to life with Bell's Theorem decades after Einstein seemed to bury it forever, and Leibniz partly restored the substantial forms though they were ruthlessly mocked by Descartes. If knowledge were really cumulative, we could establish some theories permanently and eliminate others for good. But this is precisely what Popper rejects, and Lakatos even more so. As the latter memorably puts it: "the methodology of scientific research programs does not offer instant rationality. One must treat budding research programs leniently: programs *may take decades* before they get off the ground and become empirically progressive."[813] Conversely, it may take decades before programs that seem progressive today are eventually exposed as degenerating. Both phenomena can arguably be seen in the case of string theory in physics: an interesting but obscure proposal in the 1960s, then an increasingly dominant and progressive theory beginning in the 1980s, but now the target of more-than-respectable books that say it is heading nowhere.[814] The border between progressive and degenerating in science can only be determined through the slow unfolding of the prediction of new and previously unknown facts, not circumvented by dogmatic assertions from those with vested interests in one program in particular.

The other appeal to Lakatos in a continental philosophy context of which I am aware comes from Fabio Gironi, who targets Meillassoux along with OOO. It can be found in Gironi's 2012 review of the popular anthology *The Speculative Turn*.[815] As he puts it there:

---

[813] Lakatos, *The Methodology of Scientific Research Programs*, p. 6.
[814] Lee Smolin, *The Trouble with Physics*; Richard Woit, *Not Even Wrong*.
[815] Fabio Gironi, "Between Naturalism and Rationalism"; Bryant, Srnicek, & Harman, eds., *The Speculative Turn*.

While some thinkers within [Speculative Realism] make explicit reference to Enlightenment values of rational clarity and unwavering disenchantment, others tread dangerously on the border of irrationalism and regressive metaphorizing, at times sliding down the slippery slope of uninhibited conceptual inventiveness, and turning their philosophical systems into degenerating research programs.[816]

Though the rhetoric is heated, the meaning of Gironi's critique is even vaguer than Brassier's. While no one would want to see philosophy turned into "regressive metaphorizing," the adjective here seems to be a dismissal masked as a qualifier: that is to say, Gironi seems to oppose not just "regressive" metaphorizing, but any use of metaphor in theorizing at all. In other words, he seems to think that only *literal* language can ever be appropriate for theoretical purposes: an unduly rigid view that I have criticized elsewhere.[817] In a supplemental footnote, Gironi also critiques my use of the term "weirdness" as follows: "it is hard to identify which kinds of theoretical virtues 'weirdness' is supposed to index."[818] But this claim is disingenuous, since Gironi is well aware that I define "weirdness" in a precise technical sense: as the rift between an object and its own qualities, a process central to my interpretation of the philosophies of Husserl and Heidegger as well as the literary work of H.P. Lovecraft.[819] Aside from this, while Gironi at least praises Meillassoux for endorsing "the luminous clarity of intellection," he also attacks the French philosopher for his "'divinological' forays" concerning the possible future emergence of a God who does not currently exist.[820] Yet there is no obvious reason why either an emphasis on the cognitive power of metaphor (I myself) or speculations on a virtual God (Meillassoux) should lead intrinsically to "degeneration," quite apart from the fact that Lakatos recommends lenience to new research programs for several decades.

When I followed up with Gironi about his strange use of the term "degenerating," he doubled down, insisting that he is "using the term in the Lakatosian way," which he defined as "producing too many *ad hoc*

---

[816] Gironi, "Between Naturalism and Rationalism," p. 383.

[817] Graham Harman, *Object-Oriented Ontology*, pp. 59–102.

[818] Gironi, "Between Naturalism and Rationalism," p. 380, n. 70.

[819] Graham Harman, *Guerrilla Metaphysics*; Harman, *Tool-Being*; Graham Harman, *Weird Realism*.

[820] Gironi, "Between Naturalism and Rationalism," p. 380, n. 70; Meillassoux, *After Finitude*, p. 147.

hypotheses."[821] But while Lakatos does associate degenerating research programs with *ad hoc* hypotheses, Gironi seems not to know what Lakatos — or anyone else — means by *ad hoc*. Generally speaking, to call something *ad hoc* is not the same thing as to call it "unusual" or "bizarre." Lakatos uses the phrase *ad hoc* in a very precise sense to refer to the way that a research program adds groundless auxiliary caveats to protect itself from challenge. Never does he use *ad hoc* to mean "strange-sounding" or "unlike consensus science"; nor could he do so, since he always joins Popper in appreciating "bold hypotheses." As for Meillassoux, not only is the hypothesis of a virtual God *extremely bold* in the atheist and materialist circles in which he travels, but it is not remotely *ad hoc*. Indeed, it belongs to the very core of what we might call Meillassoux's research program, and is not a shaky after-the-fact attempt to forestall critique by outsiders.[822] The same holds for "weirdness" in OOO, a philosophy based entirely on the object/quality split and the resulting turn to non-literal language: here once more, weirdness has a secure place among OOO's core theoretical tenets, and is therefore the very opposite of an *ad hoc* hypothesis.[823]

The word "degenerating" has a nice pejorative ring that lends it potent polemical force, but Lakatos meant something precise by the term that neither Brassier nor Gironi seems to understand. Given their apparent sympathies for the Hungarian thinker, how could they get him so wrong? One option might be that they simply read Lakatos in a careless manner, though I have not known them to be quite this careless in their previous work. Beyond this, both seem rather cocksure about extending Lakatos's progressive/degenerating opposition from science to philosophy, even though the philosopher tells us next to nothing about how this might be done. This is all the more baffling given that philosophy is not really in the business of "predicting novel results" or even "seeking severe tests of falsification," at least not in the same sense as natural science. Ultimately, one gets the sense that what motivates Brassier and Gironi to misapply Lakatos so hastily is the following assumption: a philosophy is progressive to the extent that it follows present-day "best science," and degenerating to the extent that it does not. As devotees of Sellars, both Brassier and Gironi are committed to the notion of a continuity between science and philosophy, both of them falling under the rubric of "knowledge."

[821] Fabio Gironi, personal communication, July 17, 2012.

[822] Quentin Meillassoux, "Spectral Dilemma"; Quentin Meillassoux, "Appendix: Excerpts from *L'Inexistence divine.*"

[823] Harman, *Guerrilla Metaphysics*, pp. 101–124.

Philosophy effectively becomes a handmaid of science, assisting it in the pursuit of what Gironi calls "Enlightenment values of rational clarity and unwavering disenchantment." Needless to say, "disenchantment" is not listed by Lakatos as one of the elements of a progressive research program: and anyway, what could be more enchanting than relativity and quantum theory? Moreover, the question of which current research program is most committed to "rational clarity" must be settled on the field of play rather than by rhetorical jabs made in advance.

Earlier, we heard Brassier's accusation that continental philosophers "equate naturalism with scientism." But his misreading of Lakatos seems guided by nothing less than flat-out *scientism*. The scientistic outlook is defined with especial candor by James Ladyman and Don Ross, who obey the following credo: "Special Relativity ought to dictate the metaphysics of time, quantum physics the metaphysics of substance, and chemistry and evolutionary biology the metaphysics of natural kinds."[824] Alternatively, as they say in their opening paragraph: "The aim of this book is to defend a radically naturalistic metaphysics. By this we mean a metaphysics that is motivated *exclusively* by attempts to unify hypotheses and theories that are *taken seriously by contemporary science*."[825] Yet this attitude is ill-advised for at least two reasons. For in the first place, given that Ladyman and Ross admit that they are not cutting-edge scientists themselves, when they say "contemporary" science this will inevitably mean *consensus* science: which is no more likely to be found at the front lines than consensus art or literature. Thus it is unclear why we should reward philosophers *a priori* for following it, any more than we should automatically praise philosophers for following the consensus *philosophy* of their time: and indeed, Ladyman and Ross have little but nastiness on offer for mainstream analytic philosophy. If Einstein had simply followed the research program of Newton and moderately extended it he could have had a solid career, but not the historic renown he now possesses.

Most importantly, by dismissing philosophies that depart from the present-day findings of science, scientism shows an authoritarian urge. Whatever the motivations for this, Lakatos simply cannot be summoned as a witness in its favor. For as he puts it: "the methodology of historiographical research programs implies a *pluralistic* system of authority, partly because

---

[824] Ladyman & Ross, *Every Thing Must Go*, p. 9. For a criticism of their theory see Graham Harman, "I Am Also of the Opinion That Materialism Must Be Destroyed."
[825] Ladyman & Ross, *Every Thing Must Go*, p. 1, emph. added.

the wisdom of the scientific jury and its case law has not been, and cannot fully be, articulated by the philosopher's statute law, and partly because the philosopher's statute law may occasionally be right when the scientists' judgment fails."[826] But there is another reason why we must not defer to scientific findings on all the traditional questions of philosophy: namely, it is by no means clear that science and philosophy are continuous. This is the subject of our next section.

C. Lakatos on Philosophical Research Programs

There is at least one publication where Lakatos does try to extend the theme of progressive and degenerating research programs from science into philosophy. Although not as well-developed as his accounts of mathematics and science, it does provide additional insights useful for our purposes. This occurs in the long and rather technical article "Changes in the Problem of Inductive Logic," where Lakatos defends Popper's falsificationism as superior to Rudolf Carnap's inductivist program.[827] [128–200] Since Popper and Carnap are philosophers rather than scientists, Lakatos is forced in this case to expand his conceptions beyond the restricted context of physical science. His opening paragraph is masterful, and deserves to be quoted in full:

A successful research program bustles with activity. There are always dozens of problems to be solved and technical questions to be answered: even if *some* of these — inevitably — are the program's own creation. But this self-propelling force of the program may carry away the research workers and cause them to forget about the problem background. They tend not to ask any more to what degree they solved the original problem, to what degree they gave up basic positions in order to cope with the internal technical difficulties. Although they may travel away from the original problem with enormous speed, they do not notice it. Problemshifts of this kind may invest research programs with a remarkable tenacity in digesting and surviving almost every criticism. [128]

---

[826] Lakatos, *The Methodology of Scientific Research Programs*, p. 137, emph. added.
[827] In what follows all page references in square brackets refer to Lakatos, *Mathematics, Science, and Epistemology*.

In the ensuing paragraph, Lakatos notes that in cases where one ends up solving problems more interesting than the original one, we can speak of a progressive problemshift. At other times, however, one ends up solving less interesting problems than the original one, or even solving nothing but self-created problems. Here, it is a matter of a degenerating problemshift. Given the stakes of this difference, Lakatos advises that "it can only do good if one occasionally stops problem-solving, and tries to recapitulate the problem background and assess the problemshift." [129] He then proceeds to unmask Carnap's research program as degenerating by contrast with Popper's.

Carnap is an *inductivist* who thinks that scientific laws can be read off of empirical facts. This also makes him a justificationist, which is precisely what Popper opposes with his anti-inductive theory of falsification. [190] Essentially, Lakatos sees Carnap's theory over time as having gone through a twofold shift, both aspects of which are degenerating rather than progressive. As Lakatos summarizes: "Carnap's shift of inductive logic from universal to particular propositions was accompanied by a parallel shift from the interpretation of inductive logic as providing primarily degrees of evidential support to its interpretation as providing primarily rational betting quotients." [151–152] Let's take each of these points in turn before asking about the more general lessons Lakatos wishes to draw.

The first concerns Carnap's shift from universal to particular statements. The logical empiricism of the Vienna Circle, of which Carnap was of course a key member, entailed a commitment to the "'reduction' of theoretical to observational terms." [130] As with every form of empiricism, "this meant that one had to start from indubitable factual propositions from which, by gradual valid induction, one could arrive at theories of ever higher order. The growth of knowledge was an accumulation of eternal truths." [131] This entails further that empiricists make "a sharp demarcation between knowledge and non-knowledge." [129] But what distinguishes logical empiricists from the classical empiricists is that the former "replaced the old idol of classical empiricists — *certainty* — by the new idol of *exactness*." [136] More importantly, Lakatos accuses Carnap of focusing too much on empirical confirmation and not enough on scientific *growth*, which is what scientific method is really about. [135–136] While Carnap was willing to concede that theories play a role in the *growth* of science — since here "nonrational factors play a role," as with "inspiration" and "good luck" — he denied that they have anything to do with scientific confirmation. [146] Thus, it seemed easy for him to ignore the role of theories in science and focus entirely on specific observations. Popper severely criticized Carnap for this, though while doing so he overplayed his own hand, misreading Carnap as denying any role for theory even in scientific growth. [147] Nonetheless, Lakatos defends Popper's central arguments. What must be appraised are not isolated facts — as Carnap holds — but *theories*. [159] After all, the determination of which facts count as relevant is heavily determined by what theories are in use. As Lakatos puts it: "in a language [such as Aristotle's] separating celestial from terrestrial phenomena, data about terrestrial projectiles may seem irrelevant to hypotheses about planetary motion. [But] in the language of Newtonian dynamics they become relevant ...." [161] Theory is ineliminable from science because evidence is simply not something that occurs in molecular form. [167] Beyond this, Carnap's turn from theories to individual observations assumes that knowledge is a matter of cumulative growth, when in fact it is not: "whole bodies of accepted evidence statements may be overthrown when a new theory throws new light on the facts." [167] Furthermore, appraisal does not even strictly concern theories, but rather the *growth* of theories: we do not evaluate a given scientific theory in isolation, but only by determining whether it explains everything explained by its rival *and more*. [176, 179] As Lakatos summarizes Popper, largely in agreement: "the only admissible evidence for a theory are the corpses of its rivals." It follows that "evidential support is a historico-methodological concept." [184] Carnap's lack of interest in theory and scientific growth goes hand in hand with a lack of sensitivity to sudden changes in science.

The second point concerns Carnap's shift of emphasis from judging evidential support in science to calculating "rational betting quotients." As Lakatos puts it: "Neoclassical empiricism [such as Carnap's theory] had a central dogma: the dogma of the identity of: (1) probabilities, (2) degrees of evidential support (or confirmation), (3) degrees of rational belief, and (4) rational betting quotients." [152] At first glance, the identity of these terms might seem entirely reasonable: our degree of conviction with respect to a given scientific theory might well appear to be something convertible into terms resembling the odds on a football or boxing match. But as Lakatos reminds us, the equation of scientific evidence with betting odds is precisely what Popper's philosophy of science annihilates. For one thing, a tautology — such as "Carnap is Carnap" — has zero evidential support, but a great deal of betting certainty: although one would never lose a wager on this proposition, there cannot possibly be any scientific evidence for it. [153–154] The problem, Lakatos explains, is that when comparing scientific evidence with rational betting quotients, "two rival and mutually inconsistent intuitions are at play." [154] The first is what Lakatos calls our "betting intuition." According to it, "any conjunction of hypotheses, whatever the evidence, is at least as risky as any of the conjuncts." [154] This is nothing more than basic probability. Let's imagine that we calculate the odds of these current national league leaders (at the time of this writing) becoming champions for the 2019–2020 season: Liverpool in the English Premier League, Bayern München in the Bundesliga, S.L. Benfica in the Primeira Liga, and FC Barcelona in La Liga.[828] Someone now offers you a *parlay* bet in which you will wager that *all four* of these current leaders will end up as champions of their respective national leagues. If we do so, our risk has obviously increased, and we will expect a larger payoff than we would for betting on any one of them: after all, the chance of *at least one* of the teams losing their lead is not that low. But as Popper argues, precisely the reverse is true with scientific evidence. In this case we are dealing with a large number of *improbable* pieces of evidence, meaning that if a theory purports to explain them all in a single stroke, the theory is *more likely* to be true than were any of its pieces when taken in isolation. For example, the precession of the perihelion of Mercury and the bending of starlight by the sun at double the rate predicted by Newton are both oddly anomalous and highly improbable facts given the general success of Newton's theory: but the fact that *both anomalies are true* makes General Relativity as a whole *more* likely. In Popper's words: "the corroborability of a theory and also the degree of corroboration of a theory ... stand both, as it were, in inverse ratio to its logical probability."[829] And in Lakatos's words: "degree of evidential support is proportional not to probability but to improbability." [155; emph. removed] In short, Carnap's "rational betting quotients" theory is not just a poor account of how science works, but *the exact opposite* of how it works.

Thus, in his effort to convert the evaluation of scientific theories into an exact procedure, Carnap ends up with an increasingly smaller and weaker theory than the one with which he started: 1. He eliminates theories in favor of local observations, and while "Occam's Razor" often receives robotic

---

[828] As it happened, although Liverpool and Bayern München did go on to win their respective leagues that season, FC Barcelona finished in second place to Real Madrid and S.L. Benfica also fell to second in favor of FC Porto. This displays the inherent risk of a parlay bet, even if it had been made midseason at the time this article was written.
[829] Popper, *The Logic of Scientific Discovery*, §83, emph. removed. Here Lakatos seems to be giving his own translation from Popper's original German.

universal praise, it is not to be recommended in cases where one is eliminating something that does have independent existence (as Occam himself fully realized).[830] There is no possibility of neutrally measuring observations without prior commitment to some theory that tells us what the facts are in the first place, and thus "Carnap's Razor" cannot eliminate theories from science. 2. He gives no account of scientific growth, other than a few throwaway concessions that it does involves some "non-rational" elements. 3. He is unable to account for the frequently murderous relation between a scientific theory and the rivals it hopes to refute, thereby losing all sense of the *historicity* of science. 4. With his dogmatic conception of knowledge as cumulative, Carnap has no way to account for scientific revolution or sudden theory-change. 5. He completely misses that scientific evidence not only cannot be converted into a matter of "rational betting quotients," but that it works in precisely the *opposite* manner. By contrast, Popper's theory can easily account for all five of these things, while all that Carnap can do is point to his reputation as a champion of exactitude and as a logical juggernaut whose machine-like intellect can easily crush "fuzzy" thinkers. Despite his air of remorseless rationality and "luminous clarity of intellect" (Gironi), Carnap gives us a theory of science with *less content* than Popper's, and therefore a research program that must be called "degenerating" by contrast.

In turn, Lakatos will argue that his own research program is even more progressive than Popper's, since it can account for the remarkable tenacity of scientists in the face of apparent refutation, and can also account for (a) *partial* refutations, and (b) merely *initial* refutations of theories followed later by startling comebacks, neither of which has any clear place in Popper's model. [177, 179] Lakatos mocks Carnap's "betting quotient" research program by acidly observing that "urn games are poor models of science." [188] But even more acid is the summary by Musgrave and Pigden in their *Stanford Encyclopedia* article on Lakatos: "Carnap starts off with the exciting problem of showing how scientific theories can be partially confirmed by empirical facts and ends up with technical papers about drawing different colored balls out of an urn. In Lakatos's opinion this does not constitute intellectual progress. Carnap had lost the plot."[831]

But what is most important about Lakatos's article on the Carnap/Popper dispute is neither his case against Carnap nor his provisional pro-Popper

---

[830] For a skillful debunking of widespread vulgar interpretations of Occam's Razor see Rondo Keele, *Ockham Explained.*

[831] Musgrave & Pigden, "Imre Lakatos."

argument. Instead, of chief interest is that he gives us a first sketch of how we might determine whether a given *philosophy* amounts to a progressive or degenerating research program. Whereas Popper emphasizes falsifications in science, we have seen that Lakatos prefers surprising predictions of facts that are either completely novel or (with Zahar's amendment to the theory) already known but not deliberately catered to by the new theory; in doing so, he sharply contradicts John Maynard Keynes's disdain for prediction. [183] But in what sense does philosophy aim to "predict new facts" in nature? In no sense, really. This is why, in judging Carnap and Popper, Lakatos says nothing about what they are respectively able or unable to predict, but only about their relative growth or restriction with respect to one another. Yet we still need to know in more detail how this might play out in philosophy specifically.

D. Gathering the Pieces

Although Lakatos departs from Popper's views on the key issue of falsification, he remains indebted to his mentor and "the magnetic field of his intellect" for a number of important ideas. In particular, it is Popper who dismissed the empiricist view that evidence is both "molecular" and "cumulative." Since Popper shifts the terrain of science from observations to theories — which Lakatos later broadens from theories to research programs — there is no question of science dealing with piecemeal facts, but only with explanatory theories that illuminate new findings and gather them under its umbrella. Nor, we have seen, can scientific evidence be "cumulative," since "whole bodies of accepted evidence statements may be overthrown when a new theory throws new light on the facts." [167] Lakatos also seems perfectly happy to retain Popper's view that newly proposed scientific theories ought to be "bold" and have "novel potential falsifiers" in comparison with the established theories they aim to replace. [170] Furthermore, Lakatos likes to emphasize — sounding more like Kuhn than he would like to admit — that a new progressive theory will not simply solve pre-existing problems, since "an interesting solution always *shifts* the problem." [169] That is to say, switching briefly to Kuhnian terminology, that while puzzle-solving is something that healthy progressive programs will always need to do, the transition to a new theory will always do much more than solve puzzles. Another feature Lakatos shares with Popper is the idea that evidence has little to do with verisimilitude. For Popper, since we proceed by way of falsifying theories rather than verifying them, there is no guarantee that corroboration of a theory means it is getting us closer to the truth. After all, "the most rigorous observance of Popperian method may lead us away from truth, accepting false and refuting true laws." [186]

One point where Lakatos pushes slightly further than Popper, though along lines the older thinker had already established, is with his notion that in identifying whether a research program is progressive, we are not considering a given theory or research program in isolation, but by comparison with its predecessor. Manuel DeLanda sounds a similar note when he stresses the importance of a theory being *improvable*.[832] Although we appraise theories in various ways both before and after they are tested, "prior and posterior appraisal appraise conjointly the growth of our knowledge produced by the theories rather than the theories in themselves." [179] For the purposes of growth it is not enough that a new theory be able to refute an established one, since "the *supreme* challenge is when [the new theory] not only claims that the challenged theory is false but that it can explain all the truth-content of the challenged theory." [176] This need not happen immediately, of course, since a new theory will not yet have had time to account for all the content painstakingly amassed by an established theory during its years of prior dominance. Thus, the ability of a new theory — or better, new research program — to account for at least some *novel* facts that the old one cannot may be taken as a good initial sign that a program is promising. But the aim of the game is ultimately the *murder* of the older theory, even if for Lakatos this happens gradually over the course of time, while for Popper it occurs with a single, sudden refutation. As Lakatos summarizes, in one of the most humorous passages of his article:

> [The] Popperian jungle [in which a theory can become a hero only through murder] contrasts starkly with Carnap's civilized society of theories. The latter is a peaceful welfare state of fallible but respectably aging theories, reliable … to different but always positive degrees, which are registered daily with pedantic precision in the office of the inductive judge. Murders are unknown — theories may be undermined but never refuted. [174]

One consequence of the murderous interpretation of theory rivalry is that we only understand the defects of a theory once we have seen its successor. Newton's shortcomings can be judged by way of Einstein's theory, "but we

---

[832] Manuel DeLanda, *Philosophical Chemistry*.

cannot give even a fallible absolute estimate of Einstein's theory itself before it, in turn, is superseded by another theory." [185] Only God could do this, the unreligious Lakatos sarcastically adds.

Lakatos does give one especially interesting criterion of theoretical boldness, making it a criterion of progressiveness as well if the bold gesture should happen to succeed. In his own words: "A theory is the bolder the more it revolutionizes our previous picture of the world: for instance, the more surprisingly it unites fields of knowledge previously regarded as distant and unconnected ...." [170] Indeed, sweeping histories of science often become heroic stories of unification, whether at the hands of Newton, Maxwell, or the "electroweak" trio of Glashow/Salam/Weinberg. But we should not neglect the opposite intuition, often stressed by DeLanda, that the history of science is at least as much about dividing previously unified scientific disciplines into new subdisciplines, in keeping with the growth of our knowledge about the multifarious regions of reality. There are also numerous examples of such crucial divisions *within* specific scientific fields. For instance, one of the most haunting passages in Richard Rhodes's classic history *The Making of the Atomic Bomb* comes when Niels Bohr is literally struck dumb at Princeton University with a sudden realization. Namely, the peculiarities of slow-neutron reactions with uranium and thorium arise from the difference between the uranium isotopes U235 and U238: the first human awareness that so-called "enriched uranium" (high in U235) would be needed for an atomic bomb to be feasible.[833]

One issue on which Lakatos's position is strikingly ambivalent is the familiar question of whether scientific theories are self-contained or directly imprinted by their socio-historical context. The latter would mark a "Hegelian" approach, and we learned from Lakatos that he was an entrenched Hegelian before coming under Popper's influence. We have already seen that Lakatos — much like Popper — holds that theories make sense only by contrast with the established theories they challenge, so that the earlier theories are in some sense part of the new ones that overthrow them. This gives us a more combative version of what Harold Bloom in literary studies calls "the anxiety of influence," meaning that a poem or novel is not self-contained in the way that literary formalists imagine, but emerges through deliberate "misreading" of its predecessor texts.[834] In related fashion, both Popper and Lakatos treat scientific theories or research

---

[833] Richard Rhodes, *The Making of the Atomic Bomb*, pp. 284–286.
[834] Harold Bloom, *The Anxiety of Influence*.

programs as emerging historically from their slain forerunners, in a manner "alien to the classical outlook." Namely: "we accept theories if they indicate *growth* in truth-content ('progressive problemshift'); we reject them if they do not ('degenerating problemshift')." [170] In this respect, it looks as if truth is contextual and historical. Yet elsewhere in Lakatos we find an opposite intuition, of a sort that would be called "formalist" in literary or art criticism: namely, the view that science is radically cut off from its socio-historical environment.[835] Lakatos expresses this most clearly in a brilliant passage late in the article on Copernicus that he co-authored with Zahar. After demonstrating that the Copernican research program was indeed superior to Ptolemy's on purely scientific grounds, the authors alert us to one of the chief consequences of this:

> Let [us] end with a trivial consequence of this exposition, which
> I hope at least *some* of you will find outrageous. Our account
> is a narrowly internalist one. No place in this account for the
> Renaissance spirit so dear to Kuhn's heart; for the turmoil
> of Reformation and Counter-reformation, no impact of the
> Churchman; no sign of any effect from the alleged or real rise of
> capitalism in the sixteenth century; no motivation from the needs of
> navigation so much cherished by Bernal. The whole development is
> narrowly internal; its progressive part could have taken place at any
> time, given a Copernican genius, between Aristotle and Ptolemy or
> in any year after, say, the 1175 translation of [Ptolemy's] *Almagest*
> into Latin, or for that matter, by an Arab astronomer in the ninth
> century. [188–189]

Far from being "trivial," this amounts to a radically anti-Hegelian claim about the relation between discoveries and the wider movement of history, one that creates interesting tension with the core Popper/Lakatos idea that the content of any theory is intimately related to the content of the theory it replaces.

While we are at it, there is another important topic where we encounter a tension between formalist and anti-formalist views of the meaning of scientific theory, one that implicates Lakatos no less than Popper. This point concerns the relation of a theory not to its historical context, but to the person who advocates it. The "formalist" side of this question appears

---

[835] Graham Harman, *Dante's Broken Hammer*; Graham Harman, *Art and Objects*.

in Popper's view that *consistency* is merely a regulative principle toward which a theory should strive, not a precondition of its being taken seriously. Thus, as Lakatos summarizes: "the body of science may be inconsistent, [and therefore] it cannot be an object of rational belief. This is yet another argument for Popper's thesis that 'belief-philosophy' has nothing to do with the philosophy of science." [176] In other words, the content of science at any given moment can be "bracketed," treated as merely the latest successful move in a game rather than as the incarnation of truth, and therefore not as something that commands our genuine credence. The scientist and philosopher of science are left in a position of ironic reserve toward the propositions they utter. Nonetheless, Popper also displays the opposite intuition, with his concern that attempts to falsify a theory must always be *sincere*. [175] And as Popper amusingly adds, "the requirement of sincerity cannot be formalized," whether in Carnap's manner or any other.[836] The reason for this is that sincerity deals with matters external to the *content* of an utterance, referring only to our specific personal attitude toward whatever scientific views we advocate.

In any case, we now sharply return to questions concerning philosophy. Other than Popper and Lakatos themselves, the main philosophical authority quoted so far is Whitehead. Earlier we cited his view that logical blunders are not the main evidence that a philosophy should be abandoned, since screw-ups of this sort are most often trivial and easily fixed. Instead, philosophies are usually abandoned when we become aware of their incoherence and inadequacy. Let's take "incoherence" to be roughly equivalent to the term "inconsistency." We have just seen that Popper is not especially bothered by this defect, since to be consistent in science is merely a "regulative" ideal in Kant's sense: a goal at which we aim without ever reaching it. We could say, more briefly, that consistency is not something to be *rushed* or *forced*. Premature attempts at consistency often cut corners or suppress ambiguity in their hastiness to make everything fit. The most famous negative assessment of consistency by a philosopher is that of Ralph Waldo Emerson in his "Self-Reliance":

> A foolish consistency is the hobgoblin of little minds, adored by
> little statesmen and philosophers and divines. With consistency a
> great soul has nothing to do. He may as well concern himself with
> the shadow on the wall. Speak what you think now in hard words,

---

[836] Popper, *The Logic of Scientific Discovery*, p. 418.

and to-morrow speak what to-morrow thinks in hard words again,
though it contradict every thing you said to-day.[837]

Whitehead does say that philosophy should be committed to "unflinching
pursuit of the two rationalist ideals, coherence and logical perfection."[838] But
the operative word is "pursuit," which merely puts Whitehead in the same
camp as Popper: consistency is a regulative idea, rather than a precondition
for any theory even to be proposed.

In any case, "adequacy" seems to be the more urgent Whiteheadian
requirement in philosophy, a pursuit whose aim is uniquely global. To deny
the existence or import of large swathes of experience simply to make one's
theory work easily is the best example of cheating in philosophy. When
Parmenides tells us that "being is, and non-being is not," it is harder to
fault him on his logic than on his simple failure to live up to the many-
colored character of reality. When physicalists simply *eliminate* anything
that cannot be explained in terms of particles, fields, or related notions,
they are choosing to address non-physical entities with the mere fiat that
no such thing can possibly exist. Sometimes individual thinkers, even
entire eras, can imprison themselves in presuppositions that take great
ingenuity even to notice. At any rate, it should be clear why the search for
adequacy is one and the same as the search for *growth*. For a philosophy
to become more adequate is to increase the amount of its content, and
therefore to become progressive. By contrast, lingering inconsistencies are
not incompatible with growth, and sometimes are the very requirement
for it: as with the ongoing incoherence, as of this writing, between General
Relativity and Quantum Theory.

On the whole, we have seen that "growth" is probably the best shorthand
criterion for what Lakatos means by a progressive research program as
opposed to a degenerating one: as long as we remember the proviso that
growth is not cumulative and does not necessarily get us "closer" to the
truth, since it may actually be leading us astray. The direction of growth
is toward greater adequacy, while coherence is a regulative ideal and thus a
less urgent question than adequacy. Our theories do not grow in a vacuum,
but only by contrast with the rival theories they supersede, whether we
view this as analogous to "murder" (Popper, according to Lakatos) or with
a more neutral term such as "influence" (Bloom). Even so, there is a further

---

[837] Ralph Waldo Emerson, *Essays and Lectures*, p. 265.
[838] Whitehead, *Process and Reality*, p. 6.

difficulty in applying Lakatos's concept of progressive growth to philosophy rather than science, and the difficulty is glaring: namely, *philosophy is something basically different in kind from science*. We have seen that Brassier and Gironi use the term "degenerating" as roughly synonymous with "at odds with present-day science," which assumes both that philosophy and science are basically continuous and that science should take the lead role in this partnership. Naturally this is true not just of Brassier and Gironi, but of much contemporary philosophy: especially the analytic variety, which is generally sympathetic to the view that science is an exemplary mode of human cognition, despite the Ladyman/Ross jeremiad against analytic philosophy for not putting science enough in control. But there are two important ways in which philosophy differs from any of the sciences, though the second will be more controversial than the first. I will conclude with a brief discussion of each.

E. First Difference: Philosophy is Not a Discipline

We begin with a passage from Kasimir Twardowski — one of the leading lights of the Brentano School — on the relation between philosophy (here, "metaphysics") and science:

> the particular sciences always deal with a more or less limited group
> of objects, a group which is formed by the natural context or a
> certain purpose .... [Yet] metaphysics is a science which considers
> all objects, physical — organic and inorganic — as well as mental,
> real as well as nonreal, existing objects as well as nonexisting objects;
> investigates those laws which objects in general obey, not just a
> certain group of objects.[839]

While not everyone will agree with Twardowski that philosophy and science deal with "objects" — though I certainly do — few will deny the basic point about philosophy having a broader scope than science. It is not only the "particular [natural] sciences" that deal with one specific and limited subject matter, but also "particular social sciences," "particular humanities disciplines," and "particular genres of the fine arts" as well. One thing that distinguishes philosophy from every other pursuit is that no particular subject matter is irrelevant to it, even if philosophy cannot be expected to

---

[839] Kasimir Twardowski, *On the Content and Object of Presentations*, p. 36.

get into the details, and is often not even welcome to do so. For instance, it is simply not relevant to physics or chemistry that film emerged as a new genre of art toward the turn of the twentieth century, except in the external sense that some applied science may be needed to produce the equipment for this art form. But film cannot fail to be relevant to philosophy, since the latter cannot avoid aesthetics as one of its topics, and also cannot avoid wondering whether film does something new and unknown by contrast with previous art.[840] The emergence or discovery of a new discipline means the appearance of a new vein of reality, and this cannot fail to be important for philosophy.

It is often said that philosophy is much like science, but "more general." Whatever this is supposed to mean, it is not enough, precisely because of the two factors now under discussion. There is a sense in which — far from being a "general" discourse of some sort — philosophy is troubled and plagued above all by the *specificity* of the different disciplines that it itself is not. These can take their own specificity for granted, despite occasional border skirmishes or foreign journeys in search of inspiration, and can find no way to account for the others unless by claiming supremacy for their own. Philosophy, surprisingly enough, is the one pursuit that cannot proclaim supremacy even in principle, since it is always surprised by the appearance of other disciplines or new kinds of beings; it always approaches these others in the position of a student. Although a "flat ontology" that treats all things as equal is a good first step in destroying received prejudices, it is not enough: precisely because the division markers between genres of beings are what philosophy must account for above all.

Much of the problem comes from the widely accepted structure of modern philosophy, which restricts our growth and is therefore "degenerating" in Lakatos's sense. Modern philosophy since Descartes basically holds that the world consists of two and only two kinds of things: (a) human thought, and (b) everything else. How absurd this situation seems, with one minor species in the cosmos granted a full half of philosophy! Of course it is not quite as stupid as it sounds, since it finds legitimation — already with Descartes — in the supposed fact that we have immediate access to our thoughts but only derivative access to everything else. *Cogito, ergo sum.* In practice, this also leads to a division of labor: philosophy — along with the social sciences and the humanities — is confined to discussing relations between human thought and the world. Meanwhile, only natural science is allowed

---

[840] See Graham Harman, "Object-Oriented Ontology."

to discuss actions *between* parts of the world, in the form of object-object interactions. It is a strange paradox that although modern philosophy claims *a priori* certainty for its meditations and only derivative certainty for claims about the world, the exactness of calculation in natural science eventually gives it the upper hand — and with it mathematics, despite their ancient dispute. Philosophers become increasingly deferential to natural science, seeing it as the most eminent of human pursuits. Again and again we restage the game of mocking philosophers and humanists who "misunderstand science," as in the 1990s Sokal Hoax.[841] (Disclaimer: unlike most people in the circles in which I run, I greatly enjoyed the Sokal Hoax, if not Sokal's own explanation of what it meant.)[842] The point is not that each discipline has its own taxonomical subject matter so that philosophy should stay away from its "misunderstandings" of nature, but that philosophy has to confront nature just as it confronts every other domain, but in its own way.

Earlier, we quoted the central credo of Ladyman/Ross scientism: "Special Relativity ought to dictate the metaphysics of time, quantum physics the metaphysics of substance, and chemistry and evolutionary biology the metaphysics of natural kinds."[843] But we can now see why this ostensibly steel-spined rationalism is little more than a degenerating research program, for it does not contribute at all to the intellectual growth that Lakatos demands. Instead, it turns philosophy into an after-the-fact encomium on the greatness of science, which is precisely what the Italian physicist Carlo Rovelli denounced: "I wish that philosophers who are interested in the scientific conceptions of the world would not confine themselves to commenting [on] and polishing the present fragmentary physical theories, but would take the risk of trying to look ahead."[844] How to look ahead? One way to do so is to avoid assuming that science is the big brother of philosophy instructing us on what to do next. This procedure assumes that there is a single continuum of human cognition, all of it called "knowledge," with the hard sciences called upon to lead the wolf pack. For as already seen, any specific discipline remains within its disciplinary walls rather than presenting itself for challenge by the very existence of other disciplines. In trying to fulfill this latter condition, we discover that we *do not want* unification, or at least not beyond a certain point. Bruno Latour was onto this issue early, when he shifted from a flat ontology of entities *translated*

[841] Sokal & Bricmont, *Fashionable Nonsense*.
[842] See Graham Harman, *Towards Speculative Realism*, pp. 67–68.
[843] James Ladyman & Don Ross, *Every Thing Must Go*, p. 9.
[844] Carlo Rovelli, "Halfway Through the Woods," p. 182.

from one form to another to the *analogy* of differing modes of existence that cannot be translated.[845]

F. Second Difference: Philosophy is Not Literal

Yet there is another reason why philosophy cannot be dominated by science or any other discipline, which is that philosophy does not even make literal statements, and therefore makes no claims to knowledge. Many readers will be familiar with the following passage from Eddington's Gifford Lectures: "I have settled down to the task of writing these lectures and have drawn up my chairs to my two tables. Two tables! Yes; there are duplicates of every object about me — two tables, two chairs, two pens."[846] The two kinds of objects in question are: (a) the object as scientifically described, made of minute particles whirling in empty space, and (b) the object as described in the context of everyday life, where it appears to be solid and has numerous macroscopic qualities. Eddington's distinction survives today in Sellars's kindred difference between the "manifest" and "scientific" images, which he assures us cannot be reduced to one another.[847] Nonetheless, despite this apparently pluralistic spirit of tolerance for both sides of the distinction, it remains far too restrictive: for it still allows the existence only of two kinds of *images*. This is no accident, since images are all that we can ever *know*, and the epistemocentrism (or "epistemism") of thinkers like Sellars is inevitably obsessed with *knowledge*, as if this were the sole form of worthwhile human cognition. But as I argued in "The Third Table," art provides one good example of a powerful cognitive force that is not primarily a kind of knowledge.[848] Artworks may now and then "teach us something," but if this were their primary purpose, they might easily be replaced with prose manifestos, though to reduce art to such statements would clearly be ridiculous. This indicates that while knowledge is crucial to human survival, it does not exhaust the sphere of human cognition.

More generally, both forms of knowing — whether in Eddington's two tables or Sellars's two images — are ways of reducing an object in two different directions. There are really only two kinds of knowledge: we can explain what something is made of, or explain what it does. The first of these reduces an object downward to its pieces ("undermining"), the

---

[845] Bruno Latour, *An Inquiry Into Modes of Existence*.

[846] Arthur Stanley Eddington, *The Nature of the Physical World*, p. ix.

[847] Wilfrid Sellars, "Philosophy and the Scientific Image of Man."

[848] Graham Harman, "The Third Table."

second reduces it upward to its effects on our minds or on other entities ("overmining"), and often enough we do both of these things simultaneously ("duomining").[849] It should be clear that none of these three procedures can exhaust any object. After all, everything that truly exists is something over and above its components ("emergence"), and always holds something in reserve beneath its current effects ("submergence"). Socrates is well aware of this, since he describes his pursuit as *philosophia* rather than *sophia*, and constantly proclaims that the only thing he knows is that he knows nothing. To behave as if everything unknowable were entirely incognizable, leading only to empty gesticulation or "negative theology," is the most un-Socratic gesture imaginable. By denying the existence of non-literalizable reality, rationalism makes the world *smaller* than it is rather than producing intellectual growth, which means that rationalism is a fine exemplar of a *degenerating* research program. (I am well aware that Lakatos called himself a "rationalist," but this was mainly in order to contrast his own position with the purportedly "irrational" ones of Feyerabend and Kuhn.) A philosophy is not supposed to call on science like a big brother to beat up its opponents, which is largely the way that scientistic authors such as Ladyman, Ross, Brassier, and Gironi proceed.

But what does it mean, exactly, for an object to be non-literalizable? When we explain something literally, we are explaining the qualities or properties that it possesses; hence, we tacitly assume that anything is equal to those qualities. Yet this is clearly not the case with artworks, since the art object is never literally present in the way that its specific qualities are, never exhausted by a literal description. We can replace the word "electron" with a textbook summary of everything that an electron has and does, but never can we replace the words *Venus of Urbino* with a prose description of the sum total of qualities of Titian's painting, if such a description were even possible. In aesthetic situations, there is only a loose relation between an object and its own qualities. This same looseness is found in the Platonic dialogues, where Socrates can never quite pin down what features belong to friendship, virtue, justice, or love. This non-literal character of reality is something never accounted for by either Popper or Lakatos, since their primary concern is *science*. Although Popper in particular ventures beyond science to talk about such matters as politics, he seems not just uninterested

---

[849] Graham Harman, "On the Undermining of Objects"; Graham Harman, "Undermining, Overmining, and Duomining."

in, but unaware of, the need to account for that which is not literalizable in prose form.

However, *it is* accounted for to some extent by one of their opponents: Kuhn. Everyone is familiar with Kuhn's distinction between paradigm-shifting science and puzzle-solving "normal" science. The reaction against Kuhn — which goes far beyond Lakatos — is linked with the view that Kuhn treats scientific change as an "irrational" matter of fashion, mob rule, or religious conversion. But Kuhn's distinction between the two kinds of science becomes more interesting if we interpret his paradigms not as meaning "sociological" rather than "rational," but as "object" rather than "quality." It should be obvious that normal science deals with the qualities of things, since it is tasked with solving puzzles or inconsistencies such as the anomalous behavior of Mercury, or more often lesser matters. It is only in times of scientific crisis or revolution that we move beyond the question of qualities and find ourselves redefining the very object under consideration: as when continents were reinterpreted as moving plates with the advent of continental drift theory and plate tectonics. Lakatos is right that Kuhn speaks too little about the simultaneous co-existence of warring paradigms, but is not generous enough to Kuhn when he treats him as an advocate of utterly irrational scientific shifts. The point is that while the majority of scientific work (like any other sort of work) deals with entities as if they were "bundles of qualities" — as in David Hume's philosophy — revolutions are something different in kind, in which the object of science is roughly pinpointed with prose descriptions but not yet entirely literalized.[850] The fact that Lakatos can state the hard core of Newton's research program as clearly as he does is possible only because Newton has already been left behind. Any living research program always has more in its hard core than can be explicitly stated or known, since — as Lakatos himself has shown — we learn the true failings of a research program only after it has been defeated by another.

When Gironi complains of a specific philosophical school (namely, OOO) that it uses "regressive metaphors," what he is apparently trying to say is that metaphor is never an appropriate technique for science. This is not true: science is riddled with *productive* metaphors and not just "regressive" ones. But let's assume for the moment that it were true, and that science should not be conducted in any medium other than that of literal statements, whether in the form of prose or of mathematical equations. If this

---

[850] David Hume, *An Enquiry Concerning Human Understanding.*

were the case, it would only follow that philosophy should have nothing to do with metaphor *provided we assume further* that philosophy is simply a spokesperson for natural science and the knowledge it produces. But this is most certainly not the case. The irreducibility of objects to bundles of qualities means that literalism is false, and that epistemism is false. Non-literalizable reality exists. And given that philosophy has a mandate to talk in some sense about *everything*, rather than "exclusively … hypotheses and theories that are taken seriously by contemporary science," (as Ladyman and Ross claim), then philosophy needs to develop tools to discuss it. This is one of the ways it grows and thereby becomes "progressive" in its research program: rather than remaining confined to the thought-world dyad, as modern philosophy has both urged and practiced.

CHAPTER 32
EXCERPTS ON UNJUSTIFIED TRUE BELIEF[851]

1. From "Fear of Reality"

As suggested by the title of his book [*Fear of Knowledge*], Paul Boghossian's strategic enemy is the relativist or constructivist thesis that "there are 'many equally valid ways of viewing the world,' with science being just one of them."[852] [2] He is hardly alone in this fight, for despite the recent prevalence of constructivist ideas in the humanities and social sciences, "there is one humanities discipline in which their hold is actually quite weak, and that is in philosophy itself, at least as it is practiced within the mainstream of analytic philosophy departments within the English-speaking world." [7] As already seen, what Boghossian advocates instead of constructivism is not the sort of highly speculative realism that Quentin Meillassoux defends. Instead, Boghossian (like so many analytic philosophers) is primarily concerned with defending the exemplary cognitive status of *science*: "for if science weren't privileged, we might well have to accord as much credibility to archaeology as to Zuni creationism, as much credibility to evolution as to Christian creationism" [4–5] The stakes here are high indeed, since if science is not

---

[851] This chapter contains excerpts from two articles. The first is "Fear of Reality," originally published in 2015 in *The Monist* 98.2, pp. 126–144. The second is "On Truth and Lie in the Object-Oriented Sense," first published in *Open Philosophy*, 5.1 (2022), pp. 437-463. For more on the topic of unjustified true belief and its paradoxical relation to knowledge see Graham Harman, *Object-Oriented Ontology*, pp. 167–193.
[852] Paul Boghossian, *Fear of Knowledge*. In the present chapter, all parenthetical page references refer to this book.

as privileged as we think, then "we have fundamentally misconceived the principles by which society ought to be organized." [5] Due to the booming prominence of constructivist ideas, we have witnessed "a growing alienation of academic philosophy from the rest of the humanities and social sciences, leading to levels of acrimony and tension on American campuses that have prompted the label 'Science Wars.'" [8] Boghossian's concern to defend the central status of *science* explains the title of his book: "Why this fear of knowledge? Whence this felt need to protect against its deliverances?" [130] For as opposed to any relativist defense of Zuni or Christian creationism, "the intuitive view [i.e., the view Boghossian finds obviously correct] is that there is a way things are that is independent of human perception, *and* that we are capable of arriving at belief about how things are that is objectively reasonable, binding on anyone capable of appreciating the relevant evidence regardless of their social or cultural perspective." [130–1; emph. added] Stated differently, "whenever we confidently judge that some belief is justified on the basis of a given piece of information, we are tacitly assuming that such facts are not only knowable but that they are known." [76]

For those of us raised in an academic world where relativist and constructivist views are taken for established wisdom, there is always something refreshing about defenses of scientific realism. For when pushed far enough, constructivist claims often border on the vacuous. In an example given by Boghossian himself, it can feel rather forced to cling to relativism in cases such as the number of moons of Jupiter. If we stipulate that someone named "Margo" believes that Jupiter has sixteen moons, "Margo's belief is true if and only if it is a *fact* that Jupiter has sixteen moons," [11] and yet "Jupiter, it turns out, has over thirty moons." [12] Any defense of a claim that Jupiter's number of moons is individually or culturally constructed would seem rather facile. There is even a certain element of bad faith in extreme forms of constructivism: as [Maurizio] Ferraris often observes, a constructivist who falls ill does not choose randomly from many "equally valid" theories of medicine, but immediately seeks the best medical care available according to widely recognized principles of medicine. All of this lends Boghossian's argument the combined moral authority of scientific method and everyday sincere human practice. Nonetheless, I hold that there are two separate problems with his standpoint: (a) He is too quick to elide the difference between justification and truth. (b) He adheres to a taxonomical distinction in which the objects of *nature* are unconstructed while the objects of *culture* are constructed. I will briefly try to show the problems with each of these views.

We have seen that Boghossian is concerned not just with reality, but with our ability to know it. Just as one would hope from a book entitled *Fear of Knowledge*, he is clear as can be in his definition of knowledge: "according to the standard, widely accepted Platonic definition of knowledge," we have knowledge in those cases where our belief "is both justified and true." [15] The problem here is the largely unaddressed gap between justification and truth. On one level Boghossian is well aware of this gap, and even embraces it as the core principle of scientific fallibilism: "one can have good reasons to believe something [that is] false. The evidence available to pre-Aristotelian Greeks made it rational for them to believe that earth was flat, even though as we may now be said to know, it is round." [15] Or again, "reasons are defeasible: one can have good reasons to believe something at one time and then, as a result of further information, cease to have good reasons to believe that proposition at a later time. The pre-Aristotelian Greeks justifiably believed earth to be flat; we justifiably believe it to be round." [15; emph. removed] But it is precisely this admirable fallibilism that brings suspicion upon Boghossian's apparent commitment to *knowledge*. For in light of the fallibilist principle that knowledge-claims are always subject to revision based on new evidence, if knowledge is justified true belief then we only ever have access to the "justified" part and never to the "true" part. That is why, throughout the book, we find Boghossian asking us to *assume for the sake of argument* that a given belief is true. For example, in the sentence just cited: "The evidence available to pre-Aristotelian Greeks made it rational for them to believe that [the] earth was flat, even though *as we may now be said to know*, it is round." [15] Or this passage: "Consider something that we now take ourselves to know — for example, that dinosaurs once roamed the earth — *and suppose that we actually know it*." [19]

I cite such examples not as an empty skeptical quibble about how any of our current beliefs might eventually turn out to be wrong. The situation is more serious than this. For given the fallibility of our knowledge, which lies at the heart of Boghossian's scientific world-view, it is impossible to imagine any scientific discovery that he would not need to preface with qualifiers of the following sort: "as we may now be said to know," or "suppose that we actually know it." It was not so long ago that Margo would have seemed correct about the sixteen moons of Jupiter, or that a top-flight scientist might easily (and wrongly) have exclaimed as follows: "Consider something that we now take ourselves to know — for example, that dinosaurs were *reptiles* — and suppose that we actually know it." Prior to James Chadwick's 1932 discovery of the neutron, we might have heard physicists say this:

"Consider something that we now take ourselves to know — for example, that atoms consist of protons and electrons — and suppose that we actually know it." Given that we can never be sure of possessing knowledge (and if this is not the chief contribution of Socrates to philosophy, then I do not know what is) we can even imagine a better title for Boghossian's book: *Fear of Justified True Belief*, a title far less compelling but perhaps more revealing than the bolder actual title.

At bottom, Boghossian is not really claiming that there is knowledge and we should govern our lives by it, but that there is scientifically justified belief and that we should govern our lives by it. He is surely right that some beliefs are "closer" to the truth than others, [31] since we do not find that all of our opinions are equally valid or useful, yet the question of what the word "closer" means remains cloudy indeed. And moreover, Boghossian is wrong to imply at the end of his book that the oppressed cannot criticize the powerful without *knowledge*. If this were true, then the future of political liberation would be in dire straits indeed, since claims that one is being politically oppressed are every bit as fallible as scientific claims. All that political liberation really needs is the ability to appeal to some *reality* of human rights or dignity beyond the current imperfect state of human affairs. If we want to say that scientists can be wrong about Jupiter's moons, then we must also admit that the protestors in Cairo's Tahrir Square in 2011 might have been wrong about Egypt's best path forward. If their case can seem so compelling, this is not because of some non-existent political "knowledge" on the Cairo streets, but because of a "justified" belief that the then-operative political system was unfair. But all this simply teaches once again the lesson of Plato's *Meno*: there is no knowledge and hence no teacher, and thus true opinion is the best that humans can hope for. What saves this from being a trite, middle-aged life lesson about never being too sure of one's beliefs? That will be one of the topics for the final section of this article. But first there is something else we need to discuss.

I said above that the second problem with Boghossian's standpoint is his *taxonomical* view that natural facts are non-constructed but cultural facts are constructed. We can all assent to Boghossian's harmless remark that "the fact that slurping your noodles is rude is not a universal fact: it holds in the [United States] but not in Japan." [13] But he goes further than this, suggesting that *all* facts involving human society are socially constructed, whereas the opposite is true of nature. For instance: "In the case of Jupiter's having over thirty moons, we can go further … [it] looks to be completely *mind-independent*: it would have obtained even if human beings had never existed." [13] Yet "the fact that there is money in the world is not a mind-independent fact — money could not have existed without persons and their intentions to exchange goods with one another." [13] But here Boghossian, like so many others, conflates two entirely different issues: whether or not humans were involved in the causal origins of a thing, and whether or not that thing is independent of the human understanding of it. Manuel DeLanda, one of the great realists of recent continental philosophy, deals with this issue wonderfully in the opening pages of *A New Philosophy of Society*.[853] What DeLanda seeks here is a realist theory of society, by which he means a theory of society in its reality apart from us. But how is this possible, given that human society is inherently constructed by humans? DeLanda answers this rhetorical question by drawing an important distinction. While on a causal level it is obviously true that human society was constructed by humans, this does not entail that human society is equivalent to what humans say or know about it. Statements in sociology, economics, history, or art criticism are every bit as fallible as those in the natural sciences, even if they are often more difficult to test with empirical precision. Thus Boghossian is wrong to claim that "there would ... be precious little point in writing a book revealing that facts about money or citizenship are cultural constructs, for this much would be obvious." [18] While I believe that such a book would be wrong, it would by no means be trivial: the point of such a book would not be that humans created society and money, but that all claims about society and money are "equally valid," a view that Boghossian and I would immediately agree in rejecting.

Why is any of this important? By assuming in advance that money and citizenship are socially constructed (which is true causally but not ontologically) while the number of moons of Jupiter is *not* socially constructed, he effectively gives the natural sciences a higher-class status in the forward progress of human inquiry. Research on money or citizenship will always seem somewhat tainted due to the contamination brought about by their human origin. In a way this is simply the pessimistic inversion of Giambattista Vico's view that since humans created society but not nature we can also *know* society better than nature.[854] Obviously this is not always or even usually the case, and neither is Boghossian's converse view. Against Vico, the causes of World War I are not inherently clearer than the causes of black holes. And against Boghossian, books such as Georg Simmel's *Philosophy of Money* or Karl Marx's *Capital* must answer to the pressure

---

853 Manuel DeLanda, *A New Philosophy of Society*.
854 Giambattista Vico, *The First New Science*.

of reality as much as any treatise on the wave-particle duality of light.[855] If someone approves of Simmel's book, or Marx's, then presumably this is because they think these authors shed light on the true nature of money, not because money is social constructed and therefore all diverse views on money have equal validity. Marxists in particular hold precisely the opposite view on this question.

Another example will prove unexpectedly helpful, this one drawn from the field of art criticism. During the generation of high modernist painting and sculpture from roughly 1948–1963, the leading standpoint in the United States was that of the formalist critic Clement Greenberg.[856] Among other things, Greenberg was devoted to the formalist (and in fact ontologically realist) principle that art is autonomous both from its socio-political and gallery context and from biographical facts about the artist. This formalist view remained central to Greenberg's one-time disciple Michael Fried, who in 1964 wrote a scathing attack on the emerging minimalist style of Donald Judd and Robert Morris.[857] This attack had two components that, as I see it, were wrongly conflated by Fried. In a first gesture, Fried rejected what he called the "literalism" of minimalist art. Rather than creating an artwork with a certain aesthetic depth beyond our personal encounter with it, the minimalists simply threw literal objects in our path in physical space: bare white concrete blocks, or mere frame-like metallic solids affixed to a wall. In a second, given that there could be no autonomous depth to such objects, Fried assumed that their whole purpose must be to generate some sort of effect on the viewer: a strategy he called "theatricality," and which he found just as lamentable as literalism, since he assumed that these two tendencies walked hand in hand.

Now, it seems to me that Fried on minimalist art makes essentially the inverse mistake of Boghossian on money and citizenship. For Boghossian, since money was created by humans the study of money cannot have the same realist status as the study of Jupiter's moons. Thus, any turn to realism must also mean a turn to natural science as a discourse privileged over anthropology and presumably over art as well. For Fried, since presenting the literal surface properties of an object does not yet constitute art, any art relying on the theatrical involvement of the human observer must also not be art. This would entail the view that art would remain art — or would

---

[855] Georg Simmel, *The Philosophy of Money*; Karl Marx, *Capital, Volume One.*
[856] Clement Greenberg, *Art and Culture: Critical Essays.*
[857] Michael Fried, "Art and Objecthood."

even be art to an eminent degree — if all humans were exterminated, which is every bit as far-fetched as claiming that money would remain money in a human-free world. Let's coin the phrase "Anti-Theatrical Fallacy" to refer to theories, such as Fried's and Boghossian's, which hold that the only way to preserve reality is to remove all human contamination from it. The problem is as follows: there exists a very large class of real objects that require human entities as a component, just as organic chemicals require carbon as a component. There is little point imagining what it would be like to have politics, society, art, chess, or basketball without humans, just as there is little point imagining an organic chemistry without carbon. It does not follow that we cannot conduct rigorously realistic investigations of politics, society, art, chess, or basketball, any more than it follows that organic chemistry is hopelessly tainted by a "carbon-centric standpoint." Just as special attention to carbon is the price of admission to organic chemistry, special attention to "theater" (i.e., human involvement) is the price of admission to human affairs, which do not thereby become irrevocably compromised by social constructionism. The root of the problem is that realism is always so severely on its guard against the human *observer*, as the one with relative standpoints that must be undercut by human-independent evidence, that it also becomes needlessly suspicious of the human as an *ingredient* in numerous situations. Thus it too quickly condemns the study of human affairs as somehow forever banished from realism, which becomes the exclusive province of the natural sciences.

There is already such biodiversity of philosophical terms for different nuances of standpoint that one hesitates to release yet another term into the wild. But given that the word "realism" is so widely associated with the Boghossian/Meillassoux assumption that realism means our ability to *know* the real, a new term is in fact needed here. This is my reason for proposing "infra-realism" as a suitable term: it retains the worthy "realism" while adding the important caveat that we are dealing with a real located beneath all knowledge-claims, and indeed beneath any access to it at all. Just as virtue is never reached by Socrates's or Meno's various statements about it, so too the black hole, Higgs boson, copperhead snake, and *Pinus strobus* family of coniferous trees remain a permanent surplus beyond all of our claims to know them at any given moment. This infra-realism does not entail a relativist free-for-all in which all viewpoints on everything are equally valid. What it does entail is a greater stress on fallibilism than we find even in the view of Boghossian, for whom the possibly incorrect character of any current knowledge-claim seems to have less weight than the obligation for everyone to follow whatever view seems most *justified* at any given moment. It also entails a more inclusive realism that does not disdain the cognitive status of the human sciences, art, and architecture simply because humans are causally linked to the very existence of these fields in a way that is not true of astronomy.

If the slogan of realism is "there is a real world, and it can be known," the motto of infra-realism is "there is a real world, and it cannot be known." The easy first reaction would be to call this a worthless insight, no better than a negative theology said to leave us empty-handed. The problem with this reaction is that it continues to ignore the achievement of Socrates, the ancestral hero of our discipline. Both etymologically and substantively, *philosophia* is neither wisdom nor ignorance but *love* of wisdom. As Socrates puts it, only a god has knowledge, and only an animal would be utterly ignorant. The human predicament is both to be and not to be in a state of wisdom. The contrary view would hold that there is either knowledge or ignorance and nothing in between, and thus no *philosophia*. This is essentially the position expressed in what is known as "Meno's paradox," though Meno himself credits it to the Sophists. According to this famous puzzle there is no point searching for anything, since you either have it or you do not have it. If you have it then there is no point searching for it, and if you do not have it then there is also no point searching for it, since you will not be able to recognize it when you find it. The argument is clearly feeble, Socrates demolishes it with little effort, and few take it seriously in this form today. Yet it remains effective even now in different, disguised forms.

One of those forms is the notion that philosophy must actually be grounded in some minimal form of *knowledge* if it is to escape being a mere fiesta of arbitrary proclamations. The topic arose earlier when we mentioned that Meillassoux and Boghossian are absolutely sure that there must be foundational principles for philosophy. In Meillassoux's case it is the correlational circle: we cannot think the unthought without turning it into a thought. There is no thinking without givenness to thought. This circle is not just an initial problem that Meillassoux challenges himself to circumvent. Instead, his philosophical conclusions remain saturated with the correlationist starting point, for which nothing exceeds the scope of thought even if much of it either precedes or outlives human thought. In Boghossian's case, as Markus Gabriel has often noted (in agreement with Boghossian), one cannot have a philosophy that denies the existence of knowledge. Why not? Because if someone says "there is no knowledge," then this statement is either knowledge or it is not. And if it is not knowledge, then it is mere opinion and can safely be ignored. If it is knowledge, then the claim that there is no knowledge has obviously contradicted itself.[858] [52–57] Hence, the only solution is that there must be some form of knowledge. The lingering consequence for Boghossian is that his is a realism about *knowledge* rather than about the real, even though he admittedly cannot be sure of when something is true and when it is merely justified without being true. The mistake at the basis of both Meillassoux's and Boghossian's objections is their shared Menoesque assumption that a philosophical view must either be knowledge or mere personal assertion, with no option in between. It is perhaps Alfred North Whitehead who has understood the stakes most clearly. As he tells us in *Process and Reality*: "after criticism, systems [of philosophy] do not exhibit mere illogicalities. They suffer from inadequacy and incoherence."[859] More famously, Whitehead claims plausibly enough that "a system of philosophy is never refuted, it is only abandoned."[860] And finally:

> the primary method of mathematics is deduction; the primary
> method of philosophy [by contrast] is descriptive generalization.
> Under the influence of mathematics, deduction has been foisted
> upon philosophy as its standard method, instead of taking its true
> place as an essential auxiliary mode of verification whereby to test the
> scope of generalities.[861]

The key to this passage is the phrase "descriptive generalization." If someone says "truth is relative" or "truth is historically determined," we can certainly always ask them if these statements themselves are merely relative or merely historically determined. As Boghossian notes:

> relativists are prone to dismissing self-refutation arguments of this
> sort as clever bits of logical trickery that have no real bearing on the
> issues at hand. That attitude, I think, is a mistake. It is always a good
> idea to know how some very general view about truth, knowledge, or
> meaning applies to itself; and few things can be more damaging to a
> view than to discover that it is false *by its own lights*. [53–54]

---

[858] Boghossian is right to say that his own defense of this principle is more nuanced than the traditional one. I am oversimplifying his position for reasons of space, though I do not think the difference between Boghossian's argument and Thomas Nagel's is as great as Boghossian thinks.

[859] Alfred North Whitehead, *Process and Reality*, p. 6.

[860] Whitehead, *Process and Reality*, p. 6.

[861] Whitehead, *Process and Reality*, p. 10.

Meillassoux makes a similar complaint about those who avoid responding to the correlational circle argument by saying that it is simply boring and empty, and that we are better served if we ignore such petty logical tricks and move on instead to some "Rich Elsewhere" of interesting concrete truths.[862] Yet there are important problems with this way of looking at things. What Meillassoux fails to admit is that appeal to the "Rich Elsewhere" is not just a rhetorically evasive stunt, but an extremely powerful factor in how seriously a philosophy is taken.[863] If Parmenides no longer has many followers for his claim that "being is and non-being is not," this is surely not due to any logical contradiction, since no contradiction is immediately obvious in the statement. Instead, Parmenidean ontology strikes us as excessively abstract, as inadequate in accounting for the diversity of experience as we know it. What Boghossian fails to recognize is that basic philosophical statements such as "truth is relative" or "truth is historically determined" are neither knowledge nor mere assertion, but something more like Whitehead's "descriptive generalization": a general sense of what the truth should be like. Each of us is committed to certain tacit first principles of what philosophy ought to look like and how it ought to proceed, but we need not claim (whether consciously or not) that these first principles represent a form of knowledge. To cite Whitehead again: "the verification of a rationalistic scheme is to be sought in its general success, and not in the peculiar clarity, or initial clarity, of its first principles."[864] Or better yet, "the accurate expression of the final generalities is the goal of discussion and not its origin."[865]

Such attempts to claim that all philosophy must rest on some minimal grain of absolute knowledge therefore fail. The same holds for the fate of knowledge on other fronts: Meillassoux did not account for the difficulty of translation between primary qualities as active in the things and primary qualities as discerned by the mind; Boghossian did not grant sufficient importance to the tension between knowledge and justification. Reality and knowledge are in some ways opposite terms, since no human theoretical, cognitive, practical, perceptual, or sensible interaction with the things is capable of directly extracting the primary qualities of things and bringing them to the mind in transparent fashion. While this raises the problem of how we seem to gain some knowledge of the world, this is precisely the sort of problem worth philosophizing about rather than short-circuiting with

---

[862] Meillassoux, in Ray Brassier et al., "Speculative Realism," p. 423.
[863] See Graham Harman, *Prince of Networks*, pp. 174 ff.
[864] Whitehead, *Process and Reality*, p. 8.
[865] Whitehead, *Process and Reality*, p. 8.

a most un-Socratic attempt to replace the love of wisdom with knowledge itself.

Yet as hinted at the outset of this article, there is another, more troubling implication of the infra-realist line of thought. The usual way of expressing realism is to call it "the view that there is a world outside of human thought." But this is only a small part of it. What realism really ought to mean is "the view that there is a world outside of any relation whatsoever." Human thought is undoubtedly more rich and complex than the experience (if any) of billiard balls, yet these same billiard balls have no more capacity to touch one another's features directly than does the human mind. We should consider here that there are at least *two* possible ways that the philosophy of Kant might be reversed. The first is the path of Meillassoux, following the German Idealists. According to this view, Kant was a great genius except for his silly archaic belief in the hidden things-in-themselves. If we simply note that to think things outside thought converts these things into a thought, then Kant is immediately flipped into the supposedly more advanced position of Fichte or Hegel. But there is another way to look at Kant, who not only defended the existence of things-in-themselves, but also mediated all relations through the central thought-world relation. For instance, we cannot talk about the collision of hailstones with a roof, but only with how this event is made present to us by way of the categories of the understanding and our pure intuition of space and time. If we were to reverse *this* aspect of Kant while retaining the things-in-themselves, we would have something more like "German Realism" than German Idealism. It would universally be the case that all objects (not just the mind, as for Brentano) make contact only with intentional objects, not real ones: that is to say, translations or caricatures of other objects, not real objects directly. It is admittedly difficult to persuade people to accept that there is no direct contact between thought and the world, no knowledge but only philosophy, and that direct causal contact between objects is just as impossible as direct human knowledge of the world. But these are the bullets that one must bite if we are to avoid *fear of reality*.

2. From "On Truth and Lie in the Object-Oriented Sense"

One of the most common philosophical definitions of knowledge is "justified true belief." The meaning of "true" in this case is that what is in our mind is adequate to what there is in the world. The word "justified" is added to ensure that one does not have true beliefs by mere luck, as if I were to randomly (and correctly) answer a stranger's question that the road to Larissa is the left fork at the crossroads, despite my having no idea of the correct route. So, a person knows when they give the correct answer *and* have good reasons for giving it. The problem in Edmund Husserl's case is that knowledge is all justification and no truth. Phenomenology makes no contact with the real except through arbitrarily dismissing the possibility that it is anything different from what appears in sensual experience. Judge Schreber could give us an excellent phenomenology of the strange voices speaking incomplete sentences to him in the "root-language" (as he calls it), and of the sun-rays with which God attempts to impregnate him.[866] But Schreber is a delusional psychotic, and hence it is obvious that none of his fine phenomologies would have the slightest contact with anything real. Husserl was no psychotic, but under the influence of certain narcotics, he might well have found himself in a living room filled with nothing but hallucinations of apples and lemons. He would be perfectly *justified* in his analyses in this hallucinatory scenario, assuming they were properly carried out, while still producing nothing but untrue statements insofar as the objects of his analysis would not even exist.

In 1963, Edmund Gettier published a famous three-page article to the effect that justified true belief is not always knowledge.[867] He offered a far-fetched but intriguing scenario in which a man named Smith is informed that his rival applicant Jones will be offered a job. For some reason, he has counted the coins in Jones's pocket and found that they number exactly ten. On this basis, he makes the perfectly justified assertion — based on what he knows — that "the man who will be hired has ten coins in his pocket." But something happens, and at the last minute the company decides to hire Smith himself rather than Jones. Smith now finds, to his surprise, that *he too* has exactly ten coins in his pocket. Therefore, the statement "the man who will be hired has ten coins in his pocket" turned out to be not only justified, but true, even though the hiring outcome was the opposite of what Smith expected. Gettier rightly notes that this is a case where we have justified true belief without anything that could convincingly be called knowledge. He thus concludes that there is a gap between justified true belief and knowledge; something more is needed.

---

[866] Daniel Paul Schreber, *Memoirs of My Nervous Illness*; Sigmund Freud, *The Schreber Case*.
[867] Edmund Gettier, "Is Justified True Belief Knowledge?" For a longer account of this article see Harman, *Object-Oriented Ontology*, pp. 178–181.

But I am not so sure that anything more is needed for knowledge to occur. It seems to me that knowledge ought to be defined simply as "justified belief," or even as "justified *untrue* belief." Knowledge-seekers are essentially seekers of justification, not of truth. For example, scientists typically scorn such notions as ghosts and even God, although it is perfectly conceivable that future breakthroughs might be able to detect and even measure paranormal or outright supernatural influences on the sphere of nature. Any scientist in the 1700s who proposed in advance an Einsteinian gravitational bending of space-time after a private brainstorm would have been dismissed as a crackpot: not because such a thing is impossible — it is the currently reigning theory of gravity — but because at the time there was no sufficient evidence for such an extravagant hypothesis. Newton's theory was basically doing fine, and was still in no need of being revolutionized out of existence. The history of science is enough to show that what sounds crazy in one decade or century can become conventional wisdom in the next. We would certainly not call Newton a crackpot for not being an Einsteinian during his lifetime, for there was simply no *evidence* for such a theory in his day, despite G.W. Leibniz's suggestive views on the relational character of space and time.[868] In Imre Lakatos we have a formidable theorist who thinks that the same holds even for mathematics, although this is a more controversial view.[869] In short, the top scientists of the present day might turn out to be terribly wrong about the universe while some lucky crank might turn out to be "right" with his guesses once quantum theory and relativity are unified with theories of dark matter and dark energy. But no future historian would call that crank a "great scientist" simply because he turned out to be right according a later phase of scientific development. Scientists are those who provide justifications according to the available evidence, and the same is true of phenomenologists. Knowledge must be justified, but it can never be true, since there is no direct access to the real. We need not be Kantian believers in the thing-in-itself in order to say this, but need only believe in the ongoing advent of scientific and philosophical changes and especially revolutions, which have happened often enough. This is the respect in which the scientific mainstream in any given era can be said to have knowledge, despite the eventual overthrow of most or all of what it thinks it currently knows. Knowledge is justified untrue belief, and therefore belongs to the realm of what Nietzsche would call "lies."

---

[868] G.W. Leibniz & Samuel Clarke, *Correspondence*.
[869] Imre Lakatos, *Proofs and Refutations*.

In recent continental philosophy, there has been a new tendency to couple "truth" not with knowledge, but with our subjective relation to the world. This is true for instance of Alain Badiou's theory of events, in which a truth is not a truth except insofar as a subject remains retroactively faithful to it.[870] Slavoj Žižek has a similar conception: "the truth that articulates itself is the truth about the failures, gaps, and inconsistencies of the big other," where "big other" is Jacques Lacan's *terme d'art* for the existing symbolic order, including everything that we call knowledge.[871] String theory sat around mostly unused for decades, until it became the topic of a collective movement that eventually became dominant in its field. The first exhibition of fauvist paintings was heckled to death by the public, yet Henri Matisse and his circle remained faithful believers in the deliriously bright-colored palette they had discovered. The word "truth" is usually employed to refer to a "submarine" state of affairs in the world that is accurately mirrored in the mind, although the story of new truths always involves an initially small group of ardent defenders of a new idea, or even one person acting alone. Søren Kierkegaard's major objection to Hegel is that his system ignores the "leap of faith" required to embrace a new outlook.[872] What all of this means is that truth requires someone embracing a new theory that is considered *unjustified* in terms of the current order of knowledge. New theories are often dismissed as crackpot productions, and this is why: existing theories have always had plenty of time to amass giant machineries of institutional justification, and new ones have difficulty competing in this environment unless they understatedly present themselves as harmless modifications of existing orthodoxy. If knowledge works by way of convincing justification, truth commonly offers fake justification to defend strange innovation. As the literary critic Harold Bloom puts it:

What intimately allies ... [Ernest] Hemingway, [F. Scott] Fitzgerald, and [William] Faulkner ... is that all of them emerge from Joseph Conrad's influence but temper it cunningly by mingling Conrad with an American precursor — Mark Twain for Hemingway, Henry James for Fitzgerald, Herman Melville for Faulkner .... strong writers have the wit to transform [their] forerunners into composite and therefore partly imaginary beings.[873]

[870] Alain Badiou, *Being and Event*; Alain Badiou, *Logics of Worlds*.
[871] Slavoj Žižek, *Less Than Nothing*, p. 518.
[872] Søren Kierkegaard, *Concluding Unscientific Postscript*, p. 340.
[873] Harold Bloom, *The Western Canon*, p. 11.

That is to say, it is better for a new novelist (or new anything else) to justify innovations by inscribing them in the circle of already recognized achievements. If a writer entirely without forerunners were even possible, they would undoubtedly fail for lack of an audience. The subjective component in philosophical truth is what Badiou calls "anti-philosophy," and he holds that philosophy must work as close to anti-philosophy as possible.[874]

If there is a truth in opposition to knowledge, it consists in discovering a hole or gap in existing theories, and of discovering something there that cannot (at least not yet) be paraphrased. A new theory initially does nothing more than *allude* to something that escapes easy definition. Heidegger's notion of "being" as that which has always been forgotten in Western philosophy is one such case, and the same holds for the essentially negative Socratic method of undercutting every definition of a thing that is attempted. But let's stay with the case of Heidegger for a moment. We have seen that he rejects both the senses and the intellect as delivering nothing but present-at-hand caricatures of the being of a thing. We do not get the apple by looking at it, nor do we get it by analyzing its eidetic qualities, or through physicalizing it as a mass located at a distinct point in space-time. These are all what Nietzsche would call "relational" conceptions of the thing, but Heidegger thinks we can gain access to something more.[875] The Heidegger of *Being and Time* thinks we can do this, initially, by focusing on the apple insofar as it *is not* directly present to us. The apple or hammer or floor in a room are, for the most part, taken for granted and therefore not present to the mind at all. In fact, none of these entities are distinguished in practical behavior for as long as we fail to notice them. Instead, they combine into a vast environmental background that enables our more explicit perceptions or thoughts in any given moment. "Taken strictly," Heidegger writes, "there 'is' no such thing as *an* equipment. To the Being of any equipment there always belongs a totality of equipment, in which it can be this equipment that it is."[876] That is to say, Heidegger tries to undercut the literal presence of individual things by arguing that they emerge not only from a non-present background, but from a background that is holistically unified.

---

[874] Alain Badiou, *Lacan: Anti-Philosophy 3*. For a favorable but partly critical review see Graham Harman, "Alain Badiou, *Lacan: Anti-Philosophy 3*."
[875] Friedrich Nietzsche, "On Truth and Lie in a Nonmoral Sense."
[876] Heidegger, *Being and Time*, p. 97.

But as argued extensively in my first book, this analysis fails on Heidegger's own terms.[877] The problem is that Heidegger is not only the philosopher of unconsciously used tools, but of *broken* tools as well. When something goes wrong — and not only in this case — we are able to become aware of *individual* items of equipment. And even if this awareness unfolds in the sphere of what is given to us, it requires a prior being of the things that is in no way given. For instance, Heidegger thinks that a hammer can become directly visible to us in such experiences as "this hammer is too heavy." What this means is that individual items of equipment are never sleekly inscribed in the "totality of equipment" in which they silently participate before something goes wrong. What contains the inconvenient quality "too heavy" is not the system of equipment as a whole, but the hammer alone. As a result, the fact that the tool-system is unconsciously taken for granted is not yet enough to escape presence-at-hand, any more than perception or the intellect were in Husserl's case. Just as the difference between perception and theory turned out to be not all that great, the same holds for the difference between these "conscious" relations and the unconsciously relied-upon ones encountered in our practical dealings with the world. Individual items like hammers, in their non-relational being that can never be fully integrated into a system, are what precede any of the relational aspects of things. Here, Heidegger allows us to catch sight of something that — contra Nietzsche — is not purely relational. While it is true that we see this by the grace of advanced philosophical theory, these withdrawn individual things are not paraphrasable, and to that extent go beyond any literalist conception.

This allows us to grasp, further, that individual entities are an unactualized surplus in relation *to each other* as well, even when no human observer is anywhere near the scene. The key difference is neither between theory and perception (Husserl) nor between praxis on one side and both theory and perception on the other (Heidegger). Instead, the key difference is the one between objects and their relations. Kantian philosophy has ruled it impossible to speak about object-object relations apart from any observer, for the eventually Hegelian reason that to speak about objects colliding with objects is already to bring them into the sphere of the human observer. But this argument is not as strong as it looks. Note that in Kantian philosophy we do not encounter our finitude *directly*. We simply experience what we experience, while a *deduction* is needed to argue that there is something behind this experience: a deduction Kant hides with the facile assertion that

---

[877] See Graham Harman, *Tool-Being*.

there cannot be appearances without something that appears. But if we can deduce human finitude this way — and I think we can — then we can also deduce the finitude of non-human entities. A red billiard ball need not be "conscious" of a blue one in order to be in a finite relation with it. All that is needed is the deduction that any interaction between two things fails to exhaust the full reality of these things, since each turns the other into a caricature, just as human experience does with whatever it makes contact.

It is in such cases, where the surplus of the in-itself hints at its existence when something goes askew on the surface, that we can speak of "truth" in opposition to knowledge. As we cited Žižek above: "the truth that articulates itself is the truth about the failures, gaps, and inconsistencies of the big other."[878] Badiou would say that certain elements *belong* to a situation without being *included* in it, and that truth occurs through an "event" in which these non-included yet belonging elements rise up and demand to be counted, as when a political underclass demands recognition, when a new artistic movement speaks a new truth that is not yet allowed for by the current situation, or when an amorous event shatters our existing world. In this respect, both Badiou and Žižek speak of the retroactive constitution of reality: that which is only now counted *will have been there all along*. The problem is that this retroactive conception borders on idealism. Badiou claims that individual things (which he terms "consistent multiplicities") retroactively generate their own surplus ("inconsistent multiplicity"), rather than this surplus having been there all along. Likewise, Žižek gives an arch-retroactive interpretation of Hegel in which each new dialectical figure emerges *ex nihilo* from a free choice at each stage, rather than having been implicitly contained in the dialectic's starting-point. Among other difficulties, this encourages an ultra-voluntarist politics that thinks itself entirely free of prior historical or geographical determinations. "Submarine" reality, as we have called it, is thus defined out of existence, and the subject's own positing of gaps and fissures in the big other is deemed sufficient to generate all the details of history. Events require a subject, and cannot occur in pre-subjective nature itself, whose very existence is vaguely conceded by the retroactivists mostly as a device for not sounding crazy. Latour takes a similar risk when he says that the Egyptian Pharaoh Ramses cannot have died of tuberculosis as present-day medical experts claim: since tuberculosis

---

[878] Slavoj Žižek, *Less Than Nothing*, p. 518.

was clinically unknown in those ancient times, it can only be posited retroactively as what killed Ramses "all along."[879]

The positive side of this paradox can be expressed as follows. If knowledge is to be defined as "justified untrue belief," then what we have called truth must be defined in the opposite way as "unjustified true belief." The reason is that truth has now been separated from any search for step-by-step justification, and takes the form of an immediate personal contact with some hole, gap, or fissure in the current state of knowledge or politics. If we call such contact "surprise," then surprise becomes "that which does not deceive," as Lacan says of anxiety, and as Badiou thinks holds for every form of "anti-philosophy."[880] Truth needs no justification, and hence is not a form of knowledge. but needs only a personal anchor in the experience of something astonishing that does not fit the current situation. I have often written that metaphor provides such a case as well. If we experience a sea that is not simply the sea of perception, theory, or practice, but a sea — reading Homer — that is a "wine-dark sea," we are immediately carried beyond the level of SO-SQ, assuming that the metaphor is effective for a given reader. Instead of a literal wine with wine-dark qualities, we are asked to think a *sea* with such qualities. This proves impossible, and the sea withdraws as something inherently ungraspable, leaving us with nothing but wine-dark qualities. But there is no such thing as objects or qualities existing without the other term, and thus some real object is needed as the support for the wine-dark qualities that have been left floating in empty space. That real object cannot be the sea, which has already been repelled into outer darkness by the impossibility of literally combining it with wine-qualities. Thus it is I myself, the reader of the poem, who must function as the substrate for wine-dark qualities, and the difficulty of doing this is what makes the aesthetic experience occur: the real I *performs* the sensual wine-qualities, which is precisely the perverse form of crossing that we needed. The term "perform" is no accident: speech act theory has long distinguished between "constative" statements that convey literal content and "performative" statements that commit our very being to what is said, whether in promises or outright aesthetic experience.[881]

This brings us back to the following comparison. What we call knowledge is what Nietzsche calls "lies," since knowledge entails phenomena grounded

---

[879] Bruno Latour, "On the Partial Existence of Existing *and* Non-Existing Objects."

[880] Jacques Lacan, *Anxiety.*

[881] J.L. Austin, *How to do Things With Words.*

in more basic phenomena, without any contact with the real ever occurring along this path. But the truth that Nietzsche calls impossible is possible indeed, with the strange implication that aesthetics is one of the primary seats of truth rather than lie. The movable host of metaphors and metonymies does not distance us from any presence of the thing-in-itself, but gives us a direct experience of truth. Granted, such "truth" can only be supermarine, since a metaphor is a reality only on the level of my performing it as a reader. The submarine reality that Nietzsche regards as inaccessible truly is inaccessible, since reality itself is not isomorphic with any trace of it that can brought into the mind. Instead of such impossible presence, we are left with truth, which deforms the space of a given situation by alluding to that which lies outside it.

PART VII
PREVIOUSLY UNPUBLISHED MATERIALS

CHAPTER 33

WITH THE SADATS IN THE DELTA[882]

As the following essay describes, I had the opportunity in December 2006 to travel to the impoverished village in the Nile Delta where former Egyptian President Anwar Sadat had grown up. It was one of the most memorable days of my sixteen years working in Egypt. After sending an email about this visit to a number of family and friends, my former professor Alphonso Lingis advised me to write up my recollections more formally and submit them to several major magazines he suggested. I did so, received nothing but rejection letters in response, and quickly forgot the idea of publishing it. But having rediscovered it recently on my computer, I think that readers of this book might enjoy it as a glimpse of Egyptian village life in the pre-Arab Spring period.

Last November, I received an email from my former student Donia el-Sadat, whose grandfather was the brother of the late President Sadat of Egypt, assassinated in 1981. Donia and her older brother Sameh, now a stock trader in Cairo, were both students of mine at the American University in Cairo, where I have been teaching since September 2000. The purpose of Donia's message was to request donations for a family project to donate bicycles to poor village children in the Nile Delta region of Monofeya, the home of Presidents Sadat and Mubarak. A special deal had been arranged with a Cairo assembly plant to provide bicycles at cost: only 200 Egyptian pounds apiece (approximately $35). I immediately responded that I would be happy to participate. My level of participation turned out to be much greater than imagined. Donia wrote back thanking me for the donation,

---

[882] This previously unpublished travel description was written in December 2006, shortly after the events it describes.

but added that I would be welcome to travel to Monofeya with the family entourage. She spoke highly of the villagers, and added that they would be excited if a foreigner were to visit. After mentioning my numerous childhood memories of President Sadat, I was also invited to visit his Delta estate, now transformed into a museum.

A few weeks later, I was informed that the next day would be bicycle day. That next day was Friday, December 8, the first of our academic weekend. I met Donia and her friend Reem in the Heliopolis neighborhood of Cairo, home to an ancient school of geometry where Plato may have studied. At the home we met Donia's mother Gehane and her cousin, the five of us joining two chauffeurs in black SUVs. The bicycles would be arriving separately, by a large truck also working at special charity rates. Much of the ride to Monofeya was spent in conversation with Gehane el-Sadat, who filled me in on the family situation. Her husband, who goes by his middle name Anwar, and Anwar's brother Talat are the two parliamentary representatives from Monofeya. (Talat was recently jailed, but retains his legislative seat.) Given the incredible esteem in which Anwar Sadat seems to be held in the region, the brothers win regular re-election with little difficulty. The Sadat family, just two generations removed from their village origins, seem emotionally attached to the region. Although Monofeya is supposedly just seventy-five miles northwest of Cairo, the drive takes more than two hours along the various winding roads. The route runs through the usual sort of Delta farmland, filled with donkeys, chickens, and deeply impoverished humans.

The Estate and Museum

Our first stop was President Anwar Sadat's countryside estate. The front building on the estate, Dar el-Salam (Hall of Peace) now serves as the museum. It contains a vast treasury of Presidential memorabilia, including photos of Sadat with dozens of foreign leaders. One of his uniforms is framed on the wall, along with a photograph of the blood-stained uniform in which he was assassinated. One also finds Sadat's toothbrush, toothpaste, combs, and other personal items, along with a television running a non-stop video loop of pundits describing the significance of Sadat in Middle East history. Jimmy Carter once sat in this room, and Henry Kissinger visited on numerous occasions. There used to be a helicopter landing pad outside, though it has now been removed — the surviving Sadat family, like President Mubarak himself, does not often travel by helicopter.

Behind the museum building is a larger mansion, a six-bedroom complex with a massive, multi-chambered living room, which is still used as the family's weekend home. A large plantation of orange trees and sugar cane lies behind the building, and a swimming pool has been installed in recent years. The younger Anwar Sadat holds political events here. After a brief stroll around the orange groves, breakfast was ready. It was a classic Egyptian breakfast, prepared by young women employed in the family's kitchen. There was *ta'amiya*, the Egyptian version of the more familiar Lebanese falafel, made from fava beans rather than chickpeas. There was *fool*, a dish similar to refried beans, but eaten most often in the morning. All of this was accompanied by newly-baked pita bread as well as fresh cucumber, tomato, cottage cheese, and even a heaping plate of biting green onion. The orange juice was squeezed from fruit grown in the yard next to us, and there was plenty of coffee as well. For dessert it was *fateer*: a thick pastry made from multiple layers of filo dough. The Sadats told me that George H.W. Bush was highly enthusiastic for fateer on his visits to Egypt. Although technically it was breakfast, Friday prayers at the mosque had just ended, so that the village minarets joined in our conversation.

The Village
The Monofeya region has a total population of approximately 400,000, including a small capital city and forty-five villages. Each of these, I was told, has an average of ten satellite "sub-villages." These satellites tend to be brutally poor, and for the day's charity work the Sadats had chosen three of the poorest. The particular one that we visited was called Kassem, with an estimated population of 4,000. Goats roam the streets along with humans, and a sizeable majority of the humans seem to be young children. Kassem is a warren of dirt roads winding back into impoverished alleys. Filthy ditches run between the farms, with donkey fodder the most important crop in the area. The background work for these visits is done by a youthful Cairene named Abdullah, a staff member of Anwar Sadat the younger. He comes to the village a day or two ahead of time to find out who has the problems that Mrs. Sadat most needs to address. It was Abdullah as well who researched which of the village children are the poorest and most studious, and hence most in need of bicycles to ride the unpaved four-mile route from the village to the nearest schoolhouse. Choosing a non-local man as the researcher seemed designed to prevent local "researchers" from possibly steering donations toward family and friends.

Along with the bicycle charity, Mrs. Sadat is hoping to develop Kassem further with a nursery for small children and a night school for adolescents. Her husband is focused on persuading the national government to pave some of the filthy mud roads and to resume building a half-completed hospital at the edge of the village. Construction was simply halted a few years ago when funds ran dry. As a result, the already sufficient number of trained MDs in the area have been left to earn their living as café waiters until the hospital is completed. On first meeting, Gehane Sadat is a friendly woman, and obviously warmer and more dynamic than most of the people one meets. Even so, her true gifts first emerged only in the village itself. From the moment she left the car in Kassem, she was surrounded and mobbed by cheering children (part rock star, part miracle worker) and even a number of elderly men. The Sadat family is clearly beloved in the region. The late President rose up from relative poverty nearby, at the beginning of his distinguished career, which helps minimize the social distance between this wealthy and celebrated family and the impoverished villagers. Without exception, each home we entered during the day contained multiple posters of the living brothers Anwar and Talat, with ghostly half-images of the late President Sadat hovering behind their shoulders.

Initially Mrs. Sadat was mobbed with such exclusive attention that Donia, Reem, and I the obvious foreigner were completely ignored. This gradually changed in my case, in a rather humorous way. Most Egyptian children, even illiterate ones, seem to know two stock English phrases: "How are you?" and "What's your name?" Whenever they ask the latter question, I always say that my name is "Harman," which is easy for Arabic-speakers to pronounce, whereas "Graham" is difficult in nearly every language other than English. When one of the Kassem children unsurprisingly asked for my name, I gave the usual "Harman" response, assuming that no one else had heard me. But word traveled quickly, and within ten minutes a group of fifty or sixty children was following me, cheering aloud: "Mr. Harman, how are you?! Mr. Harman, how are you?!" The chant was repeated every few seconds for up to an hour.

Two children in particular stand out in memory. One was the boy of about seven years old who was responsible for starting the "Mister Harman" game. He wore a sweatshirt labeled with the English word "Boxing," and bore an uncanny resemblance to my nephew in Portland, despite the Czech-Irish ancestry of my nephew. The Boxing Boy, as I later called him, loved shouting my name and title at far greater volume than the other children, as he laughed before darting off toward unnecessary hideouts. The other was a girl of about ten years old, wearing a headscarf. For whatever reason she wanted to walk side by side with me throughout the village, and I sense that such boldness is rare for Egyptian girls of the lower class. Her motivation seemed to come from something like a cosmopolitan streak, or the equivalent by sub-village standards. It could not be said that her English was especially good, and in fact I even had the sense that she was illiterate. Nonetheless, she did have command of several sophisticated English phrases, and also struck me as a clever young thinker. At one point, after another round of the "Mister Harman!" chants, one of the children corrected the other by saying "DOCTOR Harman!" (Donia had called me her "doctor" at one point, as professors are usually called in Egypt, and it must have been overheard.) After hearing the correction, the young girl turned to me and asked: "teacher, or clinic?"

The researcher, Abdullah, managed to steal me from the mob long enough to point out the future nursery/night school. But the main purpose of the sub-village tour was to visit the homes of sick people needing urgent assistance. Mrs. Sadat is sometimes able to help these people, sometimes not. But her very presence seems to transmit some sort of outside hope that someone will gain access to the outside world that might just solve their problems. I was allowed to enter each of the following houses in turn, and listen to the requests for help of the residents.

House #1. The first case was the worst of them all. A forty-year-old farmer, his head wrapped in the traditional cloth, lay in bed groaning, with a hand to his side. His wife was there, understandably worried. His daughter, a lethally cute eight-year-old with long brown pigtails, seemed to be taking everything in stride. It resembled a stock Hollywood scene of "dying peasant man." The diagnosis was hepatitis, probably the result of drinking the filthy ditchwater of the village. His liver had been completely destroyed by the disease. Although an organ transplant is technically possible, the cost of the procedure is approximately $5,000, but the average peasant income in this region is a mere $12 per month. In short, the cost of an organ transplant would work out to approximately ten years' worth of income. The Sadats seem to be doing what they can, but they cannot personally fund the dozens of organ transplants required in the various villages. Organ failure seems rampant: later in the day, I met several dignified but grim-faced men in need of kidney transplants. What Gehane is able to do is obtain needed prescriptions, and to use her connections, political status, and charming personality to negotiate discounts for numerous products and medical services. Of all the people we met that day, this poor farmer is the one I continue to worry about most.

House #2. A calm elderly man with nerve damage in one leg. He was not able to stand on the leg, since it has no feeling and he easily loses his balance. It was not clear how they planned to help him, but Gehane's arrival seemed to cheer him up.

House #3. An adolescent boy curled up on the floor with inscrutable facial expressions, stroked tenderly by his mother. The background story here was mental retardation, which doctors cannot help, but he also has some sort of abdominal pain which makes it impossible for him to sit up. The Sadats are looking into the case to see what might be done.

House #4. A young veiled woman crying inconsolably. She wanted plastic surgery for her face. Her face looked fine to me, but Donia later reported seeing severe burn marks on the left side of her face, and similar burns on her left arm.

House #5. A man whose kidney transplant had failed, leaving him on dialysis. The good news in this home was that his brother's transplant had succeeded.

House #6. We reached this house after a long walk along muddy fields, away from the village. By this point, the chanting "Mister Harman!" mob had become so insistent that one of the village elders became annoyed and chased the children away with a raised stick. Outside the home was an elderly woman suffering from depression, and I assume she can be helped. She just broke down and started crying in front of us, twice, for no apparent reason, as Donia rubbed her back in consolation. Without knowing the whole story it is difficult to be sure, but I had the sense that she might easily be treated by pharmaceutical means.

In general, I have noticed during my seven years in the country that medical privacy is no great concern to Egyptians. Often I have been startled in our university clinic to have the receptionist ask me what my problem is, in a loud voice in a full waiting room. On several occasions I have been shocked to have female students apologize that they missed my class because of diarrhea. But this apparent tendency even among the upper classes of Egyptian society was magnified beyond measure in the villages. Each of these patients announced their most intimate medical problems to us in front of fifteen to twenty of their fellow villagers, with no trace of embarrassment.

While leaving Kassem, Gehane el-Sadat pointed to another ruined sub-village nearby. It used to consist of some fourteen buildings, but last year was burned to the ground in a disastrous fire that killed dozens. The story has the ring of medieval legend, but is apparently true. It is said that a pigeon landed on top of a bread oven. As it flew away, it realized that it had some sort of burning stick or straw attached to its foot. The pigeon then panicked, landing on every roof in the village as it tried to remove the burning object. All fourteen buildings had straw roofs, and the pigeon seems to have set fire to every one of them. They caught fire so quickly that many of the peasants could not escape.

Bicycle Distribution

The time to distribute the bicycles had arrived, a more complicated operation than one would expect. A total of three hundred have been purchased so far, from both Sadat family funds and private donations such as my own. The bicycle parts come from India, and are assembled (at a Gehane-negotiated discount) in a Cairo factory. They are awfully snappy devices for $35 apiece, and come in either red or blue. The plan today was to give away fifty-two of the bicycles. The researcher, Abdullah, had drawn up a list of worthy recipients ahead of time. The major problem was how to distribute the bicycles without being attacked by a demanding mob. The Sadats initially thought that going to a vacant lot near the half-built hospital would offer sufficient secrecy, but during our mere ten minutes of waiting, there assembled a dangerously bored and curious mob of about one hundred fifty, mostly children.

At last the flatbed truck appeared, also driven from Cairo at a discount negotiated by Mrs. Sadat; the first set of fifty-two bicycles was clearly visible on the back of the truck. Yet the child-mob was such an obvious impediment to orderly handouts that she regretfully decided to cancel distribution for the day. Although she politely apologized for such a disappointing end to my Delta journey, I could only agree that the situation was far too dangerous. At this point, we decided to return to the estate/museum and pick up a few things we had left behind before returning to Cairo. The Sadat family members would come back later in the week to hand out the bicycles. At the estate, I was offered some home-grown Sadat sugar cane, along with a brief lesson on how to chew it. After a few minutes of chewing like a panda, I entered the yard to see Gehane and Donia, mother and daughter, chatting excitedly. Someone had saved the day with a brilliantly obvious idea: why not distribute the bicycles *inside* the walled-off grounds of the Sadat estate? The plan was to invite the recipients into the compound, one at a time, then let each one exit with their new bicycle through the back gate. Whoever might have made this decision, the previous crowd of children were somehow all informed of it, and seem to have sprinted *en masse* the mile or two from the unfinished hospital to the Sadat estate. A loud chanting mob could now clearly be heard outside. Sadat family security personnel, all of them well-dressed and two of them openly carrying rifles, tried to hold back the masses and only admit those into estate grounds who had one of the pre-distributed written bicycle contracts.

Before describing the giveaway itself, I should mention three things about the required arrangement for bicycle recipients:

1 Each child and his parents were required to sign a written agreement. If the conditions of the agreement are not followed, then in principle the bicycle can be seized by the Sadat family at any time in the first year and given to another child. Since the primary purpose of the bicycles is to ride to school, any child who stops attending school regularly must forfeit the gift. Furthermore, no one is allowed to sell his bike in the first year or reduce it to parts. After one year, it is private property and can be disposed of as the owner sees fit. Gehane's theory with these provisions was that any agreement lasting longer than a year would not make much sense to these children anyway, and that a year should also be enough to create a bond between the child and the bicycle that would most likely prevent unwise sale or disassembly.

2 All of today's fifty-two recipients were boys, a necessary first step. For now, the girls of Kassem will have nothing to do with riding bicycles: the very thought of wearing pants rather than their current dresses and gowns embarrasses them terribly. Gehane hopes to organize a public meeting, drafting her daughter Donia as a speaker, to develop the claim that girls should be able to wear pants just like boys. One idea for such a meeting is to show video clips of Chinese girls riding bicycles. Gehane hopes that with a bit of educational work, the Kassem girls may be ready to receive their gifts in the next wave. But I was interested to note that the younger generation on our trip, represented by Donia and her

friend Reem, were far more skeptical than Gehane and her cousin that this would succeed.

3 In response to my question about whether the bicycles come with locks, I was told that there is almost no theft in these villages whatsoever. Thus, no one involved with the charity even considered buying locks. A bigger problem seems to be that all the bicycles of each color look alike. Each boy will need to individualize his bicycle in some way, but this is sure to be done not only quickly and easily, but even ingeniously.

Apart from the choice of color, all of the bicycles looked exactly the same. Each one had a basket on the front, presumably for the transport of school supplies. The kickstands were weak enough that twenty or so bicycles fell to the ground like dominoes at one point, and I was left with the task of setting them upright again. Otherwise, I thought these were fine bicycles in view of the $35 price.

Crowd control became extremely difficult outside the Sadat compound. The chosen recipients had a hard time making their way through the chanting crowd outside. A group of children even broke through the back gate, our designated exit point, hoping to obtain bicycles for themselves from outside the official quota. The one ugly moment of the proceedings came when a group of four young adults burst in from the back and also demanded bikes. "We were with you at election time," they shouted, "and now you have to deliver for us!" Gehane simply faced them and explained that the bicycles were for children. The direct approach seemed to work: for all the violence of their shouting, the four left rather quickly when confronted.

I cannot remember all fifty-two of the bicycle recipients. In some cases, just the father or mother came in without their son. In all cases, the bicycle was not awarded until the signed agreement was handed over. Each recipient shook hands with all of us. I would say "Mabrouk!" (congratulations) and "Fursa saeeda!" (pleased to meet you) to the boys and their parents. But a few of the children remain more vividly in memory than others:

Case #1. The first boy was one of the funniest. He may have been the only one to arrive with both his mother and father. This was of course the only boy to witness the full, undepleted lineup of fifty-two bicycles, and you could sense his mouth watering. By then it was already dusk, lending an air of mystery to the proceedings. Initially he was given a red bike. He then said he'd rather have a blue one. His mother told him that this sudden change of heart was rude, but Gehane said it was fine, laughed, and gave him a blue one instead. Not twenty seconds later, he came back saying he had changed his mind yet again, and preferred a red one after all. Gehane laughed once more, as did the boy's cheerful, outgoing mother.

Case #2. A nine-year-old boy who was almost dazed with happiness. Gehane felt his chest, and had me and her daughter do the same. The little boy did not mind our feeling his chest, where we both discovered a pounding heartbeat. He rode off in a delirious trance out the back gate.

Case #3. A boy and his father. The boy's name was "Antonio," which I had never heard in Egypt before. Clearly he must have been a Coptic Christian, named after the Egyptian hermit known to us as St. Anthony. In fact, this area of the Delta is heavily Coptic. Throughout the day I had seen a number of crosses drawn on various structures, though Kassem itself seemed predominantly Muslim.

Case #4. Fathers coming in alone, multiple instances. The stated reason was always that they did not dare have their sons crushed in the tumult outside. These fathers all tended to smile and give me the heart taps made famous by Chicago Cubs baseball player Sammy Sosa as a sign of thanks, a gesture I have often encountered among the Egyptian poor.

Case #5. Two mothers entered the compound in tears. Gehane later told me that they were crying due to having been crushed by the crowd outside, an experience that rattled both of them a bit.

Case #6. With only two bicycles left, three boys entered. There seemed to have been a slight miscount, and I was worried. After the first two received the final remaining bikes, the third boy burst into tears. Gehane comforted him as though he were the victim of especially cruel bad luck. But she turned to me and whispered, in English, that the other two hundred fifty bicycles were already on the property, hidden in a storage shed. She would soon give this boy one of the hidden bikes, but first had to play out the pretense that none remained, since there were too many onlookers to safely reveal the secret presence of so many extras. Gehane waited for the crowd to file away before revealing the good news to the heartbroken final boy, who had to be left crying for more than five minutes before the onlookers departed.

Thus ended Day One of the bicycle project. Gehane el-Sadat told me that she had absorbed a number of lessons about what not to do the next time, and quickly gave me a rapid summary of possible improvements that inspired great confidence in the future of project.

I rode back to Cairo with Donia and Reem, a long but pleasant trip in the dark of night. They dropped me off outside the family residence in Heliopolis, and from there I took a taxi to the sparkling, modern Citystars mall. As I browsed in a crowded store, a hand tapped my shoulder: it was that of W____, a young architect who happens to be engaged to one of my better students at the university. This was already a more-than-minor coincidence in a city as large as Cairo. The much larger coincidence came when W____ nodded his familiarity with my report on the Sadat bicycle project: it turned out that W____ is the architect of Mrs. Sadat's proposed village nursery. The village bicycle researcher, Abdullah, is his close childhood friend.

CHAPTER 34
INTERVIEW WITH CHIARA PRINCIPE[883]

Chiara Principe: Professor Harman, first of all I would like to thank you for agreeing to make this interview happen. It is a pleasure and an honor. I would like to start by asking you: what is an object?

Graham Harman: This is the right place to start, because object-oriented ontology (OOO) has a very specific concept of the object that differs from the usual one. In modern philosophy, of course, the object is what is opposed to the human subject. But as interesting as humans may be (especially to humans themselves) I reject the modern dogma that humans deserve to make up half of the topic of philosophy: with human subjects on one side and *everything else in the universe* (animals, stars, viruses, black holes, etc.) on the other. In the end this reduces philosophy to a taxonomy of two different *kinds of beings*, which is really just a secularized version of the medieval taxonomy of Creator on one side and everything Created on the other. Since philosophy is obliged to make room for everything, philosophy must begin with a "flat ontology" that treats everything equally. Naturally, we should not *end* there, since a philosophy would be poor if it tells us only that "all entities are equally entities." But it's the only right way to begin.

---

[883] This interview was conducted in Turin, Italy during my time as a guest professor there in 2017. Although I did eventually meet Chiara Principe during my stay, the interview itself was conducted via email. It was originally intended for publication in Italian, though to my knowledge this has not yet happened.

For OOO, there are two kinds of objects: the real and the sensual. Let's start with real objects. A real object is anything that cannot be exhaustively reduced in *either* direction, downward or upward. When people speak against reductionism they are usually complaining about the downward reduction of a thing to its tinier components. This complaint is justified, since this *undermining,* as I call it, is unable to account for the emergence of a thing over and above its components. My body could not exist if it were to lose all of its atoms, for example, but it continues existing as the same body despite the constant loss of many of its specific atoms. No one living in Dante's time is still alive in Italy today, but in some sense we can still speak of the same Italy existing today as in the 1300s, despite so many changes in the meantime.

But real objects also resist reduction *upward* to their ultimate effects or appearance to the mind. This is the typical prejudice of modern philosophy: to be is to be perceived, substance is subject, the world does not exist without human Dasein, everything is caught in an endless network of signifiers. This is what I call *overmining,* and it fails because it cannot explain change. If objects are nothing more than what they are doing here and now, then how can they be doing something different a few hours or months from now? Aristotle already made this argument in the *Metaphysics* against the Megarians, who thought that everything was equal to its activity and nothing more, so that someone is a house builder only if they are building a house right now. In fact, Aristotle introduced his famous concept of potentiality in order to win this argument with the Megarians. Usually undermining and overmining strategies come as a pair, in order to cover for the weakness of each other. This is what I call *duomining,* or both forms of mining at once.[884]

The real object for OOO is that which cannot be duomined. Which is not to say that reduction is forbidden: all knowledge is reduction. When someone asks us what something is, we have only two possible responses: we can tell them what it's made of, or tell them what it does. These are the two basic forms of knowledge, and I challenge you to find a third, because there is none. And without knowledge, the human species would quickly perish. The mistake is thinking that all cognition is either knowledge or it is useless vagueness. Art is one good example of a form of cognition that is not a form of knowledge production, and *philosophia* is another: Socrates is quite serious when he denies having knowledge of any sort. But modern

---

[884] Graham Harman, "Undermining, Overmining, and Duomining."

philosophy has surrendered to the prestige of mathematics and the natural sciences and wants to be a form of knowledge too. I think this means the destruction of philosophy.

The real object for OOO is similar to Kant's famous thing-in-itself, but with at least two important differences. First difference: for Kant, the thing-in-itself only haunts human beings, who are trapped alone in their finitude. But for OOO, *any relation* is haunted by the inaccessibility of things-in-themselves. When hailstones strike a coconut tree on an uninhabited island, those hailstones only encounter a crude and oversimplified version of the tree, since hailstones are just as finite as humans in terms of what they can encounter. This by no means entails that the hailstones are "conscious"; that is a separate question altogether.

Second difference: Kant's things-in-themselves always sound otherworldly, like Plato's perfect forms, as if they belonged to one dimension and the phenomena to another. For OOO, however, real objects are not somewhere else, but here in our midst. They emerge over and above their components while withdrawing under and beneath their outward effects. Normally I would now talk about OOO's second kind of objects, sensual objects, which are our variation on Husserl's "intentional objects." But perhaps we should move instead to your next question to keep things livelier and more interesting!

Chiara Principe: You wrote that Aristotle can be considered the father of Object-Oriented Philosophy. What about his philosophy and approach is most appealing to you and how did it shape your own thinking?

Graham Harman: Aristotle is an acquired taste for most of those who love him, myself included. As a young philosophy student I, like most others, preferred "sexier" thinkers such as Nietzsche and Heidegger. But then one must also agree with Julián Marías's claim that, historically speaking, philosophy tends to become extremely fertile whenever it re-establishes intimate contact with Aristotle.[885] Unfortunately, we are not in much contact with Aristotle these days. When I began graduate study in the early 1990s, the great philosopher who was most out of fashion was Plato: everyone was supposed to "reverse" or "overturn" Plato, and to be accused of "Platonism" was the deadliest insult. Somehow that shifted, and it became fashionable to appreciate Plato again. As we speak here in 2017, I think

---

[885] Julián Marías, *History of Philosophy*, p. 372.

the least fashionable great philosophers are probably Aristotle, Thomas Aquinas, and Husserl.

We should also remember that the pre-Socratics, who are usually called the first philosophers in the West (though I think Socrates was really the first) were explicitly *anti*-object-oriented. Every pre-Socratic was an underminer, trying to reduce the mid-sized things of the world to some ultimate root. Aristotle was the first object-oriented philosopher insofar as he was the first to make perishable individual things the primary substance of philosophy. This is why I find the tradition beginning with Aristotle and ending with Leibniz to be so refreshing. (I don't think Hegel is a genuine heir of Aristotle, even though my Italian friend Alfredo Ferrarin has written an excellent book making the opposite claim.)[886] The main problem with this tradition, as I see it, is that it overvalues *nature* as a criterion of what counts as real. This is especially clear in Leibniz's overly aggressive distinction between "substances" and mere "aggregates." Leibniz would not be able to tell us much about the ontological status of an airplane or a university, and he even mocked the unity of the Dutch East India Company as an object: which is why I wrote a whole book about that company as an object, to prove him wrong![887]

Chiara Principe: You write, "while there may be an infinity of objects in the cosmos, they come in only two kinds: the real object that withdraws from all experience, and the sensual object that exists only in experience. And along with these we also have two kinds of qualities: the sensual qualities found in experience, and the real ones Husserl says are accessible intellectually rather than through sensuous intuition."[888] In the *Critique of Pure Reason*, especially in the first part where he presents the table of categories, Immanuel Kant draws explicitly from Aristotle.[889] How does this distinction between the "real object" and the "sensual object," the former being withdrawn, autonomous, and free of all relation, and the latter being available to our perception, differ from Kant's insight concerning the difference between the thing-in-itself and the objects of sense-perception, the noumena and the phenomena, put forward in his critique?

---

[886] Alfredo Ferrarin, *Hegel and Aristotle*.
[887] Graham Harman, *Immaterialism*.
[888] Graham Harman, *The Quadruple Object*, p. 49.
[889] Immanuel Kant, *Critique of Pure Reason*.

Graham Harman: There are two differences from Kant. The easier one to see is that for Kant the thing-in-itself is something that demonstrates *human* finitude. We poor humans cannot reach the in-itself, which is treated as a residue that cannot be mastered by *thought*. For OOO, however, the thing-in-itself is a residue not just of thought, but of *all relation*. Put simply, the collision between two inanimate objects is also something that occurs only on the phenomenal level. When one rock slams into another, there is also an issue with the thing-in-itself not being fully deployed in the collision. There are no doubt things that are special to thought and even to narrowly human thought, but finitude is not one of them: finitude belongs to relationality *per se*. Otherwise you would have relations that exhaust their relata, which would be a textbook case of overmining.

The second difference is subtler. OOO takes from Husserl the idea of a *sensual object* in opposition to its sensual qualities. This is what makes phenomenology possible: the blackbird that remains the same blackbird even though I view it from many different angles and in countless profiles. Phenomenology completely reverses Hume's assumption that an object is primarily a bundle of qualities. But someone might ask: doesn't Kant already accomplish this in a way? After all, he does speak of the "transcendental object=x," which is not the same thing as the noumenon, but belongs to the realm of phenomenal experience. It is an abstract idea of unity over and above any particular qualities the object might have.

However, the fact that Kant views the transcendental object=x as an abstract idea shows us how much larger Husserl's step towards object-oriented philosophy was. For Husserl the unity is in the object itself, not in the conceptual equipment of the one who perceives it. This is the "realist" side of Husserl, the side that makes people *think* he is a realist because he is so attuned to the drama underway in the specific concrete entities of experience. But it is necessary to put "realist" in quotation marks, because it's just not realism if you're rejecting the noumena outright, as Husserl does. Any "realism" in which it is possible to convert the real into some form of direct knowledge simply doesn't have enough respect for the real to be worthy of being designated as realist. Usually such "realisms" are just epistemological policing efforts that aspire to use the tools of natural science to make relativists shut up. But I chose to go into philosophy, not law enforcement.

Chiara Principe: Alfred North Whitehead could be considered as an OOOntologist *avant la lettre* on the grounds that he believes that the

world is composed of what he calls "actual occasions," the "final real things of which the world is made up," "drops of experience, complex and interdependent."[890] What has been Whitehead's contribution to the development of OOO? In his article "The Actual Volcano: Whitehead, Harman, and the Problem of Relations," Steven Shaviro wrote: "The difference between Whitehead and Harman is best understood … as a difference between the aesthetics of the beautiful and the aesthetics of the sublime."[891] Could you sum up the debate with Shaviro on this very subject matter?

Graham Harman: Let me start with your first question, about Whitehead's contribution to the development of OOO. The summer of 1997 was intellectually very important for me. I was living in the Chicago area, at the height of my sportswriting activity, and obsessively rewriting the first of the three parts of *Tool-Being*, my doctoral dissertation and eventual first book.[892] My commitment to Heidegger's philosophy was weakening, though I'm not sure anymore how conscious I was of that fact. There was a specific café near where I lived, and I would go there every day in the summer of '97 reading one of two books that had been on my shelf for a decade without my finishing them. One was Whitehead's *Process and Reality*; the other was Xavier Zubíri's *On Essence*.[893] Put those two books together and you'll have an explanation of the two ways in which I broke through the walls of Heideggerianism.

The contribution of Whitehead is pretty obvious. Whitehead tells us that his system is in many ways a recursion to the philosophies of the seventeenth century: in other words, the philosophies prior to Kant's revolution. These days Isabelle Stengers and other lovers of Whitehead seem to be in a rush to tell us that Whitehead didn't really mean it, as if somehow claiming to go back before Kant were a dangerous disqualifier.[894] But there's one very good thing Whitehead gets from going back before Kant, and that's being able to displace the human-world relation from the center of all philosophizing. In Leibniz, for instance, any relation between any two monads is treated the same way: all relations are subject to pre-established harmony. Human monads are allowed to have the title of "souls," but in terms of how they

---

[890] Alfred North Whitehead, *Process and Reality*, p. 27.
[891] Steven Shaviro, "The Actual Volcano," p. 288.
[892] Graham Harman, *Tool-Being*.
[893] Xavier Zubíri, *On Essence*.
[894] Isabelle Stengers, *Thinking With Whitehead*.

function, all human and non-human monads operate in the same fashion. With Kant that is no longer the case: we can't talk directly about how two non-human objects collide, but only about how *humans can discuss* this collision according to the transcendental conditions of our finitude. Whitehead encouraged me to go beyond such an outlook, which of course infects of all of Heidegger as well with the priority he gives to Dasein's access to the world. Heidegger would never let us talk about something happening in the inanimate world, but only about Dasein's encounter with that world. Heideggerians often behave as if this were some incredible insight on their hero's part, when really it's just Heidegger standing in the coldest portion of Kant's shadow.

I will speak more briefly of Zubíri's contribution to OOO, though it was just as profound as Whitehead's. What Zubíri sees so clearly is the way in which the essence of a thing must be the way it is in its own right, not as determined by its relations with other things (or by its "respectivity," in Zubírian terminology). This was very helpful in getting me past Heidegger's relationist misreading of his own tool-analysis in *Being and Time*. Heidegger acts as if the hammer really were nothing more than its total deployment in all the referential assignments of the equipmental system, which of course is thoroughly determined by Dasein's projection of its own possibilities of being. But this makes it impossible to understand how tools can *break*, which was always the most interesting part of Heidegger's analysis. The hammer can only break insofar as it is *not* exhausted by its referential assignments. The hammer is a *reality* that sometimes asserts itself and causes problems for the functioning of the system.

It was, rather dramatically, on Christmas morning of 1997 that I was finally able to put all of this to myself in words. Objects were non-relational, I now saw. Realists were right, but they would have to give up basing their realism on *knowledge-claims* about the real, since what characterizes the real is its impermeability to any *direct* knowledge-claims, which could only lead to idealism when it tried to make reality fully commensurable with our models of it. It was a month or so later that I started reading Bruno Latour, who wasn't enough of a realist for me, but did do a lot of other things for early OOO.[895] For example, he has a wonderful model of *translation* that goes beyond the human realm much like Whitehead did.

Your second question concerned Shaviro's claim that OOO follows Kant too closely down the rabbit hole of the sublime and ignores beauty.

---

[895] Bruno Latour, *We Have Never Been Modern*.

I love debating with Shaviro because he is blunt but somehow never offensive; I suspect this is part of why he doesn't seem to have any enemies. Nonetheless, I think his point here is incorrect. For there are at least three different things we can say about the sublime, and I don't see how any of them bolster his case:

1 The Kantian sublime is somehow impalpable. It cannot be put into words, whether we are talking about the mathematical sublime (referring to size, such as the vastness of the universe) or the dynamical sublime (referring to power, such as the overwhelming might of a tsunami). And of course, OOO frequently evokes the way in which objects are inexhaustible by any perception or paraphrase of them, and that might make it seem like we are addicts of the sublime. The problem with this point is that Kant says exactly the same thing about beauty! Here too, Kant is quite clear in the *Critique of Judgment* that the beautiful cannot be put into words. There are no discursive *criteria* for beauty; it simply has to be experienced by taste. So, Shaviro can't really imprison OOO on the side of the sublime on this first point, since Kant's point about the unparaphrasability of beauty is already enough to satisfy us.

2 For Kant the sublime is somehow about *us*, not about the amazing thing we have just encountered. The vastness of the universe and the power of the tsunami don't educate us about the cosmos as much as they teach us about our own finitude. Obviously OOO must reject this, since for us it is too subjective a way to look at aesthetics. But once again Kant's doctrine of beauty has precisely the same feature: beauty for Kant is less about the beauty of the object itself than about our own transcendental structure of judgment, shared by all humans. Since the sublime and the beautiful in Kant are both equally and surprisingly subjective in this way, OOO is not at home with either, and so once again Shaviro can't really put us on the side of the sublime any more than on the side of the beautiful.

3 Finally, we have the most important point that Shaviro misses. He should not have forgotten that for Kant the sublime is about the *infinitely* large, the *infinitely* powerful (by comparison with our own puny finitude). A tsunami strikes us as having an infinite power far exceeding our own resistance, but so too do a major earthquake, a volcano, or a black hole. None of these can really receive *individual* treatment by Kant, since they are all effectively infinite: infinite

enough to overwhelm us with amazement. But that's not what OOO's "withdrawal" is about at all. Withdrawal always has a specific finite size and specific finite qualities, even if we can never pinpoint what these are. For OOO, the real withdrawn tsunami *is not* equivalent to the real withdrawn volcano. We are fully aware that each of these is a different real object, which is precisely what the "infinity" of the Kantian sublime does not permit.

Chiara Principe: Among recent philosophical figures, Jacques Derrida and Gilles Deleuze are considered two of the most relevant. They are also two key examples for what you call undermining and overmining philosophies. What has SR in general and OOO in particular drawn from these thinkers?

Graham Harman: Let's start with Derrida. I've often mentioned the strange fact that all four members of the original Speculative Realist group (Brassier, Grant, Meillassoux, and I) only shared admiration for one author: H.P. Lovecraft, the American horror and science fiction writer, who has enjoyed a big comeback recently. But the Speculative Realists also shared another point in common: none of us has ever been very interested in Derrida, even though according to our birth years (1963 through 1968) we *should* have been Derrideans. During my own graduate school years, you really had to be working on Derrida and/or Foucault if you wanted to be at the cutting edge.

And yet, I never found Derrida very interesting. For one thing, I still cannot stand his writing style. There are far too many puns, though I understand the supposed theoretical basis for his using them. And most of his articles consist of about 10 serious pages that get to the point surrounded by another 50 or 60 pages of frivolous showboating that his followers treat as the work of genius, when I see it more as the outcome of poor literary taste. And of course there is also his rampant anti-realism, along with his refusal to come to grips with the realist aspects of Heidegger. So many people seem to love reading Derrida, but I have never understood why. For me it is a tedious and frustrating experience. I am quite sure that Derrida has not been a good influence on continental thought. Among other things, there was a whole generation of people in America who could have been good, solid, original Heidegger scholars, but who adopted too many of Derrida's own stylistic pretensions without being able to pull it off.

Deleuze is a different case. When I started graduate school in the early 1990s, he was not yet the Deleuze we know today, whom people now dare to call "the Kant of our era" and things of that sort. The Deleuze of the early 1990s was still viewed as an entertaining fringe figure, roughly on the same level as Jean Baudrillard; in fact, I first read Baudrillard and Deleuze in the same graduate seminar, and it seemed like an appropriate pairing at the time. I've always loved Deleuze's irreverence. But I think there's a good deal of truth to the old adage that Deleuze is a fusion of Spinoza and Bergson, and OOO (despite its admiration for both) is largely anti-Spinozist and anti-Bergsonian in spirit. I've also grown tired of Deleuze's alternative history of philosophy, in which we're supposed to focus on the Stoics, Duns Scotus, Hume, Nietzsche, etc., rather than on the usual pillars of the history of philosophy. I no longer find this counter-history of philosophy to be very liberating, since one now encounters it everywhere among contemporary authors. Its work has been done, and it's high time that we return to Plato, Aristotle, St. Thomas Aquinas, Hegel, and other central figures downplayed by Deleuze. That said, he has been a great breath of fresh air for the field. Let us never again lose the sense of humor that Deleuze displays when doing philosophy.

Chiara Principe: Speculative Realism seeks means of driving straight past the so-called "linguistic turn." While it is difficult to find explicit positions common to all the thinkers under the SR movement, all have certainly resisted the "traditional" focus on textual critique. Why is this so, and why do you think a realist philosophy is better equipped to tackle contemporary issues?

Graham Harman: Nonhuman entities have played a minimal role in modern philosophy, and what is called "postmodern" philosophy is just another variant on modernism. Hence my strong attraction to Latour when I first read his work in early 1998. I would not call Latour a realist in any strict sense of the term, since realism for me entails a non-relational core of the real in each and every thing, which is ruled out by Latour from the start. But his consistent practice of taking nonhumans seriously in every situation he analyzes is something we have rarely seen in the past few centuries of philosophy: certainly not since Kant, other than a few exceptions, such as Whitehead.

Modern political theory, including both Leftism and the modern conservatism that arose to combat it, is utterly saturated with philosophical idealism along with the anthropocentric bias that goes hand in hand with idealism. The right path for political theory no less than for ontology at present consists in getting back in touch with the role of nonhumans. The future will be more Latourian than Foucauldian. Foucault has had a good run as the standard footnote in the humanities and social sciences, but what sorts of tools can he really provide us in dealing with global warming, which requires us to come to terms with such entities as permafrost, algae, methane, and volcanoes? And conservatism can't help us a bit more, since it too is grounded in a theory of human nature, even if a grimmer picture of that nature than the Leftist version that can ultimately be traced back to Rousseau.[896] Human nature is not as important as it used to be, in part because humans are being swamped by nonhuman objects that are starting to lead humans along unprecedented paths.

Chiara Principe: In your own words, in your philosophy "real objects withdraw into private vacuums and make only indirect contact through metaphorical signals to one another." I find this fascinating. Could you elaborate on the concepts of "private vacuums" and "metaphorical signals."

Graham Harman: The private vacuum simply refers to the non-relational core of any real object. It has become fashionable to say that there are only relations, no relata that exist independently outside them. For me this is overmining pushed to the point of incoherence: no relation exhausts its terms, which are always a surplus outside their current relations or any possible relations. Nonetheless, objects do somehow manage to influence each other, to unleash causal forces on one another. I hold that they can only do this indirectly, through what I call "vicarious causation."[897] Two real objects affect each other only by way of a sensual mediator, and two sensual objects only by way of a real one. This concept of indirect causation is not entirely new in the history of philosophy. But the earlier versions of it always named some special entity that could engage in causal relations even though nothing else could do so: God for the Arab and French occasionalists and later Whitehead, or the human mind for Hume, Kant, and the tradition that ensued. But there is no good reason to permit one pampered super-entity (whether God or the mind) to engage in supernatural causal activity

---

[896] Jean-Jacques Rousseau, *Discourse on the Origin of Inequality.*
[897] Graham Harman, "On Vicarious Causation."

when everything else is forbidden to engage in it. Causal powers are well distributed throughout the universe, but they are indirect, just as metaphor is an indirect form of language. Causation itself is analogous to metaphor. Timothy Morton took a lot of heat for making this case in his book *Realist Magic*, but I support his efforts completely.[898]

Chiara Principe: As you mentioned above, you hold that a breakthrough in the theory of objects was made by phenomenology in contrast with the empiricist philosophers, who denied the very existence of objects, replacing them with "bundles of qualities." For Edmund Husserl each object is a unified object of experience irreducible to its sum of qualities, which keeps its evident features and unity even if it is exposed, as everything is, to ongoing shifts in its features. Martin Heidegger takes it a step further by insisting that objects are usually withdrawn into a silent background. In this respect you say the philosopher's approach is similar to that of the art critic Clement Greenberg, for "both authors make the surface too shallow and the background too deep, with the artwork's form conceived too holistically and its content too dismissively."

Graham Harman: Someday the twentieth century may be known as "the rhetorical century." I mean "rhetoric" in a very specific sense here, the one set down by Aristotle.[899] For Aristotle, rhetoric deals primarily with the *enthymeme*, the syllogism that need not be spoken directly because it is already present in the heart. Rhetoric is not primarily about making convincing literal statements, but about knowing how to address the background assumptions of an audience that are deeper and more powerful than any consciously held propositions.

This should be clear in Heidegger's case, since it is never the "ontic" or present-at-hand surface of the world that matters to him, but the being that withdraws behind all presence. Greenberg, who is not only a great art critic but also one of the very greatest prose writers, dismissed the content of painting as "literary anecdote" and says that modernism in painting is all about using the content to reflect the very flatness of painting's canvas medium: hence his view that analytic cubism was the high point

---

[898] Timothy Morton, *Realist Magic*.
[899] Aristotle, *The Art of Rhetoric*.

of twentieth-century art.[900] Greenberg, like Heidegger, is a thinker of the greatness of the background as opposed to the relative superficiality of the visible surface. Marshall McLuhan is the third member of this triad: "the medium is the message" means that the content of any medium is far less important than how the hidden structure of the medium itself transforms consciousness.[901]

Now, I am on record as saying that all three of these authors (and all are among my favorites) overstate their case. Content and surface end up playing a surprisingly crucial role for each of them. There is a revenge of the surface, but I don't think it can be understood by those who dismiss any of these figures too quickly.[902] Their contempt for content is a major theoretical breakthrough, though like all major breakthroughs it contains a good dose of exaggeration and the seeds of its own reversal. The arts in particular have suffered from a premature dismissal of Greenberg. When he fell in the 1960s he fell hard, having lost relevance to what art began to do following the abstract expressionism of which Greenberg was famously the champion. But in my view Greenberg was often reversed in the wrong ways, without having come to terms with his achievement. Eventually the arts will find their way back to Greenberg, and then past him. The point is that they are not past him yet, however old-fashioned he may seem.

Chiara Principe: I find some interesting points of intersection between your way of thinking about works of art and that of Susan Sontag's _Against Interpretation_.[903] I mean this insofar as she rejects the act of critical interpretation, first of all, as plucking a set of elements from the whole work, not considering the artwork as a whole. Secondly, there is her objection to translating the artwork or, so to speak, explaining what the artwork "really means." To her this is an attitude that has its root in "the culture of late classical antiquity, when the power and credibility of myth had been broken by the 'realistic' view of the world introduced by scientific enlightenment." Do you find this connection fitting? How does your philosophy approach thinking about art objects in a critical way?

---

[900] Clement Greenberg, _Art and Culture._
[901] Marshall McLuhan, _Understanding Media._
[902] Graham Harman, "The Revenge of the Surface."
[903] Susan Sontag, _Against Interpretation._

Graham Harman: It's funny that you should mention Sontag, since we were just reading her in my aesthetics seminar in Los Angeles a few months ago. I feel intellectually closer to Sontag's position than to those of Rosalind Krauss or Arthur Danto, to give just two examples.[904] Part of it is that Sontag has the minimal formalist instincts that I think are needed to do any justice to art at all. Her critique of interpretation is a critique of our ability to paraphrase artworks, and I'm all in favor of that. She was also more open than Greenberg or Michael Fried to some of the new trends of the 1960s, as in her positive treatment of performance art (or "happenings," to use her own contemporary term). For example, scaring the audience away with a lawnmower at the end of a show need not be as aesthetically ridiculous as the high formalists would tend to assume. I have argued that theatricality is essential to art, and not the death of art as Fried asserts. But I wouldn't be so quick to let scientific enlightenment own the word "realistic." Realism for me is not about accurate description and measurement, but about that which is so real that it is never fully captured by description or measurement. And for this reason, I think the arts (and philosophy) are the true site of realism.

Chiara Principe: What is an art object? For OOO anything is an object including computers, bicycles, gigantic international corporations, even Pizza Hut or Manchester United (in "Objects are the Root of all Philosophy").[905] In your opinion, how and when does an object become an art object?

Graham Harman: An object is not an art object just because the art world tells us that it is. For an object to become a genuine art object, it must withdraw from direct access even while its qualities remain visibly in orbit around their invisible object. As a result, I myself as the beholder must step in for the missing object and perform it myself. This is why *all* art is theatrical, contra Fried.[906] For this reason, artworks are all compounds that consist of an art object plus a beholder. We can leave open for now the question of whether the beholder needs to be human, or whether certain higher (or even lower) animals, plants, and rocks are capable of aesthetic experience.

---

[904] Rosalind Krauss, *The Originality of the Avant-Garde and Other Modern Myths*; Arthur Danto, *The Transfiguration of the Commonplace*.
[905] Graham Harman, "Objects are the Root of All Philosophy."
[906] Graham Harman, *Art and Objects*.

It's certainly the case that not even all humans will respond to all artworks all of the time. There are many pieces, even great pieces, that leave many of us completely cold, and in these cases we tend to defer to the authorities and recognize that they must be great artworks even though they do nothing for us personally. But it's also the case that not everything that gets called "art" will really prove to deserve that designation over the long haul. Just because the current social consensus recognizes Impressionism as a movement worthy of large museum and private collection expenditures does not mean that the status of Impressionism is secure for the ages. The same holds in any field, of course. Herbert Spencer was supposedly the first philosopher in world history to sell one million books, and is quoted admiringly by the likes of Henri Bergson and William James. But who reads Spencer now? Whenever I visit the van Gogh Museum in Amsterdam, I'm pretty sure I'm in the presence of artistic greatness, but if that is so, it's not so just because today's art institutions tell us that it is. The verdicts of society are every bit as falsifiable as the verdicts of science.

Chiara Principe: In a way, art has generally made it explicit that art objects can't be completely exhausted through their definition or use — they are admittedly "unparaphrasable." Somehow contemporary art makes this even more extreme for it makes use of 'things' (objects, so to speak) that may have not been previously linked to anything art-related. To quote Arthur Danto, whom you mentioned before, "with qualification, anything goes."[907] I'm especially interested in your take on the Duchampian paradigm, that is to say, the invention of the readymade as an object that becomes an artwork by the creative act of mere selection.

Graham Harman: Hasn't the Duchampian moment lasted far too long? It seems to me that his lesson has been well learned: anything put in a position where it comes to be recognized as art (such as a museum, gallery, or more offbeat art space) *can* be counted as art. But the real trick is to make it work, and that requires a power of seduction, not just of shock. When I visited Documenta in 2012 — I couldn't make it to Kassel in 2017 — there were two pieces in particular that I found seductive, in the sense that they drew me into a world and completely occupied my attention. One was Geoffrey Farmer's *Leaves of Grass*, the 124-foot-long display of people and objects

---

[907] Arthur Danto, "The Work of Art and the Historical Future."

cut from *Life* magazine and displayed on wooden sticks. That one worked by its sheer magnitude and encyclopedic character. It didn't just say: "Hey, even *Life* magazine could be taken for an artwork if we put it in a gallery!" Instead, Farmer realized that something needed to be done to the magazine to achieve a genuine aesthetic effect. The other piece that really moved me in Kassel was the filmed Crusades puppet show by Wael Shawky, whom I somehow managed not to meet during my many years in Egypt. Here we have political art at its very best: art of a sort that allows its political claims to be experienced directly and aesthetically rather than enslaving aesthetics to a literal political message.

Duchamp had a point to make, and he made it: the art object as a supposedly self-contained piece of stuff is not the whole story of aesthetics. That's why he was so undervalued by Greenberg (who nonetheless brutally exposed a number of weaknesses in Duchamp's position), and why his influence became so rampant in the 1960s once Greenberg's brand of formalism began to wane.[908] But art has been following Duchamp's star, directly or indirectly, for a few decades too long. The role of human artists and institutions in framing what counts as art is undeniably there, but someone like Danto greatly underestimates the degree to which aesthetic *mistakes* are made when this happens. It's a sort of Hobbesian argument that they have: "Might makes Art!" But Hobbes was wrong insofar as the sovereign can be wrong, and Danto was wrong because the art world can be wrong about what counts as art.

Chiara Principe: Joseph Kosuth's piece *One and Three Chairs* offers a great example (and what I believe would have been a great book cover!) for your tripartite model. As we've been discussing, philosophy and art do not and should not look to the object as something that can be reducible to its measureable or subjective properties so, in your own terminology, as something that can be *duomined*. Then how can we "read" or even relate to artistic endeavors? Based on what interpretative points can we set apart artworks that look for the third chair from those that do not?

Graham Harman: You're not the first to ask my opinion about Kosuth's piece. I don't find it uninteresting, but it doesn't speak to me in the way that many assume it will. It's true that there are "three" chairs there in

---

[908] Graham Harman, "Greenberg, Duchamp, and the Next Avant-Garde."

a certain sense: a chair, a photograph of how it is stationed in whatever exhibition it currently occupies, and a dictionary definition of chair. But notice that all three members of this tripartite distinction count as what OOO calls overmining. I don't think Kosuth gives us much ontological diversity here, despite his claim to threefold plurality. We could expand this piece indefinitely to include other overmining gestures: a holographic projection of a chair, an invitation for people to use it by sitting in it, a poster describing the socio-political impact of chair manufacturing, and so forth. In this respect, the number three in his piece is completely arbitrary and does not point to three exhaustive dimensions of chairness. There is not even an attempt at undermining the chair by describing its component pieces, let alone any presentation of the chair in a non-mined sense: the physical chair in Kosuth's piece is simply a "literal" chair in Michael Fried's sense, and that means an overmined chair. It is really a Duchampian readymade with a couple of distractions added (the photograph and the dictionary definition) so I'm not sure it takes us anywhere new. I hate to sound harsh about a piece that so many have excitedly presented as being right up my alley, but it seems to have much more in common with Derrida (whose philosophical emergence was contemporary with Kosuth's 1965 piece) than with OOO.

You also ask more generally how one should go about looking for artworks that secure a "third table" in the way that OOO demands. Since art that undermines is relatively rare, we can focus on the ways in which artworks avoid overmining. And here there are a number of principles that can be used. First of all, art that consists *entirely* in its message can be discounted; here I'm with formalists such as Greenberg and also with McLuhan. Just like Aristotelian substance, art should be paradoxical in the sense of being able to endure and sustain a large number of interpretations. It should also *not* be art that can be viewed with disinterest: this is the weakest point of Kantian aesthetics, since it arises from his doomed conception that not only should art have an autonomous value with no ulterior purpose (here I think he is right), but that such autonomy must consist in the *detachment* of thought from its object. Whether we focus only on the physical art object or only on the human faculty of judgment that assesses it, we are undermining art by reducing it to just one of its two components: which is like trying to understand water by claiming that it's all about the hydrogen or all about the oxygen. So, I think we can rightfully demand of artworks that they fascinate us in some way rather than giving rise to disinterested contemplation. Yes, this might run the risk of opening ourselves to sentimentality at times, but let's not pretend that there are no risks in the art that is with us today: we know how the contemporary art world is filled with so many empty intellectual stunts and cynical critiques.

One of the wisest remarks I've heard about contemporary art was made by J.G. Ballard, whose own fiction I admire only in part.[909] Ballard pointed out that the role of art used to be to create fictions. But in the present day, when we are all surrounded by technology and celebrity- and media-driven fictions, the artists is now called upon to create *reality*. There are a number of ways to do so, but only a handful of artists really compel our belief. So many are focused entirely on calling our beliefs into question, but is that really necessary anymore?

Chiara Principe: While talking about art critics Michael Fried and Clement Greenberg's positions in your article "Art Without Relations" you conclude that: "Aesthetics is replaced by spectacle, since the viewer is now anticipated in the structure of the artwork itself …. While the artwork must have a depth beyond how it is encountered by the spectator, the human is less a spectator than a co-constituent of the artwork itself, since non-fascinating art simply fails in a way that non-fascinating science does not …. The distinction Fried fails to make is that between humans as literalist observers of art and humans as theatrical ingredients of art."[910] In contemporary practices such as Tino Sehgal's, the artworks are exactly the situations that occur among spectators/ingredients with (supposedly) no material documentation to it. As we discussed, you hold that anything is an object, therefore can a situation count as an object, an artwork to be specific? What is, in your opinion, its ontological stance?

Graham Harman: The ban on material documentation in Sehgal's case doesn't interest me. It reminds me too much of the philosophical theories about how "events" are more primordial than substances. I find this theory weak, for reasons argued in all of my books. In fact, an artwork that is not somehow repeatable or displayable in different contexts is far less likely to be good art. The focus on events is an overmining focus, and this is the

---

[909] J.G. Ballard, *Re/Search No. 8/9.*
[910] Graham Harman, "Art Without Relations."

greatest danger for the arts just as it is for all non-scientistic contemporary philosophies.

There's also a second point, which is that it's not enough to be theatrical: it also has to be *good* theater. The fact that one's art has some intellectual underpinning to justify it (such as theories of the event) does nothing to secure its quality as art. Here I sound like Greenberg, but this is one of his valid points. I have nothing against Sehgal, but I didn't like his 2013 piece that won the Golden Lion award in Venice. It seemed like a much less interesting version of a 1960s "happening." Given his reputation, surely he must have better work that I have not yet had the privilege of experiencing.

Chiara Principe: In your articles and books you write almost exclusively about two-dimensional artworks. The only reference I could find to three-dimensional artworks is:

"Greenberg's flat canvas is not a piece of literal physical material, as it might be for Judd: it is a dematerialised two-dimensional space that all content must take into account in any truly modern, postillusionist painting. To point to the literal physical canvas is not the same as to point to the aesthetic background that the canvas enables." Could you elaborate on this point?

Graham Harman: There is one place in Michael Fried's essay "Art and Objecthood" where I think he simply gets Greenberg wrong.[911] That comes when Fried claims that, ironically, Greenberg paved the way for minimalism (a.k.a. "literalism") when he stressed the importance of the flat background canvas. Fried couples this major theme of Greenberg with what I would call a throwaway remark where Greenberg ill-advisedly concedes that a blank canvas could be an artwork. On this basis, he makes the claim — unjustifiably, in my view — that Greenberg was open to the possibility of literal objecthood as constituting art.

Why do I think Fried is wrong on this point? Because canvas as a piece of physical material is one thing, and canvas as the physical basis for a flat two-dimensional art medium is quite another. Imagine that instead of having to paint on physical canvas, nineteenth-century painters had had the technological ability to project two-dimensional scenery directly in the air in front of the viewer. In this case, by hypothesis, there would be no canvas. Yet Greenberg's critique of three-dimensional illusionism as being

---

911 Michael Fried, "Art and Objecthood."

in conflict with a two-dimensional medium would still hold good. Could we then say that Greenberg believed that the literal *air* could be an artwork? It seems to me that he could never seriously propose this, and in fact I also don't think he would have maintained that a literal piece of blank canvas could count as an artwork. My sense is that we could easily have persuaded Greenberg to retract that statement, which makes a poor fit with the rest of his thinking on art. On the whole, Greenberg is as fervent an opponent of literalism as Fried himself. I suspect that Fried was simply performing the typical gesture of distancing oneself from a mentor, and while that is always necessary to achieve a position as original as Fried's, I think it led him to unfairness in this case. Again, Greenberg's "flat canvas background" was never meant to be a literal physical material. The operative words here are "flat" and "background," not "canvas."

But your more direct question was about why I haven't said much about sculpture so far. I've actually done so in some catalog pieces about individual artists, but it's true that I haven't said anything so far about the inherent theoretical difference between two- and three-dimensional works. I will do so before long.

Chiara Principe: Apart from Joanna Malinowska, whom you mention in some lectures as being "too literal" in her approach to OOO, and a few other examples, you don't mention a lot of actual art, especially contemporary art.[912] In one of your articles, however, you feature the work of Irish artist Isabel Nolan.[913] What do you find interesting in her work in relation to OOO? What other examples would you give and what art do you generally prefer?

Graham Harman: I don't know Malinowska personally, but was greatly encouraged by her very early use of OOO in her New York show "Time of Guerrilla Metaphysics." I often used to cite her piece where she left a portable stereo, unheard, in the Arctic wastes, as an example of how an artist might deal with the non-human-centered approach of OOO.[914] What changed my mind about this (though I still thought Malinowska did a fine job) was a question someone asked at a conference in France in around 2012. The question was as follows: "What would an 'art without humans'

[912] David Coggins, "Secret Powers."
[913] Graham Harman, "It is Warm Out There/Il fait chaud là-bas."
[914] The story is told in Graham Harman, *Architecture and Objects*, pp. 95–97.

look like?" Initially puzzled by this question, I realized after several weeks of thought that it missed the point. OOO is not about a world *without* humans, but about a world in which the human encounter with things is secondary. A good example of what I mean can be found in DeLanda's realist philosophy of society.[915] The point for DeLanda is not that we need to think of human society *without humans being there*, which would be a contradictory enterprise. Instead, the point is that even though humans are a necessary ingredient of human society, society is not equivalent to what humans think they know about it, or the current ways they make use of it. We need to distinguish between humans as ingredients and humans as observers, and OOO only opposes the primacy of the latter. The former (the human ingredient) is even necessary in many cases: human society, art, chess, basketball, and so forth. No one would ask "What would water without hydrogen look like?" Well, it would simply be oxygen, not water. And for the same reason, "art without humans" would simply be pieces of canvas, pigment, or bronze in a post-apocalyptic landscape with no one there to see any of it.

I have deliberately avoided trying to become too involved in the contemporary art world, because I think it would be a mistake to prematurely choose "winners" and "losers" from a OOO standpoint. Artists will need to figure out their own ways of responding to OOO's influence, if they choose to do so, and the most fruitful ways will surely be ways I could never have thought of myself. But I have written about several contemporary artists and what I like in all of their work is their optimism, lack of cynicism, and their ability to respond to the inner magic of things. I became familiar with Isabel Nolan's work through Francis Halsall, a brilliant art writer who emailed me a few times before I met him at a conference.[916] But I continue to like everything Nolan does a great deal. I've also written catalog essays on the work of Rachel de Joode, who I think is of Dutch nationality and working in Berlin; her sculptures are filled with life and freshness.[917] The same with Reuven Israel, whom I met in New York, and who has a sort of novel twist on minimalism that I think travels a long way.[918] And then I once wrote an "emerging artists" sort of feature on Mia Feuer, a Canadian who works in Washington, D.C.[919] Here too, a deeply uncynical use of

---

[915] Manuel DeLanda, *A New Philosophy of Society*, p. 1.

[916] Francis Halsall, "Actor-Network Aesthetics."

[917] Graham Harman, "All Space is Real, All Time is Sensual."

[918] Graham Harman, "Reuven Israel's Very Unliteral Theater."

[919] Graham Harman, "Mia Feuer: Selected by Graham Harman."

color and easily recognizable everyday elements jumped out at me and left a lasting impression. More recently, I have enjoyed the paintings of Egan Frantz in the same way; we met when he invited me to speak at his show in New York in 2013.[920]

This won't be the end of it. I may have a more active phase as a critic at some point, but most likely it will only be if I'm asked to do so, since I'm not professionally involved in the art world in the way that is now true of architecture.

Chiara Principe: I would like to ask you about your definition of intentionality and the importance you believe Husserl's departure from Brentano's idea of intentionality as closely linked to the contents of experience had on philosophy in general and to OOO in particular.

Graham Harman: "Intentionality" is a term from medieval Islamic philosophy (taken from Avicenna) that was famously revived in the nineteenth century by Brentano, an ex-priest who became the teacher of Husserl and Sigmund Freud, among others. In his great book *Psychology from an Empirical Standpoint*, Brentano asks himself what the difference is between mental acts and the sorts of non-mental actions we see in the physical world.[921] His answer is to say that mental acts are "intentional," not in the everyday sense of "on purpose," but in the sense that "every mental act is directed at an object." To love or hate is to love or hate something; to judge is to judge something; to wish is to wish for something; to perceive is to perceive something. It is important to note that for Brentano, the "something" intended by all of these mental acts is an *immanent* object, one that exists in the mental sphere rather than outside it. I note this because some interpreters wrongly think intentionality refers to jumping outside the restricted sphere of the mind and making direct contact with reality itself. In fact, Brentano was not very helpful in clarifying the relation between the intentional realm of immanent objects and any reality outside the mind. This created a fertile area of dispute for his many gifted students, who other than Husserl and (to some extent) Alexius Meinong tend to be forgotten today.

In any case, Brentano's Polish student Kasimir Twardowski made a brilliant attempt to address the relation between real and mental in his

[920] Graham Harman, "Recent Paintings of Egan Frantz."
[921] Franz Brentano, *Psychology From an Empirical Standpoint*.

dissertation *On the Content and Object of Presentations*.[922] In this work, he claimed that there is an *object* outside consciousness and a *content* inside it. In some ways one could read this as a less skeptical version of Hume's position: there is a reality out there made up of objects, but inside the mental sphere all we get are sets or bundles of qualities. Now, Husserl was half a generation older than Twardowski but was in many respects less philosophically advanced at the time, having come to philosophy late after beginning in mathematics. One gets the sense when reading the young Husserl that he was somewhat obsessed with Twardowski's efforts, with which he disagreed entirely. In one famous passage, the young Husserl says that the problem with a position like Twardowski's is that it doubles up Berlin into a Berlin-object outside the mind and a Berlin-content inside the mind.[923] Husserl sees no way to cross this divide, and he worries that a Twardowskian dualism will leave us empty-handed if we seek any knowledge about Berlin, since we will be able to do nothing more than talk about the mental version of the city.

This objection to Twardowski was decisive for Husserl's entire position. He banished things-in-themselves outside the mind as a useless notion, telling his readers that the notion of an object that could not at least *in principle* be the intentional object of some consciousness is absurd. It may be that no one is in my house right now with the refrigerator open, but in principle it would not be difficult to have someone go there and look at the contents of the refrigerator and make true statements about them. In this sense, there is no refrigerator outside the mind. Now, this actually makes Husserl an idealist, since objects become a pure correlate of consciousness rather than existing outside it in any meaningful way. Husserlians regularly deny this, but that is a philosophical error that they inherit directly from their master.

Nonetheless, in Husserl's idealism lies the seed of his philosophical greatness. For even if I think Twardowski's position was closer to the truth, Husserl's voluntary confinement in the immanent mental realm forced him to work very hard to see everything that is going on in that realm: much as a king's prisoner will learn everything about the castle in which he is confined, since he is not allowed to venture elsewhere. And what Husserl accomplished through his imprisonment was to see that Twardowski's object/content distinction could be imploded *within* the mental realm. How does this

---

[922] Kasimir Twardowski, *On the Content and Object of Presentations.*
[923] Edmund Husserl, "Intentional Objects."

work? Well, Husserl notices something that escapes Hume when the latter reduces objects of experience to bundles of qualities. For it is simply not true that when I hold an apple in my hand I only encounter qualities such as red, spherical, hard, juicy, and so forth, and then arbitrarily bundle them together as "one" apple simply because they appear together so frequently. (Alain Badiou makes an analogous mistake when he says that something is one only if it is "counted" as one.)[924] The central insight of phenomenology is that the object precedes its qualities. The apple-qualities may be changing every instant, displaying what Husserl calls different "adumbrations" (*Abschattungen*), without our ever thinking that it's a different apple in each instant. What the phenomenological method asks us to do is strip away all the transient apple-qualities in our mind, in order to gain access to the essence of the apple by discovering which qualities the apple truly needs and cannot lose in order to remain the apple that it is. Husserl thinks we can do this through intellectual rather than sensual intuition, whereas I think we can do neither: the intellect is just as relational as the senses are, and the objects of OOO are explicitly non-relational. But as far as I can see, Husserl is the first philosopher to really get this division between objects and qualities right. Kant was a precursor with his notion of the "transcendental object=x," a form of objecthood immanent in the world of appearances and thus different from the thing-in-itself. But whereas Kant treats it as an empty form of unity, Husserl makes it highly concrete and specific: his intentional objects include peaches, dogs, blackbirds, centaurs, and the like.

There is a sense in which Husserl is even more important for OOO than Heidegger, since Husserl is the one who intuits *both* of the two key axes of object-oriented thought. On the one hand, he makes fully explicit the objects vs. qualities distinction. Yet on the other hand, despite his flagrant idealism, he does give us a taste of the real if we follow the spirit instead of the letter of his work. This basket of strawberries before me shifts its colors and qualities from one instant to the next, *and yet* it has numerous qualities that belong to it necessarily, which (contra Husserl) cannot be grasped directly by the intellect any more than by the senses. In other words, the strawberries have *real* qualities buried beneath their intentional ones (which OOO calls "sensual" instead). Despite rejecting the real objects of Twardowski, Husserl is driven to accept the existence of real qualities, and thus he gives us a taste of the withdrawn real, despite his misconception that this real can be made to stand naked before the mighty human intellect.

---

[924] Alain Badiou, *Being and Event*.

Chiara Principe: What allows us to understand the position of art and artworks within your metaphysical aesthetics, I believe, are the distinction between the real and the sensual and the key concept of "allure," which, in your own words, refers to "a way in which a new connection, which is still to be understood as a relation, not as an encounter with the real object itself, can be actively triggered." Could you explain the relevance of this last concept as a theory of art and, secondly, talk about OOO's second kind of object: sensual objects, which you hinted at in your first answer as being a "variation on Husserl's 'intentional objects'"?

Graham Harman: Sure. As late as 2004, two years after my debut book *Tool-Being* was published, I wasn't sure what I could say to a Husserlian if they were to claim that Husserl already knew about concealment before Heidegger did. After all, isn't the Husserlian object "withdrawn" (just as Heidegger would say) behind all the numerous profiles or adumbrations it shows to us? And it was a very important moment for me when I realized that, no, it isn't the same thing at all. For Husserl, an apple can never be withdrawn from all access; rather, the apple is already there in every adumbration of the apple, since only the apple as a whole gives meaning to each of its appearances. Hence there are always unified objects for Husserl; this is the key to his system and to phenomenology more generally. But though Husserlians want to tell us that these phenomenal/intentional/immanent objects are the only ones there are, there is a more Kantian cast to Heidegger's thought. Husserl thought things-in-themselves were an absurd notion, just as the German Idealists did. Heidegger, by contrast, weighed in on Kant's side against the German Idealists when it came to the question of human finitude and therefore of things-in-themselves as that which humans are too finite to reach. Having realized this difference, I finally had to acknowledge that there are two different kinds of objects (real and sensual) and two different kinds of qualities (again, real and sensual). The entanglement of these four poles turned out to be, for me, the key to understanding the world.

Chiara Principe: You answered one of my previous questions by writing that any "realism" which wishes or makes possible to convert the real into some form of direct knowledge simply doesn't have enough respect for the real to be worthy of the name realism. Given the alliance between art and philosophy that you wish to consecrate with your own work, as well as the alliterative title of the book you co-wrote with Mexican-

American philosopher Manuel DeLanda, Hal Foster's classic *The Return of the Real* somehow comes to mind.[925]

In his book the author discusses the development of art and theory since 1960; after the models of art-as-text in the 1970s and art-as-simulacrum in the 1980s, Foster suggests that the 1990s (when the book was published) were the witness to a return to the real, repressed in poststructuralist postmodernism, through the trauma so present in the works of artist such as Mike Kelley and Robert Gober. I find the following paragraph from Foster very interesting in relation to our discussion:

> In his seminar on the gaze Lacan retells the classical tale of the *trompe l'œil* contest between Zeuxis and Parrhasius. Zeuxis paints grapes in a way that lures birds, but Parrhasius paints a veil in a way that deceives Zeuxis, who asks to see what lies behind the veil and concedes the contest in embarrassment. For Lacan the story concerns the difference between the imaginary captures of lured animal and deceived human. Verisimilitude may have little to do with either capture: what looks like grapes to one species may not to another; the important thing is the appropriate sign for each. More significant here, the animal is lured in relation to the surface, whereas the human is deceived in relation to what lies behind. And behind the picture, for Lacan, is the gaze, the object, the real, with which "the painter as creator …. sets up a dialogue." Thus a perfect illusion is not possible, and, even if it were possible, it would not answer the question of the real, which always remains, behind and beyond, to lure us.

What is your reaction to this passage?

Graham Harman: There is another famous passage from Lacan that works in a similar direction. In it, Lacan says that whereas animals have the ability to leave a false trail to deceive predators, only humans seem able to leave a "false" trail that is actually the true one. In other words, animals can deceive, but only humans can pretend to deceive. The link with the *trompe l'œil* contest cited by Foster seems to be as follows: the Lacanian claim is that animals can mistake the surface of a thing for its reality, whereas only humans can trick themselves into thinking there is a true depth to things, when in fact there is nothing behind the veil; the veil itself is an illusion fully inscribed on the surface of the world. In Lacanese, the Real is always

---

[925] Manuel DeLanda & Graham Harman, *The Rise of Realism*; Hal Foster, *The Return of the Real*.

entwined with the Symbolic and the Imaginary, in opposition to OOO where reality is something else than its relations with either.[926]

Now, I happen to have a lot of time for Lacan. He's certainly a terrible writer in comparison with his hero Freud, but he also adds a number of important insights to Freud's work: things that Freud actually never saw. Isabelle Stengers famously compares reading Whitehead to whale watching: there are long periods of boredom interspersed with amazing leaps of whales from the ocean into the air. Whitehead's best sentences are well worth waiting for. I would give a different image for reading Lacan: it's like panning for gold. There is a lot of mud and water in Lacan as you're reading along, but when you come to the occasional gold nuggets, you'll feel that they were well worth the trouble. At his best, he was one of the sages of the twentieth century, occasionally saying things that no one had ever said before about human nature. Nonetheless, I *do not* find it to be the pinnacle of wisdom to say that the great mystery is that no mystery exists, that things are just as they seem, and so forth. This is a sort of lazy, corner-cutting, contrarian solution to the serious problem posed by the tension between reality and the human ability to come to terms with it. For similar reasons, I have always preferred Kant to Hegel.

Chiara Principe: Recently you had a big debate with another fervent Lacanian, the Slovene philosopher Slavoj Žižek.[927] Could you sum up what you believe have been the central topics of discussion which were touched upon and your general expectations in the debate?

Graham Harman: I read Žižek later than most people of my generation, not really digging into his works seriously until arriving in Egypt in 2000. There is a rare liveliness to his writing, and more importantly a willingness to make candid statements and take responsibility for them. Žižek helped make it cool to be clear again. In my youth, the standard way of writing continental philosophy was to make endless dithering evasions, call everything into question, cover both sides of the fence so as to be invulnerable to any criticism, put things in quotation marks, and mistake puns for important intellectual points. One still finds some of that around, of course, but it looks increasingly ridiculous. I credit much of this effect to Žižek. His politics are not my cup of tea, since for him

---

[926] Jacques Lacan, *The Sinthome.*
[927] Slavoj Žižek & Graham Harman, "Duel + Duet (Mar. 2017)."

it usually amounts to the old Marxist trope of blaming liberals for being hypocrites and suggesting that in many ways they are worse than the Right. While it's not entirely without value to call attention to the hypocrisies of liberals, this ultimately leads Žižek into major mistakes such as hoping Donald Trump would win the 2016 United States election. Well, here we are, and it's not as clever or funny as Žižek probably thought it was before the election. Hillary Clinton was not my first choice either (I thought we needed a Sanders-led shakeup this time) but there are some really brutal things happening in America right now that simply would not have happened under a Clinton Administration. The American electorate really blew this one, and Žižek egged it on. Blowing up liberalism is not the way to get us to a better place, but just a quick way to get us to mobs of gun-toting racists and threats to journalists. We need a generation of philosophers with the courage to defend what is great in liberalism (and not just mock its hypocrisies) rather than simply trying to outflank everyone else to the left as an easy default gesture.

But back to the main topic. Žižek sees philosophical issues with his own eyes and argues in his own words, with an unprecedented ability to identify their manifestations in popular culture. Yet as a realist, I cannot be at all happy with his general philosophical position. I don't think he takes the realist question seriously enough, but just continues to utter the word "materialism" as if that solved the problem. I'm not sure there is any passage where Žižek makes a forceful argument of his own against philosophical realism. He generally invokes Hegel and Lacan as having already solved the problem: Hegel (and a few forerunners) got rid of the annoying thing-in-itself in favor of a more sophisticated position in which the thing-in-itself exists only *as* appearance, and Lacan pulled the same move with Freud's unconscious, changing it from a real hidden force into an immanent disruption in the field of language itself. Now, this is a perfectly helpful analogy. I simply don't think it's clear that Hegel is an improvement on Kant or that Lacan is an improvement on Freud. At times Žižek seems to think it's enough that Hegel and Lacan came later than Kant and Freud, as if that settles the issue.

The funny thing about Kant is that most people agree he was a revolutionary figure, yet the general movement of post-Kantian philosophy has been to praise Kant while disdaining his central concept: the thing-in-itself! The exceptions are few in number, and they are not complete. There's a good bit of the *an sich* in Schopenhauer, and an often neglected passage in Heidegger's *Kant and the Problem of Metaphysics* where he straight-out says that the German Idealists were too quick to get rid of the in-itself.[928] It is true that Heidegger generally does not speak forcefully in favor of the thing-in-itself, though I have argued in *Tool-Being* that his tool-analysis forces this notion upon us. The existing arguments against the in-itself are surprisingly weak, and that's why the big book I've just started will begin with a wholehearted defense of it.[929]

And that brings us to what I found the most interesting part of the debate: watching the tape, you will notice that Žižek tries to claim more than once that we are in *agreement* about the object as something that is withheld from direct access. But clearly this is not true of Žižek, who sees him self as an heir of Hegel and Lacan: two great enemies of the thing-in-itself. For that reason, though I enjoyed the debate, it did not yield the sort of philosophical friction that might have made it even more interesting for viewers.

Chiara Principe: There have been some interesting experiences in art production which relate to OOO's approach which date back to the 1960s. The artists I'm referring to not only share your ontology's positions, they also relate to your philosophy via a curious assonance: they were united under the collective name OHO, a neologism derived from the Slovene words for "eye" (oko) and "ear" (uho). Through a number of media such as drawings, photographs, video, music and texts but also through their general attitude and way of life, the members of OHO wanted to develop a radically different relationship towards the world. Instead of a humanistic position, which implied a world of objects dominated by the subject, they wanted to achieve a world of things, where there would be no hierarchical (or indeed any) difference between people and things. Are you familiar with this or other similar artistic trends or movements in the history of art?

Graham Harman: Unfortunately, I do not know enough about OHO to take a position on the details of how they worked out this view of the world. So, let me just say something about why so many claims to "overcome anthropocentrism" in philosophy and the arts fall short. There are a couple of different problems that can occur. One is the Latour problem, where

---

[928] Arthur Schopenhauer, *The World as Will and Representation*, 2 vols.; Martin Heidegger, *Kant and the Problem of Metaphysics*, pp. 251–252.
[929] Graham Harman, *Infrastructure*.

after demolishing the nature/culture or world/thought ontology in *We Have Never Been Modern*, he ends up favoring the human side in spite of himself. That's because he has a tendency to think that *all* objects must be hybrids composed of *both* humans and the world, when in fact there are plenty of objects — indeed, the vast majority of all objects — that do not involve humans at all.

An even more serious problem, one that never even rises to the level of Latour's critique, is the sort that we find in Schelling and Merleau-Ponty, those perpetual "philosophers of the future" whose undeniable charms are nonetheless ill-equipped to get us to any workable future.[930] Why so? Because both of them *accept* the thought/world distinction even while trying to intertwine the two terms to a greater degree than ever happened before. That's why Merleau-Ponty overemphasizes "the body," which DeLanda amusingly describes as being similar to a token woman or minority on an otherwise all-white male corporate board.[931] If someone is talking too much about "embodiment," then that's a sign that they are too focused on the body as a bridge between thought and world, and that means they have started by accepting the modern taxonomy that needs to be abandoned if we are to leave the long shadow of Immanuel Kant, the defining giant of modernity in so many ways.

But again, I can't accuse of OHO of any of this, since I just don't know their work well enough. I'm simply trying to state some difficulties that I hope they have avoided. If so, then perhaps they are really a red-blooded aesthetic partner of OOO.

Chiara Principe: You reference Clement Greenberg quite a lot in your art analysis and believe, as you very eloquently state, that we should and will go back to reading him again. Nonetheless I was wondering, are there more recent art theoreticians and critics on your nightstand worth mentioning?

Graham Harman: Even in my own field, philosophy, I have tended to avoid what most people take to be the most recent *avant-garde*, such as Derrida and Foucault. That's because I simply don't think that the France of the 1960s was as important for philosophy as the phenomenological

---

[930] On the topic of "philosophers of the future" see Graham Harman, "The Only Exit from Modern Philosophy."
[931] DeLanda, in DeLanda & Harman, *The Rise of Realism*, p. 116.

movement of the earlier twentieth century. I've often argued that to find the real stakes of contemporary philosophy, it's necessary to go back to Husserl and Heidegger, but in a fresh way.

By analogy, I would say there are plenty of important critics writing today, but I still think the true stakes of contemporary art need to be figured out by looking at an earlier period, and at why Greenberg became such a dominant critical voice and why many eventually rejected his modernist vision. There are a number of things worth criticizing in Greenberg, but most people are too quick to think that the mere passage of years on a calendar has rendered him less important. Hardly. If you overcome formalism in the wrong way — as has largely happened — then it will continue to haunt you. I've seen this happen in philosophy, where Kantian formalism has been largely "overcome" in ways that don't overcome it at all. Greenberg's ghost haunts art today, even if usually as a scorned and rejected ghost.

However, I do try to keep up with what Boris Groys is doing.[932] We have many differences, but we met as colleagues at the European Graduate School and I find his mind congenial. Another author to whom I pay close attention is younger and less known: Robert Jackson in England, whose thoughts on art criticism evolved in personal contact with me and other OOO authors, and thus Jackson's work speaks to me much more directly than that of more famous living critics.[933] I also have a high regard for Jackson's aesthetic judgment. Perhaps the world will soon become more directly familiar with his thinking.

---

[932] Boris Groys, *Art Power*.
[933] Robert Jackson, "The Anxiousness of Objects and Artworks"; Robert Jackson, "The Anxiousness of Objects and Artworks II."

CHAPTER 35

SOME ASPECTS OF MY PHILOSOPHICAL POSITION[934]

Generally speaking, the word "ontology" is more in favor these days than "metaphysics." My own preference is to use them interchangeably, and positively, to refer to speculations concerning reality in its most basic character. This has at least two implications. The first is non-acceptance of the rampant "critiques of metaphysics" found in both the analytic and continental traditions; the second is the philosophical importance of having rich funds of synonymous terms instead of a cramped precision of mutually exclusive call signs. Let's begin with a quick review of these two points.

Heidegger's critique of metaphysics is important and basically convincing, but this is no reason to join him in disqualifying metaphysics as a usable term. The explanations by various scholars of his polemical term "ontotheology" usually hit somewhere on or near the target, though not always at the bull's eye. What ontotheology is really about is the metaphysics of presence, which Heidegger rejects. Ultimately this amounts to a rejection of phenomenology, due to Husserl's view that anything real can be intuited directly by the mind, given sufficient mental labor. Yes, Husserl also leaves room for "horizontal" intentions that are tacitly present for the mind even without our realizing it, but horizons of this sort are

934 This chapter was written in March 2022 specifically for inclusion in *The Graham Harman Reader*.

not enough to account for the Heideggerian withdrawal of being. When we merely speak of something implicit that can be made explicit, of a background that can later be consciously noticed, or of a hammer that can become openly visible as soon as it breaks, we are not venturing deep enough in the forest. What Heidegger has in mind is not that something sits in a shadowy corner of the room and can be dragged out and placed under direct lamplight whenever we please. Conscious awareness of something is never enough to bring it before us in the flesh. When we speak of Heideggerian withdrawal, we are speaking of a background of things that can never be foregrounded: to stare at a broken hammer is to notice features of this tool that we might not have noticed before, but this *does not amount* to a direct presence of the hammer. The point to hold in mind is that the hammer's visual, tactile, or even practical manifestation to us is never the same as the hammer itself. After all, a visual configuration of wooden handle and shaped metallic head is not what acts as a hammer. Knowledge is not impossible, but it cannot be a question of extracting the form of the hammer from "matter" (whatever that means) and bringing it into the mind while leaving the matter behind. Instead, the form itself is changed when it moves from one place to another, such as the hammer-form transported into the mind.

Derrida's critique of ontotheology is more radical than Heidegger's, but also more forced and less effective. For Heidegger it is enough to undercut presence with absence. Reality that exceeds its presence to human Dasein is Being, and such reality exists quite apart from how it happens to become evident to Dasein. In Derrida's eyes this is not enough, since absence would merely amount to a "self-presence," and hence we would be unable to escape the metaphysics of presence. Yet the idea of self-identity as "self-presence" is an artifact of Hegelian philosophy, with its maxim of "substance as subject." There is simply nothing "self-present" about a hammer, or a chicken, or the Himalayas. The only entity that could conceivably be "self-present" is a mind looking at itself, but even here it does not happen, since reflective consciousness and the unreflective consciousness at which it looks are not the same thing, even if both respond to the same proper name. This should be clear even from a quick taste of psychoanalysis, and the works of Lacan in particular. The best analogue to Derrida's stance in analytic philosophy is probably Graham Priest, and the two of them enter a labyrinth of "true contradictions" that they never needed to enter in the first place. Elimination of the classical law of identity will always sound unspeakably bold, like an exotic olive branch extended to Buddhist logic. But to admit contradiction into the heart of philosophy at this scale is like using anti-tank weaponry to hunt down unicycles.

The aforementioned critiques of ontotheology are both visibly descended from Kant's critique of dogmatic metaphysics in the *Critique of Pure Reason*. The finitude of human thought means that we are forever unable to intuit the thing-in-itself directly. The major difference between my position on finitude and that of Kant and Heidegger is that they regard finitude as a uniquely human burden, while for me the very structure of relationality entails inconclusive translation between any entity and those others with which it cognitively, perceptually, or causally interacts. Lazy critics will always assume that this makes OOO a "panpsychist" theory, but it is really just a matter of showing that all types of relations — human cognition, animal comportment, inanimate causation — should all be treated in terms of the more primitive fact of relationality *per se*. No doubt there are major differences between human thought and the mere interaction of lifeless chemicals, but we will not grasp them by ontologizing our commonsensical assumptions about what makes human thought unique. Furthermore, no one is in any position to claim that a philosophical discussion of object-object relations is "dogmatic" in its own right insofar as we can only discuss such relations from within the transcendental conditions of human experience. Just as analytic philosophy is most comfortable when it builds on the greatness of natural science as its rock, continental thinkers are most at home when grounding science and everything else in the transcendental encounter of two privileged entities: (1) thought, and (2) "the world." Obviously, what we call the world contains many different kinds of things, and human thought is so vastly outnumbered by them all that it hardly deserves a whole category of its own — at least not in the earliest stages of an ontology. Perhaps more to the point, the fact that we are all thinking humans does not mean that we have a more direct experience of human than inanimate finitude. Finitude must always be deduced, and is deduced as easily for fire and rainbows as it is for tortured human poets.

Levi Bryant once put it as follows, though I cannot remember where: from a OOO standpoint, withdrawal does not signify the *impossibility* of traditional metaphysics — as it does for Kant, Heidegger, Derrida — but rather the *possibility* of a non-traditional metaphysics. Now as ever, metaphysics (or ontology) refers to a theory able to account at least loosely for anything that exists. We should not be ashamed of the fact that this will be done *a priori*; empirical discoveries shape our sense of what exists, but cannot serve as foundations for metaphysics. Darwin made eternal species look permanently implausible for philosophy; Einstein effectively put an end to the notion of space and time as giant empty containers; quantum theory has poured gasoline on debates concerning the relation between thought and reality. Yet it does not follow that philosophy must restrict its speculations to limits defined by "the best science we have": we should be taking greater risks than this, for reasons of our own, and in this way we might reach a point where the best science could be half a century from now. Philosophy is useless if it aspires to nothing more than telling empirical research why it is so great, like state media in an authoritarian country: "Mr. President, how did you do such an amazing job last year, and how will you help the world even more during the coming year?" One of the reasons so many have lost their nerve with *a priori* speculation is that Kant mixes two very different notions under this heading. In the good sense, *a priori* means prior to experience, and refers to thinking about presupposed background conditions and other unnoticed prejudices. It need not only be critical in spirit, since it is quite possible for *a priori* thought to lead us to believe in more rather than less. But in the bad sense, *a priori* means "necessary." I call it bad because Kant thereby sets too high a hurdle for any philosophy to clear: permanent immunity to correction. But a new ontology of space and time is not worthless speculation just because someone eventually finds flaws in the theory, discrediting its necessity. Few today are literal believers in the philosophy of Spinoza, yet it would be odd to maintain that his philosophical career was a complete waste of time. Instead, Spinoza put another tower on the landscape that helps orient future efforts by others. That is what it means to be a classic.

Our second initial point was the desirability of having synonymous terms available whenever possible: metaphysics and ontology are just one example of this. I say this partly for stylistic reasons; no one wants to endure the hammering monotony of a single word fifty times on the same page merely because it is the right one. But there is a further, related reason: trying to pin down the exact meanings of terms before starting to discuss them is rarely a fruitful operation in philosophy. In Whitehead's marvelous words: "the accurate expression of the final generalities is the goal of discussion and not its origin."[935] There is even more to it than that. Husserl, then Kripke, showed us how names create a rift between objects and their qualities.[936] Having multiple names for the same thing does this all the more, just as

---

[935] Alfred North Whitehead, *Process and Reality*, p. 8.
[936] Edmund Husserl, *Logical Investigations*, 2 vols.; Saul Kripke, *Naming and Necessity*.

Islam's ninety-nine names of Allah only create an enhanced sense of divine unity. Yet the same holds even for the humbler entities of day-to-day life. Although OOO is closely associated with Heideggerian withdrawal, and for good reason, the true theme of object-oriented thought is the inevitably *loose* relation between an object and its own qualities, even if neither of these are withdrawn in the least. There are (hidden) real objects and (non-hidden) sensual ones, and each type of object can have both real and sensual qualities. According to OOO, the tense relations between these four poles are the basis of ontology; anything we talk about will ultimately refer to this fourfold schema of RO, RQ, SO, SQ. Space and time are produced by this schema, as are the lesser-known pair of essence and eidos.

We can also say that the quality-pole is basically continuous and the object-pole basically discrete. The puzzling co-existence of waves and stones has been a paradox for most of the history of philosophy, and not only for philosophy. Aristotle realized that he had to make room for both on the ground floor of his philosophy: the continuum is perhaps the major subject of the *Physics*, while discrete individual substances are the obvious star of his *Metaphysics*. Philosophies create major problems for themselves when they try to reduce either of these to the other. Discreteness took over the world of Islamic and later French occasionalism, so that causal interactions and even temporal endurance from one moment to the next became nearly insoluble problems. Later, at the hands of Bergson and then Deleuze, a global continuism became the fashionable model, including in architecture from roughly 1993 through 2010.[937] The most prolific young philosophy author in this tradition, Thomas Nail in the United States, often makes the argument that if you start with discrete objects, you can never get to continuity, but by starting with continuity, you can explain individual objects; thus, he opts for the latter.[938] But in fact, it is not possible to do either of these things. True enough, by starting from discreteness alone (which Nail wrongly assumes is what OOO does), one merely ends up in an occasionalist universe where constant divine intervention is needed to bridge even the tiniest gaps between one thing and another. Yet Nail is wrong to think that the opposite maneuver is possible, let alone preferable: by starting with the continuous, we attain objects only in the guise of loops, folds, swirls, and other papier-mâché surrogates of individuality. If OOO seems at first like a philosophy over-devoted to discrete entities, this is

---

[937] Stan Allen, "From Object to Field"; Greg Lynn, ed., *Folding in Architecture*.
[938] Thomas Nail, *Theory of the Object*.

only because a corrective is needed for the ongoing century-long festival of dynamic becomings. Putting wheels or wings on objects and giving them a push will not solve their philosophical problems.

As indicated above, OOO is hostile to the modern tendency to endorse the existence of two and only two basic types of things in the cosmos: (1) thought, and (2) the world. Our critical term for this is "onto-taxonomy," and any reader who has made it to the end of this book is already familiar with my case against it. But one of the worst symptoms of such onto-taxonomy is its miserable track record in attempting to punctuate the differences between various kinds of plants, animals, and humans. Even the apparently most rigorous efforts of modern (and indeed, even pre-modern) philosophy serve up little more here than heaping portions of platitudes: "animals may see objects, but they don't see them 'as' objects"; "plants only feed themselves and reproduce, but do not perceive"; "humans alone can confront the whole." Rarely do philosophers table-pound more hopelessly than when addressing such topics. Some will recommend that we simply defer to biologists and ethologists on these questions, but this cements the tired modern arrangement of letting science talk about everything specific while philosophers limit themselves to epistemological busywork along the thought-world divide.[939] Here as always, the problem is that science is by nature a pursuit of knowledge, which makes it a duomining effort to amass lists of genuine qualities of things. By contrast, philosophy is an anti-mining form of cognition, more akin to the aesthetic fields and the study of media, and therefore does not traffic in bundles of qualities. Given that philosophy has as its theme the paradoxical relation between objects and the qualities they simultaneously do and do not have, no roster of quantitative or qualitative criteria will be enough for punctuating various stations of living and non-living beings. Some progress was made on this front by Helmuth Plessner, at least to the extent that he rejects lists of qualities as sufficient ways of determining the various leaps in the plant and animal kingdoms.[940] We will know we are freed from the limitations of modern transcendental philosophy only when we witness a profusion of unprecedented ontologies — and not just sensitive ecological descriptions — of various plants, animals, fungi, and viruses.

One sometimes hears the groundless charge that OOO "never came up with a politics" or is in some sense "apolitical." Not only is this is not the

---

[939] See Ray Brassier, "Deleveling."
[940] Helmuth Plessner, *Levels of Organic Life and the Human*.

case, but clear evidence to the contrary has been available in print for nearly a decade. For many intellectuals at any given moment, and especially so in our moment, for a philosophy to "come up with a politics" means either to propose some novel permutation of Leftism, or at least to hang oneself in public honestly by veering unapologetically to the Right. "Revolution" remains the tacitly agreed-upon goal, just as "capitalism" remains the villain of emotional consensus. But as for revolution, Peter Sloterdijk notes that it "has never been concerned with an actual 'rotation' in the sense of a reversal of above and below, but rather the proliferation of top positions and their restaffing with representatives of aggressive middle classes."[941] And as for capitalism, this term is more often a moral trump card than a lantern cutting through fog. More generally, the Left-Right political spectrum is too thoroughly grounded in modern onto-taxonomy to be worth salvaging, and hence it is time to work more patiently on political questions; philosophy has never been well suited to address the urgent crises of the moment, and ought not to cave in to pressures to behave otherwise. Recently, the widely anticipated book *The Dawn of Everything* (by the late David Graeber and co-author David Wengrow) independently echoed my longstanding view that neither Rousseauian nor Hobbesian tales about human nature are the right basis for political theory.[942] Yet I am not satisfied with Graeber and Wengrow's alternative, which seems too enamored of the idea of humans as imaginative experimenters; while refreshing in many respects, it is still a story about human character and deeds. Any new political philosophy in our time will need to do a more serious job of accounting for both the stabilizing and trailblazing role of non-human objects in structuring political space. This has nothing to do with "granting human rights to chairs," as facile critics sometimes put it, but with the constraints and opportunities provided by objects that can weaken the role of human nature and sometimes even render it irrelevant.

In social philosophy, I have been disappointed in the results of all theories that prioritize events over entities; unfortunately, this standpoint still passes for avant-garde, and probably has decades more of life in it. Any theoretical outlook that treats objects in evental rather than substantive terms will always face the problem that some events are not just *relatively* unimportant compared with bigger ones, but that many have no impact on their components at all. In short, to ontologize events also means losing the

---

[941] Peter Sloterdijk, *Spheres, Vol. 3: Foams*, p. 144.
[942] David Graeber & David Wengrow, *The Dawn of Everything*.

capacity to distinguish between crucial events and trivial non-events. This point is not limited to social philosophy, but also concerns the numerous claims on behalf of "site-specific" works of art and architecture, which on closer examination always turn out to be in dialogue with no more than a half-dozen or so aspects of their site while ignoring or neglecting all others. Relations between objects occur, but they are never easy: this could be the motto of OOO as a whole. Any human or quasi-human entity will undergo a finite number of decisive events, by which I mean events that effect such entities *irreversibly*. I have borrowed the term "symbiosis" from Lynn Margulis to describe the way that entities develop through a limited number of irreversible relationships that turn them into new hybrid entities. These symbioses will tend to occur relatively early in the life of an object, which eventually takes on mature form and does not engage in further symbioses. Some mature objects (like the Dutch East India Company) are well-equipped to thrive in their environments, but for this very reason go into decline once that environment shifts (in this case favoring the English East Indies Company instead). Relational ontologies are unable to make any discoveries on this terrain, since their notion of change is so inflationary that even the tiniest hair falling from a head must qualify.

We turn in closing to the time-honored definition of knowledge as "justified true belief." It is my view that no such animal exists; justification is one thing, and truth quite another. Everything that we are accustomed to call "knowledge" is really a form of justification. Researchers have no idea what bizarre things we might learn to believe in the centuries to come. A few of today's craziest conspiracy theories will no doubt turn out to bear some relation to reality: internet sleuths in their tinfoil hats may in fact be correct about the aliens from Zeta Reticuli, and the mainstreamers who mock them may look in retrospect like sandbaggers of period-piece conventional wisdom. By contrast, the responsible scientist is more than willing to run the risk of being wrong, as long as their current views are linked closely to justifying evidence, as if to weighty alibis for inevitable error. The scientific enterprise is nothing if not fallible and corrigible, and hence there is ample reason to sail as close as possible to what is justified, not what is true. And what, after all, is the meaning of "true"? I will use it to speak, not of an impossible direct presence of reality to the mind (the intuitions of phenomenology), but of that which is taken for true on the basis of always shaky justification. Here we are in the vicinity of Kierkegaard, and thus of what Alain Badiou calls the "anti-philosophy" that haunts every philosophy. Theories and discoveries are always partial and inconclusive, and belief must outrun justification if life is to be lived rather than hedged with skeptical one-upmanship. Artists must live in garrets and activists die on barricades for what, scientifically speaking, are the flimsiest of reasons. The one modification I would suggest is reversing the referents of Badiou's "philosophy" and "anti-philosophy." For it is the enduring commitment to a certain unusual model of reality — in the face of counterexamples, inadequate proofs, and institutional harassment during one's darkest hours — that is closer to what *philosophia* has always meant. By contrast, the rational justifications used to link and prop up philosophical insights seem more deserving of the sidekick status implied by the phrase "anti-philosophy."

WORKS CITED

al-Farabi, Abu Nasr. *On the Perfect State*, trans. R. Walzer. Chicago: Kazi Publications, 1998.

al-Ghazali, Abu Hamid Muhammad. *The Incoherence of the Philosophers*, trans. M. Marmura. Provo, UT: Brigham Young University Press, 2002.

Allen, Stan. "From Object to Field," *Architectural Design* 67, nos. 5/6 (May/June 1997), pp. 24–31.

Althusser, Louis. "Le courant souterrain du matérialisme de la rencontre," in *Écrits philosophiques et politiques*, 539–579. Paris: Stock/IMEC, 1994.

Althusser, Louis. "Ideology and Ideological State Apparatuses (Notes Towards an Investigation)," in *The Anthropology of the State: A Reader*, A. Sharma & A. Gupta, eds., pp. 86–111. Oxford: Blackwell, 2006.

Altieri, Charles. "The Sensuous Dimension of Literary Experience," online. http://socrates.berkeley.edu/~altieri/manuscripts/Sensuous.html

Aristotle. *Aristotle's Physics*, trans. R. Waterfield. Oxford University Press, Oxford, 2008.

Aristotle. *The Art of Rhetoric*, trans. R. Waterfield. Oxford: Oxford University Press, 2018.

Aristotle. *Metaphysics,* trans. J. Sachs. Santa Fe, NM: Green Lion Press, 1999.

Aristotle. *Poetics*, trans. S.H. Butcher. CreateSpace, 2011.

Arnold, Dan. *Buddhists, Brahmins, and Belief: Epistemology in South Asian Philosophy of Religion.* New York: Columbia University Press, 2008.

Austin, J.L. *How to Do Things with Words.* Eastford, CT: Martino Fine Books, 2018.

Averroës (Ibn Rushd). *The Incoherence of the Philosophers*, trans. S. van den Berghe. London: Luzac & Co., 1954.

Bacon, Francis. *The New Organon.* Indianapolis: The Library of Liberal Arts, 1960.

Badiou, Alain. *Being and Event*, trans. O. Feltham. London: Continuum, 2005.

Badiou, Alain. "On the Epidemic Situation," trans. A. Toscano, *Verso* website, March 23, 2020. https://www.versobooks.com/blogs/4608-on-the-epidemic-situation

Badiou, Alain. *Lacan: Anti-Philosophy 3*, trans. K. Reinhard & S. Spitzzer. New York: Columbia University Press, 2018.

Badiou, Alain. *Logics of Worlds: Being and Event II*, trans. A. Toscano. London: Continuum, 2009.

Ballard, J.G. *Re/Search No. 8/9*. San Francisco: Re/Search Publications, 1984.

Barad, Karen. *Meeting the Universe Halfway: Quantum Physics and the Entanglement of Matter and Meaning*. Durham, NC: Duke University Press, 2007.

Barcan Marcus, Ruth. "Modalities and Intensional Languages," *Synthese*, Vol. 13, No. 4 (December 1961), pp. 303–322.

Bateson, Gregory. *Steps to an Ecology of Mind: Collected Essays in Anthropology, Psychiatry, Evolution and Epistemology*. Chicago: University of Chicago Press, 2000.

Bayard, Pierre. *Et si les oeuvres changeaient d'auteur?* Paris: Les Éditions de Minuit, 2010.

Bell, J.S. "On the Einstein Podolsky Rosen Paradox," *Physics* 1, no. 3 (1964), pp. 195–200.

Bennett, Jane. "Systems and Things: A Response to Graham Harman and Timothy Morton," *New Literary History* 43 (2012), pp. 225–233.

Bennett, Jane. *Vibrant Matter: A Political Ecology of Things*, Durham, NC: Duke University Press, 2010.

Bergmann, Gustav. *Realism: A Critique of Brentano and Meinong*. Madison, WI: University of Wisconsin Press, 1967.

Bergson, Henri. *Creative Evolution*, trans. A. Mitchell. New York: Barnes & Noble, 2005.

Bergson, Henri. *Laughter: An Essay on the Meaning of the Comic*. Rockville, MD: Wildside Press, 2008.

Bergson, Henri. *Matter and Memory*, trans. N.M. Paul & W.S. Palmer. New York: Dover, 2004.

Bergson, Henri. *Time and Free Will: An Essay on the Immediate Data of Consciousness*, trans. F.L. Pogson. New York: Dover, 2001.

Berkeley, George. *A Treatise Concerning the Principles of Human Knowledge*. New York: Cosimo Classics, 2005.

Bhaskar, Roy. *A Realist Theory of Science*. London: Verso, 2008.

Black, Max. "Metaphor," in *Models and Metaphors: Studies in Language and Philosophy*, pp. 25–47. Ithaca, NY: Cornell University Press, 1962.

Blackmore, Susan & Emily T. Troscianko. *Consciousness: An Introduction*. New York: Routledge, 2018

Blanchot, Maurice. *The Infinite Conversation*, trans. S. Hanson. Minneapolis: University of Minnesota Press, 1992.

Bloom, Harold. *The Anxiety of Influence: A Theory of Poetry*, Second Edition. Oxford: Oxford University Press, 2007.

Bloom, Harold. *The Western Canon: The Books and School of the Ages*. New York: Riverhead Books, 1994.

Boghossian, Paul. *Fear of Knowledge: Against Relativism and Constructivism*. Oxford: Clarendon Press, 2007.

Bogost, Ian. "Object-Oriented Ontology Symposium," Georgia Tech webpage, 2010. https://smartech.gatech.edu/handle/1853/33043

Bohm, David. *Wholeness and the Implicate Order*. London: Routledge, 2002.

Braidotti, Rosi. *The Posthuman*. Cambridge, UK: Polity 2013.

Brassier, Ray. *Alien Theory: The Decline of Materialism in the Name of Matter*, PhD thesis, University of Warwick, 2001. http://wrap.warwick.ac.uk/4034/

Brassier, Ray. "Concepts and Objects," in *The Speculative Turn: Continental Materialism and Realism*, L. Bryant, N. Srnicek, & G. Harman, eds., pp. 47–65. Melbourne: re.press, 2011.

Brassier, Ray. "Deleveling: Against 'Flat Ontologies,'" in *Onder invloed: Wijsgerig festival Drift 2014*, C. van Dijk, ed., pp. 64–80. Amsterdam: Drift, 2015.

Brassier, Ray. *Nihil Unbound: Enlightenment and Extinction*. London: Palgrace Macmillan, 2007.

Brassier, Ray. "Postscript: Speculative Autopsy," in Peter Wolfendale, *Object-Oriented Philosophy*, pp. 407–421. Falmouth, UK: Urbanomic, 2014.

Brassier, Ray, Iain Hamilton Grant, Graham Harman, & Quentin Meillassoux, "Speculative Realism," *Collapse* III (2007), pp. 306–449.

Braver, Lee. *A Thing of This World: A History of Continental Anti-Realism*. Evanston, IL: Northwestern University Press, 2007.

Brentano, Franz. *Psychology From an Empirical Standpoint*, trans. A.C. Rancurello, D.B. Terrell, & L. McAlister. London: Routledge, 1995.

Brockman, John, ed. *The Third Culture: Beyond the Scientific Revolution*. New York: Touchstone, 1996.

Brooks, Cleanth. *The Well Wrought Urn*. New York: Harcourt, Brace, & World, 1947.

Bryant, Levi R. *The Democracy of Objects*. Ann Arbor, MI: Open Humanities Press, 2011.

Bryant, Levi. R. "More on Withdrawn Objects," *Larval Subjects* blog post, January 5, 2012. http://larvalsubjects.wordpress.com/2012/01/05/more-on-withdrawn-objects/

Bryant, Levi R. "The Ontic Principle: Outlines of an Object-Oriented Ontology," in L. Bryant, N. Srnicek, & G. Harman, eds., *The Speculative Turn: Continental Materialism and Realism*, pp. 261–278. Melbourne: re.press, 2011.

Bryant, Levi R. *Onto-Cartography: An Ontology of Machines and Media*, Edinburgh: Edinburgh University Press, 2014.

Bryant, Levi R., Nick Srnicek, & Graham Harman, eds., *The Speculative Turn: Continental Materialism and Realism*. Melbourne: re.press, 2011.

Burke, Edmund. *Revolutionary Writings*. Cambridge, UK: Cambridge University Press, 2014.

Callon, Michel & Bruno Latour. "Unscrewing the Big Leviathan: How Actors Macro-Structure Reality and How Sociologists Help Them to Do So," in *Advances in Social Theory and Methodology: Toward an Integration of Micro- and Macro-Sociologies*, Karin Knorr-Cetina & A.V. Cicourel, eds., pp. 277–303. London: Routledge & Kegan Paul, 1981.

Caputo, John D. "For the Love of the Things Themselves: Derrida's Phenomenology of the Hyper- Real," in *Fenomenologia Hoje II: Significado e Linguagem*, ed. R. Timm de Souza & N. Fernandes de Oliveira, pp. 37–59. Porto Alegre, Brazil: EDIPUCRS, 2002.

Carew, Joseph. *Ontological Catastrophe: Žižek and the Paradoxical Metaphysics of German Idealism*. Ann Arbor, MI: University of Michigan Press, 2014.

Chalmers, David. *The Conscious Mind: In Search of a Fundamental Theory*. Oxford: Oxford University Press, 1997.

Chawla, Aditi & Deepty Sachdeva. "Impact of Duomining in Knowledge Discovery Process," Special Issue of *International Journal of Computer Science & Informatics* (IJCSI), Vol. II, Issue-1, 2 (2013), pp. 121–126.

Christov-Bakargiev, Carolyn, ed. *The Book of Books*. Ostfildern, Germany: Hatje Cantz Verlag, 2012.

Churchland, Patricia. *Neurophilosophy: Toward a Unified Science of the Mind-Brain*. Cambridge: MIT Press, 1989.

Churchland, Paul. *Scientific Realism and the Plasticity of Mind*. Cambridge, UK: Cambridge University Press, 1986.

Cogburn, Jon. "Be(ing) Here Now: Notes Towards and Indexicalist Epistemology," *Cosmos and History* 17.2 (2020), pp. 46–65.

Cogburn, Jon. *Garcian Meditations: The Dialectics of Persistence in Form and Object*. Edinburgh: Edinburgh University Press, 2017.

Cogburn, Jon & Mark Silcox. "Computability Theory and Ontological Emergence," *American Philosophical Quarterly*, 48.1 (2011), pp. 63–74.

Cogburn, Jon & Mark Silcox. *Philosophy Through Video Games*. New York: Routledge, 2008.

Coggins, David. "Secret Powers: An Interview with Joanna Malinowska," *artnet*, January 24, 2010. [Last accessed on January 13, 2022.] http://www.artnet.com/magazineus/features/coggins/joanna-malinowska1–15–10.asp

Crane, Tim. "Intentional Objects," *Ratio* 14 (2001), pp. 336–349.

Danowski, Deborah & Eduardo Viveiros de Castro. *The Ends of the World*, trans. R. Guimaraes Nunes. Cambridge: Polity Press, 2017.

Dante Alighieri. *The Divine Comedy*, trans. A. Mandelbaum. New York: Random House, 1995.

Danto, Arthur. *The Transfiguration of the Commonplace: A Philosophy of Art*. Cambridge, MA: Harvard University Press, 1983.

Danto, Arthur, Charles Altieri, Anne M. Wagner, & Anthony J. Cascardi. "The Work of Art and the Historical Future," in *"Anything Goes": The Work of Art and the Historical Future*, pp. 1–16. Berkeley, CA: University of California Press, 1998.

Davis, Zachary & Anthony Steinbock. "Max Scheler," in *The Stanford Encyclopedia of Philosophy*, E. Zalta, ed., Summer 2014. http://plato.stanford.edu/archives/sum2014/entries/scheler/

DeLanda, Manuel. *Intensive Science and Virtual Philosophy*. London: Continuum, 2002.

DeLanda, Manuel. *A New Philosophy of Society*. London: Continuum, 2006.

DeLanda, Manuel. *Philosophical Chemistry: Genealogy of a Scientific Field*. London: Bloomsbury, 2015.

DeLanda, Manuel & Graham Harman. *The Rise of Realism*. Cambridge, UK: Polity, 2017.

Deleuze, Gilles. *The Fold: Leibniz and the Baroque*, trans. T. Conley. Minneapolis: University of Minnesota Press, 1993.

Deleuze, Gilles. *Logic of Sense*, trans. M. Lester & C. Stivale. New York: Columbia University Press, 1990.

de Man, Paul. *Blindness and Insight: Essays in the Rhetoric of Contemporary Criticism*. Minneapolis: University of Minnesota Press, 1983.

Dennett, Daniel. "Real Patterns," *Journal of Philosophy* 88 (1991), pp. 27–51.

Derrida, Jacques. *Of Grammatology*, trans. G. Spivak. Baltimore: The Johns Hopkins University Press, 1988.

Derrida, Jacques. "White Mythology: Metaphor in the Text of Philosophy," in *Margins of Philosophy*, trans. A. Bass, pp. 207–271. Chicago: University of Chicago Press, 1982.

Descartes, René. *Discourse on Method*, trans. D. Cress. Indianapolis: Hackett, 1998.

Descartes, René. *Meditations on First Philosophy*, trans. D. Cress. Indianapolis: Hackett, 1993.

Dewey, John. *The Public and its Problems: An Essay in Political Inquiry*. University Park, PA: Penn State University Press, 2012.

Dreyfus, Hubert. *Being-in-the-World: A Commentary on Heidegger's* Being and Time, *Division I*. Cambridge, MA: MIT Press, 1990.

Eddington, A.S. *The Nature of the Physical World*. New York: MacMillan, 1929.

Eliot, T.S. *Four Quartets*. New York: Mariner, 1968.

Emerson, Ralph Waldo. *Essays and Lectures*. New York: Library of America, 1983.

Fakhry, Majid. *A History of Islamic Philosophy*, Third Edition. New York: Columbia University Press, 2004.

Fakhry, Majid. *Islamic Occasionalism: And its Critique by Averroes and Avicenna*. New York: Routledge, 2007.

Faulkner, William. *The Sound and the Fury*. New York: Norton, 2014.

Ferrarin, Alfredo. *Hegel and Aristotle*. Cambridge, UK: Cambridge University Press, 2007.

Ferraris, Maurizio. *Goodbye, Kant! What Still Stands of the* Critique of Pure Reason, trans. R. Davies. Albany, NY: SUNY Press, 2013.

Ferraris, Maurizio. *Introduction to New Realism*, trans. S. de Sanctis. London: Bloomsbury, 2015.

Ferraris, Maurizio. *Manifesto of New Realism*, trans. S. De Sanctis. Albany, NY: Suny Press, 2014.

Feyerabend, Paul. *Against Method*, Fourth Edition. London: Verso, 2010.

Feyerabend, Paul. *Farewell to Reason*. London: Verso, 1988.

Fichte, Johann Gottlob. *The Science of Knowledge: With the First and Second Introductions*, trans. J. Lachs & P. Heath. Cambridge, United Kingdom: Cambridge University Press, 1982.

Finkelde, Dominik & Paul Livingston, eds., *Idealism, Relativism, and Realism: New Essays on Objectivity Beyond the Analytic-Continental Divide*, pp. 259–275. Berlin: De Gruyter, 2020.

Fisher, Mark. "Fans, Vampires, Trolls, Masters" (blog post), June 12, 2009. http://k-punk.abstractdynamics.org/archives/011172.html

Foster, Hal. *The Return of the Real: The Avant-Garde at the End of the Century*. Cambridge, MA: MIT Press, 1996.

Foucault, Michel. *Discipline and Punish: The Birth of the Prison*, trans. A Sheridan. New York: Vintage, 1977.

Freud, Sigmund. *The Schreber Case*, trans. A. Webber. London: Penguin, 2003.

Fried, Michael. *Absorption and Theatricality: Painting and Beholder in the Age of Diderot*. Chicago: University of Chicago Press, 1988.

Fried, Michael. "Art and Objecthood," in *Art and Objecthood: Essays and Reviews*, pp. 148–172. Chicago: University of Chicago Press, 1998.

Fried, Michael. *Courbet's Realism*. Chicago: University of Chicago Press, 1990.

Fried, Michael. *Manet's Modernism: or, The Face of Painting in the 1860s*. Chicago: University of Chicago Press, 1996.

Gabriel, Markus. *Fields of Sense: A New Realist Ontology*. Edinburgh: Edinburgh University Press, 2015.

Gadamer, Hans-Georg. *Philosophical Apprenticeships*, trans. R. Sullivan. Cambridge, MA: MIT Press, 1985.

Garcia, Tristan. *Form and Object: A Treatise on Things*, trans. M.A. Ohm & J. Cogburn. Edinburgh: Edinburgh University Press, 2014.

Gardner, Martin. "Mathematical Games: The Fantastic Combinations of John Conway's New Solitaire Game 'Life,'" *Scientific American* 223 (October 1970), pp. 120–123.

Gardner, Sebastian. *Routledge Philosophy Guidebook to Kant and the Critique of Pure Reason*. New York: Routledge, 1999.

Garfield, Jay. *Engaging Buddhism: Why It Matters to Philosophy*. Oxford: Oxford University Press, 2014.

Garrera-Tolbert, Nicolás, Jesús Guillermo Ferrer Ortega, & Alexander Schnell, eds., *Phänomenologie und spekulativer Realismus/Phenomenology and Speculative Realism/Phénoménologie et réalisme spéculatif*, pp. 12–15. Blaufelen, Germany: Königshausen & Neumann, 2021.

Gaskill, Nicholas & Adam Nocek, eds., *The Lure of Whitehead*. Minneapolis: University of Minnesota Press, 2014.

Gettier, Edmund. "Is Justified True Belief Knowledge?" *Analysis* 23.6 (June 1963), pp. 121–123.

Gironi, Fabio. "Between Naturalism and Rationalism: A New Realist Landscape," *Journal of Critical Realism* 11, no. 3 (2012), pp. 361–387.

Gironi, Fabio. Personal communication, July 17, 2012.

Graeber, David & David Wengrow. *The Dawn of Everything: A New History of Humanity*. New York: Farrar, Straus and Giroux, 2021.

Grant, Iain Hamilton. *Philosophies of Nature After Schelling*. London: Continuum, 2006.

Greenberg, Clement. *Art and Culture: Critical Essays*. Boston: Beacon Press, 1971.

Greenberg, Clement. "Avant-Garde and Kitsch," in *The Collected Essays and Criticism, Volume 1: Perceptions and Judgments, 1939–1944*, pp. 5–22.

Greenberg, Clement. *The Collected Essays and Criticism, Volume 1: Perceptions and Judgments, 1939–1944*. Chicago: University of Chicago Press, 1986.

Greenberg, Clement. *The Collected Essays and Criticism, Volume 2: Arrogant Purpose, 1945–1949*. Chicago: University of Chicago Press, 1986.

Greenberg, Clement. *The Collected Essays and Criticism, Volume 3: Affirmations and Refusals, 1950–1956*. Chicago: University of Chicago Press, 1993.

Greenberg, Clement. *The Collected Essays and Criticism, Volume 4: Modernism with a Vengeance, 1957–1969*. Chicago: University of Chicago Press, 1993.

Greenberg, Clement. *Homemade Esthetics: Observations on Art and Taste*. Oxford: Oxford University Press, 1999.

Greenberg, Clement. *Late Writings*. Minneapolis: University of Minnesota Press, 2003.

Greenberg, Clement. "Modern and Postmodern," *Arts* 54, No. 6 (February 1980), pp. 64–66. http://www.sharecom.ca/greenberg/postmodernism.html.

Groys, Boris. *Art Power*. Cambridge, MA: MIT Press, 2013.

Halsall, Francis. "Actor-Network Aesthetics: The Conceptual Rhymes of Latour and Contemporary Art," *New Literary History* 47.2/3 (2016), pp. 439–461.

Haraway, Donna. *Staying with the Trouble: Making Kin in the Chthulucene*. Durham, NC: Duke University Press, 2016.

Harman, Graham. "Aesthetics as First Philosophy: Levinas and the Non-Human," *Naked Punch* 09, Summer/Fall 2007, pp. 21–30.

Harman, Graham. "Agential and Speculative Realism: Remarks on Barad's Ontology," *rhizomes* 30 (2016). http://www.rhizomes.net/issue30/harman.html

Harman, Graham. "Alain Badiou, *Lacan: Anti-Philosophy 3*," *Notre Dame Philosophical Reviews*, May 21, 2019. https://ndpr.nd.edu/news/lacan-anti-phil osophy3/?fbclid=IwAR3jrHD9v7NNnki8jonWRd3xU5AKB_Gm9QJdqUnII-j1QTQs7c03BTDKc-A

Harman, Graham. "All Space is Real, All Time is Sensual," in *The Hole and the Lump*, pp. 35–38, art catalog for Rachel de Joode's show at Interstate Projects, Brooklyn, New York, February 16-March 17, 2013.

Harman, Graham. *Architecture and Objects*. Minneapolis: University of Minnesota Press, 2022.

Harman, Graham. *Art and Objects*. Cambridge, UK: Polity Press, 2020.

Harman, Graham. "Art Without Relations," *ArtReview*, September 2014, No. 66, pp. 144–147.

Harman, Graham. "Autonomous Objects," *new formations*, #71 (2011), pp. 125–130.

Harman, Graham. *Bells and Whistles: More Speculative Realism*. Winchester, UK: Zero Books, 2013.

Harman, Graham. *Bruno Latour: Reassembling the Political*. London: Pluto Press, 2014.

Harman, Graham. *Circus Philosophicus*. Winchester, UK: Zero Books, 2010.

Harman, Graham. "Concerning the COVID-19 Event," *Philosophy Today* 64:4 (Fall 2020), pp. 845–849.

Harman, Graham. "The Current State of Speculative Realism," *Speculations* IV (2013), 22–28.

Harman, Graham. *Dante's Broken Hammer: The Ethics, Aesthetics, and Metaphysics of Love*. London: Repeater, 2016.

Harman, Graham. "Dolayımın İki Boyutu," trans. Mustafa Yalçınkaya, *Sabah Ülkesi*, Issue 52, July 1, 2017, pp. 18–23. http://www.sabahulkesi.com/2017/07/01/dolayimin-iki-boyutu-graham-harman/

Harman, Graham. "Fear of Reality: Realism and Infra-Realism," *The Monist*, Vol. 98, Issue 2 (2015), pp. 126–144.

Harman, Graham. "A Festival of Anti-Realism: Braver's History of Continental Thought," *Philosophy Today*, Vol. 52, No. 2 (Spring 2008), pp. 197–210.

Harman, Graham. "Filozofia zwrócona ku przedmiotom contra radykalny empiryzm," trans. K. Rosiński & M. Wiśniewski, *Kronos* 1 (20), 2012, pp. 48–61.

Harman, Graham. "The Future of Continental Realism: Heidegger's Fourfold," *Chiasma: A Site for Thought*, Issue 3 (2016), 81–98. https://westernchiasma.files.wordpress.com/2016/09/harman-the-future-of-continental-realism.pdf

Harman, Graham. "Greenberg, Duchamp, and the Next Avant-Garde," *Speculations* V (2014), pp. 251–274.

Harman, Graham. *Guerrilla Metaphysics: Phenomenology and the Carpentry of Things*. Chicago: Open Court, 2005.

Harman, Graham. "On the Horror of Phenomenology: Lovecraft and Husserl," *Collapse* IV (2008), pp. 333–364.

Harman, Graham. "I Am Also of the Opinion That Materialism Must Be Destroyed," *Environment and Planning D: Society and Space*, Vol. 28, No. 5 (2010), pp. 772–790.

Harman, Graham. *Immaterialism: Objects and Social Theory*. Cambridge, UK: Polity, 2016.

Harman, Graham. *Infrastructure: An Object-Oriented Ontology*. Edinburgh: Edinburgh University Press, forthcoming.

Harman, Graham. "It is Warm Out There/Il fait chaud là-bas," in *Intimately Unrelated/Intimement sans rapport: Isabel Nolan*, trans. Elite Traductions, pp. 58–95. Sligo, Ireland: The Model & Saint-Étienne, France: Musée de Saint-Étienne Métropole, 2011.

Harman, Graham. "Latour's Interpretation of Donald Trump," in *Nonmodern Practices: Latour and Literary Studies*, E. Arnould-Bloomfield & C. Lyu, eds., pp. 191–215. London: Bloomsbury, 2020.

Harman, Graham. "Malabou's Political Critique of Speculative Realism," *Open Philosophy*, Vol. 4, Issue 1 (2021), pp. 94–105.

Harman, Graham. "Materialism is Not the Solution: On Matter, Form, and Mimesis," *Nordic Journal of Aesthetics*, No. 47 (2014), pp. 94–110.

Harman, Graham. "Mia Feuer: Selected by Graham Harman," 2015 Future Greats series, *Art Review*, March 2015, p. 99.

Harman, Graham. "Object-Oriented Ontology," in *The Palgrave Handbook of Posthumanism in Film and Television*, M. Hauskeller, T.D. Philbeck & C.D. Carbonell, eds., pp. 401–409. London: Palgrave, 2015.

Harman, Graham. *Object-Oriented Ontology: A New Theory of Everything*. London: Pelican, 2018.

Harman, Graham. "Object-Oriented Ontology and Commodity Fetishism: Kant, Marx, Heidegger, and Things," *Eidos* 2 (2017), pp. 28–36. http://eidos.uw.edu.pl/files/pdf/eidos/2017- 02/eidos_2_harman.pdf

Harman, Graham. "Objects Are the Root of All Philosophy," in *Objects and Materials: A Routledge Companion*, ed. P. Harvey et al., pp. 238–245. London: Routledge, 2013.

Harman, Graham. *L'objet quadruple*, trans. O. Dubouclez. Paris: Presses universitaires de France, 2010.

Harman, Graham. "The Only Exit from Modern Philosophy," *Open Philosophy* 3 (2020), pp. 132–146.

Harman, Graham. "possibly the 4 most typical objections to OOO" (blog post), Object-Oriented Philosophy blog, August 2, 2011. https://doctorzamalek2.wordpress.com/2011/08/02/possibly-the-4-most-typical-objections-to-ooo/

Harman, Graham. *Prince of Modes: Bruno Latour's Later Philosophy*. Melbourne: re.press, forthcoming 2023.

Harman, Graham. *Prince of Networks: Bruno Latour and Metaphysics*. Melbourne: re.press, 2009.

Harman, Graham. "The Problem with Metzinger," *Cosmos and History*, vol. 7, no. 1 (2011), pp. 7–36.

Harman, Graham. "On Progressive and Degenerating Research Programs With Respect to Philosophy," *Revista Portuguesa de Filosofia*, Vol. 75 (4), 2019, pp. 2067–2102.

Harman, Graham. *The Quadruple Object*. Winchester, UK: Zero Books, 2011.

Harman, Graham. *Quentin Meillassoux: Philosophy in the Making*, Second Edition. Edinburgh: Edinburgh University Press, 2015.

Harman, Graham. *Die Rache der Oberfläche: Heidegger, McLuhan, Greenberg*. Köln: Verlag der Buchhandlung Walther König, 2015.

Harman, Graham. "Realism Without Hobbes and Schmitt: Assessing the Latourian Option," in *Idealism, Relativism, and Realism: New Essays on Objectivity Beyond the Analytic-Continental Divide*, D. Finkelde & P. Livingston, eds., pp. 259–275. Berlin: De Gruyter, 2020.

Harman, Graham. "Realism Without Materialism," *SubStance*, 40.2, pp. 52–72.

Harman, Graham. "Real Qualities," booklet distributed at Café Oto, London, UK, for art exhibition "CRISAP/Not for Human Consumption." November 15, 2012

Harman, Graham. "Recent Paintings of Egan Frantz," in Egan Frantz, *Words*, 4 pp. Seoul: Foundry Seoul, 2021.

Harman, Graham. "Response to Shaviro," in *The Speculative Turn: Continental Materialism and Realism*, ed. L. Bryant, N. Srnicek, & G. Harman, pp. 291–303. Melbourne: re.press, 2011.

Harman, Graham. "Reuven Israel's Very Unliteral Theater," in *Multipolarity*, pp. 11–14. New York: Fridman Gallery, 2014.

Harman, Graham. "The Revenge of the Surface: Heidegger, McLuhan, Greenberg," trans. G. Harman, *Paletten*, Issue 291/292 (2013), pp. 66–73.

Harman, Graham. *Skirmishes: With Friends, Enemies, and Neutrals*. Brooklyn, NY: Punctum, 2020.

Harman, Graham. *Speculative Realism: An Introduction*. Cambridge, UK: Polity, 2018.

Harman, Graham. "The Third Table," in *The Book of Books*, Carolyn Christov-Bakargiev, ed., pp. 540–542. Ostfildern, Germany: Hatje Cantz Verlag, 2012.

Harman, Graham. *Tool-Being: Heidegger and the Metaphysics of Objects*. Chicago: Open Court, 2002.

Harman, Graham. *Towards Speculative Realism: Essays and Lectures*. Winchester, UK: Zero Books, 2010.

Harman, Graham. "On Truth and Lie in the Object-Oriented Sense," *Open Philosophy* 5.1 (2022), pp. 437-463."

Harman, Graham. "On the Undermining of Objects: Grant, Bruno, and Radical Philosophy," in *The Speculative Turn: Continental Materialism and Realism*, L. Bryant, N. Srnicek, & G. Harman, eds., pp. 21–40. Melbourne: re.press, 2011.

Harman, Graham. "Undermining, Overmining, and Duomining: A Critique," in *ADD Metaphysics*, J. Sutela, ed., pp. 40–51. Aalto, Finland: Aalto University Design Research Laboratory, 2013.

Harman, Graham. "On Vicarious Causation," *Collapse* 2 (2007), pp. 171–205.

Harman, Graham. *Weird Realism: Lovecraft and Philosophy*. Winchester, UK: Zero Books, 2012.

Harman, Graham. "The Well-Wrought Broken Hammer: Object-Oriented Literary Criticism," *New Literary History*, 43.2 (Spring 2012), pp. 183–203.

Harman, Graham. "What the End of Modern Philosophy Would Look Like," *Los Angeles Review of Books*, October 21, 2019. http://thephilosophicalsalon.com/what-the-end-of-modern-philosophy-would-looklike/?fbclid=IwAR1XxugFZR9ski3meL_o9y7HnRiCrLSOdf31WYJbIgJmKQcuJ7GJ3HoD2nY

Harman, Graham. "Whitehead and Schools X, Y, and Z," in *The Lure of Whitehead*, ed. N. Gaskill & A. Nocek, pp. 231–248. Minneapolis: University of Minnesota Press, 2014.

Harman, Graham. "Zero-Person and the Psyche," in *Mind That Abides: Panpsychism in the New Millennium*, D. Skrbina, ed. pp. 253–282. Amsterdam: Benjamins, 2009.

Harman, Graham. "Žižek's Parallax, or The Inherent Stupidity of All Philosophical Positions," in *Parallax: The Dialectics of Mind and World*, edited by Dominik Finkelde, Christoph Menke, & Slavoj Žižek, pp. 27–38. London: Bloomsbury, 2021.

Heidegger, Martin. *Being and Time*, trans. J. Macquarrie & E. Robinson. New York: Harper, 2008.

Heidegger, Martin. *Bremer und Freiburger Vorträge*, GA Band 79. Frankfurt: Vittorio Klostermann, 1994.

Heidegger, Martin. *Contributions to Philosophy*, trans. R. Rojcewicz & D. Vallega-Neu. Bloomington, IN: Indiana University Press, 2012.

Heidegger, Martin. *Elucidations of Hölderlin's Poetry*, trans. K. Hoeller. Amherst, NY: Humanity Books, 2000.

Heidegger, Martin. *The Fundamental Concepts of Metaphysics: World, Finitude, Solitude*, trans. W. McNeill & N. Walker, Bloomington, IN: Indiana University Press, 1995.

Heidegger, Martin. *History of the Concept of Time: Prolegomena*, trans. T. Kisiel. Bloomington, IN: Indiana University Press, 2009.

Heidegger, Martin. "Insight Into That Which Is," in *Bremen and Freiburg Lectures: Insight Into That Which Is and Basic Principles of Thinking*, trans. A. Mitchell, pp. 3–76. Bloomington, IN: Indiana University Press, 2012.

Heidegger, Martin. *Kant and the Problem of Metaphysics*, trans. J. Churchill. Bloomington, IN: Indiana University Press, 1965.

Heidegger, Martin. *Metaphysical Foundations of Logic*, trans. M. Heim. Bloomington, IN: Indiana University Press, 1984.

Heidegger, Martin. *Nietzsche*, GA Band 50. Frankfurt: Vittorio Klostermann, 1990.

Heidegger, Martin. *Nietzsche, Vol. 1: The Will to Power as Art, Vol. 2: The Eternal Recurrence of the Same*, trans. D.F. Krell. New York: HarperOne, 1991.

Heidegger, Martin. *Nietzsche, Vol. 3: The Will to Power as Knowledge and as Metaphysics, Vol. 4: Nihilism*, D.F. Krell, ed. New York: HarperOne, 1991.

Heidegger, Martin. "The Origin of the Work of Art," in *Off the Beaten Track*, trans. J. Young & K. Haynes, pp. 1–56. Cambridge, UK: Cambridge University Press, 2002.

Heidegger, Martin. "The Thing," in *Poetry, Language, Thought*, trans. A. Hofstadter, pp. 161–184. New York: Harper & Row, 1971.

Heidegger, Martin. *Towards the Definition of Philosophy*, trans. T. Sadler. London: Continuum, 2008.

Heidegger, Martin. *Zur Bestimmung der Philosophie*, GA Band 56/57. Frankfurt: Vittorio Klostermann, 1987.

Heidegger, Martin. *What is Called Thinking?* trans. J. Glenn Gray. New York: Harper, 1976.

Hobbes, Thomas. *Leviathan*. Oxford: Oxford University Press, 1996.

Houellebecq, Michel. *H.P. Lovecraft: Against the World, Against Life*, trans. D. Khazeni. San Francisco: Believer Books, 2005.

Hume, David. *An Enquiry Concerning Human Understanding*. Indianapolis: Hackett, 1993.

Hume, David. *A Treatise of Human Nature*. Oxford: Oxford University Press, 1978.

Husserl, Edmund. *Ideas: General Introduction to Pure Phenomenology*, trans. W.B. Gibson. London: George Allen & Unwin Ltd., 1931.

Husserl, Edmund. *Ideas Pertaining to a Pure Phenomenology and to a Phenomenological Philosophy (Book 1)*, trans. F. Kersten. Dordrecht, The Netherlands: Springer, 1983.

Husserl, Edmund. "Intentional Objects," in Edmund Husserl, *Early Writings in the Philosophy of Logic and Mathematics*, trans. D. Willard, pp. 345–387. Dordrecht, The Netherlands: Kluwer, 1993.

Husserl, Edmund. *Logical Investigations*, 2 vols., trans. J.N. Findlay. London: Routledge & Kegan Paul, 1970.

Isutzu, Toshihiko. *Towards a Philosophy of Zen Buddhism*. Boulder: Shambhala Press, 2001.

Jackson, Robert. "The Anxiousness of Objects and Artworks: Michael Fried, Object Oriented Ontology, and Aesthetic Absorption," *Speculations* II (2011), pp. 135–168.

Jackson, Robert. "The Anxiousness of Objects and Artworks II: (Iso)Morphism, Anti-Literalism, and Presentness," *Speculations* IV (2014), pp. 311–358.

James, William. *Essays in Radical Empiricism*. New York: Longmans, Green & Co., 1958.

James, William. "Pragmatism," in *William James: Writings 1902–1910*. New York: Library of America, 1988.

James, William. *The Principles of Psychology*, 2 vols. New York: Dover, 1950.

Johnston, Adrian & Catherine Malabou, *Self and Emotional Life: Philosophy, Psychoanalysis, and Neuroscience*. New York: Columbia University Press, 2013.

Kant, Immanuel. *Critique of Judgment*, trans. W. Pluhar. Indianapolis: Hackett, 1987.

Kant, Immanuel. *Critique of Practical Reason*, trans. W. Pluhar. Indianapolis: Hackett, 2002.

Kant, Immanuel. *Critique of Pure Reason*, trans. W. Pluhar. Indianapolis: Hackett, 1996.

Kant, Immanuel. *Groundwork of the Metaphysics of Morals*, trans. M. Gregor. Cambridge, UK: Cambridge University Press, 1997.

Kant, Immanuel. *Prolegomena to Any Future Metaphysics that Will be Able to Come Forward as Science*, trans. G. Hatfield. Cambridge, UK: Cambridge University Press, 2004.

Keats, John. *The Complete Poems of John Keats*. Digireads.com, 2015.

Keele, Rondo. *Ockham Explained: From Razor to Rebellion*. Chicago: Open Court, 2010.

Kierkegaard, Søren. *Concluding Unscientific Postscript*, trans. H. Hong & E. Hong. Princeton, NJ: Princeton University Press, 1992.

Kisiel, Theodore. *The Genesis of Heidegger's Being and Time*. Berkeley, CA: University of California Press, 1995.

Kitcher, Patricia. *Kant's Transcendental Psychology*. Oxford: Oxford University Press, 1990.

Kohn, Eduardo. *How Forests Think: Toward an Anthropology Beyond the Human*. Berkeley, CA: University of California Press, 2013.

Krauss, Rosalind. *The Originality of the Avant-Garde and Other Modern Myths*. Cambridge, MA: MIT Press, 1986.

Kripke, Saul A. *Naming and Necessity*. Cambridge, MA: Harvard University Press, 1980.

Kuhn, Thomas. *The Structure of Scientific Revolutions*, Third Edition. Chicago: University of Chicago Press, 1996.

Lacan, Jacques. *Anxiety: The Seminar of Jacques Lacan, Book X*, trans. A.R. Price. Cambridge, UK: Polity, 2016.

Lacan, Jacques. *Écrits: The First Complete Edition in English*, trans. B. Fink. New York: Norton, 2007.

Lacan, Jacques. *The Object Relation: The Seminar of Jacques Lacan*, Book IV, trans. A. Price. Cambridge, UK: Polity, 2021.

Lacan, Jacques. *The Sinthome: The Seminar of Jacques Lacan, Book XXIII*, trans. A. Price. Cambridge, UK: Polity, 2018.

Ladyman, James. "Who's Afraid of Scientism? Interview with James Ladyman," *Collapse* V (2009), pp. 135–185.

Ladyman, James & Don Ross (with David Spurrett & John Collier). *Every Thing Must Go: Metaphysics Naturalized*. Oxford University Press, Oxford, 2007.

Lakatos, Imre. *Mathematics, Science, and Epistemology: Philosophical Papers*, vol. 2. Cambridge, UK: Cambridge University Press, 1978.

Lakatos, Imre. *The Methodology of Scientific Research Programmes: Philosophical Papers*, vol. 1. Cambridge, UK: Cambridge University Press, 1978.

Lakatos, Imre. *Proofs and Refutations: The Logic of Mathematical Discovery*. Cambridge, UK: Cambridge University Press, 2015.

Lapoujade, David. *William James: Empiricism and Pragmatism*, trans. T. Lamarre. Durham, NC: Duke University Press, 2019.

Laruelle, François. *Philosophy and Non-Philosophy*, trans. T. Adkins. Minneapolis: Univocal, 2013.

Laruelle, François. *Principles of Non-Philosophy*, trans. A.P. Smith. London: Bloomsbury, 2013.

Latour, Bruno. *Aramis, or the Love of Technology*, trans. C. Porter. Cambridge, MA: Harvard University Press, 1996.

Latour, Bruno. "Can We Get Our Materialism Back, Please?" *Isis* 98 (2007), pp. 138–142.

Latour, Bruno. *Down to Earth: Politics in the New Climactic Regime*. Cambridge, UK: Polity, 2018.

Latour, Bruno. *Facing Gaia: Eight Lectures on the New Climactic Regime*. Cambridge, United Kingdom: Polity, 2017.

Latour, Bruno. *An Inquiry Into Modes of Existence: An Anthropology of the Moderns*, trans. C. Porter. Cambridge, MA: Harvard University Press, 2013.

Latour, Bruno. "Irreductions," trans. J. Law, in *The Pasteurization of France*, trans. A. Sheridan & J. Law, pp. 153–238. Cambridge, MA: Harvard University Press, 1988.

Latour, Bruno. *Pandora's Hope: Essays on the Reality of Science Studies*. Cambridge, MA: Harvard University Press, 1999.

Latour, Bruno. "On the Partial Existence of Existing *and* Non-Existing Objects," in L. Daston, ed., *Biographies of Scientific Objects*, pp. 247–269. Chicago: University of Chicago Press, 2000.

Latour, Bruno. *The Pasteurization of France*, trans. A. Sheridan & J. Law, pp. 153–238. Cambridge, MA: Harvard University Press, 1988.

Latour, Bruno. *Politics of Nature: How to Bring the Sciences Into Democracy*, trans. C. Porter. Cambridge, MA: Harvard University Press.

Latour, Bruno. *Reassembling the Social: An Introduction to Actor-Network Theory*. Oxford: Oxford University Press, 2007.

Latour, Bruno. *Science in Action: How to Follow Scientists and Engineers Through Society*. Cambridge, MA: Harvard University Press, 1987.

Latour, Bruno. *We Have Never Been Modern*, trans. C. Porter. Cambridge, MA: Harvard University Press, 1993.

Latour, Bruno, Graham Harman, & Peter Erdélyi. *The Prince and the Wolf: Latour and Harman at the LSE*. Winchester, UK: Zero Books, 2011.

Leibniz, G.W. *Philosophical Essays*, trans. R. Ariew & D. Garber. Indianapolis: Hackett, 1989.

Leibniz, G.W. & Samuel Clarke. *Correspondence*, ed. R. Ariew, Indianapolis: Hackett, 2000.

Lingis, Alphonso. *The Community of Those Who Have Nothing in Common*. Bloomington, IN: Indiana University Press, 1994.

Lingis, Alphonso. *Foreign Bodies*. London: Routledge, 1994.

Lingis, Alphonso. *The Imperative*. Bloomington, IN: Indiana University Press, 1998.

Locke, John. *An Essay Concerning Human Understanding*. Oxford: Oxford University Press, 1979.

Locke, John. *A Letter Concerning Toleration*. Indianapolis: Hackett, 1983.

Lovecraft, H.P. *Collected Essays. Volume 2: Literary Criticism*, ed. S.T. Joshi. New York: Hippocampus Press, 2004.

Lovecraft, H.P. *Tales*. New York: Library of America, 2005.

Lovelock, James. *The Ages of Gaia: A Biography of Our Living Earth*. New York: Norton, 1995.

Luhmann, Niklas. *Social Systems*, trans. J. Bednarz with D. Baecker. Stanford, CA: Stanford University Press, 1995.

Lynn, Greg, ed. *Folding in Architecture*. London: 2004.

Machiavelli, Niccolò. *The Prince*, trans. W.K. Marriott, ed. R. Dillon. Plano, TX: Veroglyphic Publishing, 2009.

Malabou, Catherine. "Can We Relinquish the Transcendental?" *The Journal of Speculative Philosophy*, Vol. 28, No. 3 (2014), 242–255.

Malabou, Catherine. *The Future of Hegel: Plasticity, Temporality, and Dialectic*. London: Routledge, 2004.

Malabou, Catherine. "Le vide politique du réalisme contemporain," in *L'écho du réel*, C. Crignon, W. Laforge, & P. Nadrigny, eds., pp. 485–498.

Malabou, Catherine. *What Should We Do With Our Brain?* trans. S. Rand. New York: Fordham University Press, 2008.

Malebranche, Nicolas. *The Search After Truth: With Elucidations of the Search After Truth*, T. Lennon & P. Olscamp, eds. Cambridge, UK: Cambridge University Press, 1997.

Marder, Michael. *Plant-Thinking: A Philosophy of Vegetal Life*. New York: Columbia University Press, 2013.

Margulis, Lynn. *Symbiotic Planet: A New Look at Life on Earth*. New York: Basic Books, 1998.

Marías, Julián. *History of Philosophy*, trans. S. Appelbaum & C. Strowbridge. New York: Dover, 1967.

Marion, Jean-Luc. *Being Given: Toward a Phenomenology of Givenness*, trans. J. Kosky. Stanford, CA: Stanford University Press, 2003.

Marion, Jean-Luc. *Reduction and Givenness: Investigations of Husserl, Heidegger, and Phenomenology*, trans. T. Carlson. Evanston, IL: Northwestern University Press, 1998.

Marres, Noortje. "No Issue, No Public: Democratic Deficits After the Displacement of Politics." Ph.D. dissertation, University of Amsterdam, The Netherlands, 2005. http://dare.uva.nl/record/165542.

Marx, Karl. *Capital, Volume One: A Critique of Political Economy*. London: Penguin, 1992.

Maturana, Humberto & Francisco Varela. *Autopoiesis and Cognition: The Realization of the Living*. Dordrecht, The Netherlands: Kluwer, 1980.

McLuhan, Marshall. *The Classical Trivium: The Place of Thomas Nashe in the Learning of His Time*. Berkeley, CA: Gingko Press, 2009.

McLuhan, Marshall. *The Gutenberg Galaxy*. Toronto: University of Toronto Press, 1962.

McLuhan, Marshall. "The Playboy Interview," in *Essential McLuhan*, E. McLuhan & F. Zingrone, eds. London: Routledge, 1997.

McLuhan, Marshall. *Understanding Media: The Extensions of Man*. Cambridge, MA: MIT Press, 1994.

McLuhan, Marshall & Eric McLuhan. *Media and Formal Cause*. Seattle: NeoPoiesis Press, 2011.

McLuhan, Marshall & Eric McLuhan. *Laws of Media: The New Science*. Toronto: University of Toronto Press, 1992.

McLuhan, Marshall & Wilfred Watson. *From Cliché to Archetype*. New York: Viking Press, 1970.

Meillassoux, Quentin. *After Finitude: Essay on the Necessity of Contingency*, trans. R. Brassier. London: Continuum, 2008.

Meillassoux, Quentin. "Appendix: Excerpts from L'Inexistence Divine," trans. G. Harman, in Graham Harman, *Quentin Meillassoux: Philosophy in the Making*, Second Edition, pp. 175–238.

Meillassoux, Quentin. *Après la finitude: Essai sur la nécéssité de la contingence*. Paris: Seuil, 2006.

Meillassoux, Quentin. "Decision and Undecidability of the Event in *Being and Event* I and II," trans. A. Edlebi, *Parrhesia* 19 (2014), pp. 22–35

Meillassoux, Quentin. "Iteration, Reiteration, Repetition: A Speculative Analysis of the Sign Devoid of Meaning," trans. R. Mackay & M. Gansen, in *Genealogies of Speculation: Materialism and Subjectivity Since Structuralism*, ed. A. Avanessian & S. Malik, pp. 117–197. London: Bloomsbury, 2016.

Meillassoux, Quentin. "Potentiality and Virtuality," *Collapse* II (March 2007), pp. 55–81.

Meillassoux, Quentin. "Spectral Dilemma." *Collapse* IV (2008), pp. 261–275.

Merleau-Ponty, Maurice. *Phenomenology of Perception*, trans. C. Smith. London: Routledge, 2002.

Merleau-Ponty, Maurice. *The Visible and the Invisible*, trans. A. Lingis. Evanston, IL: Northwestern University Press, 1968.

Metzinger, Thomas. *Being No One: The Self-Model Theory of Subjectivity*. Cambridge, MA: MIT Press, 2004.

Miller, Jacques-Alain. "La Suture: Élements de la logique signifiants," in *Cahiers pour l'analyse*, Vol. 1, *La vérité* (1966), pp. 37–49.

Minkowski, Hermann. "Space and Time," Albert Einstein et al., *The Principle of Relativity*, pp. 73–91. Mineola, NY: Dover, 1952.

Mitchell, Andrew. *The Fourfold: Reading the Late Heidegger*. Evanston, IL: Northwestern University Press, 2015.

Molnar, George. *Powers: A Study in Metaphysics*. Oxford: Oxford University Press, 2003.

Moore, A.W. *The Evolution of Modern Metaphysics: Making Sense of Things*. Cambridge, UK: Cambridge University Press, 2014.

Morgenthau, Hans. *Politics Among Nations: The Struggle for Power and Peace*. New York: Knopf, 1950.

Morton, Timothy. *Hyperobjects: Philosophy and Ecology after the End of the World*. Ann Arbor, MI: Open Humanities Press, 2013.

Morton, Timothy. "An Object-Oriented Defense of Poetry," *New Literary History*, 43 (Spring 2012), pp. 205–224.

Morton, Timothy. *Realist Magic: Objects, Ontology, Causality*. Ann Arbor, MI: Open Humanities Press, 2013.

Musgrave, Alan & Charles Pigden. "Imre Lakatos," in *The Stanford Encyclopedia of Philosophy*, Winter 2016 Edition. Edited by Edward N. Zalta. https://plato.stanford.edu/archives/win2016/entries/lakatos/

Nadler, Steven. "'No Necessary Connection': The Medieval Roots of the Occasionalist Roots of Hume," *The Monist* 79 (1996), pp. 448–466.

Nadler, Steven. *Occasionalism: Causation Among the Cartesians*. Oxford: Oxford University Press, 2011.

Nagel, Thomas. "What is it Like to be a Bat?" *The Philosophical Review* 83.4 (October 1974), pp. 435–450.

Nail, Thomas. *Theory of the Object*. Edinburgh: Edinburgh University Press, 2021.

Nietzsche, Friedrich. *Ecce Homo & The Antichrist*, trans. T. Wayne. New York: Algora Publishing, 2004.

Nietzsche, Friedrich. "On Truth and Lie in a Nonmoral Sense," in *On Truth and Untruth: Selected Writings*, trans. T. Carman. New York: Harper, 2010.

Nietzsche, Friedrich. *Twilight of the Idols*, trans. R. Polt. Indianapolis: Hackett, 1997.

Okrent, Mark. *Heidegger's Pragmatism: Understanding, Being, and the Critique of Metaphysics*. Ithaca, NY: Cornell University Press, 1988.

Ortega y Gasset, José. "An Essay in Esthetics by Way of a Preface," in *Phenomenology and Art*, trans. P. Silver,, pp. 127–147. New York: Norton, 1975.

Ortega y Gasset, José. "Preface for Germans," in *Phenomenology and Art*, trans. P. Silver, pp. 17–76. New York: Norton, 1975.

Palmerston, Henry Temple 3rd Viscount of. "Treaty of Adrianople — Charges Against Viscount Palmerston," 1848. https://api.parliament.uk/historichansard/commons/1848/mar/01/treaty-of-adrianople-charges-against.

Papineau, David. "Naturalism," in *The Stanford Encyclopedia of Philosophy*, Winter 2016 Edition. Edward N. Zalta, ed. https://plato.stanford.edu/archives/win2016/entries/naturalism/

Parkinson, Gavin. *The Duchamp Book*. London: Tate Publishing, 2008.

Perler, Dominik & Ulrich Rudolph. *Occasionalismus: Theorien der Kausalität im arabaisch-islamischen und im europäischen Denken*. Göttingen: Vandenhoeck & Ruprecht Verlag, 2000.

Phillips, Wesley. "The Future of Speculation?" *Cosmos and History*, Vol. 8, No. 1 (2012), pp. 289–303.

Plato. "Meno," trans. G.M.A. Grube, rev. J. Cooper, in Five Dialogues, pp. 58–92. Indianapolis: Hackett, 2002.

Plato. *Republic*. Translated by G.M.A. Grube. Indianapolis: Hackett, 1992.

Plato. *Symposium,* trans. A. Nehamas. Indianapolis: Hackett, 1987.

Plessner, Helmuth. *Levels of Organic Life and the Human: An Introduction to Philosophical Anthropology*, trans. M. Hyatt. New York: Fordham University Press, 2019.

Plotinus. *The Enneads*, trans. G. Boys-Stones, J.M. Dillon, L. Gerson, R.A.H. King, A. Smith, & J. Wilberding, L. Gerson, eds. Cambridge, UK: Cambridge University Press, 2019.

Poe, Edgar Allan. "The Black Cat," in *Poetry and Tales*, pp. 597–606. New York: Library of America, 1984.

Popper, Karl. *Conjectures and Refutations: The Growth of Scientific Knowledge*. London: Routledge, 1992.

Popper, Karl. *The Logic of Scientific Discovery*. London: Routledge, 1992.

Pound, Ezra. *Literary Essays*. New York: New Directions, 1968.

Priest, Graham. "What is Philosophy?" *Philosophy* 81 (2006), pp. 189–207.

Quine, Willard van Orman. "Two Dogmas of Empiricism," in *From a Logical Point of View,* pp. 20–46. Cambridge, MA: Harvard University Press, 1980.

Quine, Willard van Orman. "On What There Is," in *From a Logical Point of View*, pp. 1–19. Cambridge, MA: Harvard University Press, 1980.

Rhodes, Richard. *The Making of the Atomic Bomb*. New York: Simon & Schuster, 1986.

Rocha, James. "Autonomy Within Subservient Careers," *Ethical Theory and Moral Practice* 14.3 (2011), pp. 313–328.

Rockwell, W. Teed. *Neither Brain Nor Ghost: A Nondualist Alternative to the Mind-Brain Identity Theory*. Cambridge, MA: MIT Press, 2005.

Rosen, Stanley. *The Mask of Enlightenment: Nietzsche's Zarathustra, Second Edition*. New Haven: Yale University Press, 2004.

Rousseau, Jean-Jacques. *Discourse on the Origin of Inequality*, trans. D. Cress. Indianapolis: Hackett, 1992.

Rovelli, Carlo. "Halfway Through the Woods." In *The Cosmos of Science: Essays of Exploration*, J. Earman & J.D. Norton, pp. 180–223. Pittsburgh: University of Pittsburgh Press, 1998.

Russell, Bertrand. *The Analysis of Matter*. Nottingham: Spokesman Books, 2007.

Ruy, David. "Returning to (Strange) Objects," *tarp Architecture Manual*, Spring 2012, pp. 38–42.

Sade, Donatien Alphonse François, Marquis de. *120 Days of Sodom*, trans. W. McMorran & T. Wynn. London: Penguin, 2016.

Sartre, Jean-Paul. *Nausea*, trans. L. Alexander. New York: New Directions, 2007.

Šatkauskas, Ignas. "Where is the 'Great Outdoors' in Meillassoux's Speculative Materialism?" *Open Philosophy* 3 (2020), pp. 102–118.

Scheler, Max. *Formalism in Ethics and Non-Formal Ethics of Values*, trans. M. Frings & R. Funk. Evanston, IL: Northwestern University Press, 1973.

Scheler, Max. "Ordo Amoris," in *Selected Philosophical Essays*, trans. D. Lachterman, pp. 98–135. Evanston, IL: Northwestern University Press, 1992.

Schelling, F.W.J. *Philosophical Inquiries Into the Nature of Human Freedom*, trans. J. Gutmann. Chicago: Open Court, 2003.

Schmitt, Carl. *The Concept of the Political*, trans. G. Schwab. Chicago: University of Chicago Press, 2007.

Schopenhauer, Arthur. *The World as Will and Representation*, Vol. 1, trans. E.F.J. Payne. New York: Dover, 1966.

Schopenhauer, Arthur. *The World as Will and Representation*, Vol. 2, trans. E.F.J. Payne. New York: Dover, 2012.

Schouten, Peer. "The Materiality of State Failure: Social Contract Theory, Infrastructure, and Governmental Power in Congo," in *Millennium: Journal of International Studies* 41. No. 3 (2013), pp. 553–574.

Schreber, Daniel Paul. *Memoirs of My Nervous Illness*. New York: New York Review of Books Classics, 2000.

Schumacher, Patrik. *The Autopoiesis of Architecture*, Vol. 1. London: John Wiley & Sons, 2011.

Searle, John. *Intentionality: An Essay in the Philosophy of Mind*. Cambridge, UK: Cambridge University Press, 1983.

Sellars, Wilfrid. "Philosophy and the Scientific Image of Man." In *In the Space of Reasons*, 369–408. Cambridge, MA: Harvard University Press, 2007.

Shakespeare, William. *Othello*. New York: Simon & Schuster, 2003.

Shannon, Claude E. *The Mathematical Theory of Communication*. Champaign, IL: University of Illinois Press, 1971.

Shapin, Steven & Simon Schaffer. *Leviathan and the Air-Pump: Hobbes, Boyle, and the Experimental Life*. Princeton, NJ: Princeton University Press, 2011.

Shaviro, Steven. "The Actual Volcano: Whitehead, Harman, and the Problem of Relations," in *The Speculative Turn: Continental Materialism and Realism*, ed. L. Bryant, N. Srnicek, & G. Harman, pp. 279–290. Melbourne: re.press, 2011.

Shaviro, Steven. *Without Criteria: Kant, Whitehead, Deleuze, and Aesthetics*. Cambridge, MA: MIT Press, 2009.

Siderits, Mark. *Buddhism as Philosophy: An Introduction*. Indianapolis: Hackett, 2007.

Simmel, Georg. *The Philosophy of Money*, trans. T. Bottomore & D. Frisby. New York: Routledge, 2004.

Simondon, Gilbert. *Individuation in Light of Notions of Form and Information*, 2 vols., trans. T. Adkins. Minneapolis: University of Minnesota Press, 2020.

Sinclair, Upton. *The Jungle*. New York: Doubleday, Jabber & Company, 1906.

Skrbina, David. *Panpsychism in the West*, Revised Edition. Cambridge, MA: MIT Press 2005.

Skrbina, David. Personal communication, June 27, 2007.

Skrbina, David, ed. *Mind That Abides: Panpsychism in the New Millennium*. Amsterdam: Benjamins, 2009.

Sloterdijk, Peter. *Spheres. Volume 3: Foams. Plural Spherology*, trans. W. Hoban. New York: Semiotext(e), 2016.

Smith, Barry. *Austrian Philosophy: The Legacy of Franz Brentano*. Chicago: Open Court, 1995.

Smolin, Lee. *The Trouble with Physics: The Rise of String Theory, the Fall of a Science, and What Comes Next*. New York: Houghton Mifflin Harcourt, 2006.

Snow, C.P. *The Two Cultures*. Cambridge, UK: Cambridge University Press, 1993.

Soames, Scott. *Philosophical Analysis in the Twentieth Century, Volume 1: The Dawn of Analysis*. Princeton, NJ: Princeton University Press, 2005.

Soames, Scott. *Philosophical Analysis in the Twentieth Century, Volume 2: The Age of Meaning*. Princeton, NJ: Princeton University Press, 2005.

Sokal, Alan & Jean-Luc Bricmont. *Fashionable Nonsense: Postmodern Intellectuals' Abuse of Science*. New York: Picador, 1999.

Sontag, Susan. *Against Interpretation: And Other Essays*. New York: Farar, Strauss, & Giroux, 2013.

Sparrow, Tom. *The End of Phenomenology: Metaphysics and the New Realism*. Edinburgh: Edinburgh University Press, 2014.

Stanislavski, Konstantin. *An Actor's Work*, trans. J. Benedetti. London: Routledge, 2010.

Stengers, Isabelle. *Thinking with Whitehead: A Free and Wild Creation of Concepts*, trans. M. Chase. Minneapolis: University of Minnesota Press, 2014.

Sterba, James. "From Liberty to Welfare," *Ethics* 105.1 (1994), pp. 64–98.

Strauss, Leo. "Notes on Carl Schmitt, *The Concept of the Political*," in Carl Schmitt, *The Concept of the Political*, trans. G. Schwab, pp. 99–122. Chicago: University of Chicago Press, 1996.

Strawson, Galen. "Realistic Monism," *Journal of Consciousness Studies* 13 (10–11), 2006, pp. 3–31.

Strum, S.S. & Bruno Latour. "Redefining the Social Link: From Baboons to Humans," *Social Science Information* 26. No. 4 (1987), pp. 783–802.

Suárez, Francisco, S.J. *On Efficient Causality:* Metaphysical Disputations *17, 18, and 19*, trans. A. Freddoso. New Haven, CT: Yale University Press, 1994.

Sutela, Jenna, ed. *ADD Metaphysics*. Aalto, Finland: Aalto University Design Research Laboratory, 2013.

Thacker, Eugene. *In the Dust of This Planet: Horror of Philosophy*, Vol. 1. Winchester, UK: Zero Books, 2011.

Thacker, Eugene. *Starry Speculative Corpse: Horror of Philosophy*, Vol. 2. Winchester, UK: Zero Books, 2015.

Thacker, Eugene. *Tentacles Longer Than Night: Horror of Philosophy*, Vol. 3. Winchester, UK: Zero Books, 2015.

Thomasson, Aimee. *Ordinary Objects*. Oxford: Oxford University Press, 2010.

Thucydides. *The Peloponnesian War*, trans. T. Hobbes. Chicago: University of Chicago Press, 2008.

Trotsky, Leon. "ABC of Materialist Dialectics," in *The Age of Permanent Revolution: A Trotsky Anthology*, I. Deutscher, ed. New York: Dell, 1970.

Tucker, Robert C., ed. *The Marx-Engels Reader*. New York: W.W. Norton, 1978.

Twardowski, Kasimir. *On the Content and Object of Presentations: A Psychological Investigation*, trans. R. Grossmann. The Hague: Martinus Nijhoff, 1977.

Uexküll, Jakob von. *A Foray into the Worlds of Animals and Humans with A Theory of Meaning*, trans. J.D. O'Neil. Minneapolis: University of Minnesota Press, 2010.

Vattimo, Gianni & Pier Aldo Rovatti, eds., *Weak Thought*, trans. P. Carravetta. Albany, NY: SUNY Press, 2013.

Vico, Giambattista. *The First New Science*, trans. L. Pompa. Cambridge, UK: Cambridge University Press, 2002.

Voegelin, Eric. *The New Science of Politics: An Introduction*. Chicago: University of Chicago Press, 1987.

Weisman, Alan. *The World Without Us*. New York: Picador, 2008.

Whitehead, Alfred North. *Process and Reality*. New York, Free Press, 1978.

Whitehead, Alfred North & Lucien Price. *Dialogues of Alfred North Whitehead*. New York: Mentor, 1956.

Whorf, Benjamin Lee. *Language, Thought, and Reality*. Cambridge, MA: MIT Press, 1956.

Williams, D.C. "On the Elements of Being I," *Review of Metaphysics* 7.1, pp. 3–18.

Williams, D.C. "On the Elements of Being II," *Review of Metaphysics* 7.2, pp. 171–192.

Williamson, Timothy. "In Memoriam: Ruth Barcan Marcus, 1921–2012," *The Bulletin of Symbolic Logic*, Vol. 19, No. 1 (2013), pp. 123–126.

Wilson, Edmund. *Literary Essays and Reviews of the 1930s and 1940s*. New York: Library of America, 2007.

Woit, Peter. *Not Even Wrong: The Failure of String Theory and the Search for Unity and Physical Law*. New York: Basic Books, 2007.

Young, Niki. "On Correlationism and the Philosophy of (Human) Access," *Open Philosophy* 3.1 (2020), pp. 42–52.

Young, Niki. "Object, Reduction, and Emergence: An Object-Oriented View," *Open Philosophy* 4.1 (2021), pp. 83–93

Young, Niki. "Only Two Peas in a Pod: On the Overcoming of Ontological Taxonomies," *Symposia Melitensia* 17 (2021), pp. 27–36.

Zeller, Eduard. *Outlines of the History of Greek Philosophy*, trans. L. Palmer. New York: Dover, 1980.

Žižek, Slavoj. "Carl Schmitt in the Age of Post-Politics," in Chantal Mouffe, ed. *The Challenge of Carl Schmitt*, pp 18–37. London: Verso, 1999.

Žižek, Slavoj. *Less Than Nothing: Hegel and the Shadow of Dialectical Materialism*. London: Verso, 2012.

Žižek, Slavoj. *The Parallax View*. Cambridge, MA: MIT Press, 2006.

Žižek, Slavoj. *Tarrying With the Negative: Kant, Hegel, and the Critique of Ideology*. London: Verso, 1993.

Žižek, Slavoj. *The Ticklish Subject*. London: Verso, 2000.

Žižek, Slavoj & Glyn Daly. 2003, *Conversations with Žižek*, Cambridge, UK: Polity.

Žižek, Slavoj & Graham Harman, "Duel + Duet (Mar. 2017)," YouTube, March 2, 2017. https://www.youtube.com/watch?v=r1PJo_-n2vI&t=2s

Žižek, Slavoj & F.W.J. Schelling. *The Abyss of Freedom/Ages of the World*, with the Schelling portion trans. J. Norman. Ann Arbor, MI: University of Michigan Press, 1997.

Zubíri, Xavier. *On Essence*, trans. A.R. Caponigri. Washington, DC: Catholic University Press, 1980.

INDEX

Nietzsche, 138n232
as object-oriented thinker, 106
object-quality tension, no sense of, 97
"object-type something," 135
occasionalism of, implicit, 182-188, 192, 194, 229
ontological difference, between being and beings, 126, 340
ontotheology, critic of, 88, 603
post-Heideggerian, 82, 221-222
pragmatism of, alleged, 109-112, 124-125, 127, 252, 288, 329, 469
presence-at-hand/ready-to-hand (*Vorhandenheit/Zuhandenheit*), 52, 105, 106, 108, 109, 111, 115, 116, 121, 122, 123-126, 127, 157, 184, 200, 207, 224, 268, 287, 303, 430, 457, 582
"pre-worldly something," 134
realism, critic of, 34, 128
reality treated as uncarved by, 54
resoluteness, 393
RO-SQ tension in, 116, 117, 140, 141, 229
Scheler obituary speech, 359-360
"something at all/something specific," 134, 138, 139
the thing, 126-130
thrown projection, 131
tool-analysis, 63-64, 84, 94, 105, 106-109, 111-112, 115, 118, 120-126, 128, 137, 140, 141, 145, 154, 156-157, 158, 183, 192, 193, 198, 207-208, 224, 225, 234, 251, 287, 290, 291, 303, 304, 329, 347, 457, 469, 471, 493, 599
truth as *aletheia*, 128

Towards the Definition of Philosophy (1919 War Emergency Semester), 106, 107, 120, 134, 135, 138, 139, 304, 469
veiling/unveiling, 97, 130, 131, 138, 208, 289, 448
world, 123
"world-laden something," 134
Heisenberg, Werner, 514
Hemingway, Ernest, 321, 550
Heraclitus, 12
  Heraclitean, 281
hermeneutics, 165
Hippocrates, 69
Hitler, Adolf, 292
Hobbes, Thomas, 381-398, 417
  Boyle, rivalry with, 392
  the great Leviathan, the state, 392
  Hobbesian, 422, 586, 609
  human nature, excessively oriented toward, 396
  as liberal (Strauss), 393
Hölderlin, Friedrich, 140, 216, 300, 303, 312-313, 317
holism, 70, 84, 112, 115, 123, 228, 281, 282, 288, 290, 292, 331, 333, 336, 339, 343, 346, 347, 365, 369, 431, 483, 485, 486, 551, 582
Homer, 313
  "wine-dark sea," 554
Hopi language, 72
Houellebecq, Michel, 312
Hull, David, 456
humanities, 4, 40, 330, 530, 531, 532, 581, 537
humans, 84, 88, 98, 130, 157, 161, 162, 165, 182, 185, 191, 194, 205-206, 208, 209, 217, 223, 224, 230, 231, 232, 234, 318, 337, 419,

CULTURE, SOCIETY & POLITICS

Contemporary culture has eliminated the concept and public figure of the intellectual. A cretinous anti-intellectualism presides, cheer-led by hacks in the pay of multinational corporations who reassure their bored readers that there is no need to rouse themselves from their stupor. Zer0 Books knows that another kind of discourse - intellectual without being academic, popular without being populist - is not only possible: it is already flourishing. Zer0 is convinced that in the unthinking, blandly consensual culture in which we live, critical and engaged theoretical reflection is more important than ever before.

If you have enjoyed this book, why not tell other readers by posting a review on your preferred book site.

You may also wish to
subscribe to our Zer0 Books YouTube Channel.

Bestsellers from Zer0 Books include:

Poor but Sexy
Culture Clashes in Europe East and West
Agata Pyzik
How the East stayed East and the West stayed West.
Paperback: 978-1-78099-394-2 ebook: 978-1-78099-395-9

An Anthropology of Nothing in Particular
Martin Demant Frederiksen
A journey into the social lives of meaninglessness.
Paperback: 978-1-78535-699-5 ebook: 978-1-78535-700-8

In the Dust of This Planet
Horror of Philosophy vol. 1
Eugene Thacker
In the first of a series of three books on the Horror of Philosophy,
In the Dust of This Planet offers the genre of horror as a way of
thinking about the unthinkable.
Paperback: 978-1-84694-676-9 ebook: 978-1-78099-010-1

The End of Oulipo?
An Attempt to Exhaust a Movement
Lauren Elkin, Veronica Esposito
Paperback: 978-1-78099-655-4 ebook: 978-1-78099-656-1

Capitalist Realism
Is There No Alternative?
Mark Fisher
An analysis of the ways in which capitalism has presented itself as
the only realistic political-economic system.
Paperback: 978-1-84694-317-1 ebook: 978-1-78099-734-6

Rebel Rebel
Chris O'Leary
David Bowie: every single song. Everything you want to know,
everything you didn't know.
Paperback: 978-1-78099-244-0 ebook: 978-1-78099-713-1

Sweetening the Pill
or How We Got Hooked on Hormonal Birth Control
Holly Grigg-Spall
Has contraception liberated or oppressed women?
Sweetening the Pill breaks the silence on the dark side of hormonal contraception.
Paperback: 978-1-78099-607-3 ebook: 978-1-78099-608-0

Why Are We The Good Guys?
Reclaiming Your Mind from the Delusions of Propaganda
David Cromwell
A provocative challenge to the standard ideology that Western power is a benevolent force in the world.
Paperback: 978-1-78099-365-2 ebook: 978-1-78099-366-9

The Writing on the Wall
On the Decomposition of Capitalism and its Critics
Anselm Jappe, Alastair Hemmens
A new approach to the meaning of social emancipation.
Paperback: 978-1-78535-581-3 ebook: 978-1-78535-582-0

Neglected or Misunderstood
The Radical Feminism of Shulamith Firestone
Victoria Margree
An interrogation of issues surrounding gender, biology, sexuality, work and technology, and the ways in which our imaginations continue to be in thrall to ideologies of maternity and the nuclear family.
Paperback: 978-1-78535-539-4 ebook: 978-1-78535-540-0

How to Dismantle the NHS in 10 Easy Steps (Second Edition)
Youssef El-Gingihy
The story of how your NHS was sold off and why you will have to buy private health insurance soon. A new expanded second edition with chapters on junior doctors' strikes and government blueprints for US-style healthcare.
Paperback: 978-1-78904-178-1 ebook: 978-1-78904-179-8

Digesting Recipes
The Art of Culinary Notation
Susannah Worth
A recipe is an instruction, the imperative tone of the expert, but this
constraint can offer its own kind of potential. A recipe need not be
a domestic trap but might instead offer escape – something
to fantasise about or aspire to.
Paperback: 978-1-78279-860-6 ebook: 978-1-78279-859-0

Most titles are published in paperback and as an ebook.
Paperbacks are available in traditional bookshops.
Both print and ebook formats are available online.
Follow us at:
https://www.facebook.com/ZeroBooks
https://twitter.com/Zer0Books
https://www.instagram.com/zero.books